LF

Galdós
and the Art of
the European Novel:
1867–1887

Galdós and the Art of the European Novel: 1867-1887

STEPHEN GILMAN

Princeton University Press
Princeton, New Jersey

Published by Princeton University Press, Princeton, New Jersey
In the United Kingdom: Princeton University Press, Guildford, Surrey

Library of Congress Cataloging in Publication Data will be found on the last
printed page of this book

This book has been composed in linotype Granjon

Clothbound editions of Princeton University Press books are printed on acid-
free paper, and binding materials are chosen for strength and durability

Printed in the United States of America by Princeton University Press,
Princeton, New Jersey

❧ CONTENTS

PREFACE   vii

Part I: THE HISTORICAL NOVELIST   1

CHAPTER I.   Galdós: "Life and Times"   3

CHAPTER II.   *La Fontana de Oro*   29

CHAPTER III.   From *Trafalgar* to *Doña Perfecta*   49

CHAPTER IV.   *La desheredada*   84

Part II: *FORTUNATA Y JACINTA* IN PROSPECT   131

CHAPTER V.   From *La desheredada* to *Lo prohibido*   133

CHAPTER VI.   A Colloquium of Novelists   154

CHAPTER VII.   The Novelist as Reader   187

Part III: *FORTUNATA Y JACINTA*   227

CHAPTER VIII.   The Challenge of Historical Time   229

CHAPTER IX.   The Art of Listening   248

CHAPTER X.   The Art of Genesis   291

CHAPTER XI.   The Art of Consciousness   320

CHAPTER XII.   Retrospect   356

APPENDIX.   Classical References in *Doña Perfecta*   378

INDEX   395

Critical meditation on the novel as a literary genre (not how to write one or why we should or should not read one) to a large extent began as a serious, scholarly occupation in the third decade of the present century. And, as a result, those of us who belong to the last generation to grow up on novels, to live with them and in them almost as if we were latter-day Alonso Quijanos, were introduced in our university courses to a fascinating new discipline. In the essays and books of Lubbock, Forster, Thibaudet, Ramon Fernandez, and Ortega (Lukacs was still beyond our ken) we learned to understand ourselves and the fictional experience we had accumulated at an intellectual distance. Unlike our parents and grandparents, we were living at the end of the novelistic era (a tacit sense of termination could already be detected in the novelists of our youth, Joyce, Virginia Woolf, Proust, Unamuno), but our fictional loss was in part compensated for by our critical gain.

Under these circumstances it was only natural that many of us (those of us who realized after painfully naive experimentation that we could not *be* novelists) should have chosen to teach and write about the complex variety of fiction that has meant and still means so much to us and that in a sense is a component of our identity. In many cases, admired professors (mine was Augusto Centeno at Princeton) led us into temptation, but they should not be blamed. We are directly responsible for a bibliographical flood of studies on the novel, which since the fifties has become more and more unmanageable. It is natural to regret wistfully the obsolescence of a literary form that not only gave us the time of our lives in a literal sense but also taught us how to distinguish morally between illusion and reality. But why the excess of ex-post-facto critical attention?

The obvious answer, of course, is that books about the novel or about individual novelists and novels are a form of thanksgiving, a way of expressing gratitude to the past. And in my own case, I would add the further excuse that, as an Hispanist, I have been trained, both by my reading and by my teachers, to think about novels in a way that I hope will complement the rhetorical, formal, and structuralistic approaches that have generally characterized the discussion of the novel in English, French, and other occidental languages. For those of us who take the *Quijote* as a point of departure, the novel is not really a genre at all in the traditional sense but rather a cunningly intensified passage of experience. We do not worry about meeting E. M. Forster's challenge to define the novel in such a way as to exclude *The Pilgrim's Progress,* nor do we attempt to draw justifiable frontiers between, say, novels and novellas. From our point of view almost anything, even a Shakespearean play, can be read novelistically once the habit is acquired. As Ortega, a teacher of my aforementioned teacher, said in his memorable *Ideas sobre la novela,*

> Let us observe ourselves at the moment when we finish reading a great novel. It seems as if we were emerging from another existence. . . . A moment ago we were in Parma with Count Mosca, Gina Sanseverina, Clélia, and Fabrice; we were living with them, worried by their worries, immersed in their space, their time, and their air. And now suddenly we are back in our room, our city, our date. . . . A momentary lapse may submerge us again in the universe of the novel, and with effort, as if struggling in a liquid element, we try to swim to the shores of our own existence. . . . I call the literary creation which produces this effect a novel.

Acceptance of Ortega's definition meant, perforce, abandonment of my youthful ambition to write the book on the novel. A book on the experience of living inside of a novel was all that was possible. I chose, therefore, *Fortunata y Jacinta,* the "obra predilecta" of a novelist whose "voice," according to Federico García Lorca, was "the truest and most profound" in modern Spain, and in one seminar after another my students and I have tried to understand just how it "produced its effect." The results of those years of scrutiny appeared in a series of articles on style, structure, imagery, and consciousness, which in revised form constitute the central chapters of

viii

the present book.[1] Each represents a fresh reading of the whole, and each aspires to draw closer to that "ideal implicit norm," which, according to J. V. Cunningham, may never be reached but in which we must believe.

Critical atheists, however, do exist, and those of us who talk about the novel as a passage of experience are vulnerable to the charge that we are more concerned with ourselves than with our subject. As a precaution against such criticism, therefore, and without realizing that I was anticipating the Structuralist notion of "intertextualité," I have enlarged the earlier essays with a discussion of the experiential context of *Fortunata*. By this I mean, specifically, first, Galdós' earlier novels, which he expected his readers to have read; second, novels by other novelists (primarily Cervantes, Dickens, Balzac, Zola, and Clarín), which Galdós had read and which he expected his best readers to have read; and, third, other novels, which Galdós either could not have read or had not read as far as we know (*Ulysses, Huck Finn, La Chartreuse de Parme, War and Peace, The Idiot*), but which inevitably accompany us as we read. Novelistic experience is anything but hermetic or divisible into titled compartments. Whereas the act of reading is plural in nature, as an act of communion with other novels and other readers, we need not fear the

---

[1] The following chapters contain in drastically revised form articles published separately:

Chapter I. *"La Fontana de Oro:* Historical Fable or Historical Prophecy?" *Les Cultures ibériques en devenir: Essais publiés en hommage à la memoire de Marcel Bataillon*, Paris, 1979, pp. 135–139.

Chapter II. "History as News in *La Fontana de Oro," Estudios literarios de hispanistas norteamericanos dedicados a Helmut Hatzfeld*, eds. J. Sola-Solé and Alessandro Grisafulli, Madrid, 1974, pp. 407–413.

Chapter III. "Novel and Society: *Doña Perfecta," AG*, 11, 1976, pp. 15–27.

Chapter VI. "La novela como diálogo: *La Regenta* y *Fortunata* y *Jacinta," NRFH*, 24, 1975, pp. 438–448.

Chapter VII. "Galdós as Reader," *AG*, Anejo, 1978, pp. 21–37.

Chapter VIII. "Narrative Presentation in *Fortunata* y *Jacinta," RHM*, 34, 1968, pp. 288–301.

Chapter IX. "La palabra hablada y *Fortunata* y *Jacinta," NRFH*, 15, 1961, pp. 542–560.

Chapter X. "The Birth of Fortunata," *AG*, 1, 1966, pp. 72–83.

Chapter XI. "The Consciousness of Fortunata," *AG*, 5, 1970, pp. 55–66.

Appendix. "Las referencias clásicas de *Doña Perfecta," NRFH*, 3, 1949, pp. 353–362.

charge of impressionism. We may even hope that prolonged meditation on a single novel within this larger context will enable us to achieve, at least partially, that comprehension of the novel as a generic phenomenon which I forsook many years ago.

I have been so well accompanied during the four decades that separate me from my first undergraduate essay on *Fortunata y Jacinta* that I cannot begin to list all the colleagues, friends, and students to whom I am indebted. Among the most recent, however, I can mention Roy Harvey Pearce, Judith Sklar, Stephen Graubard, Rafael Lapesa, Denah Lida, and Rodolfo Cardona, who in the last years either read portions of the manuscript or contributed helpful information. In the longer range my company divides itself into generations: Augusto, whose book this should have been, and a series of students, some of whom are already well-known "galdosistas" and others who are well on their way: Ana Fernández Seín, Peter Goldman, Leo Hoar, Diane Beth Hyman, Martha Krow-Lucal, Antonio Ruiz Salvador, Alan Smith, Chad C. Wright. I dedicate these chapters to all of them with affection and gratitude.

Cambridge, Mass.
January 26, 1979

PART I

The Historical Novelist

Galdós: "Life and Times"

1. Novel and Prophecy

In the "Preámbulo" to his first novel, *La Fontana de Oro*, Galdós comments: "Long after this book was written (since only its last pages are posterior to the September revolution) it has seemed to me to have a certain relevance to the period we are now experiencing. Probably this is the result of a relationship that may be detected between many events referred to therein and what is now going on, a relationship that undoubtedly corresponds to the similarity of the present crisis to that of the memorable years from 1820 to 1823."[1] (*10*) In so saying, the novelist defines both his overt intentions and his underlying preoccupations as political and historical. The decade of the 1860s was indeed a time of "crisis," a critical time experienced with anguished intensity by Galdós and his Madrid contemporaries. Particularly after the student riot later known as the "Noche de San Daniel" (April 1865), which was described facetiously by the novice reporter and participant, as a "descomunal batalla" (*1508*) (as readers of *Fortunata y Jacinta* may remember, there is an echo of the same tone in the first paragraph when Juanito Santa Cruz's "heroism" is recalled),[2] it became in-

---

[1] All page references (unless otherwise indicated) are to the appropriate volume of the Aguilar edition of the *Obras completas*. My collection is dated Madrid, 1950–1951, and is in 6 volumes. Page numbers are italicized to distinguish them from the notes. When necessary I have reverted to the original punctuation of the text. All translations from the Spanish and other sources are mine unless otherwise noted.

[2] The lighthearted, juvenile indignation of the original "Crónica de Madrid," published just after the event, was transmuted by the passage of decades into rueful irony: "el célebre alboroto de la noche de San Daniel." (*13*) Nevertheless, the numerous references to it throughout Galdós' works (for example, in *Angel Guerra*) seem to indicate that his participation had a more profound effect on him than his style would indicate. See J. Pérez Vidal, "Pérez Galdós y la noche de San Daniel," *RHM*, 17, 1951, pp. 94–110.

creasingly apparent that the precarious balance of forces that had propped up the regime of "la reina castiza," Isabel II, could not last for long. Ministries were increasingly short-lived; violence begot violence; the economy withered;[3] and intimations of radical change forced all concerned to choose sides. As Galdós remarked long afterwards, "In the days just prior to the revolution of '68, our disputes were passionate and formidable, since the aim was to change radically the whole of the political organism. And in effect it was changed, after being wounded in the foot [like Achilles?] and after having so opened a passage for the new ideas of our time."[4]

It was natural under these circumstances that the events of the so-called "trienio liberal" and its bloody aftermath should have been called to mind. Fear of future repression was expressed in Emilio Castelar's journal, *La Democracia* (18 April 1865), in precisely such terms:

> Reaction—yes! horrible Reaction—threatens us with its systematic violence and its entourage of evil. Auguries foretell that the tragic days of 1823, which obliged the most noble, intelligent, and high-minded Spaniards to abandon the soil of their fatherland in search of that superior fatherland called Liberty, may now be repeated.

In the face of such a grave menace, the editorial continues, prudence and circumspection rather than militance were to be strongly urged.

Castelar's analysis of the earlier historical tragedy is simple. The forces of liberty had failed during those three years of constitutional government because leftist extremists (presumably incited by royalist agents provocateurs) had stirred the masses to violence. This had now at all costs to be avoided; public order had to be maintained for the purpose of soothing the uncommitted and reassuring the powerful. It was a need so generally felt that, six days before, the liberal journals of Madrid (some eighteen in all!) had issued a joint proclamation to their readers:

---

[3] See Raymond Carr, *Spain 1808–1939*, Oxford, 1966, p. 300.

[4] See the letter dated 23 April 1894 in W. H. Shoemaker, *Las cartas desconocidas de Galdós en "La Prensa" de Buenos Aires*, Madrid, 1973, p. 520. (Hereafter cited as *Cartas*.)

4

So, be vigilant, Liberals; do not give our present enemies—our eternal enemies!—any pretext that they might use to their advantage. Order in the streets! Order everywhere! For Liberty does not need inopportune self-display in order to triumph. Nor should it react to mad provocations, if such should occur.

For the time being, at least, the appeal was heeded, and a week later *La Democracia* praised popular behavior as characterized by "la serenidad y calma de los pueblos que desean ser libres."

La Fontana de Oro, the creation of a young and liberal newspaperman whose task it was to report on each day's new and—to him—intensely interesting and hopeful segment of national history, is the direct expression of these immediate concerns. As a political fable for its time, it recreates the events from 1820 to 1823 for the purpose of preaching an alertness identical to that called for in the joint proclamation. By negative example, its readers were instructed in the dangers to be avoided and the kind of public misbehavior to be shunned. Our grandfathers, Galdós suggests, had had a chance, however slim, to free Spain from slavery to the past, and they had failed. If the present generation was to succeed not only in preserving the liberties it now possessed (far more than it realized, as any 1973 reader learns after spending a morning in the *Hemeroteca*) but also in emerging victoriously from the imminent struggle, a clear understanding of the causes of the earlier failure was essential.

In political terms, Galdós' analysis of the events of "trienio liberal" is cogent and is supported by similar moments of historical crisis in his past and in his future. As far as the past is concerned, Galdós seems to have learned a good deal from Balzac's presentation of political repression in France after 1815 in *Splendeurs et misères des courtisanes.* One of the crucial milieux of that novel is the Café David, a rendezvous for rebellious young men presided over by a caricaturesque government informer known as "le père Canquoëlle." That this personage did indeed furnish a partial model for Coletilla, Galdós' aged representative of reaction (as well as for the nameless proprietor of *La Fontana*), becomes evident when we learn that under his real name of Peyrade he formerly held the

5

ironical title of "Espion ordinaire de Sa Majesté"[5] and that (as in the case of Coletilla and his ward Clara) he keeps his beloved daughter, Lydie, and a single maidservant secluded in a camouflaged "mansard" behind a prisonlike door.[6] Turning to Galdós' future, a comparison even more apt than the similar use of provocation by our Federal Bureau of Investigation or by the Spanish police during the fifties and sixties is the strategy used to bring about the fall of Allende. In Chile, as we know now, secret agents of reaction (allegedly funded by the CIA) incited the extreme left to violence; and there, too, a past crisis, the collapse of the Balmaseda regime during the nineties, served as an explicit historical warning. This was expressed specifically in a cinema script (which was never filmed)[7] and in a comic book (which I have not seen), which both resemble La Fontana in their guiding intention.[8] In the case of the comic book, as we shall observe, there was also a strong formal resemblance to Galdós' novel.

To relate La Fontana de Oro to its immediate political context and to a possible source does not diminish its artistic originality. It is, indeed, an extraordinary accomplishment. And not because as a

[5] *La Comédie humaine,* ed. Marcel Bouteron, La Pléiade, Paris, 1962, vol. 5, p. 757. (Hereafter cited as *Comédie.*)

[6] Ibid., p. 759. The description of the pair will be familiar to any reader of *La Fontana:* "Aucun désir n'avait troublé la vie de cette enfant si pure. Svelte, belle . . . sa mise chaste, sans exageration d'aucun mode, exhalait un charmant parfum de bourgeoisie. Figurez-vous un vieux Satan, père d'un ange, et . . . vous aurez une idée de Peyrade et de sa fille." Ibid., p. 761. Marie-Claire Petit in her *Galdós et "La Fontana de Oro"* (Paris, 1972) proposes Balzac's *Pierrette* as a possible source. Certain close resemblances to the situation of Inés in the Requejo household (*El 19 de Marzo y el 2 de Mayo*) indicate that Galdós probably had read the novel. But the only specific parallel to *La Fontana* is that of Pierrette's childhood lover, Brigant, who runs after the stagecoach when she leaves Brittany on her journey to Provins. *Comédie,* vol. 3, p. 693. Thus, too, "Lázaro . . . corrió tras el coche larguísimo trecho hasta que el cansancio le obligó a detenerse." (*42*)

[7] Allende fell before the film was made. I have been informed that the role of Balmaseda had been assigned to the well-known painter Nemesio Antúnez.

[8] For a more extensive discussion of the resemblance of the political situation presented in *La Fontana* and that of Chile, see Guillermo Araya, "*La Fontana de Oro* de Galdós: cien años de lucidez política," *EFil,* 8, 1972, pp. 89–104.

first novel it was daringly conceived, conscientiously achieved, and successfully received; Dickens, after all, began with *Pickwick Papers*. Rather, it is extraordinary because, in the course of its composition, its intended fable is converted into prophecy. The conclusion, as we read it in editions available today, is not unlike those of certain political novels written by members of the Generation of '98 (for example, Baroja's *César o Nada*): the disillusioned protagonist abandons his political ambitions; returns to the provinces; marries his sweetheart; and is content with a "vida oscura, pacífica, laboriosa y honrada." (*186–187*) An examination of the manuscript and of the early editions demonstrates, however, that this may be a happy ending substituted in a lost first edition for another as an afterthought (apparently in order to offer a small measure of hope to the partisans of liberalism). The happy ending was later abandoned by Galdós in a fit of political pessimism and finally restored by publishers more concerned with pleasing the public than with historical verisimilitude. The original, handwritten and far more significant conclusion is the hero's roadside murder by his uncle, the aforementioned Coletilla. Therein lies a prophecy, which was already partially fulfilled when Galdós returned to the original ending in the second edition (1871).

As has often been pointed out, Galdós presents his predestined victim not only as an individual liberal but also as an allegorical personification of liberalism as such: Lázaro or Spain recalled to life. Therefore, his assassination, which is the inevitable result of his grave errors of judgement, can only be interpreted as a prediction of an event that had not yet occurred at the time of the writing: the lamentable, however deserved, failure of the liberal revolution of 1868, usually referred to mournfully or sardonically as "la Gloriosa." The history retold by Galdós might well have persuaded certain exalted liberals to try to avoid the mistakes of the past, but the narrative logic of the tale leads us to wonder if such efforts at self-restraint could, under the prevailing circumstances, have been successful. The point is simple: insofar as Lázaro is a typically naive liberal of the 1820s, *La Fontana* is an historical fable with a didactic moral: "Don't behave rashly like your grandparents." But insofar as he represents allegorically a political force or position, it is a tragedy in which doom cannot be avoided. What had happened in the past, Galdós foresaw, must happen again and perhaps even again and again.

In the course of chapter 1 of *La Fontana* Galdós describes the conflicting "societies" of his as yet unwritten novel as if he were intending an antithetical conclusion: "A decrepit society, but one still possessing the tenacity that characterizes certain old men, was engaged in a deadly struggle with a young, healthy, and vigorous society, which was destined to control the future." (*15*) As we come to know the paladin of the latter society, Lázaro (the symbol of national resurrection), however, we realize that the adjectives "lozano" and "vigoroso" are unsuitable. "Impractical," "hyper-imaginative," "Quixotesque," "gullible," and "easily swayed" would have been more exact. These observations should not be understood as implying that Galdós at some point reversed his original intentions and turned against his young hero and alter ego. Rather his clear novelistic insight prohibited him from writing an historical romance in which the champion of light (having undergone the trials associated with inexperience) would inevitably bring the champion of darkness to his knees. For all its sincerity and good intentions, liberalism, honestly represented as it had been in the 1820s and as it was in Galdós' own time, did not have a chance. As an enthusiastic and optimistic young partisan, Galdós may have hoped that his fable might be beneficial, but, as a novelist whose future greatness was to emerge from an inherent historical intuition, he knew better.

We have, thus, detected in *La Fontana de Oro* the first signs of a gift for prophecy, which was to grow and grace and sadden Galdós until the appropriately sightless end of his days. As we shall see, in the second series of "episodios," there are flashes of prescience that seem almost supernaturally inspired. And *La desheredada,* in particular, develops the potential for prophecy hesitantly exploited in the author's first experiment into an uncanny and systematic unfolding of future decades. Restated in a larger context: from the beginning Galdós shared that special keenness of historical vision that distinguishes a Stendhal, a Balzac, a Tolstoy, or a Dickens from their most eminent seventeenth and eighteenth century predecessors. Although at first a card-carrying liberal and later a moral radical,[9] Galdós understood Spain (just as Balzac, an unrepentant monarchist, understood France), not ideologically but historically.[10] Indeed, had he wished to encompass his works under a single title comparable to Balzac's *Comédie humaine,* none would have been better suited than that coined and abandoned by Américo Castro: *España en su historia.*

The truth that Galdós and his nineteenth-century European colleagues discovered *in fieri* and that certain past-oriented historians fail to perceive even today (as is demonstrated by their myopic attacks on Castro) is that a nation does not just *have* a history. It *is* a history. Like each one of us, it lives in time, and its collective present, emergent from the past, is headed for a future at best dimly discernible to its inhabitants. But born novelists, born into a century anxious to cater to their sensibilities and blessed or cursed with what Robert Petsch called the capability of visualizing time (presented as a "rühige Ueberschau" of what was, what is, and what will be),[11] can on occasion delineate with fearful clarity the future paths of

[9] For Galdós' radicalism in his old age, one need look no farther than the last chapter of the last of the "episodios," *Cánovas* (1912). History's short oratorical denunciation of the new Spain founded by the politicians ("hipócritas en dos bandos"), the local "caciques," the capitalists, the Church, and the army leads her to call for revolution "si no querais morir de la honda caquexia que invade el cansado cuerpo de tu nación" (*1363*). It is one of the most moving passages Galdós ever wrote.

[10] See Carlos Seco Serrano's "Los *episodios nacionales* como fuente histórica," *Homenaje a Galdós, CuH,* 250–252, 1970–1971, pp. 256–284. (The volume of essays is hereafter cited as *Homenaje.*) The critic here returns to an idea announced by Balzac in his "Avant-propos" ("Walter Scott élevait donc à la valeur philosophique de l'histoire le roman") and converted into a journalistic commonplace in Spain long before Galdós began to put it into practice. Lee Fontanella's forthcoming book on nineteenth-century Spanish journalism (to be entitled *La imprenta y las letras en la España romántica*) will cite such figures as Gil y Zárate, and Revilla to this effect. Commonplace or not, however, Seco Serrano maintains that to think of the "episodios" as historical allows us to comprehend them more deeply than if they are conceived of as a mixture of sources, which need to be discovered, and imagination, which needs to be recognized and segregated.

[11] *Wesen und Formen der Erzählkunst,* Halle, 1942, p. 164. (Hereafter cited as *Wesen und Formen.*)

their respective nations. The prophets of the Old Testament often unwillingly saw the future through the eyes of God; the novelists of the century before ours often unwittingly saw it through the eyes of History. In an indispensable article the late Carlos Clavería cites Galdós' description of how he envisaged in biological terms "la concatenación de los hechos": "El continuo engendrar de unos hechos en el vientre de otros es la Historia, hija del Ayer, hermana del Hoy, madre del mañana."[12] In this sense, one could apply to the young Galdós Merleau Ponty's definition of the central theme of Balzac: "le mystère de l'histoire comme apparition d'un sens dans le hasard des événements."[13]

Novel and Biography

Why was the nineteenth century so anxious to cater at first to historical novelists and later to novelist historians? This is a fundamental question, and it will not do to answer it with the mere assertion of Clavería that that was indeed the case: "To conclude, men of that period acquired a definitive awareness of their visceral connection with events, an awareness of being a part of the flow of historical time (which is to say, with the evolution of humanity in its constant progress), an awareness that history is the very essence of human life."[14] Or as Geoffrey Barraclough puts it: "For a century and a half, from the time of the French revolution, historical principles and historical conceptions dominated, shaped and determined the character of European thought."[15] These generalizations are true enough, but anyone who proposes to try to write about the "life and times" (meaning the historical times in which that life was lived) of a nineteenth-century novelist is duty bound to answer the question more explicitly. And if, in so doing, I seem to be heedless of the philosophical, historicistic, sociological, and ideological explana-

[12] "El pensamiento histórico de Galdós," *RNC,* 19, 1957, p. 173.
[13] *Sens et non-sens,* Paris, 1948, p. 45.
[14] "El pensamiento histórico de Galdós," p. 170.
[15] *History in a Changing World,* Oxford, 1955, p. 1. Barraclough sounds much farther removed from this faith than did Comte, who, according to Karl Löwith, was "convinced that no phenomenon can be understood philosophically unless it is understood historically." *Meaning in History,* Chicago, Ill., 1949, p. 67.

tions that are most often adduced (Hegel and Kant, the Schlegels and Marx, Comte and Taine, Romanticism and Realism, etc.), it is simply because I have convinced myself that contemplation of the new novel as a fictional biography or autobiography (our own representative title is *The Personal History and Experiences of David Copperfield the Younger*) offers a more direct path.

The notion of biography as such (whether fictional or experienced, whether in the third or first person) depends, as Dickens's title indicates, on perception of the historicity of individual lives. This perception (implicit in Clavería's use of the word "conciencia") was alien to the confessionally or celebratively inclined inhabitants of earlier centuries. The acknowledgment of sins and temptations or the exemplary song of unique deeds presented as if they were unrelated to their immediate social context was replaced in the nineteenth century by a sense of self radically interpenetrated with the rest of history. The distinction between public and private, political and personal, which had provided a Cervantes or a Fielding with marvelous opportunities for comic juxtaposition, was erased in an epoch that saw personal growth as a constituent of social change. Thus, Maurice Bardèche defines Balzac's characters as "beings charged with history,"[16] and Wilhelm Dilthey sees each life as a "germinating cell of history" ("Urzelle") "receiving influences" from its milieu and reacting in order to change it.[17] Erik Erikson's apparently paradoxical titles, e.g., *Childhood and Society* or *Ego Development and Historical Change,* are symptoms of the extent to which the nineteenth-century novelistic sense of biography has been adopted by psychologists and social scientists at their creative best.[18]

[16] *Balzac romancier,* Paris, 1940, p. 273.

[17] *El mundo histórico,* trans. E. Imaz, México, 1944, p. 278; *Gesämmelte Schriften,* ed. B. Groethuysen, Leipzig and Berlin, 1927, vol. 7, p. 246. Dilthey comprehends the novel's intimate association with biography and history, but in my opinion suggests too much of a causal relationship: "The contribution of biography to historiography was prepared by the novel." *El mundo histórico,* p. 275; *Gesämmelte Schriften,* vol. 7, p. 250.

[18] As Roy Harvey Pearce indicates in his introduction to the anthology of Américo Castro's works, Erikson provides hope for the twentieth century by reversing the nineteenth-century sense of the relationship between the individual and history. *An Idea of History,* ed. S. Gilman Jr. and E. L. King, Columbus, Ohio, 1977, p. 7. Instead of taking the historicity of individual lives as a marvelous or lamentable point of departure, Erikson proposes

At the beginning, however, and long, long before "I am a part of all that I have met" was rephrased as "Yo soy yo y mi circunstancia," the biographical sense of life was still untried and unconceptualized historically. During the second half of the eighteenth century a handful of exceptional individuals, a Rousseau, a Goethe, and later a Scott, had begun to savor their own experience in a way that would have seemed almost indecent to a Rojas or a Pepys. They remembered their private past, in particular, the "far away and long ago" of their growing up, and so began to perceive themselves autobiographically. The next step was almost a matter of course: the projection of this strange, new self-consciousness into fictional biographies, into histories of imagined selves—a Saint Preux, a Wilhelm Meister, or a Waverley, living in times and landscapes made of words. Then, after these first experiments in giving narrative shape to the newest avatar of human awareness (*Lazarillo,* for instance, has neither times nor landscape in this sense), the so-called rise of the novel was not just possible but inevitable. As Schelling first saw clearly (basing himself on *Wilhelm Meister* and a reevaluation of the *Quijote*), the epic itself, after thousands of years of abject critical veneration, was about to be replaced by this strange and not very respectable form of reading.[19]

freedom from "neurosis" through conscious acceptance of historical necessity and concludes: "Only thus can [the individual] derive ego strength (*for his generation and the next*) from the coincidence of his one and only life cycle with a particular segment of history" (*italics mine*), ibid. Later I shall express the wish that Freud had read *Fortunata y Jacinta;* now, as I append this note, I wish Erikson would.

[19] *Sämmtliche Werke,* ed. K. F. A. Schelling, Stuttgart and Augsburg, 1859, vol. 5, pp. 673–678. Such a prediction is implicit in the unprecedented seriousness of his meditation on and praise of the hitherto underestimated and indeed maligned genre. It is explicit in Friedrich Schlegel's "Brief über den Roman," which views the prospect with moderate alarm. Disapproval of the genre as immoral, untrue, and a waste of time continued all through the nineteenth century. Indeed, in some sense the very greatness of the genre depended on its *not* being canonized by official criticism as had been the tragedy and the epic. As a practicing novelist, Galdós in the tradition of Cervantes sees justifiable disesteem for the genre as a way of making his own work all the more significant. The existence and popularity of the execrable "folletines" ("siete plagas del año 65") enabled him to write and his public to comprehend the originality of *Tormento.* At the same time, production of weekly chapters (a source of revenue, which he, like Dickens, exploited) was an "excelente medio de comunicación," which created a receptive public.

Precursors are convenient, but their mere existence does not constitute a complete answer to this preliminary interrogation of the novel in terms of the nineteenth century and of the nineteenth century in terms of the novel. The remarkable interaction of history and fiction, which was achieved in France by Balzac and Zola and in Spain by Galdós and Leopoldo Alas, was not made possible because Goethe showed the way but because something had happened to history that transformed it from the record of the growth of a nation or the ascent of mankind as a whole toward the light (for which it was esteemed, when it was esteemed, in the eighteenth century)[20] into a form of personal experience. Looked at in this way (but not yet in terms of the individual lives who experienced it), the answer is quite simple: history had suddenly changed its tempo. It had suddenly accelerated, and, as a result, a Balzac or a Galdós, along with his characters and readers, was able to identify with the crises of the 1820s, the 1840s, or the 1860s, because in their century historical time seemed to be moving forward (or backwards as Balzac and a few others maintained) at roughly the same pace as biological time. Stated pedantically as a "law," the novel can only achieve the dignity of the epic, and the immense historical testimony of a Balzac, a Dickens, or a Galdós can only be recorded fictionally when the changes in ourselves are in phase with the changes in our society.

It can reasonably be maintained that in one way or another men have always been conscious, as Clavería phrased it, of being "inserted" in the flow of the times. Thus, in earlier ages entire reigns and even dynasties had constituted the human heterogeneity of

See Hans Hinterhäuser, Die "Episodios nacionales" von Benito Pérez Galdós, Hamburg, 1961, pp. 178–179. (Hereafter cited as Die "Episodios.") Perhaps the most prestigious, and so the most mistaken, expression of this condemnation is that of Thoreau in 1839 (a date too proximate for us to blame him for not having read Le Père Goriot), who complains that in "days of cheap printing" "we moderns . . . collect only the raw materials of biography and history." A Week on the Concord and Merrimack Rivers, "Sunday.") For a survey of more recent disapproval based on comparable aesthetic (rather than moral) criteria, see E. Noulet, "Literary Problems," Diogenes, no. 14, 1956, pp. 102–118.

[20] "The authentic problem of 18th century historiography was to trace the course which leads from barbarousness to the development of universal science." Dilthey, El mundo histórico, p. 367; Gesämmelte Schriften, ed. Paul Ritter, Leipzig and Berlin, 1927, vol. 3, pp. 230–231.

time. "When the King used to gamble, we were all gamblers; but now that the Queen studies, behold us all turned into students," was the wry observation of the royal chronicler of Isabel "la Católica."[21] And, conversely, in our own frantic century, history has been accelerated to a degree that far surpasses the capabilities of our tissues and our ratiocination. The observations first of Henry Adams and much later of Whitehead on the increasingly rapid tempo of change were as premonitory, if not as poetically striking, as Yeats's "widening gyre."[22] Since then, each of us has discovered personally that he or she has been evicted from the house of history, which was the dwelling, sometimes cozy, sometimes haunted, of our grandparents and their novelists. By the end of the century Galdós himself, whose historical antennae were of unsurpassed sensitivity, began to detect the difference: compared to the temporal experience of the Roman-

[21] Jugaba el Rey, éramos todos tahures; studia la Reina, somos agora studiantes." Juan de Lucena, *Epístola exhortatoria a las letras*, in *Opúsculos literarios*, Madrid, 1892, p. 216.

[22] Henry Adams, *The Tendency of History*, Washington, D.C., 1896. By graphing acceleration (mostly of invention and production) according to the law of squares, Adams finds that acceleration itself is accelerating and predicts that thought would come to the limits of its capability by 1921! See also Gerard Piel's *The Acceleration of History*, New York, 1972, for further discussion. We exiles from the century of the novel, however, are concerned less with technology than with the acceleration of experienced change: life styles, mass fears, yo-yos, value-reversals, and cataclysms descend upon us too fast for our lives to absorb. According to Alfred North Whitehead: "In the past human life was lived in a bullock cart; in the future, it will be lived in an aeroplane; and the change of speed amounts to a difference of quality." *Science and the Modern World,"* New York, 1948, p. 74. These Lowell Lectures were delivered in 1925 when Thackeray's "age of steam" still represented the intermediate velocity, which concerns us here. Daniel Halévi begins his *Essai sur l'acceleration de l'histoire* Paris, 1961, by citing Michelet's Preface to his *Historie du XIXᵉ* siècle (1872): "Un des faits les plus graves et les moins remarqués c'est que l'allure du temps a tout à fait changé. Il a doublé le pas d'une manière étrange." These steam-people obviously had no idea of what their offspring would have to face. Consider, for example, Stefan Zweig's anguished adieu to generationality as such in the Preface to his memoires: "At most, one generation had gone through a revolution, another experienced a putsch, a third a war. . . . But we who are sixty today and who, *de jure,* still have a space of time before us, what have we *not* seen, *not* suffered, *not* lived through? We have plowed through the catalogue of every conceivable catastrophe back and forth, and we have not yet come to the last page." *The World of Yesterday*, New York, 1943, p. 8.

tics and those who succeeded them (his own generation in its youth, among others), today "this social rhythm, very much like the ebb and flow of the tide, results in mutations so capriciously rapid that, if an author lets pass two or three years between projecting a work and printing it, it might well seem old-fashioned on the day of its publication."[23] Times and taste are as fugitive and capricious as "las modas de vestir."

Turning now from chronology and biology to the human agents of this new historical consciousness (the people who lived in the nineteenth century), let us take as our text Lukacs' comments on the effects of the veritable explosion of history with which it all began:

> It was the French Revolution, the revolutionary wars and the rise and fall of Napoleon, which for the first time made history a *mass experience* and moreover on a European scale. During the decades between 1789 and 1814 each nation of Europe underwent more upheavals than they had previously experienced in centuries. And the quick succession of these upheavals gives them a qualitatively distinct character, it makes their historical character far more visible than would be the case in isolated, individual instances: the masses no longer have the impression of a "natural occurrence." One need only read over Heine's reminiscences of his youth in *Buch le Grand,* to quote just one example, where it is vividly shown how the rapid change of governments affected Heine as a boy. Now if experiences such as these are linked with the knowledge that similar upheavals are taking place all over the world, this must enormously strengthen the feeling first that there is such a thing as history, that it is an uninterrupted process of changes and finally that it has a direct effect upon the life of every individual.[24]

[23] "La sociedad presente como materia novelable." (Galdós' "discurso" upon entering the Royal Academy, 1897), included in *Ensayos de crítica literaria,* ed. L. Bonet, Barcelona, 1972, p. 179. (The volume is hereafter cited as *Ensayos.*) Balzac in *Béatrix* also seems to sense acceleration itself as a phenomenon of his time: "Telle était l'opinion de nos aïeux, abandonée par une génération qui n'a plus ni signes ni distinctions, et dont les moeurs changent tous les dix ans." *Comédie,* vol. 2, p. 331. It hardly needs to be said that, along with Petsch's "Allgegenwart," a special awareness of temporality seems to be built into nineteenth-century novelists and their novels.

[24] Georg Lukacs, *The Historical Novel,* Boston, 1963, p. 23. In later sections he attributes Scott's driving intention to depict the liberation of "human

15

It is no accident, we might add, that Heine (echoing Santa Teresa, who for apparently comparable reasons calls herself a daughter of the Catholic Church) claims to be "der Sohn der Revolution."[25] Nor is it an accident that Galdós' first major literary project, the "episodios nacionales," was intended to revive for his readers the "upheavals" that ought to have made them historically conscious but that had failed to do so.

That Galdós, like Scott, Balzac, Victor Hugo, and, in his own way, Stendhal, felt that he had to begin by teaching history to his compatriots is in itself indicative of what is wrong with the kind of ex-post-facto generalizations in which Clavería, Barraclough, Lukacs, and the writer of these pages have all been indulging. The revolution in consciousness, which made possible the first biographical novels, had, like the French Revolution, leaders who with greater or less effectiveness and anticipation preached to the multitude, whom they hoped would follow them. And for this purpose they had attractive new genres—autobiographies, journalism, newly descriptive epic poetry, as well as the suddenly serious and self-important novel. Equally influential were such newspaper catchwords (indispensable to this as to all propaganda) as the two hypnotic, binary phrases "modern civilization" and "nineteenth century." This was the human, literary, and rhetorical reality behind the abstract and academic notion of historical consciousness.

Let us now listen to Balzac preaching the new gospel with marvelously ironic ambiguity in *Béatrix* (1838). In the household of Camille Maupin (a fictive name for Georges Sand) "brillaient d'autant plus les merveilles de la civilisation moderne," and her young lover, Calyste Guenic, brought up in "le monde morne et patriarcal" of rural Brittany, is hopelessly seduced by it all:

> To sum up our great nineteenth century appeared to him with its collective magnificences, its criticism, its efforts at renovation in all fields, its immense innovations and almost all of them on a scale suitable to the giant who swathed the infancy

greatness" by major historical disturbances to "the experience of the French Revolution." Ibid., p. 51. For his discussion of the "conscious sense of history" on the part of "the broadest masses," see pp. 172 ff.

[25] Heinrich Heine, *Memoiren,* ed. H. Eulenberg, Berlin-Zehlendorf, n.d., p. 179.

of that century in his battle flags and sang it anthems accompanied by the terrible bass of cannon fire.[26]

Although Balzac, in referring to Napoleon (the giant) agrees with Lukacs on the explosive birth of the century, he also sees it less as a "mass experience" than as a series of individual lessons and discoveries.

In Paris, naturally, where crowds of journalists (the madmen and con men of the new times, according to Balzac)[27] justified or condemned changes in styles, customs, and values in terms of a century that was the first to celebrate itself numerically, the birthrate of nineteenth-century identities was much higher.[28] Nevertheless,

[26] *Comédie,* vol. 2, p. 388. For the equally ironical use of the term "siglo" by Mesonero and Larra, see Rafael Lapesa, "El lenguaje literario en los años de Larra y Espronceda," *Homenaje a Julián Marías,* in press.

[27] See Philippe Bertault's discussion of Balzac's prediction that journalism will be "la folie du dix-neuvième siècle." *Balzac, l'homme et l'oeuvre,* Paris, 1946, p. 25. For a portrait of the total dishonesty of the profession, see, of course, Lucien dé Rubempré's experiences (obviously autobiographical) in *Illusions perdues.*

[28] I do not mean to say, of course, that centuries were not numbered prior to 1801. Indeed, every time a century passed the Academicians responsible for the dictionary were careful to update the illustration of their principal definition of "siècle" by changing its numerical designation. Nevertheless, although eighteenth-century intellectuals had thought of themselves as living in a very special epoch, "nôtre siècle," "le siècle des lumières," etc., and although Fontenelle (cited in Littré) had observed with prescience that "les siècles diffèrent entre eux comme les hommes; ils ont chacun leur tour d'imagination que leur est propre," they did not use the numerical designation as a kind of "shorthand" form of self-identification or as a means of setting the past apart from the new world they found themselves inhabiting. As John Stuart Mill (perhaps the first to use the term in English) explains it in his *The Spirit of the Age:* "The idea of comparing one's own age with former ages, or with our notion of those which are yet to come, had occurred to philosophers; but it never before was the dominant idea of any age." He goes on to remark that this reflects awareness of a "remarkable" distinction of his times from those that preceded and that the result is a division of men into those (usually young) "of the present" who "exult" and those (usually old) "of the past" who are "terrified." Ed. by F. A. von Hayek, Chicago, Ill., 1942, p. 1. Implicit in the very notion of a "nineteenth century" as different from the "eighteenth" or the "seventeenth" centuries was a new consciousness of "generationality." When Mill wrote this passage in 1831, he had just returned from France where he had been in contact with disciples of Saint-Simon, ibid., p. xxiii. It appears that it was Saint-Simon who in 1803 first emphasized the numerical designation when prepar-

even in that history-prone metropolis, it is probably more enlightening to conceive of the mutation of sensibility generationally than
collectively. Using the concept of the generation in the way those
developing minds were beginning to use it themselves, i.e. as a
shared awareness emerging from a common experience of major
historical events,[29] and as it has been systematized by Karl Mann-

ing his hortatory paean to the future, *Introduction aux travaux scientifiques
du XIXe siècle* (Paris, 1807). By 1814 he had taken the next logical step:
the characterization of past centuries ("Au XVIIe siècle les beaux-arts
fleurirent, et l'on vit naître les chefs-d'oeuvre de la littérature moderne,"
etc.). "De la réorganization de la société européenne, *Oeuvres de Saint
Simon,* Paris, 1868, vol. 1, p. 157. He accordingly felt compelled to harangue
the writers of the new generation as follows: "Le défaut d'institutions mène
à la destruction . . . les vieilles institutions prolongent l'ignorance. . . .
Ecrivains du XIXe siècle, a vous seuls appartient de nous ôter cette triste
alternative!" ibid., p. 158. Afterwards, journalists, historiographers, literary
critics (above all de Sanctis), and novelists took over, and the calculated
surprise of the slogan disappeared with commonplace usage. Saint-Simon's
futuristic manifesto was echoed a year later by the title of a journal listed
in E. Hatin's *Bibliographie de la presse périodique français* (Paris, 1866):
Recueil pour servir à l'histoire du 19e siècle.

[29] I find this definition more useful than that of a fixed number of years:
thirty years according to the French academicians who compiled the 1684
dictionary, but only fourteen according to Julián Marías. The latter was, of
course, inspired by Ortega, who in *El tema de nuestro tiempo* defends the
notion of hermetic generations as "el concepto más importante de la historia
. . . el gozne sobre que ésta ejecuta sus movimientos." *Obras completas,*
Madrid, 1946–1947, vol. 3, p. 147. (Hereafter cited as *Obras.*) Equally enthusiastic are Henri Peyre, who groups writers as early as the Renaissance
into discrete generations (*Les Générations littéraires,* Paris, 1949), and Réné
Jasinsky, who in his *Histoire littéraire de la France* (Paris, 1965) divides
centuries into four generations. Eduardo Nicol's cogent denial of a "ritmo
uniforme de la historia," however, *Historicismo y existencialismo,* México,
cannot be overlooked. 1969, p. 247. In contrast to the above theories, I propose that from the beginning of the nineteenth century until after World
War I there was a period of more than a hundred years when human life
and historical change possessed more or less the same tempo and when the
notion of generation (not measured in years but gathered about defeats,
regimes, and major events) was not merely meaningful but crucial to historical understanding. Anyone who has lived in our time and has coped
with what could be called the mini-generations of our university students
and with the monstrous accumulation of used history in our own lives will
understand that the concept of a generation in terms of years no longer
works. It was during this period, from *Waverley* to *Ulysses* let us say, that
the novel attained greatness. According to Virginia Woolf (remembering a
conversation with T. S. Eliot), it was Joyce who "destroyed the whole of the

heim,[30] one should imagine a few young men with an acute sensitivity to history (it is significant that Lukacs should have mentioned Heine) seeking to communicate among themselves and eventually discovering together who and when they were. It is, I think, revealing that this was how they understood what was happening to them.

Leaving aside such overtly generational novels as *Béatrix, Le Rouge et le noir,* or Turgenev's initial experiment, *Rudin* (it could be maintained fairly that *all* nineteenth-century novels, insofar as they are fictionally biographical, are in some sense generational),[31] let me illustrate the change with two reminiscences of how it felt to grow up just after the "magic spectacle" of Revolution and Empire had disappeared.[32] The locus classicus (though not the first use of the term generation in our contemporary sense) is, of course, the second chapter of Alfred de Musset's *Confessions d'un enfant du siècle:* "During the wars of the Empire when husbands and brothers were in Germany, the worried mothers brought into the world an ardent, pale, and nervous generation." And then, after France suddenly found herself to be "Caesar's widow," these children, "drops of the same blood which had flooded the earth," had an initial experience of emptiness: we "looked at the ground, at heaven, at the streets and roads; and it was all empty."[33]

---

nineteenth century." *A Writer's Diary,* ed. Leonard Woolf, New York, 1954, p. 49.

[30] "The Problem of Generations," in *Essays on the Sociology of Knowledge,* ed. P. Kecskimeti, London, 1952.

[31] The special generationality of individual novels is frequently discussed: for example, Lukacs on *Illusions perdues, Studies in European Realism,* New York, 1964, p. 49; Maurice Nadeau, who remarks that *L'Education sentimentale* is "une admirable prise de conscience par laquelle Flaubert se situe dans sa génération et situe cette génération dans son époque," *Gustave Flaubert, écrivain,* Paris, 1969, p. 18; and most recently A. D. Hutter on *A Tale of Two Cities* as structured on the French Revolution, "Nation and Generation in *A Tale of Two Cities,*" *PMLA,* 93, 1978, pp. 448–462. But a general assessment of the relationship between the rise of the novel and this variety of temporal consciousness remains to be made.

[32] "L'âme grande et noble de Félicité fût saisie par ce magique spectacle. Les commotions politiques, la féerie de cette pièce de théâtre en trois mois qui l'histoire a nommée les Cent-Jours l'occupèrent et la préservèrent de toute passion." Balzac, *Béatrix, Comédie,* vol. 2, p. 373.

[33] *The Confession of a Child of the Century,* trans. T. F. Rogerson, Philadelphia, 1899, p. 8. Georg Brandes alludes tangentially to this preliminary

Along with this intense awareness of vacancy (as Scott Fitz-gerald's alter ego, Amory Blaine, was still able to realize in 1919, to belong to a generation is to see reality in a new way),[34] there was the intuition of a new kind of time: historical time. Musset is even more expressive on this dimension: "Three elements segmented the life which offered itself to these young people: behind them a past forever destroyed; before them the dawn of an immense horizon, the first glimmerings of the future; and between these two worlds" a wasteland where past and future are intertwined and where "at every step one does not know whether he is treading on a seed or on a shard."[35] Similar testimony relating the experience of revolution, conquest, and defeat to a feeling of belonging to a generation and to a nascent sense for history not merely as a record of the past but as the circumstance of biography can easily be found in Stendhal, Vigny, Hugo, Lamartine, Heine, and others.[36] And in them all the

---

sense of sheer vacancy. In his first sentence he stresses (as does Lukacs) the "hitherto unknown force and magnitude" of the "social and political dis-turbances" with which the century began. He then goes on to call the witnesses "heirs of the 18th century," who find the "folding doors" of the nineteenth open and who have a "presentiment of what they are going to see." Georg Brandes, *Main Currents of Nineteenth-Century Literature,* London, 1901, vol. 1, pp. 1–2.

[34] When he returns from the war, Blaine realizes that "life had changed from an even progress along a road stretching ever in sight, with the scenery blending and merging, into a succession of quick unrelated scenes." *This Side of Paradise,* New York, 1920, p. 250. In contemplating this particular American Land's End of generationality, one thinks inevitably of the fondness for Baroja of both dos Passos and Hemingway. Fitzgerald also would ob-viously have appreciated Baroja. For the steep generational watershed of World War I for the British see Paul Fussell, *The Great War and Modern Memory,* New York, 1977, p. 114.

[35] *The Confession of a Child of the Century,* p. 14.

[36] Among innumerable Stendhalian examples, we all remember this simple comment: "Fabrice devint comme un autre homme" after the battle of Waterloo. For Vigny, see his self-presentation at the beginning of *Servitude et grandeur militaires:* "J'appartiens à cette génération née avec le siècle, qui nourrie de bulletins de l'empereur, avait toujours devant les yeux une épée nue, et vint la prendre au moment même où la France la remettait dans le fourreau des Bourbons." *Oeuvres,* ed. F. Baldensperger, Paris, 1914, vol. 21, p. 5. Lamartine in 1818, before his conversion to liberalism, blamed the new sense of history on the freedom of the press, which had perverted a "nouvelle génération toute entière." *Correspondance,* ed. Mme. V. de Lamartine, Paris, 1881, vol. 1, p. 352. Paul Bénichou calls my attention to the Saint-Simonien

mere fact of biological youth as against biological age is in itself irrelevant. Victor Hugo distinguishes generationally (though he does
not use the term in the immediate context) between those "who
had seen Bonaparte" and those who returned from exile.[37]

As far as the hesitant coagulation of the generation that was later
to be labeled Romantic is concerned, let me cite two sentences from
Edgar Quinet's *Histoire de mes idées*. He begins by sensing the
same vacancy: "Wherever I looked I saw a great emptyness—history, poetry, philosophy," and then adds, "I thought no one else
felt the same way." In that hypocritical and prosaic Restoration,
which most people took for granted and to which the rest paid lip

---

Théodore Jouffroy, who advocated the opposite view in his "Comment les
dogmes finissent" in *Le Globe,* 24 May 1825. He describes the coming generation as disgusted with the moral vacancy of the Restoration and on its
way towards forging "une foi nouvelle." *Le Cahier vert,* ed. Pierre Poux,
Paris, 1924, pp. 73–80. In the same year as Carlyle's *Signs of the Times* (1831),
John Stuart Mill, after contact with leading Saint-Simoniens, made his unforgettable distinction between the "new men" and the "old," who walked
on blindly straight ahead without perceiving that the road of history had
curved sharply. This was the English version of the same confident "foi
nouvelle," which, in even more simplified form, reached Galdós in the 1860s
and was echoed in the title and contents of chapter 18 of *La Fontana,* "Diálogo
entre ayer y hoy."

[37] ". . . le vieux faux goût . . . parle à une génération jeune, sévère,
puissante, qui ne le comprend pas. La queue du XVIIIe siècle traine encore
dans le XIXe; mais ce n'est pas nous, jeunes hommes qui avons vu Bonaparte
que la lui porterons." *Préface à Cromwell,* Larousse, Paris, 1949, pp. 56–57.
Hugo seems to be referring to the outmoded critical tastes and doctrines of
returned émigrés, who, having lived in exile, lacked the acute historical
sensibility of those who were on the scene. Since writing this, I have read
Paul Bénichou's splendid *Le temps des prophètes,* Paris, 1977, and Pierre
Barbéris' Marxist-oriented *Balzac et le mal du siècle,* Paris, 1970, both of
which provide abundant confirmation for the above stated thesis: the virtual
identity of historical and generational consciousness. From the latter I learn,
among other things, that I should have read Charles Dupin, Victor Cousin,
and Lamennais. As for the former, the second sentence of his conclusion
could well serve as an epigraph for this chapter: "En fait, cette epoque est,
autant qu'une autre, une epoque de doctrines, et la nouveauté de circon-
stances l'a excitée a l'être plus qu'une autre, entre un monde ancien détruit
et un avenir obscur." *Le temps des prophètes,* p. 565. Finally, I have received Vicente Llorens' "El escritor en la época romántica," *CuH,* 329–330,
1977, pp. 3–16. He cites Chateaubriand, who laments the plight of old men
surviving after the Restoration in the midst of a "race différente de l'espèce
humaine." *Memoires,* Paris, 1969, vol. 1, p. 429.

21

service, here was a young man looking into others' eyes for signs of his own despair and dissidence. How ironical, he remarks elsewhere, that just beyond his physical horizon Lamartine was also growing up. In any case the result, as we know, was a vast sensibility for history: "It was not a question of lassitude from too much living, but rather of a waiting for life. France resembled a country just emerged from a long winter, not a flower, not a leaf, but a presentment of life and history to come."[38]

Thus began a time, lasting into the twenties of our own century, when the generations of men and the mutations of styles and regimes walked hand in hand, a time when the notion of literary generations was a reality, and above all a time when the novel attained generic empery. Unlike the great novels of the past, in which individual lives are often placed in comic counterpoint with history, don Quijote's hilarious "arbitrio" for vanquishing the Turks, Tom Jones's ignominious failure to participate in the campaign against the Young Pretender, now national and personal biography were one. Not only could history determine individual lives, but, conversely, individual lives could hope to influence the course of history. As Galdós observed at the age of twenty-nine,

> We are very proud of ourselves, but that vice is no more than a slender shadow cast by the enormous achievements of our epoch. . . . The participation of everyone in public life, the justified belief that the individual can influence the future of society . . . is the greatest of all [historical] victories.[39]

Although later in life Galdós was to experience acutely the frustration that inevitably results from such "seguridad" (his private "mal de siècle"),[40] to realize that at the beginning one belonged to

---

[38] Paris, 1972, pp. 177–178.

[39] "Observaciones sobre la novela contemporánea en España," in *Ensayos,* ed. Bonet, p. 128.

[40] The contrast of the above with the pessimism of Galdós' remarks on the same subject in the 1897 Academy speech is striking: "Podría decirse que la sociedad llega a un punto de su camino en que se ve rodeada de ingentes rocas que le cierran paso . . ." *Ensayos,* ed. Bonet, p. 177. Once again Galdós was ahead of his time in foreseeing what is now only too obvious—the extent to which historical consciousness had lost its way. He had been well aware of the dilemma for at least a decade, that beginning with *Fortunata y Jacinta.*

history was an unprecedented and heady discovery. And from it there sprang a new sense that individual, family, city or province, nation, and humanity (as well as their private and collective past, present, and future) constituted a single interacting organism. This is what Dilthey meant by his succinct formulation of the object of history: "the living totality of human nature."[41] Generation would follow generation, each with its separate sense of identity according to the historical events experienced collectively by its members ("Rien n'unit les hommes comme les souvenirs communs").[42] But uniting them all on the scale of the century (in sharp contrast to our own fragmented biographies) was a profound awareness of their historicity as such. These were, indeed, nineteenth-century men and women. When Balzac, describing the effect that Camille Maupin made on her young admirer, used the term "19th century" as the subject of a sentence, he was not being entirely ironical.[43] Novelists, characters, and readers alike were biographical creatures living in their times (their milieu as well as their moment) and in time with their times. The term homo historicus would be pedantic; let us retain their formulation: they were no longer children of God but "enfants du siècle." And if later they were to sicken therefrom, their youth was a breathtaking experience.

Novel and Novelist (I)

It was to this new species that the young author of *La Fontana de Oro* belatedly (and perhaps at the beginning unwittingly) found himself belonging. As the first of his kind in Spain, he was as radically different from Fernán Caballero, Pereda, and Alarcón as Hugo had been from Voltaire. After the War of Independence, Spain had submitted herself to the grotesque, artificial, and uncharacteristically silent seventeenth century imposed by Fernando VII, "el Deseado."

[41] *El mundo histórico,* p. 408; ("die lebendigen Totalität der Menschennatur") *Gesämmelte Schriften,* ed. B. Groethuysen, Leipzig and Berlin, 1931, vol. 8, p. 166. Dilthey goes on to affirm with Viconian faith: "Die Totalität der Menschennatur ist nur in der Geschichte."

[42] André Bridoux, *Le Souvenir,* Paris, 1953, p. 29.

[43] In *Nazarín* Galdós is even more ironically emphatic in using the nineteenth century as a self-conscious subject: "El siglo décimonono ha dicho: 'No quiero conventos ni seminarios, sino tratados de comercio.'" (*1750*)

What followed (aside from a few poets and dramatists and one great Romantic ironist) were mostly timid generations of "costumbristas" and "regionalistas" intent on looking at and listening to those provinces of their native land which they considered to be most picturesque and folklorically therapeutic. Then came Galdós. Within a prose tradition that, although journalistic, was to a great extent antihistorical,[44] there suddenly appeared a writer who knew what had happened and was still happening, and was anxious to communicate what he knew.

As Spain's first authentic nineteenth-century novelist (serious imitations of Scott had never caught on), Galdós revolutionized inherited artistic techniques and reversed inherited values as decisively as a Goya, to whom he felt himself deeply akin. Indeed, such mortal leaps from mediocrity to sublimity have often occurred on the peninsula. One only has to think of the novel as Cervantes found it, or of a Fernando de Rojas suddenly appearing beside a Diego de San Pedro or a Luis de Lucena! In the case of Galdós (as is already apparent in the prophecy of *La Fontana*), the special quality behind his renovation of the novel was its historicity, its increasingly pessimistic Hispanic adaptation of the latest variety of European consciousness.

When in the search for current events the young citizen and reporter used to sally out into the streets of Madrid, remarking with

[44] This generalization is particularly unfair to Galdós' justly admired Mesonero Romanos, who (as Lee Fontanella points out in the forthcoming book already referred to) actually foresaw the future shape of the "episodios" as early as 1839. Writing in the *Semanario pintoresco* of 4 August 1839, Mesonero proposes a Spanish novel, which will combine the Scottian historical form and that achieved by Cervantes when he applied irony to marvel. He seems to have in mind an antidote to the flood of pseudohistorical "folletines" with which countless counterparts of Ido del Sagrario in the middle decades of the century falsified, and indeed "dehistoricized," Medieval and Golden Age history. Romances with such grotesque double titles as *Enrique IV (El impotente) o Memorias de una Reina* or *Don Pedro I de Castilla o el Cristo de Venganza* are, according to Enrique Tierno Galván, "novelas historicas escritas sin conciencia histórica" by authors who have no idea that they, too, are "creatures of history." "La novela histórico-folletinesca," in *Idealismo y pragmatismo en el siglo XIX español,* Madrid, 1977, p. 15. Faced with such widespread and lamentable historical "beatería" among the literate, it is no wonder that Galdós was initially both disinterested in and hostile to the centuries preceding his own.

24

mingled anticipation and resignation, "Vamos a ver la historia de España,"[45] he was speaking the language of his new species. And when he begins the "Preámbulo" of *La Fontana* with an " 'o' identificativa" (the kind of "o" which, according to Carlos Bousoño, is typical of Vicente Aleixandre)[46]—"Los hechos historicos o novelescos contados en este libro . . ."[47]—he was writing it. *La Fontana, La desheredada, Fortunata y Jacinta* and the novels in between are all founded on this same conjunctive equation, an equation founded on Galdós' nineteenth-century way of living and comprehending "lo que aquí pasa." All have as their point of departure "la historia de España," although the first novel places it in the past and the last (in which the *"hombre* del siglo" is Juanito Santa Cruz!)[48] seeks a way to transcend it and to alleviate the contemporary anguish to which it had given birth. As early as the second series of "episodios" Galdós had lost most of his illusion about the future, the same illusions that had inspired the young Musset and the young Quinet, as well as the young "krausistas" of his own time.

When Galdós was a young man, the elision of personal experience, national history, and novelistic creation was unfamiliar to Spaniards, if not to other Europeans. It is necessary to emphasize this if from our precarious vantage point in the 1970s we hope to comprehend him on his own terms. Only by trying to relive how it felt to try to lead that strange, wide-eyed, nascent, and trembling generation a little more than a hundred years ago can we describe, not the neces-

[45] Carmen Bravo Villasante, *Galdós visto por si mismo,* Madrid, 1970, p. 37. (Hereafter cited as *Galdós por si mismo.*) This masterfully assembled book exempts the present writer from having to respect literally the title of this chapter.

[46] "Un nuevo libro de Aleixandre, *Mundo a solas,*" *Ins,* 53, 1950, p. 2.

[47] That Galdós continued to believe in (and enjoy in a way comparable to the Lope of *Fuenteovejuna* and the *Caballero de Olmedo*) this equation is evident in the concluding exclamation of a letter of Fernando de Calpena to his "mother" in *Vergara:* "Madre mía, oigo a usted exclamar: 'novela, novela', y yo digo: 'historia, historia'." (977). The order has been reversed with the passage of years.

[48] Juanito's oft-underlined alternation between revolution and restoration qualifies him as the male representative of nineteenth-century history within the feminine, antihistorical novel that he inhabits. Notice the intentional variation on Musset's phrase, "enfant du siècle." It is curious that Balzac in *Béatrix* presents Camille Maupin (his fictive name for George Sand) as "une révolution" in the backwards world of Brittany.

sity, but the possibility of these novels as they emerged one from another in prodigious sequence. Galdós himself in his *Memorias de un desmemoriado* does not offer as much help. Unlike the novelist, who wrote in the heat of recent events and consequent despair, the septuagenarian memoirist professes to have lost his memory: "Ven aquí, memoria mía. . . . ¿Por qué me abandonas?" (*1661*) This may correspond in part to Sir Walter Scott's facetious notion that novelists who spend their time inventing the lives of others are themselves characterized "craniologically by an extraordinary development of the passion of delitescency."[49] Yet Galdós confesses to the same anguished mental impotence so often in title and text that it would be captious to accuse him of not wishing to remember like Cervantes. His seems to be a genuine forgetfulness, which is particularly lamentable in light of the enterprise we have undertaken.

Nonetheless, as most biographers of Galdós have stressed, in these disappointing *Memorias* there is one specific recollection of an historical occurrence prior to the composition of *La Fontana* that does reveal his state of mind. I refer, of course, to the abortive revolt of the sergeants of the "cuartel de San Gil" in 1866 and to the Draconian punishment that followed:

> The most heartrending, tragic, and sinister spectacle I have ever seen was the parade of the sergeants, two by two in carriages, up the street of Alcalá towards the walls of the old bullring, where they were to face a firing squad.
>
> Overcome with pity and grief, I and some friends watched them pass by. I had not the courage to follow the frightful procession to the place of execution, so I hurried home hoping to find some consolation in my beloved books. (*1655–1656*)

The subsequent journey in 1867 to the Exposition Universelle in Paris, a veritable celebration of progress,[50] made the brutally retrogressive events witnessed at home seem all the more heartbreaking. The enormity of the contrast of "la metrópoli del mundo civilizado"

[49] *Waverley,* Everyman's Library, London, 1937, p. 14.
[50] Among the impressive (and for him intimately depressing) man-made wonders that Galdós could well have seen was a landmark in the history of prehistory, the first exhibit of artifacts designed to illustrate the "Loi du progrès de l'humanité" from the stone age to modern times. See Glyn Daniel, *A Hundred Years of Archaeology,* London, 1975, p. 163.

with his own Madrid could not help but exacerbate Galdós' awareness of being a participant in a near hopeless form of history.

For our special purposes an even more significant recollection is Galdós' discovery in Paris of the novel as a vehicle for objectifying historical and biographical experience. According to his *Memorias,* while ambling along the quais, by chance he purchased a copy of *Eugénie Grandet,* which he devoured without delay ("me desayuné del gran novelista francés") and afterwards "conserved with religious veneration."[51] (*1656*) History, not just recorded but lived with; the novel, no longer a story of adventure or an analysis of feelings, but now a means of historical comprehension: such were the metamorphoses of consciousness he experienced and which concern us. Thus was initiated the process (consciousness, as we shall see, is not just a momentary mental phenomenon but more significantly a flow that is also an accumulation) that twenty years later was to transcend the nineteenth century itself by the creation of Fortunata. Balzac had begun by declaring himself "of all historians the most free"; Zola proposed to exploit the same generic opportunity by becoming a merciless "juge d'instruction" of the Second Empire;[52] but Galdós, when he came to understand what it meant to be a novelist-historian, used his freedom as a creator to transform the genre itself and in a fashion comparable only to the greatest of the Russians.

Let us imagine the young Galdós in the late 1860s reacting to the "crisis actual" by embarking on the epic task that had been achieved for France by Balzac, even though at the beginning he may not have been fully cognizant of where he was heading and how challenging, biography-burgeoning, and autobiography-erasing it might turn out to be. As Spain's first truly nineteenth-century novelist, he was setting forth to discover and explore his times not so much *for* as *within* his compatriots. It was an indispensable task, for, as he

[51] Rodolfo Cardona (citing an early inventory discovered in the Casa-Museo by Josette Blanquat) points out that Galdós had acquired eight novels of Balzac prior to his trip to Paris. "Apostillas a *Los episodios nacionales de Benito Pérez Galdós* de H. Hinterhäuser," *AG,* 3, 1968, pp. 119–142. For our purposes Galdós' vivid recollection of his discovery, however distorted, is more significant than the actual facts.

[52] Both quotations are from Marthe Robert's *Roman des origines et origines du roman,* Paris, 1972, p. 31. Unfortunately she does not give references.

pointed out four years before beginning it, many of his contemporaries still believed they were living under the Hapsburgs: "Pero . . . estamos en el siglo XIX, aunque muchos, cuyos nombres callo, viven o quieren vivir en aquellos felicísimos tiempos. . . ." (1516) This remark, at once rueful and lighthearted, indicates the path that awaited him once he realized the terrible gravity of Spain's historical unawareness: a path less of persuasion or rhetoric than of development in the photographic sense of the term. Minds that had been exposed to history but without realizing it (Lukacs to the contrary) had to be brought slowly through one novelistic immersion after another to a state of sharply focused, historical consciousness. Otherwise his readers would never comprehend who and *when* they were, and the violence and civil disorder into which they had been thrust would seem forever senseless, an insane phenomenon for which they bore no personal responsibility. As Hans Hinterhäuser points out, in the "episodios" the characters (among them Narváez) often compare their fatherland to "una jaula de locos furiosos."[53]

The implications of the photographic-darkroom metaphor will be dealt with in the following chapter. Galdós did not create (nor could he have created) *ex nihilo*. As he started to work on *La Fontana de Oro,* he could exploit (and he knew this) both his journalistic experience and the rudimentary, day-by-day variety of historical awareness with which his prospective readers had been infected by their avid and habitual reading of newspapers. And if he was successful, they too would discover that "la Historia no es un ser muerto, sino un ser vivo" to which they belonged organically.[54]

[53] *Die "Episodios,"* p. 84. The common view in eighteenth-century France that Spain was a nation of lunatics is surely reflected here. See Ruiz Salvador's "The 'Deverticalization Process: Spain in the 18th Century," *Reflexion,* 2, 1900, pp. 153–158.

[54] Santiago Ibero in *La de los tristes destinos (649).* Jerome Buckley's observations on the Victorian sense of history apply equally well to the whole Occidental nineteenth-century experience: "The Victorian looking outwards, could see his whole age in perpetual motion. And in this respect at least, personal time was to a high degree consonant with public time, with the actual objective history of the period." *The Triumph of Time,* Cambridge, Mass., 1966, p. 9.

CHAPTER II

La Fontana de Oro

Novel and News

It is written, or rather it used to be, that Fernán Caballero was the pathfinder of the nineteenth-century novel in Spain, and in one important sense that oft-exploded commonplace of literary history is correct. As the late José F. Montesinos and a number of others have demonstrated, novels and novelists certainly were not lacking prior to the survey-course date of 1849. But the novels worth remembering (as my teacher, F. Courtney Tarr, used to insist in his classes), the imitations of Scott attempted by Espronceda, Larra, Enrique Gil, and other estimable Romantic writers, had been written in solitude or in exile. Fernán Caballero, on the other hand, realized instinctively that the new Spanish novel, in order to function as efficiently as *Waverley* and its successors, must be written for a public—a collectivity of avid and serious readers. Such a novel, therefore, had to consider the expectations and reading habits of those to whom it was directed. Or, as Galdós himself phrased it, "el público nos pide cuentas."[1] Thus, *La Gaviota* was at once the first genuine best-seller in Spanish since the seventeenth century and a trailblazer for novelists to come, because it was directed to the new and inexperienced public that had grown rapidly with the easing of political repression during the last years of the Fernandine regime: the addicts of the weekly and daily press. Fernán Caballero's novel succeeded by giving fictional continuity to the genre of journalistic "cuadros de costumbres" (sketches of local customs), which had since 1832 (according to Mesonero) provided solace to the ever increasing numbers of city dwellers who, having left their native provinces, felt themselves to be cast out from traditional forms of existence.

[1] "La sociedad presente como materia novelable," in *Ensayos,* ed. Bonet, p. 176.

"Costumbrismo" appeared in many forms—folkloric and bourgeois, urban and rural, lyrical and satirical, photographic and nostalgic, visual and oral, olfactory and tactile, and in all of them it contributed both to Montesinos' "rediscovery of Spain" and to the possibility of fictional realism.[2] Although this assertion is by now a commonplace of Spanish literary history, we should not, because of overspecialization, forget the international character of the phenomenon. Thus, for example, the *Pickwick Papers* was first printed as a newspaper serial and reflects a tradition of costumbristic sketches (mostly of country life) going as far back as *The Spectator Papers*. And similarly, according to Bardèche, the earliest novels to be included in *La Comédie humaine,* the "Scènes de la vie privée," beginning with *La Maison du Chat-qui-pelote,* utilize and reflect the discovery of the external world of Paris and provinces in periodical articles ("scènes" and "physiognomies") and in collections such as *Les Français peints par eux mêmes* (1840–1842).[3] The Spanish counterpart with its translated title would appear a few years later,[4] but it took much longer for Spain to produce a writer comparable to Balzac or a public comparable to that which he served as an organ of perception and comprehension.

As Mary McCarthy has noted, by its very nature the nineteenth-century novel has a newspaper quality, as if novel and news were two sides of the same coin: "The novel to repeat has or has had many of the functions of the newspaper. Dickens's can be imagined in terms of headlines: 'Antique Dealer Dies by Spontaneous Combustion in Shop'; 'Financial Wizard Falls, Panic among Speculators'; 'Blackleg Miner Found Dead in Quarry.' "[5] Furthermore, according

---

[2] José F. Montesinos, *Costumbrismo y novela; ensayo sobre el redescubrimiento de la realidad española,* Valencia, 1960.

[3] *Balzac romancier,* p. 181.

[4] See Margarita Ucelay, *Los españoles pintados por si mismos,* Mexico, 1951.

[5] *On the Contrary,* New York, 1963, p. 259. Dámaso Alonso is willing to take this notion as far back as the "arte detallista" of Cervantes, an art which, he feels, is removed as far as possible from Renaissance aesthetics and which is designed to create a sense of reality: "Se diría una técnica basada en el reportaje: infundir esa confianza, esa seguridad, de no estar leyendo ficción, que tiene el lector de un diario." "La novela española y su contribución a la novela realista moderna," *CI,* 5, 1965, p. 34. In my opinion Cervantes was more irónical about his pseudo-reporting than our maestro indicates (viz. his refusal to sketch don Diego Miranda's house costumbristically); nevertheless,

to John Lukacs, the golden century of the press coincided, but not coincidentally, with that of the novel.[6] Headlines aside, however, when the intimate relationship between the writing of fiction and newspaper reporting in the nineteenth century receives the detailed scholarly attention it deserves, it is to be hoped that the sociologist of literature in charge of the project will take into account Fernán Caballero's unsophisticated, novelistic cultivation of what might be called the antinews of traditional folkways abandoned the day before yesterday. The nostalgia of recent loss; the joy of perused recovery amid what Gogol called "noise and crowds and modish dress coats"—these were the intense emotional experiences to be found in Caballero's novels and in those of such successors as Pereda and Palacio Valdés. There is a certain Grandma-Moses-like quality in the works of all three (as opposed to the lurid Dickensian headlines imagined by Mary McCarthy), which is clearly derived from journalism and which, if with less intensity, is still enjoyable today.

At this point comparison with the stepson (as we remember from the curious title, the book is *Don Quijote* and vice versa) of the founding stepfather of the novel may be useful. Just as habitual immersion in Romances of Chivalry made the *Quijote* possible, so "costumbrismo," a journalistic reading course that was in some ways even more naive, made possible not only *La Gaviota* and *Clemencia* but the Spanish nineteenth-century novel as such, those of Galdós included. The crucial difference was that, while Fernán Caballero and her followers saw in unchanging custom an antidote for what they considered to be the contamination of their times with history, Galdós' proposed therapy, as we have remarked, was antithetical. In *La Fontana* and in the "episodios" that followed, he strove to

---

Dámaso Alonso's undeniably valid point helps explain the confluence of the rise of the novel with the augmentation of journalism. Both express the new contextual aspect of nineteenth-century historical consciousness. These considerations are, of course, supplementary to the notion expressed above, that journalism provided a ready-made public with exploitable expectations, much as had the Romances of Chivalry centuries before.

[6] *Historical Consciousness, or The Remembered Past,* New York, 1968, p. 84. For further discussion of the coincidence of the rise of the novel and the growth of journalism and their mutual relationship to technical improvements in printing, see A. J. George, *Development of French Romanticism,* Syracuse, N.Y., 1955.

create indelible historical awareness and to force his unthinking public of newspaper addicts to realize that, like it or not, they were creatures of history instead of exiles from the timelessness of "la patria chica" who read about the evolution or the revolutions of the larger "patria" at best with curiosity and at worst with fanatical rejection. As slyly and as ruthlessly as a Stendhal, Galdós aspired to nothing less than the propagation of his new—for Spaniards— mode of consciousness.

The most elementary of the several techniques employed to this end in *La Fontana* was a variation of that which in Spain had first been employed in *La Gaviota*. It would be difficult to determine if Galdós was aware that Fernán Caballero (whose "cháchara pueril" he disdained) was in some ways his precursor, but it is self-evident that his first novel (as well as many of the "episodios") also strung a rosary of "cuadros de costumbres" upon a thread of intrigue. I refer, of course, not to the rural or regional, but to the urban variety produced by two of his favorite writers, Larra and Mesonero Romanos. Galdós himself had contributed rather archly to the same subgenre in the pages of *La Nación,* and he now saw in it a way of revealing the changes that had taken place in city life since the "trienio liberal," some fifty-odd years before. The description of "la carrera de San Jerónimo," of a typical political quarrel, or of the nightly oratory in *La Fontana* are manifestly costumbristic (and so familiar in style and presentation to a public of newspaper readers)[7] and at the same time long passed (and so unfamiliar). As a result, such descriptions function not only as a simple and easily-assimilated history lesson but also as a convincing demonstration that history had indeed been going on, at least in Madrid.

Galdós' remarks to the reader on the visual aspects of what was then the main street of the capital "village," the "carrera de San Jerónimo," clearly possess the latter function:

> But today, when you see streets for the most part lined with private dwellings, you cannot comprehend what a public thoroughfare, walled in almost all the way by three or four depress-

[7] Monroe Hafter in his "The Hero in Galdós *La Fontana de Oro"* discusses the contributions of "costumbrismo" to that novel. *MPh,* 57, 1959, p. 39.

ing convents, was like in those years. It is indeed impossible to imagine today the gloom that the monastery of la Victoria on one side and the dirty and decaying wall of the churchyard of Buen Suceso on the other cast over the entrance to the carrera [de San Jerónimo]. (*12*)

His added emphasis on only half a century, less than a lifetime, having passed is an added spur to temporal consciousness: ". . . cuán distinto de lo que hoy vemos era lo que veían nuestros abuelos hace medio siglo." (*11*) If neo-Scottian descriptions of castles and tournaments had failed to awaken the public to a sense of its historicity, perhaps a Spanish version of *Waverley*'s temporal sub-title (and melancholy refrain), " 'Tis Sixty Years Since," might be more effective. The description of a past at once both immediate and evanescent would supply in an elementary fashion that "felt relationship to the present" without which, according to Lukacs, "a portrayal of history is impossible."[8]

This deceptively simple combination of urban "costumbrismo" and the historical novel was Galdós' initial literary experiment. As such, it represented the appropriate beginning of a career in the course of which each succeeding novel was to be a new beginning in an unceasing effort to explore the interrelation of national history and personal experience. After finishing *La Fontana* and once underway as a professional writer, his ruthless assessment of the inadequacies of each novel after its publication (he quite properly paid little heed to the usual glowing reviews) resulted in one new experimental departure after another. Only on these terms may we attempt to comprehend the most mysterious and seemingly incomprehensible sequence among those which will concern us: how a *Fortunate y Jacinta* could possibly have been written immediately after *Lo prohibido*. Surely no one has been more concerned with this upward, zigzag path of creative evolution than the late José F. Montesinos. He begins by remarking that "las novelas se sucedieron de una manera inconsciente," but then, a few pages later on, he retracts his apparent consignment of Galdós to the category of "ingenio lego": "Galdós continually learns from his own creative experience . . . and

---

[8] *The Historical Novel*, p. 53.

for that reason among his sources one must include his own works."[9] This, in my opinion, is the most important critical statement that has been made about the art of Galdós.

Nevertheless, we should not equate Montesinos' notion of Galdós' novel-by-novel revision with Flaubert's well-known changes of course, for example, the calculated and self-conscious change in direction from *Madame Bovary* to *Salammbo*.[10] The Spanish novelist was certainly not as "inconsciente" as Montesinos makes him out to be, but, as Mesonero Romanos remarked about his disciple's grasp of history, he was usually guided by faultless intuition, and, as a result, many of the transitions between his novels are more difficult to explain critically than those of his French predecessor. The exception, of course, is *La Fontana,* which did not look back to a book with inadequacies to assess and correct but only to those in an earlier chapter. We are faced there with the simple additive or episodic experiments of the apprentice, not with the inexplicable (even to Galdós) "dialectical" dissatisfaction of a master who has just finished creating an organic whole. When the finely-tuned sensibility of Juan López-Morillas discovers in *La Fontana* a mixture of "juxtaposed" elements rather than a "unitaria creación poética," it is to this page-by-page, chapter-by-chapter innovation that he seems to refer.[11]

As we read on in *La Fontana,* then, we can observe with almost parental fatuousness how Galdós adds other, equally familiar rem-

[9] *Galdós,* Madrid, 1968, vol. 1, pp. 84–86. Montesinos typically remarks that the transition from *El audaz* to *Trafalgar* can be considered the result of a mysterious "proceso de maduración cuyas causas más profundas se ocultan porfiadamente al exámen de la crítica." ibid., p. 75.

[10] Nadeau remarks of *Salammbo:* "D'aucuns, même, s'étonnent qu'on puisse y reconnaître l'auteur de *Madame Bovary* et de *L'Education sentimentale,* comme si la grandeur de Flaubert ne résidait pas dans ce renouvellement d'inspiration et de forme avec chacun de ces ouvrages." *Gustave Flaubert, écrivain,* p. 181.

[11] "Bien sabía el novelista que para llenar el cometido que se había impuesto le era preciso fundir lo psicológico y lo histórico, lo individual y lo social. . . . En sus obras de madurez consiguió Galdós fundir estos ingredientes en un todo orgánico; pero en su primera novela se nos dan todavía yuxtapuestos, irreductibles entre sí. . . . *La Fontana de Oro* se nos antoja una armazón novelesca ensamblada trabajosamente más que una unitaria creación poética." Juan López-Morillas, "Historia y Novela en el Galdós primerizo: en torno a *La Fontana de Oro,*" *RHM,* 31, 1965, p. 274.

iniscences of newspaper prose to his initial "costumbrismo." Let us, for example, listen to the introduction of the political thesis in a speech by the moderate, young military officer, Bozmediano:

> It is deplorable, my friend, that in the imperfect realm of human life the best and most beautiful things always have drawbacks, a circumscribed penumbra, which is inevitably projected from their sphere of radiance and clarity. The most just and beneficial institutions conceived of by men for their common well-being, when first put into practice, have unexpected results, which cause those of little faith to doubt their worth and justice. Political liberty—the application of the state of the most noble of all human attributes—is the fundament of ideal government. But . . . (25)

Galdós, who at that period in his life amused himself with pastiches of various journalistic styles,[12] was well aware of the artificiality of such dialogue. "Es probable que el militar no empleara estos mismos términos, pero es seguro que las ideas eran las mismas." (25-26) It is as if he wished to call our attention to a separate section of editorial comment.

The difficulties inherent in using newspaper reading habits in the context of the historical novel are already apparent in Bozmediano's apocryphal discourse. Aside from the daily or weekly dosage of "costumbrismo" (and other specialized articles of one sort or another), politics was then, even more than it is now, the primary concern of the press. Nineteenth-century political passion ("ardente comme la flamme," according to the "Avant-propos" of the first issue of *Le Mercure du dix-neuvième siècle,* 1823) aside, it was a time (not uncommon in the Spanish-speaking world) when a given nation (say,

---

[12] Bravo Villasante, *Galdós por sí mismo,* p. 29. A more extensive meditation on the complex interrelationship of novel and news in Galdós might indicate, first, his retreat from headlines of the sort listed by Mary McCarthy into those events not considered worth printing, which Naturalists sought out (in the tradition of Fielding, who felt that the proper hunting ground for his nonprofession were "the holes and corners of the world") and which Galdós used to call "chismografía" ("gossipography"). Thus, the subtitle "historia de dos casadas." Then, having created Fortunata as the heroine of human life not only as transcending news but also history itself, he went on to contrive in *Nazarín* and *Halma* splendidly ironical encounters of timeless sanctity and newsworthiness.

Spain itself in 1976) suddenly finds itself faced with a long-forgotten freedom and with the intoxicating possibilities of political choice, which that freedom entails. The result was that, in journals such as *La Nación*, description of and comment on the political events of the day were what was expected, what was enjoyed, and what was offered. But neither opinion-shaping editorials (as we have just seen) nor political reporting could furnish more than a point of departure for Galdós' creative imagination. If editorial generalization and pomposity were unsuitable for dialogue, reportorial objectivity, or its simulation, inhibited the communication of personal experience, which by definition is the raw material of the novel. In both modes of writing belief in the biographical truth of the created character is undermined.

As an example of the incompatibility of the role of the eyewitness reporter with that of the novelist, let us read Galdós' account of the procession of defiant firebrands carrying Riego's portrait through the streets (as a sort of structuralistic substitute for a sacred image).[13] Beginning as a fictional experience ("Lázaro se mezcló en el torbellino. Sus ojos brillaron con extraordinario fulgor"), it is soon converted into an imitation news event:

> La comitiva, desordenada, siguió por la calle de Atocha y penetró en la Plaza Mayor. Allí se difundió un poco. Pero después trató de atravesar el arco de la calle de Amargura para entrar en Platerías. El gran monstruo midió de una mirada el volumen de sus miembros y la anchura del arco por donde había de pasar. El camello iba a pasar por el ojo de la aguja . . . problema de obstétrica sin duda.[14] (*64*)

[13] The same sort of substitution is obvious in *La segunda casaca* when the Madrid mob celebrates its new liberty as follows: "entre lucientes antorchas . . . llevaban . . . el libro de la Constitución, abierto e izado en un palo. La gracia de esta apoteosis consistía en hacer que todo transeúnte besase el libro, previa inclinación del palo hacía el suelo. Se obligaba a los transeúntes a ponerse de rodillas, siendo de notar que la mayor parte lo hacía de muy buen grado." (*1427–1428*) Such examples illustrate Galdós' pessimistic view of the innate fanaticism of liberals as well as conservatives.

[14] "Lázaro joined the human whirlwind. He had an extraordinary gleam in his eyes. . . . The chaotic conglomeration continued along the street of Atocha and entered the Plaza Mayor. There it spread out a bit. But afterwards it tried to pass through the arch of the street of Amargura to reach Platerías street. The enormous monster with a glance measured the size of

The combination of factual comment with wry and somewhat self-conscious imagery is typical of Galdós' initial newspaper style, a style which had its origins in his juvenile articles on the local teapot-tempests of Las Palmas.[15] Its very intrusiveness tends to diminish Lázaro's role as a witness and a participant. Here, as elsewhere, *La Fontana de Oro* resembles a Scottian historical novel less than the sort of junior high school assignment we all remember: "Describe, as if you were a reporter for the *Times,* Caesar's victory over Vercingetorix."

Galdós' use of journalistic modes of communication, however, entailed an even graver danger to fictional existence. Not only does the officious author-reporter tend to speak for and shoulder aside the individuals he is anxious to create, but also the fundamental novelistic art of cumulative characterization is inhibited. To view historical events as if they were current events inevitably foreshortens them and foreshortens those who take part in them. Why? Because the newspaper medium to which Galdós had submitted his imagination only provides daily cross-sections or slices of history. Novels pretending to be narrated chronicles, or derived from romances such as the *Amadís,* can at their best allow characters to grow and change in the course of the on-going reading experience, that is, in the course of the extended verbal time ("Vorgang"), which the reader has been trained to devour avidly. Despised by A. W. v. Schlegel as a form of sheer "restlessness,"[16] feared by Unamuno as a simulacrum of our mortal rush into the future ("Jugo de la Raza . . . felt that time was devouring him, that the artificial future of that fictional novel was swallowing him up"),[17] such obsessive tem-

---

its limbs and the width of the arch through which it wished to pass. The camel was determined to go through the needle's eye . . . a classical problem for obstetricians, to say the least."

[15] See José Pérez Vidal, *Galdós en Canarias (1843–1862),* Las Palmas, 1952.

[16] "One hears praise for the spread of the pleasure of reading in our time. But Heaven help us! What kind of a miserable reading public is it . . . that so restlessly grasps for novelty where nothing really new is to be found? Such lives must be passive, meaningless, and empty." A. W. v. Schlegel, *Vorlesungen über schöne Litteratur und Kunst,* Heilbronn, 1884, vol. 2, pp. 19–20.

[17] Unamuno, *Cómo se hace una novela,* in *Obras completas,* ed. M. García Blanco, Madrid, 1958, vol. 10, p. 871.

porality nevertheless makes novelistic greatness possible. But fiction derived from "cuadros de costumbres," editorials, and on-the-spot reporting have no such potentiality. Their characters cannot develop or be developed. Predefined once and for all in their initial presentation, they are as "flat" as E. M. Forster's most extreme examples.

Nevertheless, there are compensations. The inherent limitations of the journalistic model offer possibilities of visual vividness and striking caricature, in contrast to the "rounded" characters of other novels of whom we retain only blurred and vague physical impressions. What did Swann or Stavrogin look like? It is unlikely that such questions were asked by Galdós' early readers.[18] The cartoon as a visual aide-memoire is the natural companion of the editorial. And such are the inhabitants of this unambiguous, sharply-etched novel world: cartoon creatures all the more unforgettable because of their very inability to accumulate experience. This is not to say that they are not alive, or that they have no feelings. Rather their reactions, as schematically emphasized as their features, are discontinuous and as temporary as the daily indignation of a writer of editorials, or as the onomatopoetic nonwords ("toc," "creec," "vroom," etc.), which provide instantaneous sound effects for the rectangular temporal and spatial segments of comic books, whether political such as the Chilean one referred to previously or any other kind.

There is an obvious difference between cartoons and caricatures, which at this point should be remembered. A caricature exaggerates and flattens the features of somebody who is or was alive (for example, Fernando VII in chapter 41 of *La Fontana*), while a cartoon —I refer now to the political variety—is drawn in order to represent in positive or negative human terms contending forces and positions. It is the latter that is used to populate Galdós' earliest novel. As soon as we come to the lengthy description of Coletilla in chapter 2, we realize what awaits us visually. As the archrepresentative of reaction, he emerges from "la sombra" and poses for us so that we may

[18] With the single major exception of Fortunata (whose physical being, as we shall see, is as elusive as her consciousness), Galdós found many ways of preserving the vivid presence of his characters after he abandoned the lengthy verbal caricatures of *La Fontana*. Comparison with pictorial types and historical figures are the most obvious examples. See Joaquín Gimeno's excellent article, "La caracterización plástica del personaje en la obra de Galdós: del tipo al individuo," *AG*, 7, 1972, pp. 19–25.

inspect and interpret his face feature by feature. The implacable mechanism of the "tendones, huesos y nervios" inside the scrawny neck, the menacing eyebrows still black unlike the rest of his hair, the aggressive nose, which had once been handsome but now resembles the beak of a bird of prey, the pursed, toothless mouth, the "delicadeza timpánica" of the enormous ears, which, along with the owl-stare, can detect the slightest sign of suspicious behavior—all these taken together constitute a cartoon allegory of "una sociedad decrépita, pero conservando aún esa tenacidad incontrastable que distingue a algunos viejos." (*15*) The keen, visual imagination of Galdós' own drawings, however amateurish their execution, shows us reaction personified, physically decadent but sensorially alert, and liable to live forever.

Among the other characters, only the three Porreño sisters, representing authority, lineage, and faith (the values to which reactionary politicians are subservient, as indeed Coletilla is to them), are sketched with the same corrosive care. Yet taken as a whole, the cast of the novel was hardly unfamiliar to readers who knew by daily exposure that caricature "is allegorical in essence."[19] For example, in the liberal fortnightly *Gil Blas* (which defined itself as a "periódico político satírico") of 11 February 1865, there is a cartoon of a young officer with the word "Progreso" written on his coat; he is rescuing a young girl labeled "Política" from a sinister, hooded figure, who is so obviously "Reacción" as to need no identification. Thus also, in *La Fontana,* in contrast to the grotesque delineation of the forces of evil, there are displayed the standard or straight figures of Bozmediano (practical moderation) Lázaro (exalted liberalism), and Clara, the innocent ingénue, who, as the ward of Coletilla, is the first of Galdós' several feminine representations of Spain in captivity. In addition to the multiple incarcerations of Inés in the first series of "episodios," Rosario as a virtual prisoner of her mother, and even

---

[19] "Even when the allegory is more naturalistic, when it appropriates the language of documentary journalism, it bottles up concepts in the form of caricatures. The typical case would be a figure of 18th-century burlesque or a minor character of Dickens. . . . I would argue that caricature, as I have described it, is allegorical in essence, since it strives for the simplification of character in terms of single, predominant traits. The traits thus isolated are the iconographic 'meanings' of each agent." Angus Fletcher, *Allegory: The Theory of a Symbolic Mode,* Ithaca, N.Y., 1964, pp. 33–34.

Isidora Rufete's subjection to her own delusions of grandeur can both be understood as variations on the original cartoon.

Returning to *La Fontana,* it would probably be more accurate to identify Clara, not with Spain, but with the Spanish people. Cartoonists for such illustrated journals as *Gil Blas* or *Cascabel* usually drew Spain as a buxom matron, although if debilitated by politicians and office seekers, she could on occasion be reduced to skin and bones. (It was because of this kind of mischievousness that Galdós mentioned both periodicals by name as participating in political warfare with the "arma terrible" of caricature.) (*1501*) Clara, however, as the biological nation constantly renewed in youth, vigor, and innocence, is depicted, not as a matron, but as a victimized girl, forced to lodge in the decrepit and stagnant Porreño residence. The identification is obvious in Colletilla's own reactionary editorial: "Blessed is the nation that has such an impressionable and docile people, because even though they may go astray, those qualities allow them to be brought back into the right path; and then, with systematic repression, they will not be misled again by anyone." (*136*)

What has happened, I would propose, is that Galdós for his own purposes has split the traditional cartoon representation of Spain into two parts. The Porreños are the matrons, and their residence is a merciless allegory of the physical and historical dwelling place of all Spaniards. As Casalduero and Amado Alonso pointed out and as Chad Wright has since discussed in convincing detail, this antiquated museum of glory in decline, with its perforated religious paintings and ancestral portraits, its broken-down furniture irregularly distributed through dusty chambers, and its stopped clock (reminiscent of that of Miss Havisham in *Great Expectations*) marking the last minute of the last century, is all Spaniards have left to live in and live with.[20] Dickens was fond of describing dingy neighborhoods that have "gone down in the world,"[21] but Galdós

[20] Joaquín Casalduero's *Vida y obra de Galdós* (Madrid, 1951) (hereafter cited as *Vida y obra*) and Amado Alonso's *Materia y forma en poesía* (Madrid, 1960) are both well known and fundamental. Chad C. Wright's detailed study of the development of the house-allegory is to be found in a forthcoming article, "Artifacts and Effigies: Aspects of Symbolic Setting in Galdós' *La Fontana de Oro.*"

[21] "It is one of those squares that have been; a quarter of the town that has gone down in the world, and taken to letting lodgings." *Nicholas Nickleby,*

depicts something more sinister: "una casa-nación venida a menos" inhabited by values "venidos a menos." And Clara (if only Lázaro had been gifted with common sense!) is the only hope. Thus, Galdós not only relies on a tradition of journalistic cartoon representation but also, when he feels the need, improves upon it substantially. And in such a way as to provide the reader with crystalline comprehension (the new aim of the nineteenth-century novel as opposed to the tears and laughter sought by such predecessors as Richardson and Fielding) of how Spain was and is.

Novel and Politics

Of the several journalistic techniques just discussed, it was upon his verbal cartoons that Galdós seems to have placed his fondest hopes. From *La Fontana* through *La desheredada* he was to keep asking and answering novelistically in one way or another a single obsessive question. Stated dispassionately and without the recaptured anguish of the septuagenarian's description of the "paso de los sargentos," it is, simply, "How did Spain get where it is now?" In future years Galdós was to become increasingly preoccupied with the social and moral aspects of the inquiry, as is reflected in Juan Oleza's paraphrase: "¿Qué es, cómo es, cómo se ha formado la sociedad española?, y ¿cuál es el lugar, la misión del hombre en ella?"[22] In Galdós' first novel, however, both the examination and the diagnosis were exclusively political. Although the question was historical, the answer, i.e. the novel, was only superficially and partly historical. Sketches of customs and manners recreated archaeologically, along with imitation reporting on the current events of the "trienio," depict a Spain that was irremediably past. But cartoon characters interacting in a cartoon milieu (not only the Porreño house but also the political café, as Carroll Johnson has shown) could bind past and present together as a single reality.[23] By representing what then seemed to be immutable political forces and

---

pt. 1 in *The Works of Charles Dickens,* New York, n.d., vol. 5, p. 8. (Hereafter cited as *Works.*)

[22] *La novela del siglo XIX; Del parto a la crisis de una ideología,* Valencia, 1976, p. 91.

[23] "The Café in Galdós' *La Fontana de Oro,*" *BHS,* 42, 1965, pp. 112–117.

antagonistic positions, exaggerated visual allegory could show the reader (and the writer) the underlying identity of what was and is. Hence both the fable and the prophecy. What had originally appeared to be an exercise in historical comprehension ("How did now grow out of then?") became an alternately desperate and hopeful demonstration of a political "eternal return."

To understand profoundly Galdós' initial novelistic creation of cartoon characters within a cartoon world, we must take into account the larger metamorphosis of the genre in the nineteenth century. In the preliminary version of *Fortunata y Jacinta* Galdós describes the Madrid of the Santa Cruz family and their friends, relations, and clients as "este simulacro de la realidad que estoy haciendo."[24] Using a similar image, Mary McCarthy terms *La Comédie humaine* "a scale model of the real world."[25] What both writers have perceived is that to use the novel as a means of representing history in biographical terms and biography in historical terms required the creation of experimental replicas, which would enable the author to control and to scrutinize his otherwise incomprehensible wealth of raw material. Faced with a flood of sheer experience of a scope unknown to previous centuries (if biography is indeed history, then every fleeting impression becomes potentially significant and worth recording), the novelist could no longer limit himself to stringing together frightening or funny adventures or to tracing in morbid detail the peripeties of love. Only the calculated construction of worlds in miniature would enable him to study life's daily intercourse with history (read: politics, sociology, economics, genetics, and even meteorology) in a state of supervised simplification.

At the beginning this had been done hesitantly and intuitively (the transition from the older form to the newer one is nowhere better exemplified than by the location of Fabrice's adventures and amours in Stendhal's Parmesan tiny-town), but by the time of Zola and Galdós, the technique had been systematized and perfected. In the case of the latter, it can be fairly maintained that his so-called novelistic trajectory is composed of a series of successively more

[24] Diane Beth Hyman, "The *Fortunata y Jacinta* Manuscript of Benito Pérez Galdós," Ph.D. dissertation, Harvard University, 1972, p. 56. (Hereafter cited as "Manuscript.")

[25] *On the Contrary,* p. 258.

complex and revealing models. Even before undertaking *La Fontana,* however, he was thinking in terms of this kind of controlled experimentation, as is indicated by a "Crónica de Madrid" of 1866 entitled *Desde la veleta:*

> How wonderful it would be to visualize in a single moment the entire perspective of the streets of Madrid! How many things might we see in one instant if we could, despite the natural weight and gravity of the human condition, pin ourselves atop the bell tower of Santa Cruz like a weather vane! What a magnificent point of view would be a weather vane for taking the pulse of the capital of Spain. We recommend to the avid novelists of our time this most elevated desk chair, where they can dip their pens into the gall necessary for the bitter seasoning that today seems indispensable to their genre. Let them climb towers, and there . . . they will be in a position to create a soaring narrative, which from now on we dare baptize with the name of weather-vane literature.[26]   (*1548*)

Aside from the interesting conjunction of irony ("gall") and distance in this miniature manifesto, it is significant for our present purposes in showing that the Lucianesque ascension of the novelist inevitably results in the miniaturization of the social organism, Madrid, which he proposes to study. In light of this the beginning of *La Regenta* takes on additional meaning when Fermín de Pas examines "su pasión y su presa," Vetusta ("más que una ciudad . . . una casa con calles" according to Galdós) (*1449*), through a telescope from the cathedral steeple.

The first and simplest model, the cartoon Madrid of *La Fontana,* had, as we have seen, inherent drawbacks of the most pernicious sort. A cast of flattened drawings inhabiting allegorical milieux can only be presented in a series of rigid ideological tableaux (comparable to the framed squares of the comics): well-intentioned forces

[26] Anyone seriously interested in the future development of *Galdós* should read the article in full and take time to meditate on the quantity of thematic concerns therein predicated: love affairs, political intrigue, domestic dissension, prostitution, commerce, ecclesiastical customs, death, and birth. A similar vertical point of view is to be found in the 1870 sketch "Mi calle," which was recently discovered and edited by Leo J. Hoar. "Mi calle," *Symp.,* 24, 1970, pp. 128–147.

of Public Order intervene to prevent the confrontation of Reaction with Mob Violence (Bozmediano, Coletilla, and the three ruffians who want to be "menistros"); Chivalrous Moderation woos the Spanish People under the nose of Reaction (Bozmediano talking in undertones to Clara while Coletilla is in a state of shock); Reaction threatens Imprisoned Liberalism (Coletilla's visit to Lázaro's dungeon in the chapter entitled "Diálogo entre ayer y hoy"). There is no need to continue. Rereaders of *La Fontana* will have little difficulty in finding as many examples as they choose to look for. And in all of them, as in all cartoons, the meaning is predetermined, sharply outlined, and held still for inspection. Strung out one after another, scenes such as these build a novel that can never be a *working* model. It cannot grow from its original premises and so come to provide—as *Fortunata y Jacinta* was to provide—ever deeper and only partially planned comprehension.

That Galdós was fully aware of the paralysis imposed on his narrative by the techniques of his borrowed medium is manifest at the beginning of the second of the examples just cited, when Coletilla does not intervene in the conversation of Bozmediano with his ward. After sketching the heroine as she first appeared to the young officer, the author feels obliged to comment: "The searching glance of the soldier lasted much less than the time it took us to describe the young lady. For a few seconds the three characters were immobile, each facing the others without saying a word." (27) The cartoon has been drawn with precision, and it must be exhibited for a moment before its figures begin to speak and react to each other's presence. Galdós, in fact, is so committed to his ideological juxtaposition that, even when Moderation begins openly to flirt with the People, he invents a rather unconvincing interval of rage and alienation to keep Reaction from interfering as long as possible.

The same dilemma is even more apparent in the preceding cartoon in which Coletilla is threatened with mayhem for refusing to cry "¡Viva la Constitución!" That this master dissembler, this stealthy secret agent, this archconspirator, should risk his life and the success of his future intrigues for a piddling matter of principle is totally incredible. And again the only possible explanation is that Galdós wants us to witness the confrontation as long as possible, to hold it motionless so that we may grasp its full visual significance. Both episodes reveal a fundamental narrative contradiction, that of the pictorial expression of a static allegorical message imposing itself on the temporal progression of happening. Political stances drawn in two dimensional space have defeated the temporality both of language and of life. Galdós' success in building a model for political analysis has inhibited a deeper comprehension of history and has subverted the already flat cartoon of his principal politician.

It could be reasonably argued that these contradictions are more the fault of the subject, political history, than of the journalistic medium. The introduction of politics into the novel, as both Stendhal and "les bons stendhaliens" have enjoyed repeating, "c'est comme un coup de pistolet dans un concert." The introduction of politics produces exactly the sort of sudden narrative paralysis that we have observed in *La Fontana*. The truth, however, is that there is no conflict between the two explanations. Stendhal was thinking of politics as a chess game in which contending forces confront each other statically: Fabio Conti, Mosca, the Prince, Ferrante Palla. In contrast to the changing, vulnerable, and passionate hero engaged in essentially novelistic amours and adventures, these four characters, in accord with Pedro Laín Entralgo's definition of politics, are "petrified by the final exteriorization of their interior conflictive life."[27] They have, thus, become caricatures of themselves, and their behavior and encounters are better suited for satire or partisan journalism than for the flow of biographical experience, a combined flow of sentiments and chance, according to Stendhal's most famous contemporary, which carries the reader pleasantly or excitedly downstream.[28] After all, Stendhal was better known to his fellow countrymen as a satirical journalist (as well as a popular historian of the arts) than as a novelist.

The foregoing discussion of the difficulties encountered by Galdós in trying to introduce the political novel to a public as yet only exposed to "costumbrista" novels was not intended critically. It would be absurd to demand that the twenty-three-year-old author should have begun with *La desheredada* (a novel based on a more profound understanding of the dynamic identity of politics and

---

[27] *A qué llamamos España,* Madrid, 1972, p. 126.
[28] I refer, of course, to Goethe's fundamental generic differentiation of the novel and the drama in chapter 7, book 5 of *Wilhelm Meisters Lehrjahre.*

45

social change), or that he should have rediscovered Stendhal's ironical contrast of sheer aliveness with political petrifaction. After all, Galdós was a youth committed to the cause of liberalism, whereas the aging Stendhal had lost all political illusions long before writing *La Chartreuse*. Rather, if I have insisted at such length on the vital and temporal inverisimilitude of Galdós' first experiment, it is because his subsequent attempts to correct himself ultimately were to lead to *Fortunata y Jacinta*. The course of his journey to Parnassus was, as it were, set by the remedial steps taken at the beginning, after realizing that *La Fontana* had failed as a working model. Unlike Mark Twain, who was never sure when and why he was great, Galdós, once underway, knew half-consciously and half-instinctively where he wanted to go. As well as how best to get there!

As we have already lamented, Galdós has not bequeathed us an explicit account of his continual dissatisfaction and self-criticism. Nevertheless, to sum up what has been proposed thus far with an admittedly far-fetched comparison (suggested by Clarín's Heraclitean interpretation of Balzac),[29] cannot the dilemma posed by *La Fontana* be understood in terms of pre-Socratic philosophy? Galdós had to choose—but at the same time could not choose—between Parmenides and Heraclitus. For the novel to provide clear and valid comprehension it had repeatedly to bring its own forward movement to a standstill. And in that sense it could be said that the clock of the Porreño sisters, which "marcaba las doce de la noche del 31 de diciembre de 1800," not only stands for their rejection of history but also for Galdós' failure to capture the dynamism of his century novelistically. Unlike Scott and Balzac, Galdós' journalistic and Aesopian choice of Parmenides prevented him from representing historical change as an experience at once collective and personal.

Thus, the indecision about the ending is also explicable. As noted

[29] "Obsérvese la imitación de la manera de moverse la vida, de la sucesión de fenómenos en libros como *Un ménage de garçon, Los empleados, Eugenia Grandet,* y otros muchos de Balzac, y se verá qué es lo que el arte puede alcanzar en esta ilusión de parecerse a la realidad, no quieta, para ser retratada, sino moviéndose, fluyendo, como diría Heráclito." Sergio Beser, *Leopoldo Alas: Teoría y crítica de la novela española,* Barcelona, 1972, p. 145. (Hereafter cited as *Leopoldo Alas.*) Clarín goes on to single out *L'Assommoir* and *La Fortune des Rougons* as continuing Balzac's technique.

earlier, the manuscript ended with a gloomy prophecy, the murder of Lázaro predicting the future collapse of "la Gloriosa," which belied the political lesson ("Be moderate in order to prevail") that had initially been intended. Then, in what I believe to be a lost first edition (1870), Galdós, apparently feeling that it would be better to encourage rather than discourage his embattled liberal readers, replaced in the proofs the catastrophe with the happy ending with which we are familiar. That later editions reject murder in favor of marriage should be attributed to their editors, who were of course primarily concerned with selling books by pleasing the public. Galdós himself, apparently, did not agree. After 1867 political history had continued on its remorseless course, and, as Joaquín Gimeno suggests, the assassination of Prim (described in *La desheredada* as the moral watershed of nineteenth-century Spain) caused Galdós to "interrupt" the conclusion in the second edition (1871) because of new evidence supplied by a "testigo presencial" and to return (one assumes definitively) to the manuscript prophecy.[30] As a novelist who presents history as if he were a political reporter, Galdós is not in control of his subject but rather is controlled by it. The next day's

[30] I am greatly indebted to don Benito Verde, the grandson of Galdós, for permission to examine the MS of *La Fontana,* which he has retained in his possession and which is not, therefore, in the extensive collection now conserved in the Biblioteca Nacional (BN). The manuscript does not contain the pregnant interruption that is to be found at the end of the first known edition (1871): "Al llegar a este punto de nuestra historia, el autor se ve en el caso de interrumpirla para hacer una advertencia importante . . . desgraciadamente la colaboración de un testigo presencial . . . le obligó a desviarse de este buen propósito dando a la historia el fin que realmente tuvo." From this I think it is not unreasonable to conclude that, when Galdós sent his manuscript to the printers, he might have considered the original, tragic ending too discouraging for his liberal readers, and he therefore used his powers as a miniature divinity to save Lázaro. This is the ending I believe was used in a lost first edition. Then, after the assassination of Prim, he returned to his original, prophetic pessimism, justifying the change with the above sentence. I say "lost first edition" because, as Walter Pattison predicted, the "1870" Guirnalda copy in the BN is, according to my student Alan Smith, typographically identical to the 1892 edition. Carlos Seco Serrano states (without specifying the source of his information) that one "logical" ending contemplated by Galdós while adding the final pages long after the completion of the rest was Lázaro should die "a manos del populacho." "Los *episodios nacionales,*" p. 309, n. 45.

events may compel him to reverse the end and so alter the significance of the whole.[31] He is a prisoner of his own technique.

Conversely, whenever Galdós as a creator of lives rather than as a political pundit allows himself to be fascinated by biographical change, preassigned meanings are washed away, as if unexpectedly caught up in the Heraclitean stream. The one striking example in *La Fontana* is doña Paulita Porreño, who, when she falls in love with Lázaro, can no longer maintain her wax-museum representation of stultified religiosity. Instead of meekly conforming to her preassigned allegorical role she rebels violently against it. As a drastically simplified novelistic, rather than cartoon, character, she cannot bear her own image.[32] Almost in spite of himself, Galdós has modified a key inhabitant of his political diorama in such a way as to present us with a precursor of Isidora, Fortunata, and the rest of his future Quixotesque heroines. In the middle, human-interest section of the one-man newspaper we perceive the gestation of the novelist.

[31] This is in no way comparable to Galdós' felicitous modification of the ending of *Doña Perfecta*, which eliminates the "Grand Guignol" anticlimax he had first envisaged. See C. A. Jones, "Galdós' Second Thoughts on *Doña Perfecta*," *MLR*, 54, 1959, pp. 570–573.

[32] Salvador de Madariaga does not cite doña Paulita's excruciating and revealing self-analysis, a passage which confirms his view of the cyclical repression and explosion of Galdosian heroines and antiheroines. *De Galdós a Lorca*, Buenos Aires, 1960, p. 93. Later crises are predicted in these words: "¡Ay de aquellos que no se han conocido, que se han engañado a si mismos y han dejado torcerse a la naturaleza y falsificarse el carácter sin reparar en ello!" etc., etc. (*129*) No less a personage than Nazarín himself expresses the same preoccupation with excessive religious self-dedication in *Halma:* "'Llegará día, si no toma la señora otro rumbo, en que todo ese misticismo se le convierta en un nido de pasiones, que podrían ser buenas, y también podrían ser malas.'" (*1869*) Just as in the case of Cervantes, Galdós achieves greatness by turning over his theses to his characters and then watching ironically to see what they make of them.

CHAPTER III

From *Trafalgar* to *Doña Perfecta*

Novel and History (I)

Confronted with the pre-Socratic dilemma posed by *La Fontana de Oro*, Galdós moved forward boldly in two opposed but complementary directions. After a second novel (*El audaz*, 1871) conceived of as a newspaper history of revolutionary fanaticism (another political fable for his time),[1] he began in 1873 the first series of "episodios nacionales" with *Trafalgar*. Only three years later, he launched his "novelas españolas contemporáneas" with *Doña Perfecta*. The advantages and indeed the necessity of this double undertaking should be evident to perceptive readers of *La Fontana* and *El audaz*. In the "episodios" Galdós could follow the inevitable course of history from the past towards the present, while in *Doña Perfecta* and its successors he could build contemporary models of Spanish society, which would provide deeper comprehension than politically-oriented cartoon sequences. The bifurcation of Galdós' creative path was, therefore, his initial solution to the mutual interference of movement and meaning (fascination with historical mutability as such and the compelling need to freeze it in order to comprehend it), which had crippled the newspaper novels. Only in *Fortunata y Jacinta* would the definitive synthesis be achieved. But even some fifteen years earlier, Galdós' profound preoccupation with what we shall see to be the crucial dilemma of his art of the novel was patent.

The "episodios" resemble *La Fontana* in that both eschew the more remote sources of the Heraclitean stream. Unlike Scott and his followers, Galdós was not at all enchanted with the time long past,

---

[1] See the excellent senior honors paper of Russell Thomas in the Harvard Library archives, "Benito Pérez Galdós, 1865–1871; Journalist and Novelist," 1969.

49

as Amado Alonso has observed.[2] Spain's Middle Ages and Golden
Age, with their escutcheons, monuments, and faded glories (upon
which Ido del Sagrario and his innumerable colleagues fattened or
starved themselves), seemed to him as ridiculously irrelevant as
Camelot did to Mark Twain. We remember, to cite a minimal
example, his amusement at the Porreño family motto: "En la Puente
de Lebrixa perescí con Lope Díaz." The only difference was that
in Spain, unlike Missouri, the past was present not only in archi-
tecture and slogans but also in the minds and habits of most of the
population. As such, it constituted an intolerable weight on "una
sociedad lozana y vigorosa llamada a la posesión del porvenir," which
could not be spoofed or ignored. Galdós, therefore, wisely chose to
begin with a symbolic end (just as *La desheredada* begins with "el
final de otra novela"): Trafalgar, the last imperial gasp of preterite
Spain. In his *Memorias de un desmemoriado* Galdós attributes the
choice to an inexplicable "obsesión del pensamiento" (*1660*), but
perhaps more decisive was that in 1873 the catastrophic defeat of
Spain's own ancien régime could still be remembered by a handful
of survivors. The historical reality of Trafalgar was still, although
just barely, biographical.

Galdós goes on to mention having met by chance one such decrepit
veteran while vacationing in Santander, but, in addition, he could
hardly have been unaware of the "solemne acto" in memory of
Gravina, which had taken place in the Madrid church of San Francisco el Grande. In reporting on that event of the week, *La Ilustración Española y Americana* (5 November 1870) had included
engravings of other participants still living. Trafalgar was, in fact,
perfect for Galdós' new purpose. It recalled the grandiose under-
takings of the dying Empire (follies mirrored by those of Clara's
mother); it suggested the "raíces vivas" of the heroism and patrio-
tism of episodes to come; and, above all, it was still available to the
nascent historical consciousness of his public. It was what his future
readers were willing to call "History" with a capital "H." Journalistic
celebration along with private reminiscences had kept Trafalgar
alive in the same fashion that Gettysburg was still alive during my

[2] "Lejos de presentar Galdós un pasado como pasado y caducado, lo que
hace es mostrar las raíces vivas de la sociedad actual." *Materia y forma en
poesía,* p. 198.

childhood. The memories of the aged Gabriel Araceli could in all verisimilitude actually have been written.[3]

The confluence of historical and biographical time, which distinguished the nineteenth century, was, then, the point of departure for the first two series of "episodios." In *La Fontana* Galdós' intentional contrast of past and present customs had been limited by his use of cartoon models for unchanging political behavior. But now he was free to undertake narration of national history in its own historical terms. In comparing the consciousness of the Generation of '98 to that of Larra and Galdós, Luis Cernuda remarks with justified astonishment on the latter pair's lack of anguished realization that Fernando "el Deseado" had carelessly lost the world's largest empire almost overnight.[4] It was precisely this lack of historical conscious-

---

[3] Hans Hinterhäuser mentions several other possible motives: (1) H. C. Berkowitz's unsupported statement that the young Galdós had planned to write a drama on the Trafalgar theme; (2) Eugenio Ochoa had written a letter, published in the *Ilustración de Madrid* of 30 September 1871, praising Galdós' first two newspaper novels and pointing to the defeat of Trafalgar as symptomatic of Spain's decline: and (3) depiction of naval battles (important because the following "episodios" were all to be essentially land-locked) was a favorite subject for panoramic historical painting in the 1860s and 1870s as well as later. This last statement is, like the first possible motive, unsupported, and it could well be that Galdós' novel helped to stimulate such pictorial interest. Hinterhäuser, *Die "Episodios,"* p. 22. What cannot be denied is that Trafalgar was in the historical air of the early 1870s and seemed to be a more estimable, magnificent, and properly ordered battle than others recently remembered, not only Carlist guerrilla warfare but also the shameful recent naval bombardment of Callao, against which Galdós reacted with scathing journalistic contempt. Trafalgar was remembered in spite of, or even because of, its being lost on a large scale. In any case, it is clear that the "episodios" had to begin artistically with an officially-recognized epic event. The lesser and private aspects of those turbulent years would then naturally follow in its wake.

[4] "Ni Larra ni Galdós, quienes, aunque tan diferentes, tenían una conciencia igualmente clara, se preocuparon nunca por estas otras tierras de raigambre española. Ante su desgarramiento peninsular, Larra, contemporáneo, Galdós, casi contemporáneo, guardian silencio. ¿Por qué? A la visión nacional que uno y otro nos ofrecen, le falta así algo; algo que históricamente había sido parte de nuestra vida, y que se desintegra de ella durante el siglo mismo que ambos vivieron y escribieron." Luis Cernuda, *Prosa completa,* eds. Derek Harris and Luis Maristany, Barcelona, 1975, p. 113. Cernuda is correct in suggesting that Galdós did not agonize over the amputation of the Empire, but to imply that he ignored it merely means that the poet has forgotten his childhood reading of *La segunda casaca* with its acute analysis of the deteriora-

ness, however, even among those who spent their time reading or writing popular romances about medieval Spain, that the new series was designed to remedy. Instead of watching poor Lázaro (a hero almost as inept as Pepe Rey) make his inevitable blunders, Galdós' readers could now participate novelistically in the skill and daring of Gabriel Araceli and Salvador Monsalud in coping with the hazards of history. They were to be enticed into reliving the exploits, hardships, errors of judgment, and narrow escapes of their immediate forebears. They would learn by reading who they had been and, little by little, what they had become—for better or worse.

The intention just attributed to Galdós may well be compared to the aging Américo Castro's epic attempt at national psychotherapy, although the techniques employed and the notion of what had gone wrong were entirely different. Galdós wanted simply to exchange an irrelevant and dead, official past for one that would be alive and meaningful, whereas Castro hoped to comprehend and teach others to comprehend the Hispanic experience as a whole, from the birth of Castile to the violent regimes of the twentieth century. In any case, Galdós' exclusive attention to the "raices vivas del presente" succeeded in its aims. Generations of his readers did discard their costumbristic view of themselves as outcasts from tradition; grudgingly or enthusiastically they did come to realize that they themselves were participants in the freshly-minted history "de una España nueva"; and the nineteenth century did become transformed from a newspaper commonplace, "estamos en el siglo XIX,"[5] into a

---

tion that led to the collapse of the imperial edifice. It is a masterful study of the total lack of political awareness that characterized the pompous and corrupt regime of Fernando VII. See, for example, page *1378* where Galdós in a sense answers Cernuda's question. With such a regime what else could have been expected? One cannot agonize over the inevitable. "Despidámonos de las Américas," as Fernando VII remarks with a shrug in *Memorias de un cortesano de 1815. (1329)*

[5] See Galdós' amused and rueful comments on those who were ignorant of "when" they "were" (page 28). The task of teaching them not history but their own historicity led to the sudden amplification of his narrative efforts. At first this was not very complex, and by the time of *Fortunata y Jacinta* he was to meet the challenge that, according to Donald Fanger, "alternately exhilarated and paralyzed Gogol. . . . Russia was awaiting the advent of a work of prose art in which it might at length recognize its own features and its own voice." *The Creation of Nicolai Gogol*, Cambridge, Mass., 1979, p. 35.

meaningful reality.[6] As Clara Lida has pointed out, history mattered to Galdós, not for its own sake (he was the opposite of don Cayetano), but as "clásica *magistra vitae*."[7] Historians and reporters had done their work; patiently compiled chronicles and newspaper sources were waiting; it only required the magic of the novel for conversion of the known into formative experience.

Emphasizing the same abstract noun, experience, Montesinos exclaims admiringly at the magnitude of Galdós' undertaking: "rehace la experiencia de su nación y su siglo."[8] Yet I think his verb, "rehacer," also deserves our attention. In the first place, it indicates the immeasurable distance that separates epic "episodios" such as *Zaragoza* or *La batalla de los Arapiles* from the battle of Waterloo as presented by Stendhal in *La Chartreuse de Parme*. For it could be said not unfairly that what Stendhal is attempting in this potential "episodio" is to *"deshacer* la experiencia de su nación y su siglo."* Only Tolstoy's genius could depict the great military encounters of the nineteenth century at once epically and novelistically. In the second place, the notion of "remaking" implies changing, the adaptation of history to one's own magisterial and humanistic necessities. In the later series we constantly find Galdós wrestling with his material, trying to tell us how Spanish history should have been, or would have been if. . . .[9] *El abuelo* amounts

[6] This was explained perceptively by the young Azorín in his 1912 essay on Galdós included in *Lecturas españolas*. Azorín qualifies Galdós as the first Spaniard to experiment with "contemporary realism," which "establece [una relación] entre el hecho real, visible, ostensible y la serie de causas y concausas que lo han determinado." As a result he was instrumental in creating "una conciencia nacional" and in putting "la nueva generación de escritores" in existential debt for "lo más íntimo y profundo de su ser." *Obras Completas,* ed. Angel Cruz Rueda, Madrid, 1947, vol. 2, pp. 627–630. For similar appreciation see also the essay on the Generation of '98 included in his *Clásicos y modernos*, 1913. Although he did not use the terminology employed here, Azorín clearly recognized Galdós' application of neo-Romantic historical consciousness to earlier naive costumbristic observation of rural and metropolitan life. That is, the nineteenth-century novel was born in Spain by a process of midwifery that will not be unfamiliar to students of other national literatures.

[7] "Galdós y los *Episodios nacionales:* una historia del liberalismo español," *AG,* 3, 1968, p. 62.

[8] *Galdós,* vol. 1, p. xv.

[9] Joaquín Casalduero describes these last "episodios" as follows: "Galdós, en lugar de la 'historia de lo que fue', cree que hubiera tenido que escribir la

essentially to a conscious manifesto in favor of recreating rather than merely reproducing history. We cannot, therefore, help but suspect that even in the first two series Montesinos' apparently innocent verb, "rehacer," implies both imaginative salvation and imaginative condemnation of the past. Except for the novels themselves, the reticent author does not provide us with a single clue to his intentions.

When in his *Memorias* Galdós recalls the gestation of the first series, his modesty seems almost complacent: "In my memory the years '70 and '71 pass by without leaving a trace behind, but at about the middle of '72 I return to life and I discover that without knowing why—or why not—I was at work on a series of brief and agreeable historical novels."[10] (*1660*) Awareness after both his commercial success and his achieving exactly what he had wanted to achieve, nothing less than the creation of the Spanish nineteenth century, resulted in self-camouflage. That Galdós' "sin saber por qué sí ni por qué no" was indeed disingenuous is demonstrated by his calculated and radical modifications of the traditional shape of historical novels. The "episodios" differ from the Scottian model not only in being "agreeable" and "brief," although both qualifications are correct, but in their very conception. Today we would term them "nouveaux

---

'historia de lo que debía haber sido'. No una historia imaginaria, sino una utopía del pasado; no una historia normativa, sino combativa, esto es, junto al diagnóstico, la manera de vencer el mal. Mostrar lo que era doña Perfecta y su sociedad; junto a ello haber indicado cómo había que combatirla." "Historia y novela," *Homenaje,* p. 139. At this Land's End of historical consciousness, the inescapable and unforgettable horrors that had really happened (for example, the execution of the sergeants in *La de los tristes destinos*) appear almost as if they were dreams, or nightmares (*650*)

[10] It is undoubtedly true that, as Montesinos remarks somewhat superciliously, Galdós' initial cultivation of the historical genre was produced by "experiencias y meditaciones suscitadas por las zaragatas de la Gloriosa." *Galdós,* vol. 1, p. 75. That is, the "episodios" continued to express in a more systematic way the fear and pessimism of the *La Fontana* manuscript. This generalization, however, is ostensibly more supported by the pessimistic second series (which was clearly *not* "amena") than by the more celebrative and optimistic didacticism of the first. In the latter, Galdós was engaged in therapeutic meditation on possibilities of generational renewal as well as in analyzing failure and expressing disappointment. He seems to have been trying to resist and to help others to resist "el desaliento," which, according to Juan López-Morillas, "que por aquellos días roía a las almas que más se preciaban de temple y serenidad." *El krausismo español,* México, 1956, p. 27.

romans" and expect from their author an appropriate amount of polemical self-display. Galdós, as usual, preferred to let what he had written speak for itself.

Galdós' generic innovations modify profoundly both terms of the hybrid, or perhaps it would be better to say redundant, classification "historical novel." But since recent critics have attended at length to the adjective, i.e. the redefinition of history in the "episodios," only two points need to be added for our purposes. First, the use of advertisements from the *Diario de avisos* and other such research as a means of surrounding military and political events with "la vida ordinaria" clearly continues the journalistic and costumbristic composition of *La Fontana*. And, second, as Hans Hinterhäuser has pointed out, Galdós uses these scraps of realism to communicate the endless flow of "la marejada del tiempo." Like the reappearing characters (it would be difficult to overemphasize how much of Balzac was compounded with Scott in the genesis of the genre), who in successive novels appear older, changed in appearance and intentions, and in different states of health, an endless flux of styles, slang, occupations, and distractions shapes Galdós' new temporal design,[11] specifically, the seamless integration of the time of political and military history with the time of personal memory. "We used to do this"; "'We used to wear that." The preference for Heraclitus over Parmenides is consistent at every level.

It is in his metamorphosis of the genre as such that Galdós' purposefulness is most apparent. Ricardo Gullón begins his important essay on the art of *Trafalgar* (understood as a new novelistic departure and not as a juvenile classic to be taken for granted) by remarking that the narrator-protagonist, Gabriel Araceli, is a "muchacho gris, personaje sin relieve."[12] This is perhaps too negative

[11] Hans Hinterhäuser's enlightening explication of these and other techniques for communicating the march of time in nineteenth-century Spain does not fully take into consideration Galdós' apprenticeship as a reader of Balzac and Dickens. Maurice Bardèche explains how Balzac used reappearing characters for exactly the same purpose: "Des omissions calculées, des périodes d'obscurité ou d'absence lui servent ensuite à opposer avec plus de relief deux profils choisis à des moments différents." This is compared to Proust and termed "la 'troisième dimension' des personnages imaginaires." *Balzac romancier*, pp. 360–361. See also Harry Levin, *The Gates of Horn*, New York, 1963, p. 201. (Hereafter cited as *The Gates*.)

[12] "Los *Episodios*, La primera serie," *PhQ*, 51, 1972, p. 292.

a view. Gabriel's immediate actions and reactions combined with his series-long "Bildung" result in trust and sympathy. Sharing, as we do, his essentially healthy and clear consciousness, we know him not as a mere camera eye but as an old friend, who can be counted on to tell us truly not only what happened but also (according to Castro's definition of the novel) how it felt to exist within the happening.[13] But he is not a d'Artagnan, an Ivanhoe, nor even the Lázaro of *La Fontana,* for he seldom occupies the historical foreground. At once a naive witness and an experienced judge (Gullón's analysis of Galdós' dual use of the first-person point of view is extremely illuminating), his life *is* the history he experiences, or at the very least a private extension of it. In that sense Gabriel is a human precision-instrument specially designed for Galdós' experiment with historical time. Or, reversing the metaphor, he is a laboratory demonstration of the lasting compatibility, not to say love affair, of the novel and the nineteenth century.

The intended effect of these innovations can best be grasped in terms of the reader. As a general rule it can be said that avid consumers of historical novels learn about history in the same way that readers of detective stories learn about the law. In the process of identifying themselves with another and more flamboyant life, they absorb without effort or full awareness the author's view of the historical background. Adventure and intrigue provide a momentary escape from the humdrum, an escape as harmless as it is useless, but the costumes, customs, politics, and milieux, which give such novels imaginative shape, are not so quickly forgotten. Most of us, I suspect, know more about the age of Richelieu or of Richard the Lion-Hearted from such reading than we ever learned in school, although, admittedly, if we had paid better attention in class, our notions of those portions of the past would be less nostalgic.

The point of this elementary critical catechism is that Galdós, a hopelessly addicted reader himself, was as aware as Cervantes of the marvelous opportunities offered by the habit. The difference was, of course, that the former, at least at this point in his career, saw these opportunities as primarily didactic rather than satirical. He proposed to involve Gabriel in just enough adventure and intrigue

---

[13] Castro's definition, which I have frequently referred to and will again on these pages, is to be found in *De la edad conflictiva,* Madrid, 1961, p. 202.

to keep the process of automatic assimilation underway and, at the same time, to present history, not as exotic background, but as something alive in an individual life. Heroism not merely as a quality of action but redesigned to allow for clear perception and illuminating meditation; history carefully investigated and recreated as a "circunstancia" (to use Ortega's most famous word)—these were the creative audacities that made the "episodios" possible. By their means, and notwithstanding that he was not yet the novelist he was to become, Galdós succeeded in providing for his Spain what Rojas, Cervantes, Goya, and the "juglar" of the *Poema del Cid* had provided for theirs—renewed self-understanding.

One more thing needs to be said about the intended readers of the first series as opposed to the later ones: quite clearly Galdós seems to have had mainly a juvenile public in mind.[14] I assert this not only because of the age of the protagonist and certain aspects of intrigue and style but also because of Galdós' awareness of the possibilities of amelioration that were inherent in the generationality of the nineteenth century. Like the founders of the "Residencia de Estudiantes" and Ortega himself, Galdós aspired to exempt children from the sins of their fathers, to launch a generation that, knowing the authentic history of its nation, would know what to save and what to discard in the future. That Galdós was, indeed, conscious that this possibility of self-therapy was a distinctive feature of his century is manifest in *Los apostólicos,* in which he describes the deliquescence of the reign of Fernando VII and the tentative emergence of Spain's first young literary generation, that of Espronceda and Larra. As he phrases it, "Youth was opening its eyes, glimpsing in the distance the future greatness of its destinies. Oh valiant generation; you were born in a propitious hour!" (*119*) Like Musset and his fellows a decade before, "they all believed in the presage that they were the beginning and foundation of a fecund generation." (*120*) The next step for Galdós was to create novelistically his own generation, not Romantic but moderate, tolerant,

[14] Martin Green in his recent *Dreams of Adventure, Deeds of Empire* points out that a major sociological change in the nineteenth-century reading public was the literacy of boys, and as a result there was a host of boys' novels written in order to form their character: "For the books which shape ourselves as a nation or as a class are surely the books we read as children." New York, 1979, p. 110.

responsible, and courageous young men of good will modeled on Gabriel Araceli.

But Galdós was not satisfied as he never was to be satisfied. However vivid his fresh awareness of his youthful public might be, the meaning of the proffered experience was ambiguous, as history must be by definition. In certain episodes of high heroism, such as *Zaragoza* or *La batalla de los Arapiles,* where the uphill charge of the English infantry is as moving as the best of Hugo, epic certainly is approached.[15] Such behavior under such circumstances could only be celebrated. But in others, *Cádiz,* for example, there is an antithetical presentation of the explosive mixture of reactionary fanaticism and liberal candor, which (as we saw in *La Fontana*) was eventually to confiscate the spiritual rewards of the immense, popular self-sacrifice. Even worse, even in the epic novels doubts and reservations creep in. Did Palafox know anything at all about strategy? Was doña Francisca correct in her condemnation of Gravina's fatal indecision? After all, by definition Galdós was concerned as much with the judgment as with the patriotic enthusiasm of his generation of young readers. Much later in *La de los tristes destinos* he introduces a young Alonso Quijano, Vicentito Halcón, addicted to reading about the great epic moments of the Spanish past, and concludes that such history is a "ciencia superficial y fragmentaria, portentosa para un cerebro de tan corta edad." (*647*)

Heine once remarked that to "demand their history from the hand of the poet" is a "strange whim of the people."[16] Galdós was quite obviously determined not to cater to that "whim" on the part of his young people; he would neither glorify the past rhetorically nor repeat *La Fontana* by sketching its protagonists as if they were the black and white inhabitants of a motionless and so immediately comprehensible cartoon world. Furthermore, if he was determined to exhibit the epic flaws of epic achievement, he was also capable of appreciating redeeming qualities in otherwise deplorable men and institutions, the totally impractical Cortes of Cádiz and even that royal villain, Fernando VII.

Speaking of the "constitucionalistas de 1812" in *Memorias de un*

[15] See my "Realism and the Epic in Galdós' *Zaragoza*," *Homenaje a Archer M. Huntington,* Wellesley, Mass., 1952, pp. 171–192.
[16] Cited by Lukacs in *The Historical Novel,* p. 56.

cortesano de 1815, Galdós (using Gabriel Araceli, briefly reintro-
duced for the purpose, as his spokesman) typically emits the following dispassionate mixture of praise and condemnation:

> Their errors were enormous. They stumbled from one mistake
> to another as, dazzled by their ideals, they attempted the impos-
> sible. Yes, they were blind, but their blindness was caused by
> gazing at the sun. They made mistakes; they were passionate,
> intemporate, rash, and unrealistic, but they were impelled by an
> idea. To create was their banner; their valor enabled them to
> face the task of reconstructing a crumbled society during the
> uproar of a hundred battles. . . . One can even affirm that they
> were wrong in everything that had to do with method, because
> what they said sagely they carried out childishly. (*1333*)

This particular history lesson (repeated in *Los apostólicos, 111*) is
typical of the second series and was badly needed by Galdós' still
passionately polarized contemporaries. It should also be heeded by
Spaniards in 1978 since it indicates that the unifying theme of the
first series, the inadequate leadership of popular heroism (which,
according to Lukacs, is also manifest in certain Scottian novels),[17]
is ambiguous.[18] We must avoid the temptation to oversimplify either
Galdós or Spanish politics.

There is, of course, a more positive aspect of the discrepancy
between the good intentions and catastrophic results of leadership.
I refer to Joaquín Casalduero's well-known interpretation of the
gradual emergence from below of new leaders embodying new
values and patterns of behavior as a bourgeois "redención del pícaro."
But as was indicated in our previous discussion of the "episodios"

---

[17] "Scott very often shows in a humorous, satirical or tragic manner the
weakness, the human and moral degeneration of the upper strata. Admittedly
the Pretender in *Waverly* [and others] exhibit humanly attractive and win-
ning features, but the chief tendency in their portrayal is to show their inability to fulfill their historic missions. In such cases Scott achieves his poetry
by conveying to us the objectively historical, social reasons via the atmosphere
of the whole, without pedantic analysis." ibid., p. 55. One might object that
both Scott (Fergus MacIvor) and Galdós (el Empecinado) were in this connection equally concerned with character analysis, which is not surprising as
they were after all, primarily novelists.

[18] "¡Singular dialéctica en que alternan lo mitologizante y lo desmitifi-
cador!" Gullón, "Los *Episodios,* La primera serie," p. 307.

as a form of generational education, this was more a program than a genuine historical development. The "paso de los sargentos" *had* happened, and, after the ten-volume reading experience is over, such thematic optimism does not enable us fully to comprehend its possibility. As for the more urgent problem—how to analyze what was wrong with Spanish society convincingly enough to deter Galdós' compatriots from similar atrocities in the future—neither criticism of the old leadership nor celebration of the new could offer a solution. The *Quijote* itself, despite the profundity of its sociological castigation and the therapy of its laughter, had not done better in the short run.

Thus, Galdós, at the beginning of his epic undertaking, as a creator was almost as naive as his creature, the young Gabriel. On the one hand, he expected too much from the novel as a means of comprehension and amelioration. And, on the other, he had not yet realized the truth that Lionel Trilling expresses succinctly: the novel, as "the pedagogic genre par excellence," is the "chief opponent of the heroic view of life."[19] It was a creative lesson he was to learn with admirable rapidity. We can only be grateful, however, for Galdós' characteristic cycle of fecund confidence and relentless self-criticism. Without the first, he never would have undertaken the "episodios"; without the second, he would have been content to repeat his success. The same dual impulse applies to the initiation of every novel he ever wrote, with the single and logical exception of *La Fontana*.

The second series, which narrates events posterior to the defeat of the French (1812–1834), transforms the ambiguous celebration of the first series into a ten-volume exhibition of the bleakest sort of historical pessimism. It is as if Spain, the author, and the protagonist had all three suddenly been nipped by the first autumnal frost of their biographical and historical maturity. Galdós does not quite reach the point of saying "A plague on both your houses!" The pen portraits of Fernando VII, his minions, and the "apostolic" future

[19] *Sincerity and Authenticity*, Cambridge, Mass., 1973, p. 84. He is indirectly quoting Jacques Barzun, but is unable to locate the original reference. Tolstoy's achievement in surpassing this dilemma is admirably analyzed by Isaiah Berlin in *The Hedgehog and the Fox*, New York, 1957, pp. 48ff.

"carlistas" are far too Goyesque for that.[20] Nevertheless, Galdós' description of their opponents could be almost as scathing. For example, in *El Grande Oriente,* written in the same year as *Doña Perfecta,* Galdós' presentation of the stupidity, small-mindedness, unscrupulousness, and self-defeating envy of the rival lodges or orders (Masons and "Comuneros") constitutes an historical analysis far harsher than that of the Cortes of Cádiz we have just listened to and one with which the matron of Orbajosa herself would have agreed. Instead of deluded and idealistic liberals and a well-intentioned moderate government (as in *La Fontana*), fools, knaves, and cowards are the only political leaders concerned with the future. And instead of being composed of comic or picturesque popular types, "el pueblo de Madrid" is bloody, capricious, and cruelly vengeful. Only the protagonist, Salvador Monsalud, who in the later novels of the series emerges as a kind of Larra figure, stands above the mêlée in his corrosive yet clear-sighted discouragement.

As Montesinos observes, these novels are more powerful than their predecessors in their ability to communicate experience as well as in their more sophisticated narrative techniques. They possess a command of chiaroscuro, a perception of depth, and a capacity for describing movement, which enables their scenes of bravura (the Masonic meeting, the death of the King, or the massacre of the regular clergy in *Un faccioso más*) to engrave themselves on our minds in a fashion that neither the cartoons of *La Fontana* nor the panoramic battles of the previous "episodios" could achieve. As specific examples of Galdós' technical improvement we may cite the portrait of José Manuel Regato (a far more oily and convincing agent

---

[20] Scott closes *Waverley* with an evocation of Raeburn's Highland Chiefs and was perhaps the first to use the pictorial technique, which, as Hinterhäuser shows, was fundamental to the "episodios." The presence of Goya in the second series is at best implicit in the atmosphere of certain scenes rather than explicit in verbal reproductions of specific paintings or etchings (as, for example, in the case of the *El 19 de Marzo y el 2 de Mayo*). Thus, we might compare the sinister reunions in the dark and precarious dwelling of don Felicísimo Carnicero to the painter's vision of the *Inquisition* or the *Council of the Indies*. Galdós' familiarity with Goya is obvious in any case, in contrast to Larra's single reference to him in *¿Entre qué gentes estamos?* I have been told by Professor Edith Helman that during Larra's lifetime Goya's work was not easily seen.

provocateur than his prickly predecessor, Coletilla) and the cartoon dwelling of don Felicísimo Carnicero, which represents reaction far more effectively than that of the Porreño sisters.[21] The latter, as we remember, was static and forever petrified, while the former with its flickering lamps (evoking the repeated cry, "¡Luz, luz!") its disintegrating ceiling, and its final collapse (like the Clennam house in *Little Dorrit*)[22] just after the King's death is announced reveals its meaning in a way that would not have displeased Lessing.

In spite of the increase in technical skill, the conclusions reached by Salvador Monsalud (conclusions corresponding to Galdós' own anguish at the assassination of Prim and the catastrophic dénouement of "la Gloriosa") offer little in the way of precise historical comprehension. To say, as Monsalud and Galdós say in one voice, "despotism lies in the heart of Spain and flows through its veins. That is its character; that is its humor, a leprosy inherited from past centuries, which can only be cured by the medicine of future centuries"[23] (*177–178*), amounts only to recognition and resignation.

[21] Don Felicísimo, like his dwelling, is just as caricaturesque as Coletilla. The difference is that the Galdós of the second series (in contrast to the novice author of *La Fontana*) has learned to depict both resident and residence in movement, almost as if he were creating an animated cartoon for the cinema. It is true that the features of don Felicísimo "habían tomado desde muy atrás un acartonamiento o petrificación que le ponía, sin que él lo sospechara, en los dominios de la paleontología" (*149*), but when we see him pick up one fat thigh with his hands in order to be able to cross his legs, the evolution of Galdós' narrative technique is evident.

[22] Another precursor might conceivably have been the house of Usher (Galdós had read Poe in French), but the equally gloomy Clennam house with its creaking murmurs, its flaking walls and ceilings, and the constant need for its candles and lamps to be procured seems much more likely as an unconscious or semiconscious model for don Felicísimo's collapsing dwelling. As for the portion dedicated to his profession (the archives of dusty parchments recording injustices legalized in forgotten centuries), an obvious precursor is Mr. Spenlow's "monkish attorney's" office in Doctors' Commons, "where they administer what is called ecclesiastical law and play all kinds of tricks with obsolete old monsters of Acts of Parliament, which three-fourths of the world know nothing about, and the other fourth supposes to have been dug up in a fossil state in the days of the Edwards." *David Copperfield, Works*, vol. 1, p. 378. For a discussion of Galdós' way of adapting memories of past reading to his immediate creative purpose, see chapter 7.

[23] Such pessimistic comments are abundant throughout the second series: "estos fenómenos políticos, expresión morbosa de nuestra miseria" (*Un faccioso más, 238*); "Pero, amigo mío, ya he visto que los que creía gigantes

What Galdós wanted to know and what he needed desperately to comprehend were the social mechanisms, the human typologies at once noxious and sincere, the underground communal continuities, which connected the fierce partisanship of preterite strife to the hypocritical politics, the encysted prejudice, and the latent, fitfully explosive violence of the history he himself had witnessed. And since the Heraclitean stream was not providing satisfactory answers, in 1876, when the second series was about half-finished, Galdós embarked on a new series of sociological—Parmenidean?—novels: *Doña Perfecta, Gloria, La familia de León Roch*.

Novel and Society (*I*)

Aware of the inadequacy of the historical approach, Galdós had recourse to a solution he was to perfect in later years, which for the moment may be termed "double dialogue."[24] By this I mean that in the act of creation he was at once "talking" to himself and to another novelist. Specifically, he was concerned with responding to the problems that had been left unresolved in the "episodios" and at the same time with adapting to his own creative needs possibilities suggested by his experience as a reader of the novels of his colleagues both native and foreign. In the particular case of *Doña Perfecta* the other novelist was Balzac and the reading was a "scène de province" and a "scène de campagne": *Eugénie Grandet* and *Les Paysans*. The dialogue with the first of these has been admirably studied by Juana Truel in a recent article;[25] here was a novel that Galdós remembered having absorbed as hungrily as if it were

---

eran molinos de viento y aquí concluye mi caballería andante" (*La segunda casaca, 1419*); "Este afán de renovación periódica del personal político, que en otras partes se hace por razón de ideas de aspiraciones elevadas, se suele hacer aquí . . . por el turno tumultuoso de las nóminas" (*El Grande Oriente, 1501*); etc.

[24] As we shall see in chapters 6 and 7, one aspect of Galdós' growth as a novelist is the increasing complexity (and the addition of multiple inter-locutors) of his inter-novel "dialogue."

[25] "La huella de *Eugénie Grandet* en *Doña Perfecta*," *Sin Nombre*, 7, 3, 1976, pp. 105–115. Professor Truel points out that although Galdós' recollection of first reading Balzac after purchasing a copy of *Eugénie Grandet* on the quais is inaccurate (see chapter 1, note 51), the reminiscence does indicate the special importance of that novel for Galdós.

a good breakfast ("me desayuné del gran novelador francés") (*1656*) just before beginning *La Fontana*. It had above all solved the problem of presenting a static rural milieu, not as a costumbristic or pastoral story, but in terms of the nineteenth century novel—the new novel far more at home in dynamic urban or historical circumstances. Simply have an attractive outsider from the capital woo a repressed provincial girl and record the catastrophic but revealing local reactions.[26] The pattern in both cases is identical.[27]

The notion of dialogue, however, implies discrepancy even more than it does equivalence. *Eugénie Grandet* may have provided Galdós with a narrative approach, but it also posed a crucial ques-

[26] As Professor Truel further observes, the use of this pattern does not stop with Galdós. Pereda clearly uses it to "reply" to *Doña Perfecta* by having the intruder from the city import corruption into the innocent society of "la Montaña." It was a reply that did not disturb Galdós at all when read aloud to him by Pereda before publication. From the tone of his letter on the subject, it seems to have amused him: "El éxito de ese libro será completo, y podrá V. contemplar con júbilo el destrozo que su caballero hará en las falanges progresistas. Si la sátira antiprogresista es como me la figuro, y como recuerdo por lo que de la obra me leyó V., no la creo injusta." Carmen Bravo Villasante, "28 cartas de Galdós a Pereda," *Homenaje*, p. 27. (Hereafter cited as "28 cartas.") For Rómulo Gallegos' adaptation of the pattern in *Doña Bárbara*, see D. L. Sisto, *"Doña Perfecta and Doña Bárbara,"* H, 36, 1953, pp. 167–170, and Ulrich Leo, *Rómulo Gallegos, estudio sobre el arte de novelar*, Caracas, 1954, pp. 73–98. The description of rural misery in *Fathers and Sons*, which Vernon Chamberlin and Jack Weiner believe to have influenced chapter 1 of *Doña Perfecta*, is probably only coincidentally similar. See "Galdós' *Doña Perfecta* and Turgenev's *Fathers and Sons*," *PMLA*, 86, 1971, pp. 19–24. Whatever his flaws, Pepe Rey is no Bazarov, and, knowing Galdós, I believe that he would have absorbed, transformed, and adapted other aspects had he read such a fascinating and sophisticated novel.

[27] Balzac was an admirably fecund inventor of narrative patterns indispensable for the further growth of the new novel. In addition to the disturbing arrival of an outsider into a closed society (a pattern springing naturally from the dichotomy of Paris and provinces as can be seen at the beginning of *Béatrix*), I am thinking of the pattern of a heterogenous group that interreacts after being brought together by chance within a tense but temporarily lasting situation as in *Jésus Christ en Flandres* of which the first derivation (or reinvention) was Maupassant's *Boule de Suif*. Never used by linear narrators prior to Balzac, it has since become a mainstay both of the novel (*Ship of Fools*) and above all of the cinema. Related and just as important is Balzac's invention of the pattern of the "family" novel (first adapted by Galdós in *León Roch*): "Aussi regarde-je la Famille et non l'Individu comme le véritable élément social." "Avant-propos," *Comedie*, vol. 1, p. 9. Discussed by Bardèche, *Balzac romancier*, p. 299.

tion about Spanish provincial society as contrasted to that of France. What characteristic vice of rural Spaniards might correspond to the sordid avarice of old Grandet and his fellows? The terrible answer must have been present in Galdós' mind even as he was reading Balzac's novel for the first time: his traditionally and ostensively generous country cousins (famous for their patriarchal distribution of roast suckling pigs and ink-dark wine) were murderously fanatical. It is as if Galdós were asking himself, not what history can tell us about the way we Spaniards are, but rather what is the atrocious failure of our human coexistence as a society unwillingly submitted to history. And, as noted above, how can I, Galdós, find a way to communicate in narrative form my deeply pessimistic conclusions?

Eugénie Grandet, however, was not the sole Balzacian interlocutor to participate in Galdós' novelistic conversation with non-Parisian "scènes." As we shall see (in Appendix I), *Les Paysans* may have suggested to him the use of classical imagery as a means of expressing provincial degeneration thematically. But it also taught him something even more important: in France social antagonism was an expression of class differences and oppressed economic interests, whereas in Spain those who cling to provincial folkways tend to reject outsiders unanimously and without reference to station or wealth. Instead of rebellious and avaricious "paysans" conspiring against their exploiters, all of Orbajosa, from the lady of quality to the peasant, bands together against Pepe Rey, as if he represented to them an alien caste. The contrast between the two societies could not have been more striking.[28]

In his Preface to *Les Paysans* Balzac differentiates himself from Rousseau, whom he regards as having contributed to the absurd deification of "le Prolétaire." In so doing, he indicates the profound discrepancy between his "campagne" and Orbajosa: "J. J. Rousseau mit en tête de la *Nouvelle Héloise:* 'J'ai vu les moeurs de mon temps, et j'ai publié ces lettres.' Ne puis-je pas vous dire. . . . J'étudie la marche de mon époque, et je publie cet ouvrage."[29] Balzac sees rural

[28] Balzac's distinction between "province" and "campagne" (two of his six varieties of "scènes") was pointless for an author mortally concerned with "las dos Españas."

[29] *Comédie,* vol. 8, p. 11.

France during the Restoration as undergoing a relentless, agonizing, yet not immediately perceptible process of social change and class conflict. Hence, Lukacs' Marxist interpretation of the novel, in spite of its author's explicit antagonism to the historical change he is concerned to "study."[30] In Spain, on the other hand, the social agony, although just as inexorable as in France, was in addition shocking in its violence: "Nuestro mapa no es una carta geográfica sino el plano estratégico de una batalla sin fin." (*122*) To Galdós, what was occurring in Spain was not just a matter of social and economic tension but rather a conspiracy on the part of more than half of the population to assassinate the nineteenth century itself. Salvador Monsalud, Pepe Rey, "los sargentos de San Gil," and ultimately Prim himself were the new "judíos," who had replaced "los franceses" in that undesirable role.[31]

Two contrasting encounters will illustrate the difference. Balzac's Père Fourchon, a sort of latter-day "villano del Danubio," confronts the well-mannered and upwardly-mobile bourgeoisie who now possess the Chateau of "les Aigues" with a demand for an authentic revolution: "*Aujourd'hui* n'est que le cadet d'*Hier*. Allez! Mettez ça dans *voute journiau!* Est-ce que nous sommes affranchis? Nous appartenons toujours au même village, et le seigneur est toujours là, je l'appelle Travail."[32] But when Pepe Rey, as a "revolutionary" landowner, confronts doña Perfecta, it is more a matter of totally irreconcilable "moeurs" than the inevitable "marche de son siècle": "I think neither of us is in the right. There is violence and injustice in you, and in me there is violence and injustice. We've become each as barbarous as the other, and we fight and wound each other without compassion." (*466*) It is true, or course, that the lawsuits and encroachments of "el tío Licurgo" and his peasant companions against the Rey estate do emulate the behavior of "les infatigables sapeurs" or "maraudeurs" who nourish themselves parasitically on the forest of "les Aigues," but in the Spanish novel this

---

[30] See chapter 1 in Lukacs' *Studies in European Realism*.

[31] Extrapolating "structuralistically," one could interpret Galdós as saying that fanatical Spaniards *need* "Jews" to blame, to burn, or to expel. See for example, *Los cien mil hijos de San Luis* (*1648*) and *La segunda casaca* (*1421*) for the extended use of the term.

[32] *Comédie,* vol. 8, p. 82.

is less an historical process than a secondary aspect of the provincial crusade led by doña Perfecta.

In a recent essay dedicated to the same problem that tormented Galdós—violence as an Hispanic phenomenon—Pedro Laín Entralgo proposes an historical explanation. Thinking along lines suggested by Américo Castro, he remarks specifically on "el carácter más conflictivo que problemático que en España poseen las tensiones socioeconómicas."[33] Although the basic sources of discord may have been identical to those of Balzac's France, the structure of their expression even in the nineteenth and twentieth centuries continues to resemble that of the "edad conflictiva," which terminated the caste coexistence of the earlier Middle Ages.[34] The secular struggle for preeminence or mere survival, which had ended abruptly for the "moriscos" in the time of Cervantes and for the converted Jews ("conversos") after centuries of agonizingly slow assimilation, was suddenly renewed for liberals and "afrancesados" after the Napoleonic invasion. As Laín presents it, it was as if Spain had been condemned to redream its nightmare past—and the rest of the Hispanic world too, as the recent history of Argentina, Chile, and Uruguay demonstrates.

In the Spain represented in *Doña Perfecta,* the traditionalists (who, when they termed themselves "castellanos viejos," echoed significantly the earlier caste designation "cristianos viejos") viewed the new liberal ideologies in their midst as heresies and properly subject to inquisitorial extirpation. Political opponents were not just adversaries to be refuted or attracted to one's cause but noxious, human weeds to be plucked out by the roots from the flower bed of society, or, as Costa Gavras' colonel expressed it, a kind of parasitical fungus living off the national grape arbor, which can only be eliminated by the use of chemical sprays. As in the so-called "siglos de oro," the "dimensión social" (or, if the reader prefers, Sartre's "l'être pour autrui") tended to invade the individual's intimate life and to convert him into an inhuman being as implacable and intransigent as a Torquemada or a Robespierre. Galdós laments in *La segunda casaca* (as we shall see in a moment, the "episodio" the

---

[33] *A qué llamamos España,* p. 144.

[34] For the complex mixture of motives underlying certain aspects of Castro's "edad conflictiva" see my *The Spain of Fernando de Rojas,* Princeton, 1972, pp. 184 ff.

internal contradictions of which provoked the new novelistic departure) that both sides ("las dos Españas") were guilty; "In this country there's nothing but absolutism in its pure form, in all classes and in all regions. The majority of liberals speak and think of revolution, but their hearts, without their being aware of it, overflow with despotism." (*1419*)

Galdós had already imagined the life and catastrophic death of a potential Spanish Robespierre (Martín Muriel in *El audaz*), and now in *Doña Perfecta* it was the turn of the less pathetically isolated and vulnerable fanaticism of the right. In so doing, he showed himself to be essentially in accord with my oversimplified paraphrase of Laín. As we observed, the inhabitants of Orbajosa do indeed think and behave "conflictively" in the sense that their class divisions and several varieties of economic self-interest do not directly affect their politics,[35] that is, if we can even conceive of the "politics" of a collectivity dedicated to the abolition of history itself. As instinctively hostile as antibodies confronted with a transplanted heart, "los orbajosenses" are as one in their rejection of the historically "infected" outsider, and unaware that their aggresiveness must ultimately be self-destructive. What was occurring in Madrid as represented by Pepe Rey should not be merely opposed or quarantined; it had to be eradicated. It was not simply a question of traditional resistance to change; history itself was the newest form of heresy.

The most interesting result of reading *Doña Perfecta* in the light of *De la edad conflictiva* is a bolder understanding of the former's thematic innovation. As we journey through the second series of "episodios," we sense that Galdós was becoming increasingly impatient with his own work. As before, he obviously sought to present his reactionaries and liberals as precursors of those of his time and to discover in them a key to the meaning of his own political and social experience. This was not a great problem with

---

[35] Angel del Río noticed this solidarity but did not come to Laín's grave conclusions: "Galdós percibió—mientras historiaba la sociedad de las primeras décadas del siglo, de la época fernandina—que la pugna siempre activa entre lo antiguo y lo nuevo estaba radicado en lo religioso, en las creencias tanto o más que en los intereses y en la división de clases." *Historia de la literatura española,* New York, 1963, vol. 2, p. 202. Montesinos makes similar observations, *Galdós,* vol. 1, p. 124.

the liberals, who from his point of view had not changed very much. It is, in fact, plausible that Galdós' devastating portraiture of the Masonic hierarchy was partially inspired by the venal and incompetent politicians who had successively betrayed Amadeo and the First Republic. But the conservative leaders, whose rule he had witnessed, an O'Donnell and later Cánovas and his band of trimmers, did not resemble the fanatical "apostólicos" of the past. (Galdós' intentional exception to this generalization was the ubiquitous Juan Bragas, who on one occasion defines the Restoration *avant la lettre*.)[36] How was he to account, then, for the grass-roots persistence of reaction in the older sense, a persistence which had much to do with both the possibility and the future of the new regime?

The difficulty of comprehending present reaction in terms of the past was due not only to political and social changes in Madrid but also to the genre of the "episodios." In contrast to the stream of history within which don Felicísimo Carnicero and his associates live novelistically, their fundamental changelessness and mechanical movements are comic by Bergsonian definition. Masks that no longer frighten, they seem as clownlike and bound to lose as don Rodrigo, the ridiculously quixotic reactionary in *Cádiz*. Even their predecessor and miraculously reincarnated colleague Coletilla, when taken out of his cartoon world, is no longer frightening.[37] Yet this appearance of absurdity and futility was completely misleading both in their case and in that of their true-blue provincial descendents, and Galdós knew it. Something more than comic perversity, vain stubbornness, and self-defeating wickedness must have characterized their commitment, and to find out what it was the novelist realized that he must complement his contemplation of the present in the past with an investigation of the past as it lived on in the present.

The exact moment when the decision was made to undertake the new novelistic voyage cannot be determined, but I would surmise that it occurred at some point during the composition of *La segunda*

---

[36] ". . . una cosa teatral y de mentirijillas que no alterara nada en el fondo, sino en la superficie, y que contentándose con fórmulas verificase un razonable y justo cambio de personas, que es, al fin y al postre, lo más conveniente." *La segunda casaca* (*1419*) Galdós, as usual, is, as students used to say a few years ago, relevant.

[37] See chapter 7, note 40.

casaca, which was completed in January 1876. The description therein of the two archabsolutists, Carlos Navarro and his father-in-law, d. Miguel de Baraona, involved a valiant but ultimately unsatisfactory attempt to understand their undoubtedly sincere convictions. Of the former Galdós remarks in agreement with Laín Entralgo, "he regarded liberalism as a kind of horrendous heresy even more worthy of cleansing by fire than those of Luther and Calvin. He identified religion and politics, concentrating all his [political] beliefs into a single faith [and those of the liberals] into a single sin." (*1349*) That this explanation, however true, was nonetheless incomplete is indicated by Monsalud's later efforts at a more ample historical analysis. Spain, he says, is "un pueblo de costumbres absolutistas," and customs, like mountains, are the lasting results of time. Thus arises the hopelessness that distinguishes him from his predecessor, Gabriel Araceli. The fault, as Galdós and his spokesman insist time and again, was that of the nation as a whole and not of just one of the two contending ideologies.

The problem—the terrible problem—had at last been posed directly, but it still had not been comprehended in depth, let alone solved. Where to look for enlightenment? The answer may seem obvious once proposed, but at the time it represented extraordinary insight: in those hermetic local societies where customs ("costumbres absolutistas") had not yet been distorted or adulterated by history. Madrid would come later, but now, and here Monsalud presents the next project of his creator, "los pueblos del campo y las pequeñas ciudades" had to be examined. Only there can the novelist and his readers experience "la nación desnuda y entregada a si misma obrando por su propio impulso." (*1429*) So too had believed Fernán Caballero, Pereda, and their followers, with the result that Galdós' unprecedented "menosprecio de aldea" designed to display the unsuspected corruption of the children of "nature" must have been all the more shocking. Only readers of Balzac's "scènes de province" and "scènes de campagne" were to a certain extent prepared for what they would find in *Doña Perfecta.*

Without presuming to invent the literary memoirs that Galdós never undertook seriously (all he says is: "Interrumpí esta serie con nuevos trabajos"), such were, I believe, the immediate circumstances of the genesis of *Doña Perfecta.* The representatives of antihistorical fanaticism in the "episodios" could never be fully understood in historical terms. They were alien to a milieu composed of narrative time. But their contemporary counterparts inhabiting a more or less functioning provincial society (and, later on, Madrid enclaves) were available for close scrutiny. And they had to be scrutinized closely, or the Restoration's sterile compromise would be accepted at face value as a promising new era, and the appalling dangers lurking in the future (the threat that became a reality sixteen years after Galdós' death) would be ignored blindly. Thus, the decision to initiate a new series of novels dedicated to answering the question: what kind of human community could seriously and with iron determination undertake to defy history? Having presumably discovered themselves as nineteenth-century men and women, Galdós' readers were now to contemplate the hostile consciousness of their adversaries, those who, like both Jenara and doña Perfecta, were disposed to solve human problems with one simple command: "¡Mátale!" And if, in so contemplating, they should detect relics of the same degenerate "dimensión imperativa" (as Castro was to call it) in themselves, so much the better!

A radical change in narrative techniques necessarily accompanied the change in human focus. In a novel dedicated to the portrayal of social stasis Galdós could now construct an intricate and exact model without the necessity of allowing for the ambiguities of historical change or of individual growth and decline. In other words, by substituting Parmenides for Heraclitus, he could at long last attain the precise novelistic comprehension that had eluded him for a decade. The objection frequently raised that *Doña Perfecta* is a petrified novel, a narrative tragedy, which conceals far more of its action than it reveals, would be hard to refute. Yet that very reticence is also the condition of its efficacy. After reading it and coming to know its denizens in their society, we realize that we have been led to comprehend certain fundamental characteristics of Spanish interpersonal relations far more profoundly than in the "episodios." Presented without superimposed intrigue, resistance to history has been held up for our close inspection long enough for the meditation it deserves.

Aside from deceleration, the representational superiority of *Doña Perfecta* as compared to *La Fontana* emerges from its characterization. If Coletilla was expertly drawn as the personification of a political stance or force (the notion of party is, of course, alien to him), doña Perfecta is the perfected exemplar of a thousand and one of her kind living throughout provincial Spain. Rather than a decrepit yet frightening verbal cartoon, she is an archetype, an archetype all the more vigorous and dangerous because it feeds on the lives it represents. And the same thing is true of her "august" fellow citizens in that their social typifications, wily peasant, stallion-like "cacique," and so on, are immediately recognizable. A sketched personification *represents* an idea and is correspondingly fixed and flat, but these beings *are* the stagnation of Spanish society. Their "who" is identical to the "how" of their nation. Hence, their inherent stasis is not that of a succession of cartoon postures and juxtapositions; it is rather a pregnant, potentially explosive self-containment, which a "krausista" critic at the time described perceptively as "sculpturesque."[38] Doña Perfecta and her friends, unlike Coletilla, can and do move around physically, but the willed paralysis of their souls strikes us as defectively monumental. Centering their lives around a magnificent but crumbling cathedral, they themselves incarnate a petty monumentality that betrays the grandiosity of earlier centuries.[39]

The assertion that in *Doña Perfecta* social types are transformed into archetypes may be misleading. I am thinking less in terms of Molière and Jung than of Erwin Goffman and (as already noted) Américo Castro. The latent past that lives outside historical records

[38] Urbano González Serrano, review of *Doña Perfecta* in *El Imparcial*, 31 July 1876, p. 4. The passage in question is as follows: "Pero donde revela su estilo verdaderamente escultural Pérez Galdós es en la descripción de los caracteres, en el bosquejo de sus tipos y en la pintura de sus personajes, convertidos todos en *Doña Perfecta* en centros, a que converge constantemente toda la complexión de la obra."

[39] Hence, their overweening municipal pride and self-satisfaction. Orbajosa as a provincial social entity is not only characterized by an apparent lack of class conflict (we need not speak here of its beggars or of its evidently desperate and starving bandits summarily executed by the "Guardia Civil" any more than does Galdós) but also by the lack of desire in its inhabitants to emigrate. The Chekhovian generalization of Albert Thibaudet ("une petite ville . . . c'est le désir d'être ailleurs") is totally inapplicable to our cast of characters. *Gustave Flaubert*, Paris, 1935, p. 98. The possible exception may be "las niñas de Troya," who may or may not have been aware that they might have found "novios" in Madrid.

and does its best to determine the present of our customs, values, and sense of identity was called by a Fernán Caballero and a Pereda "la santa tradición." Galdós, however, saw it in Orbajosa as a repertory of petrified roles, which, although necessary and even admirable in the Middle Ages, were now either superfluous (don Cayetano) or noxious. Doña Perfecta, in other words, is anything but a caricature of reaction; she is a noble, well-intentioned, and even attractive lady whose inherited role (that of being an exemplar of communal values or, as is said in English, a pillar of society) shackles and ultimately destroys her as well as all the lives around her. As such a self-conscious archetype, she is far more a captive of her own virtue than the Porreño sisters, who end by groveling for spilled coins. For if they are caricaturesque in pictorial conception and comic in Bergsonian action, doña Perfecta is fated tragically to hold erect a traditional statue of herself.

In an earlier essay (revised here as an Appendix) I meditated on Galdós' cunning employment of classical references in the creation of such imposing beings. And now, having observed how *La Fontana*'s two-dimensional political model of Spain has been converted into a three-dimensional social model, we must pause again to consider the more abstract problem of the novel as an experimental genre. This notion, as everybody knows, is usually associated with Zola and with his self-conscious exploitation of techniques of social analysis first used in *La Comédie humaine*.[40] As observed previously,

---

[40] One of the major differences between the nineteenth-century novel and its predecessors is its consciousness of the representational dimension of its private lives. Thus, for example, an Evan Dhu Maccombich was created to represent *the* upright clansman, while a Sancho Panza or a Squire Western, who are more or less typical (and so comic), are taken for granted insofar as they exaggerate the traits of given segments of society or historical forces, i.e. the caste of pork-eating "cristianos viejos" or the class of beef-eating rural landowners. For a Cervantes or a Fielding it was extreme typification *within* the social segment that was interesting: Squire Allworthy as opposed to Western; Juan Haldudo el Rico as opposed to Sancho. One cannot imagine Cervantes saying about don Quijote what Balzac says of César Birotteau and his brother: "En saissant bien le sens de cette composition, on reconnaîtra que jusqu'alors les historiens en ont attaché aux événements de la vie la vie individuelle, à leurs causes et à leurs principes autant d'importance que jusqu'alors les historiens en ont attaché aux événements de la vie publique des nations. . . . Les infortunes des *Birotteau,* le prêtre et le parfumeur, sont pour moi celles de l'humanité." "Avant-propos," *Comédie,*

Realism and Naturalism have in common the painstaking construction of miniature worlds, which in their interaction with fictional biographies enabled writer and public to comprehend the novelty of inhabiting the nineteenth century. But Galdós, who ultimately cannot be classified as either a Realist or a Naturalist, was even more boldly experimental. His miniature societies not only were laboratory reproductions to be observed as if they were "natural" or "real" but were also populated by beings whose larger significance (the Spanish people, the ancien régime or whatever) had been preassigned. Such representational characters in their carefully worked-out chess moves along the course of the novel were clearly intended to provide, in addition to comprehension, exact diagnosis.

I suppose that most habitual readers of Galdós are at best only dimly aware of the latent allegorical or representational dimensions of his fiction. To scan a page as a reading experience (meaning, paradoxically, importation of the reader's experience into the novel) is by definition a vivification of particulars—person, event, scene.[41]

---

vol. 1, p. 13. Humanity is seen through the particularities of milieu, occupation, historical generation, etc. From this Bardèche concludes that although many of Balzac's secondary characters may seem "mal rattachés à l'action," by a process of "transmutation" they become "les symboles de toute une réalité sociale, ils expliquent tout déjà par leur presence." *Balzac romancier,* p. 185. It was this new consciousness that first Zola and later Galdós went on to systematize and develop in their different ways. Lukacs indicates that a principal stimulus for this consciousness was German Romanticism with its theories of epic and dramatic art: "These essential features and all important laws of life must appear in a new immediacy as the unique personal features and connections of concrete human beings and concrete situations." *The Historical Novel,* p. 92.

[41] See my "The Novelist and His Readers; Meditations on a Stendhalian Metaphor," *Interpretation: Theory and Practice,* ed. Charles S. Singleton, Baltimore, Md., 1969, pp. 153–173. At the time I had forgotten the immensely pertinent observation of Marcel Proust in *Le Temps retrouvé:* "Car ils ne seraient pas, selon moi, mes lecteurs, mais les propres lecteurs d'eux mêmes, mon livre n'étant qu'une sorte de ces verres grossissants comme ceux que tendait a une acheteur l'opticien de Combray; mon livre grâce auquel je leur fournirais le moyen de lire en eux mêmes." La Pléiade, Paris, 1954, vol. 3, p. 1033. The Stendhalian metaphor of the reader as a violin, which provides the sound while the novelist plays, has been carried one step further. Since writing the above, I have further learned that Bergson in 1889 described the function of the novel as essentially that of bringing us

Nevertheless, unlike Balzac, Flaubert, and Zola, whose representational dimensions of significance (as we shall see in further detail in our discussion of *La desheredada*) are to a greater or lesser extent ex post facto, the casts of every one of Galdós' novels prior to 1887 were microcosms explicitly designed to communicate (or, as we said previously, to "develop") an understanding of the macrocosms, specifically, Spain's nineteenth-century experience. And if this be dismissed as antiscientific because foregone conclusions are imposed on the experiment, two answers can be given. The first is that *all* novelistic experiments (as critics of Zola never fail to point out) are necessarily prearranged, and Galdós has, at least, the honesty not to pretend otherwise. Instead, like Stendhal, he seems to be looking for readers perceptive enough to join him in his novelistic game.

My second answer, suggested by Montesinos, is less apologetic: Galdós' experimentation is indeed genuine, for each novel is a revision and reexamination of the preceding one. In *Doña Perfecta* the change of focus from politics to society adds a third dimension to the cartoons of *La Fontana* and the intrigues of the "episodios." In *La desheredada* the representational model is studied in time, as if it were history in miniature. And finally in *Fortunata y Jacinta* an immensely complex "simulacro de la realidad" uses allegorical rapprochement of biography and history as a potent source of irony. Nor does Galdós' microcosmic experimentation stop there by any means. In fact, it is the fundamental weakness of much of his theater.

So to observe may help define the problem, but it does not offer a solution. Why and whence this constant variable—or varying constant—in the lifelong creation of the world we love? To return to the beginning, we attributed the cartoon of Coletilla and the allegory of Clara's foster home to the writer's journalistic apprenticeship. This was true, but it may not have been the whole truth. Perhaps we should also have taken into consideration Galdós' recent experience as a student. He may have been as bored as his biographers indicate with studying law, but he was well aware that the University he had been sent so far from home to attend was engaged in a process

---

back "into our own presence." *Time and Free Will,* New York, 1960, p. 134. Cited by Robert Penn Warren, *Democracy and Poetry,* Cambridge, Mass., 1975, p. 71.

of radical self-regeneration inspired by the peculiarly Spanish movement of reform called "krausismo."

As this point I must appeal to my own readers for collaboration, for it is reasonable to assume that they (being by definition interested in Galdós) must know at least as much as I do concerning the origins of the movement (the discovery of the doctrine of Karl C. F. Krause by the future professor of philosophy, Julián Sanz del Río, while holding Spain's first government fellowship to Germany in the 1840s), its tenets (at once neo-Hegelian and transcendentalist), and its phenomenal influence (direct or indirect responsibility for almost everything that has since been estimable in doña Perfecta's native land). If by chance they do not, they would be well advised to scan the standard references.[42] For a good case can be made for the proposition that Galdós' intimate contact with "krausismo" and with leading "krausistas" while attending the University of Madrid was primarily responsible for the allegorical point of departure of his novelistic art.

The characteristic "krausista" justification of literature as a means of education, reform, and regeneration is clearly applicable to the early novels of Galdós. Juan López-Morillas in his indispensable survey of the movement remarks that the "new novel" that it proposed for the future was not to be "realistic" but "idealistic" in the sense that it was to be "alimentada por ese deseo de que las cosas sean distintas de lo que son."[43] From this general aesthetic credo to the specific political and social fables for Galdós' time that have concerned us, *La Fontana* and *Doña Perfecta,* was a very short step. And in fables, whether those of an ancient and cynical slave or of a young and anguished (but not yet desperate) reporter, the standard approach is to teach by means of representation. Galdós in later years was to learn far more about the novel and its possibilities than he could even have suspected in the 1860s and the 1870s, but he continued to be "idealistic" to the extent that his passion to change "things as they are" remained constant.

[42] A representative selection would include: Pierre Jobit, *Les Educateurs de l'Espagne contemporaine,* Paris, 1936; Juan López-Morillas, *El krausismo español,* already mentioned; and, more recently, Elías Díaz, *La filosofía social del krausismo español,* Madrid, 1973. The last contains an extensive bibliography.

[43] *El krausismo español,* p. 138.

A great North American contemporary of Galdós once pierced prevailing political rhetoric with the following riddle: "If you call a tail a leg, how many legs has a dog?" The answer is, of course, four, "because calling a tail a leg doesn't make it a leg." And in the same way calling a novel a fable does not make it a fable. The comparison may be more or less apt for *La Fontana* and *Doña Perfecta*, but it would be more exact to say that both Galdós and the "krausistas" knew that, before history could be transformed into fable and the appropriate moral derived therefrom, "things as they are" had first to be comprehended in that unsatisfactory state. Realism had to precede idealism. These were avid and questing minds and they had learned, if not from Krause, from their reading of Balzac and Scott that art in general and the novel in particular provided the truest form of historical understanding, the least distorted means of grasping what Giner de los Ríos called "el sentir común de nuestra edad."[44]

According to López-Morillas, "krausista" criticism had first placed its hope in the drama as the most immediately influential and most direct variety of creative communication. By 1876, however, in a review of *Doña Perfecta,* Urbano González Serrano, one of the group's most distinguished critics, had come to the conclusion that the novel, because of its capacity to portray "circumstancias reales y objetivas" and because of its "espíritu crítico," was "el género literario más adecuado al espíritu y tendencias de los tiempos presentes."[45] González Serrano understood that the novel's new nineteenth-century avatar as a model of "things as they are" could serve not only for comprehension but also for diagnosis and therapy. He conceived of the novel much as Balzac had, but, in view of its capacity for "critical" correction, he wanted it to accomplish a special task for Spain. He wanted the novel to function as a fable, and *Doña Perfecta,* with its remarkable presentation of social archetypes, had shown how that was possible.

How had Galdós effected the transformation? Quite simply, I

[44] Francisco Giner de los Ríos, "Del género de poesía más propio del siglo," in *Ensayos,* ed. Juan López-Morillas, Madrid, 1969, p. 45. In Giner's essay on the epic and the failure of nineteenth-century poets to echo Homer's all-embracing historical voice one can sense the inevitability of this not yet specified conclusion.

[45] Cited by López-Morillas, *El krausismo español,* pp. 136–137.

would propose, by applying representational techniques derived not only from political cartoons but also from the basic tenets of "krausista" social theory. The belief, reminiscent of the traditional wisdom of China, that the moral and intellectual reform of the individual was the only path to the moral and intellectual reform of society had as its necessary corollary the nondissimilarity of whole and part. A typical Sanz del Río comparison begins: "Así como el hombre es organizado en el espíritu y en el cuerpo . . . , así también la sociedad es orgánica."[46] The hoary notion of microcosm and macrocosm, thus, remains implicit in the "krausista" quest for "el racionalism armónico," a complicated way of saying that biography and history can and must be brought to a state of perfection together! Thus, too, the allure of novelistic representation. For if the whole could be cured piecemeal, its ills could also be diagnosed piecemeal, understood by analogy and represented by allegory. As was suddenly patent in *Doña Perfecta,* theoretical discussion and novelistic practice were two sides of the same coin.[47]

[46] *Textos escogidos,* ed. Eloy Terrón, Barcelona, 1968, pp. 92–93. Cited by Elías Díaz, *La filosofía social del krausismo español,* p. 62. A copious collection of such quotations could be gathered from the writings of Sanz del Río and his followers as well as from their reading. The doctrine of the organic harmony of the individual with ever larger collectivities is central to Krause's thought and is expressed in many places and ways in his writings. Thus, for example, "Sehen wir endlich darauf, dass jeder einzelne Mensch ein organisches Glied zunächst höherer menschlicher Gesellschaften ist." *Lebenlehre oder Philosophie der Geschichte,* ed. P. Hohlfeld and A. Wünsche, Leipzig, 1904, p. 170. Or again at more length, "Fünfter Lehrsatz. Das Leben des Einzelmenschen wird bestimmt und soll bestimmt werden nach der Idee des Organismus, wonach der Einzelmensch das unterste, aber doch ein unendlich würdevolles Glied ist in der Ganzen Menschheit." The familiar hierarchy from person to family, to "Volke," and to humanity then follows. ibid., p. 309. One should add that later this notion became a commonplace of nineteenth-century sociology. Jerónimo Vida in his discussion of Albert E. F. Schäffle's *Bau und Leben des socialen Koerpers* ("en donde la comparación entre la sociedad y el organismo individual se lleva a sus últimos límites") holds that Schäffle's ultimate precursor was Schelling but it was mainly Krause and his disciples who converted the ancient metaphor into a "verdad experimental." Jerónimo Vida, "La familia como célula social," *Revista de España,* 109, 1886, p. 183.

[47] Francisco Giner de los Ríos, who dispensed with much of his master's metaphysical terminology, retained the organic image of society with its concomitant "toda persona se constituye necesariamente como Estado." Cited by Díaz, *La filosofía social del krausismo español,* p. 84. Thus, on the one

A comparison with something more familiar to us than Confucianism may help us to understand the matter at hand. Like Christian Science, another errant stream from the same fountain of nineteenth-century German idealism, "krausismo," by maintaining that evil is illusory, an apparition derived from "irrational disharmony," equated the good with health.[48] Society, therefore, was a body, which could be healed cell by cell (meaning individual by

hand, his Bronson-Alcott-like belief that education and the ethical reform of individuals must eventually redeem, one after another, the concentric collectivities of family, nation, and humanity. And, on the other, his judgment of the value of art according to its degree of realization of "esa feliz armonía de lo general con el individual que es el *summum* de la representación sensible." Giner de los Ríos, *Estudios de literatura y arte,* Madrid, 1876, p. 169. Combining these two articles of faith, it follows that because they are ordered in an identical fashion to their times, literature and art are the best means ("el más firme camino") for comprehending history and society. Indeed, as in the case of Galdós, they can be created specifically for this purpose.

[48] A comparison of the two movements, Christian Science and "krausismo," must necessarily take into account Castro's concept of "vividura," the inherent structure of collective preferences and rejections, which distinguish the continuing life of a people. Specifically, the "idealism" of Christian Science is American because "it works," or at least claims to work, while "krausismo" is a new form of an ethical preoccupation that goes back to the *Poema del Cid* and the "ome en si" of don Juan Manuel. Rejecting degenerate forms of that millenary "hombría" ("machismo" and all that it represents), the "krausistas" proposed and indeed incarnated an ideal of inner ethical strength. In this light it is curious to read Giner's scathing review with its attack on the weakness, irresolution, inexperience, cowardice, and complacency of the supposedly "krausist" protagonist. "Sobre *La familia de León Roch,*" in *Ensayos,* ed. López-Morillas, pp. 64–77. In Krause's works we find statements that would have pleased Mary Baker Eddy and her disciples: "Auch selbst die Pflege der Gesundheit und Herstellung der gestörten Gesundheit wird durch den Einfluss des Geistes, durch seine Wissenschaft und Kunst möglich; einmal, indem jeder Geist selbst auf seinen Leib heilend einwirken kann, dann durch die Heilkunst überhaupt, welche sowohl die Kräfte der Natur, als auch die Kräfte des Geistes kunstgemäss zur Heilung anwendet und leitet." *Vorlesungen über psychische Anthropologie,* ed. P. Hohlfeld and A. Wünsche, Leipzig, 1905, p. 245. I should add immediately that this is only a minor aspect of Krause's belief that evil is abnormal and anomalous and that the essence of man is infinite spiritual perfectibility. Furthermore, a brief investigation indicates that those who have sought out the hidden "sources" of Christian Science never mention Krause as a possibility. Galdós in *La desheredada* only mentions mind sickness ("El pensamiento se pone malo, como las muelas y el pulmón" *1086*), but we should not forget the "miracles" of Nazarín.

individual), and the novelist was nothing less than its wise faith healer (or witch doctor). In other words, "krausista" optimism (to us so alien!) was based on the notion that the nineteenth century was sick spiritually as if it were a person. This in turn implied the possibility of *choosing* to be saved (or rather cured) spiritually, a possibility eventually personified by Fortunata on her deathbed. As Galdós phrased it many years later, even the corrupt society of the Restoration might be redeemed by "impulsos que nazcan de su propio seno."[49] (*1447*) As late as 1904, he was still conceiving of society as possessing a "breast!"

It was no accident, therefore, that it should be Galdós' favorite "krausista," Máximo Manso, who expressed most revealingly this aspect of his poetics: "It is interesting to study the philosophy of history in the individual, in the corpuscle, in the cell. As in the exact sciences, that approach also demands use of a microscope." (*1203*) This fascinating possibility was further explained by Manso's author in his Discourse on the occasion of Pereda's entering the Royal Academy: "The society in which we are born confers our own being upon us; one might say that it deals or distributes its basic qualities in order that we may be what it is."[50] Lest we interpret this as a manifesto of determinism, let us listen to Galdós, as a critic, interpreting Ana de Ozores' downfall: "The manner and nature of her perdition correspond to a subtle, symbolic relationship to the history of our nation."[51] (*1450*) Ana is not doomed by heredity and environment; rather as an individual she *is* symbolically the failed fervor of Spanish history.

It would not be difficult to compile a copious anthology of Galdosian observations on the mysterious correlation of individual and society, of private lives and historical events.[52] As we have already

[49] "Prólogo a la tercera edición de *La Regenta.*"

[50] *Ensayos,* ed. Bonet, p. 191.

[51] He goes on to characterize Fermín de Pas as representing "el estado eclesiástico con sus grandezas y sus desfallecimientos." (*1450*)

[52] One of my favorites is a metaphor for Galdós' own creative process cited by Hinterhäuser (who compiles a minor anthology of his own) from *Montes de Oca:* "Los íntimos enredos y lances entre personas, que no aspiraron al juicio de la posteridad, son ramas del mismo árbol que da la madera histórica con que armamos el aparato de la vida externa de los pueblos, de sus príncipes, alteraciones, estatutos, guerras y paces. Con una y otra madera, levantamos el alto andamiaje desde donde vemos en luminosa perspectiva el

observed and as attentive readers need not be told, this is the constantly reappearing skein running through the whole of his work. And I believe that Manso's categorical explanation of how to use the correlation experimentally should be sufficient for our purposes. Galdós' choice of him as a spokesman amounts to a tacit acknowledgment of indebtedness to "krausismo" for his initial innovation in the theory and practice of the nineteenth-century novel.[53]

This is not meant to imply that Galdós was an orthodox (or an unorthodox) "krausista." In fact, he was not a "krausista" at all any more than in 1887 he was a disciple of Hegel, although certain aspects of the structure of *Fortunata y Jacinta* strangely resemble Hegel's *Philosophy of Mind*. Although he had absorbed and learned to use creatively certain of the underlying preoccupations and preconceptions of "krausismo" (its way of thinking and of seeing man and society), he did not belong to the movement. Nor, being the sort of novelist he was, could he have belonged to it. Conversely, as the portraits of Manso and León Roch (his two ostensible "krausista" protagonists) suggest, they themselves could never be novelists. They lack the gift—or curse—of irony, the very irony with which their author delivers them at birth. These are didactic lives deeply immersed in their own sincerity as against the writer of novels, who stands apart, views from a distance, and in the very same words simultaneously praises and blames, admires and ridicules.[54] Novelists do not adhere to movements or schools, however concerned they may be, if only because they watch themselves creating in the very act of creation.

Friedrich Schlegel explains Romantic irony in precisely these terms, that is, as corresponding to the awareness of the artist, who, like a miniature God, smiles both at his own capabilities and his

---

alma, cuerpo, y humores de una nación." (*761*) Carmen Bravo Villasante cites a comparable example from the same novel, which is apparently a good hunting ground. *Galdós por sí mismo*, p. 106.

[53] See chapter 4 for the differences between Galdosian and Zolaesque representation.

[54] In a related discussion Denah Lida reaches a perceptive conclusion: "Hay que ahondar . . . en cada novela . . . para apreciar con justeza la muy sutil escala de adhesiones y rechazos con que respondió Galdós a lo que sólo en sentido muy elástico puede llamarse 'krausismo.'" "Sobre el 'krausismo' de Galdós," *AG*, 2, 1967, pp. 20–21.

own limitations.[55] And if present in *all* latter-day, modern, and non-naive creators, such conscious distance is particularly apparent among novelists, in Zola as well as in Stendhal and Flaubert. As for Galdós, as we have seen, even in his least quixotically ambivalent novel, a novel of social tragedy from which "locos-cuerdos" and "sabios-simples" are rigorously excluded, the tragic hero is also a pompous ass. Galdós does not adhere to any "-ism," and he cannot write tracts even when he wants to, which is, I think, the real reason why don Francisco Giner was so disappointed in the portrayal of León Roch.[56]

Perhaps without meaning to (if he was referring only to his ironic surrogate, Cide Hamete), Cervantes gave definitive expression to this novelistic posture when he termed himself the step-father (or "padrastro") of don Quijote. Instead of being the solicitous father of his human creation (or loving mentor, as Manso is for Manuel Peña), he is removed, even cruel if need be. It is precisely because he is not intimately committed to his creature (although not necessarily unaffectionate) that his stepfatherly mind can appropriate and give wings of imagination to the main intellectual currents of his time. Not the dated commonplaces (although they too have a novelistic function, as we shall see), but the major meditations. Galdós' early association with "krausismo," in other words, is not unlike the relations of certain of his past and future colleagues to a Pinciano, a Claude Bernard, or a Freud.

For our present purposes Galdosian "krausismo" is significant because it helps us to understand the evolutionary advance from *La Fontana* to *Doña Perfecta*. The element of continuity that is inherent in the concept of evolution is easily discernible. Both novels resemble fables for their time; both combine an analysis of the negative forces operative in Spanish nineteenth-century history (its "irrational disharmony") with a warning of the tragic results of their underestimation; and both "study the philosophy of history in the individual." And yet, as we read on from the first into the sec-

[55] Although there is interesting recent work on the subject, the clearest exposition of Schlegel's concept that I have seen is R. Immerwahr's "The Subjectivity or Objectivity of Friedrich Schlegel's Poetic Irony," *GR*, 26, 1951, pp. 173–191. A convenient bibliography is provided by Réné Bourgeois in his *L'Ironie romantique*, Grenoble, 1974.

[56] See note 48.

ond, we realize, continuing the biological metaphor, that we have climbed from the level, let us say, of the mollusk to that of the fish. The increase in thematic complexity and technical mastery that had been achieved by Galdós in a single decade was in its way no less prodigious than that achieved by the natural selection over a span of eons. That Cervantes should have followed *La Galatea* with the *Quijote* may amaze us more, but this relentless and consequential evolution of a single intention also deserves due reverence.

Thus, a two-dimensional political novel of youth against age, progress against reaction, and good against evil has been replaced by a deep, sociological comprehension of the implacable conflict of inherited roles with continuing history. Cartoon characters are now rounded archetypes, all the more alive and threatening because of their very inability to exist in any other way than their ancestors had. The postcard background of "cuadros de costumbres de antaño" has disappeared and been replaced by a virtually invisible Orbajosa composed of forces and attitudes, a collective "hado social" to be sensed rather than seen. And, finally, the jerky, stop-and-go movement of the narrative has subsided into a throbbing stasis, a gathering tragedy so ominous that the final catastrophe seems almost anticlimactic.

Representation, in other words, has at last in *Doña Perfecta* accomplished all that Galdós hoped it might: a comprehensive and indeed virtually irrefutable diagnosis of the social sickness that had made possible "el paso de los sargentos." On one occasion in the course of the "episodio" entitled *El 7 de Julio,* the candid liberal and "bon bourgeois" don Benigno Cordero wonders with plaintive naiveté: "I can't figure out why people like that don't love Liberty, such a self-evident, clear, unarguable good." (*1604*) Had don Benigno been able to read *Doña Perfecta,* he would have found the answer that could not be provided by his own literary circumstance, the historical novel. As don Francisco Giner pointed out, "it is natural that history, understood as a mere narrative of what occurred in the past, cannot enable us to comprehend its essential nature."[57]

---

[57] Cited by López-Morillas, p. 128. *El krausismo español,* p. 128.

CHAPTER IV

La desheredada

Novel and History and Society

The bifurcation of narrative paths, one leading to the "episodios" and the other to *Doña Perfecta* and the "novelas contemporáneas," which immediately followed it, was not a solution to the problem of the incompatibility of movement and meaning, which had handicapped *La Fontana de Oro*. Rather in one sense it was an expression of helpless acquiescence. Galdós' creative mastery of both the enigmatic time of history and the stark timelessness of provincial society is itself an illustration of the gravity of the problem. The dilemma was, in fact, so apparently insuperable that *La desheredada's* unforeseen synthesis of representation with biography and history dumbfounded the public then and still today seems almost miraculous. The reuniting of what had been put asunder, definitively it had seemed, in 1873 and 1876 could only have been achieved by an experimenter at once determined and profoundly intuitive. Galdós was never acquiescent for long; in fact, as far as rigorous judgment of his own art is concerned, he may well have been the least acquiescent of all nineteenth-century novelists, Flaubert included.

In this sense *La desheredada* is prodigious. If the increase in organic complexity achieved during the decade 1867–1876, which separated *La Fontana* from *Doña Perfecta,* could be compared to that which distinguishes fish from mollusks, *La desheredada,* written only five years later, reaches up to our own supposedly exalted limb of the evolutionary tree. Uneven, repetitive, overemphatic, and humanly unconvincing when read for the first time, it is nevertheless the crucial novel for anyone concerned with Galdós' creative evolution. That he was aware of its particular claim to importance is demonstrated by his classification of it as the earliest of his mature "novelas españolas contemporáneas" as opposed to those labeled "de primera época" (*Doña Perfecta* and the two successive novels of intolerance).

In a frequently cited reply to Giner de los Ríos, who had praised it highly,[1] Galdós remarks: "In effect, in this work I have tried to explore new paths, or perhaps I should say, as artists do, to initiate my second or third "period." I wrote it with special determination, and, when I finished it, I judged it to be better than anything I had done before."[2] An even more intimate revelation of Galdós' acute consciousness of having embarked on an unprecedented novelistic adventure is to be found in an 1879 letter to Pereda:

> I now have a great project. For some time my imagination has been simmering with a novel, which I had intended to write later on in order to be able to work on it slowly and carefully. But in view of the mediocre success of my last one [*León Roch*] . . . I want to attack it now. I shall need a year or a year and a half. The subject is . . . political in part and does not rub religion the wrong way at all. If it works out, it will be the last I shall write before undertaking my long desired trip through Europe, which I hope will be in your company. We'll go to see the Pope if you like.[3]

Galdós was not alone in this realization. That his public and the critics who advised it on what to read were also aware of the dis-

[1] "Es no solo la mejor novela que V. ha escrito, sino la mejor que en nuestro tiempo se ha escrito en España. Nada ha hecho ninguno de nuestros novelistas mejores, V. inclusive, que se parezca a este admirable libro: único además que acaba con un arte extremado y lleva un desarrollo de primera fuerza. Esto se llaman caracteres, y sucesos, y descripciones y trabajar a conciencia: estoy encantado con la obra, llena de verdad, de vigor y de vida. Creo señala una nueva etapa en la historia de sus obras. Adelante y *excelsior!* . . . *La desheredada* es la *única* novela moderna española que puede saltar el Pirineo sin inferioridad alguna a lo mejor extranjero." W. H. Shoemaker, "Sol y sombra de Giner en Galdós," in *Homenaje al profesor Rodríguez Moñino,* Madrid, 1966, pp. 12–13. (Hereafter cited as "Sol y sombra.") This judgment was repeated orally to Clarín, who quoted Giner on the subject in his 1882 article on Naturalism: "Es *Pepita Jiménez* una obra maestra y, sin embargo, como novela, sería absurdo compararla con *La desheredada. La desheredada* es la mejor novela, la *más* novela que del *Quijote* acá se ha escrito en castellano." Beser, *Leopoldo Alas,* p. 140.

[2] M[anuel] B[artolomé] C[ossío], "Galdós y Giner, una carta de Galdós," *La Lectura,* 1, 1920, p. 257.

[3] Villasante, "28 cartas," pp. 31–32.

concerting innovation of *La desheredada* can fairly be deduced from the unprecedented silence that followed its publication, for by this time Galdós was used to being fêted in the press after the appearance of each novel. The letter to Giner goes on to remark ruefully on this "frialdad,"[4] and that the complaint was justified is indicated by Clarín's indignation at the failure of reviewers even to attack the new novel: ". . . nadie ha dicho a *La desheredada,* 'por ahí te pudras' . . . Ya ni el escándalo hace ruido."[5] Such is the fate of many novels written at moments of transition from one "manera" to another: their unexpected novelty confounds both critics and public at the moment of their appearance, while future generations of readers are acutely conscious of their imperfections as compared to cherished later masterpieces. Thus, *La desheredada,* when compared to *Fortunata y Jacinta* or *Misericordia,* strikes us as lacking in narrative intensity and human conviction. And so must it have seemed to Galdós himself in later years. But he also knew that it was at that point that he had at last overcome those hindrances to creation that would have impeded his ascent to Parnassus.

In order to comprehend the possibility of Galdós' reunion of the "episodios" and the earlier "novelas contemporáneas," we may best begin by observing that *La desheredada* presents a vision of

[4] "Pero como nadie me había dicho nada, y, por el contrario he encontrado cierta frialdad en el público y en la crítica, casi me sentía inclinado a variar de rumbo" C[ossío], "Galdós y Giner, una carta de Galdós," p. 257. And he would surely have so decided, he goes on to say, had not Giner's generous encouragement kept him on the path that was to lead to *Fortunata y Jacinta* and *Misericordia.*

[5] Clarín's angry paragraph begins as follows: "Y si el silencio fuese la muerte para el ingenio, para la fama del que ha de vivir en sus obras mucho más de lo que puede durar esta generación hipócrita y sin gusto, bien muerto estaría Galdós, o por lo menos *La desheredada.* ¿Saben ustedes algo de lo que se ha dicho la crítica acerca de *La desheredada?* ¿Han escrito los periódicos populares, con motivo de este libro artículos *de sensación,* de los que tienen un titulejo o rótulo especial para cada párrafo? Nada, el silencio" Beser, *Leopoldo Alas,* p. 232. See also Leo J. Hoar, "Pérez Galdós and his Critics," Ph.D. dissertation, Harvard University, 1965. (Hereafter cited as "Critics.") Curiously enough when Galdós in the prologue to *Los condenados* (1894) comments sadly on the paucity of journalistic attention paid to the novel as contrasted to the theater, he refers to the former genre as being itself "disinherited": "La novela ha sido, durante mucho tiempo, una inféliz desheredada, y su existencia un verdadero milagro del Señor, que milagro es vivir sin calor, sin movimiento y hasta sin atmósfera." (*701*)

Spain in its history that is quite different from that to be found in the 1876 novels, *Doña Perfecta* and *La segunda casaca,* as well as their immediate sequels. Although it is true that these latter were written after the Bourbon restoration (1874), they still represented ("en toda la extensión de la palabra") the anguished preoccupations of the preceding decade. Galdós was still obsessed by the failure of "la Gloriosa" and the fall of the First Republic, events which he had both seen and foreseen. The tacit prophecy of *La Fontana,* however, had been inaccurate in its historical analysis. As we saw, during the course of the second series of "episodios," the author realized that the quixotic idealism and the imprudent enthusiasm of the Lázaros of 1868 were less to blame than the sordid self-interest of power-hungry politicians and the unrestrained passions of their violent followers. Such were Galdós' tormented meditations prior to beginning *La desheredada.*

Salvador Monsalud speaks for his author in a disillusioned "political" valedictory written when the second series was approaching its end (*Los apostólicos,* written during "mayo-junio de 1879"): "In the course of my life I have observed in those around me few generous motivations and many, very many insane ambitions, insatiable desires, and hatreds, all of which differ from despotism only in name." Affecting liberals as well as reactionaries (as the above sentence, makes explicit), this was "la herencia leprosa de los siglos," and now Spain in condemned to at least "a century of experimentation, tryouts, agonies, and terrible convulsions." (*176–178*) There is a double prediction in this pessimistic conclusion. The first is that of Galdós' surrogate, Monsalud, whose hundred years of future national misery began in 1831 and so was partially verifiable for liberal readers who in 1879 had just lived through the collapse of their hopes. And the second prediction was that of Galdós himself as he finished the somber second series. No longer confident in inevitable historical progress (or in "rational harmonization"), he projected the failures of both the distant and the immediate past well into the twentieth century.

If Monsalud's prophecy was verified by history lived through, that of Galdós must have seemed grievously erroneous to those of his readers (and they must have constituted a large majority!) who were impressed with the wonders of the Bourbon restoration. Had not the new, young king in the so-called Declaration of Sandhurst reconciled by royal fiat an antagonism that was two centuries old by declaring himself "como todos mis antepasados, buen católico; como hombre del siglo, verdaderamente liberal"? Had not the writer of the phrase, the new, middle-aged Prime Minister, Antonio Cánovas del Castillo, implemented the reconciliation with a British-style parliamentary government admirably designed to give all acceptable politicians their turn at the public trough?[6] And were not the Carlists finally relegated to the domain of folklore? Indeed it seemed, especially to the newly prosperous, that Spain was entering a new era as a European nation dedicated to the order and the progress that had been conspicuous by their absence during the preceding decades. And the new era was to endure, curiously enough— until 1931 when after exactly a century Galdós' gloomy prognostication would be fulfilled. Beginning with the "tentativas" and "ensayos" of the Second Republic, "dolores y convulsiones terribles" were shortly to follow in their wake.

The ultimate justification of Galdós' pessimism matters less to us now than his capacity to see behind the façade of Spain's particularly gaudy and feverish gilded age. Almost twenty years before the young men of 1898 began to try to teach their compatriots that the true Spain was polar to the new Spain,[7] Galdós has his antiheroine, Isidora Rufete, gaze with rapt admiration at a map of the peninsula replete with ascending graphs, arrows indicating shipping routes, and an elaborate frieze on top on which "menudeaban las locomotoras, los vapores, los faros, y, además muelles llenos de fardos, chimeneas de fábricas, ruedas dentadas, globos geográficos, todo presidido por un melenudo y furioso león y una señora con las

[6] In *La desheredada*, particularly in part 2, Galdós anticipates Ortega's slashing 1914 analysis of Cánovas' system. See Ortega's "Vieja y nueva política," in *Obras*, vol. 1, pp. 279–285.

[7] For a reestimation of Galdós' relationship with the Generation of '98 see Ricardo Gullón's "Cuestiones galdosianas," *CuH*, 34, 1958, pp. 237–254. In general it can be said that Unamuno is waspish and irresponsible in his incomprehension: "La vida pasional, palpitante, profunda de España había que buscarla donde la halló Pereda en *Sotileza*, o Blasco Ibáñez en *La Barraca*, en las naturalezas bravías y elementales del pueblo del mar o del campo." "Nuestra impresion de Galdós," in *Obras completas*, ed. M. García Blanco, Madrid, 1952, vol. 5, p. 369. This is compensated for by Azorín's finely focused admiration. See chapter 3, note 6.

carnes más descubiertas de lo que la honestidad exige." (*974*) Hung on the wall of the waiting room of a madhouse, this was the initial emblem of *La desheredada,* a novel designed to chronicle and to comprehend the special folly of the Restoration. If in the "episodios" Galdós often compared the historical behavior of his compatriots to unrestrained madness, now he presents them peacefully shut up in an asylum, classified according to the kind of living conditions they could afford, and supposedly encouraged by a graphic exhibition of progress.

To put it even more bluntly, the alternately patriotic or desperate, hopeful or desolate, novels we have so far attended to were no longer relevant for a time that had replaced passionate commitment to ideology with a nonviolent but sordid commitment to money-making and social climbing. And Galdós, by this time a mature and "sickened" "enfant" of Spain's belated nineteenth century, realized it. Analysis of intolerance and its attendant hypocrisy (*La familia de León Roch* had appeared two years before) could not diagnose the deeper falsification of values, which afflicted the inhabitants of the strange new Spain that had just been born.[8] Salvation of the most recent generation would not only be more difficult; it would have to be attempted in an entirely different way.

What was necessary novelistically was not in itself mysterious. A means had to be found to combine the crystalline social insight of *Doña Perfecta* and its two sequels with the dynamic historical comprehension of the best of the "episodios." Only a novel that could treat society and history without distinction and that could discern

[8] In his 1897 address to the Academy, Galdós, agreeing with Balzac, remarks that the nineteenth-century processes of "urbanización" and "nivelación," with all the new social uncertainties they entail, are profoundly favorable to the novel as a genre. *Ensayos,* ed. Bonet, pp. 173–188. In a sense he was defining both his public and the human raw material of the "segunda o tercera manera." In marked contrast to Galdós, Becquer rejects the possibility of artistic interest in those who have surrendered themselves to historical time: "gente febril e inquieta [que] oscila al compás de los sucesos políticos, vive en los círculos, en los cafés . . . se desespera en la antesala del ministro y lleva . . . su dificil digestión a los bufos o su ayuno a los bancos de los paseos públicos . . . turba dorada o miserable de banqueros, títulos, oradores, empleados, escritores, artistas, cesantes y vagos." "Escenas de Madrid," in *Obras completas,* Madrid, 1949, pp. 998–999. This typical cast of a Galdosian novel is opposed by Becquer to those who still live in the authentic world of customary and liturgical time.

the meaning of movement could reveal the guilt beneath the gilt. Contemporary Madrid, seen not as an indistinct background for intolerance and domestic infelicity (as in *León Roch*) but as a living entity in continuous mutation, had now to be discovered, that is, created. Galdós was no longer asking, "Who are we?" and "Why did we become what we are?" but rather "Where are we now?" and, above all, "How are we going to be in the future?" To find the answers he could only turn to his own experience as a writer of novels and try to invent a new sort of "episodio" in which the protagonist would not only experience contemporary history (the abdication of Amadeo, the mistakes of the Republic, the advent of the Restoration) but also represent society as effectively as doña Perfecta.

Although the fictional biography of Isidora Rufete joined the two previously separated narrative paths into a single creative conquest, for purposes of explication let us for the moment preserve their separateness. Let us try to conceive of that poor, fluttering, crippled bird called Isidora as a kind of Republic-and-Restoration Gabriel Araceli. Antonio Ruiz Salvador has interpreted the renunciation of the "episodios" on the last page of *Un faccioso más y algunos frailes menos* as really a disguised project for their continuation and metamorphosis.[9] The ostensible reasons offered by Galdós —"The years which followed 1834 are too close to us. . . . There is a spark of life in them which hurts and quivers when touched with the scalpel" (*317*)—should not be interpreted as a decision to avoid pain by mirroring blander years. On the contrary, as a veritable connoisseur of agony, the future author of *Tormento* and *Torquemada en la hoguera* moved forward in time in order to enable its plenary expression. However much he may have wept for Marianela in his old age, Galdós was, like Cervantes, Mark Twain, and Stendhal, a genuine stepfather. The image of kindly wisdom—"good gray novelists"—that all of them with the exception of Stendhal liked to cultivate was a deception designed to ingratiate themselves with sentimental readers. Even the jolly Dickens of *Pickwick Papers* enjoyed contemplating pain, as we remember from the interpolated tales.

[9] "La función del trasfondo histórico en *La desheredada*," *AG,* 1, 1966, pp. 53–62. (Hereafter cited as "La función.")

From this point of view *La desheredada* is an "episodio," which narrates events so recently lived through by Galdós and his readers that scar tissue had not yet covered the wounds. Furthermore, in addition to the pleasure of probing the exposed nerves of unhealed history (for example, the assassination of Prim in chapter 17) as a means of intensifying novelistic experience, masochistic observation from below of exactly how "la Gloriosa" had become "la Ignominiosa" could lead to comprehension of the present and future.[10] Thus, the techniques developed in the "episodios" for presenting historical change on every level from politics to fashion were re-applied to the contemporary world. A girl younger than her author arrives in Madrid and, in the course of her tormented experiences there, leads the reader into reliving his own life in the same time and place. The great cycle of metropolitan novels was now under way. Galdós' Madrid could now take its place alongside the Paris of Balzac and the London of Dickens.

If Balzac in the "Avant-propos" to the *Comédie* was explicit about his application of the techniques of the historical novel to his own times (the decisive innovation that inaugurated the great period of the nineteenth-century novel), Galdós as usual was not. Indeed, it is probable that the puzzled readers of the first edition of *La desheredada* were unaware of the continuity pointed out by Ruiz Salvador. Galdós hints at it by having two comically wretched conspirators from the second series of "episodios," Canencia and Tomás

---

[10] Here, as elsewhere, Galdós employs a rich repertoire of words for physical pain. The description of Rufete's shower "en brazos de la Inquisición" with its "lanzazos," "azotes," etc., serves as a verbal introduction to seemingly infinite varieties of pain, which will give "reality" to this and to all the novels to follow. So it is that Máximo Manso (in the tradition of both Lázaro de Tormes and Lazare Chanteau) discovers that he is real through "el dolor." Perhaps the earliest expression of this *Lazarillo*-like variety of "realism" is to be found in a characteristically humorous occasional piece about Galdós' initial impressions of urban existence: "Después otro pasa junto a mí de la misma manera y después otro y otro. . . . ¿qué es esto? ¿quién soy yo? . . . ¿Qué es de mi cuerpo? . . . Pasa un bárbaro junto a mí, y me da un pisotón; el dolor me revela mi personalidad." *Madrid,* ed. J. Pérez Vidal, Madrid, 1957, p. 48. For some of its inhabitants the presence of the city is a reassurance of their reality (as we shall see, a Rosalía de Bringas or a Barbarita); for Galdós, who characteristically vacillated between fantasy and observation, the opposite was the case. Only a blow or a kick could save him from the fate of the narrator of *La novela en el tranvía.*

Rufete, turn up as inmates of the insane asylum.[11] Their appearance, however, could just as validly be interpreted as an indication of the changed intention. The ideological passions of former years, Galdós seems to be suggesting, were anachronistic and deranged in the new historical context. How to compare, in other words, the fiercely "conflictive" politics of the 1820s and 1830s with a regime governed alternately by "peces" and "pájaros" on the basis, at once peaceful and cynical, of Harold Lasswell's sarcastic title for a treatise on "political science"—*Who Gets What: When, How*.[12]

Even more unfamiliar to "episodio" addicts, or to those who were used to the relatively bare stages of the novels of intolerance, was the immeasurably increased attention paid to society in all its levels and ramifications. Unlike the novels of Scott and Cooper, which had served Balzac as models, the "episodios" had been comparatively restrained in their description of milieux. As already remarked, their use of "costumbrismo," based on the memories of Mesonero Romanos and others as well as on personal research, was restricted by the time of history with its concomitant stress on flux. But now Galdós, without sacrificing the basic correlation of history and biography, succumbed to what Lukacs considers the inherent "temptation" of the historical novel—the desire "to try to produce an extensively complete totality."[13]

How was this achieved? The answer that would surely have been given by those readers of *La desheredada* who had been curious or prurient enough to have purchased one of the translations that had just appeared of the recent French literary sensation, *L'Assommoir,*

---

[11] There are grave problems of age and identity involved, because we are asked to imagine them more than thirty years later, and in the case of Canencia apparently after his death. (See chapter 7, note 40.) Their earlier eccentricities along with their names, however, allow us to classify them at least as pseudoreappearing characters of the sort referred to by Galdós in the closing statement of the second series: "Pero los personajes novelescos que han quedado vivos en esta dilatadísima jornada, los guardo, como legítimo pertenencia mía, y los conservaré para casta de tipos contemporáneos." (*318*)

[12] Ruiz Salvador explains the historical background of the Pez surname and image in terms of the sarcastically nicknamed "Ministerio de los Pájaros." "La función," p. 59. As we shall see, there are other literary sources.

[13] *The Historical Novel,* p. 42. Balzac is, of course, the obvious example.

was that Galdós had surrendered to Naturalism.[14] This was the "cuestión palpitante" of those years, and, without participating in the implicit censure of the verb "surrender," we cannot refute their answer. It was precisely Zola's new descriptive techniques that enabled Galdós to revise the "episodio" formula in such a way that it could deal with social history. Let us put it in this way: the twin crises that beset the novelist—the aesthetic (the incompatibility of movement and meaning) and the historical (the disconcerting metamorphosis of nineteenth-century Spain)—had both come to a head at a propitious moment, that is, at the very moment when the Naturalistic transformation of the novel could point a way to their resolution. Or, as Harry Levin phrases it elegantly, when Galdós could learn from Zola how to substitute "Bernard's *comment*" for "Balzac's *pourquoi*."[15]

Thus it was, as recent critics, contemporary colleagues (Clarín, Palacio Valdés and doña Emilia Pardo Bazán), and Galdós himself have all affirmed, that Galdós' "segunda o tercera manera" was inaugurated Naturalistically.[16] But *La desheredada* was neither an imitation nor, as has often been stated, a mixture of French innovation and Spanish tradition. Rather it was a carefully calculated experiment in cross-breeding, an experiment designed to bring together the narrative lines that had been put asunder in the 1870s and to show Spaniards what they had now become. Perhaps the best way to counter the stultifying concept of influence is to insist again on the notion of massive novel-to-novel dialogue, which we broached in connection with *Doña Perfecta, Eugénie Grandet* and *Les Paysans* and which we shall return to in more detail when discussing the conception of *Fortunata y Jacinta*. To be specific I pro-

[14] According to Walter T. Pattison there were two translations of *L'Assommoir* in 1880 along with one of *Nana* and another of *Une Page d'amour. El naturalismo español*, Madrid, 1965, p. 52. Also according to Pattison, Galdós had begun to read Zola in French two years previously, as is indicated by his private library. ibid., p. 91.

[15] *The Gates*, p. 321.

[16] For Clarín see the article in his *Galdós*, Madrid, 1912, p. 97; for Palacio Valdés and doña Emilia, see Pattison, *El naturalismo español*, pp. 39 and 92; for Galdós see the Prologue to *La Regenta*: "Escribió Alas su obra en tiempos no lejanos, cuando andábamos en aquella procesión del naturalismo. . . ." (*1447*)

pose that *La desheredada* presents its frivolous, spendthrift, and corrupt Madrid as a reply to the drunken and bestial Paris of *L'Assommoir,* each novel representing its own variety of descent into hopeless historical prostitution. Naturalism for Galdós was not an end in itself or a fad to be copied but a new possibility of comprehension. It was, to change the image, the sire, not of a sterile hybrid, but of a new and admirably fecund "episodio contemporáneo."

For a mind deeply preoccupied with the latest and in some ways the most depressing avatar of nineteenth-century Spain, the chronicle of "une famille sous le second Empire" must have been a revelation. Unlike Balzac's Restoration, which had fascinated both Galdós and Clarín with its preservation of a residual capacity for eighteenth-century intrigue, this was new, freshly-minted, prosaically sordid history of the sort the two Spaniards had themselves witnessed. All of Zola's twenty volumes were in their own way "episodios nacionales" of an immediate past, which in its pretentiousness, hollow grandiosity, social injustice, and flagrant trivialization of values was not dissimilar to Spain's own belated Bourbon Restoration. Eugène Rougon, with his symbiotic circle of office seekers, was a rich country's version of Galdós' dispenser of bureaucratic largesse, don Manuel José Ramón del Pez (although the Barnacle family in *Little Dorrit* must also have contributed their name and their bit).[17] And Gervaise's daughter Nana was a more corrupt, seductive, and perilous predecessor (by a year) of the Isidora of part 2. Here, indeed, was a sequence of novels made to order for Galdós' effort to present society historically and history socially.

Novel and Speech

It was above all in *L'Assommoir* that Zola showed Galdós how to create in words the world of Madrid. I do not refer now to the lat-

17 This was noted by E. L. Erickson, "The Influence of Charles Dickens on the Novels of Galdós," *H,* 19, 1936, pp. 421–430. See also Balzac's *Le Bal de Sceaux* in which there is a more delicate comparison to silkworms: "Grâce au bon sens, à l'esprit et à l'addresse de monsieur le comte de Fontaine, chaque membre de sa nombreuse famille, quelque jeune qu'il fût, finit, ainsi qu'il le disait plaisamment à son maître, par se poser comme un ver-à-soie sur les feuilles du budget." *Comédie,* vol. 1, p. 76. Balzac goes on to give details of the different posts: magistrate, général, "sous-préfêt," etc.

ter's use of the end of that novel as a referential point of departure, which, as we shall see, it manifestly was. Rather Galdós was most impressed by Zola's boldly experimental use of the "bas fonds" of spoken French and his ruthless vivisection of the most degraded oral milieux; according to the critics, use of the language of taverns and tenements in *L'Assommoir* represented a novelistic break-through within the Rougon-Marquart series.[18] Zola showed the way to full exploitation of a gift that had been displayed more and more vividly during the apprenticeship of the second series of "episodios," i.e. Galdós' extraordinary ear for speech.[19] The transcription of the comic dispute of Tablas with "la Pimentosa" in *Un faccioso más* is a final example of his oral development of a "costumbrismo" that had

---

[18] For Zola's own special pride in his oral achievement, see Levin, *The Gates,* pp. 347–348. F. W. J. Hemmings is emphatic in this regard. *Emile Zola,* Oxford, 1966, p. 120.

[19] For a perceptive discussion see Villasante, *Galdós por sí mismo,* pp. 26–29. The author does not emphasize that such sensibility seems to have been a common characteristic of nineteenth-century novelists, at last totally relieved from the interfering demands of rhetorical decorum. I am not, of course, denying that a Rojas, a Cervantes, and a Fielding obtained some of their most felicitous and comic effects by combining the conventional with the overhearable. As writers of dialogue must, they all had sharply perceptive ears and a shared joy in language as a phenomenon. What I am suggesting is that Balzac, Flaubert, Zola, Dickens, Twain, as well as Galdós participated to-gether in a consciousness of liberation from inherited standards of proper writing. They could at last exploit to the limit of their own capacities the infinite possibilities of the spoken languages in which they were immersed. On the one hand, the experience of living in the nineteenth century, how-ever depressing to reactionary Romantics, was often one of amazement at the discovery of the seemingly limitless possibilities of creative freedom. Everything was there waiting to be heard, written, built, seen, understood. And, on the other, that very intermixture of classes, which was the favorite theme of the new novelists (see chapter 6, note 26) and which Becquer de-tested ardently, brought with it a thousand and one new oral combinations capable at once of delighting the ear and feeding the bottomless sociological curiosity of these professional auditors of their times. Obviously this does not mean that their styles are in any sense imitations or reproductions of what they had heard. Rather, as Albert Thibaudet says with reference to Flaubert: "avoir un style, c'est avoir fait une coupe originale dans ce complexe qu'est le langage parlé." *Gustave Flaubert,* p. 249. The prerequisite of the new art was to be a listening genius. Carmen Bravo Villasante is at her best and most intuitive when she discusses Galdós' initial provincial enchantment with the multiple oral reality of the capital. But we should also remember that this attention (the ability, say, to write *The Celebrated Jumping Frog,* or tran-scribe the speech of "la Pimentosa") was only the commencement.

begun with a more visual emphasis. Yet, like that of John Mucklewrath and his Jacobite wife in *Waverley,* it is still costumbristic in
the sense that it is tangential to the thrust of the narrative, a
"cuadro" (perhaps it would be more exact to call it an "audition"),
which provides a moment of comic relief from and domestic parody
of the civil war. In *La desheredada,* on the other hand, the spoken
medium captures the message, although the transformation was
still tentative if compared to the full sonority of *Fortunata y Jacinta.*
Zola's example had enabled Galdós to make the most of an ability
to hear popular speech, to reproduce it effectively and to exploit it
artistically that was superior even to Dickens's and only equaled by
Mark Twain at his best.[20]

How did the oral novel emerge from the oral interlude? At the
risk of grievously foreshortening Naturalistic theory and practice, I
shall give two complementary answers. In the first place, although
the narrative presence of Galdós in *La desheredada* is far more evident than that of Zola in *L'Assommoir,* it has receded considerably
as compared to the storytellers (the author and his several surrogates) of the "episodios." And as Galdós' voice fades, the focus of
Isidora's encounters with certain milieux, for example, "el barrio
de las Peñuelas," increasingly centers on the intonations, the
rhythms, the inventiveness or triteness of their speech as a coherent
language on its own terms.[21] Cervantes and Fernando de Rojas had

[20] It is, I think, significant that it was Zola's ruthless and somewhat pedantic (he is known to have had occasional recourse to a dictionary of argot)
exploration and exploitation of the lowest depths of speech that finally freed
Galdós from his costumbristic heritage: the mere reproduction of salty, expressive, or comic excerpts of popular speech. It was not, of course, a question of imitation. The endless repetitiousness, the devaluated obscenity, the
pathetic mispronunciation, and the gauche malice of much of what the
Lantiers and their acquaintances have to say to each other are echoed only in-
frequently in the 1880 novels, for instance, Pecado's "¡Estarvus quietos! . . .
Vus voy a reventar!" (*1005*) Rather Zola showed Galdós how an author
could convert spoken language as such into an expressive instrument or, as
Thibaudet would have it, a "style." Its eventual result was the incredible
novel-long dialectic of expressiveness and inexpressiveness that becomes the
linguistic "reality" of *Fortunata y Jacinta.*

[21] The contrast is not only with Galdós' earlier oral "costumbrismo" and
with that of his self-conscious predecessors (particularly Fernán Caballero
and Estébanez Calderón) but also with Eugène Sue, who reproduced the
lowest depths of Parisian argot from without, as if it were a picturesque
antistyle.

used their own superlative aural sensitivity for the purpose of sustaining dialogue overheard as essentially comic. Indeed, there are many reminiscences of the *Quijote* scattered throughout *La desheredada*.[22] What Zola added, however, and what Galdós was learning how to utilize creatively was the essentially serious exploration of language as a social phenomenon, a documented pursuit of speech, class by class and zone by zone. Determinism in the novel, as in life, is linguistic as well as economic, and it is therefore appropriate that Isidora's definitive "death" is presented by her adoption of the speech of her sister prostitutes: "¡Qué puño! . . . Si pudiera desbautizarme y no oir más con estas orejas el nombre de Isidora, lo haría." (*1160*)

Zola's lesson was only gradually assimilated by Galdós, which in itself explains part of the awkwardness of *La desheredada*. At the beginning oral interchange, for example, the dialogue of Isidora with her aunt, "la Sanguijüelera," is still displayed more or less as an amusing sideshow. But, as we read on, we find it functioning more and more as a means of integrating the lives of the characters with a narrative world alive in its speech. The dichotomy of foreground and background, event and scene, which had prevailed in the "episodios" and had abbreviated the Madrid of *La familia de León Roch,* was gradually superseded by milieu.[23] And milieu, although it is composed of smells, surfaces, sights, and taste sensations, was, at least in *L'Assommoir,* primarily the realm of spoken language in which we all live, as it were, osmotically. How fervid

[22] "esos librotes que llaman novelas" (*984*); "¡Leoncitos a mí!" (*989*); "tan desnudo de saber como vestido de presunción" (*1015*); "donde ardieron con chisporroteo, que parecía protesta contra la Inquisición, papeles varios" (*1027*); "La calentura le abrasó los sesos" (*1132*); etc.

[23] Ana Fernández Seín in her forthcoming book on *La desheredada* will demonstrate how substitution of a metropolitan milieu in *León Roch* for the classically bare stage of *Doña Perfecta* did, in effect, permit family scenes and a modicum of urban history to disguise the "conflictive" inertness of the subject with an appearance of novelistic forward movement, in this case, the forward movement of urban change. One can sense therein the uncomfortable groping of the novelist for the new creative formula of *La desheredada*. But Madrid's immense advantage over Orbajosa (its visible "history of Spain") has been reduced to a simple dialectic of tolerance and intolerance. In other words, the Madrid of *Los apostólicos* with its clear-cut political division between butchers and sheep (don Felicísimo Carnicero versus don Benito Cordero) is no longer a working model.

an adherent Galdós was eventually to become to this crucial novelistic revolution is exemplified in *Fortunata y Jacinta*. There traces of Mesonero, Larra, and Cervantes are almost entirely absorbed, as the giant organism of speech and speaking lives flows on to its inevitable conclusion—Fortunata's final, angelic silence.

In the second place, in addition to the discovery that speech could be used to create a living model of the world, the self-awareness of the characters is integrated into that world by Galdós' adaptation of Zola's characteristic "dialogue indirecte libre" or, in German, "erlebte Rede." This self-conscious "innovation"[24] permits the moment-to-moment consciousness of a given individual as it shapes itself in

---

[24] Medieval examples of the technique exist, but were not systematically exploited. I suspect that English and American criticism of this technique has been in some way foreshortened by our lack of an imperfect tense as well as by our corresponding need to employ less expressive verbal periphrases: "he used to meditate"; "he was meditating"; etc. Even the specific terminology used by Robert Humphrey, "indirect interior monologue," refers to one of several subtechniques for rendering free association. *Stream of Consciousness in the Modern Novel,* Berkeley and Los Angeles, 1958, p. 29. Nor does Humphrey examine it historically in terms of Thibaudet's Flaubertian watershed. See Thibaudet's fundamental discussion on Flaubert's perfection of the technique in *Gustave Flaubert,* pp. 205–264. National study of literature, as opposed to comparative study, is often lamentably hermetic and misleading. Just as Roland Barthes after a public lecture in Princeton stated that he saw no relationship between the innovations of the "Nouveau Roman" and Joyce and Virginia Woolf (which he admitted not knowing well), so Humphrey fails to consider the importance of Flaubert, Zola, and Proust for the interiorization (Erich Kahler's "Innerwendung") of the novel as a genre. I, therefore, have preferred the historically significant French and German terms, which were coined, as far as I can determine, by Charles Bally and Eugen Lerch in 1912 and 1914, respectively, in articles in the *GRM.* For studies of the medieval use of the stylistic potentialities of the imperfect tense, see Eugen Lerch, "Das Imperfektum als Ausdruck der lebhaften Vorstellung," *ZRPh,* 42, 1922, pp. 311–331 and 385–425. Further bibliography may be found in the notes to chapter 8 of my *Tiempo y formas temporales en el "Poema del Cid,"* Madrid, 1961, and in Harald Weinrich, *Estructura y función de los tiempos en el lenguaje,* Madrid, 1968. Grammatical theory clarifying the relationship between the imperfect tense and the narrative technique is provided by J. Damourette and E. Pichon, *Des Mots à la pensée,* 5 vols., Paris, 1911-1940. For consideration of nineteenth-century exploitation of the oral potentialities of the imperfect, see Thibaudet's *Gustave Flaubert* and his 1919–1920 "discussion" with Proust in the *NRF;* M. Lips, *Le Style indirect libre,* Paris, 1926; and Stephen Ullman, *Style in the French Novel,* Cambridge, 1957. For a more recent discussion with more recent examples, see Dorrit Cohn's *Transparent Minds,* Princeton, 1978.

personalized yet silent speech to invade the third-person narration of the author. Or it can be explained from the opposite perspective. As Clarín, an equally skilled practitioner, observes, "Another technique which Galdós uses . . . is . . . to substitute for the comments which the author customarily offers on his own account concerning the situation of a character the thoughts of the character himself. He uses the character's style but not as if it were a monologue; instead it is as if the author were inside the character and as if the novel were being created in his consciousness."[25] Dialogue in the third person had been first perfected artistically by Flaubert as an aspect of his experimentation with the nontemporal expressive capabilities, ignored by traditional grammarians, of the imperfect tense and became a routine form of narration for Zola. The depressing and banal thoughts of a Gervaise or a Lantier were far better documented in this fashion than if reproduced in direct dialogue. Had they been quoted "audibly" they would ultimately have become so monotonous as to be intolerable.

The decisive advantage of "dialogue indirecte libre" is that lives so expressed both prove and exemplify Zola's fundamental doctrine of the indifferentiation of the individual from his surroundings. The innermost soul of the character comes from the outside, from the language learned in a given milieu, and can go back outside without hindrance into the language of the narrative. Opening *L'Assommoir* at random, we find a description of Gervaise calculating laundry bills while one of her assistants comments in obscene terms on the private lives of each of the clients: "Quant à Gervaise, sérieuse, à son affaire, elle semblait ne pas entendre. Tout en écrivant, elle suivait les pièces d'un régard attentif, pour les reconnaître au passage; et elle ne se trompait jamais, elle mettait un nom sur chacune, au flair, à la couleur." Then abruptly, without punctuated pause or syntactic warning, we realize while reading on that we have begun to think her thoughts and hear her language: "Ces

---

[25] Beser, *Leopoldo Alas,* p. 231. Tomás Navarro Tomás gives a curiously similar description: "Parece que Galdós fue el primero en emplear en España ese procedimiento explicativo que consiste en revelar el estado de ánimo de un personaje o las circunstancias de un asunto como si el autor se situara en el interior de los personajes mismos, encomendando a las propias reflexiones de estos la marcha y progreso de la acción." "La lengua de Galdós," *RHM,* 9, 1943, p. 292.

serviettes-la appartenaient aux Goujet; ça sautait aux yeux, elles n'avaient pas servi a essuyer le cul des poélons. Voilà un taie d'oreiller qui venait certainement des Boche."[26] Whose words are these? Gervaise's or Zola's? It would be equally difficult to discern exactly where the transition takes place. Perhaps Gervaise was also thinking: "elle ne se trompait jamais."

I have cited this routine example of Zolaesque soul-documentation in order to emphasize Galdós' very different use of the same technique. For him it provided both unexpected access into what Rojas terms the "atribulados imaginamientos" of his characters and, above all, the possibility of conducting hitherto impossible or at least awkward experiments with point of view. In such "episodios" as *Los cien mil hijos de San Luis* we do find a shifting back and forth from the third to the first person and occasional, self-conscious play with the author's omniscience or pretended lack thereof.[27] But now in *La desheredada* concealment and revelation, internal monologue and theatrical dialogue, straight narration and "dialogue indirecte libre" provide innumerable variations in the story line. Paradoxically I dare propose that the linguistic breach opened by Zola into previously hermetic intimacy brought out more of the Cervantes latent in Galdós than ever before. If previously he would have had to describe in his own words what a character was feeling ("Don Benigno heard all this ecstatically, promising himself seriously that he would see to the reforms [suggested by his fiancée]")

---

[26] "As for Gervaise, serious, tending to her business, she seemed to pay no heed. As she made out [the laundry lists], she bestowed on each item an attentive look in order to recognize them as they were disposed of; and she never made a mistake; she could name the owner of each one by noticing style and color. Those napkins there belonged to the Goujet; that was obvious—they'd never been used to dry the bottoms of pans. And now here was a pillowcase, which certainly came from the Boche." *Les Rougon-Macquart,* ed. A. Lanoux and H. Mitterand, La Pléiade, Paris, 1961, vol. 2, p. 507.

[27] When speaking in *Un faccioso más* of don Benigno Cordero's indignation at the massacre of friars and at the official cowardice of Rufete, Galdós excuses himself for not recording his outraged comments but adds in order to console us: "Puede ser que todos estos dichos sean recogidos escrupulosamente por algún cachazudo historiador que los perpetúe, como sin duda merecen." (*314*) Thus, archness of tone and self-consciousness in the act of intervention continue until the very end of the second series but disappear entirely two years later when a reborn Rufete reaps his final retribution. Galdós can now enter or leave as he likes without apology or preamble.

or, at best, following Rojas' example, arrange for self-betrayal in dialogue, now he could weave milieu and consciousness together in ever-varying patterns.

Granting that Naturalism was, surprisingly enough, a form of novelistic liberation for Galdós, we should not be further surprised to observe that, rather than using "dialogue indirecte libre" without calculation, he often saves it strategically for maximum narrative effect. We all remember the climactic passage of the last chapter of part 1, which occurs after Isidora's pretensions have been rejected definitively by the Marquesa de Aransis, when, in the tradition of Florence Dombey and of every Galdosian heroine from Clara to Fortunata, she wanders forth frantically into the maze of city streets.[28] As in the case of Clara, political change is in the air. Amadeo has abdicated; and Isidora associates her own disillusion with that of the disappointed monarch: "Y como la humana soberbia afecta desdeñar lo que no puede obtener, en su interior hizo un gesto de desprecio a todo el pasado de ilusiones despedazadas y muertas. *Ella también despreciaba una corona. También ella era una reina que se iba.*"[29] (Italics mine.) (*1058*) Galdós has waited patiently to give us our first hint of Isidora's representational significance, and, when he does, it is with the Zolaesque flourish just underlined. At the precise moment of their betrothal, history and

---

[28] I had originally related Isidora's urban Odyssey to that of poor Gervaise looking for a paying lover on the "trottoirs" of Paris, if only because of the Naturalistic and sexual connotations of both haphazard itineraries through named streets. And I still think there is such a relationship. But Galdós is not a man of sources but of intricate combinations, and in this case he also draws upon his own creation of Clara as representing helpless Spain exposed to a night of political upheaval. Then, in addition, probably still present in his mind was the strikingly similar chapter from *Dombey and Son* entitled "The Flight of Florence" in which the castout, like Clara, is accompanied by a dog (Diogenes in the one case, Batilo in the other). Further, when Florence finds shelter, it is in order to become the "little housekeeper" (a favorite nineteenth-century fantasy figure) of the aged Captain Cuttle. Similarly Sola, who wanders through Madrid on the night of "el 7 de Julio" searching for "el batallón Sagrado," occupies herself domestically with several codgers including her father's enemy, don Patricio Sarmiento.

[29] "And since pride, which is characteristic of humankind, pretends to disdain what it cannot obtain, within herself she made a scornful mental gesture at her whole past of broken and dead illusions. *She too scorned a crown; she too was a departing queen.*"

biography celebrate their new union with another betrothal, that of the first person with the third in "dialogue indirecte libre."

The result of these two lessons, one social and the other individual, in the novelistic use of spoken language was an immense increase in creative freedom. Zola's exploration of speech as milieu had showed Galdós how to narrate a city. At the same time, the availability of "dialogue indirecte libre" had allowed him to undermine typification and sculpturesque characterization and to explore consciousness in its temporal flux. This is not to imply that Galdós was a Spanish precursor of Joyce or that Isidora's recurrent night thoughts are more than remotely comparable to those of Molly Bloom. Nevertheless, *La desheredada* represented a long step forward toward a kind of novel that would have one crucial feature in common with *Ulysses:* submersion of the author in the spoken language of his people to such an extent that it often appears that it, and not he, is in charge. Galdós had now begun to discover his mature rhythm, the rhythm of speech, which could at long last integrate society and the self, or in more properly Galdosian terms, the time of life and the time of history.

Novel and Myth

Decisive integration was not to be achieved until after the passage of five years and five novels. But before we dare begin to meditate on *Fortunata y Jacinta,* the next prodigious phase of Galdós' novelistic revolution, we must return to the demanding questions we chose to avoid at the outset of the present essay. In what sense is Isidora representational? How did *La desheredada* manage to reconcile its unceasing historical and biographical flow with representation? How, in other words, could the "documentary" case history of an Isidora Rufete *be* Spain for purposes of fable or prophecy in the sense that Clara is a cartoon creature implicitly labeled "the Spanish people," or that doña Perfecta is the sculpturesque archetype of Spain's virtuous and murderous resistance to history? Cartoons and archetypes hold still for inspection of their significance, but Naturalistic lives do not come to rest until they reach their ultimate degradation. Again Zola provided an answer so profound and so efficacious that Galdós never needed to seek another: the elevation of a life clinically recorded to the stature of myth. Or, as Montesinos puts it, "la segunda manera" represented "una expansión casi explosiva del poder mitográfico del autor."[30]

In his illuminating comments on this aspect of Zola's incessant journeying through the gates of horn, Harry Levin translates the praise of Anatole France: "His grand and simple genius creates symbols and brings to birth new myths."[31] Galdós perceived this intuitively and went on to achieve it for himself in *La desheredada*. For myths, whether they are characterized by the Delphic obscurity of a Hesiod or by the crystal-clear representation sought for by Galdós, present meaning in the unfolding of their narratives. Defined in elementary terms, they are stories (perhaps it would be better to say happenings), which create significance in the process of their telling (or happening). Fables and allegories are also stories (or plays), but since they are designed to teach us ahead of time, we sense the rigidity of their design long before they reach their predetermined conclusion. Myths, on the other hand, involve us and our lives in the making of what they mean. Only afterwards do we withdraw and begin to realize what they have indeed meant to us and how we have changed. This in essence is what Galdós discovered.

In the case of *Madame Bovary*, the mythical potential had to wait (as far as I have been able to determine) for Albert Thibaudet to intuit that the heroine, in addition to being Flaubert himself, is France.[32] Zola, on the other hand, as a reader of his own writing, came to a comparable conclusion without outside help. After

[30] José F. Montesinos, Madrid, 1969, vol. 2, p. xiii. Montesinos' critical intuition is keen, as usual, but he tends unfortunately to see Galdós as a kind of hermetic creator and not in fecund relationship with the nineteenth-century novel as a genre.

[31] *The Gates*, p. 325. Although Curtius opens his *Balzac* (Bern, 1951) by announcing "modern myths are even less understood than ancient myths," Anatole France was not alone in his insight. Flaubert, too, in an 1880 letter remarked that "Nana turns to myth without ceasing to be real," and much later Thomas Mann observed that Zola's Naturalism "has close kinship with the mythical." Cited by Haskell Block, *Naturalistic Tryptich*, New York, 1970, pp. 21 and 31. These more or less intuitive tributes were later converted into standard critical doctrine. See, for example, "Les Procédés épiques; les allégories et les mythes," chapter 27 of Guy Robert's *"La Terre" d'Emile Zola*, Paris, 1952.

[32] *Réflexions sur le roman*, Paris, 1938, p. 32.

finishing *Nana* and meditating on the meaning of what he had just made public, he wrote to his translator into Dutch that "her recumbent body prefigures 'France in the agonies of the Second Empire.' "[33] If Zola possessed such immediate critical clairvoyance, Galdós' conscious realization of the immense opportunities that could be exploited through creative emulation is not surprising. He had learned from his predecessor's experiment.

We seem, in other words, to be witnessing what Thibaudet terms "une logique intérieur [du] roman" comparable to that which at once unites and differentiates the tragic visions of Corneille and Racine.[34] First Flaubert, without realizing it, creates a potential myth of France as a self-indulgent and doomed woman; then Zola realizes that he has done the same thing in different terms; and finally Galdós, prepared by his previous use of other more direct forms of representation, sets out intentionally to fabricate his own version of the same myth or antimyth for Spain. As usual, he does not announce his purpose (to do so in this case would have spoiled everything), but he does let us glimpse the cards in his hand when he comments ironically that one of Isidora's lovers looks at her as if she were a "religiosa o mitológica visíon." (*1098*) After agonizing for years over the incompatibility of free movement and fixed meaning, Galdós could now essay the original pre-Socratic solution.

This interpretation would surely have seemed far-fetched to those opening the just published novel for the first time, for in the early chapters of *La desheredada* they would find little to indicate any such intention. The familiar nineteenth-century pattern of a young person from the provinces arriving in a great city with even greater expectations led Galdós' readers, with the usual mélange of sympathy, hope, and concern, deeper and deeper into the reading experience.[35] But when they reached the penultimate chapter of part 1,

[33] Levin, *The Gates,* p. 356.

[34] *Gustave Flaubert,* p. 93. He is referring specifically to Flaubert's possible realization after learning of the death of Balzac that there was "une succession ouverte et une suite à prendre."

[35] Galdós' awareness that Madrid was a vast conglomeration of émigrés from the provinces (in this and other novels often, ironically, from "la Mancha") is also characteristic of Zola (who remarks, for example, that Mignot is one of the "rare parisiens" employed at "Au Bonheur des Dames") and was anticipated by Balzac as early as 1829, when in *Le Bal de Sceaux*

"Igualdad. Suicidio de Isidora," they must have suddenly realized that their habitual identification with the heroine had misled them and that Galdós all along had had something more than storytelling in mind. As Isidora wanders through the streets of Madrid on the eve of the First Republic, the rapport of her disillusion with the historical change she is witnessing is designed to make the reader discover for himself that what until then had seemed to be private annals had in truth concealed a public dimension. Isidora's impracticality, her helpless extravagance, her love of luxury, her good intentions, her capacity for corruption, and above all her illusions about her own identity, known to the reader directly from shared past experience, had all along represented Spain. Not the ferocious, chiaroscuro Spain of Salvador Monsalud, but the Spain Galdós had actually lived in.[36] There is another distinction equally important: unlike Clara, Inés, and Rosario, Isidora is no passive and innocent victim of reaction; she and the nation for which her biography was the latter-day myth were victims of themselves.

The preceding chapter in which Isidora is turned away "unrecognized" by the Marquesa de Aransis had been ironically entitled "Anagnorisis." The true self-recognition, the "suicide" of her illusions, was yet to come, and only when she achieves it do we in our turn recognize her. The beginning of her generational "rebirth," with its sudden discovery that history and biography are one, is a shattering of her sense of identity: "ella misma era punto menos que otra persona." (*1056*) Along with this, her surroundings appear changed and estranged as if undergoing a parallel crisis: "El mundo era de otro modo; la naturaleza, el aire y la luz era de

---

he calls Paris "la moderne Babylone où tous les gens de province finissent par perdre leur rudesse." *Comédie,* vol. 1, p. 78. For these three metropolitan novelists (I suspect it is less true of Dickens) the city was fascinating not just physically but as an immense ingathering, a province of provinces, where individuals no longer rooted traditionally in regional class structures encounter history and cope with it as best they can. See Aurée d'Esneval, *Balzac et la provenciale a Paris,* Paris, 1976.

[36] Although written during the Restoration, *La desheredada* is not *about* the Restoration until the birth of Riquín in part 2. Galdós is clearly projecting back his current disillusionment onto the period that had filled him with hope and fear as a younger man. The Republic's folly and corruption inevitably resulted in the later and manifestly spurious avatar of national consciousness.

otro modo. La gente y las casas también se habían transformado."
Then, unexpectedly, she overhears a political slogan:

> De una taberna, donde vociferaban media docena de hombres
> entre humo y vapores alcohólicos, salió una exclamación que
> así decía: "Ya todos somos iguales," cuya frase hirió de tal
> modo el oído, y por el oído el alma de Isidora, que dió algunos
> pasos atrás para mirar el interior del despacho de vinos.
>
> "Se confirma lo que mañana se decía," murmuró don José,
> demonstrando una gran pesadumbre. "El rey se va, renuncia
> a la corona, y a mí no hay quien me quite de la cabeza que es
> la persona más decente . . ."
>
> "Todos somos iguales," afirmó Isidora repitiendo la frase. Y
> la frase parecía volar multiplicada, como una bandada de
> frases, porque a cada paso oían: "Todos somos iguales. . . .
> El rey se va."[37] (1057)

For the lowbrow winebibbers the phrase resounds with inane optimism, but for a quixotic social climber such as Isidora it is a
devastating realization.

As long as Isidora (along with the reader) believed herself to be
unique, not only as an individual but also as a chosen victim of
noble disinheritance, Galdós uncharacteristically refrained from
suggesting historical parallels to her biography. But when, after
hearing a chance exclamation uttered in the Madrid equivalent of
an "assommoir," she perceives the community of her "revolutionary" soul to that of Spaniards in their contemporary history, such
references appear in abundance. Both her life and her novel are

---

[37] "The world had changed; nature, air, and even light were different.
People and houses were transformed. . . . Out of the door of a tavern,
where half a dozen men were talking loudly amid tobacco smoke and alcoholic vapor, the exclamation 'We're all equal now!' could be heard clearly.
The phrase shocked the ears and—through the ears—the soul of Isidora, and
she walked back a few steps in order to peer into the place.
'That confirms what they were talking about yesterday,' don José mut-
tered with visible grief. 'The King is leaving; he has abdicated, and nobody
can convince me he wasn't as decent as they come. . . .'
'We're all equal,' Isidora asserted, repeating the phrase she had just heard,
and the same phrase was on every lip, multiplied as if it were a flight of
birds. Because every step they took they kept hearing: 'We're all equal. . . .
The King's leaving.' "

abruptly transformed, realigned, impregnated with new significance. She now knows that "todos somos iguales," and we now know that she represents Spain in political crisis. And if we stop to remember what we have read, we realize further that all along she has been doing precisely that.

The unsuspected capacity for representation appears in two different forms. Emerging from within Isidora's errant consciousness, passages of "dialogue indirecte libre" allow us to overhear her own anguished and inexperienced attempts at personal myth making. In addition to "También ella era una reina que se iba" (*1058*), she plays with another pathetic self-portrayal: "ella echaría a su abuela del trono. Venían días a propósito para esto. ¿No éramos ya todos iguales?"[38] (*1059*) These contradictory and childish fantasies of a new historical identity are immediately vitiated by a surge of unfamiliar sensations. Desires and feelings that had found no place in her earlier dream of herself and had therefore been repressed are brought to the surface by the physical aggression (jostling crowds, redolent taverns, blood dripping from the "carros de carne") of the immediate experience. On the one hand, she feels "a pain so piercing that she even felt that she did not want to live any longer," but, on the other, she has a sudden appeite for sensual fulfillment, which brings with it an uncontrollable desire for life: "The contact with the multitude, that magnetic fluid which served to conduct mysterious desires and was transmitted from body to body by the touching of shoulders and arms, entered through her pores and agitated her profoundly."[39] (*1059*)

Galdós, the Naturalist and observer of the natural impulses of his creature, now takes over and proves himself to be a far more talented mythographer than she. The result of the eruption of sensuality within Isidora is her decision to give herself to Joaquinito

[38] "She would dethrone her grandmother. The time was now ripe for that. Weren't we all equal now?"

[39] One of Galdós' first sensations upon being exposed to the city must have been precisely this galvanic effect of compressed humanity. As he expresses it in one of his early newspaper articles, "irradiación eléctrica en los contactos fortuitos." (*1519*) From my own experience I would say that such contacts, particularly visual, are much more intense, provocative, or haughty in Madrid than in Paris or London, but O. Henry does have similar impressions of New York.

Pez, a decision equivalent to moral suicide as the title of the chapter indicates. The fact of surrender, however, is less significant than how it takes place: as Antonio Ruiz Salvador pointed out in a brilliant essay, Isidora's surrender is an iconographic reenactment of the assassination of Prim.[40] The three men who emerge from the portals "del Congreso," where Isidora is waiting without knowing why, clearly are intended to recall Prim himself ("Uno de ellos se distinguía por su gabán claro"), Sagasta, and Herreros de Tejada. They walk together followed by Isidora and her squire, don José Relimpio, to the "calle del Turco," where don José observes: "Here don Juan Prim was killed. You can still see on the wall the traces of the bullets." (*1060*) Then, at that very moment, Isidora rushes into the arms of Joaquinito, who is actually wearing the "gaban claro." The fatal deed is done, and it only remains for don José to weep for the loss of his "ahijada": "with his face turned away . . . perhaps with a tear he moistened the wall on which gunfire had written the most shameful page of our contemporary history." (*1060*)

The representational significance of these events is not at all ambiguous. Beneath the superficial change of regime, presented in terms of gossip ("El rey se aburre, el rey se va"; "La República, la República"; "Ya, todos somos iguales") and exploited by Isidora for her private myth, Galdós sees a far deeper mutation. At the time, the fate of Prim had seemed to him so fraught with national foreboding that it may have caused him to abandon the happy, that is, patiently optimistic, ending of *La Fontana* and to return to the grim augury of the manuscript. But now he presents it as nothing less than the moral watershed of the whole of Spain's nineteenth century. Galdós did not interpret the assassination as an isolated catastrophe; rather, like recent political murders in the United States, it was a symptom of profound historical demoralization. As he himself stated it in 1909 with rhetoric appropriate to *España trágica:* "Historical fatality . . . commands with the tone of an infallible oracle: 'Spaniards, assassinate Prim!'" (*945*) Hence, the representation of the deed in terms of the degraded moral suicide of Isidora, whom we have just discovered to *be* that moment of Spanish history.

[40] See "La función," p. 56.

Suicide like sexual surrender is, of course, a metaphor for what Galdós believed to be the turning point of the nineteenth century. As he presented them, the Spaniards who had inhabited the second series of "episodios" may have been either intransigent fanatics or venal turncoats, but at least the former were spiritually incandescent and ready for self-sacrifice, as Ortega was later to insist.[41] Now, after their departure from the scene of history, a debilitating loss of commitment was perceptible. Prim had been the last and best of the old leaders, and those who replaced him (represented by Joaquinito and the succession of subsequent lovers in part 2) could offer, at best, either a temporary simulacrum of prosperity or the consoling but empty rhetoric of theatrical oratory. Two years later Galdós was to make the comparision with the theater explicit: "nuestra politica [me parece] case siempre, y hoy más que nunca, una mala comedia representada por regulares cómicos."[42] Let the reader of *La desheredada* take heed. Galdós did not begin both parts of the first edition with a theatrical cast of characters by chance. Although the two chapters in part 2 that are composed entirely of stage dialogue and entitled "escenas" may at first appear to satirize neo-Romantic melodramas, in reality they are intended to express the melodramatic, meaning simply fake, relationship of the nation with its government.

Our hypothetical answer to the question of how Galdós' adaptation of Naturalism enabled him to bring together the concerns and narrative structure of the "episodios" with those of the early "novelas contemporáneas" can now be made more precise. On the one hand, he had learned how to use his gifted ear for spoken language in order to integrate community and individual, city and citizens, into a narrative world. And on the other, he could wait patiently (as Zola had waited, but perhaps not so intentionally and certainly not so slyly as Galdós) during sixteen long chapters for Isidora's private case history to accumulate a charge of potential meaning strong enough for myth making. The procedure was the opposite of that employed in *La Fontana*. Instead of beginning with fixed and im-

---

41 "Vieja y nueva política," in *Obras,* vol. 1, pp. 265–308. He refers, for example, to the Spain recorded in the second and third series as possessing "los esplendores de un incendio de energías." ibid., p. 280.

42 Shoemaker, *Cartas,* p. 43.

posed cartoons, Galdós sought to lure his unsuspecting readers into participating in the task of exegesis. Myths, after all, as Socrates knew, are the oldest and most efficient form of education, because participation is of their essence. Galdós had at last discovered how to juxtapose the narration of ceaselessly moving history with rigorous and perspicuous comprehension of society.

Novel and Reader

The notion of reader participation in the process of Naturalistic myth fabrication returns us to the problem of the paradoxical collaboration of Zola and Cervantes in the composition of *Le desheredada*. The art of Cervantes depended, and still does, on ironical play with the habits and expectations of the reader, while the art of Zola, in spite of its poetry and its occasional black humor, is one of straightforward documentation, not literary reflections and refractions, but every detail smelled, observed, heard, which together make up the "train-train" of daily existence. How could two such antithetical kinds of narration be reconciled, enticed to collaborate in the creation of a new species of novel?

This was the formidable question faced by Galdós upon initiating his "segunda o tercera manera," and he answered it characteristically, not after perplexed critical meditation, but by getting immediately to work. As early as the writing of *Trafalgar,* as we saw, he had realized that the habit of reading so-called historical novels could be usefully exploited, and in 1880 he was determined not to lose that advantage. He would naturalize Naturalism and make it subservient to his special purpose (nothing less than the redemption of his readers!) by combining it with techniques he had learned from the *Quijote.* After all, Cervantes, too, had made a myth superbly designed for the comprehension of Spain, and, if certain of his methods could be applied to nineteenth-century history and society, the resulting novel might at long last tell author and public all they so desperately needed to know, that is, what was happening to them and how they might avoid the same in the future.

This experiment, at once bolder and more delicate than any Galdós had yet dared attempt, had to be protected by initial concealment. To begin at the beginning, the title is intentionally misleading. We may suspect irony or be disconcerted by occasional hints, the broadest of which, as Martha Krow-Lucal has shown, is the philippic of "la Sanguijuelera."[43] But until chapter 16 there is no explicit indication that Isidora has not been "disinherited," that she is a Rufete and not an Aransis.[44] Galdós' play with the expectations of his readers (specifically their habitual, sentimental support for such heroines as Eugène Sue's unwitting "desheredada," Fleur-de-Marie), is, therefore, the basis of his intentional delay in revealing Isidora's representational significance.[45] Only when the reader realizes that she is *not* what she thinks she is and *never* can become what she aspires to be can her life be understood as representing contemporary Spain.

Isidora is attractive and pathetic; her excesses of generosity and imprudence harm no one but herself; and it is only human to hope that *her* novel will be the true one. So too did Byron, Heine, and Unamuno (but not Stendhal!) prefer the Romance of Chivalry that don Quijote never ceases to invent for himself and Sancho to the novel of Cervantes. The nineteenth-century reader, having recognized the telltale presence of Naturalism, may have feared a horrifying, Zolaesque denouement, but, as a devotee of modern romances of society, he would naturally hope against hope. He or she need not necessarily have been an addict of Sue or Fernández y González, whose absurd *Los desheredados,* published in 1865, seems to have provided Galdós with his title.[46] Such reputable authors as

---

[43] "The Evolution of Encarnación Guillén in *La desheredada*," *AG*, 12, 1977, pp. 21–29.

[44] Robert Russell goes so far as to suggest, at least by implication, that both she and we are justified in believing that she is in fact "disinherited": "Part I puts Isidora through a series of experiences which serve largely to confirm her illusions about herself." "The Structure of *La desheredada*," *MLN*, 76, 1961, p. 796. Personally, I think Galdós is a little fairer to his readers than that, but Russell's reaction is interesting because it reveals how cunningly Galdós feeds our desire to believe.

[45] In addition to Eugène Sue's heroine, one might also mention the various Dickensian versions including the authentic "desheredada," Florence Dombey, who ends up by "adopting" her father!

[46] The two long volumes of *Los desheredados* (Madrid, 1865), clearly modeled on the format of Eugène Sue, are replete with authentic "desheredados" (one of whom, as we shall see in chapter 7, note 49, resembles Maxi in a number of ways) and "desheredadas." Another likely fictional presence, which comes to my attention after writing the above is Faustina Saez de

Valera, Dickens, and Balzac (Esther Gobseck's biography is in some ways parallel to that of Isidora) had all, whenever they felt like it, combined realism with Romance.[47] So why not Galdós? Hadn't he done the same thing frequently in the "episodios"? And then, when the reader has almost convinced himself that the heartless Marquesa de Aransis (appropriately related to both doña Perfecta and the Condesa de Rumblar, as Martha Krow-Lucal has pointed out)[48] has turned her granddaughter away because of her fanaticism and aristocratic pride, Galdós disabuses him with the shocking Cervan-

---

Melgar's *La Cruz del Olivar,* which appeared in the *Correo de la Moda* in 1867. According to Alicia Graciela Andreu, who discusses the novel in her suggestive and well-researched "La *Mujer Virtuosa;* Galdós y la literatura popular," this is exactly the kind of "roman rose" to which Isidora must have been addicted. Ph.D. dissertation, University of Oregon, 1978. Unlike Ayguals de Izco, who identifies poverty with virtue (Ido's version of Amparito), here virtue is the companion of social success, elegant clothing, romantic love, and plenty of money. It seems to be a perfect example of the "literatura de salones," which Galdós "hated." (See chapter 10, note 24.)

[47] We have already seen in chapter 1, note 6 the curious contribution of *Splendeurs et misères des courtisanes* to *La Fontana de Oro,* and later on we shall have occasion to discuss its dialogue with both *La Regenta* and *Fortunata y Jacinta.* In *La desheredada,* I propose, Galdós echoes Balzac's ebullient and unrepentant Romanticism as a novelistic means of provoking our identification with Isidora and so enticing us into his Naturalistic snare. Esther's biography parallels Isidora's up to a point, since the former *is* an unwilling prostitute capable of sublime suicide for the sake of love. Other specific resemblances are evident. (1) Both heroines are abandoned by Romantic lovers "plein[s] de tendresse dans le coeur et de lâcheté dans le caractère" whom they have supported. *Comédie,* vol. 5, p. 790. (2) Both furnish their houses with an "ensemble de choses lugubres et joyeuses, miserables et riches, qui frappait le régard." ibid., p. 674. (3) Both are forced to sell themselves to rich but repulsive and avaricious protectors, and (4) both experience seizures of their personal property as the result of unpaid debts. Balzac sums up such lives in a way that applies directly to the theme of *La desheredada:* "Ces femmes tombent donc avec une effroyable rapidité d'une opulence effrontée à une profonde misère. Elles se jettent alors dans les bras de la marchande de la toilette, elles vendent a vils prix des bijoux exquis, elles font des dettes. . . . Ces hauts et bas de leur vie expliquent assez bien la cherté d'une liaison . . . ménagée." ibid., p. 843. But far more interesting than these parallels is Galdós' cunning and effective play with the readers' expectations and with their addiction to the various novelistic schools of the nineteenth century.

[48] "The Marquesa de Aransis: A Galdosian Reprise," in *Essays in Honor of Jorge Guillén on the Occasion of his 85th Year,* ed. M. Krow-Lucal, Cambridge, Mass., 1977, pp. 20–31.

tine conclusion: "Ultimos consejos de mi tío el canónigo." Like Isidora herself, the reader discovers that he is the victim of an elaborate and cruel practical joke. Isidora has been trained for her delusion by the eccentric uncle, while the reader has been enticed (or at the very least allowed) by the author to identify himself sentimentally with a deranged existence.

Galdós, like the inventor of the novel, may have been the wicked "padrastro" both of his brainchildren and his readers, but it would not be fair to accuse him of sadism. The pain he inflicts is intended to be therapeutic. It is precisely the reader's chagrin, his feeling of having been betrayed and made to look like a fool, that prepares him for his bitter medicine. Having found out that all along he has been duped and that by identifying himself with her life he too has been an Isidora, he may at last also be prepared to admit that as a Spanish citizen he has allowed himself to be deceived. If, in the first place, Isidora is a representation of the Spain of her time and if, in the second place, her whole existence has been as much of a sham as the map of progress in the anteroom of Leganés (the twin discoveries that are made at the end of part 1), then a civic identity crisis is in order. Isidora has been misled and brought to moral suicide by the eccentric pseudocanon and, as we learn later, by her mad father, while the reader's untrustworthy mentors have been Cánovas and the other silver-tongued leaders, whose instant remedies and false optimism were so satisfying to believe. Coldly, cruelly, and deliberately, Galdós has written an ironical object lesson in historical illusion and disillusion.

And yet in so saying, are we not also, although unintentionally, being cruel and lacking in sympathetic understanding? When Galdós was writing *La desheredada* and living the life of Isidora in his mind, was he not in fact engaged in what Kenneth Burke would call a quest for relief from an intolerable burden? The salutory chagrin that is prepared for the reader is at the same time a confession on the part of the writer that he too has been gulled politically. Seen in this way, the novel can be fairly interpreted not only as a carefully prepared myth but also as an expression of Galdós' own feelings about "la Gloriosa" and its aftermath. In the late 1860s and early 1870s, when he was working on *La Fontana* and the first series of "episodios," he had been almost as much of

113

an Isidora as his readers, but now he could see clearly how ill-conceived, corrupt, and doomed to early failure had been the reality behind his illusions. He could see how shallow certain aspects of his youthful vision of Spanish history had been.

This was not a sudden revelation. Galdós' historical pessimism had had a long gestation and was born full grown in the second series of "episodios." What was unprecedented in *La desheredada* was the means of its expression. Galdós realized that having Salvador Monsalud speak for him and explain what was wrong at length to his surprised and patriotic readers had not provided the kind of relief he required. Now, on the other hand, as suggested by Flaubert's famous equation, "Madame Bovary, c'est moi," he discovered how to relive his life (and, in so doing, how to purge himself) in Isidora and as Isidora. Was not Cervantes alluding to the same kind of liberating identification when his pen affirms oratorically, "Para mí sola nació don Quijote, y yo para él; él supo obrar y yo escribir; solos los dos somos para en uno"?[49]

Such questions are speculative, but what can be affirmed and analyzed critically are the techniques used consciously by Galdós first to incite and then to shatter our sentimental participation in Isidora's hopes and fears, illusions and disappointments. I refer now specifically to the calculated stress at the beginning and end of part 1 on the Cervantine enhancement of Naturalistic myth making. It is as if the author wanted to touch our hearts with his presentation of the pathetic circumstances of the bereaved foster daughter and at the same time to warn us tacitly not to be taken in. For when we discover at the end our humiliating gullibility, he can gloat all the more at our failure to heed his veiled warning.

The title of chapter 1, "Final de otra novela," ostensibly refers to the past life of Rufete, fragments of which we remember from

---

[49] Rodolfo Cardona in his "Nuevos enfoques críticos con referencia a la obra de Galdós" meditates on the probability that in *El doctor Centeno* Galdós engaged in what I have called a creative "dialogue" with Goethe's *Wilhelm Meister* (which he owned in a French translation): "Como novelista, Galdós mata simbólicamente al joven dramaturgo de su propia juventud, encarnado en Alejandro Miquis." *Homenaje,* p. 70. If so, this would constitute a parallel example and so would confirm our speculation that "Isidora c'était lui" in addition to being Spain. Cardona does not mention Javier, "el Doctrino," in *La Fontana* as a precursor of Miquis.

the second series of "episodios." And as far as we can tell from our earlier reading (and from all that we gradually learn about him in *La desheredada*), if a novel about Rufete had ever been written, it would have been both comparable to that of his daughter and intimately entwined with it. The notion of the novelist as a compiler of "documents humains" necessarily implies, first, that every life is a potential novel and, second, that all lives commingle in a kind of total novel. In addition to this, as Ana Fernández Seín will show in her forthcoming study of *La desheredada,* half-concealed references in the same chapter also recall the specific "finales" of two novels by other authors, novels that were intimately familiar to his readers. Galdós' double game, his almost Stendhalian "catch me if you can," is already under way.

For us the hardest to detect is, of course, the "final" of *L'Assommoir.* Yet it is there and must have been more evident to readers of the period. The ravings of Rufete, his water imagery, the kindly if somewhat dispassionate behavior of the physicians (as a general rule all nineteenth-century novelists are fond of doctors), and the scene of horror and degradation witnessed by a poverty-stricken female member of the family all taken together echo beyond any doubt the terminal delirium tremens of Coupeau, an episode that was considered especially shocking at the time.[50] Even don Juan Valera (replying to doña Emilia Pardo Bazán), though repelled both by the school and the novel ("el heroe es el aguardiente"), had to admit that Zola's ending was "admirablemente descrito."[51] It was not alcohol, however, that had destroyed Rufete. His addiction was not physiological but to a genre of "fiction" as habit forming and far more dangerous to the mind than Romances of

[50] Coupeau's delirium tremens results in an hallucination that concludes in a way that will be familiar to readers of *La desheredada:* "Ça pisse de partout, des fontaines, des cascades, de l'eau qui chante, oh! d'une voix d'enfant de choeur. . . . Épatant! les cascades!

"Et il se redressait, comme pour mieux entendre la chanson délicieuse de l'eau; il aspira l'air fortement, croyant boire la pluie fraîche envolée des fontaines." *Les Rougon-Macquart,* vol. 2, p. 783. Perhaps Galdós' own apparent enjoyment of water spectacles should be taken into account. In addition to the cleansing of the Plaza Mayor as observed by Fortunata, see the description of "la Granja" in *Los apostólicos* as a "manicomio de rios."

[51] "Apuntes sobre el nuevo arte de escribir novelas," *Revista de España,* 111, 1886, p. 383.

Chivalry, the fiction of politics and bureaucracy, which earlier had warped the mind of Gogol's Proprischin.[52] Galdós is revealing as overtly as a novelist can the ingredients of his experimental recipe.

The second of his allusive "finales" is that of the *Quijote*. Rufete on his Naturalistic deathbed recovers an Alonso Quijano-like lucidity that Coupeau had lost forever: "The patient sighed loudly, opened his eyes, and looked at them all one by one, but not violently and without spasms of madness or irate recriminations. Rather he spoke in a low, tranquil, sorrowful voice full of self-pity, saying, 'Gentlemen, is my guess true? . . . Am I really in Leganés?'" (976) At the very least, we have been given an inkling that, along with "race, milieu, et moment," endemic national folly is in charge of *La desheredada*.

By the end Cervantine component is obvious and is used in such a way as to make us acutely aware of our own foolish performance as readers. The pseudo-Canon's name, Santiago Quijano-Quijada, which appears as a kind of closing pseudosignature (he is after all the fabricator of the plot), cannot be misinterpreted. The creator of Isidora's dream romance is a Quixotesque eccentric, an individual so absurd and so spurious that it is all the more humiliating to have been taken in by him, to have hoped, as Galdós wanted us to hope, that the mysterious documents might be authentic and that Isidora would eventually be embraced by her fanatical grandmother.[53] If Cide Hamete Benengeli is a liar, the letter from

---

[52] One of Galdós' most intriguing journalistic series is entitled "El manicomio politico-social." See W. H. Shoemaker's edition of *Los artículos de Galdós en "La Nación,"* Madrid, 1972. (Hereafter cited as *Los artículos*.) These consist of mad monologues in many ways similar to that of Rufete. Thus, the "Neo" in the "jaula primero" concludes: "padezco horribles tormentos; porque no tengo a quien quemar. Me han quitado los fósforos." Ibid., p. 449. A possible inspiration for these pieces (as well as a very probable "tercer final de novela" for the first chapter of *La desheredada*), which came to my attention after completion of my MS, is Gogol's *Diary of a Madman*, which had been translated into French in 1845. A mad bureaucrat, under the delusion that he is the King of Spain, who believes his "loqueros" are Inquisitors (Galdós calls them "inquisidores del disparate") and who is doused in cold water, is certainly familiar.

[53] As Martha Krow-Lucal suggests in her dissertation on *La desheredada*, in many ways Galdós is closer to the vision of the spurious *Quijote* of Avellaneda than to the genuine article, although he was probably not aware of it. Not only do both madmen end in asylums but also, with a few exceptions,

Tomelloso could only have been written by a crackpot. Of all the unhappy endings Galdós ever wrote, and they were a specialty of his, this is perhaps the most bitter, because it affects not only the character but also the reader and the writer.

I am well aware that these conclusions conflict with the standard interpretations of *La desheredada*. Galdós' literary play with Zola and Cervantes has usually been explained in terms of the debate on Naturalism, which was the so-called "cuestión palpitante" of the period.[54] Naturalism was not in the least new to Spain, patriotic critics were fond of asserting. The superior native variety was at least as old as the *Lazarillo,* and its definitive achievement, far more humanly significant than any sordid product of the latest French fad, was, of course, the *Quijote.* And, the argument continues, Galdós intended to demonstrate the superiority of the older school, while adapting useful, recent techniques for the purpose of depicting nineteenth-century society. Yet in the context of *La desheredada,* this facile historical explanation of the mélange seems to me misleading. Galdós did not share the view held by "most Spanish critics" and first expressed in English by William Dean Howells that Zola's brand of Naturalism should be rejected as "deterministic and pessimistic" and that Cervantes provided an optimistic antidote.[55] Fully

---

the inhabitants of the two novels are characterized as spurious. "Theory and Practice of Character Usage in Galdós. A study of *La desheredada,"* Ph.D. dissertation, Harvard University, 1979.

[54] A documented survey of this critical effort simultaneously to assimilate and to reject, to repatriate and to excoriate the new art of narration is to be found in Pattison's *El naturalismo español.*

[55] For the view held by "most Spanish critics" see Eamonn Rodgers, "Galdós' *La desheredada* and Naturalism," *BHS,* 45, 1968, p. 285. Galdós does say in his prologue to *La Regenta:* "Francia, con su poder incontrastable, nos imponía una reforma de nuestra propia obra, sin saber que era nuestra; aceptémosla nosotros restaurando el naturalismo y devolviéndole lo que le habían quitado, el humorismo, y empleando éste en las formas narrativa y descriptiva conforme a la tradición cervantesca." (*1448*) An attentive reading of *La desheredada,* however, will not allow us to equate these statements to those of William Dean Howells when he describes Zola's subject matter as "simply abhorrent" and wanting in the endearing humor that is the "quintessence" of the Spaniards' (Galdós and Palacio Valdés) "charm." See *My Literary Passions,* New York, 1895, pp. 245–246. Galdós' notion of past and present Spanish "humorismo," unlike that of Rodgers and Howells, is pitch-black.

as bitter about his nation and his times as his French master about the Second Empire, Galdós sought, not to soften the historical diagnosis of *L'Assommoir* and *Nana,* but rather to apply it to Spain and make it recognizable to Spaniards.

For this purpose the *Quijote* could be of great help. As Casalduero has pointed out, in 1881 Galdós still conceived of its author as a myth maker as negative and caustic as Zola and of its hero as a representative of what had gone wrong with Spain.[56] Thus, when he has his "malditos Rufetes, maldita ralea de chiflados," originate in "la Mancha," he hopes his reader will recognize the resemblance to the Provence of the Rougon-Macquarts and at the same time perceive the relevance to himself, i.e. that he is a member by right of birth of a mad tradition and that Spain has its own spiritual heredity fully as noxious as the biological variety of Zola. Galdós, in other words, in preparing for the future revelation of Isidora's life as possessing a "sutil parentesco simbólico" with modern Spain, reinforces the new Naturalistic myth of the prostituted nation with that of don Quijote interpreted as a personification of his country's traditional rejection of reality.

In *Fortunata y Jacinta,* as we shall see, Galdós was to demonstrate a far more profound comprehension of the *Quijote,* and even then in 1880 and 1881 certain exploitations of Cervantine narrative techniques (liberated dialogue, play with point of view, and so on) represented more positive professional hommage. Yet within the experimental parameters of *La desheredada,* Galdós is ruthless in his rejection of those aspects of Cervantes that do not suit his intention. How, for example, can the murder of Zarapicos by Pecado be explained other than as a victory of crude Naturalistic brutality over the master's mellow revision of the picaresque mode? The point is that Zarapicos and his companion Gonzalete both in their occupation (they are juvenile sharpers) and in the rhythm and rhyme of their names intentionally recall Rinconete and Cortadillo. And when one of them is murdered by the modern, sociological variety of marginal youth, a juvenile delinquent, the message is unambiguous. What Galdós is telling us in the chapter entitled

[56] *Vida y obra,* p. 83.

"¡Hombres!" (aside from the prediction of civil war)[57] is that the Cervantes of the *Novelas ejemplares,* the humorous and tolerant "manco sano," who said of *La Celestina,* "libro a mi ver divino, si encubriera más lo humano," will no longer serve as a model. Spain was entering an age not only of self-deception and spurious values (Isidora) but also of political assassination and latent violence determined by "race" and "milieu" (Pecado). Cervantine tolerance and humor are all right in their place, but a Galdosian "episodio" of the Republic and the Restoration centered on such siblings as these was not their place. Only that other Cervantes, the percipient and caustic outsider, who, according to Galdós, predicted the national future by having his stepson sent home encaged, could serve as a foil to Zola.[58]

Once Santiago Quijano-Quijada (not the descendant of Cervantes' creation but rather the reflection of Galdós' jaundiced view of him in 1880) has given the coup de grâce to our last hopes for a happy ending, there seems to be no reason for the novel to continue. Indeed, as Ana Fernández Seín discovered in the manuscript, one preliminary notion for the ending was Isidora's suicidal leap from the recently constructed "Viaducto" of the Calle de Segovia.[59] Such

[57] In *Montes de Oca,* Galdós recalls this chapter but reverses the comparison. In the Basque provinces, he says, "las generaciones han jugado a la guerra civil, movidas de ideales vanos, y se han desgarrado las carnes y se han partido los huesos, no menos ilusos que los niños jugando a la tropa con gorros de papel y bayonetas de junco." (*1135*) The organic contribution of the "novelas contemporáneas de segunda época" to the later "episodios" is once again borne out.

[58] The young Galdós' interpretation in 1868 of the end of part 1 of the *Quijote* speaks more to his own initial art of the novel than to that of Cervantes and, therefore, is all the more interesting to us: "La ruina venía desde atrás, pero al morir Felipe II, dos años antes de concluirse el gran siglo de la preponderancia, aún los secretos males de la monarquía no habían presentado tristísimas señales exteriores, como sucedió algo después. Se presentía el descenso: no estaba lejos la jaula encantada que había de traer encerrados a todos aquellos andantes." Peter B. Goldman, "Galdós and Cervantes: Two Articles and a Fragment," *AG,* 6, 1971, p. 101.

[59] From both Ana Fernández Seín and Martha Krow-Lucal, who have examined the *La desheredada* MS in detail (one in the residence of doña María Galdós and the other in the BN), I learn that it does not contain on the reverse side of its pages as complete a preliminary version as that of *Fortunata y Jacinta* now in the Houghton Library. But apparently there are

an ending would have been psychologically convincing, eminently Naturalistic, and familiar to a public of newspaper readers.[60] Nevertheless, in view of the concluding revelation of the heroine's representation of modern Spain in its history, to persist with this ending would have been out of the question. If nations are extraordinarily difficult to bury (in spite of Khrushchev's optimism on that score), so also must be their symbolic representatives.

But we need not view Galdós' dilemma in apocalyptic, contemporary terms. The possibility and impossibility of the death of Spain was a preoccupation not without precedent in the nineteenth century. As opposed to Larra, who in his *Día de difuntos* saw the nation as unaware that it was already dead, Jaime Balmes, whose notion of what had gone wrong was antithetical, compared its history to "las angustias y dolores de un enfermo que sufre."[61] But, he consoles himself, "neither does it seem to us that society will once again descend into chaos and its suffering breast be exposed pitilessly to the buzzard's beak." [62] This painful, collective application of the facile proverb "While there is life, there is hope" is rephrased cynically by no less a personage than Juanito Santa Cruz in the preliminary version of *Fortunata y Jacinta:* "The republic is here and so what? . . . Nations don't die. . . . The buildings of Madrid

---

clear indications that the physical, as against the allegorical, "suicidio de Isidora" was seriously contemplated by the fledgling Naturalist at one point in his labors. For me what is extraordinary is Galdós' conversion of that too facile, Naturalistic, physical suicide into his complex representation of contemporary history at the end of part 1.

[60] From the contemporary press one gathers that there was a kind of suicidal fad in connection with the "Viaducto" comparable to that which accompanied the opening of the Brooklyn and Golden Gate bridges. At the end of *Fortunata y Jacinta,* "Maxi . . . Ido, Refugio y otras personas" in a conversation on current events mention "la frecuencia con que se tiraba gente por el Viaducto de la calle de Segovia." (*489*)

[61] Jaime Balmes, "Le ciencia y la sociedad," in *Antología del pensamiento de lengua española,* ed. José Gaos, México, 1945, p. 131. (Hereafter cited as *Antología.*)

[62] Ibid., p. 121. Curiously Marcelino Menéndez Pelayo in his "Dos palabras sobre el centenario de Balmes" uses the same image: "Hoy presenciamos el lento suicidio de un pueblo que, engañado mil veces por garrulos sofistas, . . . contempla con ojos estúpidos la destrucción de la única España . . . cuyo recuerdo tiene virtud bastante para retardar nuestra agonía." *Antología,* ed. Gaos, p. 877. Principal among these "sofistas" he goes on to indicate is the "secta lóbrega y esteril" of the "krausistas."

will still be worth what they are worth now. Whatever happens rent will still be collected."[63] This means implicitly that Galdós, even more desperate than Balmes, has concluded that a nation that has so debased itself ought to die but unfortunately cannot. And so it is with Isidora. If even a novel of private life must begin at the "final de otra novela," it follows that a nation's novel cannot come to an end or at least to a climactic end. It is for that very reason that Galdós continues to play ironically during part 2 with Isidora's various potential deaths, by assassination at the hands of her son or by a final "consent" polar to that of don Rodrigo Manrique.

By the time the reader finishes the last chapter of part 2 entitled "Muerte de Isidora—Conclusión de los Rufetes," he realizes that Galdós, unlike Larra and Balmes, has throughout been using the image of national death in order to castigate national life. His point is that, even if Spain could voluntarily and feasibly choose not to be, the Spain represented by Isidora Rufete would be as unlikely to make such a choice as that of Juanito Santa Cruz. To Galdós, the worst thing about the new era was its self-satisfaction, its lack of awareness of its own spiritual sickness. On the contrary, a rage to live lavishly, a joy in spending as much as could be borrowed on imposing façades and impotent battle cruisers, a reckless willingness to mortgage an authentic and modest future in order to keep up appearances ("el aparentar") as a European nation were the order of the day. Not suicide, not death, but prostitution, at first genteel but by the end grotesquely sordid, was the true counterpart of Restoration Spain in the biographical microcosm.[64] The reader

[63] Hyman, "Manuscript," p. 173. In the published text this commonplace is transferred to the dialogue of the fatuous and pompous Marqués de la Casa Muñoz: ". . . habrá un poco de república; pero ya saben ustedes que las naciones no mueren." (*81*)

[64] Seco Serrano discusses Galdós' bitter memories of the inception of the Restoration as expressed in *Cánovas,* the last of the "episodios" and written ten years before his death. It is worth noting that much of that post-1898 analysis is already present in *La desheredada.* "Los *episodios nacionales,"* p. 283. The aging novelist significantly returns to his earlier images of national sickness and death. Spaniards, he exhorts, become revolutionaries, "si no queréis morir de la honda caquexia que invade el cansado cuerpo de tu nación." (*1363*) Spain's condition, of course, was only one national reflection of a far more widespread malaise of Western civilization, which became apparent towards the end of the century and which was explained by Max Scheler as derived from a metaphysical vacancy (the "oquedad" that pre-

121

has not merely been "warned" as in certain romances of horror; he has discovered by identifying himself with Isidora, who he is and what his descendants are likely to become in the future.[65]

In profound agreement with the somberness of its prophetic theme, *La desheredada,* as we look back on it, is the most dimly-lighted novel Galdós ever wrote. A fitting companion to *Little Dorrit* (doubly centered on the Usher-like Clennam house and on the Marshallsea prison), it begins in a madhouse and ends in a jail. And its style, as if emerging from the description of the final

---

occupied the Generation of '98), which was the inevitable result both of historicism and positivism and which infiltrated into the tastes and social relations of the self-satisfied inhabitants of the end of the century. *Philosophische Weltanschauung,* Munich, 1954, p. 6. Marx, on the other hand, according to Edmund Wilson, was intent "in the middle years" on demonstrating that a system based on ruthlessness covered with moral pretense "with its wholesale encouragement of cant [Torquemada's speech at the banquet?] was an inherent and irremediable feature of the economic structure itself." *Eight Essays,* New York, 1954, p. 35. The choice between moral cant and Isidora's "aparentar" presumably corresponds to Castro's notion of "vividura," but both have in common the covering up of an inner hollowness and sense of unreality. Or as Flaubert is said to have phrased it, "Tout était faux sous l'Empire [de Napoleon le Petit], des cocottes jusqu'a la littérature." Nadeau, *Gustave Flaubert, écrivain,* p. 16.

[65] Even I am shocked slightly when I read in Clarín's review: "Galdós se ha echado a la corriente; ha publicado su programa de literatura incendiaria, su programa naturalista; ha escrito en quinientas páginas la historia de una prostituta." Cited by Carlos Rovetta, "El Naturalismo de Galdós en *La desheredada,"* Nos, 8, 1943, p. 279. Galdós does not let the reader judge his antiheroine at the social distance that Zola creates for Nana. And yet the reader knows at the same time that she is one more prostitute, or even worse than a prostitute, for one can hardly make for her the same eloquent defense that Casalduero makes for "la Tal," Dulce, "la Peri," and the grotesque women who follow Nazarín: "Incluso en estas últimas lo que sobresale es esa hondura humana que las hace, al margen de la Sociedad y de la legalidad, verdaderamente dignas. Con la dignidad de lo que vive verdaderamente. No sujetas a los prejuicios, convencionalismos e intereses; ni siquiera arrastradas por la compasión y la conmiseración, sino ligadas al ser humano por ser sencillamente eso, un ser humano." Casalduero, "Conjunción y divergencia de vida y arte en Galdós," *H,* 53, 1970, p. 830. Rovetta sees *La desheredada* as reproduciendo "con no pocas variantes la historía de Nana en París." "El Naturalismo de Galdós en *La desheredada,"* p. 279. To the extent that this is true, for example, the deformed child, for reasons both of dating and subject matter it applies to part 2 rather than part 1. It also overlooks the contribution thereto of *Splendeurs et misères des courtisanes.* See note 47.

agony of Rufete, clouds our eyes with images of physical, spiritual, and national death. Even more, the central deception of its plot, the delayed revelation of the fundamental spuriousness of most of those who inhabit it (whether father, daughter, uncle, politician, or marchioness), is premised on the art of obscuring vision. This was detected by the irreproachable sensibility of Ricardo Gullón, when he remarked that certain characters "are illuminated only partially and in flashes. The whole is mysteriously dim as if keeping a secret as a consequence of this lack of illumination."[66] What an extraordinary achievement to have thus portrayed, from within the inner darkness and dry rot, a gilded age devoted to the gaiety of exhibiting its contrived effulgence! Our initial spur-of-the-moment criticism, repetitiousness, overemphasis, etc., has succumbed to admiration.

Novel and Fatality

Part 2 of *La desheredada,* the chronicle of Isidora's step-by-step descent into the "bas fonds" of society, was thus the result of Galdós' realization that the unveiling of the myth had left him with nothing less than a key to the future, or risking a second mixed metaphor, with prophetic antennae so delicate that they could detect what was to happen not only in a few years (as in *La Fontana*) but in more than six decades. The essays of Wright and Ruiz Salvador have called attention to the most important revelations.[67] First is the succession of ever more squalid and cynical lovers (future governments), then the rejection of simplistic but salutary revolution (the honorable pretensions of Juan Bou), and last, the macrocephalic child addicted to ecclesiastic and military games (the Restoration), who will one day execute his mother.[68] The violent

---

[66] "Desdoblamiento interior en *La desheredada,*" *Ins,* 300–301, 1971, p. 9.

[67] Ruiz Salvador, "La función." Chad C. Wright, "The Representational Qualities of Isidora," *RF,* 83, 1971, pp. 230–244.

[68] This particular abnormality is presented with an ample dose of Galdosian ambiguity. Wright interprets it, on the one hand, as an hereditary deformity typical of Naturalism. And indeed it seems comparable to that of Louiset, Nana's miserable child, who suffers from a "carie des os du crâne." *Les Rougon-Macquart,* vol. 2, p. 1359. The deformity is also comparable to that of Torquemada's second son. On the other hand, also according to Wright, it is representational, a symbol among other things of the "over-centralization of power in Madrid." As early as 1783 London was similarly compared

conclusion of the period represented by Isidora is visualized in a characteristically prophetic dream, which deserves much more admiration than it has so far received:

> Sometimes in her dreams Riquín appeared with his enormous head and pretty face leaning to one side, a rifle on his shoulder and marching like a soldier. And that little rascal of an antichrist would look at her, take aim with childish winsomeness and—*pow!* He would fire a shot that would kill her on the spot. Then other children would come, Riquín's little friends, and with boisterous laughs they would take hold of her and drag her through the streets. Jeers and uproar from the infantile multitude, which would cry out in unison: "the Marquesa, the Marquesa!" (*1131*)

If in part 1 the clash of juvenile gangs had been explicitly interpreted by Galdós as anticipating "la discordia del porvenir," prediction in part 2 is so central to the novel that it needs no explanations. The very act of imputing historical significance to a life in its biographical time (in contrast to a cartoon creature or a living statue) enabled projection of that life into history that had not yet happened. How incredibly accurate this kind of novelistic vaticination could be is demonstrated by the final abyss of unabashed public prostitution that was the fate of Isidora and for which she (unlike poor Gervaise) felt "una atracción invencible." The only quibble I have to offer as I write this now in 1974 is that business is far more flourishing than Isidora's final appearance and manner of speaking might have led us to expect.

---

to "a monster with a head enormously large." Raymond Williams, *The Country and the City*, New York, 1973, p. 146. Larra in *Los barateros* (a likely source) suggests a slightly different reading of the allegory based on the well-known Roman parable: "llámanme ahora sociedad y cuerpo, pero soy un cuerpo truncado: ¿Y no ves que no tengo sino cabeza, que es la nobleza, y brazos que es la curia, y una espada ceñida, que es mi fuerza militar? Pero, ¿no ves que me falta la base del cuerpo, que es el pueblo? . . . ¿No ves que no soy la sociedad, sino un monstruo de sociedad?" *Obras*, ed. C. Seco Serrano, BAE, Madrid, 1960, vol. 2, p. 2066. Robert Ricard calls attention to a Dickensian parallel, that of Mr. Chillips's "heavy-headed" and "goggle-eyed" baby, who appears in chapters 22 and 31 of *David Copperfield*. *Aspects de Galdós*, Paris, 1963, p. 30, note 1.

As the potential for prophecy found in *La Fontana* becomes fully realized in *La desheredada,* the element of fable becomes vestigial. It is still present in the initial dedication and the closing "moraleja" (as in all evolutionary ascents, Galdós never completely abandons earlier solutions), but despite being so prominently displayed, it is apparent that the lesson we are supposed to have learned has little to do with what we have read. As far as the dedication to the nation's true physicians, "los maestros de escuela," is concerned, to try to imagine Isidora having been brought up by Máximo Manso instead of Santiago Quijano-Quijada would amount to imagining another novel altogether.[69] How she was to be educated was simply not a question posed to her by this novel (her mad indoctrination has taken place before we begin to read) or by society (her uncle and father represent the fatal "heredity" of centuries).

When we come to the closing recommendation that we use a ladder if we wish to climb up to "una difícil y escabrosa altura" and not "alas postizas," the tone is so brutal and sardonic (borrowed

[69] The crucial role of the "Instituteur" in French nation-building and of the "maestro de escuela" in Spanish nation-rebuilding was a commonplace of the time. Strange as it may sound today, Pierre Nora in his "Ernest Lavisse: son rôle dans la formation du sentiment national" remarks that teachers and army officers are "les piliers jumeaux de la patrie." *Révue historique,* July–September 1852. Cited by Aimé Dupuy, "La guerre de 1870 et les manuels scolaires de la Troisième," *Le Monde,* 3 September 1970, p. 7. Perhaps the moderate young "militar," Bozmediano, and Máximo Manso have more in common conceptually than is apparent at the end of the twentieth century. Of direct relevance to *La desheredada* is a text of Concepción Arenal, for which I am indebted to Antonio Ruiz Salvador; "No vemos otro medio de combatir eso que se llama la frivolidad de la mujer, su sed de lujo, la importancia que da a las cosas pequeñas, el desconocimiento de las cosas grandes, los extravíos de la veleidad inquieta de su hastío, los peligros de su actividad que no se dirige, las monstruosidades de su desesperación, ni las ignominias corruptoras de su envilecimiento no vemos defensa contra tantos enemigos sino en la instrucción." Arenal, *La instrucción del pueblo, Memoria premiada con accesit por la Real Academia de Ciencias Morales y Políticos en el concurso ordinario de 1878,* Madrid, 1881, p. 18. That this was indeed another "cuestión palpitante" at the time is attested to by the articles of Pedro de Alcántara García on various aspects of the education of women. *Revista de España,* 106 and 112, 1885–1886. Hemmings refers to a letter of Zola's in *La Vie littéraire* of 22 February 1877 in which he invites critics of *L'Assommoir* to support school building. *Emile Zola,* p. 124. And in that context he must have meant for both sexes!

125

directly from Larra in one of his didactic moods, according to Ruiz Salvador) that we almost feel indignant with the writer.[70] We have been too caught up in Isidora's tale of woe to accept the abrupt, Icarian postscript as relevant. The deeper truth, however, is that Galdós, who may at times seem heartless but who invariably shuns pedantry, has realized that his newly-acquired determinism has undermined the whole concept of the fable and, along with it, the concept of the helpful "moraleja." Fables traditionally are a harsh genre, but, at the same time, are premised on elementary free choice between prudence or rashness, cunning or (as in the case of Lázaro) gullibility. It is precisely this simple option, demonstrated by her pathetic Little Dora-like attempts to mend her ways and to keep double-entry books, that is denied to Isidora by her biography. A hopeless situation, in other words, ends with a helpless moral.

Having presented Galdós' novel-by-novel evolution as a ceaseless dialectic of problem and solution, dissatisfaction and new departure, it is fitting that we close our discussion of *La desheredada* with a few remarks on the novel that appeared a year later, *El amigo Manso*. There, if anywhere, we should be able to detect how Galdós himself viewed the major experiment that preceded it. As far as the theme of the new novel is concerned, it has often been observed that Galdós was concerned about presenting the kind of "maestro de escuela" who could have taught Isidora the *"Aritmética, Lógica, Moral y Sentido común,"* which in the Dedication he cites as her most glaring lacunae. Having finished the biography of Isidora and having harshly chastised therein the "Quijano-Quijada" tradition, which predominated among Spanish "filósofos y políticos," it was now up to him to provide a novelistic version of a one-man "institución libre de enseñanza." That this was accomplished with a

---

[70] Speaking about "la poca solidez de la instrucción de los jóvenes del día" and about those who try to imitate French innovations without beginning at the national grass roots, Larra in *Los barateros* concludes: "Para esta clase hemos escrito nuestro artículo; hemos pintado los resultados de esta despreocupación superficial de querer tomar simplemente los efectos, sin acordarse de que es preciso empezar por las causas; de intentar, en fin, subir la escalera a tramos. Subámosla tranquilos, escalón por escalón, si queremos llegar arriba." This text is missing in the 1835 edition but is to be found in the anthology *Clásicos castellanos,* ed. J. R. Lomba y Pedraja, Madrid, 1959, vol. 1, p. 72.

mixture of irony, pessimism, and affection, as Carlos Blanco Aguinaga has recently pointed out, should not surprise us.[71] However
great may have been the mutual esteem of Galdós and don Francisco
Giner de los Ríos, Pepe Rey, Isidora, and Máximo Manso all had
the same "padrastro." What Galdós called ironically "el gran asunto
de la educación" (*1165*) might be beneficial, but it was not going to
cure the Madrid of *La desheredada* in the ephemeral span of a
single generation.[72]

At present, however, I am less concerned with the thematic continuity and discontinuity of the two novels than with Galdós' calculated attempt to reintroduce a semblance of free will into the
structure of the narrative. After contemplating the implacable determinism of imposed history and heredity during the course of
two long volumes, Galdós was now anxious to design a novel that
would permit its protagonist not only to make choices but also, and
more importantly, to make genuine mistakes. For that purpose he
returned to the first person and had his story told by what is called
today an "autonomous" character, that is, a consciousness liberated
by authorial fiat both from the dictation of its biographical circumstances and from that of the plot. Isidora has to do what her life
(the perverted childhood she comes from, the perverted Madrid she
goes to) demands; Máximo Manso, on the other hand, presents
himself in terms of a continual capacity for decision. In his own
mind he is as free as Alonso Quijano was when he decided to show
up Avellaneda by going to Barcelona instead of Zaragoza. This is
fine until, like the rest of us, he discovers that there are feelings
and situations (the most serious being his love for Irene) beyond
rational control. It is precisely at that point, at the juncture of
freedom and servitude, that the novel gets under way and that
Galdós tries to redress the one-sidedness of his biography of Isidora.

Critics have frequently commented on Galdós' debt to Cervantes
in contriving autonomy.[73] This is true, but it should be added that,

[71] *"El amigo Manso* y el 'ciclo céntrico de la sociedad'," *NRFH,* 24, 1975,
pp. 419–437.

[72] For a discussion of the equation of Giner with Manso, see Shoemaker,
"Sol y sombra."

[73] See, for example, Leon Livingston, "Interior Duplication and the Problem of Form in the Modern Spanish Novel," *PMLA,* 73, 1958, pp. 393–406.
Monroe Hafter, however, makes an interesting case for Anatole France's *Le*

whereas don Quijote's belief in his self-determination grows organically and slowly from the deepest postulates of Cervantes' creative vision, Máximo Manso shocks us by introducing himself as a human, or inhuman, answer to Naturalism. To begin the novel with the paradoxical assertion "Yo no existo" and to close it with an ironically celestial view of "las desgraciadas figurillas" who had been involved in Manso's moment of feigned residence on earth is essentially a means of undermining the notion of documentation and recovering that element of doubt about its own reality, that element of play, which is an inherent possibility of the novel and which Zola and his followers chose not to exploit. The mind of Manso is not free in the sense that it can do or accomplish whatever it chooses, but it is not a product of its milieu, and it can contemplate its novelistic circumstances accurately or erroneously, with illusion or with disgust, from a distance. In other words, Galdós used the device of autonomy, not for its own sake, but as a means of severing the fatal nexus of self with heredity and environment.

El amigo Manso is, thus, a initial experiment in breaking the fetters of Naturalistic theory and practice. It shows Galdós' full awareness of the stultifying effects of determinism not only in *La desheredada* but also in the novel as such. In his own initial experiment with the imported techniques, he had resolved the fourteen-year-old problem of the incompatibility of movement and meaning, which had worried him so much; he had created the city novel in Spanish terms; and above all he had developed the prophetic capacity of the parvenu genre to an extent never rivaled by any other novelist I can mention. But he had not, and he knew it, endowed Isidora with that freedom to react, to grow, and to change that gave meaning to the lives of don Quitote and Sancho. Nor, despite his intentions, did he really do so in *El amigo Manso*, for this was a patently artificial experiment relying on self-conscious authorial

---

Crime de Sylvestre Bonnard, which has significant plot resemblances to *El amigo Manso* and whose hero reflects significantly on the figure of don Quijote, whom he imagines explaining to him, "sache que la pensée est la seule réalité du monde." Even more suggestive is that Manso's initial "Yo no existo" is said to Bonnard in a dream by a fairy: "C'est vous qui n'existez pas." *"Le Crime de Sylvestre Bonnard, a possible source for El amigo Manso,"* Symp, 17, 1963, pp. 123–129. Once again there appears to be a convincing case for Galdós' characteristic "double dialogue."

management. The strained and affected humor of Manso's account of his relations with "un amigo que ha incurrido por sus pecados, que deben de ser tantos en número como las arenas de la mar, en la pena infamante de escribir novelas" (*1165*) is in itself an indication of artificiality. Galdós' first truly autonomous character, autonomous in the deepest Cervantine sense of "inner-directed" authenticity, was to be Fortunata.

One question concerning the definition of Isidora's fate remains unanswered. Certain critics (Casalduero, Montesinos, and, most explicitly, Rodgers) have mentioned the incompatibility of the two varieties of heredity, traditional and biological, as a telltale flaw. I disagree for two reasons. In the first place, to insist on the dichotomy foreshortens the art of Zola, who was centrally preoccupied with the interaction of culture and genes and whose ultimate aim (as Harry Levin has demonstrated eloquently) was the same as Galdós': the enlargement and health of consciousness. In the second place, as we have seen, in this particular experiment *L'Assommoir* and the *Quijote* are set purposefully in ironical counterpoint. Reversing the phrase attributed to Samuel Barnum, it is almost impossible to overestimate the cunning of Galdós, that is, the extent of his awareness of what he was up to in every novel from *Trafalgar* to *La razón de la sin razón*. And to insist critically on fissures, flaws, and incongruities amounts to the opposite—gross underestimation. As a literary organism, *La desheredada* accomplishes exactly what it was supposed to accomplish. What is lacking in it is what was not *put* into it, what could not be put into it—genuine self-determination. That would have to wait.

PART II

Fortunata y Jacinta in Prospect

CHAPTER V

From *La desheredada* to *Lo prohibido*

Novel and Dialectics

In addition to professors, beloved and unbeloved, four classmates accompany Juanito Santa Cruz in the opening paragraph of *Fortunata y Jacinta:* Jacinto María Villalonga, Joaquinito Pez, Alejandro Miquis, and Zalamero, whose surname sufficed for an author who was not fond of "flatterers" or teachers' pets. For Galdós' reading public they are old acquaintances, reappearing, young representatives of middle-class Madrid, perhaps comparable to the young Parisian dandies encountered by Lucien de Rubempré at the "bal de l'Opéra."[1] And if some members of that public felt hesitant to take the plunge into the ocean of the new, four-volume novel, they might well have been enticed into so doing by vivid memories of these four in *La desheredada, El doctor Centeno,* and *Lo prohibido.* As Galdós surely intended, the reader's encounter with lives not too long ago relived in print is comparable to recognizing familiar faces while standing uncertainly on the threshold of an enormous and forbidding social gathering. Critics of Balzac are unquestionably right in insisting on the contribution of reappearing characters to our belief in fictional worlds, to the growth of Paris as a "true" milieu through one novel after another. In addition, however, mentioned so abruptly at the outset, the familiar four names help to put us at ease in the face of the vast accumulation of human experience that awaits us. If these old friends of ours are also the friends of Juanito Santa Cruz, we already feel comfortable as we enter his world.[2]

---

[1] At the beginning of *Splendeurs et misères,* of course.

[2] The reappearance of characters provides indispensable support for the nineteenth-century novel's pretense of historical truth (Balzac's "le vrai"), while at the same time reflecting the ever-increasing "novelization" of consciousness among both authors and readers. Among the critics who have discussed the paradox, Félicien Marçeau, in his classic *Balzac et son monde,*

Although encouraged to continue reading by the presence of these remembered companions, an inevitable question occurs: which among his friends does Juanito resemble? Is he committed to a vocation like the diligent Zalamero or the idealistic Miquis, or is he one more useless "señorito" like the other two. The latter is, of course, the case, as we learn before the first paragraph is finished, but there is a crucial distinction to be made: "Although, when first meeting Juanito Santa Cruz, we might believe him to resemble Joaquinito Pez, upon getting to know him, we would remark rather on their profound differences, because the Pez kid with his irresponsible character and inconsequential mind was nothing but a show-off. ('botarate')" (15) Galdós is clearly warning us in no uncertain terms that the two are only superficially alike. We should not dismiss this latest version of the plumed, young bourgeois as a mere reincarnation of the Pez caricature, a caricature we have already learned to disdain.

At the same time that Galdós corrects this possibility of misapprehension, he alludes implicitly to what we shall eventually discover to be a 180-degree change of novelistic course. By including Joaquinito among Juanito's cohort (the diminutive is stressed even more for the latter) and by insisting on their enormous discrepancy in human worth, Galdós buttresses the notion, advanced in chapter 4, that *Fortunata y Jacinta* was initially conceived of as an antithesis to the Naturalistic thesis of *La desheredada*.[3] The sequence of creative problems and solutions, which we have hitherto referred to as a form of "dialogue" with his own novels and those of others, is so manifest, overt, and influential in this case that it can be understood as "dialectical."

As an answer to Joaquinito's poor showing in the role of the "señorito" as seducer (he actually uses the title "Marqués viudo de

---

most explicitly refers to the above advantage of the device. The "nouveau personnage," he says, validates his existence through his friends and ours, who reappear "chargés de souvenirs." Paris, 1955, pp. 21–22.

[3] The notion of an underground continuity joining the two characters Joaquinito and Juanito is further supported by a passing remark in *La desheredada*. Isidora has been imprisoned for presenting forged documents in her suit, and she typically compares herself with Marie Antoinette in the Conciergerie: "El día lo pasó en estas cavilaciones, acordándose mucho del Delfín, de Joaquín Pez y de otras personas." (*1129*)

Saldeoro" on his calling cards!), Juanito will possess a physical and oral charm so genuine as to render him the plausible beloved of the two most adorable women in Madrid. By the end we may despise him all the more, but we must not underestimate him. He is definitely *not* a "botarate." Similarly, as we learn much later on, Fortunata is a creature capable of profound and altruistic passion antithetical to the Romantic and socially self-serving infatuation of Isidora.[4] Otherwise, she too would have descended into what Galdós might have termed "el infierno social": "despeñada en voraginoso laberinto de las calles." (*1161*)

In spite of, or perhaps because of, his consciousness of a dialectical intention, it is probable that at the moment of beginning chapter 1 of the preliminary manuscript Galdós, like Cervantes before him, had not the remotest idea of the human depths into which he was to plunge, or of the angelic heights into which he was to soar. An examination of the *Fortunata* manuscript clearly reveals that initial ignorance through the contrast it offers with what was finally achieved. For in the completed version, the introduction, not of Cervantine irony (already present in the juvenile pieces written in Las Palmas), but of Cervantine "incitation" into the humdrum, contextual, milieu-oriented documentation of Zola was to produce an unprecedented "naturalismo espiritual" capable of exploring regions of consciousness comparable only to those known to readers of Dostoievsky and Melville.[5]

---

[4] The continuity that joins the two women as well as the profound difference between them is particularly evident when we take into account certain aspects of Isidora's ororverbalized and so rationalized image of herself: "Mi corazón es de una sola pieza. No puedo amar sino a uno solo y amarle siempre. . . . Uno solo me ha conquistado, y de ése soy. Venga lo que viniere a mi amor me atengo. No sé cómo hay mujeres que adoran hoy a éste y mañana al otro. Yo no soy así. (*Con tristeza*) ¿No es verdad que nací para ser honrada?" And a few lines later on: "No hay nada que me cautive tanto, que tanto interese mi alma, como un acto de estos atrevidos y difíciles, en que entren la generosidad y el peligro." (*1087*)

[5] The oxymoron "naturalismo espiritual" is, of course, used by Galdós as the title of part 3, chapter 6, which contains, on the one hand, the Zolaesque death of Mauricia surrounded by the pious but somewhat childish rites and decorations organized by doña Guillermina and, on the other, the beginning of that inner transformation in Fortunata that was to result in the "pícara idea" of the following chapter. As we shall see, the end of the novel constitutes one of those moments of Hegelian synthesis (Fortunata absorbs "la

The artifice of autonomous characterization employed in *El amigo Manso,* which was Galdós' initial response to the determinism of *La desheredada,* had only resulted in intellectual play with the confrontation "ego versus Madrid." But now as Fortunata creates her own, genuine autonomy in the course of this veritable novelistic Gulf Stream, her range and profundity of experience will come to surpass that normally afforded to human life. In the intense encounters of part 4, for example, the final meeting of the married couple, we sense, just as we sense while immersed in *The Brothers Karamazov,* that we are in the presence of beings so passionately conscious and so inextricably interlocked in mutual yet conflictive experience as to belong to some unknowable, and probably never-to-be-born, future species descended from mankind.[6] In Spain only the great series of episodes, which begin with the discovery by don Quijote and Sancho that part 1 of their novel has been published and widely read, offer a comparable revelation of amplified human meaning as well as a comparable imperviousness to exegesis.

If this means, as it does, that *Fortunata y Jacinta* will elude our most cunning stratagems for its critical capture, it does not necessarily follow that the path traced thus far leads only to awed silence in the face of the ineffable. Galdós in such later novels as *Misericordia* was to attain equal or perhaps even greater insight into the soul. But only in the case of *Fortunata y Jacinta* is it possible to follow him from initial intention to final achievement. In later chapters I shall try with due humility and as closely as I can to discuss the portent of that novel, but for the moment I am only concerned to view from a distance the whence and the whither of a narrative that begins with documentation and ends with transfiguration.

---

rata eclesiástica" "como si la hubiera tomado en comunión") with which Galdós enjoyed playing ironically in the manner of his Spanish master. The adjective "espiritual" should be understood not only in Christian terms but also as referring to "Geist." Casalduero in his pioneering *Vida y obra* sees the same confrontation ("materia" versus "esprítu") as characteristic of the novels written during the crucial central period of Galdós' artistic evolution.

[6] Such characters are referred to by Robert Petsch as "epische Menschen" as opposed to "Alltagsmenschen." Because they are creatures of a common creator, they share in his omniscience and therefore possess the ability to peer into each other's "letzten Tiefen." *Wesen und Formen,* p. 119.

136

Unlike the major novels of Dostoievsky, Galdós' first masterpiece does not delve into the sublime and the deranged ab initio. Rather, in a way comparable to the Melville of *Moby Dick,* he only dared transcribe the words of his incited creatures after a calculated and lengthy process of first creating Juanito's Naturalistic milieu and afterwards slowly peeling it off. It was a double process, which, to the extent that I understand it, gave dialectical precision to the spontaneous and intuitive novel-to-novel (or in *La desheredada* part-to-part) dialogue to which we have attended thus far. Once he had discovered that method, Galdós was equipped for a major voyage of exploration. *Fortunata y Jacinta,* first conceived of as an antithesis of the Naturalistic thesis of *La desheredada,* continues to operate dialectically in such a way as to prepare both author and reader for our awesome encounter with "spirit" ("Geist") finally unveiled and in the flesh. Before we are done, at least a tentative discussion of the novel's Cervantine play with Hegelian phenomenology will be unavoidable.

As we pointed out a moment ago, confirmation of the dialectical contribution of the biographical "failure" of Isidora Rufete and the autobiographical "failure" of Máximo Manso to the creation of Fortunata is provided by the first draft. Written, as seems to have been Galdós' usual practice, on the reverse side of the pages of the version destined for the printers, these "materias reunidas" constitute an independent if fragmentary novel of their own.[7] When the

---

[7] My conclusions on Galdós' mode of composition are based on Robert J. Weber's *The "Miau" Manuscript of Benito Pérez Galdós,* Berkeley and Los Angeles, 1964; Walter T. Pattison, *Etapas preliminares de "Gloria",* Barcelona, 1979; the reports of those who have worked on the MS of *La desheredada* (see chapter 4, note 59); and my own examination of a xerox copy of the *Doña Perfecta* MS in the BN. The last contains a fairly long fragment of a preliminary version on the reverse side of its pages in addition to what appears to be a translation of an English novel identified (by Chad C. Wright in a personal letter) as Dickens's *The Battle of Life. La Fontana,* on the other hand, is written, without a preliminary version, on both sides of the pages. From the fragmentary evidence thereby provided, I strongly suspect that Galdós composed ever more elaborate preliminary versions as he became more experienced in his profession. (One thing is certain: his penchant for saving paper by composing final drafts, subject, of course, to extensive changes in the proofs, on the reverse side of pages of preparatory notes and tentative narration will bring both headaches and opportunities to future scholars.) If Galdós felt obliged to rewrite his second version as well, thus

impeccably transcribed edition of the *Fortunata* MS by Diane Beth Hyman appears, we shall have been given a priceless gift: a revelation of Galdós's initial intention so clear as to make the mystery of his achievement all the more worthy of reverence. We shall be able to read for ourselves a remarkable text, an unambiguous *Fortunata y Jacinta* displaying exactly what Galdós had in mind when embarking on his most memorable voyage.

Understood in these terms, the aspect of the preliminary version of *Fortunata y Jacinta* that is most interesting to us is its emphasis on Naturalistic determinism. Fortunata in the ample tradition of the Rougon-Macquarts is afflicted with hereditary epilepsy;[8] she describes herself as an "hija del acaso . . . traída y llevada;"[9] she fears that her ultimate destiny will inevitably be "el fango;"[10] and so on. Galdós, thinking dialectically, was concerned about emphasizing the enormous handicaps to be overcome before the redemptive legacy of an heir was possible. He did not know exactly how the novel should end (a possibility jotted down on the last page is Fortunata's suicide after giving birth), but from the text it appears that he was fully aware of the message he intended to send both to his public and to posterity. Fortunata, as Naturalistically pre-

---

leaving both sides of the same page filled with unusable material, he consigned those pages to the wastebasket and left lamentable gaps in the preliminary MS. I have therefore been unable to read his initial formulation of the meeting of Juanito and Fortunata in part 1, to my great personal regret. That part must have been intensively worked over. The *Fortunata y Jacinta* MS is in the Houghton Library collection at Harvard and available to qualified scholars. A microfilm has been purchased by the Casa-Museo in Las Palmas.

Despite the lacunae in the MSS, it is fascinating to observe the essentially narrative nature of Galdós' creative imagination. Even in his notes he often tells himself what he is planning to write as if it were a story.

[8] "La lectura de aquella carta produjo a Fortunata una de aquellas crisis epilépticas, que rara vez le acometían." Hyman, "Manuscript," p. 419. Robert Ricard comments on the common subjection to this disease of Maxi, Mauricia, and Fortunata, although in the case of the last, he admits that it may well be "une simple comparaison." *Aspects de Galdós,* p. 31, n. 1). He is right. The related passage in the published edition seems to be a veiled, metaphorical reminiscence of the earlier version: "De repente cual movida por un impulso epiléptico, Fortunata se incorporó en el lecho." (*525*)

[9] Hyman, "Manuscript," p. 460.

[10] Ibid., p. 400.

destined as Isidora, or even more so, was to save herself by a totally generous exercise of free will. Or to rearrange the phrase already cited from the prologue to *La Regenta,* "por un inesperado impulso que naciera de su propio seno."

Novel and Disease

Although the dialectical interdependence of *Fortunata y Jacinta* and *La desheredada* is apparent at the level of story in their similarities and dissimilarities, Galdós did not embark immediately on the major task of creative re-creation. Before the crucial dilemma posed by Isidora's biography, the possibility of freedom in a history-obsessed century, could be faced novelistically, a period of further experimentation was indispensable. In the six-year interval between the twilit enunciation of the thesis and the epic undertaking of the antithesis, *El amigo Manso,* the Centeno-Bringas trilogy, and *Lo prohibido* appeared in rapid succession and constituted a secondary pattern of novelistic questions and answers. Specifically, after Galdós perceived that the point-of-view coquetry of *El amigo Manso* amounted to relinquishing the major achievement of *La desheredada,* the possibility of systematically creating and exploring urban milieux, he drew back. He returned to audition and observation in the third person singular and in the next three novels escorted his public on a guided, Naturalistic expedition through the wilds of Madrid.

Beginning with the sordid lodgings of students, prostitutes, and impoverished priests, Galdós continues by showing us the shoddily pretentious oil cloth of cramped bourgeois apartments and ends with a backstairs excursion into the Palacio Real itself. There is, however, one characteristic that is shared equally by these diverse habitats. In contrast to the comfort and luxury of the Santa Cruz residence (the "palace" of the new "nobleza del dinero"), misery, anguish, and squalor are their common condition.[11] A few valiant or self-deluded spirits, an Amparito Emperador or a Felipe Centeno, may on occasion try to flutter upwards on their own, but essentially the

---

[11] If this seems a strange thing to say about the Palacio Real, we only have to remember Dickens's similar description of Hampton Court in *Little Dorrit,* a description which may well have suggested to Galdós an exploration of Spain's comparable milieu.

Madrid of the trilogy is as Naturalistically presented as Zola's Paris. It would seem that from 1882 to 1886 Galdós abandoned his first experimental reaction against the movement and was instead intent on seeing what he might make of it.

The display of painfully diseased minds in these novels (as contrasted to Fortunata's immune consciousness) is remarkable for its diversity and perversity, but perhaps the sickest mind of all is that of Rosalía Pipaón de la Barca, otherwise known as "la de Bringas."[12] A middle-aged and emphatically corseted avatar of Isidora (her seducer is don Manuel María José de Pez, identified by Galdós as the father of Joaquinito), she has none of the redeeming charm and youthful spontaneity of her predecessor.[13] On the contrary, her ingrained bourgeois money-consciousness is accompanied by a hypocrisy so tawdry that we actually enjoy her final series of humiliations. As a result, when the lady, following the representational example of Isidora, converts herself into a symbol of national degeneration by surrendering to Pez "père" a few days before the collapse of the monarchy, the reader feels no personal involvement.[14] Late nineteenth-century Spain may, indeed, be represented not unfairly by a presumptuous, surreptitious, and, worst of all, morally self-righteous whore, but the *reader* has never sympathised with her.

[12] This title, like that of *La regenta,* which was being written in the same year (1884), instead of merely suggesting a fictional biography in an historical milieu, evokes that milieu as a self-conscious collectivity dedicated to what Galdós called "chismografía" ("gossipography"). Both titles are substitute names conferred ironically on the ladies in question by the societies in which they live. They, thus, suggest exposure to ready-made, nineteenth-century community malice rather than to a careless universe, as in the case of a Lazarillo or a Pleberio.

[13] The variation in the seducer's name (in *La desheredada* he is called don Manuel José Ramón del Pez) corresponds, as Martha Krow-Lucal has shown in her dissertation on that novel's characterization, not to carelessness, but to a desire to depersonalize the figure. Every time he reappears his given names seem to change. In the trilogy, however, he is specifically identified as the father of Joaquinito.

[14] It could be argued plausibly that the hypocritical—"married"—prostitution of Rosalía is supposed to represent "la farsa y licencia de la reina castiza," i.e. the old regime, as compared to Isidora, whose "lovers" are the successive governments that followed the departure of Isabel II. Although it seems to become a continuing way of life for Rosalía, as well as a concealed modus vivendi for the Bringas family, the point I try to make in the text is not therefore vitiated.

Nor has Galdós tricked him into identifying with her. He can share in the satirical denunciation and avoid personal responsibility, a comforting situation that had not been offered to the reader of *La desheredada*.

At the very end, however, if Galdós' supposedly complacent and scandalized reader reads closely enough, he is due for a shock. The hitherto more or less invisible narrator openly confesses that he, too, secretly has been a client of the fallen bourgeoise, a client all the more despicable when he refuses, for ostensibly moral reasons, to continue to assist her financially:

> From her eloquent eyes one could detect proud self-assurance, her consciousness of being the cornerstone of a home undergoing such terrible trials.
>
> In specific terms I heard the same thing from her own lips later on during a very private interview. She desired me to join her once more in our—for me—far too expensive relationship, but I quickly called a halt. For if it seemed to her only natural to take over the burden of maintaining the out-of-office family, I saw no reason why I should help her and defy the exigencies both of morality and of my own personal budget. (*1671*)

The implications of this offhand confession will not puzzle connoisseurs of Galdós: if the narrator, who in style and episode has prompted us all along to despise his heroine, finally admits unashamedly his sordid commerce with her, ought not the reader begin to wonder about his own possible participation and responsibility? If Rosalía represents a moment in Spanish contemporary history, do not both the narrator and his public belong to the same clientele? Or to rephrase the humiliating interrogation, had not most of the Spaniards who were likely to read the novel sought and received favors from one corrupt regime or another? And had they not also, like the narrator in the course of his narration, tried to camouflage their complicity with moral reprobation? Nor should North American readers some ninety years later consider themselves exempt from this tacit censure. In our terms Galdós' satirical admission would apply to those of us who have denounced a Secretary of State or of Defense as a war criminal at a cocktail party instead of from behind bars.

The allegorical and moral impact of the anticlimax of *La de Bringas* is devastating. But for our present purposes its implications for the novel to come, which immediately preceded *Fortunata y Jacinta,* are particularly significant. To be specific, a complementary and equally valid way of interpreting the narrator's shameful admission is that it springs from a realization on the part of the author (our contemporary theorists insist that the two be strictly segregated, but Galdós, at least during this phase, seems rather to enjoy the cohabitation) that he has been unfair. Why should weak and venal women always be chosen to represent the corruption of the body politic, when it is clear that men, who legally control society, are at least as responsible? Is not the stingy and secretive yet inwardly unabashed and fatuous male client more reprehensible than the female merchant forced by circumstances to debase herself and to become her own merchandise? And, therefore, was not Galdós morally obliged to amplify the brief masculine confession of the closing paragraph into a new novel, which would contemplate directly the diseased consciousness of a domesticated, frock-coated, nineteenth-century don Juan Tenorio?

The result was, of course, *Lo prohibido,* the novel of a "super-señorito," who buys or seeks to buy (he is so self-consciously a man of means that, unlike the miserly narrator of *La de Bringas,* he seems to enjoy listing his extravagances) the favors of his three married cousins. The act of novelistic penitence on Galdós' part is laudable; there is much psychological truth (based on the writer's merciless self-scrutiny?) in the perversity examined, but *Lo prohibido* in my opinion is one of the least successful of the later "novelas contemporáneas." The underlying difficulty is that the questions just mentioned impelled Galdós in a direction that was more provocative than novelistic in the full, nineteenth-century sense. The new biography lacked an historical dimension. Such a subject might well have served a faithful and unimaginative disciple of Zola intent on converting the genre of Cervantes into an exercise in social documentation, but for an author on the verge of creating a Maxi and a Fortunata in their Madrid, the sordid private life of an antihero pompously baptized José María Bueno de Guzmán was uninspiring.

To begin with, there is the problem of form. The fact that honest answers to Galdós' perhaps somewhat masochistic questions about

142

male sexual consciousness could best be given in the first person gave rise to grave difficulties. The ironical gap between what a neo-picaresque narrator intends to say and the antithetical insight of the reader, which Galdós had exploited rather crudely in *Memorias de un cortesano de 1815,* is here out of the question.[15] If we are told confessional truth, we must accept it and believe all we read on its own terms. Nor can Galdós resort convincingly to the wry, self-deprecatory humor of Máximo Manso's account of his own life. The thinly veiled baseness of Bueno de Guzmán's obsessions renders such gentle mockery, when it is attempted, incongruous. The novel's most fundamental contradiction, however, has to do with verisimilitude. Everything we learn about the narrator's shameless behavior (the consequence of a Naturalistic "mal de familia," presented comically but by definition far more Zolaesque than the Manchegan curse of the Rufetes) makes the very fact of confession improbable. Unlike Guzmán de Alfarache, ostensibly intent on purging himself of sin, Lázaro de Tormes, who wants to make "vuestra merced" (and all the "vuestras mercedes" of the reading public) squirm, or Gabriel Araceli, who tries to draw hopeful conclusions for Spain from the historical dimension of his autobiography, such a human being as Bueno de Guzmán has no believable or even conceivable reason for making his self-awareness public.

These irresolvable formal problems all derive from the failure of *Lo prohibido* to present a genuine confession in which accumulated wisdom allows for a comprehension of the sins, follies, trials, and naive reactions of the past. Instead of providing us with that essential perspective, Bueno de Guzmán as narrator has a dear-diarylike tendency to run on and on, writing down everything that occurs to him in a kind of pseudopresent. He proceeds gaily, on some occasions wryly, from one unsavory recollection to another without the reflection and the interpretation that enable other fictional autobiographers to perceive or create meaningful order in "le temps retrouvé." Unlike the narrator of *Fortunata y Jacinta,* he is a mere chronicler of time, a drummer in contrast to a Toscanini.

[15] See M. Baquero Goyanés, "Perspectivismo irónico en Galdós," *Homenaje,* pp. 143–160. Goyanés discusses Galdós' use of the neo-picaresque *Cartas del pobrecito holgazán* of Sebastán de Miñano (1820) as a model for the first-person irony of this particular "episodio."

Galdós was not unaware of what was wrong, as is indicated at the end by an awkward effort to supply the missing motive for using up so much ink. Bueno de Guzmán, we finally learn, authentically concerned with his own human inauthenticity, has all along wanted to leave an utterly truthful "esquela" for posterity. He proposes to strip himself of all social camouflage and to reveal for whatever it may be worth "son coeur mis a nu." This is a variety of Romantic self-display in which from time to time many of us are tempted to indulge (usually while intoxicated!), but, in order to sustain a two-volume narrative, the narrator had better be a Poe or a Baudelaire and not a trivial Naturalistic rake. The self-portrait of the total invalid hiring Ido del Sagrario (of all people!) as his amanuensis in mortal haste to retrieve truth from memory is a splendid Galdosian flourish. But this belated reason for writing, however believable, cannot be applied retroactively to the bulk of the novel, which is supposedly recorded before the stroke of apoplexy and when the writer obviously had no intention of ever dying. There, feverish documentation of money spent, assignations arranged, and ankles observed constitutes a one-way stream of personal time, which might well have titillated Spanish nineteenth-century sexual repression but which does not throw much light on the human condition.[16]

In addition to formal and psychological deficiencies, the disappearance of the tacit representational significance, which had deepened the private lives of Isidora and Rosalía in spite of their shallowness as case histories, is a manifest loss. As Bueno de Guzmán tells us himself, his only intention is "to relate without rhetoric my prosaic adventures from the Autumn of '80 to the Summer of '84, events which are in no way different from those which make up

---

[16] Arthur Terry suggests that there is a tacit equation here: "Galdós is touching on an assumption which governs most serious 19th-century thinking on the subject of sex, the idea that sexual vitality and economic prosperity obey the same kind of laws. Once the equation is made, the metaphors follow: sexual energy becomes a matter of spending or conserving; promiscuity may be compared to rash investments." He also cites Steven Marcus to the effect that "the body is regarded as a productive system with only a limited amount of material at its disposal." Terry, *"Lo prohibido:* Unreliable Narrative and Untruthful Narrator," in *Galdós Studies* (I), ed. J. E. Varey, London, 1970, p. 75. (The volume is cited as *Galdós Studies* (I).) Marcus, *The Other Victorians,* London, 1966, p. 22.

the lives of other men." (*1888*) Galdós, among other things a pitilessly self-observant male, clearly found the endless sequence of desire and satisfaction, which he shared biologically with "otros hombres," to be both inevitable and insignificant. Hence, exactly as in the case of Fernando de Rojas, the evident superiority of his feminine over his masculine characters. The latter, unless they transcend the sequence vocationally, only represent themselves.

In addition, in the specific case of Bueno de Guzmán, we should add that the possibility of male myth-making of the sort achieved by Tirso de Molina and his successors did not exist in Restoration society. An authentic don Juan, as Clarín implies in *La Regenta* (also finished in 1885) when he contrasts Zorrilla's Tenorio to his own antihero, represents what used to be called the life force. He is more than a sexual champion; he incarnates, by destroying fictions and mocking conventions, our inherent biological antagonism to social order. But the "señorito" who works from within the system is at best a "botarate" (Joaquinito) and at worst a sneak (don Alvaro Mesía and Juanito). Bueno de Guzmán is a bit of both and a spendthrift as well. After paying through the nose, he enjoys his disappointing pleasures secretly and above all avoids challenging stony guests. His libidinous imperative, or, as Galdó phrases it, his "comezón," can never find either satisfaction or invigorating danger. On the contrary, when his misbehavior is suspected or virtually discovered, it is ignored or condoned. In a society fully as trivial as its antihero, whatever is prohibited is also covered up. And most reprehensible of all is the special consideration given to nattily dressed young men with substantial bank accounts and influential friends.

From what has just been said it follows that, if Tirso and Zorrilla perceived society as an essentially masculine entity in which honor was fragile and infractions physically dangerous, Galdós and Clarín (who had to invent an extravagant pseudo-Quijote to make his duel at all plausible) perceived the Spanish society of their time as essentially female. Stated more simply, Restoration Madrid, like Edwardian London, was a happy hunting ground for aggressive philanderers, each dedicated to augmenting his individual tally of so-called victims, but, seen as a social collectivity, its characteristic vices were feminine.[17] Naturally, I do not mean feminine in an absolute sense (if indeed there *is* any such meaning) but rather in the nineteenth-century novelistic terms archetypically represented by Emma Bovary: a passion for luxury, an inability to keep accounts, a dedication to appearances rather than to reality, all premised on self-indulgence and a lack of moral principles. Thus, although *Lo prohibido* may have been a praiseworthy act of reparation on Galdós' part, from the point of view of using the novel as a means of comprehending the whole in the part, it was necessarily a failure. Restoration society, in terms of representation, was a woman, not a man, and Bueno de Guzmán could not, therefore, be consecrated novelistically in the same fashion as Galdós' earlier antiheroines.

These comments should not be interpreted to mean that I think all novels must contain an intentional allegory in order to be worthy of esteem. The novel has many ways of presenting the lasting and universal significance of private experiences, those of Huck Finn, Prince Bolkonski, or Fortunata for instance. Nor would I be inclined to defend Galdós' approximation to allegory unreservedly. Not only in *La Fontana* and *Doña Perfecta* but also in *La desheredada* and some of the later novels there is a tendency to allow pressing historical preoccupations to foreshorten and at times even to distort narrated lives. No! It is not the mere lack of a representative dimension that causes our and Galdós' dissatisfaction with *Lo prohibido*. Rather, I think, it is our suspicion that that novel could well be a *mis*representation. Here we detect the influence of Zola at its most pervasive, for an identical suspicion of sociological prevarication remains after a reading of "documents humains" such as *Nana* and *Pot Bouille*. The notion of the organic relationship between individual and society that is inherent in Naturalistic poetics was, we surmise, capable of leading both the French founder and his Spanish disciple astray.

[17] Michel Foucault in his *Histoire de la sexualité,* vol. 1, *La Volunté de savoir* (Paris, 1976) makes a number of points that contribute to our comprehension of *Lo prohibido.* He stresses the special sexual consciousness of the nineteenth century and above all its tendency to talk "exhaustively" about its "secret life." The anonymous author of the remarkable annals that bear that title would, thus, be an historical counterpart to Galdós' fictional alter ego. Foucault is also pertinent when he examines fascination with incest and horror of hereditary infirmities as concomitant to the cult of the family.

The problem emerges from our two authors' nineteenth-century obsession with sexual transgression. F. W. J. Hemmings and others have suggested that Zola's personal feelings about sex (fascination, fear, repulsion) are responsible for its presentation in his novels as "un ferment de destruction," which must eventually corrupt and undermine French civilization. Yet does not this rather far-fetched alarm (civilization has always seemed to thrive on a certain degree of sexual freedom) really emerge from the natural tendency of Naturalistic novelists to believe in their own mythography?[18] The fallacious logic that lies beneath the excessive novelistic attention paid to Octave Mouret and Bueno de Guzmán seems to be as follows: if, as in *Madame Bovary, Nana,* and *La desheredada,* individual lives can be revealingly presented as representing the whole of society at a given historical moment, it follows that the reverse must also be true. The sexual license and perversion of private transgressors must necessarily infect the body politic. In this both "krausistas" and Naturalists find themselves in full agreement. And if moral contamination is indeed a threat to family, society, and mankind, it is well worth worrying about and exposing relentlessly in long, documentary novels.

Thus, Zola and Galdós, by confusing a means of social comprehension, which was used successfully for certain female protagonists, with what they believed to be a social disease, misrepresented the true ills of their times. For all its scientific palaver, there is something primitive and superstitious about the Naturalistic cosmos, a macro- and microcosmos within which illicit sexual intercourse, if no longer a sin, was something far worse—the violation of a tabu.[19] Zola may

[18] Jared Wenger in an undeservedly forgotten article anticipated the mythographic school of criticism by explaining the function of human archetypes in the nineteenth-century novel. He points out that the major novelists of that century (in contrast with Galdós and his conscious and purposeful myth-construction in *La desheredada*) communicated with the public in terms of tacit myth-figures, the little mother, and the fascinating bitch, etc., which could be both recognized and reappraised in the course of the reading. "By these means," he says, "the novelist arrived at a mythology and left a tradition the banality of which should not blind us to its virtues." "Character-Types of Scott, Balzac, Dickens, Zola," *PMLA,* 62, 1947, p. 227.

[19] According to Bardèche, the origins of this sociological superstitution are to be found already in Balzac. Speaking specifically of *Le Père Goriot* in his conclusion, he remarks: "le mouvement implacable vers l'or et le plaisir est

indeed have suffered from crippling inhibitions, but Galdós, as recent documentary evidence has vividly revealed, had very few. Nevertheless, he, too, was impelled by the doctrine he had borrowed and embraced prior to the definitive apostasy of *Fortunata y Jacinta* to warn us as solemnly as his temperament allowed against the perils of "lo prohibido." He, too, found himself writing a novel in two parts dedicated to nothing more important than discovering "pourquoi monsieur Un tel commèttait où ne commèttait pas l'adultère avac madame Une telle." So remarked Huysmans in a 1903 preface to *A Rebours* in which he confesses his own past misrepresentations and recalls his growing disillusionment with Naturalism. In the middle eighties he was, like Galdós, "seeking to escape from the cul-de-sac in which he was suffocating."[20]

Novel and Health

The author of *Fortunata y Jacinta* reacted far more decisively and fruitfully than Huysmans. His incomparable genius for self-criticism was to provide us not merely with a "nuevo modo de vida" (the definition of the Romances of Chivalry suggested by Cervantes' Canon) but rather with a spiritual rejuvenation, which I believe will be as lasting as that of the *Quijote*. Although judged at long range the new novel was clearly intended to be a dialectical response to *La desheredada*, Galdós' acute awareness of the patent triviality of the unmotivated and ingrown confessions of Bueno de Guzmán provided the immediate impulse for the radical reversal of creative direction that was to give birth to Fortunata. As Galdós fully realized, he had reached the dead-end of Naturalism, at about the same time Huysmans and many of his fellow novelists (Zola was the not unsurprising exception) were coming to the same conclusion.[21] The discontinuity, however, between what had just been completed and what was in prospect (a discontinuity even more startling than that

---

la loi d'usure de la société, c'est le germe de mort que porte en elle toute société considérée comme une organisme. La société est, en quelque sorte, un être collectif qui est épuisé lui assui par le désir." *Balzac romancier*, p. 377.

[20] See Michel Raimond, *La Crise du roman: Des lendemains du Naturalisme aux années vingt*, Paris, 1967, p. 29. (Hereafter cited as *La Crise du roman*.)

[21] Ibid., pp. 25–43.

which separated *La desheredada* from *La familia de León Roch*)
did not preclude at least one element of continuity. In fact, as Hegel
discovered, without some inner continuity a truly dialectical response is impossible. In the case of *Lo prohibido* that essential element is nothing less than the creation of a positive precursor (Isidora
was, of course, the negative one) of Fortunata.

In the course of exploring the diseased consciousness and dissolute
compulsions of Bueno de Guzmán, Galdós was led, particularly in
part 2, to confront him with a feminine antagonist completely
uninterested in "las travesuras más sabrosas cuanto más anormales."
(*1714*) She is, readers will remember, the narrator's youngest cousin,
Camila, whose careless disregard of his advances is as ultimately fatal
to him as Jacinta's was to be to his novelistic reincarnation, Moreno
Isla. Camila's uncomplicated and natural virtue, "mitad virtud,
mitad salud," was, according to Clarín, "lo más bello del libro." If
the novel had focused on her, Clarín goes on to imply, it would have
been far more worthwhile.[22] And that Galdós agreed with him
before the fact is indicated by closing remarks no less indicative than
those of *La de Bringas*. Once again the character and the author
meet, and once again we are playfully alerted to the narrative right-
about-face, which we are to expect and which is going to be expected
of us: "As Ido had suggested, I showed the manuscript to a friend
of his and of mine who spends his time on such pastimes and even
earns his living from them. Today the fellow came to see me; we
had a chat. I proposed that he write the biography of "la Prójima"
(the "Wench"?), of which all I have completed is only the prologue, to which he replied that it would certainly be worth while to
attempt it." (*1890*)

The meaning of this interview is again not elusive. The "amigo

---

[22] *Galdós*, p. 144. Clarín's first review was in *El Globo*, 30 June 1885. In the
second letter to Clarín cited in note 23 below Galdós seems to anticipate his
friend's reaction: "Le diré con completa sinceridad lo que es este libro. En él
hay una veta buena: ya ve V. que le hablo con inmodestia. No le digo a V.
cuál es esta veta, porque V. la ha de conocer en cuanto llegue al segundo
tomo, y si no la concoce, es que me equivoco. . . ." Two of the other reviewers, Ortega y Munilla, who praised it, and the hostile "Orlando"
(Francisco Izquierdo Trol), agreed with Clarín on this point. For the former,
Camila "es la verdadera heroina." *Lunes del Imparcial*, 11 May 1885. For
the latter, she is "lo mejor de la novela." *Revista de España*, 104, 1885, p. 298.
Hoar, "Critics," pp. 175–188.

suyo y mío" is, of course, Galdós himself, as usual no more reluctant to play ironical games with the "documentary pretense" of his "documents humains" than his greatest master. And when he accepts Bueno de Guzmán's suggestion that his next novel should continue the history of "la Prójima" (a somewhat vulgar nickname for Camila later applied to Fortunata), he reveals that even in the course of writing *Lo prohibido* he had decided to change his novelistic tack. Personally, I do not believe that Galdós ever intended seriously to compose a sequel devoted to the married life of Camila and Miquis (characters as flat as Dickens's flattest). Rather he seems to be planning to continue his creative meditation on that health of consciousness that served as a foil to the diseased awareness of the narrator and was Camila's raison d'être.

Galdós, in other words, was concerned both with indicating to his readers the new territory he intended to explore and with confessing frankly his disappointment with the novel just completed. Indeed, long before finishing he acknowledged privately to Pereda that in opening up the inner world of Bueno de Guzmán he had drained the cup of nasty tasting medicine called Naturalism to the dregs. As he explains to him in colloquial Castilian in a letter dated 24 February 1885:

> Dates: I calculate that I shall have finished by April, but in the second half of the month rather than the first. I already have some proofs [four "pliegos" or signatures]. But there are going to be two volumes. I'm at the end of my rope. Why the devil did I get involved in such fancy doings? I'm up to my neck in goo. And it isn't working out. There are boudoir scenes naturally, but no problems. . . . That is, there are only the kinds of problems that adultery and other such trifles create. In a word, I deeply repent having gotten myself into this bedlam, but there is nothing for it but to get out of it as well as I can and swear that I won't let it happen again.[23]

[23] Villasante, "28 cartas," p. 35. In the letters to Clarín recently published by Dionisio Gamallo Fierros concerning Galdós' initial reactions to *La Regenta,* Galdós on several occasions refers to *Lo prohibido* with cogent self-criticism: ". . . hoy por hoy mi cabeza está llena de las peores impresiones respecto a este libro. Lo que sea lo dirán los que lo lean. Creo que el asunto no es malo; pero la ejecución no corresponde al asunto. Sin embargo he hecho

It is not necessary to provide an "explication de texte" for the euphemistic phrase "I'm up to my neck in goo" ("Ya estoy de caramelo hasta donde puede figurarse") in order to comprehend the disgust, which the closing paragraph at once conceals and reveals.

Was it not now time, therefore, to accept once again the challenge of *La desheredada?* Was it not now time to replace hereditary sickness with newborn health and determinism with freedom? Or to say the same thing in terms of the century, to find a way of saving souls from helpless subjection to history? Máximo Manso's archly-programmed intellectual autonomy had only provided momentary relief from the numbing pressures of "race, milieu et moment." Perhaps a new version of Camila, a Camila submitted to a fate even more wretched and apparently invincible than that which had doomed Isidora, might somehow find a free and fully voluntary response. And perhaps that response, that defiance de profundis, would enable her not only to save herself as a person but also, by representational magic, her society. As we remember from his remarks in the Prologue to *La Regenta,* Galdós was never able fully to believe in the absolute inevitability of the national perdition that on so many occasions he had accurately prophesied.[24] To that extent he seems to have been influenced by his "krausista" friends.

It is necessary to stress the contributions of both *La desheredada* and *Lo prohibido* to the gestation of *Fortunata y Jacinta* not only for the sake of understanding its possibility but also in order to avoid one of its most frequent misinterpretations. Unlike Dostoievsky when beginning *The Idiot* after just finishing *Crime and Punishment,* Galdós was not attempting to explore that most challenging of novelistic themes, the possibility of saintliness in modern times. That was to come later, with *Misericordia* as its most profound expression. But Fortunata, as perceptive readers soon discern, is not necessarily good, certainly not always good, and, above all, not

---

lo que he podido más." (6 April 1885) (*La Voz de Asturias,* 17 August, 1978). Or again: "Así es que el conjunto vale poco, esto dicho como se deben decir las cosas entre sastres. Lo que si resulta es de una moralidad gruesa que salta a la vista hasta de los más ciegos. Por eso quizá le he tomado tirria a este libro, pues no me gusta que la moral de una obra sea de las que están al alcance de todas las rétinas." (5 May 1885) (*La Voz,* 27 August, 1978). Fortunata and Jacinta are in the wings!

[24] See chapter 3, note 49.

progressively better. It is during the final interview with Maxi when he proposes she join him in his "sainthood" that she is most authentically diabolical.[25] Rather, as a three- or four-dimensional re-creation of Camila, Fortunata is spiritually and until the very end physically healthy, and she possesses to a superb degree the natural freedom that health alone can supply.

It is, of course, true that just before and after her death she is or was an angel. But we should not be misled by the comparison. Angels are not the same as saints, and not only because some of them are fallen. Belief in their existence is not hagiographical; it does not spring from a dubious Golden Legend of miracles and conspicuous charity. Rather it arises from our innate conviction that consciousness by its very nature can and indeed must attain far higher degrees of intensity than are normally available to our mortality or our habitual self-centered myopia. Health aside, it is this that distinguishes Fortunata from the other inhabitants of her novel, particularly from "la santa moderna," doña Guillermina, who is cunningly paired with her in order to suggest the difference. This suggests something about the inherent capabilities of the genre itself: the greatest novels, those of a don Quijote, a Huck Finn, or a Fabrice del Dongo, while emergent from the comic tradition, discover in human life intensities comparable to those of tragedy. The difference is that, instead of ready-made great characters initiating a process of mass release or catharsis, we individually incarnate the angelic heroes or heroic angels, because in the act of reading we provide them as far as we are able with the pulsating raw material of our own experience.[26]

If not a tale of goodness and evil or of innocence and perversion, *Fortunata y Jacinta* was conceived of as an exhibition of how the freedom of one individual could vanquish what Galdós had termed eight years earlier "el hado social." That is, how that freedom could reduce the immense mercantile, materialistic, and erotic collectivity of Madrid to its proper size and divest it of its capacity for harm.

[25] "Ahí tienes la maravillosa arma de la lógica humana, con la cual te hiero para sanarte. Más vale morir aprendiendo que vivir ignorando. Esta lección terrible puede llevarte hasta la santidad, que es el estado en que yo me encuentro." *(510)* In a sense the entire end of the novel may be interpreted as a battle to the death between the saintly and the angelic.

[26] See the discussion in chapter 3, note 41.

That an angel, in the sense just defined, was to be born in the process was surely unforeseen by Galdós, if we can judge by the wretched heroine he sketched for himself in the preliminary version. But the potentiality of the new experiment was as great as its daring. The increment of Cervantine "incitation" and of an invulnerably healthy free will brought completely unexpected possibilities of meaning to the *La desheredada* story of externally imposed fatality. Instead of an artificially constructed myth designed to catch the conscience of the readers, Galdós was now to create a latter-day, yet completely authentic, pre-Socratic myth, with all the depth, mystery, and endlessly suggestive ambiguity that that implies. Galdós, in other words, has transcended allegory. Movement and meaning, at long last fused, endow the novel, as they will endow those yet to come, with a spiritual altitude and a spiritual profundity that is only limited by each individual reader's capacity for participation.

CHAPTER VI

A Colloquium of Novelists

Novel and Incitation

The metamorphosis in Galdós' art of the novel that is predicted in the sincerely rueful closing paragraph of *Lo prohibido* and concealed by the deceptively casual opening gambit that we encounter upon first looking into *Fortunata y Jacinta* ("Las noticias más remotas que tengo . . .") cannot be fully explained either by the proposition that the new heroine was intended to be the antithesis of Isidora or by the broad hint that she was to continue the therapy offered by the example of Camila's healthy consciousness. Both derivations are true, I believe, but to approach the change only in terms of the author's initial intention, its calculated dialectical conception and structure, is to confine ourselves within the closed frontiers of Galdós' works, whereas he, as a nineteenth-century European novelist, was open to the genre as a whole, as susceptible as Cervantes to all that he read.

So let us now return to the notion of a spontaneous and intuitive dialogue with other novelists, which was proposed in our discussions of *Doña Perfecta* and *La desheredada*. As we remember, when Galdós was dissatisfied with a work just completed, he frequently would recall novels by colleagues, which he hoped would provide him with a remedy for what had gone wrong, or would at least indicate a new direction to follow. And now, just after finishing *Lo prohibido* and feeling himself immersed in "caramelo hasta donde puede figurarse," he took the trouble to listen closely and to reply imaginatively not to one other but to four other major artists who had celebrated, deplored, and diagnosed the nineteenth century in a genre that had previously been considered frivolous. Cervantes presided as usual, but it was a new Cervantes, freshly understood in terms of Galdós' meditations on Clarín, Flaubert, Balzac, and, once again, although this time at one remove, Zola.

In the foregoing essays on the evolution of Galdós' narrative art three assumptions were made about his internovel dialogue, which should now be made explicit. The terrain we are about to survey is treacherous and demands meticulous preparation on the part of the surveyor. In the first place, unlike, say, Pereda when he answers *Doña Perfecta* with *Don Gonzalo González de la Gonzalera* (an answer that amused Galdós almost as much as the title must have), the dialogue that is audible in Galdós' novels is always positive and never polemical. Galdós was less interested in answering back than in learning how his colleagues went about their business. As he explained it, "To visit a colleague's workshop . . . allows one to recreate onself through appreciation of works that are not one's own, to comprehend how they are made, the procedures of their achievement. One can seek out and catch unawares the difficulties that have been overcome, the easy solutions and those arrived at with great effort." (*1446*)

In the second place, as Juana Truel points out in connection with Galdós' crucial reading of *Eugénie Grandet,* in addition to professional and technical appreciation, Galdós was profoundly interested in the way the themes of other novels could be adapted to his own experience at once personal and national.[1] Having discovered as a reader a new and possibly reusable narrative pattern, he would then "translate" the foreign meaning there presented in terms of his vision of nineteenth-century Spain. In so saying, we must not oversimplify: the phrase *"his* vision" should be understood as including both the conventional vision that he attributed to his public and that which he hoped to impress upon it. Trilling's perception of the inherent didacticism of the novel in *all* its manifestations, whether major or minor, profound or shallow, is undeniable.

In the third place, we should not insist on a rigid before-and-after sequence for such dialogue. Using *Doña Perfecta* again as a typical example, it would seem that its use of the outsider-as-a-catalyst pattern did not occur to Galdós upon first reading *Eugénie Grandet.*

---

[1] Truel, "La huella de *Eugénie Grandet* en *Doña Perfecta,*" p. 107.

Rather, I surmise, he was reminded of it by a second and more immediate reading experience, an experience of the sort that revives memories of earlier novels and imparts unsuspected relevance to them. To be specific, it might well have been the conflict between city and country in *Les Paysans,* a novel which is present only tangentially in Galdós' denunciation of rural intransigence, that caused, in Stendhal's words, "a crowd of memories" of *Eugénie Grandet,* Balzac's first fully Balzacian novel, "to besiege his consciousness."[2] Or, conversely, it does not seem unreasonable to suppose that it was Galdós' excited reading of *L'Assommoir* and in particular of Coupeau's frightening and vivid death scene that brought to his mind the antithetical death of don Quijote and eventually resulted in the replacement of the empty Madrid of León Roch with the verbally dense milieu with which his "disinherited" refugee from "la Mancha" could not cope.

In the conception of *Fortunata y Jacinta,* however, it was a Spanish novel that precipitated a multiple and far more complex process of dialogue. Appearing at just the right time (1885) and esteemed and enjoyed by Galdós far more than anything written by Zola, *La Regenta* triggered a radical change of creative course. As Galdós said about that major achievement of Spanish Naturalism by his friend and devotee, Leopoldo Alas (already well known by his pseudonym, Clarín, to the newspaper public), "admiration, even more than pleasure, [is] an absolute necessity in every profession or trade, since I consider that to admire constitutes the breath of art. Whoever does not admire anything runs the risk of death by asphyxiation." (*1446*) In a moment we shall see in detail just how Clarín threw open all the windows of Galdós' novelistic dwelling.

Let us first observe how Galdós expressed his reaction. While on her honeymoon, Virginia Woolf wrote to a friend that she and Leonard were spending their time reading novels "like tigers."[3]

[2] Ibid. See the discussion in chapter 3, note 25. Stendhal's phrase, indicative of the intensity of consciousness possessed by major novelists, is used for both Fabrice and his author. See my *The Tower as Emblem,* Frankfurt, 1967, p. 38.

[3] *The Letters of Virginia Woolf,* ed. Nigel Nicolson and Joanne Trautmann, New York, 1976, vol. 2, pp. 3–4. She continues to remind us of every authentic novelist from Cervantes on in the next letter: "My God! You cannot think with what a fury we fall on printed matter." ibid., p. 5.

And the aptness of this comparison for the carnivorous excitement with which Galdós savored and devoured *La Regenta* is suggested by Clarín's reply to a lost letter of acknowledgement: "May I remind you that you have used very strong language, that you have employed oriental adjectives, and that that sentence about feeling yourself haunted (you, Galdós!) by the characters and events of *La Regenta* is enough to make a novice fatuous for the rest of his life?"[4] Nor were these "oriental adjectives" an expression of momentary enthusiasm. The extent to which Galdós' admiration for Clarín's achievement was lasting is testified to in his recollection of his first reading in his 1903 prologue to the novel (the beginning of which was cited earlier): "For my part I dare say that I have read very few works of such profound interest with such truthful characters and such living language that I have so completely forgotten its considerable length. Rather, upon finishing it, I felt disconsolate at no longer being able to look forward to a sequel to its events and a new sally—or reincarnation—of its characters." (*1499*)

Judging by the relatively few letters of Galdós that have been published as well as by the many received by him and conserved in the Casa-Museo in Las Palmas, we may conclude that Galdós was characteristically generous with his praise. A letter to Pereda concerning *Sotileza* and written about the same time as the comments which flustered Clarín is typical: "I have read it at intervals at night in bed . . . and I can tell that it has given me joy."[5] But his reactions upon immersing himself in *La Regenta* seem to have been,

---

[4] *Cartas a Galdós,* ed. Soledad Ortega, Madrid, 1964, p. 227. Only now, two years after publication, do I learn (through the kindness and initiative of my student, Francisca González Arias) that Dionisio Gamallo Fierros has published in *La Voz de Asturias* (July 30, 1978) Galdós' original letter. The paragraph to which Clarín refers reads as follows: "Pues desde que empecé a leer su novela, hasta ahora, los personajes me persiguen de tal manera que van conmigo adondequiera que voy, me acometen desde que abro los ojos, y no me dejan hasta que los cierra. Si yo soñara, no sueño nunca, soñaría con ellos. Crea Vd. que su obra la tengo metida entre ceja y ceja, en términos que no me deja vivir, ni trabajar, ni pensar en nada que no sea ella. Y vea Vd. en esto, juntamente con las impresiones del lector, las del autor, las del oficio. ¿Quiere Vd. más?" The letter is undated, but according to Gamallo Fierros, it must have been written in February 1885.

[5] Villasante, "28 cartas," p. 36.

as we might have expected, far more intense. If we can judge by the remarks just cited, it was not read "a ratos" or "entre sábanas."

Aside from the sheer voluptuousness of transport, I suggest that what Galdós admired most about this particular "taller ajeno" was Clarín's superb display of a skill that he himself had mastered by 1884 when he finished the Bringas trilogy but that he had somehow lost while bogged down in *Lo prohibido*. As we saw, the more or less unmotivated confessional mode of that novel impeded the ironical control of characterization and narrative progression, which was part of Cervantes' priceless legacy to his nineteenth-century heirs. How startling, then, and how gratifying it must have been to read Clarín's superbly confected mélange of Cervantes and Zola, of Argamasilla and, as we shall see later, Plassans. Here was a novel that had found a way ironically to manage, and so to save, Naturalism, an even more elegant answer to the "cuestión palpitante" posed by doña Emilia Pardo Bazán than his own *La desheredada*. But odious comparisons aside, at the very least *La Regenta* was a chefd'oeuvre propitiously timed for the lasting benefit of a momentarily distracted disciple of the same pair of masters.

Before returning to the testimony of the two texts, *La Regenta* and *Fortunata y Jacinta,* let us continue to speculate on the nature of Galdós' reaction. The *Quijote* has always provided novelist-readers with far more than they seek therein, but at times, as in the case of Fielding and the English novelists, or perhaps of Gogol and the Russians, new and unexpected creative comprehension emerges from observing a second novelist explore what Cervantes had wrought. Such, I think, was the impact of *La Regenta* upon Galdós. If previously Galdós had admired Cervantes as a master of point-of-view manipulation and ironical communication with the reader over the heads of the characters, he had not had, as Casalduero observes, much sympathy for the numerous latter-day Quijotes who inhabit the first two series of "episodios" and the early "novelas contemporáneas." I refer, of course, to Lázaro as well as his uncle, to Isidora as well as her father, to the Sarmientos and Navarros, and in general to all those who oppose fanaticism to moderation or eccentric enthusiasms and ambitions to bourgeois common sense. At best they were figures of fun, or of fun mixed with compassion, and at worst they were negative myths, as they were in a different way for

Gogol, representing the degradation of the author's native land.[6] But after seeing what Clarín had harvested from the *Quijote,* these ridiculous or disheartening reincarnations of the mind behind the Rueful Countenance vanish abruptly. Thenceforth, in novel after novel, Galdós was able to emulate with complete originality that marvelous combination of endless profundity and clear equanimity, which characterizes the so-called comic spirit of the world's proto-novelist.

Let us now see whether the two texts will support these generalizations. While completing the chronicle of a supremely trivial life dedicated entirely to its own satisfaction and hence *neither* moderate *nor* fanatical, Galdós had absorbed a novel in which two passionately committed characters, Ana de Ozores and Fermín de Pas, are contrasted to the cynical dandyism of don Alvaro Mesía as well as to the superficial and ingrown provincial society, which looks on him as a kind of nineteenth-century Amadís.[7] The reflection of this confrontation of two against one (plus everybody else) is apparent in *Fortunata y Jacinta:* Juanito Santa Cruz, the idolized drone of commercial Madrid (his superficial sensuality and expensive self-indulgence are the ultimate raison d'etre of the busy, money-secreting, urban beehive) is opposed to the sublime outcasts, Maxi and Fortunata, who take spiritual charge and impel the novel onwards and upwards. Influence and imitation have long been unfashionable and unworthy notions, but if understood as a form of dialogue not only between the two novels as technical achievements but also between

---

[6] Gogol clearly takes the side of "El caballero del verde gabán" in one of the fragmentary chapters that remains from part 2 of *Dead Souls.* His quixotic characters, accordingly, resemble more closely those of the young Galdós.

[7] The likeness of Ana de Ozores to Fermín de Pas was noted in the only extensive contemporary review of the novel, which was signed by "Orlando": "Logran fijar la atención desde el primer instante Ana Ozores y D. Fermín de Pas . . . no solo porque ellos dan orígen a la parte más sustancial de la novela, sino porque entre ambos existen bastantes puntos de semejanza. De sentimientos profundos uno y otro, su educación respectiva y su buen talento los reprimen. *Revista de España,* 106, 1885, p. 127. I am indebted to Professor Gloria Ortiz for this information.

Clarín's concluding verbal castigation of don Alvaro as possessing an "alma insubstancial sosa y hueca," which "se habia enamorado de la ropa del sastre" reminds us all the more of Galdós' own "hombre de trapo." *Obras,* ed. J. M. Martínez Cachero, Barcelona, 1963, vol. 1, p. 824.

disparate novelistic meditations on "What Men Live by" (the titular interrogation of Tolstoy that preoccupied the dying patients of *The Cancer Ward*), Galdós' remodeling of Clarín's triangle of commitment and selfishness was crucial. It marks the moment of the former's steepest ascent in his journey to Parnassus.

If don Alvaro Mesía is in many ways a more plausible precursor of Juanito Santa Cruz (Galdós playfully echoes the former's name when he refers to the latter as "el Mesías") than Joaquinito Pez, who half believed in his own sentimental effusions, the others, Maxi and the Magistral, Fortunata and "la Regenta," aside from their flaming souls, seem to have nothing in common.[8] No matter; it is not in the characters or in the situations but rather in the sheer incitation of these four consciousnesses that we may overhear the dialogue between the two novels and eventually detect their common ancestry. Setting Fortunata and the Magistral aside for later consideration, it is apparent that Maxi does share with Ana, as well as with don Víctor, his counterpart in marital impotence, a common addiction. All three are readers, avid Alonso Quijano-like readers, who in their rapprochement of life and literature record for us the kind of intensified experience that makes novels work and that by definition is out of the question for a don Alvaro Mesía, a Juanito, or a Sansón Carrasco.

In addition, we must not forget that not only do they read passionately but they are themselves read passionately, with the result that we as readers partake in their separate varieties of exaltation. This is what matters, for exaltation, in that it corresponds to an expansion of consciousness, provides far more insight into the human condition than the blind "tormento" of a Pedro Polo or the erotic "comezón" of a Bueno de Guzmán. The result was that, after reading *La Regenta* and participating in the supercharged lives that inhabit it, Galdós could no longer interpret the *Quijote* merely as a model for political and social caricature or as a myth of Spanish decadence; instead, in the knight's unique amalgamation of adventure and experience, he glimpsed unforeseen and immensely exciting avenues for novelistic exploration.

Ana de Ozores is the crucial creation, and, before returning to the

---

[8] "Orlando" speaks of "las llamas que consumen el corazón del magistral." *Revista de España*, 106, 1885, p. 139.

prospect of *Fortunata y Jacinta*, it would be well to consider who she is and how she came to be. This immediately turns our attention to Clarín's own exemplary "cervantista," Flaubert. As Robert Jackson has shown convincingly, Ana, in spite of Clarín's ironical remarks in *Mis plagios*, is indeed in certain ways a human reply to Emma Bovary.[9] Jackson naturally rejects the foolish and malevolent charges of Luis Bonafoux (as we shall see, it was fortunate for Clarín that Bonafoux had not read *La Conquête de Plassans*) and demonstrates instead the importance of *Madame Bovary* as a living lesson in how to comprehend and utilize the *Quijote* in the nineteenth century. In our terms, this means simply that Maxi, Ana, Emma, and Alonso Quijano constitute an ascending genealogy of insatiable and more or less deranged readers.[10] Thus, Ana's sur-

---

[9] " 'Cervantismo' in the Creative Process of Clarín's *La Regenta*," *MLN*, 74, 1969, pp. 208–227.

[10] In addition to Scott's young alter ego, Waverley, another obvious precursor is Augustine Guillaume, who appears in the earliest piece of fiction to be included in *La Comédie humaine*, *La Maison du Chat-qui-pelote* (1829) and whose undesirable marriage resulted from reading such novels as *Hyppolyte comte de Douglas*. Balzac, however, although bitingly ironical in his assessment of motives and blissful in his enjoyment of unexpected details, was always too close to the "truth" ("le vrai") that he was intent on creating to exploit and explore fully this particular pattern. He was less a "padrastro" than a "padre" and, therefore, better equipped to use the kind of incitation that impels a Vautrin or a Goriot. When Lukacs verges on the notion of incitation by describing novel heroes as "problematical" individuals whose ideas have turned into "ideals," who engage in "self-quest," and who give life to the novel-world through the "erlebenden Innerlichkeit" derived from being lost therein, he was obviously thinking of don Quijote. *Die Theorie des Romans*, Berlin-Spandau, 1963, pp. 76–77. (Hereafter cited as *Die Theorie*.) This formulation is especially significant because it posits the inner impetus of the novelistic personage upon vulnerable exposure to a hostile and careless world where all lives are "criadas en contienda y batalla." Thus, Stendhal portrays his heroes actively incited (Julien Sorel's *Amadís* is the *Memorial de Sainte Hélène*) and at the same time "passively" exposed "aux coups de marteau du sort." Cited by Maurice Bardèche, *Stendhal romancier*, Paris, 1947, p. 277. Goethe, on the other hand, only stresses receptiveness and passivity in his comments on Wilhelm Meister, and there are similar comments by Hardy in *The Return of the Native*: the new hero views life as a "thing to be put up with." In the Cervantine tradition, however, it is only by *both* charging windmills and then suffering the consequences that an individual can perform the essential novelistic task described by Merleau Ponty as communicating "une expérience du monde, un contact . . . qui précède toute pensée sur le monde." *Sens et non-sens*, p. 49.

render to mystical works as well as her susceptibility to *El Tenorio* (in which doña Inés provided her with a role model for the justification of her love affair) is not a borrowed device or technique. Rather both enthusiasms underscore Clarín's comprehension of the profound Cervantine potentialities lying beneath Emma Bovary's fictionally motivated and comparatively superficial deviation from what the reader is free to interpret as morality, respectability, common sense, or the reality principle. The Spanish novelist's fresh insight into the deeper significance of the national masterpiece is confirmed somewhat paradoxically by the presence of don Víctor, whose shallow, Calderonian honor fantasies (their echo in those of Ido is a kind of novelistic salute, the parody of a parody) are presented in calculated contrast to those of his wife. His ridiculous caricature of don Quijote (reminiscent of such early Galdosian types as don Rodrigo in *Cádiz*) provides a measure for *her* relevance as a genuine nineteenth-century version of Cervantes' stepchild. But without the prior existence of Emma . . . ?

The two heroines, Ana and Emma, could not have been more different in profundity of consciousness or nobility of aspirations; yet their shared susceptibility to the written or the printed word is at once a calculated tribute to Cervantes and a spontaneous declaration of adherence to what Ortega would call his "posture towards life." By this I mean adherence to Cervantes' preference for characters vulnerable to what Américo Castro first termed in 1947 "la incitación"—"*in*citation," the conscious *in*corporation of *ex*citement. At the time Castro was only referring to Cervantes' creative concern with " 'the interreality' of the aspirations of the spirit and the process of incorporating them into one's individual life."[11] Accordingly, "the fantasy-laden Romances of Chivalry become an integral part of the existence of don Quijote," while his author, hardly less mad according to Manuel Azaña,[12] reveals an "extraña preferencia . . . por los desequilibrados de toda laya [por los incitados]."[13] Don Quijote is anything but a solitary Romantic hero; his life is

[11] La estructure del *Quijote*," in *Hacia Cervantes,* Madrid, 1957, pp. 245–246.

[12] "La invención del Quijote," in *Obras completas,* ed. Juan Marichal, México, 1966, vol. 1, p. 1106.

[13] Castro, "La estructura del *Quijote*," p. 246.

intertwined with other lives like his, lives typical of a century at once incited and stultified.

We must, therefore, take care not to praise this fundamental innovation in the art of the novel as uniquely Cervantine, nor to consider it (as did Unamuno) an autonomous expression of don Quijote's heroism. Rather the *Quijote* demonstrated for the first time that only by attending to incited lives can prose fiction, previously a vehicle for imaginary chivalric adventure, vicarious pastoral sentimentality, or picaresque humor and social criticism, eventually dare to challenge the supremacy of the epic. Only in this way could the romance be transformed as if by magic into the novel. This, of course, does not mean that all novels resemble *Don Quijote, Madame Bovary,* or *Moby Dick* either in significance or in artistry, but rather that ever since Cervantes, and above all in the nineteenth century, we have been aware generically of worthy novels in terms of the incited self-propulsion of their protagonists in a milieu that is at best resistant and at worst hostile.

In other words, the "casos máximos de vida," as Castro calls them, which we encounter during the second and third sallies, represent something more than an unprecedented cast of characters; they constitute a new way of understanding human life. As we read the *Quijote,* we are nothing less than witnesses to a narrative revolution as radical as that which gave birth to "La Première République," or, changing metaphors, to a narrative mutation, which spawned a new human species: "To live in a Cervantine way is to allow one's soul to be transfixed by every kind of incitation and to live or die therefrom."[14]

While reading these crucial essays of 1947 we should remember that what Castro had in mind is not fictional presentation of explosive passion, extreme sentimental distress, or unbearable pain. The static, emotional self-torture of Leriano and Sireno, the carnal misery of Lazarillo, and the "machista" jubilance of Oriana's lover when he cries out "¡Soy Amadís!" upon returning to battle after self-exile in "la Peña Pobre," a virtual allegory of alienation, all lack that participation in "el mismo hacerse de la vida" that is inherent in Cervantine fictional biographies as well as in the future

---

[14] Ibid., p. 252.

novels that were to spring from them. I suppose it could be said that listening to the chanted predictions of the three witches "incited" Macbeth to trespass against feudal order. But I think that Castro would answer that the agony and ambition to which he was afterwards submitted are not presented in terms of an ongoing, daily process of self-fabrication. It is precisely the creeping "petty pace from day to day" that Macbeth, unlike don Quijote and Sancho, can least abide or endure.

If in the two quadricentennial essays Castro limited his discussion of the new literary species to the *Quijote,* in the indispensable introduction to the Porrúa edition of that novel he comments at length on the second coming of "incitation" in the nineteenth century.[15] According to this later view, the Cervantine revolution or mutation was, after an interval of two centuries, to establish the novel as a major literary form. To mention only a few of the very greatest, Captain Ahab, Vautrin, Huck Finn, Julien Sorel, the Karamazov brothers, and perhaps even Doctor Faust (genre notwithstanding) all live and in some cases die in a fashion comparable to that of don Quijote. In spite of each one's uniqueness, all of them fight their giants with a heroic folly, a sublime impetuosity, and a sly naiveté neither less absurd nor less admirable than the vocational conduct of their predecessor.

Not all of them were fervent book lovers (although only Huck shares Fortunata's illiteracy), nor were their authors necessarily aware of a debt to the seventeenth century. The revolution in novelistic consciousness was by that time too widespread to be attributed to a single mind or book, or to facilitate recognition of remote origins. Reminders of the proto-novelist are everywhere (a challenge for comparativists and a solace for "cervantistas"), but only in exceptional cases such as those which now concern us, Flaubert, Clarín, and Galdós, ordered in sequence, do nineteenth-century novelists engage in conscious dialogue with their founding father. Castro explains the long-delayed impact of the *Quijote* as due to certain aspects of that extraordinary metamorphosis of European

---

[15] *Don Quijote,* México, 1960. This text is available in English in The Ohio State University Press anthology of Castro's works entitled *An Idea of History,* ed. S. Gilman and E. L. King. Columbus, O., 1977, pp. 77–143.

consciousness commonly known and dismissed as Romanticism.[16] Authors and readers were now ready, on the one hand, to comprehend and to recreate Cervantine comedy in somewhat more serious nineteenth-century terms (Stendhal, Gogol, Mark Twain) and, on the other, to invent their own new forms of incitation and irony (Goethe, Balzac, Dickens).[17] Both direct irradiation and independent re-creation, however, are more generic in nature than they are self-conscious, unlike the calculated tuning in of the authors who here concern us. By this I mean specifically the exploitation of their characters' lust for literature.

To sum up, in spite of patriotic critics, who prated about the traditional Spanish Naturalism of picaresque narratives and above all of the *Quijote*,[18] the genuine Cervantine fecundation of the Spanish nineteenth-century novel came from abroad, specifically, as

[16] This paraphrase is obviously a gross oversimplification. What Castro is really saying is much more subtle: "El curso dinámico del vivir, haciéndose en enlace con el mundo en torno, es irreductible a conceptuaciones quietas y cerradas, pues nos encontramos así con que lo obturado y detenido por un lado, brinca y se escapa por otro. Me imagino que este inmenso panorama de atracciones y conflictos fue lo que hizo abrir los ojos al *Quijote* a los educados en el pensar y sentir románticos." *Don Quijote,* p. xxi. There is no point in going on. This most profound and enlightening of all Castro's studies of the *Quijote* should be read not only by students of Cervantes but also by anyone concerned with the rise of the novel in the nineteenth century. *Waverley* really began it all, and Scott's quixotic presentation of his alter ego needs to be thought about. Castro's essay also goes into illuminating philosophical corollaries.

[17] Stendhal, Gogol, and Twain did not approach the task entirely seriously, of course, but they show an easily recognizable pretense of concern and sympathy, which differentiates them from the most eminent eighteenth-century representatives of the Cervantine tradition: Fielding, Sterne, and the Diderot of *Jacques le fataliste.* There are certainly Cervantine echoes in *Wilhelm Meister,* in *Pickwick Papers,* and, as we have just seen, here and there in Balzac. But these three authors were ultimately more concerned with experience derived from Lionel Trilling's "sincerity" and not from the deranged "authenticity-inauthenticity" of the "loco-cuerdo." As I correct these notes, it occurs to me that our last genuine (but only 14-carat) example of intentionally Cervantine incitation is that of Henderson, the Rain King.

[18] Galdós' own affirmation of this commonplace was an easy evasion for a self-confessed noncritic. He is far more interesting when he discusses his (and Clarín's) "re-Quixotization" of the "analytical" power of the French movement. Personally, I believe it was tactfulness that kept him from mentioning Flaubert. See the discussion in chapter 4, note 55.

Robert Jackson points out, from Flaubert, who both in his letters and his fiction ranks as one of the great "cervantistas" of all time. Then Clarín, a fascinated reader of *Madame Bovary* as well as the *Correspondence,* answers in his turn Flaubert's nineteenth-century answer to the *Quijote*.[19] And like all such answers, his was also a question; not the simple question of what an Emma would have been like in priest-ridden provincial Spain rather than in Yonville, which would at best have resulted in a *Doña Perfecta*–like novel of some sort, but rather how could her quixotism be recreated in Spanish provincial terms.

It had been centuries since the *Quijote* had provided the land of its birth with subversive relief from conventionality and social dogmatism. Those forces had long ago won the war in Spain and in the course of history had converted their printed antagonist into a castrated official classic, at best read by reverent scholars and their obedient or reluctant students. What was necessary was to revive it in modern terms, to create biographies for those nineteenth-century avatars of Alonso Quijano, who, like Virginia Woolf's Orlando, had unaccountably been turned into women, that is, into discontented housewives, who found in their own insatiable reading what the idle "hidalgo" had discovered in the *Amadís:* not just escape, but genuine incitation, an incitation which could be used ironically to provoke their local societies into unwitting self-betrayal.

Such was Ana de Ozores, neither a continuation nor a copy but a deeply moving as well as living and breathing reply to Emma Bovary's quixotism. And so Galdós understood her. Naturally, he had also read Flaubert, and, in creating Isidora, he had played with the same possibility. He did not develop it to any degree, however, for he was well aware that romances of sentiment or of society, trashy as they might have been, were relatively innocuous, at least as far as Spain was concerned. Although in the form of "folletines," both native and translated (as we remarked previously, Sue's Fleur-

[19] In a letter to Galdós on 8 April 1884 Clarín mentions having read the first volume of the *Correspondence,* which appeared in that year. He goes on to describe the novel as a "forma revolucionaria" the seriousness of which begins "en Flaubert, en Zola y en Vd." The names that are missing are interesting from the generational standpoint: Balzac and Dickens, who were apparently considered old-fashioned, and the Russians, who had not yet been read. *Cartas a Galdós,* ed. Ortega, pp. 216–217.

de-Marie and Fernández y González' Gaspar Media-noche are genuine "desheredados" whose high station is attested to by authentic documents), such fiction may have misled more than a few middle- or working-class women, it did not endanger the national spirit in a fashion comparable to that feared by Cervantes when he contemplated the scary mass culture of his century. The true counterpart of that age-old threat in the nineteenth century, Galdós believed, was the language of politics and bureaucracy. Hence, his initial stress on the insane oratory of poor Tomás Rufete, which served as a fitting introduction to the socio-political allegory and prophecy that were to come.

The intense experience of reliving Ana de Ozores' life seems to have taught Galdós something completely unexpected about his own tradition. As the remorseless author of such novels as *Los apostólicos* and *Doña Perfecta,* he had maintained in public print as late as the beginning of 1885 that Spain, in spite of, or because of, outward appearances, was the least "spiritual" country in Europe.[20] Religious fervor, he seems to have concluded, was in reality a pious disguise for blind and selfish political fervor, and the nineteenth century was in that sense the opposite of the seventeenth. But in that very same year novelistic exposure to Ana's undeniable spiritual altitude, to her utter lack of triviality and hypocrisy, and to her helpless folly was apparently a revelation. On the verge of *Fortunata y Jacinta* Galdós had suddenly perceived the perils and "high possibilities" (as Castro was to phrase it) of being Spanish in a fashion far more novelistically fecund. We can easily criticize and then forgive Ana (Clarín leads us ironically to believe that we are more sophisticated) for not seeing through don Alvaro, but her book-inspired religious incitation is as admirably noble and absurd as don Quijote's intoxication with chivalrous heroism. We revere as we smile.

Anticlericalism was now beside the point, although it cannot be said that either author changed his opinions about the Church and

[20] Shoemaker, *Cartas,* pp. 152–153. The statement is devastating: "En resumen, que hoy la gran mayoría de los españoles no creemos ni pensamos. . . . Todo está en el aire, las creencias minadas, el culto reducido a pura práctica de fórmula . . . España, la hija predilecta de la Iglesia, la que tuvo por estandarte la cruz, es uno de los países más descreídos del Globo." Earlier the same views were attributed to Daniel Morton in *Gloria.*

its civic behavior. Instead, Galdós learned from Clarín that the enduring spirituality of Spain was at once a priceless legacy and a potentially catastrophic form of irrationality. Even more, he perceived how it could enable the creation of novelistic characters who, in spite of the banality of contemporary history and society, were apt for incitation of the most intense variety, apt, like their Russian counterparts, to take to the road figuratively or literally after incorporation of the word. Witness, as Castro has suggested, the peculiarities of Spanish anarchism, and witness as well Bakunin's fervent passion for the *Quijote*.[21] Religiously motivated characters in the earlier novels had been typically odious (María Egipciaca), ominous (doña Perfecta), or, at best, spurious (doña Paulita). But now Galdós envisaged the possibility of a deeper exploration, if not of martyrdom (*Nazarín* and *Misericordia* were yet to come), at least of full, spiritual self-commitment.

The result was the creation of Galdós' first (at the beginning of part 2 Fortunata had still to create herself) great incited character, Maximiliano Rubín. As has been suggested, the addiction to literature of this self-appointed "redentor" may well reflect that of Ana de Ozores. True, he has no Magistral to force feed him on mystical treatises, but his awakening soul is precociously susceptible to the great classics of world literature. Goethe and Shakespeare operate in him in a fashion comparable to the way Saint Teresa and Thomas-a-Kempis operate in Ana.[22] It is worth noting that for both of them

[21] Castro, *La realidad histórica,* México, 1962, p. 309. Castro notes here that "cuando al español se le cierra una vía de creencia, se inventa inmediatamente otra." Peter Heinz cites Bakunin's *Beichte* (confessions) as follows: "Ein Grundübel meiner Natur war stets die Liebe zum Phantastischen, zu ungewöhnlicen und unerhörten Abenteurn, zu Unternehmungen, die eine grenzenlosen Horizont eröffnen. . . . In mir war sehr viel vom Don Quijote." Pure incitation! *Anarchismus und Gegenwart,* Zürich, 1951, p. 19.

[22] As Maxi's madness grows, his choice of books becomes more eccentric, as we learn when Segismundo Ballester catches him reading *La pluralidad de los mundos habitados* of Flammarion in the pharmacy. (*415*) Arthur Holmberg documents a number of significant resemblances between Maxi and Louis Lambert. "Louis Lambert and Maximiliano Rubín: the Inner Vision and the Outer Man," *HR,* 46, 1978, pp. 119–136. (Hereafter cited as "Louis Lambert and Maximiliano Rubín.") I am not convinced by Holmberg's explanation of this title, along with *Errores de la teogonía egipcia y persa* (*422*), as a reference to Swedenborg via Balzac. Don Víctor in *La Regenta* also seems to have been an aficionado of Flammarion. *Obras,* vol. 1,

the absurd fictional romances that had incited both Alonso Quijano and Emma Bovary have been replaced by inspiration derived from nonnovelistic texts of recognized worth and profundity. There is, however, a very important difference between the two protagonist-readers. Maxi, as a nineteenth-century "loco-cuerdo" Naturalistically handicapped to the point of being grotesque, if at times appealing and even admirable, is ridiculous. He is a creature of caricature, who, like poor don Víctor, resembles his laugh-provoking Manchegan forebear during his first sally much more than he does Ana. For she, even at her most absurd, as when she submits to barefoot public penitence, provokes sympathy rather than amusement. In the case of Maxi, far more a stepchild even than don Quijote, our reactions (pity, horror, laughter, even scorn . . .) are far less warm.

At present we are only concerned with incitation, with the Cervantine portion of Maxi's literary heritage, which we are meant to recognize immediately. At the beginning in the boring pharmacy class (a modern version of "un lugar de la Mancha"), "he began to titillate his imagination and to kindle his illusions" (*161*), and then a page later we encounter the following telltale description of his evening walks: "once he had wound himself up and got going, his brain began heating up and the mental pressure got higher and higher—to such an extent that the 'adolescent errant' imagined that he was involved in adventures and that he was a completely different person." Maxi is now ready for the following chapter in which he will meet Fortunata. And finally, when with trembling limbs and criminal desperation he smashes the "hucha," he experiences and we experience with him the same immensely comic and immensely exciting initiation of adventure converted into experience that we remember from our ride over "el antiguo y conocido campo de Montiel." After the seemingly endless construction of commercial Madrid, the real novel is at last underway.

But a point of departure does not define a journey. In spite of doña Emilia Pardo Bazán's well-known description of the novel as "la admirable epopeya de Maxi Rubín," his role is essentially to

p. 504. Judging from the three (at least) editions in translation listed in the BN catalogue that were available to Maxi, it is not surprising that he should have participated in the apparent fad. Galdós' copy in French is listed by Berkowitz in *La biblioteca de Benito Pérez Galdós*, Las Palmas, 1951, p. 38.

serve as a foil or point of comparison for Fortunata's spiritually healthy incitation. Even more, and even though he destroys her at the end, his ultimate justification lies in having launched Fortunata on her way to self-transcendence. Without her marriage to him and without his redemptive aspirations for her, her consciousness could never have flowered. I surmise that this is what Galdós intended to teach Clarín in return for all he had learned from him. To state the lesson explicitly: even in the *Quijote,* as deeply rooted as it is in Cervantes' preoccupation with literary folly, windmill jousting is eventually absorbed by a higher and nobler variety of incitation. Life inside great novels must be lived not just at full tilt; it must also be lived significantly in such a way as to grow and to surpass its initial invention.

It is tempting to speculate on how Cervantes might have reacted had he been able to read these novels and to take part in their dialogue with his own. One possible clue is furnished by the episode of Marcela, for it suggests that he, too, was capable of creating a feminine protagonist determined to transform her pastoral image into lifelong pursuit of a "pícara idea." Or perhaps I should say "pastoril idea"! My personal suspicion is that he would have found the endings of *Madame Bovary* and *La Regenta* depressing and the life of Fortunata blurred by too much detail. Conceivably he would have perferred Lamiel, the most compulsive reader of them all, if only because trenchant Stendhalian irony would not have eluded a charter member of the Happy Few. On the other hand, the reservations expressed about *La Celestina* might also have reappeared. In any case, guessing games aside, we know that what Cervantes learned from experience, Galdós rediscovered with his assistance: the kind of incitation that is solely provoked by reading is limited and ultimately self-defeating. It is a marvelous and comic means of converting romances into novels, but if overused, the end result may be caricature and mock romance. Don Quijote's behavior upon being brought back from his first sally and the shallow Tom Sawyer of *The Adventures of Huckleberry Finn* are familiar examples.[23] Indeed the only possible justification for Tom's presence on the

[23] It was this tendency that Cervantes was at once lamenting and excusing when in the Preface to part 2 of the *Quijote* he discussed the necessity of introducing non-Quixotesque narrative patterns into the second half of part 1.

scene is that just proposed for Maxi: to start Huck off on his journey to novelistic salvation. It is this same function that in a very different fashion the cudgeled, cozened, caged (again like Maxi), and chronicled don Quijote of part 1 performed for the don Quijote of part 2.

To return for a moment to Emma and Ana, we may now surmise that their spiritual and carnal perdition, like that of Isidora, resulted not only from the Naturalistic determinism that destroyed Gervaise but also from their inability to reconcile literature with life, plot with time, illusion with reality. Ana's aspirations are nobler and more value-charged, but both of them were laid low by the whirling vanes of nineteenth-century existence. Their authors either could not or would not cure them of the self-imposed blindness of their initial bookish incitation. In contrast, and in light of their literary condemnation to a wretched fate, Galdós' intentional juxtaposition of Maxi's fervent reading with Fortunata's translucent illiteracy reveals the depths of his excavation into the Cervantine mother lode. His only peers, in my opinion, are the Dostoievsky of *The Idiot* and Mark Twain, when in his one truly great novel he also reversed the contrast of literacy and illiteracy inherited from Cervantes. The crucial difference, however, is that after *Fortunata y Jacinta,* Galdós' systematic excavation of the treasures of his own tradition was to continue for years to come in one major creation after another.

Thus, Ana can be understood in terms of Clarín's dialogue with the quixotism of *Madame Bovary,* but Galdós' dialogue with Ana was not limited in turn to Maxi's fondness for great books. Fortunata, too, in her own way constitutes an answer not just to the self-centered folly but to the failed nobility of Ana's aspirations, an answer so daring and unexpected that it surely left the author himself breathless. Salvation of the spirit in the nineteenth century (that it was still conceivable leaves a bitter taste in twentieth-century mouths) may have been as difficult as the passage of a camel through the eye of a needle. But nevertheless, Galdós sensed keenly, the horrid, Naturalistic toad-kiss of Clarín's punitive closing sentence was neither novelistically inevitable nor a retribution devoutly to be wished. Stated in general terms, Maxi may be understood as a Naturalistic caricature of the defeated and too often ri-

171

diculous don Quijote of part 1, while Fortunata in her vocational autonomy renews that of the catastrophically ennobled don Quijote of part 2. And like him, only she (unlike Emma, Ana, and Maxi) was able to complete the long, circular journey home, there to die with dignity and meaning.[24]

Novel and Society (II)

But what about Fermín de Pas? If Maxi and Fortunata can be interpreted as "prospective" answers to the Quixotesque incitation of Ana de Ozores (by which I mean their initial conception as characters and not their final states of consciousness), how did Galdós react to her confessor? Can we find in *Fortunata* any indications of an intentional response to Fermín de Pas' repressed and potentially explosive variety of incitation, an incitation manifestly not derived from *his* reading?[25] A reasonable answer might be that both he and Fortunata are human beings whose invincible passions are implacably shackled by "the social fate" of role or class. This is far too common a resemblance, however, to qualify as inter-novel dialogue. The nineteenth-century proliferation of the genre corresponded to the appearance of a seemingly limitless congregation of hot-eyed Julien Sorels and Becky Sharpes, whose undeniable talents and limitless ambitions are agonizingly thwarted, though not necessarily forever squelched, by their station. A partial, unfamiliar, and indeed grudging relaxation of social inevitability had provided a new and potent source of incitation and was, as both Balzac and Galdós affirmed explicitly, the major factor in the so-called rise of the novel.[26]

[24] Home in this case, as we shall see, means the building on the Plaza Mayor.

[25] Fermín's incitation, however, may well have been derived from Clarín's reading, as we shall see.

[26] It was, of course, first Stendhal who, while meditating on Napoleon's "bonne éducation, imagination ardente et pauvreté extrême," had the genius to see the relationship of a certain relaxation of the class structure to new possibilities of novelistic incitation. See Maurice Bardèche's discussion in *Stendhal romancier*, p. 167. To have fallen in love with a lady who by definition is unattainable (the situation of troubadours and of Saint Preux) is not the same thing as the new form of incitation discovered in the nineteenth century; the earlier impossibility leads not to the novel but to lyric

This is not to say that such plots were not age-old. As Marthe Robert observes, the novel, which by definition is a stirrer-up of life "in order to redistribute its elements and ceaselessly create new situations, . . . needs love as a powerful motor capable of effecting great transformations of existence which then become 'pseudo-états civils'."[27] Nevertheless, this fundamental variety of fictional novelty affected readers of previous centuries in a way quite alien to the nineteenth-century publics of Balzac and Galdós. What still had the charm and unreality of a fairy tale to those who listened to the story of Dorotea achieved lachrymose seriousness in novels such as *Pamela* and the *Nouvelle Héloïse*.[28] And if cynics such as Voltaire and Fielding reacted with mocking laughter, it was because they recognized both the sentimental self-indulgence of the tears of their contemporaries and the virtual impossibility of such aspirations.[29]

After the revolutions, however, love and marriage in defiance of propriety and property came to constitute an infinitely varied source

---

and romance. A consciousness of the unfairness of society's prohibition as well as of the uncertainty of one's own social place ("Am I Lucien de Rubempré or Lucien Chardon?" "Am I M. Balssa, Balzac, or de Balzac?") is indispensable. For Balzac's discussion of the novelistic advantages of the new mobility of the "social animal," see the beginning of the "Avant-propos." For Galdós' further meditations on "la sociedad presente como materia novelable," we have the Academy address already cited in *Ensayos,* ed. Bonet. The best critical discussions I have seen are Bardèche, *Balzac romancier,* p. 343; Lukacs, *The Historical Novel,* p. 383; Levin, *The Gates,* p. 86 (where he comments on the Stendhalian term "agitation") and p. 203; and on the England of Jane Austen, Raymond Williams, *The Country and the City,* pp. 108ff. Ian Watt's *The Rise of the Novel* is indispensable, even though for my purposes another approach seems more appropriate.

[27] *Roman des origines et origines du roman,* pp. 37–38.

[28] In the *Quijote* there is a marvelous ambivalence about the fairy-tale quality of the story both told to and witnessed by don Quijote's companions and about Cervantes' own implicit criticism of Dorotea's Quixotesque aspirations as a "cristiana vieja" and "villana" who lets herself be seduced by and then aspires to matrimony with an aristocrat whose past misbehavior, cruelty, and treachery hardly can be interpreted as indicating future matrimonial concord. See my "Los inquisidores literarios de Cervantes," *Actas del Tercer Congreso Internacional de Hispanistas,* México, 1970, pp. 3–25.

[29] I refer, of course, to Fielding's murderous parody, *Shamela,* and to Voltaire's sardonic comments on *Clarissa Harlowe* in his letter dated 12 April 1760 to Mme. du Deffand.

of human interest for realists, Naturalists, and fabricators of feuilletons alike. It is probable that one of the reasons we have been talking so much in recent years about the decline of the novel is that such situations are not as novel as they used to be. As money inundates our society, neither Baron Nucingen is quite as funny nor Gobseck quite as scary as they were to nineteenth-century readers. And in the course of the resultant erosion of our social restrictions, Dickens's tacit indignation at the overt indignation of Henry Gowan's mother because of his marriage to "Pet" Meagles in *Little Dorrit* becomes harder to share. This is not said in order to deny the stubbornly vestigial importance of class distinctions among us, nor the success of *Love Story* as a nostalgic replay of social imperatives the weakening of which we regret somewhat perversely. Rather I am trying to recapture an aspect of Galdós' irony that was surely more audible to his public than it is to us: when the narrator mimics the characteristic bland tone of his society and expatiates on its unprecedented form of equality based on "la dichosa confusión de todas las clases" leading to "un socialismo atenuado e inofensivo" (*65*), he is preparing us ironically for the thematic bleakness of the rest of the novel.[30] Jacinta may be a bourgeoise

---

[30] John Sinnigen makes the same distinction between the narrator and the author and observes that the former presents himself as belonging to the Madrid of the Santa Cruz and their friends and relations. Conversely, he seems to feel superior to and less intimately familiar with the "petty bourgeois" ambiance of the doña Lupe and her nephews. As a result, "in spite of the narrator's recognition of the flaws of this society, he affirms strongly its innately positive nature: 'Insensiblemente con la ayuda de la burocracia, de la pobreza y de la educación académica que todos los españoles reciben, se han ido compenetrando las clases todas, y sus miembros se introducen de una en otra, tejiendo una red espesa que amarra y solidifica la masa nacional. El nacimiento no significa nada entre nosotros.'" "Individual, Class, and Society in *Fortunata y Jacinta*," in *Galdós Studies* (II), ed. R. J. Weber, London, 1974, pp. 49–68. (*65*) The narrator continues by asserting that there are justified differences among individuals because of inevitable "desigualdades del espíritu humano," thereby at once announcing and denying the theme of the whole. Fortunata's superiority of spirit unrecognized by society (which by definition cares nothing about that variety) because of her anonymous "nacimiento." Sinnigen's undeniable conclusion that the creator of Fortunata simply *could not* have believed that "la educación académica" was available to *all* Spaniards seems necessarily to posit two levels of irony. First is that intended by the narrator, who in such phrases as "célebre *alboroto*" communicates his humorous newspaper-skepticism about char-

Cinderella, but not Fortunata. The phrase "dichosa confusión" means simply that that society was engaged in a ferocious battle not only offensively among its rival climbers but also defensively against those who threatened from below in any way, whether rebels, outcasts, idealists, trespassers, or victims whose only weapon is the pity they inspire. Rosalía de Bringas' treatment of Amparito Sánchez Emperador is but one example.

Thus, Fortunata's two antithetical "ideas," "la blanca" (social conformity) and "la pícara" (moral revolution), were the offspring not only of inner meditation but also of agonized exposure to collective injustice. If tragic drama is only meaningful in epochs separating metaphysical certainty from skepticism (Karl Jaspers' fruitful "Zwischensein"),[31] so too the novel, emergent from the comic tradition, acquires the elevation and intensity of tragedy in a century that had lost its social certainty and had not attained our own degree of social skepticism, or our pretense of it. The serious, and to us rather surprising, attention paid by such Naturalists as Zola,

---

acters and current events, and second is that of the author, Galdós, who in part 1 watches wryly the repeated self-betrayal of his narrator. Thus, the narrator, having claimed that nothing can be done about poverty because "la otra determinación positiva de clase, el dinero, está fundada en principios económicos tan inmutables como las leyes físicas . . . ," goes on to describe the Santa Cruz family as surrounded by friends and relations of whom the most admired are dedicated to usury, profiteering, and conspicuous consumption. For a theoretical discussion of this variety of irony, see Seymour Chatman, *Story and Discourse,* Ithaca, N.Y., 1978, pp. 233–235. It seems to me, however, after literally years of meditation that the fatuous editorials of chapters 6 and 7 of part 1 correspond less to a double-tiered elaboration of ironies than to a fecund and self-mocking utilization of Galdós' own ambivalence towards his society, that is, towards the Spain which he hoped against hope might save itself and the Spain the future of which seemed to him so hopeless. Thus, if in *La desheredada* he comments caustically that "la confusión de clases es la moneda falsa de la igualdad" (*1019*), in a newspaper article written three years later he provides ammunition for his future Marxist critics by praising "la España futura, la generación fresca" because in the University there is an "ejército inmenso de muchachos de todas las clases sociales, pues allí se confunden el hijo del prócer con el del artesano, y todos se tutean, todos son amigos." Shoemaker, *Cartas,* p. 134.

31 "The greatest phenomena of 'Geistesgeschichte' are transitional. . . . They have the quality of being intermediate ['Zwischensein'] . . . and are unrepeatable and inimitable. Human greatness occurs only on such terms." *Vom Ursprung und Ziel der Geschichte,* Frankfurt, 1955, p. 234.

Galdós, Clarín and Eça de Queiros to a subject previously suited only for medieval and eighteenth-century satire, clerical celibacy, is simply another path for investigation of the same "mal du siècle."[32] Both Fortunata and Fermín de Pas can be interpreted as representing in antithetical fashion the "novelistic condition of man" in the nineteenth century. Their incitation is the result of the confrontation of their half-liberated, newly conceivable personal aspirations with a society all the more determined to keep them in their place. It does not result from (as in the case of Ana), a dialogue among nineteenth-century authors or their shared exploration of literary tradition.

Nevertheless, even considering that many apparent resemblances among nineteenth-century novels are generic and historical in nature, a case can be made for a subtle comic reply to Clarín's priest in *Fortunata y Jacinta.* But in order to overhear and understand what Galdós is saying to his friend, two more novelist-interlocutors must be taken into account: the Balzac of *Splendeurs et misères des courtisanes* and the Zola of *La Conquête de Plassans.* The first was a novel that Galdós had absorbed more eagerly and profitably than any other in the whole *Comédie.* Reminiscences of it, as we remember, are unmistakable both in *La Fontana* and *La desheredada* where memories of Esther Gobseck help entice readers into identifying themselves with Isidora's tribulations. And in *Fortunata y Jacinta,* what can only be interpreted as a scene intentionally allusive to the same novel is used to an even more subtle purpose. As I shall try to show, Galdós, while reading *La Regenta,* perceived that Fermín de Pas was a "naturalized" (in both senses of the word) don Carlos Herrera, Vautrin's penultimate role in *Splendeurs et misères* as a Macchiavellian Spanish Jesuit. And while writing his own novel, Galdós apparently could not resist the temptation to in-

---

[32] Pierre Barbéris distinguishes a novelistic (meaning also bourgeois) variety of this historical disease of the spirit from the lyrical melancholy to which the phrase usually refers. The latter, the result of having been thrust unwillingly into prosaic history, is typically represented not only by Baudelaire but also by Lamennais. *Balzac et le mal du siècle,* vol. 1, p. 58. The former variety, however, "comme le dira magnifiquement Balzac" is characterized by "impatience d'avenir." Ibid., p. 59. One felt an anguishing gap between what one aspired to accomplish or become and what implacable tradition allowed.

sert an episode that would let Clarín know he had been overheard.

Since this tripartite novelistic relationship is both complex and highly speculative, it will be well to proceed cautiously. To begin with, although the contained passion of Fermín de Pas may well have been a response to that of Vautrin (the one's forbidden love for Ana and the other's for Lucien echo each other uncannily), nineteenth-century scholars would not have considered *Splendeurs et misères* to be a "source" for such a dissimilar novel as *La Regenta*. That dubious category should have been assigned to the second of the novels just mentioned, Zola's *La Conquête de Plassans*.[33] How would our academic forebears have studied the relationship between the two? Probably they would have started, in deference to Naturalistic doctrine, by looking at their milieux. Plassans with its provincial presumption, its ecclesiastical rivalries and intrigues, its passive bishop, its congealed political factions, and its coterie of bourgeois "beatas" vying for confessional gratification and seeking social credit by supporting pious causes will be familiar to readers of Clarín.[34] It is evidently a far more exact prefiguration of Vetusta than Galdós' Orbajosa, Balzac's Tours, or Flaubert's Yonville.

The principal characters in the two novels also resemble each other to a suspicious extent. Marthe Mouret, the feminine protagonist (and mother of our future novelistic "fellow travelers," Serge and Octave), exhibits symptoms of hyper-emotional devotion very much like those of Ana de Ozores. It is true that, not being addicted to mystical treatises, she lacks the neo-Cervantine incitation that her successor shares with Madame Bovary. Nor does she appeal to us

[33] After writing the first version of this chapter for publication in the *NRFH*, I discovered with some chagrin that Clarín's use of *La Conquête de Plassans* was mentioned in passing by Werner Küpper. *Leopoldo Alas, "Clarín," und der französische Naturalismus in Spanien,* Cologne, 1958, p. 107. Nor do my observations above at all cover the ground. There are so many more similarities and echoes that separate study would seem to be indicated. And again now, just before correcting this note, I have read Gonzalo Sobejano's cogent discussion of the same resemblances in his edition of *La Regenta* (Barcelona, 1976). Neither notes that Clarín praised *La conquista de Plasance* for its *lack* of "composición armónica" in his review of *El amigo Manso* in *El Día,* 19 June 1882. Hoar, "Critics," p. 130.

[34] The bishop in Zola's novel may have been a partial model not only for don Fortunato but also for Ripamilán in view of their mutual love of Latin poetry.

through sincere efforts to understand herself and come to terms with an unmentionable sexual frustration. She is a fool, and her husband, at worst the sort of Frenchman who protests crossly about "les courants d'air," seems to be as virile at least as his fatherhood requires. Nevertheless, when we read about her "tristesses sans cause, de ses secrètes joies, de ses besoins d'être guidée," it all sounds strangely familiar.[35] If Emma provided the form or manner of Ana's incitation, Marthe Mouret's eccentricities seem to have suggested its particular direction.

But it is Marthe's mentor, the enigmatic and stealthy "conqueror of Plassans," l'abbé Faujas, who confirms the intimacy of the two novels. Everything he does and represents (unscrupulousness, thirst for power, capacity for intrigue, iron will, physical fitness, and even an abnormal relationship with his mother) reappears in Fermín de Pas. What is missing in his rather phlegmatic temperament is the passionate capacity for both adoration and anguish, which distinguish the Magistral from the other more placid males of Vetusta. The truth, I think, is that Clarín's male protagonist is a literary hybrid (in the same fashion that his beloved recalls both Emma Bovary and Marthe Mouret) and that (Zolaesque inspiration aside) his special form of incitation was kindled by that of Vautrin in the role of Herrera. Both Vautrin and de Pas are characterized by that apparently antithetical juncture of metal-cold calculation and incandescent energy that is admirably analyzed by Jean-Pierre Richard in his essay on Balzac.[36] Thus, Ana's tortured confessor constitutes a simultaneous answer to both Zola's and Balzac's priestly protagonists. His "source," his social identity, and his role or self-image may be derived from *La Conquête de Plassans,* but in his soul he is a worthy heir of perhaps the most fascinating personage of the entire *Comédie humaine.*

That this cannot be dismissed as mere speculation is attested to novelistically by Clarín's patent adaptation of one of the more melodramatic scenes of the first part of Balzac's novel entitled *Comment*

---

[35] *Les Rougon-Macquart,* vol. 1, p. 1010.

[36] *Etudes sur le Romantisme, Paris,* 1970. Richard comments in his chapter entitled "Corps et décors balzaciens": "Toute grande passion ici est éruptive." Ibid., p. 9. "Dureté, froideur, maigreur, rigidité, tout cela rêvé a travers l'image désespérante du métal." Ibid., p. 37.

aiment les filles. I refer to the scene in which Herrera (his true identity has not yet been revealed to the reader) heartlessly refuses to heed medical advice that Esther will die within a month if her enforced seclusion in a religious institution is continued. So, too, chapter 12 of *La Regenta* reveals the depths of ecclesiastical baseness to which Fermín de Pas has descended by chronicling an identical refusal. As we remember, for no better reason than avoidance of a possible anticlerical scandal, he refuses to advise the Carraspiques to have their ailing daughter, Rosa, removed from her damp and unsanitary cell in Las Salesas. In so refusing, he defies the professional authority and personal indignation of the family physician, don Robustiano Somoza, who, in this case correctly, predicts her imminent death. Clarín, who as a narrator was as maliciously ironical as Stendhal, knew exactly what he was up to. Although the general pattern of the relationship of Ana and her mentor had been borrowed without advertisement from Zola and recreated in Asturian terms, he copies this particular villainy of Herrera's almost literally in the hope that well read readers will participate in his dialogue with Balzac. And if they are especially perceptive, they may thereby be led to appreciate the way his novel aerates Naturalistic documentation with a cunning counterpoint of Ana's Cervantine and Fermín de Pas' Balzacian varieties of incitation.

With all this in mind, we may return to *Fortunata y Jacinta* in prospect. For in its future author, Clarín found, as he knew he would, his ideal reader. Not only had Galdós already experimented successfully with the juxtaposition of seventeenth- and nineteenth-century narrative techniques (the probability of dialogue between *La Regenta* and Galdós' previous Naturalistic novels remains to be explored) but also he had read about the splendors and miseries of Lucien, Esther, and Vautrin as voraciously as Clarín. It is not surprising, therefore, that he should have recognized the affiliation of Fermín de Pas' at once passionate and unscrupulous character with that of Vautrin. In addition, he could not have helped noticing the origin and appreciating the dialogic irony of the Rosa Carraspique episode. Otherwise why should he, too, have borrowed (both in the preliminary and final versions of *Fortunata y Jacinta*) the scene from *Splendeurs et misères* that immediately precedes the spurious Jesuit's refusal to heed the alarmed physician? The two intentional "plagiarisms" are so alike that Clarín must have smiled to himself when he finished reading part 2, chapter 4, section 4.

A brief description of the Balzacian episode will allow those familiar with Galdós' version to judge for themselves. We are near the beginning of the novel; Vautrin, as immersed in his ecclesiastical role as if he had been trained by Stanislavski, is intent on guarding his protégé, Lucien de Rubempré (for whom he hopes to arrange an advantageous marriage), from the scandal that the latter's love for the prostitute Esther Gobseck has already begun to create in Parisian society. When he visits her, however, in spite of himself he gives up his notion of appealing to her generosity and persuading her to relinquish Lucien. Instead, he proposes a sojourn in a "maison religieuse," where he will be prohibited from seeing her until she emerges "chaste, pure, et bien élevée."[37] The tone is admittedly different (sinister in the one case, ironical in the other), and the two pairs of characters are totally unlike each other, but the situational parallel of this interview with that of Nicolás Rubín and Fortunata is undeniable.

As recent readers may remember, Fortunata, naturally unaware of the real novelistic origins of her future brother-in-law's plea, is reminded of another probable literary echo of the same Balzacian episode: the visit of M. Du Val to Marguerite Gautier in *La Dame aux camélias*, which she had "heard read aloud." But this at best is a Cervantine red herring, Cervantine in the sense that Fortunata, like don Quijote, discovers her own "source" in the most popular romance of the time. In this, Galdós alludes specifically to the fact that such situations are topical in the sentimental fiction of his century and further suggests that we withhold our tears. But implicitly, I dare suggest, he is saying something quite different: you, Clarín, must realize that by my referring playfully to an erroneous parallel, I have found you out. Since you have chosen to reveal the dialogue of *La Regenta* with *Splendeurs et misères* by openly substituting Fermín de Pas for don Carlos Herrera in an unforgettable episode, I shall now demonstrate how closely I have read both novels by a

---

[37] *Comédie,* vol. 5, p. 684. Arthur Holmberg has noticed the resemblance independently and offers a more detailed comparison. His interpretation, however, is very different from mine. "Balzac and Galdós: *Comment aiment les filles,*" *CL,* 29, 1977, pp. 109–123.

comic adaptation of the part of Balzac's story that occurs just prior to the one you borrowed yourself.

With parody in mind, Galdós proceeds to underline the similarities as well as the reversal in tone. The pious language of the priestly emissary, the idea of committing the fallen woman to a religious reformatory, and even character-mimicry all point intentionally to the original. As far as the last is concerned, Nicolás Rubín's doltish complacency in his role of "zurcidor moral" echoes that fatuous moment when Herrera gets carried away by his own rhetoric: "Does it not bring us near to the angels charged to bring back the erring into the path of right; to purify a creature such as this . . . is it not to create? What an incentive to unite moral beauty to physical beauty! *Quelle jouissance d'orgueil, si l'on réussit!*"[38] And Esther in her portion of the conversation reveals an abysmal ignorance of the most elementary matters that is only comparable to that of Fortunata; she is a "fille qui n'a réçu ni le baptème de l'Eglise ni celui de la science, qui ne sait ni lire, ni écrire, ni prier."[39] Her ignorance is innocence, and when purified she will be compared by the diabolic Vautrin to an angel. No, it was not Dumas-fils but Balzac's pathetic scene Galdós had chosen to play with.

Having gone this far, one final speculation cannot be avoided: Galdós' tacit comparison of Fermín de Pas and Nicholás Rubín was not solely intended as a wry professional salute. By sending into the novelistic game a genuine priest, as a substitute for the sinister Balzacian impostor, as cloddish and unincited as his predecessor had been steely and fiery he comments indirectly on Clarín's choice of Herrera as a model for portraying the social harmfulness of which the Spanish clergy was capable. And he may even have had a professional reason for doing so. Clarín, who had finished reading *La familia de León Roch* not long before undertaking *La Regenta,* apparently felt that Galdós had exaggerated the fanatical intervention of Padre Paoletti, María Egipciaca's confessor, into the private life of the Roch family (or antifamily), and he took pains to specify the far greater subtlety of Fermín de Pas' domestic meddling: "And in view of all this should we therefore wear sack cloth and always look with pious affection at the floor? Should we torment our husband

---

[38] *Comédie,* vol. 5, p. 683.
[39] Ibid., p. 687.

with our domestic inquisition, refusing to leave the house to go for walks or to accept social invitations? God forbid, Ana, God forbid! . . . Domestic harmony is nothing to trifle with."[40]

When or if Galdós noticed this passage, I would guess that he accepted the correction. On the other hand, he does not seem to have been convinced that Hispanization of Balzac's romantic mystery priest was novelistically convincing. And his answer was the creation of Nicolás Rubín. He is saying, in effect, that a Fermín de Pas, for all his lasciviousness, unscrupulous ambition, and driving passion, was no more dangerous and a lot less true to life than the erotically frigid, well-meaning, insensitive, and run-of-the-mill priests who were more often than not to be found in Spanish pulpits. True, Nicolás in his gluttony and in his hirsute exuberance is as much a Naturalistic caricature as his brother, and in that sense he is also an exaggeration. But is not this Galdós' point? To give such an exceptionally gross and spiritually void creature a role identical to that played by Clarín's model for the Magistral is at once a comic tour de force and an appropriate reply to Clarín's earlier tacit criticism of Paoletti's lack of verisimilitude.

In conclusion, within the overall pattern of resemblance (the triangle of two incited characters opposed to and eventually destroyed by a hollow, nineteenth-century avatar of don Juan Tenorio), we have overheard in *Fortunata y Jacinta* two specific comments on the art of *La Regenta,* one positive and the other negative. The first is, of course, the new comprehension of the *Quijote,* which Flaubert had taught to Clarín and which both Spaniards, each in his own way, went on further to explore in the context of their contemporary society. In the case of Galdós, who had been a devotee of Cervantes since childhood, the lesson was revolutionary in its effects, an authentic turning point in his career. He had suddenly grasped creatively the full significance of Cervantes' achievement. As already suggested, he had read it prior to 1885 as a masterpiece of ironical word management ("Wortkunstwerk") and as a devastating satire of national irrationality. But now, thanks both to Clarín and to his own professional maturity, he understood how don Quijote and Sancho, once born in print, in the course of their continued existence eventually surpassed their simplified introduc-

---

[40] *La Regenta,* in *Obras,* vol. 1, p. 467.

tory caricatures, just as his own future offspring, Fortunata, Benina, and even Torquemada, were to do. In addition, he began to realize something far more profound than Clarín could have taught him: how the knight and squire in their vocational consciousness were eventually liberated from the intentional control both of their author and of their "race, milieu, et moment." Like the Dostoievsky of *The Idiot,* the Mark Twain of *Huck Finn,* and the Stendhal of *Le Rouge et le noir,* Galdós had unexpectedly been granted a vision of the fathomless nature of the human condition, at once determined and free. His long apprenticeship was over.

The second comment is that Vautrin, who had served Balzac so well earlier in the century, was no longer susceptible to revealing, novelistic re-creation. Galdós' society was stodgy and gossipy, pretentious and unjust, and the more spurious the value, the more fervent the reverence of his contemporaries. But it was not a fascinating game of cops and robbers, government spies and revolutionaries, Hurons and "courreurs du bois," as both Stendhal and Balzac, with a certain amount of romantic overemphasis, had portrayed their Restoration. In Galdós' own terms, there were no "apostólicos," no "comuneros," and no Coletillas or José Manuel Regatos to worry about. Unlike the French Restoration, which relied on the police for containing the historical effervescence that remained after 1815, the Spanish version during the 1880s and 1890s offered greater personal freedom than do most late twentieth-century societies, a freedom particularly pleasant for those who, like Juanito Santa Cruz or Galdós himself for that matter, had enough money to enjoy it. Vautrin would have been, as they say, out of phase in the Spain of Cánovas.

I willingly admit that the novelistic depiction of Fermín de Pas' Vetusta and Leon Roch's Madrid as social straitjackets within which individuals writhed impotently is not a misrepresentation of either. But it was a blind alley as far as comprehension of the true illness of the Bourbon Restoration was concerned. The essentially isolated intensity of the Magistral's imprisonment in his cassock rendered his private experience far less historically revealing than that of his beloved Ana, whose wrong choices emerged from day-to-day contact with the world in which she lived. It never would have occurred to her, any more than it would have to Fortunata, to engage

183

in telescopic espionage from on high. Galdós, in other words, as he envisioned his future novel was not only going to abandon Zola but also the Balzac of *Splendeurs et misères*. And in doing so he inevitably reminds us of Dostoievsky's manifest consciousness of the alternate isolation or affective participation ("convivencia") of his own creations: Raskolnikov as against Myshkin, Alyosha as against Stavrogin. After all, Cervantes, too, was not lacking in sympathy for the solitary passion of Marcela, but he sensed that it was only don Quijote who, in the oral company of Sancho (and everyone else he encountered) could lead the way in that first, unprecedented expedition into the wilderness of daily experience at once private and historical.

Novel and Novelists

It should now be clear that inter-novel dialogue, whenever it is not limited to direct debate or to the overt polemic of opposing theses, tends to be polyphonic. The voice of each novelist interlocutor is accompanied by the voices of all those other novelists to whom he has listened most attentively in the past. Thus, in the dialogue of Galdós and Clarín, we detected the tacit presence of Cervantes, Flaubert, Balzac, and, at one remove, Zola. Nor should we be surprised at the subtlety of the game. Ever since the *Quijote,* which is literally composed of conversations with characters from other works of fiction as well as with other authors, such dialogue has been crucial to this innately sophisticated form of literature. The narrator of a romance is the single dominating voice of the story, but the novelist, as we have seen, trains us to participate, to see through his sly deceptions, to watch him watch himself at work (Cervantine irony being the origin of Romantic irony) by utilizing in large part our expectations and habits as readers.[41]

The result is that, in comprehending critically novels in the Cervantine tradition, we must pay continual attention to the following: (1) what the characters say they have read; (2) what the au-

[41] For a discussion of Romantic irony see the admirably lucid article of R. Immerwahr, "The Subjectivity or Objectivity of Friedrich Schlegel's Poetic Irony."

thor reveals he has read both implicitly and explicitly; (3) what he believes the authors he has read to have read; and (4) what he expects us to have read, whether we have done so or not. All four are crucial factors in the conducting of novels, conceived of as mental symphonies, which become ever more elaborate with the passage of generations. And if this is valid for a Fielding or a Stendhal (who specialized in ironical epigraphs), imagine the possibilites offered to a Clarín or a Galdós who in the eighties of their century took delight in spending lavishly the immense novelistic treasure accumulated during the previous decades!

A final word of warning as much to myself as to my readers: by bringing to the surface and making explicit a literary polyphony that in *Fortunata y Jacinta* and *La Regenta* is subterranean and tacit, we betray both novels. We are in danger of converting them into the sort of calculated, fictional legerdemain in which such writers as Nabokov and Borges take their delight. As a result the consciousnesses of Ana and Fortunata, Maxi and the Magistral appear subordinated to the artifice of the artist. They come to resemble pieces in a chess game or answers to a complex quiz in literary history more than lives in time. This should not be construed as a criticism of the endlessly fascinating art of Nabokov and Borges; instead, I suggest that the sophistication of novels such as *La Regenta* and *Fortunata y Jacinta* is of an altogether different kind. We are not supposed to be initially mystified or finally classified either as cognoscenti or as hopeless lowbrows. Rather the fundamental Cervantine equation of consciousness with reading—our past reading, the character's past reading, the author's past reading, all tacitly present in *this* reading— is designed to engage us in the seemingly autonomous experience of another person in another place to the extent that our age, sensibility, and past dedication to literacy will permit.

Thus, the inter-novel dialogue with which we have been concerned is in a sense more "biological" than intellectual. It is nothing less than a means of conception, gestation, childbirth, and growth not just in creating the printed page but *in* the reader of the printed page as well. One is provoked by reading and a memory of reading to surrender the best one has lived through ("erlebt") and read through to a fictional life and thereby to become more than one has been, or as Proust, turning the notion around, phrased it, to make us more profound "readers of ourselves."[42] This is not a paradox; rather the implication is that, once apprenticeship was completed and the nineteenth-century reader had settled into reading and the habit of life creation (surely without full awareness of having been seduced into it by tacit inter-novel dialogue), he or she too became novelistic. One understood oneself novelistically; one behaved novelistically; and one was ready to participate fully in what we shall call in the following essay the novelistic consciousness of one's age. As we shall see, submersion succeeds sophistication, and Quixotesque belief, Cervantine play.[43]

[42] See chapter 3, note 41.

[43] Among the numerous minor and probably unwitting similarities between *La Regenta* and *Fortunata,* we may note just a few. (1) Anacleto, the name of the "familiar del Obispo," was the name chosen for Nicolás Rubín in the manuscript version of *Fortunata y Jacinta. Obras,* vol. 1, p. 9. (2) Don Cayetano's habitual gesture when speaking of theology ("formaba un anteojo con el dedo pulgar y el índice") resembles that of Torquemada. Ibid., p. 38. (3) Doña Anuncia customarily shops for food with the help of an eccentric "catedrático" who advises her on quality and helps bargain. Ibid., p. 109. (4) There is an insistence on the close or distant blood relationship of all the Vetustenses as revealed in interminable discussions of genealogy ("Y como las cerezas, salían enganchados por el parentesco casi todos los vetustenses"). Ibid., p. 142. (5) Consider also the "flamenco" affectation in clothes and self-presentation of Joaquinito Orgaz and other young "señoritos." (6) Fermín de Pas' self-serving confession to Ana closely resembles those of Juanito to Jacinta: "La confesion del Magistral se pareció a las de muchos autores que en vez de contar sus pecados aprovechan la ocasión de pintarse en si mismos como héroes, echando al mundo la culpa de sus males, y quedándose con faltas leves, por confesar algo." Ibid., p. 588. (7) The superficial "materialist" reading of don Alvaro resembles that of Juan Pablo. Ibid., p. 222. I dare not insist on the abundance of bird imagery in both novels, or their use of mechanical imagery to represent psychological change, for they reflect basic tenets of Naturalism and so go beyond the frontiers of this particular "dialogue."

CHAPTER VII

The Novelist as Reader

Novel and Consciousness

The notion just presented of the novel as a form of dialogue is again true but insufficient. As in the case of our previous hypothesis that the prospect of *Fortunata y Jacinta* was "dialectically" contingent upon Galdós' critical dissatisfaction, first, with *La desheredada* and, second (and more immediately and acutely), with *Lo prohibido,* the metaphor of corrective inter-novel "dialogue" is also limited to what the critic believes to be at least the semiconscious intention of the novelist. In effect, the gestation of the novel-to-be in terms of its author's intimate conversation with *La Regenta* and *Splendeurs et misères des courtisanes,* when made explicit, resembled a kind of prearranged chess problem, a literary game of the sort that Cervantes played with the pastoral, the picaresque, and the chivalresque. What such an interpretation does not and indeed cannot take into account is the undetermined, living interaction of consciousnesses, which my teacher, Augusto Centeno, has called, as opposed to "intention," "intent" and "extent."[1] By this he meant *all* that the writer calls up out of himself in the process of creation (intent) and *all* his text calls up out of *all* of its readers in the process of their re-creation (extent). If books as long as the *Quijote* or *Fortunata y Jacinta* are worth the time it takes to read them, it is not because of their authors' theses or half-formulated intentions (susceptible to recapitulation by critics, scholars, and teachers) but rather because they create new consciousness endlessly.

Let me explain my sense of the insufficiency of what has so far been said about the prospect of Galdós' novelistic maturity. As remarked earlier, the dialogue that may be detected in Galdós' novels is double in nature: the novelist listens attentively to his own voice

[1] See the Introduction to *The Intent of the Artist,* Princeton, 1941.

emergent from the unsatisfactory past of the preceding novel and at the same time appeals for help to another novelist, or perhaps an entire "colloquium" of precursors assembled in the Parnassus of his memory, who may be able to guide him in preparing the novel in prospect. As we have seen at the conclusions of both *La de Bringas* and *Lo prohibido,* he intentionally converts both himself and his colleagues into members of the fiction. But this is not all. It is obvious that the notion of the novelist as listener cannot by itself justify use of the term "dialogue." He must also speak and be heard, which means he must have *his* listeners. Frequently in the case of Galdós this was a living colleague to whom he directed himself more or less slyly and to whom he may even have sent a complimentary copy. Hence, our conjecture that Nicolás Rubín's assumption of the role of Balzac's spurious Abbé was directed to Clarín. And hence Carmen Bravo Villasante concludes from doña Emilia Pardo Bazán's love letters to Galdós that *Memorias de un solterón* (1891) and *Tristana* (1892) are "novelas que se complementan o se contrastan en réplica."[2]

The listeners who matter, however, are those who overhear, the public of past and present readers (and even "los no nacidos" as in the ballad of Diego Ordóñez), who were, are, or will be expert enough in their favorite genre to be able to participate in what is at stake in the dialogue. And once that process gets underway, such notions as intention or conscious interpretation no longer apply. Whether or not Clarín got the point of the substitution of Nicolás Rubín for Fermín de Pas is a pointless question because unanswerable (personally I am positive he did), but whether or not the reader proceeds from vague or precise awareness of literature reflecting literature to unconditional surrender to the "new mode of life" is crucial. Thus, the terms proposed by Centeno, "intent" and "extent" (the one corresponding to the author and the other to the readers or "apprehenders"), can be understood as synonymous with the notion of an overarching "novelistic" comprehension of self and world. Beyond, beneath, above, or perhaps *through* the words on the page, it is this shared consciousness that converts author, character, and reader into a trinity and enables the third member—instead of

[2] Carmen Bravo Villasante, *Cartas a Galdós; Emilia Pardo Bazán,* Madrid, 1975, p. 9. (Hereafter cited as *Cartas a Galdós.*)

having to annotate specific reminiscences of past reading on his or her mind's margin—to absorb paragraph after paragraph meaningfully and with the proper velocity.[3] One submits oneself, offers oneself, to fictional experience and validates it with one's own store accumulated simultaneously from living and reading.[4]

Seen in this way, the very possibility of the kind of "dialogue" of which we spoke in the preceding chapter depends on the existence of a generic "language" (in the sense that language constitutes shared consciousness and shared reassurance that reality is real) known to both novelists and readers. As such, it consists of an ever-expanding vocabulary of adventures and experiences in the form of biographical patterns, milieux, and particular situations, which has been learned so well and so intimately that neither speaker nor listener can be aware of the full extent of his latent knowledge. As such, too, it describes the communion of reader and writer, as well as of reading and writing, which enabled the rise of the novel in the nineteenth century and expresses it far better than the musical metaphors (symphonic form, polyphony of voices) usually used when speaking of the intention of the author. I am aware, of course, that theories of language (along with synchronic techniques for its study) have in recent years been widely and at times irresponsibly applied to other fields, among them the novel. What I now propose,

---

[3] S. Bacarisse remarks correctly that we should read Galdós' novels for content "and without concern for style." "The Realism of Galdós; Some Reflections on Language and the Perception of Reality," *BHS*, 42, 1965, pp. 239–240. He does not seem to recognize, however, that the whole process of absorption of this kind of novelistic experience is a question of matching velocities, of surrendering our mind to the rhythm of sentence-by-sentence and page-by-page growth. So also one should read Stendhal and Balzac but not (in my experience) Flaubert or Hemingway.

[4] In this sense it is hard to imagine how a youth of our time can begin his reading of novels with a *Fortunata y Jacinta* or others of its length and depth, although it certainly *is* done. During the great period of novelistic consciousness, apprenticeship was institutionalized in the form of gradually more complex juvenile reading, overheard conversation among grown-ups, and indeed family experience itself. Individual novelists seem to have sensed this; *Tom Sawyer* must precede *Huck Finn* in exactly the same way that the "episodios" precede *La desheredada*. And even Virginia Woolf (who inaugurated her career in *The Voyage Out* with relatively greater complexity), by having characters in *To the Lighthouse* discuss *Waverley*, hints strongly that all novel readers might best start with Scott.

however, is neither hermetic nor antihistoricistic. Rather it corresponds to a specifically and typically nineteenth-century manifestation of Georg Lukacs' youthful theory of "novelistic consciousness."[5]

I am willing to stipulate that the almost four-hundred-year-old genre of the novel (the *Quijote,* premised on demythification, was as central to Lukacs' initial meditations as it had been to Schelling's) at once expresses and is made possible by the alienation of the modern or Western consciousness. But it is, I think, equally true that its nineteenth-century triumph was founded on its thitherto unexploited ability to *relieve* the alienation of a vast public of avid readers by providing, not just other, more gratifying lives with which to identify (as in the case of romance), but rather whole cities, countries, and epochs of the mind for communal belief and cohabitation. Each reader of a Balzac, a Dickens, or a Galdós knows, without necessarily knowing that he does, that he is accompanied in mass rapport by all the enriched consciousnesses (both novelists and fellow readers) who have lent their treasures of personal experience to the genre and that he himself is immeasurably enriched thereby.[6] Hence the propriety of the comparison with language. On a far smaller scale and within a comic frame of reference, don Quijote can converse with Dorotea, the literate Canon, and many others (thereby relieving his feeling of "Obdachlosigkeit," "rooflessness," Lukacs' first novelistic and pre-Marxist version of alienation), because in their common condition as reader-believers they possess an identical "chivalresque consciousness." They literally speak the same language.

Mention of the *Quijote,* which presented novelistic consciousness as simultaneously voluptuous and ridiculous, reminds us again forcefully of the historical peculiarity of Galdós as a reader-writer and of nineteenth-century reading and writing in general. Perhaps it is only now, when all sorts of "hot" and "cold" visual and oral media have replaced the printed page and have supposedly converted us into global villagers, that we possess the perspective necessary to

[5] For a penetrating critical discussion of this and other aspects of *Die Theorie des Romans,* see Paul de Man, "Georg Lukacs's *Theory of the Novel,*" *MLN,* 81, 1966, pp. 527–534.

[6] For more detailed discussion see my "The Novelist and His Readers; Meditations on a Stendhalian Metaphor."

be fully aware of and (in spite of Marshall McLuhan) to regret the belief we are losing, the companionship we need no longer, and the language we have half-forgotten. As a sign of the times, I would point to a recent cartoon in the *New Yorker*. The setting is a bookstore; a notice on the counter announces the availability of the latest and last Agatha Christie novel. The clerk standing behind the counter is wearing a black armband; a matronly client has apparently just asked him why, and the reply is the caption: "Hercule Poirot, il est mort."[7] In contrast, when Balzac on his deathbed cried out for Doctor Bianchon, or when the blind Galdós, having been escorted to a performance of the dramatic version of *Marianela* and hearing her speak, exclaimed, "¡Es mi Nela! ¡Es mi Nela!" nobody laughed. The two anecdotes (and many others like them) may or may not be true, but one thing is certain: they were told repeatedly and interpreted reverently as pathetic cases of novelistic consciousness in extremis and not as examples of comic senility.

Here again the reader and the writer must be understood without ontological distinction. Fiction was, in fact, so alive for our grandparents and their grandparents that they not only learned how to cope with life in their unprecedented century from novels, as David Riesman remarks,[8] but they also felt, with only a tinge of comic

---

[7] The earlier version of the present chapter begins with a discussion of this cartoon from the issue of 17 November 1975.

[8] "I think not so much of the novel's use as a device for reform . . . as of its less obvious use as a device by which people might prepare themselves for novel contacts and novel life-situations—anticipatory socialization, that is, a preparation in imagination for playing roles that might emerge in one's later career. . . . The novel of the 19th century doubtless disoriented many chambermaids and a few duchesses, but on many more occasions it helped prepare individuals for their careers in a disorienting world of rapid industrialization and urbanization—where fictional moves and actual ones were not so unlike, life and art could almost imitate one another." David Riesman, "The Oral and Written Traditions," *Explorations,* 6, 1956, p. 26. Riesman has given us, I think, a sociological definition of "novelistic consciousness." This, I should like to add, gives indispensable historical frontiers to the generic approach of Jonathan Culler, who cites Philippe Sollers: " 'Le roman est la manière dont cette société se parle.' More than any other literary form, more perhaps than any other type of writing, the novel serves as the model by which society conceives of itself, the discourse in and through which it articulates the world. . . . For the basic convention which governs the novel . . . is our expectation that [it] will produce a world." And, thus, an identity for ourselves. *Structuralist Poetics,* Ithaca, N.Y., 1975, p. 189.

paradox, that people in books were more real and important than people outside them. Readers who read "like tigers," or "like Woolfs," both believed in and got fat on what they digested. We do not need Marañón to tell us that Galdós in his later years spoke of his characters "como si hubieran tenido existencia humana,"[9] nor do we need the future novelist, who had just finished translating *Pickwick Papers,* to proclaim, echoing Balzac, that "la vida que existe y se manifiesta en las páginas de un libro es más importante y digna de ser conocido que los innumerables accidentes domésticos que en nada distinguen a un hombre de la vulgar multitud."[10] All we need do is follow Jorge Manrique's advice to look into our own lives and remember the conversations about books of the grandparents we have loved and lost. I myself was at once moved and disconcerted when I encountered that passage in *To Kill a Mockingbird* in which the children act out the roles of Tom Swift and his friends in an endless game of communal reading. Why? Because I suddenly remembered having been engaged for weeks and months in the same form of recreation, literally re-creation. And then I realized that, far from having forgotten how to talk "Tom Swiftian," those prefabricated, mass-produced, utterly flat fictional lives remain with me far more vividly than those of my flesh-and-blood childhood friends and fellow readers.

Now that novelistic consciousness is becoming obsolete, it may console us to remember that the greatest of all novels and more than a bookcase full of others providing lasting fascination were written before the nineteenth-century ascension of the genre. And this despite grave impediments. For as we know, the nascent phe-

---

Culler goes on to cite Sollers again. " 'How do others see us if not as a character from a novel?' " ibid. Sollers, *Logiques,* Paris, 1968, p. 228.

[9] Gregorio Marañón, *Elogio y nostalgia de Toledo,* Madrid, 1958, p. 144. Cited by J. C. Ullman and G. H. Allison, "Galdós as Psychiatrist in *Fortunata y Jacinta,*" *AG,* 9, 1974, p. 24. (Hereafter cited as "Galdós as Psychiatrist.")

[10] In the introduction to his forthcoming serial translation of *Pickwick Papers,* Galdós was addressing the readers of *La Nación,* 9 March 1868. The young Galdós' acute comprehension of Dickens's characteristic descriptive techniques results in one of the most cogent pages of criticism to have emerged from his pen. See Shoemaker, *Los artículos,* p. 452. In his "Avant-propos," Balzac lists a wide assortment of previous characters (among them "Don Quichotte") "dont l'éxistence est plus authentique que celles des générations au milieu desquelles on les fait naître." *Comédie,* vol. 1, p. 6.

nomenon of novelistic consciousness (the Gutenberg malady), if diagnosed as ridiculous by Cervantes, was castigated as mortally sinful by the oratorical pen of Fray Pedro Malón de Chaide and by a host of other ascetics and moralists.[11] Even worse, in its own birthplace it was soon submerged by a rival variety: the oral consciousness of the theater, shared and celebrated by all,[12] except for a few who could easily be dismissed as intellectual snobs and grouches.[13] Afterwards, of course, Cervantes' view prevailed in England and France; those who were entertained by *Tristram Shandy, Joseph Andrews,* and *Jacques le fataliste* would, like the readers of the *New Yorker,* have found the mourning of a bookseller for his merchandise not immoral but delightfully absurd.

Curiously, a clear intimation of the revolution that was to come is to be found in the correspondence of Diderot himself. Writing to Mme. de Vindeul in 1781, he facetiously recommends submersion in novel-reading (*Gil Blas, Manon Lescaut,* and the *Quijote* among others) as a form of therapy for the mournful soul comparable to mineral baths. But when he mentions Richardson elsewhere, his reaction is antithetical to that of Voltaire and Fielding. This is not trashy or at best amusing fiction, he declares, but truth itself; *Pamela* and *Clarissa Harlowe* should therefore *not* be classified as "romans." The next step was to be Scott's description of himself (in the persona of Waverley) as a youthful bookworm: "young Waverley drove through the sea of books like a vessel without a pilot or a rudder."[14] Admittedly there is a certain amount of self-mockery and self-criticism in this portrait of the artist as younger than a

[11] See Américo Castro, *El pensamiento de Cervantes,* Madrid, 1972, pp. 60–62, and Edward Glaser, "Nuevos datos sobre la crítica de los libros de caballerías en los siglos XVI and XVII," *AEM,* 3, 1966, pp. 393–410.

[12] Marcos Moríñigo, "El teatro como sustituto de la novela en el Siglo de Oro," *RUBA,* 2, 1957, pp. 41–61.

[13] I refer to the impatient tone of the defenders of Lope cited by Menéndez Pelayo in his *Historia de las ideas estéticas,* Madrid, 1962, vol. 2, chap. 10. In the particular case of Cervantes as "mal contentadizo," see my *Cervantes y Avellaneda,* México, 1951, pp. 50–63.

[14] *Waverley,* p. 76. Diderot, *Oeuvres complètes,* Paris, 1972, vol. 13, pp. 990–991. In the well-known "Eloge" Diderot confessed to identifying with Richardson's novels so seriously and so enthusiastically that he refused to classify them as "romans." *Oeuvres Complètes,* Paris, 1875, p. 213. In this isolated, critical perception of 1761 of the work and himself as reader one can begin to sense the shape of things to come.

young man. Yet also, and perhaps for the first time, believed-in reading is presented with tender, autobiographical concern. It is as if Scott foresaw all that he himself was virtually to inaugurate!

From these remarks we may draw two conclusions. The first is not to succumb to despair. Even though many of our far-too-self-consciously intellectual contemporary novels present themselves as obscure parables or insoluble puzzles, as if purposefully designed to antagonize the reader, greatness within the genre is surely as feasible now as during the centuries before last. García Márquez' comments on the success of *Cien años de soledad* are in this sense revealing: "According to what they tell me, my book has a strange power: when anyone reads it, he wants to talk about it. It is given to friends in order to be able to be talked about. And they in their turn buy it, give it away, and talk about it. A chain of buyers is thus formed. After it was published, one of my friends bought 250 copies and gave them away as Christmas presents: 'This is going to be the best year of my life; I'm going to spend it talking about *Cien años de soledad.*' "[15] The second conclusion is perhaps ultimately less important but for us more pertinent. As twentieth-century "galdosistas" concerned with the possibility of *Fortunata y Jacinta,* it is essential that we comprehend the special quality of nineteenth-century reading. We must try to relive historically a time when whole cultures, English, French, German, and afterwards Russian and Spanish, behaved and talked as if they were collective Alonso Quijanos.

Novel and History (II)

Fernán Caballero and "Perico Alarcón" (as he is referred to in the "episodios") aside, it was Galdós who single-handedly endowed Spain with what we have called novelistic consciousness. In the process of teaching his compatriots "when they were" (as we phrased it previously), he also taught them to comprehend experience from

[15] I have translated the French of the interviewer, Claude Couffon. *L'Express,* 17–23 January 1977, no. 1332, p. 117. Couffon remarks on his own that on the occasion of his preliminary visit to Aracataca he was shown by "la maîtresse des lieux" various places mentioned in the novel—always a suggestive indication of the conquest of reality by reading. ibid., p. 101. The Aracataca Irregulars are on their way!

their reading and in terms of their reading. Of course, those two, Alarcón and Fernán Caballero, and many others had written novels that were widely popular. Furthermore, as Montesinos stresses, translations of foreign novels (usually French or from French translations) had appeared and were appearing in ever greater numbers. And finally, as was emphasized in our discussion of *La Fontana de Oro,* without the mushroom growth of the periodical press, there would have been no potential public.[16] Galdós' achievement would have been otherwise inconceivable.

All this is true, but nevertheless I cannot bring myself to believe that economic, technical, and sociological explanations (growth of the middle class, more widely available education, increased leisure time, kerosene lamps, improvements in printing, statistics of supply and demand) will enable us to understand meaningfully how the previously marginal genres of epic in prose, comic romance, or imitation chronicle suddenly captured the mind of the century. Instead, I hope to show, not (as in the discussion of Galdós' "times") how the novel reflected and expressed historical consciousness, but rather how it first captured and then transformed that consciousness into the unprecedented communion or language just described. For this purpose we had best begin with Balzac, for his role in France (what he *did to* France) blazed the trail that Galdós was to follow.

Relinquishment of cause-and-effect statistics (comprehension based on the gradual increment of favorable social and physical conditions) virtually compels us to propose a precise moment for the symbolic birth of the new form of consciousness. My choice is that day in 1833 when Balzac (a charter member of the Scott and Cooper fan clubs and already well into the creation of what was later to become *La Comédie humaine*) realized he had created a "world" and wrote to his sister, Laure, that he was on his way to becoming "a genius."[17]

---

[16] The survey of that same press (the word journalism is inapplicable) at the end of the eighteenth century reveals extreme poverty and asphyxiating censorship (as compared to France and England) prior to the liberation of the new medium. See Paul-J. Guinard, *La Presse espagnole de 1737 à 1791: Formation et signification d'un genre,* Paris, 1973.

[17] Both Bardèche and André Bellesort comment on this moment but give very different versions. The former has Balzac "se précipiter chez les Surville" and cry out: "J'ai trouvé une idée merveilleuse. Je serai un homme de génie." *Balzac romancier,* p. 351. The latter, on the other hand, cites a letter to the

Five years earlier, just before beginning his epoch-making "Scènes de la vie privée," he had described with surprise changes in his own subjective consciousness since becoming a novelist: "A world of people [Tout ce monde] lives, loves, suffers, and squirms inside my head, but if God lets me live long enough, it will all be ordered, classified, labeled in books, and wonderful books at that."[18] What Balzac learned after having accomplished this ambitious program was that the act of transferring "the world . . . inside his head" on to the printed page, the act of sharing his consciousness with a society of readers, amounted to its objectification.

Instead of the personal, mind-to-mind, "We share-a-secret" communication with the Happy Few sought for by Stendhal in a few cryptic novels appearing one after another, Balzac and his public collaborated in converting Paris and the provinces into a fictitious France encompassing any number of novels all at once. In other words, one can begin reading *La Comédie humaine* at any point and go on exploring in any direction. The task of ordering, classifying, and labeling planned in 1828 resembles that of a museum director setting up a series of exhibits, each related to the other and all designed for a multitude of simultaneous visitors moving from one to another freely and without a preordained "sens de la visite."[19] And when Balzac had accomplished it, when visitors had come en masse and had so accepted and absorbed his vision of reality that

---

sister, Laure Surville, in 1833 as follows: "Saluez moi, car je suis tout bonnement en train de devenir un génie." *Balzac et son oeuvre,* Paris, 1924, p. 98. Perhaps both versions are factual, but the situation is further complicated by the disagreement over time of day between Marcel Bouteron and Bardèche. Bouteron refers to the Surville visit as occurring on "un beau matin." *Comédie,* vol. 1., p. xix. Bardèche speaks of "un soir de 1833, au moment où Balzac allait commencer *le Père Goriot."* The crucial moment seems to have accumulated the uncertainty that always accompanies moments of legendary significance.

[18] Bellesort, *Balzac et son oeuvre,* p. 69. For critical comments on this sense of habitation, see Bardèche, *Balzac romancier,* p. 371.

[19] Félicien Marçeau makes the same point explicitly when he observes that the author's consciousness of the past of the reappearing characters is not necessarily the same as that of the reader's (obviously, since the sequence of the composition is not the same as the order of appearance) and that, therefore, it is perfectly permissible to read *"la Comédie humaine* dans l'ordre que nous plait." *Balzac et son monde,* p. 19.

they saw in their own world a replica of the museum (rather than the other way around), novelistic consciousness was born.

The museum comparison is woefully inadequate in one respect; dioramas (the favorite word of the lodgers at the Maison Vauquer) are as still as death, while novels are alive. But the comparison does suggest another similarity: natural history museums are supposed to exhibit only the truth; their visitors are supposed to believe in them. And in the same way the Balzacian revolution in the history of prose fiction consisted precisely in replacing believability with belief. Using Balzac's own term, the teasing verisimilitude of Cervantes and his followers and the revered verity of Neo-Classicism was replaced by insistent assertion of "le vrai." In this sense, as Lukacs explains the metamorphosis, Scott had shown the way by converting what previously had been presented as inert background into the contextual protagonist of his novels.[20] Despite the title, the real hero of *Ivanhoe* is Plantagenet England faithfully restored to life. The individual champion may be fictitious, but the novel is true. *He* is at best "vraisemblant"; *it* is "vrai."

Balzac left Scott far behind, however, when he discovered how to systematize the latter's tacit reversal of the roles of fictional biography and historical milieu by using his (Balzac's) own and his readers' more or less vivid recollections of previous novels (experienced as if they were real) in order to construct a "truer" present world than that into which we have the fortune (or, according to Segismundo, the guilt) of having been born. As we remarked earlier, it is axiomatic that shared memory is the best guarantee of truth.[21] It was therefore possible, Balzac suddenly realized, for fictitious shared memories, vivified and focused by the novelist's craft, to create truth. The result was a collective dream of, or conviction about, reality, which surpassed the individual novels that contributed to it. Here was not a novel but an entire "monde-oeuvre," which possessed, according to Marcel Bouteron, "une unité foncière, organique."[22]

"A great step forward," Balzac wrote in 1834 just after finish-

---

[20] *The Historical Novel*, p. 35. See also the chapter entitled "L'art du roman en 1820" in Bardèche, *Balzac romancier.*

[21] See Bridoux, *Le Souvenir.*

[22] Introduction to *Comédie,* vol. 1, p. xx.

ing *Le Père Goriot,"* has just been taken. On seeing certain previously created characters reappear . . . the public has understood
one of the most daring of the author's purposes, that of giving
life and movement to 'tout un monde fictif' whose inhabitants
will still exist when a great majority of their models are dead
and forgotten."[23] Reappearing characters as such, however, were
less a cause than an advertisement of the metamorphosis that
had taken place. Instead of individual, imitation histories, we have
been introduced to a world-history, which we can consume with
our eyes and which in some fashion, perhaps because of the consolation that is inherent in any act of belief, makes the unpredictable
variety that threatens us from without (the 19th "saeculum" in
all its new and disconcerting dynamism) seem more comprehensible
and humane. Bleak though certain novels and episodes may be,[24]
there is still a great deal of comfort to be derived from *La Comédie
humaine,* just as there is from Dickens and also, even though he
often seems to be doing his best to prevent it, from Galdós.

Balzac's repeated acknowledgment of his indebtedness to Scott
supports the contention that the nascent novelistic consciousness
(which knew itself in him jubilantly in 1833 and which his "public
understood" after reading *Le Père Goriot* in the following year)
had been sired by the prevalent historical consciousness of the new
century. Balzac's use of the word "monde" had first occurred in
the expression "tout ce monde," which alluded to a chaotic collection
of half-invented lives clamoring impatiently for printed release from
inside the mind of the budding novelist. But his later use of the
word in the expression "tout *un* monde" implies not only classification and organization but also the incorporation of individual existences, each bearing the temporal burden of its own biographical
novel, into collective time. Balzac's ultimate "monde," as he himself
understood it, is really a synonym for history. If Cervantes and Defoe thought of themselves as "play historians" or "sham historians,"

---

[23] Ibid.

[24] Barbéris cites a naive character from *Pot Bouille,* Marie Pichon, who
spurns Balzac as "triste" and "désagréable," because "ça ressemble trop à la
vie." Being essentially a romance reader with a yearning to escape, she cannot participate in the salvation of reality that the novel makes possible and
that Zola aspired to emulate, experimental theories aside. *Balzac et le mal
du siècle,* vol. 1, p. 128.

the new novelists *are* historians, and their novels possess "le valeur philosophique de l'histoire."[25] In fact, Balzac goes on to assert in the "Avant-propos," they are the only true historians, which is demonstrated by the great characters of fiction whose existences are authenticated by gestation in the "entrailles de leur siècle" rather than in a mere womb of flesh.[26]

The terms history and historian are, of course, equivocal.[27] Judging not only by our previous presentation of nineteenth-century historical consciousness but also by our reading of Scott, Saint-Simon, and Hugo, we may interpret Balzac as intending to suggest that each "siècle" is a giant organism composed of an infinite number of individual lives and events and at the same time defined by a single nature or character of its own. As a result, it is the achievement and privilege of the novelist-genius to provide that organism with consciousness, or, as we paraphrased Bardèche a moment ago, to transform it into a protagonist. That such a seeming miracle could happen, that historical context could become self-conscious, that this consciousness could then become public, and that the novel could as a result become a means of comprehension and a vehicle for communication (a language), depended on a series of circumstances and changes, some of which we have discussed and others of which we have, either purposefully or ignorantly, overlooked.

But there is no need now for worried repetition or futile apologies. What matters to the urgent task of examining the prospect (or possibility) of *Fortunata y Jacinta* is to comprehend *La Comédie humaine* not just as a revolution in the art of the novel (which it

---

[25] "Avant-propos," *Comédie*, vol. 1, p. 6.

[26] Ibid.

[27] Thus, Stendhal, who was as generationally concerned with history as Balzac, still conceived of it in moral terms; that is, as Bardèche points out, in terms of hypocrisy and sincerity or of true and false values. *Stendhal romancier*, p. 262. It is characteristic of Stendhal to remark that Julien Sorel "en temps de l'Empereur eût été un fort honnête homme." Balzac, however much he may have disapproved of his century, could not have written such a nostalgic sentence any more than Galdós could have; for both of them "le vrai" meant historical truth. When Stendhal writes in the margin of his own copy of *Le Rouge et le noir*, "M. de Tracy told me that truth could only be attained by means of the novel," he means the truth of *who* men and women are, as well as what they are worth. Cited by Levin, *The Gates*, p. 104.

was) but also as the product of a monumental metamorphosis of nineteenth-century consciousness. When Galdós tells us with a half-smile that the very first step in his career as a novelist consisted in eating Balzac for breakfast, we should take him at his word. For by the time he wrote those *Memorias,* he had understood profoundly and professionally how his French precursor's "great step forward" depended on serious exploitation of the alimentary nature of the reading process, in contrast to Fielding's comic remarks on the subject.[28] In order to create and so to surpass history (as he was to do in the years 1887 to 1897) as contrasted to writing historical novels, Galdós, too, had to begin not only by digesting Balzac but also by allowing himself to be eaten for breakfast, lunch, and dinner by his compatriots. Both were acts of communion and so of belief and new truth.[29]

We must keep in mind, of course, that by the seventies when Galdós, as an eager apprentice, was reading and writing with an avidity and energy as remarkable as his major predecessors, novelistic consciousness had become institutional outside of Spain. Beyond the Pyrenees, above the Bay of Biscay, and even across the Atlantic the century had become comfortably novelistic, and its inhabitants had come to understand the world and their lives in it as if it and they had been created by a well-intentioned author. If today our students of "Siglo de Oro" literature tend to be disconcerted when confronted by German critics with Lope's osmotic "Literaturisierung des Lebens," it is because their own involvement with a variety of media is not apparent to them and because they are unaware of how acutely readers only two generations ago were aware of the intercourse between fictional and biographical experience. Thus, Galdós as a European reader presents novelistic consciousness as if it were

---

[28] For example, "The Introduction to the Work, or Bill of Fare to the Feast." In the same "18th-century" comic vein, Galdós in *Un viaje redondo* addresses his readers as "lector gastrónomo." Cited by H. C. Berkowitz, "The Youthful Writings of Benito Pérez Galdós," *HR,* 1, 1933, p. 105.

[29] Giuseppe di Lampedusa in his "Notes sur Stendhal" was surely thinking more of his own, still surviving, novelistic consciousness than he was of Stendhal when he speaks of "la fusion totale de l'auteur, du personnage et du lecteur." *Stendhal Club,* 2, 1960, p. 157. Stendhal still enjoyed playing the Cervantine (and eighteenth-century) ironical game of catch-me-if-you-can instead of immersing himself and us within the world of fiction.

commonplace in his 1870 newspaper essay "Observaciones sobre la novela contemporánea": "The truth is that the novel is a world. In every imagination there is a memory, a vision of a society we have only known through reading, and we are intimately familiar with this imaginary world. Indeed, it exists in us with all the color and solidity of reality, in spite of the fact that its innumerable inhabitants have never been alive [in the way we are alive]."[30] Anyone concerned with the achievement of Galdós must never forget that he began by being a reader of Balzac and Dickens as lucid as he was enthusiastic.

Novel and Novelist (II)

As we read Galdós' early texts, in which his voice and feelings are far more audible than he will allow them to be later on, our impression that his mind was particularly receptive to the reading experience receives increasing confirmation. For example, the jocosely ironical (yet inwardly frightened) story entitled *La novela en el tranvía* is an overt confession of his fervent delight in (and vulnerability to) novels. As a precursor of Ido del Sagrario (whose ironical relationship to his creator is partially comparable to that of Tomé de Burguillos to his),[31] the anonymous, first-person narrator

---

[30] *Madrid*, p. 230.

[31] For a study of this character in his various avatars, see the classic article of W. H. Shoemaker (to whom we are all indebted in so many ways), "Galdós' Literary Creativity: Don José Ido del Sagrario," *HR*, 19, 1951, pp. 204-237. In general, I think it can be said that Ido represents a way of objectifying and so standing at a distance from Galdós' own consciousness of irrepressible imagination. He is not an alter ego like Juan de Mairena or a lying historian like Cide Hamete, but rather a comic personification (hence the comparison to Tomé de Burguillos) of how it feels to be a rampant fictioneer and hence of how it felt to be Galdós in one aspect. Perhaps it would be better to say that Ido is a way of observing ironically Galdós' own "espíritu turbado e inquieto." According to F. Ruiz Ramón, who does not give the source, it was thus that Galdós contrasted himself to Pereda. *Tres personajes galdosianos*, Madrid, 1964, p. 222. Ido's Calderonian delusions are referred to only in *Fortunata y Jacinta*, which confirms the probability that they purposefully echo those of don Víctor. Both Clarín and Galdós would have agreed with Vicente de la Fuente's critique of the passionate blindness of many Spaniards (he is referring to no less an academic villain than León de Castro): "Hay hombres que, enamorados de mujeres feas y hasta re-

"sentía una sobreexcitación espiritual espantosa," which led to a hopeless confusion of fictional and real experience. As a result and like Balzac in 1828, his "entendimiento [está] empeñado en fuerte lucha con un ejercito de sombras." (*495–496*) There is, perhaps, not a grain of autobiography in this youthful and overcontrived novella, but I dare say that it can be read as an urgent attempt to communicate how it felt to be the young Galdós suspended between the entrancing oral and visual immediacy of Madrid and the "alivio [de sus] amados libros"[32] (*1656*), or, in other terms, between intense perception and vivid imagination.

This self-awareness of the novelist as inhabited is again remembered in a passage from the *Memorias,* written when Galdós' interior lodgings had long since begun to turn away guests:

Feeling abandoned by my memory, I call out to it; I question it . . .

"Are you asleep? Are you momentarily absent-minded?"

"You're the absent-minded person. For years now you've been immersed in the task of making up characters and events. You hardly have finished one novel before you begin another. You live in an imaginary world."

"The fact is that whatever is imaginary gives me far more pleasure than anything real."

"Well, since I am nourished only by reality, I shall not conceal

---

pugnantes, tienen con todo eso horribles celos y hay hombres que, enamorados de ideas secas y deformes se apasionan por ellas. . . . En España nuestro carácter impetuoso y poco tolerante nos ha inclinado siempre a tales exageraciones." Vincente de la Fuente, *Historia de las universidades,* Madrid, 1885, vol. 2, p. 301.

[32] Complementary to Galdós' half-amused, half-appalled consciousness of his own rampaging imagination, there was also, as we have seen, a sense of inner estrangement, of unreality, as if he, like Manso, were somehow removed from "moment et milieu" and dependent on pain to return to Earth. In the last analysis, it is this inner, psychic irony that makes his realism both possible and aesthetically important, in contrast to the naive variety of Fernán Caballero. As a systematic investigation of circumstance by "psychic outsiders," this new form of "distance," experienced by Balzac, Dickens, and Galdós alike, constitutes an invaluable nineteenth-century adjunct to the earlier, satirical apartness from society and its asserted values felt by Fielding, Sterne, or Diderot. It also differentiates the former group from doctrinaire Naturalists.

the fact that I am bored in the shadowy chamber of your brain populated by phantasms, and I escape through the first breach I can find." (*1661*)

As remarked earlier, I think we should interpret the admission literally. Granted that Galdós was a gentleman (and not a loquacious don Alvaro Mesía or a compulsive scribbler like Bueno de Guzmán) and that he scrupulously concealed those portions of his past life that remain most vividly in the minds of most men and women, surely his unconditional surrender to novelistic consciousness must have smudged (Scott's "delitescency"?) the outline of events and half-erased entire years from the long past. Precisely because his imaginary world was so tangibly present and because he had given himself to so many lives, his own seemed strange and far away.

It is this vivid presence that differentiates the inner population of a Balzac, a Dickens, or a Galdós from that of the Romantics as described by Albert Béguin and best exemplified in Spain by Gustavo Adolfo Becquer, like Galdós an ardent reader of Hoffmann, Heine, and perhaps Poe.[33] Becquer, too, testified to an awareness that he was not alone, although, in his case, the rebellious inner population was both embryonic ("desnudos y disformes") and visionary (products of "el insomnio y la fantasía"). As such "fantasmas de la imaginación," they necessarily lacked the precision of physiognomy, intonation, and turn of phrase as well as the shared intimacy that result from novelistic derivation.[34] Galdós could never have written "conozco a muchas gentes a quienes no conozco." His cerebral guests were neither half-created nor in search of an author; they were individuals, more "there-and-then" and more sharply outlined than the flesh-and-blood clients of his café of the moment. As a professionally inhabited—rather than hallucinated—man, he knew his inhabitants as well as we as children, generations ago, knew Tom Swift and his friends or the members of *The Swiss Family Robinson*.[35] And he could judge them far more perceptively.

[33] In particular, see Béguin on Brentano and Nerval. *L'Ame romantique et le rêve,* Paris, 1946, pp. 281 and 361.

[34] Becquer, *Obras completas,* pp. 36–38.

[35] Notice the precision of the narrator's recognition of the fictional major-domo: "En un segundo le examiné de pies a cabeza y reconocí las facciones cuya descripción había leído. No podía ser otro: hasta los más

The archness of the dialogue in the *Memorias* between Galdós and his errant memory is even more annoying a few pages further on, when he describes his return to *Fortunata y Jacinta* after a summer vacation. But we should not dismiss what Galdós is trying to tell us because we disapprove of his stylistic self-indulgence (as compared to the trenchant self-control of most of his fictional prose), or because the characters seem blander in recollection (notice that he cannot bear to mention Maxi) than on the pages of the novel.[36] In its description of the way direct observation is indistinguishable from novelistic consciousness, the passage is an invaluable revelation of Galdós' creative process:

> At the end of the summer I returned to Madrid, and I'd hardly entered the house when I was treated to the visit of my friend, the notable gentleman don José Ido del Sagrario, who brought me news of the doings of Juanito Santa Cruz and his wife, Jacinta, of doña Lupe la de los Pavos (the "turkey woman"), of Mauricia la Dura (the "tough one"), of pretty Fortunata, and finally of that famous fellow, Estupiñá.
>
> All these characters belonging to the world of my imagination and left behind during my summer travels once again took command of my will. I visited doña Lupe in her home on Cuchilleros street, and I chatted with the moneylender, Tor-

---

insignificantes detalles de su vestido indicaban claramente que era él. Reconocí la tez morena y lustrosa; los cabellos indomables, cuyas mechas surgían en opuestas direcciones, como las culebras de Medusa (and perhaps also like those of Nicolás Rubín!); los ojos hundidos bajo la espesura de unas agrestes cejas; las barbas no menos revueltas e incultas que el pelo; los pies torcidos hacia dentro, como los de los loros, y, en fin, la misma mirada, el mismo hombre en el aspecto, en el traje, en el respirar en el toser, hasta en el modo de meterse la mano en el bolsillo para pagar." (*489*) It is this visual and auditory exactness that characterizes the novelistic imagination as against the poetic studied by Béguin. Both may seem equally strange today, but they are not identical. Hence, I would disagree with Philippe Bertault's over-Romantic description of Balzac's "intériorité": "Compagnes chéries de ses veilles, les ombres accourent, elles affluent, elles grouillent sous ses yeux hallucinés." *Balzac, l'homme et l'oeuvre*, p. 64.

[36] It is as if Galdós could not bear facing Maxi at the time of writing his *Memorias*. Was his absence due to Galdós' remorse at having created such a personage, to repugnance, to resentment at the lethal role Maxi had played at the end, or perhaps to a combination of all three? In any case, his very omission is an indication of his "reality."

quemada, and the maid, Papitos. I spent interminable hours in the Café del Gallo, where I was entertained by the conversation of the carters and provisioners of the markets specializing in chickens and other domestic fowl. I went up and down the steps of the passageway twenty times a day, and the square of Puerta Cerrada was the headquarters of my observations. In the Plaza Mayor I spent agreeable intervals talking to the store-keeper José Luengo, whom I had baptized Estupiñá. Here is at least one character faithfully reproduced from reality. (*1663*)

Thus, whether derived from past creation (the characters mentioned by that personification of the fictional imagination, Ido del Sagrario) or present reality (José Luengo and the "trajinantes y abastecedores"), whether remembered from an unfinished text or observed and overheard in the Café del Gallo, Galdós' inhabitants cannot be sorted out categorically one from the other. They are lives, at times reawakened, at times enlisted, which populate his mind, exactly as he inhabits and explores their Madrid as an urban chronicler. For an art premised on the lack of recognizable frontiers between the objective and the subjective, photographic notions of realism are totally inadequate.[37] Galdós went about creating the Madrid of Isabel II, the First Republic, and the Restoration almost as uninhibitedly as Lope created the reign of Pedro "el Cruel" (or "el Justiciero") according to the poetic needs of each individual "comedia." Like the London of Dickens or the Paris of Balzac, Galdós' Madrid was born in his consciousness, its only city limits corresponding to the fact that his readers also lived there and that some of them had "seen" the same portion of "la historia de España." This is to say, the novelist could dream as he pleased, but he could not alter the names and locations of the streets and the sequence of

[37] Of course, Galdós did observe and gather documentation, and his novels do constitute a report on reality, as he himself tells us on more than several occasions. In so doing, however, it is necessarily in terms of a projection of his creative consciousness. Cf. Bardèche, *Balzac romancier,* p. 380. Thus, too, according to George Gissing, Dickens invented "the squalid mystery and terror . . . the grimly grotesque reality . . . the labyrinthine obscurity and lurid fascination" of his London. *Critical Studies of the Works of Charles Dickens,* New York, 1924, p. 53. Cited by Donald Fanger, *Dostoievsky and Romantic Realism,* Cambridge, Mass., 1965, p. 85.

public events as reported in the newspapers. Ido, when he comes to visit Galdós in his lodgings, is at once inside and outside, exactly like José Luengo Estupiñá.

The first conclusion to emerge from Galdós' slightly senile description of how he felt in the act of giving birth to *Fortunata y Jacinta* has already been suggested: the characters who appear, disappear, and reappear in the mind-cities of Zola and Galdós and later on in the mind-regions of Valle-Inclán and Faulkner should not be dismissed as imitations of those of Balzac.[38] They are not merely products of a borrowed technique; instead they should be understood as the natural offspring of a special form of consciousness, which all of the authors shared with their readers and which was synonymous with "les entrailles de leur siècle."

Specifically, what Galdós is trying to tell us is that Ido and doña Lupe returned to his mind ("se adueñaron nuevamente de su voluntad") in exactly the same way that Canencia and Rufete, last seen in the second series of "episodios," "reappeared" at the beginning of *La desheredada*. Characters ("lives" is the more exact term) reappear not only because their authors adhere to the Balzacian tradition but also because they are waiting for a chance to do so perhaps in a way comparable to the submerged personalities of schizophrenics). So too the lives which had invaded Galdós and remained with him "between eyebrow and eyebrow" from morning to night upon first reading *La Regenta* later seemed to him to share the same desire to be allowed a "new sally or reincarnation."[39]

In a hitherto little known prologue to the second series (which will be edited and published by Alan Smith in a forthcoming issue of *Anales galdosianos*) Galdós expresses himself even more emphatically:

> Almost all the men and women who were still alive at the end of the first series will appear in the second, and, as I have learned

[38] See Roberta Salper de Tortella, "Repeated Characters in Valle-Inclán," Ph.D. dissertation, Harvard University, 1967.

[39] I quote both the 1885 letter (see chapter VI, note 4) and the 1901 review. (*1449*) Lukacs verges on the same notion when he remarks that Balzac's characters "cannot fully unfold their personality within a single novel. . . . They protrude beyond the framework of one novel and demand another." *Studies in European Realism*, p. 54.

recently, they are already getting dressed in order to appear on stage. I have to restrain their impatience and order them not to scream in my ears, not to make me dizzy with their threatening faces, nor to drive me crazy with their constant pleading that I open the door once more and return them to their former selves and situations in the great theater of the world.

As Smith will point out, the truth is that very few characters from the first series actually reappear in the second, but nevertheless the description of their turbulent eagerness to do so is vivid.

Galdós, in other words, does not distinguish critically or categorically among "characters" from other novels, from earlier novels, from earlier chapters of the same novel, or from the Café del Gallo. If not created equal, they are equal creatively, taken from life in a more radical sense than mere observation and audition. No matter where they came from or whether they are as "linda" as Fortunata, as physically underprivileged as Maxi, or as spiritually perverse as Bueno de Guzmán, they are all made out of his (and our) life and so share in a programmed urge to go on living, to reappear as often and as long as possible. In fact, one particularly sly and stubborn individual managed to contrive not merely reappearance but actual reincarnation. As we remember, Coletilla died of "profunda hipocondría" at the end of *La Fontana*. His tenacious soul must have quickly rebelled, however, for he reappears as an "apostólico" and survives long after the date of his earlier death.[40]

---

[40] As we saw in the case of Coletilla, Galdós' characters are not bound by normal biological necessities, nor subject to the sometimes ineffective efforts at systematization attempted occasionally by Balzac. For example, Canencia, who was dragged through the streets (and presumably killed) in *Los cien mil hijos de San Luis,* is described in that novel as "muy viejo." Had he been made of flesh and blood, he could not possibly have reappeared in *La desheredada*. Martha Krow-Lucal has examined a number of other less flagrant but equally unsystematic instances in her dissertation. The typical case of Joaquinito Pez as a lover of Isidora's and a classmate of Juanito's, according to Martha Krow-Lucal's calculations, involves a discrepancy of some seven years. Galdós apparently felt perfectly free to adjust the lives that inhabited him to the needs of the individual novel. Yet the effect is never disconcerting to the reader, for in his life he, too, constantly encounters reappearing "characters of uncertain age." The very untidyness of this technique is what makes these novels "épouser . . . étroitement la vie," to use the expression of Félicien Marçeau. *Balzac et son monde*, p. 24.

It follows, therefore, that we should not confuse the familiar, novelistic benefits of the device of reappearance with the historical and psychic conditions that made it possible or necessary. To encounter used lives in new narratives is, as we saw in discussing the opening sentence of *Fortunata y Jacinta,* an effective way of making the reader feel at home in a strange novelistic world; it also imparts a sense of time passing and time past, as we remarked in connection with the "episodios"; and, above all, it is a means of endowing what Bardèche calls "la réalité romanesque" with the sense of permanence and amplitude that are indispensable for genuine confidence in its truth.[41] On the one hand, the possibility of "replaying" Rastignac and Vautrin that is implicit even in the briefest of their reappearances renders this variety of history, "toujours vivant," far more satisfactory than the other kind. And on the other, such reminders of previous novelistic experience have a cumulative effect, which at once reinforces present illusion with past illusion and, at the same time, creates a world of multiple human vistas, provinces, professions, districts, classes, generations, which, however ultimately self-enclosed, seems to possess the limitlessness that believed-in worlds must have.

For all this, we as readers should be deeply grateful. But if we heed the confessions of a Galdós or a Balzac, reappearance often seems less a matter of authorial strategy than of the willful self-imposition of the characters. Neither novelist is a genuine divinity, who kills those whom he has created for sport (as Gloucester and Pleberio would have it); rather they are inhabited men partially controlled by their inhabitants. Indeed, it seems to have been difficult for novelists of this sort to abandon characters for good (surrogate suicide?). Elaborate ceremony as in the case of Mauricia la Dura, stylistic emphasis as in that of Moreno Isla, or, at the very least, a detailed record of the reminiscences of those who mourned for Fortunata seems to be called for. As we remember, Cervantes was quite conscious of the problem at the end of the *Quijote.* Novelistic

---

[41] *Balzac romancier,* p. 363. His use of this term for what we have here called novelistic consciousness is expressed as follows: "La réalité romanesque s'empare du romancier. Elle est pour lui non seulement un refuge, mais un rêve perpétuel, une création continue. Elle est plus vrais, plus présente pour lui que la réalité véritable."

208

"geniuses" (in contrast to the majority of readers, who tend to flatten even the most profound characters) infuse their creativity into their creations. And such incited lives want above all to go on creating themselves.

Novel and the Unconscious

Considerations such as these are more proper for those who concern themselves with an Unamuno writing at the Land's End of novelistic consciousness and with his terminal speculations on the theology of the author-character relationship than they are for students of Galdós. Our problem, stated as simply as possible, is one of velocity. How was it possible to create a novel not just as long but as massive and consequential as *Fortunata y Jacinta* in a few months of composition "sin freno"? The phrase is from an 1876 letter to Pereda and indicates that Galdós even then was conscious of his increasing acceleration.[42] Anyone who has tried to transcribe one of Galdós' later manuscripts has faced this question directly at its point of origin. Not that Galdós was so hasty as to be careless and even vulgar (as was maintained during his eclipse in the first decades of our century), for every paragraph reveals how carefully and often he revised previous versions both in his own impatient handwriting and in the proofs. It is rather the sheer eagerness of the invention, the ever-faster pace both of his imagination and his pen, that constitutes the mystery of his narrative impetus. Everything, even his preliminary notes to himself, is expressed in story form; one event grows out of another in exactly the same way that one novel grows out of another; and the whole races into the future without skipping a single detail, like a time-lapse motion picture of the life cycle of a plant from seedling to flower. The frequently puzzled transcriber (Galdós' handwriting becomes more and more illegible

---

[42] "Así es que los artículos críticos son para mí de una dificultad abrumadora. Me he acostumbrado a fantasear, y todo lo que no sea escribir fantaseando me cuesta más que escribir sin freno." Villasante, "28 cartas," p. 12. A year later, speaking of part 2 of *Gloria,* he writes: "yo cuando empiezo una obra con empeño, pongo tanto por concluirla que no puedo dejarla de la mano. Me parece que si pierdo un instante se me han de ir las ideas y si para mi trabajo siento una gran pesadumbre." Ibid., p. 21. The marvel is that ten years later he had learned to control and so to utilize his own velocity.

as his hand moves faster in the mature novels, as contrasted to, say *Doña Perfecta*) is the privileged witness, not of a meditation on freedom expressed paradoxically as in *El amigo Manso,* but of the visible pen-and-ink record of a breathless eruption of freedom.

To conclude from this that Galdós was a genius (as Balzac, with every justification, naively termed himself) or a "monstruo de la naturaleza" (as Cervantes, with every justification, ironically termed Lope de Vega) is to avoid the problem. And to attribute his speed to a talent for borrowing from his predecessors would be a gratuitous insult of the most unpardonable sort. Let us instead admit the possibility that all the metaphors we have been hiding behind (Ortega defines proverbs as oral "almenas" or crenelations) have as their least common denominator the fact that Galdós, who lived and breathed novelistically, wrote in the same way that he read and read in the same way that he wrote. He read himself in the act of writing, and, in the act of reading, if his lips did not move (as did those of Fernando de Rojas), his fingers surely twitched. Both operations were characterized by an identical voracity. All this may grant us a more intimate understanding of how his characters, and those of others, were able to reappear out of nowhere whenever the burgeoning story gave them a chance to do so.

To be a Galdós, then, was to possess a marvelous reservoir waiting to be tapped, an immense wealth of assimilated living (types, gestures, phrases, reactions, situations, and events) immediately available for new creation. It goes without saying, of course, that to point out such minor resemblances is not to question Galdós' originality or lack of it. Judging by my own velocity, had those I am about to mention been "sources" that Galdós had had to hunt for (in the way Rojas hunted for quotations from Petrarch), he would at best have finished three or four novels. But no; as we have seen, Cervantes, Clarín, Balzac, Zola, Dickens, and above all his own novelistic past (with its inhabitants clamoring for resuscitation) were in his mind and in his readers' minds too (though perhaps less vividly), waiting to be used and adapted to his ever more profound vision. As we said before, to engage in conscious dialogue presupposes first knowing the language. And as Spain's first great nineteenth-century reader (despite his weak English and lack of

German), Galdós was that nation's first native speaker-writer of novels.

Having returned to the metaphor of language, we must now take into account a fundamental aspect that has hitherto been carefully skirted: in the course of speaking or writing (or reading, too, for that matter) at any given moment we are by definition not conscious of the words we are *not* using.[43] Galdós was, of course, aware that Nicolás Rubín was a negative image of Fermín de Pas, and he certainly was well acquainted with the reappearing lives that demanded his attention. They had, as it were, signed the guest register of his mental boarding house. But, as in the case of language, beneath that level Galdós' creative velocity and spontaneity depended on a vast latent vocabulary, an enormous nether warehouse of ready-made narrative raw material (I refuse on principle to talk about narremes),[44] the contents of which summoned each other— invoked each other—in the process of composition.

The comparison is risky, but I think there is a certain resemblance between the phenomenon we are about to examine and the epic recitation of the South Slavic "singers of tales" described by Milman Parry and Albert Lord. If we can conceive of an assembly of human formulae derived from reading as taking the place of metrically regular verbal formulae, we may try to diagnose that "fiebre novelística" which Galdós remembered being possessed by in later

---

[43] Culler points out that in literary creation as in language "the line between the conscious and the unconscious is highly variable, impossible to identify, and supremely uninteresting." The last two statements strike me as dubious, but I cannot help but agree that the phenomena we are about to examine do support the comparison. In fact, they may be considered to be specific examples of the abstract notion of "intertextualité" that seems to be fundamental to Structuralist poetics. Culler, *Structuralist Poetics*, p. 118.

[44] As I understand it, narremes are (as their suffix implies) standardized, narrative building blocks. Unlike Structuralists, who prefer to talk about texts in and of themselves, I am still concerned with a problem that may seem old-fashioned but nevertheless in the case of Galdós (in contrast to his major nineteenth-century colleagues) has not yet received the extensive meditation it deserves: how was a novel such as *Fortunata y Jacinta* possible? What do we already know (and what can we find out) about Galdós' times, life, opinions, and methods that may help explain that incredibly realized possibility? Such questions cannot be answered "scientifically," but, even so, they have to be asked sooner or later by anyone concerned with literature as an expression of human experience.

years.[45] In other words, while he probably would not have denied the literary antecedents heretofore discussed (my premise is that as they were more or less intentional he would have willingly acknowledged them), some of the resemblances now to be proposed might well have surprised and annoyed him had they been mentioned in a contemporary book review.

The notion of novelistic consciousness, then, is incomplete if we do not conceive of it as operating in constant symbiosis with what might be called—at the risk of both impropriety and anachronism—the "novelistic unconscious." Having penetrated as far as I could (and perhaps farther than I should) into this shaky terrain (where there is not a single derivation that is demonstrably from a unique source), let me begin with what I hope will be my most convincing example, the "appearance" of Camille Raquin when Galdós was beginning part 2 of *Fortunata y Jacinta*. Readers of "la admirable epopeya de Maxi Rubín" will find much that seems strangely familiar in Zola's early pen-portrait (published in the same year as *La Fontana*) of a typical Naturalistic cuckold: "Il était petit, chétif, d'allure languissante; les cheveux d'un blonde fade, la barbe rare, le visage couvert de taches de rousseur, il ressemblait à un enfant malade et gâté."[46] In addition, Camille does his unsatisfactory best in a "cours d'un école de commerce," and he is prey to "toutes les maladies imaginables," in spite of the solicitous care of Madame Raquin. At home he reads pedantically and attempts in vain to communicate his poorly digested learning to Thérèse. In so doing he displays that special complacency, at once presumptuous and inane, that is so irritating in Maxi: "Moi, je suis de l'avis de M. Grivet, dit-il avec une importance bête."[47]

Yet how can the equally complacent hunter for sources be sure that Camille is Maxi's only predecessor, given the existence of a double (Zola had his own inner population), Théophile Vabré, who plays the same wretched role in *Pot Bouille*? Galdós had probably read the latter (it appeared in 1882) more recently than

---

[45] "Después de *La familia de León Roch,* y sin respiro, *La desheredada,* en seguida me metí con *El amigo Manso.* . . . Hallábame yo por entonces en la plenitud de la fiebre novelesca." (*1660*)

[46] *Thérèse Raquin,* ed. H. Mitterand, Paris, 1970, p. 68.

[47] Ibid., p. 111.

Thérèse Raquin. And in addition, there are such suggestive similarities as Théophile's grotesque scenes of jealousy and his brother's recurrent attacks of migraine.[48] It would, indeed, seem likely that Maxi was conceived from a confluence of the two in Galdós' mind, and this supposition immediately suggests the possibility of other, unknown tributaries.[49] Even a critic who had carefully examined every book Galdós is known to have read could not be certain. Galdós surely did not look up given passages or descriptions to see if they might be useful; rather he seems to have drawn intuitively from an inventory of novelistic formulae so complex and so intertwined that our only safeguard is a far from blissful awareness of our own ignorance.[50]

[48] We must not forget that elements of autobiographical experience are also utilized and in such a way as to collaborate intimately with that derived from reading. In this connection, the following paragraph in a letter to Pereda is most curious: "Yo me encuentro hoy con la cabeza recién salida de esos horribles huracanes de jaquecas que me dan cada cierto tiempo. El último ha sido de los más tremendos y puede V. creer que me ha dejado idiota." Villasante, "28 cartas," p. 16. In a letter written in 1888, eleven years later, he refers again to the same torment. Doña Emilia also refers to her lover's migraine in a letter, which concludes "Ojalá no haya jaqueca." Villasante, *Cartas a Galdós,* p. 45.

[49] Arthur Holmberg mentions significant resemblances between Maxi's later biography and that of Louis Lambert. See "Louis Lambert and Maximiliano Rubín." Although the initial conception of caricature of Maxi seems to have been derived from Zola's preordained cuckold, later associations with other fictional lives are almost inevitable. After writing the above I find in Fernández y González' *Los desheredados* the pitiful hunchback, Gaspar Media-noche, whose beautiful bride is willing to marry him for the one reason that gave Maxi hope: "¿Y porqué no he de amarle yo—dijo—si tiene el alma más hermosa del mundo?" And the results of the two matches were identical: "La felicidad de Gaspar no pasó de la iglesia y no salió de ella." *Los desheredados,* vol. 1, pp. 25 and 27. From the very beginning, Maxi seems to have provoked a search for both literary and non-literary precedents. Thus, in an anonymous review of *Fortunata,* the reviewer (possibly don Eduardo himself) comments: "Maximiliano Rubín es una creación prodigiosa. Es el espíritu noble dentro de un cuerpo ridículo, un Quasimodo de la facultad de farmacia." *El Lunes del Imparcial,* 25 April 1887. Attempts to trace the development of his madness according to the psychology of the time also may be relevant, for Galdós was certainly aware of contemporary theory and demonstrably interested in it. The latest article on the subject, by J. C. Ullman and G. H. Allison, "Galdós as Psychiatrist," exemplifies the difficulty of distinguishing what Galdós learned from what he intuited.

[50] This, I think, is the crucial flaw in Marie-Claire Petit's proposal of *Béatrix* as the major source for *Fortunata y Jacinta.* Thanks to her I have

The case of the "matrimonio," don Baldomero and doña Barbarita, illustrates even more tellingly the perils of these games of erudite solitaire. At first glance, their ideally happy, bourgeois married life and their years of well-deserved commercial success recall the "éternelle lune de miel" of César Birotteau and his wife. The former, distinguished for his "probité et bonté," for his speech "farci de lieux communs," and for his benevolence to subordinates,

---

had the pleasure of reading the Balzacian "roman à clef" about Georges Sand, and I am sorry to say I cannot discern any overall similarity or possibility of inter-novel dialogue. If there is anyone more unlike Juanito than Calyste Guénic or more unlike Fortunata than the two women he loved prior to marriage, they would be hard to find. But what *is* in *Béatrix* and what seems to have misled Professor Petit are certain formulae, which clearly contributed to the creation of Jacinta as well as to her honeymoon preoccupation with Fortunata. Petit, *Galdós et "La Fontana de Oro,"* pp. 106–118. Readers of Galdós' novel will perceive immediately the significance of the following citations from the "Troisième Partie" of *Béatrix* entitled "Un Adultère rétrospectif." Calyste has submitted to an arranged marriage with Sabine; he is a "fils unique" and "enfant gâté" while she is "d'un esprit fin et délicat, pieuse, aimante et attachée uniquement à lui, d'une douceur angélique encore attendrie par l'amour." *Comédie,* vol. 2, p. 546. And on her honeymoon she insists on hearing the story of his passionate love for Mme. de Rochefide: "Ce fut entre nous l'objet d'un petit débat qui dura pendant trois relais." And when he finally tells all, he concludes "le poème de ses souvenirs par le plus chaleureuse protestation d'un entier oubli de ce qu'il a nommé sa folie," ibid., pp. 526–527. This is, of course, a lie and one which she sees through or rather smells through as a result of perfume on his cravat. A son is born, who "chercha le sein à travers la robe" and who is described as "le plus belle enfant que jamais race royale eût pu désirer pour hériter présomptif." Ibid., pp. 562 and 566. (We remember that Joaquinito Pez was also associated with "el Delfín." See chapter 5, note 3.) The notion of bourgeois and professional "royautés" is again discussed on page 592 and may have been in Galdós' mind when he wrote his "Crónica de Madrid" of 9 July 1865 (see chapter 10, page 303), which I was first to cite in relation to *Fortunata y Jacinta.* All of us, therefore, should be grateful to Professor Petit, for if she had not called our attention to *Béatrix,* we should have been as ignorant of that precious vein of novelistic raw material as doubtless we are of many others. Nevertheless, the logic of "sources" and "influences" is not applicable to a novelist of Galdós' caliber. For example, thinking in those terms, another tempting but misleading possibility in relation to Jacinta would be the *Mémoires de deux jeunes mariées,* not because the title resembles the Spanish subtitle, but because of its laments for childlessness and its expressions of worship of children. My reading of the two novels, however, leads me to classify such resemblances as shared themes at best rather than recollection and reelaboration of specific formulae.

seems to be a particularly suitable model.[51] But when we learn that, along with uxoriousness, Birotteau had had a moment of military glory, things get more complicated. Perhaps he had also contributed to an earlier affectionate caricature of the "buen burgués," don Benigno Cordero, otherwise known as "el héroe de Boteros." Cordero was not only, and significantly, the grandfather of Jacinta but also, as we remember from the second series of "episodios, an ideal husband (when widowed, his role changes to that of don Diego in *El sí de las niñas*) and an honorable dry-goods merchant. Could not, as in the case of Maxi, two characters, both Birotteau and Cordero, have been present when don Baldomero and his wife were conceived?

The question becomes even harder to answer if we glance at the earliest novel to be included in the *Comédie, La Maison du Chat-qui-pelote,* where M. and Mme. Guillaume (the parents of the Quixotesque Augustine mentioned earlier) present an exceedingly convincing claim to participation.[52] Although Balzac does not stress their cloying marital bliss (Mme. Guillaume "était laide"), Guillaume, like don Baldomero and don Benigno, was a dry-goods merchant (Birotteau was, of course, a "parfumeur") "dont la probité commerciale ne soffrait pas le moindre soupçon."[53] Furthermore, just as in *Fortunata y Jacinta,* Guillaume's novelette deals with two generations of proprietors and examines their changing relationships with employees and apprentices ("commis" in the one case, "horteras" in the other), as well as the historical evolution of

---

[51] *Comédie,* vol. 5, pp. 354 and 356. Readers of Galdós will also find significant the description of Birotteau's behavior while courting: "il était demeuré niais comme un mouton; l'amour l'enniaisait encore davantage, il n'osa pas dire un mot." ibid., p. 347. When the action begins, Birotteau's wife is thirty-seven years old and "ressemblait . . . parfaitement à la Vénus de Milo." ibid., p. 366. As for Barbarita's "chifladura de las compras," it might well reflect Zola's presentation of the psychology of those who patronized "Au Bonheur des Dames," the most extreme case of substitution of store for church being Mme. Marty. Aside from such resemblances, I think Barbarita can also be understood in terms of an intentional antithesis with "la de Bringas." It is stressed that the former needs no corsets, that she is generous (being rich enough not to have to think about money), and, above all, that she is a perfect lady and a loving wife.

[52] See chapter 6, note 10.

[53] *Comédie,* vol. 1, p. 22.

retail trade in cloth. M. Guillaume's "antique despotisme" and paternalism was a school "de moeurs et de probité," whereas his successor "marchait avec son siècle," thereby reminding us both of don Baldomero's complacent maxim ("el mundo marcha") and that of M. Homais ("Il faut marcher avec son siècle"). As a result, the new proprietor relaxed the rules to the extent of allowing his dependents to talk during meals and stay for dessert. It thus seems probable that this exemplary establishment contributed directly to the creation of the firm of "Sobrinos de Santa Cruz." And then, when we realize that it must also have played a part in the gestation of *Au Bonheur des Dames,* which in its turn certainly suggested to Galdós that he undertake an exhaustive exploration of the economic history of Spanish commerce in cloth and clothing, we begin to appreciate just how labyrinthine this approach can be.

The largest number of novelistic reminiscences in *Fortunata y Jacinta* proceed, not from Zola's *Au Bonheur des Dames* or any of the others just mentioned, but from his *Le Ventre de Paris.*[54] This is not as surprising as it may seem at first glance. There is a social congruence between the world of "les Halles" and the Madrid of Fortunata that is lacking in the Paris of Gervaise Lantier or in that of Eugène Rougon, insofar as *Le Ventre de Paris* presents in meat-and-potato terms a panorama of the infinite gradations of the lower middle class. Galdós found in that novel exactly the kind of literary experience that he needed to supplement his more abstract disquisitions on the cloth trade: he found there all the eating, conversation, charged atmospheres, and eccentric characters that would in turn evoke living Madrid counterparts in the Café del Gallo and elsewhere.

To regress for a moment, we may safely speculate that, when Galdós finally decided to undertake a major offensive against the

[54] Aside from the general scheme of the inter-novel dialogue, which accounts for such reminiscences of *Au Bonheur des Dames* as the new vogue for white goods, the competition of national and foreign industries, the joy in place names—"lainage d'Angleterre, toile de Flandre, les calicots d'Alsace," the changes in style and color, etc., the only possible specific reminiscences that I have seen in that novel are the references to a counter for Oriental imports (Barbarita's "monerías"?) and the meeting of Mouret with Valagnose during which they remember youthful pranks comparable to those of Juanito and his companions at the university. In short, nothing to speak of.

Naturalism he had previously espoused, he realized that he would have to present "race, milieu, et moment" in terms at once more concrete and more menacing than he had done in *La desheredada,* the Bringas trilogy, and *Lo prohibido.* He had to create, as it were, a social giant that would be a worthy antagonist for Fortunata. Galdós' previous experiments with Naturalism had been, at first, relentlessly representational and, later, unconvincingly private in their diagnoses of social disease; now he would have to examine the larger implications of Zola's vision of the nineteenth century. And perhaps the best way to do that would be to engage in intentional novelistic dialogue with Zola's department-store epic and to set about gathering the materials necessary for constructing an answer in Spanish terms. In Madrid, however, large-scale retail commerce did not yet exist, and in the course of writing, specific episodes, scenes, and individuals from the most atmospheric and olfactory novel in the Rougon-Macquart series, *Le Ventre de Paris,* kept coming to mind. The treatise on the history of cloth and clothing (a history at once commercial and, because of the evolution of styles, social) was, thus, surrounded with more immediate alimentary experience.

Returning to specific examples, let us consider "el falso Pituso," whose most obvious precursor is Muche, the sprite of "les Halles." The combination in both infants of innocence and external corruption is, indeed, strikingly similar: "Muche in his seventh year was a little fellow as pretty as an angel and as foulmouthed as a carter. He had thick curly chestnut hair, a tender look in his beautiful eyes, a perfect mouth given to blasphemy and to swearing in a way that would have rasped the throat of a policeman."[55] Of course, being older than "el Pituso," Muche is more verbally adept; instead of merely screaming "putain" at his grandmother (Galdós surpasses himself in linguistic daring when he allows "el Pituso" to call Jacinta a "putona"), he insults her with a barrage of profanity: "Alors les 'salopes,' les 'catins,' les 'va donc moucher ton homme,' les 'combien on te paye, ta peau?' passaient dans le filet de cristal d'enfant de choeur."[56] But it is above all the children's Renoir-like complexions that both authors admire. If "el Pituso" is described

[55] *Les Rougon-Macquart,* vol. 1, p. 724.
[56] Ibid., p. 724.

as possessing "ese rosicler puro y celestial que tiene la infancia al salir del agua" (*135*), the arms of Muche's friend Pauline are revealed by her short sleeves as "nus et roses . . . adorable d'enfance." A few moments later she is as smudged as the "diablillos" who had painted themselves with Ido's "betún."[57]

There is, however, another child described in another language who also seems to have played a part. I refer now to the orphaned grandchild of Betty Higden in *Our Mutual Friend,* whom the newly rich Boffins wish to adopt.[58] Like Jacinta and doña Guillermina, Mrs. Boffin and her husband's secretary (the mysterious "mutual friend") undertake a journey to one of London's many suburbs populated by the English "cuarto estado," "muddy Brentford," where they have heard of infants worthy of their charity. The news of their plan gets around Brentford with results that allow Dickens to display his genius for exaggeration:

"it was found impossible to complete the philanthropic transaction without buying the orphan. For, the instant it became known that anybody wanted the orphan, up started some affectionate relative of the orphan who put a price upon the orphan's

[57] Ibid., pp. 815 and 817. Another relevant presence in Galdós' novelistic consciousness at the moment of creating "el pitusín" surely was Jacinta's great uncle, Juan Jacobo Cordero, who as a robust child in *Los apostólicos* (chapter X) smeared his face with paint."

[58] Again we encounter a complication impossible to resolve, because in addition to the Dickensian infant discussed above, there could also have been a Balzacian precursor. Zola's Muche may very well have been a reincarnation (of exactly the sort with which we have here been concerned) of the equally liberated (what a shame that Galdós could not have read *Huck Finn!*) rural child in *Les Paysans,* whose name, Mouche, seems to have suggested his. Furthermore, Mouche is the loving companion of his grandfather, "le Père Fourchon," whose fractured French dialect and whose violently revolutionary sentiments we overheard in chapter 3, page 66. Galdós may well have recognized this. If the deceitful old peasant did indeed play a part in the genesis of José Izquierdo, the three-way relationship of the children is a good illustration of the intricate workings of novelistic consciousness. As if that were not enough, we can again bring Dickens into play by remembering the patriarchal physiognomy attractive to painters and sculptors of the scoundrel in *Little Dorrit* called Christopher Casby. From his case Dickens draws a general conclusion quite applicable to Izquierdo: "In the Royal academy some evil old Ruffian of a dog stealer will annually be found embodying all the cardinal virtues on account of his eyelashes, his chin or his legs." *Works,* vol. 1, p. 169.

head. The suddenness of an orphan's rise in the market was not to be paralleled by the maddest records of the Stock Exchange. He would be at five thousand percent discount, out at nurse, making a mud pie at nine in the morning, and (being inquired for) would go up to five thousand per cent premium before noon. The market was rigged in various artful ways. Counterfeit stock got into circulation. . . . the uniform principle at the root of all these various operations was bargain and sale."[59]

Who knows? It is possible, even probable, that Galdós was partially aware after the fact that "el Pituso" was conceived through association of these disparate recollections. But that is as it should be. In order to function creatively the novelistic unconscious must interact with consciousness.

Let us now turn to the emblematic situation that, like don Quijote and the windmills, has come to represent *Fortunata y Jacinta* as a whole: Juanito's first sight of Fortunata through a doorway from a landing above number 11, Cava de San Miguel. It is a very Naturalistic encounter, and not just because of the raw egg. Juanito as a predatory "señorito" has, as we have seen, a series of predecessors whose behavior is as "natural" as his (Joaquinito Pez, Bueno de Guzmán, don Alvaro Mesía), but the one who concerns us now is Zola's Octave Mouret. At the beginning of *Pot Bouille* the apparition of one of Octave's future mistresses is identical in its structure, if not in its content, to the one we know so well. Octave's friend, the architect Campardon, is showing him the new apartment house where he plans to live and which will be the scene of his sordid, erotic adventures:.

After the third floor, the red carpet stopped and was replaced by a plain gray mat. Octave reacted to this with slightly hurt pride. Little by little the staircase had filled him with respect; he was impressed and moved by the prospect of living in such a splendid residence, as the architect had expressed it. As he followed him in the corridor which led to his room, through a half open door he perceived a young woman standing in front of a cradle. She raised her head at the noise. She was blond with

[59] *Works,* vol. 1, p. 222.

clear empty eyes; and what he took away with him was that very distinctive look.[60]

The Zolaesque origin of Juanito's and Fortunata's love at first sight is also indicated by a complementary episode in *Le Ventre de Paris:* that is, the attempted seduction of "la belle" Lisa in the "caves" beneath Gavard's "pavillon de la volaille," a milieu remarkably similar to the "tienda de aves," which Juanito had passed through on his way upstairs. There "les femmes, assises, plumaient,"[61] and afterwards the naked creatures "montraient leur poitrine charnue, tendue par l'arête du bréchet." Furthermore, in the underground storage place various concessionaires keep their still-living merchandise in "des boîtes plates à claire-voie," through which their pathetic "coups de bec" (Galdós' "picotazos") are visible. The next installation is the "abatoire," where blood flows copiously and where a woman performs the murderous task of Galdós' "sicario."[62]

To the argument that these minor details of resemblance are the result of parallel Naturalistic observation, I would reply that that is, of course, the case, but that the notion of gathering such "materias reunidas" was suggested by reading Zola. There are obvious differences: Madrid's "vientre" was bloated only at Christmas time, and, as against the delicious prosperity of "les Halles," it was nourished by marginal middle-men and poverty-prone retail vendors. But it is not coincidental that both documentary investigations of the commerce in domestic fowl were overtures for erotic encounters. Galdós' "tienda de aves" was the Naturalistic point of departure for nothing less than a re-creation of the classical myth of the birth of Eros.

In the case of Zola, the activities, not surprisingly, appear to be less mythological than zoological. Young Marjolin, Gavard's assistant (again, both their complexions remind us of Renoir), escorts "la belle" Lisa on a guided tour of the premises. As they enter ever deeper into the connecting caves that lie beneath the market, Marjolin's hands begin to tremble and his breath quickens:

[60] *Les Rougon-Macquart,* vol. 3, p. 7. Throughout the novel Octave engages in intense visual encounters with female neighbors and future mistresses. On this particular occasion it is the location (stairway, landing, and open door) that is significant for us.

[61] Ibid., vol. 1, p. 663.

[62] Ibid., pp. 789–794.

Marjolin in that recess redolent with odors said nothing. There was the alcaline aggression (rudesse) of guano. But he, he seemed wakened and stimulated. His nostrils twitched, he breathed heavily as if rediscovering immensities of appetite. During the quarter of an hour that he had spent in that basement with "la belle" Lisa, that odor, that body heat of living creatures, had gone to his head. Now he was not timid any more, he was full of a rutting urge emergent from the heat of the manure in the coops, there under the broken vault darkened with shadows.[63]

Those who cannot abide not knowing what happens next are advised to read the end of the fourth part of Zola's novel. It would be hard to imagine a more vivid demonstration of the miracle of Galdós' narrative art than a comparison of the two episodes. Juanito, like Marjolin, may have been stimulated by the unfamiliar earthiness of the "olor de corral," but the author and his heroine react by soaring: the one on wings of imagination and the other on wings of devotion.

To conclude, we have been concerned with a remarkable phenomenon, novelistic consciousness, historically more than half a century old and intensely alive, nourished on feverish reading, in an author at the height of his creative powers. Although novelistic consciousness was shared by earlier novelists and by generations of readers literally driven out of their minds by fictional biography, the consciousness of Galdós when *Fortunata y Jacinta* was in prospect was unique in its incandescence and potential fecundity. Like Fernando de Rojas' "palabra del hombre science," it was about to "echar de sí crecidos ramos y hojas" on a scale that was unprecedented even for him. Using an apparently inexhaustible supply of narrative formulae, which in turn stimulated fresh observation of urban reality, Galdós was now to create with scurrying pen a world at once familiar and astonishingly new. So new in fact that, unlike the nameless and quintessentially Castilian city of *La Celestina* (it just could not have been Seville, "navíos" to the contrary!) where perdition was inevitable, the virtual Madrid that was about to be

---

[63] Ibid., pp. 794–795.

born was to be a place where spiritual salvation would be at least conceivable.

Novel and Observation

At this point we are still concerned, not with *Fortunata y Jacinta* as a completed work of art, but with its possibility. By way of epilogue, therefore, it is necessary to discuss briefly the aspect of Galdós' creative process that was just referred to, that is, the way reading can retrieve half-forgotten documentation and go on to stimulate new observation. Again, *Le Ventre de Paris* offers a useful example. Florent, the novel's hero and victim, returns habitually to the café of M. Lebigre; Zola's description of his feelings will be familiar to any reader who has reached part 3 of our "dos historias de casadas":

> The odor of the room, that liquorish odor, warm with tobacco smoke, went to his head, provided him with special happiness (une béatitude particulière), a self-abandonment and sense of consolation that made it possible to accept without difficulty great provocations. He came to love the faces of the steady customers who were there, to look for them and wait for them with the pleasure of habit. . . . They entered his life and occupied an ever larger place in it. When he put his hand on the copper doorknob of the room, it seemed to him to be alive, to warm his fingers, to turn of its own volition; he could not have had a more vivid sensation if he had been holding the supple hand of a woman.[64]

The Galdosian café addict of whom we are reminded, Maxi's ideologically petulant brother, Juan Pablo, bears no genuine resemblance to Florent, whose nightly conversations reveal sincere revolutionary fervor.[65] Serious source hunters would hardly consider worth mentioning their one manifest similarity: the satisfaction of each with the familiar smell of the café, with the reassuring faces of the "parroquianos fijos," and with the customary artifacts in a state of

[64] Ibid., pp. 745–746.
[65] In Juan Pablo Rubín one senses (in addition to don Alvaro) the tacit presence of Ana de Ozores' verbose and irresponsible father.

Pomboesque animation. What matters greatly to those concerned with how Galdós created novels is the strong probability that this unobtrusive and unemphasized passage from *Le Ventre de Paris* was the seed of nothing less than Galdós' marvelous, full-length exploration of Madrid café life. A minor narrative formula amplified with remembered experience and fresh observation grew into one of our favorite chapters, that entitled "Costumbres turcas."

At this point it may help to contrast Galdós with such a totally different novelist as Ernest Hemingway. The raw material of the latter, as we know, was imported from the widest possible assortment of milieux: northern Michigan, Paris, Pamplona, the trenches of Italy, the waters off Cuba, central Africa, almost everywhere but the suburbs of Chicago. These alien sources of experience had to be observed closely, scanned for misinterpretation, evaluated correctly, and only then transformed with excruciating care into language. Hemingway was not always successful in these endeavors, but we can only admire the care used to make consciousness, the world of words, correspond exactly to the world of the senses.

Galdós, on the other hand, fed on experience derived from reading, experience that entered the mind without mediation and as a whole, experience shaped and prepared for residence there by prior verbal existence. Afterwards, such book memories might lie dormant for an indefinite period, but when one fragment or another in the course of novel fabrication was, as it were, summoned from the unconscious, it incited the novelist to rediscover with wide-eyed appreciation the Madrid he already knew so well, the Madrid he had savored for so many years. Certified by Zola's or Dickens's authority, remembered reading confers new value on remembered living. Unlike Hemingway's constant and at times anguished awareness of the schism between words and experience, a writer whose consciousness resembles that of Alonso Quijano makes no difference between the two. As suggested earlier, basically Galdós could not tell, or could barely, the difference between Estupiñá and José Luengo.

"Amplificatio" of inherited narrative formulae, was, of course, immensely facilitated by the oral nature of novelistic consciousness. From Cervantes through Fielding and Sterne to the major nineteenth-century masters, a tide of printed speech has flowed through

223

the main channel of the genre. Unlike Hemingway, who had to content himself with tasting, smelling, looking, and touching because he understood imperfectly the languages spoken in most of the places he wrote about, novelists in the Cervantine tradition "observed" through their ears as much or more than they did through their eyes, noses, fingertips, and taste buds.[66] Thus, when Galdós, having in a literal sense, "recalled" Zola's brief description of Florent's "jouissance" upon entering his café, went on to a full-length essay on the function of that institution in Spain, he also recalled all the endless conversations he had listened to there night after night. The borrowed fragment, reshaped in the unconscious and without doubt translated into potential Spanish, found that language ready and waiting for a new, far longer, and more impressive narrative reincarnation.

Instead of having to search for the one right word to communicate a sensory impression of an unfamiliar place (Hemingway kept writing *Salammbo* over and over again), words orginally read mesh with words originally heard as together they tell the truth, "le vrai." Once titillated by Paris, Madrid speaks for itself as Galdós takes dictation. No doubt, too, that once the process was underway, the writer, having finished his day's labor, would sally forth to one café or another in order to give his novelistic consciousness the exercise it needed. It does not take much imagination on our part to visualize his half-smile upon overhearing some particularly pungent and usable interchange. In his own way he must have shared the private pleasures of Florent and Juan Pablo.

Elimination of the familiar, but ultimately misleading, critical dichotomy of literary "sources" as against documented "reality" calls into question another familiar dichotomy, that of intention and inspiration. For as we have seen, novelistic consciousness can only be conceived of as interacting, or existing in a state of interdependence, with what we have called the novelistic unconscious. As mentioned earlier, when Galdós in his *Memorias* tried to recapture

[66] That Hemingway was aware of the Cervantine tradition and perhaps too of its uselessness to him is indicated by his sardonic presentation of the novelistic consciousness (founded primarily on W. H. Hudson's *The Purple Land*) of Robert Cohen, whose name constitutes the abrupt beginning of *The Sun Also Rises*.

that interval of "lost time" when he was most aware of being aware both as a writer and as a reader, he availed himself of two physiological metaphors, fever and appetite. Compulsion from within, hungry assimilation of sentences served from without—both comparisons allude to the participation in the creative process of an underworld, which complements that of intention. Fever is the result of unperceived and unavoidable contagion (other novels being the carriers), while appetite, having been awakened by the irresistable savor of the printed page, has as its result the more lasting pleasure of absorbing its life. As against inspiration, which classically descends from above, Galdós clearly suggests that his conscious intentions are implemented by the welling upwards or outwards of the literate unconscious.

It is impossible to establish clear-cut categories in matters as delicate and subjective as this one. Nevertheless, and allowing for infinite gradation, I think that Centeno's distinction between "intention" and "intent" (as well as extent), which was our point of departure, proves valid. It is possible to differentiate roughly between a reading experience kept clearly in mind and used as a basis for inter-novel dialogue, that is, a reading experience that contributes to what Percy Lubbock was to call "the shape of the whole," and the dismembered fragments of life and situations, which we have just been discussing. Instead of a distinctive necklace exhibiting the special art of the jeweler, these latter are random narrative beads whose thread has been broken, or flotsam from lost derelicts adrift in the Sargasso Sea of the unconscious. When recalled by the needs or opportunities of the ongoing story, they emerge, not just one at a time as if stored in a card catalogue or commonplace book, but tangled together and sea-changed from within.

During their stay inside Galdós a gradual and unsuspected process of reclassification and metamorphosis has been going on, and it is in this altered state that they enter the creative flow and contribute to the gestation of many novels. But now let us contemplate directly his first great masterpiece, *Fortunata y Jacinta,* in my opinion the most mysterious and profound of them all. Let us contemplate the paradoxical truth that in spite of its elaborately calculated structure, in spite of the foreordained conclusion that is explicit (in several

225

variants) in the preliminary version, and in spite of the use made of an immense wealth of prior reading experience, it is as fresh on every page as the morning snow on the Plaza Mayor. The "source" itself refreshens. After witnessing the pathetic deathbed scene of Lalie, Gervaise goes out to find Paris covered with snow: "Rien ne tombait, mais il y avait un gros silence en l'air, qui apprêtait pour Paris un déguisement complet, une jolie robe de bal, blanche et neuve."[67]

[67] *Les Rougon-Macquart,* vol. 2, p. 760. After writing the above, Martha Krow-Lucal has called my attention to Mark Twain's remarks on his own "Art of Composition." Although he speaks of "sentences" rather than narrative fragments, his approach encourages me: "Let us guess that whenever we read a sentence and like it, we unconsciously store it away in our model-chamber; and it goes with the myriad of its fellows to the building brick by brick. . . . If I have subjected myself to any training process, and no doubt I have, it must have been in this unconscious or half-conscious fashion. . . . Yes, and likely enough when the structure is at last pretty well up, and attracts attention *you* feel complemented, whereas you didn't build it, and didn't even consciously superintend." *Life as I Find It,* ed. Charles Neider, New York, 1961, p. 227.

PART III

Fortunata y Jacinta

CHAPTER VIII

The Challenge of Historical Time

Since both Marxism and the so-called rise of the novel are manifestations of nineteenth-century historicism, it is natural that Marxist critics should be preoccupied with Sir Walter Scott, Balzac, and their successors. And it is equally natural that Spanish Marxist critics should be preoccupied with the "episodios" and, among the "novelas contemporáneas," with *Fortunata y Jacinta*.[1] This is all to the good, for their approach poses directly a fundamental problem, which from other points of view is often overlooked: how did novelists in that century transform raw material that is largely social and historical, and therefore by definition transitory, into lasting works of art? Or to rephrase the question in more familiar terms: why are the Naturalistic and realistic novels that are still worth reading anything but "human documents?" Once having aided us by posing the problem, however, Marxist critics, at least in the case of *Fortunata y Jacinta,* offer an incorrect solution. Here is a story, in their view, of an innocent, proletarian victim caught in the "engrenage" of an immense and complex bourgeois society, which literally cries for a revolution. All of Galdós' social and historical "materias reunidas" are justifiable artistically because they are "socially realistic" and show us vividly the mechanisms of corruption and exploitation.

Why is this, at first glance, apparently reasonable interpretation of our novel, an interpretation that might well be applied, say, to *Tormento,* "incorrect"? The answer is simply because the way the novel ends makes Galdós appear to be a kind of toadying Estupiñá dedicated to providing the Santa Cruz fortune with an heir. When the enormous river of the novel finally reaches its delta, it seems

---

[1] I refer specifically to Carlos Blanco Aguinaga's "On the Birth of Fortunata," *AG,* 3, 1968, pp. 13–24, and to Julio Rodríguez Puértolas' *Galdós: Burguesía y revolución,* Madrid, 1975.

to have been converted into a benediction of the bourgeois values and institutions it began by criticizing. From the point of view of "socialist realism," it is an immense exercise in insincerity. Read as a treatise or "human document," *Fortunata y Jacinta* can teach us about social injustice and class conflict in nineteenth-century Madrid, but read as a novel in which all parts join to form an organic whole, it is a failure. Because of its strongly emphasized and ostensibly counterrevolutionary ending, it cannot convert its historical and social raw material into a coherent work of art.

Discussion of what Galdós intended and what he in fact achieved in the creation of his masterpiece must wait until a step-by-step exploration, from style, through poetic imagery, into Fortunata's consciousness, is completed in the chapters to follow. Naturally, Marxist readers will not be convinced, insofar as they are committed to a definition of what novels are (and should be) antithetical to that of Galdós. This is precisely my justification for beginning part 3 of this book with these introductory pages. I should like to try to answer the question posed by the Marxist approach: how are the social and historical raw materials to be found in one nineteenth-century novel after another transmuted artistically in *Fortunata y Jacinta?* In so doing, I intend to take advantage of our familiarity with Cervantes' novelistic practice, as well as what we may have learned about that of Galdós in preceding chapters, in order to try to define the genre as the latter might have when he undertook his four-volume "dialectical" response to *La desheredada* and *Lo prohibido.*

Let me begin with a distinction with which every student of the *Quijote,* whatever his or her ideological commitments may be, is familiar: the distinction between novel and romance. Alonso Quijano is a reader of romances; they are fictional, often grotesquely fictional; yet he comes to believe that they are true. Does he do this only because he is addlepated? No. Aside from possible predisposition to romance, there is something about the way such fiction is written and read that helps to addle his pate. What is it? Simply that they seem vividly present, more real than reality, socialist or otherwise, to the transported reader. Even though their verb tenses are usually past (historical presents are infrequent) and their syntax not manifestly different from a story written about something that happened long ago, they are absorbed rapidly by the skilled reader of print as a substitute-life lived now, which, having escaped breathlessly from one hermetic adventure, immediately rushes into another and then another.

At this point I could, and should, cite Marshall McLuhan and George Simmel, whose respective meditations on the revolution in reading and on the nature of adventure as a hermetic phenomenon are important for Cervantes. But since I have done so elsewhere,[2] let me recall instead the description offered by Ortega's teacher at Marburg, Hermann Cohen, of the way music "creates" new time: "The movement grasps forward beyond its previous point of departure; it anticipates; it emerges from itself and merges with what it will be; it creates its present as an intimation of futurity."[3] So too the printed romance creates velocity. No wonder the poor "hidalgo" bookworm lost track of the snaillike daily time of his domestic routine, or rather was carried away by the Babieca-like fictional time of his chivalric reading. As Cervantes' Canon observes shrewdly, romances constitute a "nuevo modo de vida," a possibly heretical form of "expérience vécue."

But what about the novel? When Käthe Hamburger in her much discussed *Die Logik der Dichtung* concludes that all third-person narrative tenses are really present,[4] she fails to make a distinction between the Cervantine tradition and the romances Cervantes loved and laughed at. For in the *Quijote,* as we all know, the temporal paradox that is inherent in the very act of narration—the words are said *now,* while the events narrated happened *then*—is exploited to the limit, just as it was to be later on by Fielding and Sterne. Everything that happens seems to be present, because we have trained ourselves to read breathlessly and believe candidly, but at the same time past, because Cervantes, his Morisco translator, and

[2] See my "The Novelist and His Readers; Meditations on a Stendhalian Metaphor."

[3] "Die Bewegung aber greift überall über ihrer jeweiligen Zustand hinaus, sie greift vor, sie taucht auf und nimmt vorweg; sie schafft sich ihre Gegenwart stets in der Antizipation der Zukunft." Hermann Cohen, *Aestetick des reinen Gefühls,* Berlin, 1912, pt. 3, p. 143. In this context Vernon Chamberlin's musical interpretation makes perfect sense. *Galdós and Beethoven: "Fortunata y Jacinta," a Symphonic Novel,* London, 1977.

[4] Stuttgart, 1957.

Cide Hamete keep interrupting the movement forward and remind us impertinently that the story is over. It is no accident that the *Quijote* gets underway as a novel (as against a possible "novela ejemplar" inspired by the *Entremés de los romances*) when two things occur: when don Quijote and the "vizcaíno" are halted with their swords in the air in the midst of their chivalric encounter (thereby abruptly returning the reader to the present he shares with the printed page) and when the new "author" is introduced. Like the seemingly infinite variety of interruptions that constitute the structure of the novel, Cide Hamete's probable prevarication causes us to doubt what we are being told and thus inhibits our surrender to fictional time, specifically, to the time of "It is now; therefore, it is true."

In a moment we shall review the two immense, artistic conquests made possible by this strategy. But before doing so, proper recital of this catechism for Hispanists directs our attention to a paradox resulting from the identification of "nowness" with "trueness," which does not exist for illiterates. For example, when the boring and pious Miss Watson tells him the story of Moses and the bullrushers, Huck loses all interest as soon as he learns when that event (which ironically predicts his own future on the raft) was supposed to have happened: "I didn't care no more about him, because I don't take no stock in dead people." Addicts of the printing press, however, the learned Canon or the owner of "el más delicado entendimiento en toda la Mancha" prior to his self-transformation (after which he never reads again), are more perverse. To accept romance as true and to live it as a now, they demand fictional reassurance derived from an ostensibly nonfictional past, such as an ancient chronicle, a mysterious document (either found carelessly in the street or solemnly in a sealed leaden coffer), or even a voice from beyond the grave. In contrast to Huck, the habitual reader *only* takes stock in dead people.

The paradox is still with us. The invented present of an author pretending to authority as an historian (an archaeologist of feudal society, a Romantic witness of half-forgotten folkways, or a conscientious compiler of a "document humain" on the misery of the proletariat) is a precondition for forgetting his existence as we read on and on. We, too, need help, documentary reassurance, in order to be able to pretend what we want to pretend: that fiction is true. It is precisely this kind of artificial help that the candid listener to the celebrative oral ritual of the *Poema del Cid* (which is so faithfully believed that every "now" is an implicit "once again") did not need at all. Even now, literate descendants of the insatiable readers of *Waverley* and its progeny continue to require what they required. The printed present has to appear to be historically past in order to function as such a present; fiction has to be camouflaged as nonfiction in order to perform as it is supposed to perform.

This is what Cervantes and those who follow him reject. The very basis of Cervantes' invention of the novel lies in having compelled first the reader and later the characters to contemplate the fictionality of fiction pretending to be nonfiction. Such conventional camouflage as the playful "no ha mucho tiempo que vivía" or the self-important "las noticias más remotas que tengo" may be believed at the beginning. But both the *Quijoe* and *Fortunata y Jacinta* before long surpass the simple transition, or simple game, of "and then," "and then," "and then" becoming "now," "now," "now," and their readers become instead participants in the larger self-consciousness of the creative process. Cervantes and Galdós in intimately related but historically different modes exploit the temporal paradox of fiction (or the fictional paradox of time) in order, not just to make us laugh or to attract our attention, but to make us aware of who we are and who we could be or should be, to lead us to become, as it were, working members of the "Wortkunstwerk," whose consciousness of society and self is heightened and changed by that membership. A Stendhal aspired to nothing less than the colonization of his best future readers with his own consciousness, readers who would belong to the immortal band of the Happy Few!

To return to what we have learned from the *Quijote,* the immense artistic advantage gained by the narrator's ironical interruption of the narrative process (reminding the readers that what seems to be happening happened and that what seems to be true is fictional) is the initial creation of a semblance of freedom for don Quijote and Sancho, freedom from both the ever present control of the narrator and enforced involvement in the implacable (meaning "uninterruptable") sequence of one episode after another. In the classroom formula of my teacher, Augusto Centeno, what Cervantes achieved was the capability of converting adventures (the proper stuff of romance) into experience (the proper stuff of the novel). Don Quijote and Sancho (in this first novel their mutual presence is indispensable) can now take time out to react each in his own way, can sit down to talk over what just took place, and can even relax enough in order to try to reconcile their separate perspectives. The "lives and experiences" of knight and squire may be comically caricaturesque rather than sentimentally replete in the manner of David Copperfield, but they are indisputably the first and in my opinion the best. No night has ever been as dark, or experienced as darkly, as that of the "batanes." And the result is that the dialogue of the *Quijote* is authentically present as contrasted to the illusory fictional present created by the suspense of Amadís' breathless quest.

The second advantage of Cervantine interruption may be less obvious to first readers, but it is just as important in novelistic terms: the reading of the *Quijote* constitutes for the reading public and the characters a postgraduate course in distinguishing what is fictional from what is real. It is nothing less than a marvelous workbook or exercise book, which trains the reader in the perception of the fictional, that is, the fake, the put-on, the obsolete, the social, both in its demands and its pretenses, in a word, all that is not true to life in the profoundest sense of the expression.

We all, of course, remember the increasing perceptivity of don Quijote after undergoing the harsh training of part 1: not only does he *not* convert inns into castles in his imagination but he even senses shrewdly that the proprietors of genuine castles have certain innkeeperlike characteristics. Indeed, as is often pointed out, his final autonomy is gained by freeing himself from fiction, the fiction he had told himself and that had been told about him in part 1. For our part, as just remarked, the *Quijote's* invitation to consciousness of fictionality extends to the fictions imposed upon us by society and culture. Not just the fictions of Cervantes' times (for example, the cult of "honra" and lineage) but of all times so that we come to comprehend the collectivity to which we belong and our relationship to it in a new way after reading the *Quijote,* the *Chartreuse de Parme,* or *Huck Finn.* To join the sophisticated game of such novels leads to the discovery of how to "work" ourselves "free," as

Virginia Woolf phrased it in her journal,[5] or, as suggested by the titular image of Pérez de Ayala's *La pata de la raposa,* how to gnaw off the trapped paw.

It was, I propose, to this notion of the novel that Galdós returned in *Fortunata y Jacinta.* But three centuries had passed, and the expectations of the reading public, which he intended to exploit ironically, had changed. Although then, as now, there were a host of contemporary romances offering serviceable conventions (as in the case of *La desheredada*), the new novel, in spite of minor echoes of Sue and Fernández y González, was after far bigger game: nothing less than the central tradition of nineteenth-century fiction extending from Scott through Balzac to Zola. As we remember, these novelists and their colleagues (with the tangential exception of Stendhal) no longer played games with the temporal paradox inherent in the act of narration. And it was precisely this, the solemnity of their validation of fiction by presenting it as if it were nonfiction, that Galdós now intended to subvert. Nineteenth-century replacement of the documentary pretense of printed romances with what might be called the historical pretense had to be questioned if Fortunata was ever to work herself "free" and in so doing show her readers the way.

When Voltaire had meditated on the historicity of time ("Be sure that your madness corresponds with the return and temper of your age"), he had understood it as tragicomically as Fernando de Rojas. But for Scott and his post-Romantic heirs (among them the young Galdós) it represented a new and eminently serious way of comprehending the human condition. As a result, their novels display a common pattern: a long introductory section is devoted to historical reconstruction of milieux (the past as past or the present as if it were past), which, as the action gradually accelerates, is converted into the fictional present of a protagonist who experiences and copes with it. Such nineteenth-century authors, in other words,

---

[5] She is speaking of her own task of "working free" from ready-made language and grammar in the process of writing *Jacob's Room.* But the inevitable corollary is that the reader in the process of reading her liberates himself, and not only from linguistic habit but also from commonplace ideas and explanations. *A Writer's Diary,* ed. Leonard Woolf, New York, 1954, p. 51.

gravely foreswore the joys of being an enchanter (who intervenes at will) or an "historiador arábigo" (who changes truth at will); they were instead the only genuine historians, and they had to prove themselves worthy of their task. For this reason they constructed at the beginning such intricate, preliminary models as the establishment of Cedric the Saxon or the Maison Vauquer.

Galdós, as Marxist critics correctly observe, does not in *Fortunata y Jacinta* redeem his social and historical raw material in this classic nineteenth-century fashion. Nor does he imitate Cervantes directly, even though on the very first page Cervantine reminiscences and turns of phrase ("Otras muchas tonterías *de este jaez* cuenta Villalonga") are at least subliminally recognizable to Spanish readers. Such stylistic allusions, along with the intermittent intervention of a fictional narrator (whose critical but bland judgment of society and events, as we have seen, is not always trustworthy), function rather as a warning to the reader that the customary narrative pattern has been undermined ironically. Both the construction of the initial historical model and the subsequent presentation of personal experience, although they may at first look familiar, are as profoundly transformed in *Fortunata y Jacinta* as chivalric adventures are in the *Quijote,* and for identical reasons.

To begin with, the historical and social introduction is more ample than any the reader had ever seen or could conceivably ever see, with the exception of *Moby Dick* (which justifies its unceasing documentation with a transcendental irony possible only in Melville's tradition) and perhaps of *Nostromo.*[6] Furthermore, unlike the preliminary background construction of Scott and Balzac, only a few of these infinite genealogical and commercial "pormenores" are indispensable to the later development of the novel. After the

[6] Zola, as we know, abandons the Cedric-the-Saxon and Maison-Vauquer tradition of long preliminary description in favor of communicating the milieu through the natural movement and daily and seasonal rhythms of his experimental creatures. In the same fashion Galdós in his Naturalistic period no longer relies on the panoramas and pen-portraits that had characterized *La Fontana* and the first two series of "episodios." It is therefore all the more noteworthy that he should have returned at such length in 1886 to the earlier "realistic" technique. William Risley corrects Gustavo Correa's contrary view. Correa *Realidad, ficción y símbolo en las novelas de Galdós,* Bogotá, 1967, pp. 34 and 39. Risley, "Setting in the Galdosian Novel," *HR,* 46, 1978, pp. 27–28.

first part is finally completed, the Rubín family and the semisordid milieu that it inhabits (the scene of the happening that really matters) are introduced hastily as if they were afterthoughts. Yet it is precisely within that sketchy milieu that we learn most vividly and most lengthily how it felt "to exist within the happening" of *Fortunata y Jacinta*. We are aware that the Madrid of the Santa Cruz and their friends and relations continues to function historically on the periphery of Fortunata's life, and occasionally the one impinges on the other with explosive results. But it can hardly be said that Galdós in part 1 emulates the art of gradual acceleration that Bardèche admires in the novels of Scott,[7] that is, the patient presentation of infinite details all of which contribute to, or are drawn into, the posterior and ever faster rush of happening.

The most noteworthy modification of the traditional pattern of documentary introduction lies in Galdós' contemptuous estimation of contemporary history. To dismiss part 1 as merely "la gloriosa historia de la sastrería moderna" (*18*) would be inexcusably misleading, but the years chronicled in *Fortunata y Jacinta* do seem to justify the comparison of both Restoration politics and the evolution of Restoration society with Juanito's capricious mutability. In *Aita Tettauen,* written long afterwards (1904), the aged Jerónimo Ansúrez remarks that the only real difference between "moros" and "cristianos," aside from religion and language, is that among the former there do not exist "lo que aquí llamamos modas." He then goes on to express his disillusion with progress by favorably contrasting Moorish historical changelessness with the incessant and pointless innovation of later nineteenth-century Spain, a brand new Spain for him but one which his author had lived in and through. It is as if Ansúrez were describing our experience as readers of *Fortunata y Jacinta*:

> Here, on the other hand, mutability reigns continuously over everything: fashions in clothing, fashions in politics, fashions in religion, fashions in philosophy, fashions in poetry. Both art and ideas suffer the effects of this delirious mania for change. Today you wear a necktie in this shape; tomorrow it will be the oppo-

---

[7] See the chapter entitled "L'Art du roman en 1820," in Bardèche, *Balzac romancier.*

site shape. Philosophers and hats, poets and hairdressers every fifteen years find a new style and a new model to imitate. *(233)*

Change for change's sake, progress without genuine growth, fair sharing, or spiritual improvement, monuments as fictitious as that immortalized by Cervantes, a simulation of historical life without the rhythmic continuity of a beating heart, all implicit in 1886 and 1887, became explicit after 1898.

In order to avoid generational anachronism, let us remember that the Spain described in part 1 was still ostensibly alive and apparently moving into the future when the first readers cut the pages of the first edition. As late as 1947 in Valladolid I myself recognized, not without tenderness, remnants of the same, now vanished commercial society. The point that Galdós was intent on making in 1887 (ambivalently since his irony is as usual creatively Cervantine and not destructively Quevedesque) is that there is a kind of inherent "pastness" in the milieu of don Baldomero and his clan. The patent unimportance of so much self-importance makes every event seem "remote" (the key word of the opening sentence) as soon as it happens. It is as if Galdós in his mature wisdom had reached a devastating conclusion comparable to that of Mark Twain's naive narrator: he took "no stock" in dead Madrids. Instead of celebrating historical time as a means of comprehending human life novelistically, as he had done earlier in the grand novelistic tradition that had grown with the young century, he now denigrated it ironically as a medium for the stultification of that same human life. Just as *Fortunata y Jacinta* is an intentional "reply" to the conventions of the Naturalistic novel, so it is also an intentional "reply" to those of the historical novel from which Naturalism had emerged.

Having described Galdós' introduction to the social and historical milieu of Madrid as tediously ample, apparently pointless (if compared to Balzac's novel-long exploitation of the Maison Vauquer or Scott's of the Lowlands and Highlands), and hopelessly disillusioned, have I not then come to the same incorrect conclusion for which I reproached the Marxist interpreters? That is to say, the implicit conclusion that Galdós, well-meaning as he may have been, simply does not convert his social and historical "materias reunidas" into a work of art? Such criticism would certainly be justified if part 1 were the whole of the novel and the "Final que viene a ser principio" were simply the "Final." But it is not. If as experienced readers of Galdós we realize that with a daring worthy of the circus he has subverted the conventional structure of the nineteenth-century novel just as Cervantes almost three centuries before had subverted that of the Romances of Chivalry, we shall also realize that the apparently excessive attention paid to the past-prone, time-fraught Madrid of the Santa Cruz family was indispensable. The very preteriteness of its documentation introduces by contrast the next phase of the customary narrative sequence: that in which a character in his or her fictional and therefore believed-in present copes with historical and social determinism.

Part 1 of *Fortunata y Jacinta* corresponds to the Cervantine technique of incessant interruption. It is nothing less than an enormous invitation to self-consciousness, a demonstration of the fictional nature of the history and sociology upon which his public heedlessly premised its believed-in realism. Galdós wanted to show his readers not only that their society was unjust but also, and more importantly, that the history and progress in which they had so much faith was literally worm-eaten with fiction. And even though we inhabit a far more pessimistic and catastrophic age, we too must accept the invitation and pay attention to the lesson. For only after immersing ourselves in that most remote of all possible Madrids can we prepare ourselves to participate in the liberating, therapeutic, "true-now" experience of a heroine who, like don Quijote and Fabrice del Dongo, is not determined by "race, milieu et moment." Truth and fiction have once again been purposefully turned about.

Although Maxi and to a lesser extent Jacinta and even Ido are also "incited," only through Fortunata can Galdós communicate what her fellow citizens ignore or accept without question. Madrid is replete with babblers, "señoritos," cynics, self-satisfied successes, self-pitying failures, madmen, misers, spendthrifts, and any number of other ailing and deformed lives. They fill the pages of the novel, but their ample assortment of eccentric reactions to their metropolitan milieu amounts at best to "costumbrismo" on a grand scale. Fortunata, on the other, is nothing less than a perfectly designed, human instrument, a kind of ultimate novelistic heroine, who provides us with clear, wide-focused illumination of all she encounters.

An ostensibly similar observation was made earlier in relation to Gabriel Araceli as a perfectly designed hero-witness-narrator of history. But in the case of Fortunata, history-subservience and history-immunity aside, there is a fundamental difference: Gabriel is an intermediary between past and public, whereas the quality of Fortunata's experience first affects those who know her inside the novel. She fascinates nearly everyone she meets, although only a very few are perceptive enough to understand even dimly how or why. Apart from physical beauty, Fortunata's irresistible attraction (ironically enough poor Maxi expected to be loved because of "la atracción de *su* alma"!) resides not just in her superb body but in the sheer health of her consciousness. As a result, proud, presumptuous, and morally moribund Madrid (as socially sick and addicted to pre-varication as Mark Twain's Old South) ignores the fact that its hope to be remembered in future centuries depends on what Fortunata does with her life and death. As a true reporter and, without knowing it, a remorseless judge, she may also be in her own novelistic way a savior.

Castro, as we remember, remarked that a novel must tell us not only what happened but also how it feels to exist within the happening. After comparing the experiences of Fortunata to those of Maxi or Jacinta, we should add that *who* is feeling him or herself existing therein is equally important. Fortunata in these terms is not merely a purveyor of the present emergent from the historical past (as are all novelistic protagonists); she is or becomes a *presence,* a being that is human but at the same time more than human, at once alien and comforting like don Quijote, Huck Finn, Fabrice del Dongo, or the Cid. Many of the others among our best-loved fictional beings—a Saint-Preux, a Wilhelm Meister, a Waverley, a Rastignac, a Gervaise, or an Amparito Emperador—are as marginal as Fortunata and they may even be as victimized. But they nonetheless conform to their societies and times in a way that don Quijote and his epic ancestors and novelistic descendants do not. Fortunata, who appears from nowhere and ends nowhere, belongs to a privileged class. Her presence is always, and, as a result in her novel, as in the *Quijote,* everything else is open to question.

By way of introductory illustration, let us consider Galdós' introduction of Fortunata's consciousness in the chapter entitled *"Las*

Micaelas por dentro." As we remember, the other inmates either fight the system (the "anarchist" Mauricia) or truckle to it (the "beatas" Belén and Felisa), but only through Fortunata's experience, most vividly expressed in the imaginary but moving dialogue with the host, which results in "la idea blanca," can we judge truly how it feels and what it means to be inside such an institution. Prior to that completely private and deeply moving moment of truth, however, there is another moment when Fortunata has not yet been distinguished from the others, when her experience is (as indeed most experience is) shared with those who share her situation: the first view of the sunset over the Guadarrama. It is in that description that we are first given an inkling of what the novel has in store for us.

Like shipwreck, superstition, and jealousy, incarceration is a classic novelistic device for intensifying experience. In this case, one side of the building of "las Micaelas" has a "corredor alto" from which can be seen, as a consolation to the encaged, a wealth of landscape: ". . . los tonos severos del paisaje de la Moncloa y el admirable horizonte que parece el mar, líneas ligeramente onduladas, en cuya aparente inquietud parece balancearse, como la vela de un barco, la torre de Aravaca . . ."[8] (*240*) Fortunata and her companions had surely never before looked at a view, except when she was briefly and somewhat pedantically prepared for this one by Maxi. (*226*) But now Galdós, merging his sensibility imaginatively with that of the forlorn inmates he had created, comments on their spontaneously Romantic projection of feeling into vision: "la recortadas nubes oscuras hacían figuras extrañas, acomodándose al pensamiento o a la melancolía de los que las miraban."[9] (*240*)

Quite unlike Fabrice del Dongo in his Citadel spiritually transported by crystalline and timeless Alps, Fortunata and her sister victims endow the landscape with the freedom to move that they themselves are denied: the horizon is restless; the tower rocks

---

[8] ". . . the sober shading of the landscape of the common land of Moncloa and the admirable horizon which resembles that of the sea, slightly undulating lines with an illusion of movement where the tower of Aravaca seems to rock as if it were the mast of a ship . . ."

[9] "The dark silhouetted clouds took on strange shapes, which adapted themselves to the thoughts or the melancholy feelings of those who contemplated them."

gently; the clouds form transitory shapes. And by the end of the evocation (itself progressing in time as the sunset comes to its apogee and begins to fade) the day itself, compared by implication to a wild animal, is at last free to escape: "la claridad blanda, cola del día fugitivo, la cual lentamente también se iba."[10] (*240–241*) Galdós, however, is not content with this, and he cruelly contrives to accentuate the combined experience of space and time by having a wall under construction slowly rise to blot out the landscape:

> Cada día, la creciente masa de ladrillos tapaba una línea del paisaje. Parecía que los albañiles, al poner cada hilada, no construían, sino borraban. De abajo arriba, el panorama iba desapareciendo como un mundo que se anega. Hundiéronse las casas del paseo de Santa Engracia, el Depósito de Aguas, después el Cementerio. Cuando los ladrillos rozaban ya la bellísima línea del horizonte, aun sobresalían las lejanas torres de Humera y las puntas de los cipreses del Campo Santo. . . . Por fin la techumbre se lo tragó todo, sólo se pudo ver la claridad del crepúsculo, la cola del día arrastrada por el cielo.[11] (*241*)

Although corrections in the manuscript indicate the care with which Galdós composed this collectively perceived erasure, let us consider it only as our first direct communication from Fortunata. Novelistic experience is primarily temporal in nature, a moment-to-moment sense of time of one's life in its interconnection with that of the turning world, which in Galdós, as in other novelists (Proust, Joyce, and Mark Twain spring to my mind), is often expressed in water imagery. Fortunata's feeling of her own existence as artificially channeled and restrained—institutionalized—is, thus, inseparable

[10] "The bland evening light, tail of the escaping day, also was slowly departing."

[11] Every day the growing barrier of bricks covered up a portion of the landscape. It seemed as if the bricklayers, as they added each new row, were not building but rather erasing. Higher and higher it went, and the view kept disappearing like a drowning world. The buildings along the path of Santa Engracia, the reservoir, and afterwards the cemetery all sank one after another. When the bricks finally scraped against the beautiful line of the horizon, the distant towers of Humera and the cypresses of the burial ground still stood out. . . . Finally, the top with its tiles swallowed everything up; only the light of the sunset, the train of the day's wedding dress sliding along the sky, remained to be seen."

from the rising wall, which appears to her and to her sister inmates as gradually submerging liberty itself. The envied freedom of the distant mountain-waves in the preceding paragraph has been changed to an image of hydraulic servitude, of helplessness in the face of implacably rising waters. And as we read, we too intuit the damming up of a soul's natural flow, the construction of a conventional dike, which will only burst in an "estallido de infinitas ansias" with the return to Juanito at the end of part 2.[12]

It is, thus, the presence of Fortunata as a perfect conductor of experience (as contrasted to Maxi's anguished distortion of reality and Mauricia's hallucinations) that captures our present and differentiates the rest of the novel from part 1 and from its unrelenting narration, at once critical and nostalgic, of historical time. In so saying, we are reminded of Käthe Hamburger and her notion of the inner metamorphosis of narrative tenses. Far more radically than Alonso Quijano's voluptuous surrender to the present of romance, the novelistic symbiosis of the rise of the wall with Fortunata's own process of "pensamiento o melancolía" subverts the preterites and imperfects of the foregoing experience. To read them as past would be to "kill" Fortunata in the same way that Miss Watson's pious recital of the legend of his birth "killed" Moses for Huck Finn. As in all authentic novels, whenever an event, scene, or encounter is narrated not "an sich" but as an emblem of consciousness, the character's *presence* inevitably prevails over the grammatical *present* of the narrator, whether a persona or the novelist himself, telling us about the long ago of yesterday or of the thirteenth century. In *Fortunata y Jacinta,* however, the temporal contrast is aggravated. A past that is more past than our own (or those of other novels) creates by contrast a present that is more present than our own (or those of other novels, although in so affirming I can almost hear the ironical indignation of Stendhal), and the subservient tenses of the verbs behave themselves accordingly.

The result for the reader of Galdós' neo-Cervantine reconstitution of the nineteenth-century novel is confidence that a life capable of transmitting the flow of sheer experience we have just had the privi-

[12] Madariaga, curiously enough, does not mention this extreme example of repression and explosion in his illuminating discussion of the importance of such cycles for Galdosian "psychology." See chapter 2, note 32.

lege of re-reading cannot be drowned, no matter how "englouti" may be the world into which it has been thrown. For, as we all know, the present and past of novels encounter each other not only in the act of narration but also and far more importantly in the lives of their inhabitants. Who am I? What meaning can I find or create for my life in a world that is historically self-conscious, that solemnly affirms tradition and at the same time believes secretly and fatuously that all values are relative? How can I account for myself as a person in society? Or more abstractly paraphrased: How can I defeat the fatality of the past (both the person I used to be and the person others were brought up to think that I am) with what I feel myself to be now and what I aspire to become in the future? Such are the questions posed thematically by novelistic characters ever since Alonso Quijano, and Fortunata is certainly not exempt from them. Nevertheless, as she stands there in "las Micaelas" watching the masonry wall ascend tier after tier like a symbolic representation of her surrender to society, we know that in the end she will not succumb as did Lucien de Rubempré, Emma Bovary, Ana de Ozores, and Isidora Rufete. The sheer presence of Fortunata, even at this moment of her loss of freedom, is as manifest and in its own way as reassuring as that of the Cid in his *Poema*. After reading the above description of the ascending wall we cannot doubt that she will answer her questions and will create for herself a new and far more meaningful freedom. The trajectory of Fortunata's biography is one of ascension, and by the end she will soar far higher than any wall that history and society are capable of building.

Reference to the end of Fortunata's life confronts us again with the problem with which we began: her exercise of freedom in bequeathing her son to Jacinta. As I shall argue (although it is not an argument that Marxist critics who do not live in Marxist societies are likely to agree with), Galdós intended to show us that salvation is possible. Of course, the historical injustice and social evil of the complacent world of the Santa Cruz will continue to fester and will surely, as Galdós had predicted years before, become more and more inflamed. In contrast to the saga of the Rougon-Macquarts, however, here the miserable fate of the Barcelona factory girls or even that of Fortunata's wretched ex-colleagues in "la casa de la Paca" is thematically tangential. It is only who Fortunata is and who she becomes, when "concentrándose en una sola idea, *se determinaba* con desusado vigor y fortaleza" (Italics mine) (536), that matters.[13]

Although Galdós' surrogate narrator (through whose somewhat rose-tinted glasses we have already surveyed the Madrid social scene) seems to flirt with the possibility from time to time, allegorical hope for the reconciliation of the "cuarto estado" and "la nobleza del dinero" does not spring from the gift of the baby. From what we know of his future family and of his new mother, it is easy to predict that he will grow up to be one more "señorito" and that Spain's ancient, genealogical curse will not yet be exorcized. Nevertheless, the act of giving (like Huck Finn's anguished decision to tell the truth to Miss Mary Jane, Fabrice's return to the Citadel, or Prince Myshkin's departure from Russia) can only be considered a final, self-justifying epic deed, an autonomous affirmation of humanity in the very teeth of history. As such and although only a handful of citizens care enough about Fortunata to attend her funeral, pretentious Madrid history and pretentious Madrid society are saved from the oblivion they seemed so richly to deserve, saved in exactly the same way that the obscure hamlet of Vivar was saved —by having given birth to a heroine. Thus, in the greatest nineteenth-century novels (and *Fortunata y Jacinta* is surely one of them), after the scrupulous documentation of social illness and the poetic expression of intensely lived experience have been completed, "then" and "now" become "forever."

Galdós is not trying to excuse nor does he still aspire (as does Zola) to cure the diseased society portrayed in the novel. Like Mark Twain's Mississippi shores, Stendhal's Parma, or Cervantes' "la Mancha," it is both unjustifiable and in its own terms chronically ill, but Galdós does see, with the clear, distant vision with which great novelists are blessed, the ironical interdependence and interaction of society (sick almost by definition) with those rare incited souls who inhabit it but are immune to its debasement and who at the end find their individual paths to a reevaluation of the human

---

[13] This sentence was added in the proofs in order to ensure that readers in love with Fortunata (and as a result bemused) would get the point. See the forthcoming article of James Whiston in the *Actas* of the second "Congreso Internacional Galdosiano."

condition. The further paradox that we as readers, having shared their lives in their milieux, are left with a kind of residual affection and nostalgia for these novelistic worlds is the result, I think, of a kind of final structural transformation. As we look back after the deed is accomplished, all that was so reprehensible seems somehow changed, illuminated in an unexpected way. In contrast, novels that end without heroism, for example, *L'Assommoir* or *Madame Bovary,* leave us with a sense of sadness and distaste for their milieux. Let the reader compare his own recollections of the Madrid of the Santa Cruz family with those he retains of Emma's Yonville or Gervaise's Paris.

In the earlier version of this essay mentioned in the Preface I indulged in the kind of comparison of narrative structure with sentence structure that is taken so seriously and has become so complicated today. I have since grown more and more skeptical of such abstract equations, but considered as a metaphor such a comparison may help us to comprehend the difference between Galdós' masterpiece and *Madame Bovary*. Part 1 of *Fortunata* (corresponding to what Ramón Fernandez in his essay on Balzac in *Messages* terms "le récit")[14] functions as a preparatory and informative first "clause": "In Madrid there used to live an idle and dissolute prince. . . ." Then follows the second "clause" (Fernandez' "roman"), which provides the expectant listener with the action and emotion without which the sentence would be pointless: "who charmed and betrayed an innocent peasant girl." From imperfect to preterite, from situation to suspense, from past described as past to past experienced as present, such is the structure of fictional narratives in prose whether they be stories or novels, whether heard and transcribed by Grimm or composed by Balzac. The only difference is in quantity and proportion.

In the case of *Fortunata y Jacinta* and the others just mentioned, however, the silence after the "sentence" has been completed does not merely signify the termination of happening, talking, and living. There is, I postulated, though the analogy is admittedly forced, a third "clause," which transforms all that has gone on before and constitutes what Frank Kermode would call the "sense of the end-

[14] Paris, 1926.

ing."[15] As we close these books, just as when we close the *Quijote,* the silence is as pregnant as that which, according to Octavio Paz, surrounds a poem. We have witnessed nothing less than the salvation of the spirit in purely human terms. In the case of Fortunata in particular, this was done less by the gift as such than by the willingness to forgive, which the gift implies. Although Fortunata herself thinks of the legacy in terms of sisterly love for Jacinta, she has really forgiven Madrid and its history. We may well think that neither of them deserves it (even though the iniquities of the Restoration seem pallid compared to those of the unpardonable regimes of Fernando VII and his twentieth-century disciple), but nonetheless we cannot fail to be moved by her nobility.

[15] *The Sense of an Ending,* New York, 1967.

CHAPTER IX

The Art of Listening

Speech and Posterity

When Dorio de Gádex, the brash and effete young poet in *Luces de Bohemia,* refers superciliously to Galdós as "don Benito el Garbancero," the epithet is clearly a critique of his style, which that still-beardless generation found to be irretrievably vulgar: that is, as vulgar in a literary narrative as "garbanzos" (the chick peas that were Torquemada's favorite vegetable) on a restaurant menu. Twenty-six years before, in 1898, Valle-Inclán had written a glowing review of *Angel Guerra,* remarking only at the end that "a producir con menos facilidad, Galdós sería no más novelista, pero sí más literato."[1] But now, perhaps in part because of a personal grievance,[2] he seems to participate in the ebullient rejection of the literary past as such that constituted the implicit program of the second or third generation of newly fledged "Modernistas," who in the early 1920s were beginning to succumb ecstatically to "Ultraismo," "Futurismo," and whatever other brand new "—ism" happened to attract their attention.

Valle's slur was a sign of the times. Just after his death, Galdós' reputation underwent not merely a decline but a virtual hiatus, which was to last for over two decades, a hiatus which is perhaps best explained in "La deshumanización del arte." Ortega y Gasset, who had appointed himself as the intellectual attorney for the defense of the flesh-and-blood counterparts of Dorio de Gádex and his

---

[1] In *El Globo,* 13 August 1891, and reprinted in W. L. Fichter, *Publicaciones periodísticas de Don Ramón María del Valle-Inclán anteriores a 1895,* México, 1952, pp. 56–59.

[2] According to Francisco Yndurain (who heard of the episode from José María de Cossío, who was present), Valle-Inclán, offended by Galdós' supposed role in the rejection of *El embrujado* by "el Español," attacked him in a speech at the Ateneo. No date is given. Francisco Yndurain, *Clásicos modernos,* Madrid, 1969, p. 174.

adherents, felt duty bound to express his "hostility" to the nineteenth century as if it were a kind of viral disease still infecting his generation.[3] As for Galdós, he remarks, like Dickens, Sorolla, and almost all other artists of that century, he lacks "style"; his virtues are limited to "character," that is, limited to "content," which is significant only because of its illusion of human reality. If the poets and painters of the most recent vintage and those who were to come are "dehumanized" (read: "highly stylized"), Galdós is typical of a period that had hopelessly strayed from "el camino real del arte," the path of style.[4] There is no qualitative difference separating *Fortunata y Jacinta* from *El tren expreso* or *¿Quién supiera escribir?*[5]

It is not my present intention to attempt to refute these opinions (only apparently dissonant, for in the last analysis Ortega and Dorio de Gádex are saying the same thing) but rather to try to understand them. For there is, indeed, something about Galdós' style that has been a hindrance to his recognition as a major world

---

[3] "Nada 'moderno' y 'muy siglo XX,'" *El Espectador,* 1916. "Este es, pues, el verdadero, el único enemigo. Lo llevamos dentro de nosotros. . . ." *Obras,* vol. 2, p. 21.

[4] "El realismo . . . , invitando el artista a seguir dócilmente la forma de las cosas, le invita a no tener estilo. Por eso, el entusiasta de Zurbarán, no sabiendo qué decir, dice que sus cuadros tienen 'carácter', como tienen carácter, y no estilo, Dickens o Galdós." "La deshumanización del arte," in *Obras,* vol. 3, p. 368. For reference to similar criticism during the same period by José Bergamín and Antonio Espina, see J. E. Varey, "Galdós in the Light of Recent Criticism," in *Galdós Studies* (I). Espina asserts: "Galdós no es ni siquiera[!] un Balzac . . ." Ibid., p. 1. See also Melchor Fernández Almagro (who was later to become a fervent "galdosista"), who commented: "Pero ninguno gana el pleito y todos quedan en el lugar común." "La prosa de los antepenúltimos," *RevOcc,* 18, 1926, p. 258.

[5] The last reflections of this outdated attitude are to be found in Torrente Ballester's incredibly imperceptive *Panorama de la literatura española,* in the course of which he remarks benevolently, "No es tampoco un gran escritor, aunque no sea tan malo como suele decirse." Madrid, 1956, p. 63. See also José María Valverde's "Actualidad y vejez de Galdós," *Revista* (Barcelona), 6 September 1956, which I have not read. Cortázar seems to be trying to inaugurate a second period of disesteem: in *Rayuela* he mingles a paragraph from the beginning of *Lo prohibido* with his own stylistic critique ("una lengua hecha de frases preacuñadas ideas archipodridas, las monedas de mano en mano, de generación en generación . . ."). Buenos Aires, 1963, p. 227. Enough of Galdós is cited to justify a lawsuit by his heirs!

writer. Let us begin by allowing Galdós to speak in his own defense. Like Stendhal and Flaubert, he reacted strongly against the lush oratorical stylization to which as a nineteenth-century man he had been incessantly subjected.[6] Or as he phrased it, "la excesiva cosecha de oradores . . . que nos ahoga, obstruye y embaraza de continuo."[7] As a result, his professed goal as a writer was to transcribe "la emisión fácil y sincera de la verdad"[8] in "roman paladino / en cual suele el pueblo fablar con su vecino," as Berceo would have it, or in "roman garbancero," as Dorio de Gádex would have it. Thus, Galdós' self-defense in a way seems to justify the attacks of later critics.

We must, therefore, admit and, if possible, accept, enjoy, and admire the conversational tone of the major novels. Galdós simply and intentionally wrote not only in the language he himself spoke but more and more, once Zola had showed him the way, in the language he heard spoken in Madrid. As he remarked a year after finishing *La desheredada,*

> One of the greatest difficulties facing the novel in Spain is the relative lack of preparation of our literary language for rendering the shades and nuances of ordinary conversation. Orators and poets cling to traditional academic patterns and defend them from the inroads of Spanish as it is spoken. The rigid "protectionism" of those who consider themselves cultured forbids linguistic flexibility. Furthermore, the public press, with very few exceptions, has not distinguished itself for its capacity to utilize the expressiveness of oral Spanish. As a result, the stale antipathies of rhetoric and conversation, of academy and editorial desk are so irreconcilable that they can be considered the fatal stumbling block of would-be novelists. (*1429*)

[6] Dickens and Mark Twain also reacted in the same way, if we can judge by the oratory they reproduce. Indeed, it could be argued plausibly that the revival of the novel as a vehicle for ordinary, overheard speech can be understood as a reaction against contemporary political rhetoric. Jean Pierre Richard in his penetrating essay on Stendhal comments on his feeling of repugnance at the stylistic fundament of oratory, "la multiplicité vicieuse des *synonymes." Littérature et sensation,* Paris, 1954, p. 22.

[7] Shoemaker, *Cartas,* p. 52.

[8] *Lo prohibido, 1888.*

Desperation and shipwreck, possibly, but also, as we have seen and shall now see again, a challenge and an opportunity.

Galdós surely would not have changed the course of his stylistic exploration even if he had been able to foresee a future loss of esteem even more catastrophic than that suffered more or less simultaneously by his beloved Dickens. Indeed, in later years he must have been encouraged by the admiration of the Generation of '98, which (with the exception of Unamuno, who not untypically blew both hot and cold) perceived ancestral kinship in his critique of the Restoration and in his gifted ear.[9] Nevertheless, during at least two decades, the crucial 1920s and 1930s, when Stendhal, Flaubert, and the Russians were triumphant internationally, Galdós' way with words seemed to young Spanish readers careless, distasteful, and unartistic. He had long been underrated, even attacked, by traditionalists, sentimentalists, and spiritual academicians, who for their different reasons preferred Pereda, Palacio Valdés, or Valera. But now more acute sensibilities than these lost interest in his novels and failed to perceive the irony and profundity that lay behind the apparent vulgarity of his narrative language. The phenomenon was perhaps comparable to the overrefined aesthetic intolerance that one senses in Nabokov when he berates Dostoievsky, or comparable to Virginia Woolf's initial rejection of Joyce as "vulgar"!

This is a fact about Galdós' literary reputation that ought not to be ignored by later critics who believe themselves to be blessed with deeper insight. And above all, it ought not to be ignored by those of us who hope to persuade foreign readers that they have overlooked a novelist of major importance. As Hispanists, we dare not dismiss such heresy out of hand, because the supposedly antiartistic transcription of spoken language, which grated on sensitive Spanish nerves before the Civil War, is precisely the impediment faced now by would-be translators. When Galdós, for example, calls

[9] For Azorín, see chapter 3, note 6. For Unamuno see his "Nuestra impresión de Galdós," in *Obras completas*, vol. 5, pp. 367–369. Further favorable and unfavorable criticism by Unamuno is given in résumé by Theodore Sackett, *Pérez Galdós, An Annotated Bibliography*, Albuquerque, N.M., 1968, p. 119. Perhaps his most unjust comments are in a speech given at the Salamanca Ateneo in March 1920. Cited by F. Chueca Goitia in "La ciudad galdosiana," *Homenaje*, pp. 86–87.

a "vieux beau" a "galán fiambre" (a comic phrase from Madrid slang meaning roughly "preserved-meat gallant"), I for one cannot possibly find the appropriate equivalent in English. And I imagine that French and Italian translators, too, would be stumped by the oral hermeticism of the phrase, a viciously comic hermeticism even more hermetic than that which characterizes all argot by definition.

As we know, Galdós the novelist, as opposed to Galdós the dramatist, has in more recent years been rehabilitated with almost Chinese spectacularity. Beginning in the early 1940s (the 1943 centenary was naturally feted more abroad than in Spain), critic after critic, sensing the revived relevance of Galdós' vision of man in society to their tormented decade, expressed their surprise and admiration at the world they had begun to explore. Unlike Keats's Cortez, such major figures as Madariaga, Amado Alonso, Alfonso Reyes, Federico de Onís, María Zambrano, and Joaquín Casalduero (in his unfortunately foreshortened book) raised their voices in wonder (followed by cogent praise) and, in so doing, dispelled the stylistic incomprehension of the immediate past.[10] Then, in the 1950s and after, aside from the self-evident merit of the major works, a series of external factors, the gradual relaxation of censorship, the increasing alienation of young Spanish readers, the editorial explosion, the neo-realistic resuscitation of the novel, and the cinematographic adaptations of Luis Buñuel, contributed to the momentum of the resurgence. At the very least, Galdós has now been given tenure in the Spanish section of Parnassus. It is an appropriate reward for his heroic "character." For as Clarín remarked in 1890, long before Galdós' years of critical ostracism, "Few people realize the strength of character, the iron will, the self-sacrifice, and the authentic modesty that are necessary if one is to run counter to ready-made opinions, official pomposity, and conceited blather."

---

[10] The essays of Reyes, Onís, and Zambrano, which have not been previously cited, may be found in any bibliography of Galdós. I refer to Casalduero's *Vida y Obra* as "foreshortened" because he has informed me that he had originally completed almost one thousand typewritten pages when Amado Alonso asked him in 1942 to publish the present, greatly abbreviated version in the Losada Biblioteca contemporánea. It is fervently to be hoped that his work has not been lost and will eventually appear in its complete fórm.

This single comment from a "Palique" published on 28 June 1890 in *Madrid cómico* reveals more about what the two novelists were forced to live through than would a record of their personal finances or a survey of their reviews. The problem was not to withstand attacks but to create a public.

Speech and Commonplace

Amid the rapidly increasing accumulation of critical bibliography that has accompanied the rehabilitation, only a 1956 essay by Joaquín Gimeno, "El tópico en la obra de Galdós," has attempted to elucidate from within the stylistic malaise that his prose awakened in pre-Civil War sensibilities. The problem, according to Gimeno, lies primarily in Galdós' use of the commonplaces of oral interchange as a major source of narrative raw material.[11] If, on the one hand, this choice seems to rule out personal stylization (the prose of the Modernist and of the Generation of '98), on the other (as in all Naturalistic documentation), it gives printed recognition to the emptiness of social and political history in the nineteenth century. Or, as it was expressed more picturesquely in *Mendizábal:* "Just talking! Damned words. They're our country's chronic itch. Spain will reach the end of the century without having accomplished anything but scratching, by which I mean chattering." (*439*) Yet, in spite of such criticism, Galdós' superbly professional capacity for accurate listening effectively preserved a verbose Spain, which later generations were intent on abandoning for good.[12]

In this connection, we should not ignore that Galdós, in addition to making use of salty idioms typical of "la época chulesca . . .

[11] This approach was first used in Gimeno's "Galdós y el Naturalismo," Ph.D. dissertation, Murcia, 1955, and appeared later as the above mentioned article, "El tópico en la obra de Galdós," which Tierno Galván published in the almost unobtainable *Boletín Informativo del Seminario de Derecho Político de la Universidad de Salamanca,* January-April, 1956, pp. 35-52.

[12] Elsewhere Galdós remarks that, however intolerable this "océano de palabras" may seem, it is far better than "el silencio torvo del régimen absoluto." Shoemaker, *Cartas,* p. 237. It seems probable that one aspect of his rehabilitation is that he presented to the silenced generations of the 1940s and 1950s the refreshment and jubilance of oral freedom.

galán y expresivo" with its "inventiva fecunda" and its "léxico rico" as he says in a 1915 lecture entitled "Madrid" (*1495–1496*), did not reject commonplaces derived from extremely questionable sources. This was an era of osmosis between printed language and spoken language comparable, although on a far larger scale, to that of Fernando de Rojas. And the result was that, along with violent or trite sermons and silver-tongued political oratory (both of which Galdós exploited and disdained), bureaucratic officialese of the sort that drove poor Tomás Rufete mad and the pseudointellectualisms of newspaper reporting (often translated mot-à-mot from French and even word-for-word from English) also provided Galdós and his readers with ready-made phrases. In *Fortunata y Jacinta,* then, we are confronted with a mixture of suggestive popular invention, semicultured repetition, and trite adaptation, which together constitute a new and virtually untranslatable language.

The reading experience that is offered by the mature novels is, in consequence, immensely comic and secretly alarming. We are exposed to an unprecedented assortment of apparently antiliterary varieties of Spanish, the café, "tertulia," and madhouse languages, which at once anaesthetized and betrayed the triviality of the inhabitants of Restoration Madrid. Galdós "observes," Gimeno comments, "how nineteenth-century society is nourished on topics; its inhabitants can only feel, think, and express themselves topically,"[13] or as Sartre phrases it, "le lieu commun" is etymologically "le lieu de rencontre de la communauté."[14] From this we can only conclude that Galdós' novels in stylistic terms were dedicated to recording and, it must be admitted, exaggerating and enjoying a socio-linguistic state of degeneration far more serious and alarming than the superficial "affectation" humorously castigated by Henry Fielding. Even worse, this, seen at close range, has the apparent effect of binding the author irrevocably to his times.

Let us, therefore, try to step back to a more revealing distance. As both Clarín and Sartre indicate, and as Zola demonstrates with the ambiance-laden poetry of his prose, mere reproduction of topical language is at best a point of departure, whereas we need to com-

13 "El tópico en la obra de Galdós," p. 45.
14 Préface to Natalie Sarraute's *Portrait d'un inconnu,* Paris, 1956, p. 9.

prehend Galdós' planned destination.[15] Gimeno's essay suggests two complementary possibilities. In the first place, pompous and worn-out commonplaces (whether derived from press or podium) constitute a vehicle for irony in a tradition that extends at least as far into Cervantes' past as *La Celestina* and the *Lazarillo de Tormes*. It also extended well into Galdós' own past, for one of his student essays in Las Palmas was apparently a critique of the rhetorical commonplaces to which he had been subjected.[16] In the second place, Gimeno proposes, from a sociological point of view, those classes that are not "ociosas" season the novels with suggestive phrases "llenas de jugosidad, de vida y de gracia." This proposition seems questionable to me, particularly after having read Galdós' enthusiastic and penetrating historical analysis of "el léxico popular" in the 1915 lecture mentioned earlier. The truth is that such an eminently respectable respresentative of "la burguesía trabajadora y emprendedora" (which, according to Gimeno, Galdós believed to be the class responsible for linguistic revitalization)[17] as doña Lupe "la de los pavos" typically mixes stale formulae, "en toda la extensión de la palabra," with salty rhetoric: "Sosiégate; tú eres así, o la apatía andando o la pura pólvora. . . . Eso es ahora, que antes para mover un pie le pedías licencia al otro." (*181*) Nevertheless, we can only be grateful to Gimeno for clearly defining the problem.

Admittedly Galdós, unlike Fernán Cabellero, Estébanez Calderón, and Pereda, did not believe that the unique recipe for the salvation of prose style was folklore, and "lo chulesco" is not necessarily "gracioso," as the speech of a series of characters ranging from

---

[15] In his article on *Torquemada en el purgatorio,* Clarín remarks on Galdós' special, personalized, philological study of "las transformaciones del lenguaje y el estilo del insigne prestamista." *Galdós,* p. 268. Galdós in 1885 had already praised Clarín for his satirical utilization of commonplaces: "Lo que es verdaderamente maravilloso y único en su obra de V. es la vena satírica, aquella gracia digna de Quevedo con que persigue los lugares comunes de la conversación, de la literatura, del periodismo." First cited by Edith Fishtine from an unpublished letter dated 30 April 1885 in "Clarín in his early writing," *RR,* 29, 1939, p. 326. Although Galdós goes on to say that he plans to follow Clarín's example, his own style is far less Flaubert-like in this respect.

[16] J. Pérez Vidal, *Galdós en Canarias (1843–1862),* p. 102.

[17] Gimeno attributed this aspect of his approach to E. Tierno Galván. See the latter's "El tópico, fenómeno sociológico," *REP,* 45, 1952, pp. 111–131.

"Tres Pesetas" and his friends to José Izquierdo clearly demonstrates.[18] But the listening artist certainly did not exclude that traditional variety of oral enrichment.[19] When Torquemada begins a
sentence with "Partiendo del principio . . ." and "la tía Roma"
answers him by saying, "Don Francisco, usted está malo de la
jícara," Gimeno's two varieties of commonplaces are clearly audible
but in a fashion more in accordance with Cervantine decorum than
the sociological hypothesis seems to predict. No, we should not
identify Galdós' auditory delight in "el español medio" (a richly
hybrid idiom, alternately flat and effervescent, which mixes in ever-
varying combinations printed triteness with the creative spontaneity
of the "Volksgeist") with his earlier hope that Spanish history would
be redeemed by the proliferation of middle-class values.

That hope, at best, was a hope against hope. Our own personal
salvation is to join Galdós in listening directly, as the major novels
enable us to do, to the "confusión evolutiva" of metropolitan society.
As we have seen, it was only by offering this possibility that the
genre of the novel, according to both Balzac and his Spanish prophet,
could reach its apogee in the nineteenth century. When "las picantes
frases castizas" invade polite society,[20] and when sophisticated
rhetoric descends to the marketplace, the reader's own social identity
is, as it were, both questioned and enlarged. Or as Philippe Sollers

---

[18] Galdós' special disdain for Izquierdo may be understood in part in the
context of the latter's apparently apocryphal participation in the "cantón" of
Cartagena, which the former judged to be "la página más vergonzosa de
nuestra historia." Shoemaker, Cartas, p. 173. In the next sentence he also
mentions the assassination of Prim, described, as we have seen in La
desheredada, in similar terms. These two events evidently seemed to Galdós
to have been the most conspicuous contributing factors to the collapse of
his liberal hopes.

[19] Hinterhäuser cites the following description from Bodas reales: ". . . en
vez del castellano relamido y desazonado que en el centro hablaban los
señores, oíanse los tonos vigorosos de la lengua madre, caliente, vibrante y
fiera, con las inflexiones más robustas, el silbar de las eses, el rodar de las
erres, la dureza de las jotas, todo con cebolla y ajo abundantes, bien cargado
de guindilla." (1256) Die "Episodios," p. 101. Carmen Bravo Villasante describes admirably the enormous social range of Galdós' auditory attention as
well as the delighted and fascinated reaction of the young provincial to the
oral riches offered by the capital. Galdós por sí mismo, pp. 23–34.

[20] This passage from Lo prohibido (1724) is cited by Robert Ricard, Galdós
et ses romans, Paris, 1961, p. 81.

put it, "le roman est la manière dont cette societé se parle."[21] In the case of Galdós, the Madrid that speaks to itself in his 1880 novels is a very curious society, and its language encompasses a seemingly limitless range of decorum, an unceasingly fascinating encounter of styles. Linguistic petrifaction, mocking irony, and irresistible humor are at once the frontiers and the consolations of Galdós' addiction to the topoi of his culture. And if he in his role as secretary pretends only to have used a "nonstyle" or "antistyle," we must keep firmly in mind that the social and biographical truths "emitted sincerely and easily" therewith are probably more complex than any we are likely to experience on our own.

Within these ample boundaries, the incredible linguistic richness of Galdós' prose, a cornucopia that surpasses even the poetry of Lope, pours out unceasingly. Ricardo Gullón cites Unamuno's vivid description of the phenomenon: "Galdós' language—which is his supreme work of art—flows along slowly, solidly, vastly, compactly without cataracts or shoals, without whirlpools, and without ebbing either," and in a similar fashion Raymond Williams attributes "the greatness of *Ulysses*" to a "positive flow of . . . wider human speech."[22]

But what are the tributaries of Galdós' epic river of language? The notion of topicality is at once too general and too vague. So let us listen to a contemporary authority, Galdós' dear friend and colleague, doña Emilia Pardo Bazán: "In Galdós' novels there is a lexical treasure of expressions, words, and idioms—the language of the back alleys and of salons, the oratory of folklore, the jargon of politics and parliaments, transitory and traditional

---

[21] *Logiques*, p. 228.

[22] Unamuno, "Galdós en 1901," in *Obras completas*, vol. 5, p. 366. Cited by Gullón in his Introduction to *Miau*. The context of Williams's assertion seems to me to be relevant for *Fortunata y Jacinta:* "Yet what also should be said, as we see this new structure, is that the most deeply known human community is language itself. It is a paradox that in *Ulysses*, through its patterns of loss and frustration, there is not only search but discovery: of an ordinary language, heard more clearly than anywhere in the realist novel before it; a positive flow of that wider human speech which had been screened and strained by the prevailing social conventions. . . . The greatness of *Ulysses* is this community of speech." *The Country and the City*, p. 245.

ways of talking."[23] Unamuno stresses the oral flow of "la lengua *corriente"*; doña Emilia, the lexicographical *summa;* and together they confirm the title of the present chapter. We listen as we read (not literally as in *La Celestina,* which is only fully understood by those who have had practice reading aloud to their children), and what we hear is what Galdós has listened to accelerated and concentrated artistically. As Gullón observes, without moving our lips we perceive the inflections, the tone, and the resonances of "la palabra hablada." If we know how, we too can "do the police in different voices"[24]—but in our minds.

Galdós' oral commonplaces, therefore, cannot be truly understood when abstracted from what I can only describe awkwardly as the speaking-listening-writing-reading-listening that is built into every sentence. To catalogue, to compare, and to laugh or sneer at the ready-made phrases that constitute the "caudal léxico" may be tempting, but it is also dangerous. For spoken words, even more stubbornly than their written counterparts, resist removal from context. They are spoken by somebody to somebody else and always within and in terms of specific situations, and as a result, to understand them, to grasp what they are really saying, we must know where and when and by whom and to whom they are said. Unlike oratory constructed rhetorically in order to reach and influence the widest possible audience, the spoken words of Galdós seem to fly as spontaneously as birds from a speaker here to a listener there (or to a group of listeners there) alive in their biographies and in their shared history. Perhaps this is why Homer employed the epithet "wingéd." In Galdós' prosaic, provincial, presumptuous, and utterly unheroic Madrid, Homeric ἔπεα πτερόεντα could by virtue of his art be reincarnated as τόποι πτερόεντες, as airy, accurate, and at times as palpitating as their Achaian predecessors.

Galdós, of course, was not alone. During the nineteenth century one novelist after another had listened attentively to the commonplaces and ever-changing slang of their several languages. And then

---

[23] "El estudio de Galdós en Madrid," in *Nuevo Teatro Crítico,* 8, 1891, pp. 57–59.

[24] So Betty Higden described Sloppy's skill at reading aloud crime reporting in the newspapers. *Our Mutual Friend, Works,* vol. 1, p. 225. The phrase was, of course, a favorite of T. S. Eliot's.

in the act of ostensible transcription each one found his own un-precedented and entirely nonrhetorical (as contrasted to a Rojas, a Cervantes, or a Fielding) way of creating lives—individuals as members of the linguistic collectivity—out of spoken words. A recognized pioneer among these auditory explorers, who was in a sense antithetical to Galdós, was Flaubert. As an intellectual "cousin" to the "dandy," according to Roger Kempf, Flaubert was intent on chastising bourgeois society by maliciously polishing and displaying, as if they were precious stones, its most banal commonplaces.[25] And so he was understood by Baudelaire, who also "manipul[ait] [les lieux communs] à la barbe du siècle."[26] Galdós, on the other hand, is closer to Dickens and Mark Twain because, depending on the specific oral situation, he alternately or even simultaneously chastises the banality and saves the poetry of his novelistic language.

We are the overhearers, and it is up to us to listen with sense and sensibility. Otherwise we shall fail completely to grasp Galdós' renovation of even those commonplaces that, heard out of context, sound most worn out and ready for disposal. Two examples will have to suffice. The first is uttered by Isabel Cordero when she de-scribes her convoying of seven ravishing but undowried daughters to church in the language of her husband's trade as "concurriendo con su género."[27] Naturalistic reproduction, ironical amusement, and a kind of wry tenderness have been combined in the resuscitation of the moribund phrase. The second is funnier and more obvious, and because the speaker is not aware of the situational incongruity, it illustrates the point all the more clearly. Mauricia la Dura, having been expelled from don León Pintado's captive audience of "Fil-omenas" and wandering drunkenly through the streets pursued by

---

[25] R. Kempf, *Dandies, Baudelaire et Cie,* Paris, 1977, p. 67.

[26] Ibid. A Russian critic cited by Donald Fanger describes Gogol's way with language with an image that could be appropriately applied to that of Galdós: "Gogol opens up techniques of writing undiscovered by anyone else, saturating the verbal texture with a rain of popular, colloquial, occupational, and local words polished into pearls of language." *The Creation of Nicolai Gogol,* p. 22.

[27] She does not actually say this, but, as we shall see, the italicized phrases often constitute a special variety of "dialogue indirecte libre": "Era forzoso *hacer el artículo,* y aquella gran mujer, negociante en hijas, no tenía más remedio que vestirse y concurrir con su *género. . . ." (33)*

little boys, suddenly turns upon her tormentors and transfixes them with the exclamation "¡Apóstoles del error!" (*260*) An apostrophe musty with the insufferable boredom of ten thousand sermons has suddenly been reclaimed in the same fashion that Gypsies in "el Rastro" "seleccionan, limpian, ordenan y clasifican los abandonados desechos para imprimirles nueva utilidad y vida nueva" (*1494*), or in twentieth-century terms, in the same fashion that a Picasso incorporates an abandoned and broken cogwheel into a sculpture. In the act of making such a comparison we suddenly realize how generationally deaf both Ortega and Dorio de Gádex must have been.

The two examples to which we have just listened could never be found in the prose of Moratín (about whom Galdós said, "tiene el arte de ennoblecer las expresiones bajas y groseras")[28] or in that of Zola (about whom Mallarmé said, "many often inept modes of expression take on the value of the most beautiful literary forms."[29] There is obviously a procedural resemblance, but both Moratín and Zola lack the oral irony by means of which Galdós achieved the fundamental task of the artist of words as defined by Abel Martín: to utilize "lo humano que la palabra como tal contiene" to create "valor cualitativo" and above all "nueva significación."[30] As such an "objeto único," *Fortunata y Jacinta* does not confront its reader with two sealed warehouses of topics, the ones stale and the others just out of the oven. For even the most trite of the former, no matter how badly corroded by communal usage, can become as fresh as the latter in the appropriate human situation. Galdós might well have thought the dictum of his younger contemporary, Karl Kraus—"my language is the universal whore whom I have to make into a virgin"—to be either pompous or effete.[31] But he could not have disagreed, for the style of *Fortunata y Jacinta* corresponds organically, as all authentic styles must, to its vision of life. Both

[28] Cited by J. Menéndez y Arranz, *Un aspecto de la novela "Fortunata y Jacinta,"* Madrid, 1952, p. 59. From *De Moratín y su época* (1886), which I have not been able to read.

[29] Cited by Haskell Block, *Naturalistic Tryptich,* p. 26.

[30] Antonio Machado, "De un cancionero apócrifo," in *Obras completas,* ed. José Bergamín, México, 1940, p. 379.

[31] Cited by W. H. Auden, *The Dyer's Hand,* New York, 1962, p. 23.

on the level of style and on the level of theme Galdós expresses a faith that redemption is never impossible for whores. Nor even, as we have already observed, for the far more reprehensible society or "communauté," which prostituted both words and women.

Speech and Society

In order to comprehend the possibilities and limitations of Galdós' situational irony let us consider it as a phenomenon; or in more pedantic terms, let us meditate on the fundamental "situationality" of his narration. Taking *Fortunata y Jacinta* (his linguistic *summa summarum*) as an example, we recollect immediately an enormous and elaborate tapestry of conversational milieux, milieux which furnish situational contexts for all the kinds of spoken expression mentioned by doña Emilia and many more besides. The book is a seemingly limitless oral history of Madrid, the record of a thousand and one interchanges in as many locations. Furthermore, most of what is said is multilateral in nature, the indispensable "jarabe de pico" of people gathered in cafés, "tertulias," private homes, or around counters of retail stores.[32] We have already touched tangentially on Galdós' sociological observation of Madrid café life as the "natural environment" of Juan Pablo Rubín and as an amplification at once ironical and original of a paragraph from Zola. Yet, contrary to Unamuno's snide generalization ("Sus novelas parecen contadas en un café de Madrid, de sobremesa"),[33] the café as such is only the primus inter pares of the many quasi-institutional oral situations in Galdós' extensive repertory of "costumbres turcas." At the bottom of the social scale we find Segunda Izquierdo's "horita de tertulia que solía pasar en el puesto de la carne" (533), and as we look upward towards the regal bourgeois "sobremesa" of the Santa Cruz household, it becomes clear that a census of such situations would be time consuming. Some of the gatherings are special-

---

[32] Carmen Bravo Villasante offers a similar list in biographical terms. *Galdós por sí mismo,* p. 25. The link between cafés, politics, and conversation is a recurrent theme beginning in *La Fontana* and evident in the "episodios." Hinterhäuser mentions *Un faccioso más* in this connection. *Die "Episodios,"* p. 83.

[33] "Nuestra impresión de Galdós," in *Obras completas,* vol. 5, p. 370.

ized, and in them we overhear the vocabularies of "cesantes," "mus" addicts, apprentice pharmacists, and others. But more often than not it is ordinary, topical, conversational Spanish to which we listen. In either case, an abundance of repeated oral situations is a basic condition of the art of *Fortunata y Jacinta*.[34]

Taken as a whole, then, the language of this novel and of Galdós' novels in general is social and semipublic, a language located somewhere between oratory and the verbal intimacy of a stream of consciousness. Forged in group comment (Cervantes' "corrillos") and argument, more often than not it impoverishes the aspirations to sublimity of certain individuals, a Maxi and later a Fortunata, who are obliged to use it in their dialogue. And yet, in the case of the latter, her ability to make it communicate matters for which it is not adept (for example, the dialogue with conscience, which results in "la idea blanca") is both revealing and touching. Language here must, thus, perform two tasks: it must give voice to Madrid (certainly with as much pleasure as censure) and communicate "the difficulty of being" a "madrileño" or "madrileña," who during the latter part of the nineteenth century was determined to do something more humanly significant than "comer, dormir, digerir la comida, y pasear[se]."(*201*) As we shall see, one way to explain what *Fortunata y Jacinta* is about is to compare it to what *Huck Finn* is about: what it means to live an authentic life, which, in spite of Lionel Trilling, implies the utmost sincerity at crucial moments, in an entertaining oral society that is nonetheless a colossal prevarication.

Let us continue now our general description of Galdós' language. Humorous, stale, violent, sententious, but never boring, the tone of "las palabras calientes de los vivos" rises and falls according to the speakers, their profession and class (the cast is a population segmented both vertically and horizontally), and their infinite varieties of personal relationships. Topics, as we have seen, are ever present, but they are not there only because Galdós heard people saying them, or only to provide him with occasions for irony. Instead, each

[34] See the inventory of such situations in Hinterhäuser, *Die "Episodios,"* p. 122. In *Fortunata y Jacinta* the list would include, in addition to the above, such specialized meetings as "las veladas de los Samaniegos," "la inmemorial tertulia de la tienda de Arnaiz," "las jaranas" of Izquierdo, etc.

of them can be considered to be a "word" in the lexicon of a metropolitan world. These topics or commonplaces, that is, phrases repeated over and over and given conventional meanings and implications, are characteristic of limited groups. Within the English-speaking world, we are all only too familiar with such diverse topic speakers as those who lived through the Gay Nineties, those afflicted with Brooklynese, or professional teachers of literature. In any case, Galdós uses such groups with superbly comic art to invoke not only Madrid, as if it were one of the allegorical figures of *La Numancia* ("esos grandes individuos que se llaman Roma, París, o Madrid"),[35] but also the particular milieux that constitute the parts of its body. In saying this, however, we necessarily return to the question we have all along been asking and struggling to answer: why invoke this Madrid and its milieux if this city (unlike that of *La Dorotea* or even that of the earlier "episodios"), although amusing to listen to, has nothing important to say? As we remember, it was this that had hindered Galdós in his previous novel.

Formulated in this way, the problem is susceptible to a more specific solution than the true but vague notions of redemption and authenticity so far suggested. What I now propose is that the topical language (accompanied by topical meaning and topical values), which Galdós knew how to reproduce and manipulate masterfully, functions in much the same way that chivalric commonplaces function in the second part of the *Quijote*.[36] Coffee-house chatter caught on the wing not only creates milieux but also confronts the reader and those characters who care enough about its tacit suppositions with the challenge of validation. The ennobled don Quijote of the third sally can no longer ask (within its situation it is perhaps the

[35] Shoemaker, *Los artículos*, p. 445.

[36] The title of the earlier version of this chapter (given in the Preface) for this reason intentionally recalls that of Américo Castro's fundamental essay, "La palabra escrita y el *Quijote*," in *Hacía Cervantes*, pp. 267–300. As far as I know, Pérez de Ayala was the first to compare Galdós' attack on decorum with that of Cervantes and to note the comparable narrative enrichment that resulted. *Las máscaras*, Madrid, 1917, p. 62. Galdós was at least as ambivalent towards the spoken language of Madrid for all its use of stale topics as was Cervantes towards the prose of the Romances of Chivalry. The novelists' well-known sentimental comments on the café as an oral institution are at once moving and representative. (*297*)

funniest question ever asked by anybody): "si en seco hago esto, ¿qué hiciera en mojado?" And Maxi and Fortunata, who, unlike everybody else, are usually silent until provoked, find themselves living in a society that pays tireless lip service to the very beliefs they aspire to incorporate in their lives. But instead of repeating commonplace assertions "en seco" like everybody else, they have chosen to live them "en mojado."

In the world of our novel, amid a great deal of idle gossip (one of Galdós' favorite journalistic neologisms was "chismografía") about the theater, the weather, and the scandal, politics, and business that constituted Madrid's humdrum version of the wheel of fortune, communication through commonplaces corresponded to the commonplace nature of the values accepted by all good citizens. As we saw in the Declaration of Sandhurst, some values were traditional—faith, love, honor, loyalty, virtue, thrift, charity, self-sacrifice, and others corresponded to the recent history of Europe—liberty, equality, order, and above all progress. We are not concerned now with the contradictions inherent in the list, for having been reduced to commonplace expression, they were seldom put into practice, no matter how candidly or violently they may have been asserted by the likes of a don Baldomero or a don León Pintado. But to try to live in deed by such principles was to be a revolutionary in the profoundest sense, as Bakunin perceived when he identified himself with don Quijote.

Thus, in *Fortunata y Jacinta* the language of company and the silent truth of solitude engage in continual thematic encounter. The familiar theme of the nineteenth-century novel, society versus the self, is here presented orally. By this I do not mean that Fortunata cares very much about "el qué dirán" (as contrasted to her passionate query "¿quién soy yo?"), or that her constant oral worry about how she may sound to others really matters, except in the case of Jacinta, who in this respect *is* society for her. What matters is her epic effort to understand and to create herself in terms of the debased language, decayed values, and rationalizations that her society (in this respect represented by Juanito) have to offer. It was this that Galdós had in mind when he (like Mark Twain, sick and tired of his own tendency towards Tom Sawyerism) rejected "style" in *Tormento:* "El estilo es la mentira; la verdad mira y calla." (*1448*)

In order to comprehend this puzzling defense of silence on the part of one of the world's great artists of the spoken word, let us remember our earlier distinction between literary and vocational varieties of incitation. In *Tormento* Galdós, like the Cervantes of part 1 of the *Quijote* used as a point of departure the encounter of literature and life—the quiet truth of Amparito's love and penance as against the novels of the stylist, Ido del Sagrario. But now the spoken language he was learning to write during this period (with the help of Zola) finally enabled him to create, not a bourgeois victim, but an oral and axiological heroine from the "pueblo," who will insist (just as do popular etymologies) that language is real, a vehicle for truth, and that, accordingly, values are not *mere* words. When Galdós wrote years later in *España trágica,* "Oh I was bookish all right, but a while ago I became "humanish"; I've taken the pulse of life and my books now are the people" (*946*),[37] he expresses his continuing hope (a desperate and even absurd vocational hope, not unlike that which underlies the pessimism of part 2 of the *Quijote*) that the insecure and pretentious society that spoke Spanish might learn from someone how to tell the truth and in so doing learn how to reclaim its history-submerged nobility. Linguistic regeneration and moral regeneration (two sides of the same coin) might regenerate what is called (grotesquely) "la raza" and enable it to become once again what Américo Castro was to term "una alta posibilidad de ser hombre." Fortunata in this sense can be thought of as Galdós' latter-day linguistic reincarnation of Lope's Laurencia.

Speech and Characterization

These social and national aspects of Galdós' use of speech are complemented by his capacity to reproduce intimate interchange and the tones and styles of individual characters. Elementary in this connection is his frequent introduction of new characters as voices, and not only Fortunata's *"yiá voy"* with its atypical (we have no reason to believe she always squeals) "vibración agudísima de una

---

[37] Cited in Hinterhäuser, *Die "Episodios,"* p. 101.

hoja de acero" (*41*) but also Izquierdo's growl, Nicolás Rubín's "voz cavernosa de sacerdote" (*211*), Adoración's "metal de voz argentino" (*119*), and Ido's theatrical elocution. But perhaps the two most effective examples of this technique are the end of Mauricia's initial description ("But as soon as Mauricia opened her mouth, forget your illusions. Her voice was hoarse, more like a man's than a woman's") (*234*) and the introduction of Villaamil as if he were a disembodied voice: " 'Well, as for me,' murmured a voice, which sounded as if emerging from a bottle." (*297*) Equally elementary, although nowhere near as mechanically persistent as in Dickens,[38] are the familiar tags: Torquemada's comic misuse of the word "materialismo," doña Lupe's emphatic "en toda la extensión de la palabra," or Aurora Samaniego's curiously meaningless insertion of "por ejemplo" into the middle of her sentences.[39]

The next step is just as familiar, although less obvious. As a master of his métier, Galdós carefully orchestrates his multiple voices in terms of his remarkable ability to represent individual identities in transcribed patterns of speech. The inhabitants of this oral world are (as we are too, according to Buffon) creatures of style, or perhaps it would be more truthful to say, creatures who depend for their very lives on what they say, creatures whose flesh and blood is style. Doña Guillermina Pacheco speaks pointedly and her words drive to the heart of the matter as well as to that of the listener. Nicolás betrays his pretentious stupidity through the rhetoric and the second-person plurals of the incurable sermonizer. The two

---

[38] As Bardèche points out, it was Scott rather than Dickens who first exploited this technique systematically. Balzac apparently disapproved of it as an obvious sign of imitation. *Balzac romancier*, p. 39.

[39] This apparently represents a Hispanization of the "par exemple" with which the conversation of Gervaise and her friends is replete. Similarly, when we hear Aurora say, "Me pareció a mí, por ciertas cosas que vi y oí, que al *buen hombre* le gustaba demasiado Jacinta" (*435*), the echo of "bonhomme" may well be audible. It is characteristic of Galdós' art that he should not (as Rojas did not) explain or emphasize such calculated cases of oral subtlety. But that he knew what he was doing is indicated by the appearance twenty years later of a Fenelon (the name, but not the biography, is identical to that of Aurora's husband) in *La vuelta al mundo en la "Numancia,"* whose speech is punctuated by italicized "por ejemplos." (*454ff.*) Novelistic consciousness is indeed curious, as Lewis Carroll's heroine might have remarked.

styles, the one sharp and the other dull, reveal the antithesis of their religious vocations. But perhaps the most striking of the several styles of falsification (what Fielding, as already noted, more mildly termed "affectation") is that of Torquemada. In this Galdosian masterpiece of verbal caricature, we can hear the honeyed words ("melosidad"), the rising and falling of the voice, his underlying heartlessness, the transparent disguise of meaning with manner. Yes, for such a man, "el estilo es la mentira."[40]

Galdós, however, is at his novelistic best when he submits these creatures of style to unfamiliar situations, which are at once revealed and shaped by their verbal reactions. Doña Guillermina's crucial interview with Fortunata is a striking example. As we remember, "la santa" has been unable to prevent Jacinta from hiding in the closet in order to eavesdrop. That failure is fatal for her usual oral command: "Pero lo verdaderamente singular era que Guillermina, tan dueña de su palabra normalmente, estaba también azorada aquel día, y no sabía como desenvolverse." She begins in her usual fashion: "Tengamos sinceridad, y̌ hablemos claro." But a few sentences later when Fortunata, just as sincerely and clearly as she, reveals "la pícara idea" ("Esposa que no tiene hijos no es tal esposa"), her only recourse is exclamatory moral condemnation: "Por Diós . . . cállese usted . . . No he visto otro caso . . . ¡Qué idea! . . . ¡Qué atrevimiento! Está usted condenada."[41] (*401-405*) As Galdós presents the situation, a central peripety of the plot is determined orally: if doña Guillermina had been able to speak freely, she might

---

[40] As an example of this masterpiece of oral caricature, see the extraordinary discourse beginning "Mire usted señora: estos señores disolutos son buenos parroquianos. . . ." (*195*) Moreno Isla, Ballester, and even Juan Pablo Rubín also offer comparable examples of characterization through speech.

[41] "But the really singular thing was that doña Guillermina, normally in full command of words, was so upset that day that she didn't know how to explain herself."

"Let us be honest and speak plainly."

"For heaven's sake! . . . Not another word! . . . I have never heard of such a thing. . . . What kind of an idea. . . . How do you dare . . . ? You'll be damned for sure."

In reading the third passage it is important to note that the "puntos suspensivos" all belong to Galdós. I have omitted nothing.

267

have been able to dissuade Fortunata from carrying out the project demanded by her incitation, that is, bearing Juanito Santa Cruz' second child.

Another example, less decisive but more typical, is the change in doña Lupe's speech when in the presence of "la santa moderna." The strong impression made on the former by the latter (far more because of her position in society than because of her good works) finds a vivid reflection in the grotesque politesse of leave-taking: "Amiga de mi alma, la obligación me llama a mi choza." Doña Lupe's usual sharp tongue both minimizes ("choza") and inflates ("la obligación") as she seeks the complicity, at once stylistic and social, of her interlocutor. This combination (which doña Guillermina demolishes in the intonation of her reply, "Sí, sí, . . . la obligación antes que nada. Hasta luego.") (*381*), precisely because of its manifest use of topical insincerity, creates a miniature and subtle situational comedy.[42]

There are two important characters, Estupiñá and Fortunata, whose speech is presented in a very different way from that of their fellows. The former may be considered a kind of familiar spirit or tutelar deity of this special world: "Estupiñá suffered from an hereditary and chronic vice, which all the willpower he had at his command was powerless to remedy, a vice which, although apparently inoffensive, enslaved him hopelessly. It wasn't alcohol, sex, gambling, or spending money. It was conversation." (*35*) As a seemingly ageless incarnation of what is at once "la sarna" and "la gracia" of his country, he dispenses his "jarabe de pico" (syrup of chirping) whenever and wherever he can find more or less attentive listeners. More conspicuous at the beginning and the end (because of his residential proximity to the beginning and the end of Fortunata's passionate biography), Estupiñá's incontinence introduces us to and reminds us of the special nature of Galdós' narrative art. In this sense, he can be thought of as providing a flat oral frame for a three-dimensional oral world, a function which enables us to understand

---

[42] "My dear friend, my obligations recall me to my humble abode (literally "hut")."

"Of course, of course . . . obligations come first. See you later."

why Galdós usually prefers to talk about his talkativeness rather than transcribe literally what he says.[43]

In addition to being an ideal family retainer and a possibly indiscreet family confidant, Estupiñá has witnessed attentively (but without insight) the major historical events of nineteenth-century Spain. His penchant for reminiscence is, in fact, so emphasized that we may well suspect that his secondary function is to remind the readers of 1886 and 1887 that their pseudomonumental Spain was also time-fraught. In other words, all Estupiñá has to say about the remembered past is so anecdotal and picturesque that it seems to have no more importance than Galdós conceded to the apparently harmless imitation history to which Spain had been submitted by Cánovas. Furthermore, as was pointed out in connection with the allegory of Isidora, in retrospect Galdós was no longer persuaded that the 1860s and 1870s (prior to Cánovas' "continuation" of the true past of the nation) were, for all their alarms and excursions, more significant historically than the Restoration.

Biographically speaking, with the terrible exceptions of the "paseo de los sargentos" and the assassination of Prim, most of the "historia de España" that Galdós had "seen" with great concern as a young man now seemed to him to have been "una mala comedia representada por regulares cómicos,"[44] that is, as overinflated as the "célebre alboroto de la noche de San Daniel," which is mentioned maliciously in the first paragraph of *Fortunata y Jacinta* as the one occasion when Juanito behaved as a proper hero.[45] Compared to the heroic and grim history retold in the first two series of "episodios,"

---

[43] Only at the end in an amusing scene in which he does not want to speak to his tenant Fortunata, but cannot refrain from doing so when provoked, are we given a sizable sample of his chatter.

[44] Shoemaker, *Cartas,* p. 43.

[45] The tone of Galdós' journalistic account of the affair (see chapter 1, note 2) is at once blithe, sarcastic, and indignant. That he was not on that occasion "transido de dolor" is confirmed by a personal album in the collection of the Casa-Museo Pérez Galdós, which celebrates the confrontation with "aleluyas" accompanied as usual by cartoon sketches. See J. Pérez Vidal, "Galdós y la noche de San Daniel." At the time of writing *Fortunata y Jacinta,* his memories of the event and of his reaction to it may have been refreshed by his similar account of the "agitación escolar," which occurred in Madrid in November 1884. Shoemaker, *Cartas,* p. 135.

later events appeared to the novelist to be as petulant as those recorded in the more recent annals of our own universities. For Estupiñá and his circle of open-mouthed auditors such distinctions would have been out of the question. As Rojas implied in the speech of Sempronio's beginning, "¿Qué dices de sirvientes?" (Act III), oral history by its very nature is inconsequential and can therefore be used to remind perceptive readers of all it cannot evaluate or account for.

Galdós, thus, uses his character's cheerfully anecdotal history to communicate his own bleak historical disillusion. Like Stendhal, concerned with challenging ironically the public of his own earlier Restoration, unrelenting presentation of contemporary history as gossip (the gossipers being not only Estupiñá but also Juanito, his coterie of "señoritos," and everybody else, the narrator included) must be understood as a training in judgment and insight. This is, it is worth repeating, what novelists do when they do what they are supposed to do—from Cervantes through Fielding and Jane Austen to Flaubert and his nineteenth-century colleagues. In this particular novel Galdós thoughtfully provides us with a conspicuous negative example specially designed to provoke the reactions he desires, Estupiñá. As we learn to know him, we realize that this smuggler turned equerry (like the Restoration of which he approves) is at once the antithesis of Fortunata (whose being was created as history-free) and of Gabriel Araceli (whose parallel life was created in order to transmit the meaning of history). Galdós must have been fascinated, yet perhaps not without some justifiable degree of literate melancholy, by Estupiñá's flesh-and-blood counterpart, "el tendero José Luengo."[46]

[46] Geoffrey Ribbans has observed that the date of Estupiñá's birth is the same as that of Galdós' mentor, Mesonero Romanos: 19 July 1803. "Contemporary History in the Structure and Characterization of *Fortunata y Jacinta*," in *Galdós Studies* (I), p. 92. This does not mean, of course, that one was modeled on the other, but rather that both were loquacious witnesses of the same century of national history. Galdós' remarks on Mesonero in an 1868 newspaper article could in part apply to Estupiñá: "*El curioso parlante* es un objeto (permítasenos la palabra) complementario de esta villa. Es su historia personificada, es la representación viviente de su vida interior y de esa otra vida lenta, casi perdurable, en que las poblaciones nacen, crecen, se desarrollan y mueren; de esa vida determinada por las demoliciones, los embellecimientos . . . el plantel y construcción de nuevos

If Estupiñá provides oral and historical boundaries for this immense fictional world, Fortunata, because of her rejection by society and afterwards of society, for the most part exists silently at its hub. As a consequence, unlike her upstairs neighbor, whenever she does speak, it is in a new and unexpected way. She exists in a constant state of linguistic metamorphosis. And one aspect of her attractiveness to the other characters lies precisely in this, in her lack of oral formation and typification. At the beginning, Fortunata seems hardly able to speak at all. The first time we hear her her speech consists of a few rudimentary sentences and a "yiá voy" so high in pitch that it more resembles bird song than human utterance. And during the rest of part 1 (as far as we can tell at second hand through Juanito's memory), she continues to exist at about the level of a talking animal.[47] Later on, certain conversations, particularly some

---

edificios, el arbolado, el riego. . . ." Shoemaker, *Los artículos,* p. 445. Nevertheless, instead of being a caricature of Mesonero (although both are "parlantes"), I would suggest that Juanito's confidant and Izquierdo, taken as a pair, constitute an ironic rejection of Galdós' own "episodio" approach to history. Estupiñá is the verbalizer, while the basely incoherent Izquierdo rents out his noble visage as an artist's model (Galdós was apparently remembering the identical métier of Christopher Casby in *Little Dorrit,* see chapter 7, note 58) for exactly the sort of panoramic historical paintings that were imitated verbally in the first series. The references in this early newspaper article to municipal water supply and to urban construction and demolishment are worthy of note because they indicate the young Galdós' attention to the kind of history that was to be his principal concern in the creation of *Fortunata y Jacinta.*

[47] Thus, Juanito thinks of her as "un animalito muy mono," "un animal; pero buen corazón" (*50*), and, more generously in his cups, as a "paloma madre" who can coo "rorróo" convincingly but who mispronounces "indulgencias" as "indilugencias" and "volver" as "golver." Montesinos is correct, however, when he points out that Galdós goes out of his way to avoid oral typification of his heroine. *Galdós,* vol. 2, p. 228. In a brief rereading of pertinent passages, I cannot find a transcription of any utterance of hers more unsavory than "¡pa chasco!" (*180*), although it is remarked that her "pintoresco lenguaje" "arrojaba luz vivísima" upon the story of her sordid life after being deserted by Juanito. (*175*) Jacinta, too, though more compassionate than her husband, imagines her rival substituting "diquialuego" ("de aquí a luego") for "hasta luego." (*52*) See Américo Castro, "*De aquí a = hasta. Surto. Guelte,*" *RFE,* 3, 1916, pp. 68–69. It is, however, an expression she never actually uses. As we shall see later, this lack of oral characterization corresponds to an intentional and exceedingly careful lack of physical description.

with Maxi, seem to indicate that the novel is going to become a Shavian "Bildungsroman" with Fortunata in the role of Eliza Doolittle. Her husband's pedantic pleasure in teaching her new words and in correcting her pronunciation also recalls another well-known pair of conversationalists. And although Fortunata lacks the ready wit of Sancho in oral response, it cannot be denied that during the course of her short life she quickly learns first how to talk to herself eloquently and later to others, as well as much else.

Nevertheless, to present the novel on these terms would be grievously misleading. It is only Fortunata's lovers and protectors, who hear her from without, who think of her as tongue-tied and rude. As Galdós remarks, "one of the things about Fortunata that pleased [doña Lupe] the most was her timidity in expressing herself . . . because uninhibited language would have been a sign of an uncontrollable will." (223) Little did doña Lupe or Maxi know, for as early as her sojourn in "las Micaelas" Fortunata demonstrates in the discovery of "la idea blanca" a capacity for straightforward and intelligent mental discourse that they, as well as we, should envy. Throughout the course of the novel, we encounter the same alternation between apparent speechlessness, basically an inability for small talk and for commonplaces, which pour out of the mouths of everybody else, and a combination of devastating cogency and overwhelming passion. We can never be sure how Fortunata will talk, because she is so intensely alive.

At this point we must pause and remember that the evolutionary metaphor used earlier is only a metaphor. Fortunata's feelings, her reasoning, and her consciousness of herself do not belong to another order of being. She is a woman, and if at the end some of those who have lived with her remember her as an angel, she certainly is not one during the allotted span of her biography. What distinguishes her from her fellow citizens (and, I dare say, from most of us) is that she is a whole, seamless, and (as Galdós implicitly predicted when he agreed to try to continue the novel of Camila) a completely healthy human being. This is her only inheritance, her single advantage in a world that offers her no privileges at all, and it is this that characterizes her dialogue. Fortunata says what is necessary and what she feels, a practice that on some occasions may sound rudimentary and, on others, inspired. She is, thus, as orally exceptional as Estupiñá, but if the one is social, historical, and voluble, the other is personal, vital, and cogent. It is a contrast that is crucial to the novel's profoundly Cervantine transformation of its language from a medium for narration into meaning (what the work of art is made of becomes what it is about) and challenge.

The challenge is to each one of us. When Jacinto María Villalonga encounters Fortunata dressed fashionably (as we remember, she was even wearing a hat!) and the first question that occurs to him is "¿Cómo hablará?" (*152*), he is thinking only of vulgarity and refinement. Yet the same question never ceases to concern those of us who, as fellow human beings engaged in dialogue, hope that the life we share with her may help us recover, not our innocence (the impossible dream of American white people, according to James Baldwin), but our ability to express what we think, what we have experienced, and what we feel truthfully and clearly. This is not meant to imply that Fortunata is an unwitting yet naturally gifted teacher of rhetoric (as are, say, Celestina or doña Guillermina) but rather that her oral integrity reveals by contrast all the evasions and self-deceits with which we try to conceal what has been variously described as our hollowness, our civilized discontents, our alienation, or our intimate war between reason and passions.

To conclude, in a novel thematically concerned with plain-spokenness and prevarication in which the characters literally *are* their speech it is not surprising that the author should reduce substantially his earlier experimentation with "dialogue indirecte libre."[48] As compared to *La desheredada, Fortunata y Jacinta* is

---

[48] Exclamations and italicized expressions recognizably typical of the person under discussion are among the most frequent forms of "dialogue indirecte libre" in the novel. For an example of the first we may recall Juan Pablo Rubín in the café ". . . hablando de la situación, ¡siempre de la situación, de la guerra y de lo infames, indecentes y mamarrachos que son los políticos españoles! ¡Duro con ellos!" (*159*) Typical of the second the following: "No se pueden contar las faltas que cometió [Papitos] en una hora. Bien decía doña Lupe que tenía todos los demonios metidos en el cuerpo y que era mala, pero mala de veras, una mal criada y una calamidad . . ., *en toda la extensión de la palabra.*" (*182*) Once in a while a suffix used ostensibly by the narrator (but really corresponding to the person whose actions or reactions are the subject of the narration) produces the same effect:

much more like the *Quijote* or *Pickwick Papers* in its varied display of dialogue directly reproduced. Of course, as we have seen, Madrid as a collectivity speaks through its inhabitants in a common, communal language. But unlike the deadening linguistic milieu that determines from within the souls of the inhabitants of *L'Assommoir,* that of the inhabitants of Madrid usually *sounds* through their "many voices" and their personal preferences in the selection of topics. The decision to turn away from Naturalism necessarily meant a partial abandonment of its most conspicuous technique. Particularly in the case of Fortunata, as compared not only to Isidora but also to Maxi, insofar as he began as a Naturalistic caricature,[49] we come to know her to a great extent through what we hear her say.

This does not mean that Galdós relinquished his hard-won ability to penetrate within what Rojas called the "atribulados imaginamientos" of his characters, or that even in the case of Fortunata he does

---

"Cuando iban visitas a la casa, [doña Lupe] enseñaba [la hucha] como una cosa rara, sonándola y dando a probar el peso, para que todos se pasmaran de lo arregladito y previsor que era el niño." (*168*) In a novel in which the author writes the language in which the characters speak, such momentary transferences of identity seem to occur spontaneously. The consistent use of "dialogue indirecte libre" by Flaubert, Zola, and Galdós (in *La desheredada*), on the other hand, implies an otherwise impassible ironical gap between author and character. In this sense, Naturalism appears far more self-conscious than the new art Galdós had discovered.

[49] I refer not only to Maxi's physical (and situational) resemblance to Camille Raquin but also to Galdós' play with the hereditary headaches Maxi shared with his brothers and the equally hereditary traits that, corresponding to different fathers, distinguish the three so strikingly each from the other. Later, as Arthur Holmberg has shown, Maxi's incitation encompasses not only his original Naturalistic caricature of Quixotism but also expands to include that of Balzac's Louis Lambert. "Louis Lambert and Maximiliano Rubín." See also the discussion in chapter 7, note 49. At the same time, Maxi's speech directly reproduced becomes more and more extravagant and even frightening. At the beginning, however, his one sustained passage of "dialogue indirecte libre" is the paragraph that follows the "assassination" of "la hucha": "No había tiempo que perder. Sentía pasos. ¿Subiría doña Lupe? No, no era ella. . . ." (*170*) Galdós is obviously intent on teasing both Naturalism and its principal stylistic device. It is a way of illustrating by contrast the new direction he is engaged in exploring. In her most Naturalistic movement (the confession of her relationship with Juárez "el negro") Fortunata's speech is also presented indirectly.

274

not occasionally resort to fragments or brief passages of "dialogue indirecte libre." On many occasions, however, I have noticed that she tends to revert automatically to speech in the first person: "Después soñaba que era ella la esposa y Jacinta la querida del tal, unas veces abandonada, otras no. La manceba era la que deseaba los chiquillos y la esposa la que los tenía. 'Hasta que un día . . . *me daba* tanta lástima, que le dije, digo: Bueno, pues tome usted una criatura para que no llore más.' "[50] (Italics mine.) (*247*) But far more important and more interesting than these remnants of Naturalistic technique are the several innovations to be examined in chapters to follow: the uncannily proto-Freudian use of dreams; the direct interior monologue of conscience resulting in "la idea blanca"; the recording of unspoken dialogue ("'Oh! If you only knew who is sitting beside you!' Fortunata was thinking") (*375*); and, above all, those descriptions of experience in which Galdós enters the sensibility of Fortunata and supplies her with the words and concepts she needs.[51] The building of the wall damming up the view of the "Filomenas" and "Josefinas" has already been discussed; the snowfall of the Plaza Mayor will be examined later as a concluding "scene of consciousness," and there are many other examples. Galdós is experimenting with a form of rapprochement between narrator and character, which is significantly antithetical to "dialogue indirecte libre" and marvelously adapted for interior characterization.

[50] Afterwards she would dream that she was his wife and Jacinta his mistress—and sometimes deserted by him too. The concubine was the one that longed for children while the wife had a family. "Until one day . . . I felt so sorry for her that I said to her, 'All right, take one of my babies and stop crying.' "

The MS and the first edition are punctuated as above. The editor of the so-called Aguilar *Obras completas,* however, corrects the apparent illogic by initiating a new paragraph for the direct quotation. Other examples are frequent. Two from part 3, chapter 6 ("Naturalismo espiritual"), may be found on pages *391* and *400*. In the first example, the Aguilar editor once again clumsily interrupts the flow of language on the printed page.

[51] The consciousness of Galdosian characters, in other words, exists in a constant state of transition between third-person narration, fragments of "dialogue indirecte libre," and direct dialogue, both mental and actually pronounced. For an enlightening discussion of Galdós' further development of this technique in *Misericordia,* see Denah Lida, "De Almudena y su lenguaje," *NRFH,* 15, 1961, pp. 307–308.

Speech and Communication

In a novel devoted to the contemplation of its own oral medium, we should not be surprised to discover that we experience the narrative world as if we were partially deaf and trying hard to listen. Both what we overhear and fail to overhear constitute what contemporary critics might term the structure of our avid absorption of the Madrid of Fortunata. Galdós guides our reading by means of continual concern with the limits or frontiers of speech, that is, by means of unremitting attention to those areas or situations where speaking as such begins, ceases, or becomes inaudible. We have just seen how Fortunata oscillates between extremes of oral poverty and wealth, and so, too, her author almost obsessively probes the limits, not of language as such (he is neither a Joyce nor a Huidobro, needless to say), but of that familiar expression of consciousness known as talking. In the novel (as against the epic, in which everything is pronounced emphatically and heard clearly) oral artistry necessarily depends on the interaction of speech with its own form of the "unconscious"; in this case, what is not audible or, although audible, not comprehensible.

Exactly what and where are the frontiers of spoken language? The easiest and most apparent answer is to be found in Jorge Guillén's "The Complete Afternoon": "Pervasive sound! Footsteps/And cries, which aspire to dialogue,/are mixed together. /Music is mere noise." Some of Galdós' most intense moments of acoustic experience are constructed in precisely this way. A strong desire to listen or speak is hindered by noise, noise which is often as annoying as the buzz of voices in a café or the sound of wheels in the street but which also can be such ordinarily agreeable distractions as bird song or music.[52] When, for example, Maxi feeds

---

[52] Noise here functions in a fashion comparable to the distance and the physical barriers used by Rojas. These too, however, are necessarily present in the novel because they impede aural comprehension, as, for example, when doña Lupe tries to overhear the discussion of Maxi and Nicolás through their bedroom door. (*211*) But even in this case, noise (the creaking of the bed) contributes to the problem. Unlike *La Celestina,* in which the human voice emerges from silence, the dialogue of the novel is integrated into auditory experience as such. Experimentation with the use of noise as a limit of speech is also present in the later series of the "episodios" and constitutes

doña Desdémona's canaries, "they all began to chirp and sing at the same time and nobody near them could hear anybody else. Doña Desdémona was reduced to gestures." (*492*) Again, a few pages later on, Maxi tries to overhear a conversation of Aurora Samaniego with her mother in order to confirm his suspicions that the former is having an affair with Juanito:

> Maxi, pretending to be wrapped up in the piece Olimpia was playing, actually didn't miss a word of that domestic squabble. It was lucky that it took place when the girl was caressing the *andante cantabile molto expresivo,* because if it had coincided with the *allegro agitato,* the Good Lord Himself couldn't have made out a single syllable of what the mother and daughter were saying. While the *presto con fuoco* was going on, Maxi said to himself: "How could I possibly have doubted for an instant that it was absolutely true." (*496–497*)

In a world thematically centered on speech, all music, whether natural or human, is likely to be heard as noise.[53]

---

one of their fundamental technical differences from the first two. Thus, for example, Pedro Hillo's vain attempts to make sense of "el rumor oratorio" from "los pasillos del Estamento" in *Mendizabal.* (*504*) It is such new possibilities, developed during the course of writing "las novelas contemporáneas," that Hinterhäuser overlooks in his otherwise eminent book, by far the most serious scholarly presentation of Galdós as a novelist of history. The problem Galdós has now solved is how to communicate the atmosphere of a parliamentary debate without describing the speeches or, what would be even worse, transcribing them.

[53] The conversion of music into noise can also be oneiric, as is demonstrated by two curious examples. The first is a part of the dream-journey to the depths of Fortunata's psyche (the structural counterpart to Jacinta's Dantesque and Quevedesque "vista al Cuarto Estado") when incited by "la pícara idea." She has just met the shade of Juanito: "tiembla Fortunata, y él la coge de una mano preguntándole por su salud. Como el pianito sigue tocando, ambos tienen que alzar la voz para hacerse oir." (*410*) The second occurs just before Jacinta is lulled to sleep while listening to Wagner: "la orquesta hacía un rumor semejante al de las trompetillas con que los mosquitos diviertan al hombre en las noches de verano." (*86–87*) As we remember, she is about to descend into a dream equally as Freudian in its own way as Fortunata's. Comparable examples can, of course, be found in the works of other novelists (Clarín notes how the "gritos gárrulos y agudos" of birds increase the noise of a party in *La Regenta,* chapter 13, but nevertheless the persistent development and the many variations on this technique in *Fortunata y Jacinta* deserve special attention.

The ironical smile, which we can imagine accompanying the writing of the above passage, has disappeared when Galdós utilizes the same situational impediment for the last time. Fortunata is on her deathbed, trying feebly to listen to a conversation. Its meaning eludes her, however, not only because of her semiconsciousness but also because "bird song . . . echoed from those somber walls along with the cries of Juan Evaristo for his bottle." (*536*) Bird song is a fitting requiem for Fortunata and a fitting accompaniment for the crying of her "polluelo"; but above all, just as it was for doña Desdémona, it is an auditory hindrance. Galdós, thus, is not only interested in situations in which talking is possible, expected, and arranged for (cafés, "tertulias," and the rest) but also and equally as much in situations that render it difficult or impossible. The latter complement the former because the reader's awareness of the novel's wealth of auditory experience is enhanced by the special intensity of spoken language when confronted with its impossibility, or even the mere possibility of its impossibility.

When one of Dickens's tone-deaf characters remarks that music is "respectable,"[54] he implies that, even though it may be an interruption, it cannot properly be objected to; it has to be waited out. The author of *Pickwick Papers* was himself enamoured of sound effects for their own sake and used them far more decoratively and musically than Galdós—jingling bells, whistling wind, the clopping of horses' hooves, and the rest. Galdós, on the contrary, often indicates sound effects when they impede what one wants to hear, or possess a significance of their own, a message without words. Thus, for example, "el ligero ruido estridente que hace el papel al ser desdoblado," which at once bothers and "attracts the attention" of Fortunata (Galdós' most sensitive acoustical instrument) when Maxi during the night opens his "papeletas" containing poison. (*438*) Thus, too, to cite another random example, Sor Marcela's panic when she hears "en la soledad de su celda el bullebulle del maldecido animal," specifically the tiny "bullebulle" of the monastic mouse, which plays a paradoxically major role in the plot. (*249*)

At other times, meaning is projected into the noise, as in the case

---

[54] *Our Mutual Friend, Works,* vol. 1, p. 146.

of Fortunata's (and our) climactic auditory experience on the night after the snowfall on the Plaza Mayor. Again, most of the words belong to Galdós, but the projection of maternal experience is totally hers:

En el estado incierto del crepúsculo cerebral, imaginaba Fortunata que el viento venía a la plaza a jugar con la hora. Cuando el reloj empezaba a darla, el viento la cogía en sus brazos, y se la llevaba lejos, muy lejos. . . . Después volvía para acá, describiendo una onda grandísima, y retumbaba, ¡plam!, tan fuerte como si el sonoro metal estuviera dentro de la casa. El viento pasaba con la hora en brazos por encima de la Plaza Mayor, y se iba hasta palacio, y aún más allá, cual si fuera mostrando la hora por toda la villa y diciendo a sus habitantes: "Aquí tenéis las doce tan guapas." Y luego tornaba para acá, ¡plam! . . . ay, era la última! El viento entonces se largaba refunfuñando."[55] (483-484)

Could anything be more antithetical to Isidora's bell-punctuated and totally self-centered "Insomnio número cincuenta y tantos"? Speaking in general terms, we have been led to participate in an aural world in which noises ranging from the barely perceptible to the deafening are woven into the context of words. Furthermore, we perceive in their juncture unexpected and strangely suggestive meanings.

To return to the frontiers of language, a second and equally obvious one, suggested by doña Desdémona's frantic "señas" at bird-feeding time, is marked by the gestures used by the characters

[55] "In the uncertainty of her mental twilight, Fortunata imagined that the wind had come to the plaza to play games with the striking hours. When the bell of the great clock began to sound, the wind would take the exact time in its arms and would carry it far, far away. . . . And then it would come back in a great circle and would resound—bonggg!—as loudly as if the sonorous metal were in her room. The wind went across the Plaza Mayor with the time in its arms, reached the Royal Palace, and further on still as if it were showing it off to everyone in town and saying, 'Look at the twelve little hours all so cute. And then it would come back—bonggg—and —what a pity!—then it was all over. The wind then blew itself away sulking and grumbling." Galdós goes on to recreate Fortunata's fantasy of a dialogue or argument between the striking hours of the several belfries, which are audible in her apartment and ring at slightly different times.

279

to accentuate meaning they feel incapable of articulating adequately. My readers will undoubtedly remember (I have intentionally limited myself to the most conspicuous examples) Torquemada's circled thumb and forefinger (identical to that of don Cayetano in *La Regenta*), Nicolás Rubín's handmade screen for eructations, Papitos' defiant tongue, doña Lupe's imperative tapping with her fan, Nicolás and don León Pintado, who gossip about Church bureaucracy "cogiéndose recíprocamente las borlas de sus manteos" (*229*), as well as many others I have omitted. Intimately related to these are what could be called "oral gestures," the exclamations and expletives that in novelistic language (as in ours) are called upon when communication fails: "psch," "chist," "eh," "plaf," "pun," "ea," "ji ji ji," "ja ja ja," "ju ju," etc. Gestures and onomatopoetic transcriptions are, of course, the companions and the seasoning of all authentic dialogue from *La Celestina* to the novels of our time. I only propose here that Galdós emphasizes them much as he emphasizes noise, as a means of intensifying our attention to printed speech.[56]

Characterization, too—that is, the innate ignorance, inexperience, and inability to communicate of given individuals—constitutes a frontier, which Galdós explores with particular care. His prime example is, of course, José Izquierdo, who represents the wretched oral milieu from which Fortunata emerges. As we remember, among other subcostumbristic aspects of his way of life, the infamous language (at once profane and incomprehensible grammatically) with which he "converses" with his comrades titillates the two "señoritos," Juanito and Villalonga, in their maiden voyage to the lower depths. Juanito, as a result, is not above showing off his man-of-experience command of such expressions to Jacinta during their honeymoon, thereby providing a properly grotesque contrast to the intolerable baby talk of the loving couple. It could even be said that use of

---

[56] Perhaps I am mistaken, but in this novel, as in the *Poema del Cid,* all gestures seem either to be inhibiting to speech or a form of speech. As an example of the first I would offer Aurora Samaniego's use of pins (*464–465*). As for the second, notice the menacing way Sor Natividad inspects the floor that Fortunata and Mauricia have just polished: "ladeando la cara como los pájaros cuando miran al suelo." (*235*) It is curious that in *Los apostólicos* Crucita checks on things in exactly the same way. Another miniature formula!

the language of one class by a member of another is in itself a form of characterization, just as is the effort to refrain (as does Mauricia on her deathbed) from one's normal mode of speech.

In the case of Juanito, however, after a while, as he explains it to his bride, physical and linguistic satiety together led him to abandon Fortunata and her family: "Me parece que oigo aquellas finuras: '¡Indecente cabrón, *najabao, randa, murcia* . . . !' No era posible semejante vida. Di que no. El hastío era ya irresistible. La misma *Pitusa* me era odiosa, como las palabras inmundas." (*61*) Juanito does not realize and never will realize (even when Fortunata's self-creation has been fully achieved and is clearly manifest even to the likes of a Segismundo Ballester) that his victim has not been determined by her background.[57] Because he is who he is, he cannot possibly hear her soar above the wretched frontier of speech that persists in his memory. Cervantes (like Galdós) could free Sancho from oral determinism when he chose to, but Juanito, had he possessed the patience and ambition necessary for writing a novel, would, for all his talent, have been at best a second-rate Naturalist. Fortunata, on the other hand, possesses the potentiality of being a great oral novelist in the tradition of Dickens and Mark Twain, as Galdós implies when he remarks that she reproduces mentally her final quarrel with Juanito "with the words, the gestures, and the most insignificant inflections of their dialogue." (*462*) She can literally "re-hear" how "self-love and pride came in torrents out of his mouth." (*463*)

And, one might add in passing, Fortunata also reveals a sense of what we called earlier novelistic "habitation" when Feijóo suggests that she return to the Rubín household:

Thus, thus as in those dissolving pictures in which images fade out and others begin to appear (at the beginning only as a vague suspicion of the emerging form and afterwards outlines, colors, and complete graphic definition) from that time on in the mind

---

[57] As for the others, it is true in general terms that those in the same class tend to communicate at the same level of decorum as far as grammar, vocabulary, pronunciation, etc., are concerned. Despite this kind of linguistic determinism, however, the occasional cogency and profane eloquence of a Mauricia contrast sharply with the incomprehensible monologues transcribed for Izquierdo. See, for example, pages *109–110*.

of Fortunata—like shapes gradually recalled from a nebulous dream—Maxi, doña Lupe, and even *Papitos* herself began to be visible. They invaded her first as if they were specters but then became real with life, body, and voice.

We cannot help being reminded of Galdós' description in his *Memorias* of his return to the half-finished novel!

Mention of the cloying, honeymoon baby talk reminds us of Galdós' unremitting attention to that sector of the communicative frontier. Examples run from the infantile improprieties of "el falso Pituso" to the Feijóo's last senile mumbling. The most charming are Fortunata's cajoling of her pigeons and her tender consolation of her second baby, "el rey de España," and the most frightening is Maxi's linguistic degeneration during fits of insanity: "His laughter horrified the two ladies, and at the end they couldn't understand a single word of the many that trampled on each other on the way out of his mouth and that were pronounced primitively as if by a child just learning to speak." (*471*) Finally, although not as close to the borders of incoherence, the language of children is also given due attention. The intonations and mispronunciations of Papitos are carefully rendered, as are those of the urchins encountered by Jacinta during her "visita al cuarto estado."[58] In the latter case biological and social handicaps (the children are neighbors of Izquierdo) mingle: "Por el vestido se diferenciaban poco, y menos aún por el lenguaje, que era duro con inflexiones dejosas. 'Chicooo. . . . *miá*

---

[58] Another well-developed example is the dialogue of Barbarita and her little friends in chapter 2 of part 1, which constitutes Galdós' first excursion (in this novel) into oral realism. Galdós' exploration of this oral terrain, as far as I can remember, began with his transcription of the conversation of "el Majito" and his friends in *La desheredada,* a transcription introduced as follows: "Hablaba el lenguaje de su edad, con graciosos solecismos, comiéndose medio idioma y deshuesando el otro medio. Si en el cielo hay algún idioma o dialecto, el oir como le destrozan los ángeles será el mayor regocijo y entretenimiento del Padre Eterno." (*998*) Galdós' somewhat less sentimental approach to the problem in *Fortunata y Jacinta* as well as his effort at phonetic reproduction (not just words but sound) coincide with Antonio Machado y Alvarez' observations on juvenile language in his articles on 'El folklore del niño," which appeared in the 1880s in the *Revista de España.* The earliest example I have seen in Spanish ("la niña de nuef años" speaks like a "juglar") occurs in the *Lisandro y Roselia* of Sancho de Muñón, ed. J. López Barbadillo, Madrid, 1918, p. 114.

este. . . . Que te rompo la cara. . . . ¿sabeees . . . ?' "[59] (*99–100*)
In such transcriptions as these the sensation of pointlessness and
loudness—Guillén's "gritos que deben ser diálogos"—is reminiscent
of the frontier of speech—sheer noise—with which we began.[60] The
multiple enclosures surrounding Galdós' oral world once again make
us conscious of its thematic and technical self-consciousness.[61]

In addition to the situational, social, and biological boundaries
just discussed, the moment-to-moment feelings of the speakers frequently incapacitate them verbally. In states of excitement or passion, communication is interrupted. Maxi, in particular, although
at times glib, is speechless at climactic moments. When Fortunata
at long last offers her love to him (if he murders Juanito and
Aurora!), "Maxi, stupified and mute, looked at her, and after a
moment his eyes filled with tears. . . . He was literally melting. He
tried to speak, and he couldn't. He sounded as if he were gargling."[62]

---

[59] "They were dressed in more or less the same way, but they were even
more identical in their language, which was harsh with dragged-out intonations. 'Bud*deee*. . . . Look at him. . . . I'll knock your block off. . . .
Watch *iiit!*'"

[60] Ultimately the novel as a whole is enclosed in the equally profound yet
radically heterogeneous silences of the womb and the coffin. The individual
pages are, however, as it were, framed in noise: the screaming children, the
mewing kittens, the bells, and the rest. Even in dreams, particularly that of
Fortunata which accompanies the "pícara idea," deafening sound effects are
vivid: "Como el pianito sigue tocando y los carreteros blasfemando, ambos
tienen que alzar la voz para hacerse oir." And when she wakes up, the
shouting is converted into "la voz de doña Lupe [que] ensordece la casa
riñendo a Papitos." (*410*)

[61] One frontier Galdós neglects to explore in depth in *Fortunata y Jacinta*
is the Spanish of foreigners (always excepting the Gallicisms of Aurora
Samaniego). The only two examples I have noticed are the few words of
the drunken Englishman in the hotel in Seville and Guillermina's even
briefer miming of d. Amadeo's "erre": "Mando que dieran seis mil *gueales.*"
(*78*) It is a lack he was amply to make up for in *Misericordia.* R. Ricard
comments on Galdós' description of the peculiar Spanish of Gibraltar. *Aspects
de Galdós,* p. 83.

[62] In the same way, Jacinta, when overcome by her "rabia de paloma"
after overhearing Fortunata's exposition of her "pícara idea," ". . . no
podía hablar . . . , se ahogaba. Tuvo que hacer como que escupía las palabras
para poder decir con gritos intermitentes: "Bribona . . . , infame. . . .'"
(*407*) A complete inventory of such cases of momentary incapacity for speech
would be very long indeed. They are obviously complementary to the prev-
alence of direct dialogue.

(525) If the speaker is not completely silenced by an uncontrollable surge of feeling, his speech is often reduced in volume: thus, the "ahilada voz" (tremulous and falsetto) of Maxi after being beaten by Juanito, recalling those of don Quijote ("tono afeminado y doliente") and Sancho ("voz enferma y lastimada") after their encounter with the Yangüeses. Thus, too, that of Fortunata when she replies "ténuemente" to the harsh questioning of Nicolás in the same chapter.

On other occasions, however, an excess of passion results in animal-like vocal metamorphoses, and the introductory verb "dice" is replaced by "ruge," "muge," "gruñe," and "brama." One step more and words themselves are replaced by "berridos," "chillidos," "aullidos," or even "ronquidos . . . cual monólogo de un cerdo." (506) Although it may seem reasonable to interpret these cries, grunts, and roars as testimony of Galdós' continued interest in the art of the creator of *La Bête humaine,* the truth is that, with the exception of Izquierdo, most instances of this sort correspond to momentary passions or aberrations, rather than resulting from heredity or environment. The point is, not to shock the reader with a revelation of what human life is really like, but to show by contrast the normal identity of speech and consciousness.

The ultimate frontier of language in this sense must then be death, for sleep is by definition a mere parenthesis and in some cases (for example, Jacinta's baby talk during her dream at the opera) not without words. As Casalduero notes, *Fortunata y Jacinta* is among other things a latter-day *Danza de la muerte* with recurrent mortality symbols as well as many actual funerals. We must not forget, however, that in the most vivid death scenes dying is portrayed as a termination of speech.[63] Mauricia's final oaths seem to emerge "del hueco de un cántaro muy hondo y sonaban como lejos."[64] (393) And Moreno Isla, cut off in the middle of one of

[63] F. Ruiz Ramón comments briefly on the theme of silence as death in *Tres personajes galdosianos,* p. 170. When Tsvetan Todorov (unaware that he is mimicking Unamuno) remarks that in the *Arabian Nights* "absence of narration" is death, he makes an ingenious critical point, which does not apply to the agony of Galdós' creatures. *Littérature et signification,* Paris, 1967, p. 86. Cited by Culler, *Structuralist Poetics,* p. 109–110.

[64] As described by doña Lupe. Her second version, "una voz que parecía venir por un tubo, del sótano de la casa" (393), is equally vivid.

his interminable interior monologues, above all suffers the terrible imposition of speechlessness:

> "All right then, I'll come back in April, and I'm sure that by then . . ."
>
> He had to hold himself rigid, because from the center of his body up through his chest he felt an immense swelling rising towards his throat. It was like a wave, and it wouldn't let him breathe. He stretched out his arm as if it were a gesture accompanying an exclamation, but the exclamation—perhaps an expression of anguish or perhaps a cry for help—could not make its way past his lips. The wave grew and grew; he felt it inundate his throat and then grow some more. Now he was blind. He put both hands on the edge of the table and, dropping his head, let it rest on them with a muffled groan. There he let himself stay, immobile, silenced. (*461*)

I assume it is not necessary to print the relevant words and phrases in italics in order to make apparent Galdós' careful use of contrast in order to prepare us for the climactic death scene of Fortunata.

Among all the things that here have been and will be said (along with the many others that could and should be said), about this "Final," only its oral nature now concerns us, by which I mean Fortunata's (and our) acute anguish at her loss of speech. After pardoning Juanito by gestures, "her tired efforts to breathe were indicative of her desire to conquer the physical impediments that hampered her speech." But doña Guillermina reassures her:

> "You don't have to say anything . . . just answer with a nod of your head. Do you forgive Aurora? . . ." The dying woman moved her head in a way that could be interpreted as affirmative, but half-heartedly, as if her soul were not entirely convinced.
>
> "Make it clearer."
>
> Fortunata tried again a little more emphatically, and tears came to her eyes.
>
> "That's the way."
>
> Then the face of unfortunate Señora de Rubín began to glow as if she were in a state of poetic inspiration or religious ecstasy,

and, having gained incredible mastery over her state of prostration, she found the energy and the vocabulary to say the following: "Me too . . . Didn't you know? . . . I'm an angel . . ." She tried to say something else but her words were once more unintelligible . . .

Afterwards Fortunata manages to stammer "soy ángel" twice more, but then her voice fades away forever: "¿Había dicho algo? Sí, pero Nones no pudo enterarse." (*540–541*)

What we have just listened to is the breaking of the link between consciousness and consciousness. The frail bridge of words we live by has collapsed, and, as Hamlet remarked on a similar occasion, "the rest is silence." Such is the natural and necessary end of the gigantic oral edifice called *Fortunata y Jacinta,* a title that in its very duality seems about to speak,[65] even though the "dos casadas," each so profoundly concerned with the other, actually exchange no more than a few words. But if ended, this one human voice is not necessarily defeated. These final fragments of speech at the very frontier of mortality, rather than constituting a meaningless rupture (as in the case of Moreno Isla), are charged with all that has been said since the by now appropriately "remote" opening sentence. What Fortunata cannot say and what she manages to say validates and gives a sense of significant completion to all we have read and heard.

Speech and Salvation

At this point we may return to the fastidious younger generation, who did not like either to eat "garbanzos" or to read the prose of those who did, although some of them (including Aleixandre and García Lorca) seem secretly to have suffered from and surrendered themselves voluptuously to an addiction to Galdós contracted while still children.[66] On the basis of the foregoing discussion, their fun-

---

[65] The two popular expressions most frequently used for speaking in the novel are "soltar la palabra" and "pegar la hebra." Each corresponds to a fundamental oral mode: to let the word fly like an arrow towards the listener, or to involve (literally "weave in") him or her in the web of a conversation.

[66] "Alguna vez he contado la sensación de gozo y sorpresa que tuvimos cuando, almorzando un día en una tabernilla madrileña con Federico García

damental objection to his novels may now be expressed interroga-
tively. Is not language and particularly topical language a variety
of determinism fully as implacable as that proposed by the Naturalists? And are not characters who speak it as irremediably "agar-
banzados" (Galdós used the adjective in *La de los tristes destinos*
(*641*) to describe Isabel II in her last years) as their author was ac-
cused of being? My answer, more fervently given now, is the same
as it was before. Words, however topical, may be ready-made and
given to us by society, but they are not necessarily inflexible molds
for consciousness. They are, instead, always capable of being rede-
fined and refreshed in appropriate situations and in the mouths and
minds of appropriate speakers. They are capable of salvation.

The decisive example of this capability in *Fortunata y Jacinta* is
the expression "un rasgo," literally a generous or brave act, which
because of its lack of self-interest and its spontaneity represents an
authentically noble "trait" of character. As used in the course of
the narrative, however, it is a commonplace infected with all the
falseness, triteness, and hollowness of frequent journalistic and theatrical usage. It is surely not accidental that the first speaker to avail
himself of the expression should be Juanito Santa Cruz,[67] whose
participation in a minor historical event, "la noche de San Daniel,"
triggered by Castelar's attack on the Queen in an aggressively sarcastic article entitled "El rasgo," constitutes the opening of the
novel.[68] In attempting to retrieve his reputation in the eyes of

---

Lorca, nos descubrimos ambos admiradores apasionados de Galdós ¡en
aquell época! y amigos 'vividos' y sin falla desde chicos de Jacinta, de la
Peri, de Orozco, del León de Albrit." Vicente Aleixandre, "Revisión de
Galdós," *Ins,* 82, 1952, p. 3. In 1935 Lorca was to declare that "aquel hombre
maravilloso . . . tenía la voz más verdadera y profunda de España." *Obras
completas,* ed., Arturo del Hoyo, Madrid, 1960, p. 1737.

[67] Actually Galdós uses it first in a passage of indirect dialogue reflecting
doña Lupe's surprise at her nephew's rebellion. In her mind it is merely the
appropriate commonplace.

[68] In an editorial so entitled in *La Democracia,* Castelar exposed the
Queen's false generosity in ceding her royal patrimony to the state with
limitations "las cuales convertían el 'rasgo' de la reina en beneficio pecuniario
suyo." *Diccionario de historia de España,* Madrid, 1952, vol. 1, p. 602. The
results were that, along with the "rector," Castelar was deprived of his chair
in the university; a number of colleagues resigned in protest; and student
agitation was violently suppressed on the aforesaid "noche" (10 April 1865).

Jacinta (who has just learned of his renewed affair with Fortunata), he seeks to portray his actions in a favorable light and remarks to himself: "Aquí me viene bien un rasgo." (313) Instead of excusing himself, he will show Jacinta how nobly he had behaved in "rescuing" Fortunata!

Juanito's commonplace cynicism is later matched by Feijóo's well-meant but patronizing course in "filosofía práctica" during which, on several occasions, he warns Fortunata against her propensity for "rasgos." His at once rational and affectionate sarcasm is audible in the word: "Conque déjese usted de *rasgos* si no quiere que la silbe porque esas simplezas no se ven más ya que en las comedias malas." (327) Just as Castelar had found in the overtones of prevarication and pompous exaggeration that had adhered to the expression a means of unmasking the hypocritical generosity of "la reina castiza," so Feijóo uses them to educate Fortunata. But at the end, when she has given her son to Jacinta and doña Guillermina describes her act as "un rasgo feliz y cristiano," the little word suddenly is cleansed and recovers its full meaning. Like the heroine herself, the topic is saved at the moment of oral culmination. Both the Naturalistic determinism that Zola felt was built into language and the devaluation that results from overuse have been transcended.

As Américo Castro pointed out in the indispensable introduction to the Porrúa edition of the *Quijote* mentioned earlier,[69] one way to comprehend the rise of the nineteenth-century novel is in terms of Romantic reading and interpretation of Cervantes. Although previously we attended to the redefinition of heroism and incitation, novelistic language was equally affected by the same reevaluation. For if Cervantes and Fielding undermined chivalric pomposity and social affectation with comic glee, the Romantics, as Roy Harvey Pearce phrases it, wondered instead: "How might language be made to transcend language? Or, how might man break out of the confines of language and see what he must see?"[70] Or in our terms, confronted with the language of a nineteenth-century society that

---

The word is also used ironically several times in chapters 7 and 8 of part 1 of *Halma*.

[69] See chapter 6, note 15.

[70] "The Burden of Romanticism: Toward the New Poetry," *Iowa Review*, 2, 1971, p. 110.

was "absolument usée,—pire qu'usée,—abrutie et goulue,"[71] how and what to write? The answers of Flaubert and Baudelaire to these seemingly unanswerable questions are poetically superb but ultimately as despairing and ironical as Clarín's. But Galdós, a non-believer, nevertheless allowed Fortunata's consciousness of salvation —for him a metaphor—to answer for him. If she (like Benina, who was to come later) can see what she must see, be whom she must be, do what she must do, and say what she must say. . . .

In order to sense the mystery that Galdós wants us to sense, it is essential to observe that the inspiration that led to Fortunata's "rasgo" came to her "cuando estaba sin habla." (537) As we have seen, the oral structure of the novel is founded on the continuing confrontation of spoken language not just with silence (as in the *Romancero* or Machado's "Palacio buen amigo")[72] but above all with nonlanguage or substitute language. By the latter I mean Galdós' special attention to regions (human situations as well as social milieux) within which speech is either impotent or impossible. Thus, his constant probing of the frontiers of expression and communication, and thus, too, his delineation of characters known through speech who, nevertheless, when they are most authentically themselves, live in dreams and visions. Or die climactically in a state of mute inspiration. As a nineteenth-century novel in the Cervantine tradition, the theme of *Fortunata y Jacinta* is necessarily that of the individual who strives to know himself and be himself in alien social and stylistic contexts. Every novelist and novel has to develop this theme in his own way, and in the present case the alien stylistic context is spoken language, the language of commonplaces. Thus, when Fortunata achieves personal plenitude in the speechlessness of dying ("cuando estaba sin habla"), all of our accumulated reading-listening experience (intensified by trying to

---

[71] From Baudelaire's essay on *Madame Bovary. L'Art romantique,* in *Oeuvres complètes,* Paris, 1868, vol. 2, p. 413. Roger Kempf comments: "Rien de plus excitant que la banalité . . . rien de plus fertile. Curieusement, le lieu commun rapporte en fonction de son indigence; mais, pour decoller le néant, il oblige a la prouesse. C'est en ce sens que Baudelaire étudie le matériau et l'avènement de *Madame Bovary.*" *Dandies, Baudelaire et Cie,* pp. 67–68.

[72] See Claudio Guillén, "Stylistics of Silence," in *Literature as System,* Princeton, 1971, pp. 221–279.

listen to what we cannot hear) also reaches its plenitude. As a structuralist might say it, Galdós employs speechlessness ("le degré zero" of speech) as a means of providing language with its maximum possibility of functioning.

CHAPTER X

The Art of Genesis

The Birth of a Society

In his 1897 address to the Royal Academy Galdós went out of his way to refute a notion of realism that might well be described today as "socialist": "el arte se avalora sólo con dar a los seres imaginarios vida más humana que social."[1] Nevertheless, as we have seen, his public had been nourished by a creative diet of contextuality and, as a result, believed unquestioningly that "to give human life to imaginary beings" required their prior situation in a social and historical milieu. And now they were going to get more than they needed or ever had been given before. Unlike a Racine concerned more with the verity than the reality of ancient Athens or a Cervantes who laughed at "la Mancha" as a sort of negative "environment" and demanded gratitude from his readers for *not* describing its households, Galdós begins his definitive novel with the construction of an ironically enormous world of streets, houses, professions, classes, current events, and above all conversation and noises. Will Rogers' movie version of *The Connecticut Yankee* begins with the operation of an acoustic sensor capable of amplifying and making audible the residual sound waves of Camelot; but we need no such science fiction device for recapturing the 1880s in Madrid. Part 1 of *Fortunata y Jacinta* is a perfect time machine, perhaps the most complex and detailed world ever to be constructed within the frontiers of a single novel. And once it was completed, Galdós, in spite of his intention to subvert historicism, realism, and Naturalism, nevertheless must have experienced a sense of satisfaction comparable to that of Balzac when in the "Avant-propos" he claimed to have preserved the France he knew in a fashion never

[1] *Ensayos,* ed. Bonet, p. 180.

before achieved or even attempted by any past historian for any culture or period.

As we pointed out, however, in the case of *Fortunata y Jacinta* the *imitatio mundi* is at once too big and too trivial to be taken seriously. Like Stendhal, Tolstoy, and Dickens, Galdós was primarily concerned with "vida más humana que social." The immense diorama of bourgeois Madrid may be understood as the milieu of Jacinta's novel, but for the life "history" of the other titular "casada," it is only an ironical overture. And, indeed, as we look back over the completed reading experience, we perceive that all we are told in part 1 was less designed to construct an urban model than to provide a point of departure for a network of interlaced Stendhalian "chemins" running their common biological course from birth to death. Birth is the major happening of the beginning, just as death (Mauricia la Dura, Feijóo, Moreno Isla, and Fortunata) is the major happening of the closing chapters. That moment of mortal contemplation at the end of part 3 during which Fortunata from the "esplanada del Portillo de Gilimón" sees a panoramic Madrid landscape accentuated by several simultaneous funeral processions and at the same time hears "la campana de San Justo que anunciaba cadáver" (*411–412*) is moving both in itself and as a preparation for what is to come.

As we have seen, Casalduero (like Albert Béguin discussing *Les Splendeurs et misères des courtisanes*)[2] interprets this aspect of the novel as a nineteenth-century Dance of Death and comments perceptively on this and other recurrent emblems of human annihilation.[3] He fails to comment, however, on the complementary role played by biological replacement, the provision of new lives for the mortal pilgrimage. Galdós, of course, does not look on the way of all flesh with the glee, at once subversive and didactic, of the poets of the fifteenth century. Rather he contemplates it, as we see and hear beside the cradles and deathbeds of the principal characters, with the relentless aplomb of the experienced "naturalist" in the older sense of the word. The borrowed literary technique (which

[2] *Balzac lu et relu,* Paris, 1965, p. 174. For Galdós' slightly morbid fascination with death, cemeteries, and funeral ceremonies see the November 1886 article in Shoemaker, *Cartas,* pp. 202–210.

[3] *Vida y obra,* p. 109.

had produced the grotesque and Zolaesque "Final de otra novela") has been transmuted into serene observation of the human condition.

Serenity, on the other hand, need not be heartless. Neither Galdós nor Cervantes confirms Ortega's vision of a "dehumanized" artist rendering a death scene.[4] Neither removes himself from shared mortality or from the pity and terror that it awakens in us all. Even Estupiñá, the flattest, the most comically Dickensian, and therefore the most ostensibly invulnerable of all the characters, is our brother. When Galdós tells us that on the day before Christmas in 1873 he beats, not his "pious breast," but "la caja del tórax" (136), we suddenly realize that, in spite of his historical durability and his resemblance to a timeless "estampa de Rossini," he too is a fragile mechanism of flesh and bone. He, too, has emerged from a womb and is destined for a grave.

But for now we are concerned only with the beginning of mortality. In part 1 in addition to the birth of Juanito Santa Cruz, Galdós narrates in greater or lesser detail the entrance into the world of his first son, his mother, his sixteen brothers-in-law and sisters-in-law, the innumerable progeny of "el cuarto estado," and a family of cats.[5] It would almost seem that the authentic heroine of this lengthy overture is neither Jacinta nor Fortunata but doña Isabel Cordero, whose incessant fecundity makes the former's sterility all the harder to bear. In fact, Galdós describes the daughter of our old friend don Benigno, "el heroe de Boteros," in just such epic terms, mingling admiration and pity with irony. During her "campaña prolífica desde el 38 al 60," each birth is accompanied by a well-known historical event. The newly born infants, Galdós implies by this not unfamiliar technique of representational rapprochement,[6] are in their own right genuine "episodios nacionales."

---

[4] "La deshumanización del arte," in *Obras,* vol. 3, pp. 360–363.

[5] The feline motherhood instinct, which leads Jacinta to demand frantically the rescue of the kittens, is alluded to later on by Juanito in connection with her desire to adopt "el Pitusín": "Estás como las gatas paridas, escondiéndo las crías hoy aquí, mañana allá." (149) A metaphorical contrast with Fortunata's birdlike nature is, thus, hinted at.

[6] A technique that had been serious and central from *La Fontana* through *La desheredada* is now ironical and tangential, which confirms our belief that *Fortunata y Jacinta* is not only *not* a "political novel," but rather an "answer" to Galdós' political novels.

And after the arduous campaign is over, the haggard and spent mother devotes equivalent brio to her "combate social": the bringing up and marrying off of her seven surviving—and undowried—daughters. Thus, doña Isabel, unlike her royal namesake,[7] represents the daily heroism of Spanish womanhood, and the product of such stamina and biological prowess as hers is nothing less than the society of Madrid.

As a result the first fourth of the novel may be understood not only as a critique of Restoration history and society but also as a book of genesis. The linear series of Biblical "begats" takes on a social and horizontal dimension when Galdós describes a family tree for the entire city: "The friends and relations of the Santa Cruz and Arnaiz families can be considered an example of that happy jumble of social classes; but where is the hero who would be brave enough to dare to try to derive statistics from the branches of that enormous and labyrinthine genealogical tree? In fact, it is really more like an ivy covered wall than a tree with shoots that climb up and down and get lost in the dense foliage." (60) The answer to the question is, of course, the narrator himself, who unrelentingly provides us with more details than we want to know or can possibly remember regarding the wealth, the avocations, and the relationships of the Arnaiz, the Samaniegos, the Morenos, the Trujillos, and other branches of the tree. I say the narrator and not the author, because, as we have seen in connection with the adjective "dichosa" (in the complacent phrase "dichosa confusión de todas las clases"), the latter would hardly have agreed that Restoration society could be defined as a *"feliz* revoltijo de todas las clases sociales."

To the question of why Galdós exploits his fictional narrator's reportorial verbosity and allows him to supply so many apparently

[7] Galdós underlines the moral contrast between the two "tocayas" by contrasting the one's childbearing to the historical events of the other's reign and, above all, by having Isabel Cordero's death coincide with the assassination of Prim, her namesake's heroic antagonist. It should also be noted that, although Galdós specifies the relationship of Isabel and her father, "el heroe de Boteros," (". . . casó Gumersindo con Isabel Cordero, hija de don Benigno Cordero . . .") (28), in Los apostólicos, where the Cordero family is enumerated, the only daughter mentioned is an Elena, grown up and married. The point is that Galdós intentionally invented for her the "heroic" lineage of which she is so worthy. The contrast with the blander bourgeois "royalty" of the Santa Cruz is not insisted upon but is nevertheless apparent.

unnecessary and seemingly endless "pormenores," several answers have been and will be proposed. Among them, one that is obvious, reasonable, and pertinent to our present concerns is that Galdós wants us to realize that the human collectivity called Madrid and not urban topography or abstract social categories constitutes the living body both of the city and the novel. A work that is to end with the grafting of the Izquierdos onto the stem of the Santa Cruz begins with an appropriate allegory af alliance and fecundity, the intricate and endless burgeoning of the gigantic human tree from which the individual characters have sprouted and from which they will fall with Homeric inevitability ("old leaves cast on the ground by wind") and be replaced.[8] When Moreno Isla dies, the same emblem is recalled as a simultaneous image of birth and death: "The stem that attached him to humanity was broken. The completely withered leaf, which had only been held in place by the thinnest of fibers, now fell from the great tree. The tree with its immense branches felt nothing. Here and there at the same time many other useless leaves were falling; but the next morning's sun would shine on innumerable new and fresh buds." (461) The wealth of individual adventures and experiences, which (accompanied by historical time) constitute the sequence of the narrative, are supported novelistically by our underlying awareness of an endless and seamless biological and social "intrahistory," as Unamuno would have called it.

In addition to the arboreal allegory,[9] which remains with us subconsciously as we read, daily prayer is a recurrent recognition of the continuity of human endings and beginnings. It is particularly in their repetition of the *Ave Maria* that the inhabitants (again both of Madrid and the novel) remind themselves of the eternal mystery of procreation. Galdós himself, however, is sardonic rather than pious

[8] "Very like leaves upon this earth are the generations of men— / old leaves cast on the ground by wind, young leaves / the greening forest bears when spring comes in. / So mortals pass; one generation flowers / even as another dies away." *Iliad,* trans. Robert Fitzgerald, Garden City, N. Y., p. 146.

[9] The image is age old, but Galdós' sociological version is more original than most. For a comparable example of poetic renovation of the figure "family tree," see Lope's ironical comparison of human reproduction and the grafting of fruit trees. *La buena guarda,* Act 3, lines 136–175.

when he transcribes the devotions of Barbarita and Estupiñá, in the course of which reverence for the heavenly origin of life is interrupted by whispered comments on the way it is sustained three times a day on earth:

> La señora rezaba en voz baja, moviendo los labios. Plácido tenía que decirle muchas cosas y entrecortaba su rezo para irlas desembuchando. "Va a salir la de don Germán de la capilla de los Dolores . . . Hoy reciben congrío en la casa de Martínez; me han enseñado los despachos de Laredo . . . llena eres de gracia; el señor es contigo . . . coliflor no hay, porque no han venido los arrieros de Villaviciosa por estar perdidos los caminos . . . ¡Con estas malditas aguas! . . . Y bendito es el fruto de tu vientre, Jesús . . ."[10] (73)

Not only does Galdós employ his mastery of the art of interruption to allow us to overhear the grotesque mixture of spiritual and material values that characterized his Madrid even more than Balzac's Paris in spite of a comparable observation in La Maison Nucingen,[11] but also he suggests the thematic pertinence of the prayer of the Annunciation as a daily litany of fecundity.

But once again, as in the case of speech and its several varieties of impossibility, it is Jacinta's awareness of her own sterility and her frustrated maternal incitation that most effectively and pathetically communicate the opening theme.[12] Who can forget her frenzied

---

[10] "The lady was praying in a low voice, moving her lips visibly. Plácido had many things to tell her and from time to time broke into the prayer in order to get them off his chest.

'Don Germán's wife is just coming out of the Chapel of Our Lady of Sorrows. . . . Today there's going to be a shipment of fresh conger eel at Martínez, the fish monger; they just showed me the bill of lading from Laredo . . . full of grace; the Lord is with thee. . . . There's no cauliflower at all in the market, because the drovers from Villaviciosa can't make it over the roads. . . . with all the cursed rain we've been having . . . Blessed is the fruit of thy womb, Jesus . . .'"

[11] "Sur cent personnes qui rendent les derniers devoirs à un pauvre diable de mort, quatre-vingt-dix-neuf parlent d'affairs et de plaisirs en pleine église." Comédie, vol. 5, p. 620.

[12] In my opinion Galdós agrees with Juanito's description of a hypothetical novel presenting such a problem as irredeemably sentimental. As we remember, the latter accuses his wife of having, in Cervantine language, "calentado la cabeza de Barbarita" and then concludes: "como historia el

urge to rescue the drowning kittens, or her spiritually painful descent into the teeming biological hell (or heaven) of "el cuarto estado"? As Galdós points out:

> *She paid exclusive attention* to the children she kept on encountering one after another. The lady called Santa Cruz was amazed that there were so many mothers in that part of town, since every time she took a step it seemed that she would run across one carrying a baby snugly wrapped in the end of her shawl. The only part of these future citizens that one could see was the head looking over its mother's shoulder. Some were looking backwards, exhibiting a round little face encircled by a bonnet, bright eyes, and a gurgle for each passer-by. Others scowled, like people already disillusioned at the very beginning of life. Jacinta also saw not just one but two or three on their way to the cemetery. She thought their waxen faces looked tranquil inside the little coffin, which some fellow was carrying carelessly on his shoulder as if it were a gun. (Italics mine.) (*99*)

After this a seemingly endless procession of similar intimations of nativity continues to torment her. For example, when she hears a hoarse song sung by a blind child, the words begin: "A Pepa la gitanilla, cuando la parió su madre . . ." (*114*) Or again when she sees a group of women, the one she most envies "tenía cinco hijos y vísperas de lo que daba fe el promontorio que le alzaba las faldas media vara del suelo." (*119*) All aspects of the unfamiliar milieu seem to have conspired for the purpose of reminding Jacinta of the motherhood that has been denied her.

Jacinta's obsession with childbearing—the unique source of novelistic movement forward prior to the appearance of Maxi and Fortunata—is also expressed in "alucinaciones y desvaríos": "Some nights just after falling asleep, she would feel a warm mouth on one of her nipples intent on nursing. The licking tongue would wake her up with a start, leaving her with the tragic knowledge

---

caso es falso, como novela es cursi." (*145*) Galdós, perversely using Juanito as his spokesman, predicts that only Fortunata's exalted incitation can save "esa maldita novela del niño encontrado." Jacinta's mother-cat maternal instincts are at once too shortsighted and too pathetic.

that it wasn't true. Then she would sigh loudly, and her husband would ask from the other bed, 'What's wrong, little girl? Another nightmare?' " (*86*) Such oneiric revelations of interiority are, as we know, frequent in the "novelas contemporáneas," but *Fortunata y Jacinta* stands out among them for its remarkable proto-Freudian dream descriptions, one of which occurs while Jacinta drowses during a performance of Wagner. It is too long for full citation here, but since it is crucial for comprehension of the human contrast of the titular rivals, my readers are urgently advised to reread it in the text.[13]

The central figure of the dream is an homunculus, a "niño-hombre," resembling Juanito, who appears to Jacinta in the white satin environment (like her own family, as well as the Santa Cruz, she, too, lives in a world of cloth) of an enormous layette:

> Jacinta was conscious of being in a place that was not her house but at the same time was. . . . It was all lined with white satin with embroidered flowers exactly like the material she and Barbarita had looked at in Sobrino's shop the day before. . . . She was seated on an ottoman, and a lovely baby boy was trying to climb on her lap; he rubbed her face at first, but then he put his hand into her bosom. "No, no, stop that. . . . that's stinky. . . . it'll make you sick. . . . We'll give it to the cat." But the boy persisted. He had nothing on but a chemise of chambray, and his smooth skin rubbed against the silk peignoir of his mother. (*87*)

The child's later refusal of her surrendered bosom and conversion into a plaster image indicates the extent to which frustrated sexual desire for Jacinta, as for Yerma, some of whose fantasies are also characterized by cloth imagery, is maternal. How different is this expensively upholstered nightmare from the aggressively phallic dreams of her rival, which will be considered in a later chapter. For the daughter of doña Isabel Cordero motherhood and not sex is the

[13] As we shall see, instead of satin and infantile intimacies, Fortunata dreams of undeniably phallic symbols. The contrast of the two is also implicit in Galdós' description of Jacinta's virginal timidity on her wedding night ("aquel frío invencible y aquella pavorosa expectación que la hacían estremecer') (*47*) as against Fortunata's reaction to Juanito's initial proposition ("La respuesta fué coger el mantón y decirme: 'vamos'"). (*51*)

only authentic fulfillment. In spite of, or perhaps because of, her Virgin-like compassion, Jacinta is incapable not just of sharing but even of understanding Fortunata's passion.

Although Jacinta's incitation is less explosive than that of Fortunata and although it leads her to coddle her husband in infantile language (here reality imitates dreaming), which is cloying to readers whose appetite for novels exposes them to transcription of her "vida intima," it is nonetheless authentic. It impels her to descend into the hell of the "cuarto estado," and at the same time it torments her with the empty heaven of the nursery.[14] Galdós, seem-

[14] Although comparison of the "cuarto estado" with Hell is not overt, Galdós' intentions are nonetheless obvious. Isidora Rufete's "abismo" (or "voraginoso laberinto de las calles") first appears to Jacinta as a kind of "infierno comercial" (the lower depths of the dry-goods trade) where brilliant colored cloth (as opposed to her own "pardessus color de pasa") is a form of torture, where the "horteras" "braceaban, como si nadaban en un mar de pañuelos," and where "juegos de calzón y camisas de bayeta parecían personajes de azufre." (99) Later it becomes an "infierno social" where poor children die in batches and are carried carelessly "camino del cementerio" with waxen faces, while those who are alive paint themselves to resemble "micos, diablillos, o engendros infernales." (102) It is also appropriately enough an "infierno oral," where sounds (cries, quarrels, insults, shrill songs, and harsh popular accents) torment the ear with their "bulla infernal" (105), and an "inferno zolaesco" ("Una puerta sí y otra no, taberna. De aquí salen todos los crímenes)." (99) Among the most recognizable and specific references are the "pucheros armados sobre las ascuas" that are visible in certain "círculos" (101); the "espectros" on the walls of Ido's abode; his collection of outdated almanacs, which are "los años muertos"; and the jaded joke, which converts his family into condemned "luteranos," reminding us of Quevedo's treatment of Luther. In general it can be said that the word play that is used in this section so repeatedly, as my colleague Raimundo Lida suggested, reminds us far more of the *Sueños* than of the *Divine Comedy*. On the other hand, the resemblance of doña Guillermina's role as guide to that of Virgil is obvious. Moreover, unlike Quevedo, Galdós' intention is not to fabricate an infernal frame for rhetorical self-display and social satire. As the title of the chapter indicates, Jacinta undertakes nothing less than a mythological "viaje" to the underworld, a self-testing by means of which she seeks, in vain, for personal salvation. The passage may also be compared to Balzac's famous description (at the beginning of *La Fille aux yeux d'or*) of Paris: "Peu de mots sufriront pour justifier physiologiquement la teinte presque infernale des figures parisiennes, car ce n'est past pour plaisantérie que Paris a été nommé un enfer. Tenez ce mot pour vrai. Là tout fume, tout brûle, tout brille, tout bouillonne, tout flambe, s'évapore, s'éteint, réallume, étincelle, pétille et se consume." *Comédie,* vol. 5, p. 255. What Galdós does, then, is to adapt Balzac's vision of the metropolis as Hell and combine it to

ingly affected by Jacinta's obsession, abandons irony for tenderness (we have already noticed the resemblance to the paintings of Zola's friend, Renoir) when he describes the first bath of the spurious "Pituso":

> The torture finally came to an end, and the infant was wrapped in an enormous bath towel. Jacinta drew him to her bosom, informing him that now he really was handsome. The warmth soothed him; his screams changed to sobs; and his cleanliness, along with his physical reaction [to the unprecedented bath], illumined his face, tinting it with that special dawn-pink color children have when they emerge from the water. They rubbed him dry, and his shapely arms and his perfectly formed body caused one admiring exclamation after another. (*135*)

Although, as just remarked, Jacinta's obsession with motherhood is comparable to that of Yerma, the two women differ in one respect. In the one case it is the baby that is longed for, and in the other it is fertility. For the wife of Juanito the possession and nurture of an infant, whether by birth or by adoption, is what really matters.[15] Severiana, whose offspring are all stillborn (Galdós relentlessly explores every biological possibility), explains to Jacinta the solace she finds in her niece, the abandoned daughter of Mauricia la Dura. She loves the little girl, she says, "como si la hubiese parido." The avowal is perfectly comprehensible to Jacinta, willing as she is to accept either physical discomfort or social embarrassment in exchange for just such felicity. To bear or at least to bring up a child is for the daughter of doña Isabel Cordero the ultimate good, the caress and palpitation of life in a world of cloth and brick.

---

the well-known tradition of the Orphic voyage. As we shall see, within the frontiers of this novel Jacinta's journey is balanced structurally against Fortunata's oneiric exploration of her unconscious conceived of as a midnight city, an exploration from which she returns humanly triumphant and all the more sure of her "pícara idea."

[15] The verb "criar" is central to the occupation and preoccupation of many of the characters we meet in part 1: Barbarita "criaba a Jacinta para nuera" (*45*); Fortunata "criaba los palomos a sus pechos" (*60*); doña Guillermina does the same for her "veintitres pequeñuelos de Dios" (*77*); Jacinta tells Izquierdo "que usted no . . . puede criar ni educar al *Pituso*," and he answers, "colóqueme a mí y yo lo criaré" (*117*); etc.

Thus, aside from the intentional contrast of her incitation with that of Fortunata, society, Galdós seems also to be saying, may be studied more or less profoundly by novelists and sociologists and guided more or less intelligently by politicians, but the soil from which it grows is maternity.

The Birth of a Prince

Although a professional bachelor, in comments such as that just indicated Galdós reveals the extent to which he shared in his culture's worship of babies and children. Moreover, in addition to comprehending his patriarchal (and matriarchal) countrymen, as a recent disciple of Zola he was Naturalistically preoccupied with the theme of infantile innocence as contrasted to the adult guilt that results from social infection. In *Fortunata y Jacinta*, accordingly, the first serious question to be posed is, simply, to what avail the marvel of infancy if the grown-up product is stunted or worthless? The birth and upbringing of Juanito Santa Cruz, an adorable baby (in everyone's opinion), a prodigious child (in the eyes of his mother), and a prince of a fellow (according to his comrades), is, thus, the crucial case history of this book of genesis. And, as we study it, we come to admire more and more the irony with which Galdós unravels the heroic mantle, which readers of popular fiction had been trained to wrap around male protagonists and which Restoration society instinctively wrapped around scions of wealthy families. The rhetorical strategy becomes far more interesting than the human end product. Once stripped, like the Emperor in the fairy tale, Juanito is not even conspicuously perverse like his immediate predecessor, José María Bueno de Guzmán; he is a nonentity.

Instead of the uninteresting, fictional human being, let us now consider the royal image, the Sartrian "être pour autrui," which justifies Juanito in his own eyes (as well as in those of his admirers) and which he quite understandably devotes his life to cherishing. From the point of view of popular literature, the heir of don Baldomero II is, of course, a prince, who descends from his "highness" into Fortunata's life imbued with all the marvel and mystery with which Rodolphe impressed Fleur-de-Marie in *Les Mystères de Paris*. As Pierre-Emmanuel Main points out in his 1977 introductory essay to that novel: "After all, what could have been more banal in the year 1842 than to read a novel about a somber and desperate prince with all the virtues of chivalry who by chance in the course of his errant path meets a pure-hearted prostitute?"[16] In his ironical utilization of this standard fictional pattern, Galdós departs from the practice of Cervantes in the early chapters of part 1 of the *Quijote*. As far as we know, neither Juanito nor Fortunata has read Eugène Sue, and their roles are obviously divergent. By the time Fortunata eventually does become, if not a pure-hearted, at least a healthy-minded prostitute, Juanito's responsibility for her Naturalistic fall has been made perfectly clear. Furthermore, it is poor Maxi and not the handsome prince who proposes to be her "redentor."[17]

Accordingly, I do not propose that Galdós intentionally took advantage of such Romantic expectations on the part of his public in order to conduct it on a guided tour of the spurious realities that lay behind the pretentious social façade of those wealthy bourgeois families that seemed to have usurped the function of royalty. He was more concerned with their distortion of values. Thus, in contrast to Jacinta's authentic worship of children and deep sense of maternal failure, he pinpointed the social concern on the part of the "court," including Estupiñá and doña Guillermina, with providing that fortune with a legitimate heir. As Fortunata preceives at the end, from the point of view of the dehumanized Santa Cruz dynasty (in spite of its exterior bonhommie) her only value as a fellow human being lies in having provided it with a "verídico nieto natural": "I know perfectly well that I can never be accepted by the family, because I am as common as they come and they are the real upper crust; what I want is for it to be perfectly clear—yes, clear to everyone—that their humble servant is the mother of the heir." (*504*) The Santa Cruz pay for an elaborate hearse, but only Estupiñá goes to her funeral.

[16] Eugène Sue, *Les Mystères de Paris,* Paris, 1977, vol. 1, p. 10.

[17] If Galdós was indeed playing intentionally with reader expectations derived from this nineteenth-century, socially committed *Amadís,* his choice of poor Maxi for the role of "redentor" was ironical to the point of cruelty. For as we remember, in *Les Mystères* it is the heroic prince himself who saves Fleur-de-Marie: "Rodolphe sentait qu'il y avait quelque chose de solennel, d'auguste dans cette espèce de rédemption d'une âme arrachée au vice." ibid., p. 94.

Before beginning his career as a novelist, Galdós had commented on the same fundamental change in social estimation in his 1865 "Crónica de Madrid":

The royal court has departed for the summer palace of the Granja . . . but in the vicinity of that court other courts and other thrones have come into being. Alongside our old-fashioned aristocracy founded on [genealogies recorded on] parchment, new aristocracies have arisen. If inherited nobility follows the royal court, the nobility of wealth remains in Madrid. Fashionable stores are still open offering the public their varied merchandise. Luxury and fashion never abdicate, nor are they ever dethroned; their courtiers wait on them every day of the year. (*1516*)

Then, in *La desheredada,* as already noted, Isidora's Romantic imagination had momentarily associated her absent lover, Joaquinito, with the Dauphin, whose mysterious disappearance had entranced generations of fatuous or conniving would-be "desheredados." And now the two strands merge in a dynasty of dry-goods merchants (kings not only in their wealth but in their command of fashion) founded by don Baldomero I, presently prospering under don Baldomero II, and eventually to become the property (but not the business) of the Romantic "Delfín," Juanito.[18] In the novel that title is bestowed on him by his faithful equerry, Estupiñá, and is afterwards emphasized ironically by the narrator. Even a reader imbued with the values of his epoch (and as a result impervious to

---

[18] Aside from the probable contributions of *La Maison du Chat-qui-pelote* and *Au Bonheur des Dames,* Galdós' interest in clothing as an industry and as a form of human identity was at once perverse and abiding. It extended from doña Ambrosia's dry-goods store in *La Fontana* through the "episodios" into all parts of the "novelas contemporáneas." We remember, for instance, the lush wardrobe of "la de Bringas" and the observation in *Halma* that "la ropa es como una segunda piel, en cuya composición y pátina tanta parte tiene lo de dentro como lo de fuera" (*1783*); etc. It is only in part 1 of *Fortunata y Jacinta,* however, that the whole complex of changing styles, evolving commerce, and acute consciousness of personal appearance is studied in all its—for Galdós—distasteful depth. This was apparently first observed critically in a forgotten article by Kasabal (José Gutiérrez Abascal), "Los trajes de un siglo, 1794–1894," *La Correspondencia de España,* 10 January 1895, p. 1. Cited in Hoar, "Critics," p. 216.

irony), however, soon realizes from Juanito's behavior the extent to which he has betrayed the promise of his childhood. One does not have to be exceptionally clever to draw the obvious conclusion: a society that reveres such an individual as its crown prince is in bad shape.

The contrast between image and reality, inside and outside, opinion and merit could not be more striking. Juanito was born with every advantage, not only those accompanying his bourgeois "rank" but also those endowed by nature: good fortune, good looks, good taste, good health, a good mind, and even a good disposition. Conceived of with traditional delay, he was therefore much better suited for comparison with the Messiah than poor, allegorical Riquín ("la Restauración cabezuda"): "Los felices esposos contaban con él este mes, el que viene y el otro, viéndole venir y deseándole como los judíos al Mesías." (*26*) "Considerado como un ser bajado del cielo" (*46*) (the contrast with Fortunata's angelic ascent thereto is deliberate), his birth was accompanied with the appropriate omens: Barbarita's dreams and Arnaiz' unwitting reference to future events. I refer to his characteristically heavy humor at the baptism: "A mí no me la das tú. Aquí ha habido matute. Este ternero lo has traído de la Inclusa para engañarnos. . . . ¡Ah! Estos proteccionistas no son más que contrabandistas."[19] (*27*) And at the same time, as an archetype (not an allegory) of the hero of "la Restauración," Juanito is a "señorito" incarnate, a "fils à papa" dedicated only to the polishing of his shoes and his image and above all to the discreet satisfaction of his biological urges. Or, according

---

[19] This first suggestion of the future role of Estupiñá (who as an ex-"contrabandista" will, in fact, smuggle the genuine heir under his cloak from Fortunata's rooms into his own) is followed by similar foreshadowings. For example, he supplies the Santa Cruz family with untaxed cigars and cigarettes, and "cuando atravesaba las calles de Madrid con las cajas debajo de su capa verde, el corazón le palpitaba de gozo . . ." (*75*) Later, he brings the "nacimiento" (at once a symbol of Jacinta's craving and a present for the child) into the house in the same fashion. But the most explicit, although unwitting, prediction is that of Juanito when he criticizes Jacinta's way of acquiring the child: "esto hija de mi alma no se debe ir a buscar a las tiendas, ni lo debe traer Estupiñá debajo de la capa como las cajas de cigarros." (*194*) It is clear that this event was in Galdós' mind from the beginning. But Galdós is also a master of misleading predictions. For example, when "el Pituso" is first set down on a sack of money, we are led to believe in his authenticity, that is, that he *is* the heir.

to Pereda, "sin otra ocupación que la de regalarse el cuerpo."[20] Juanito is, thus, justly described as an "hombre de trapo" (Galdós alludes both to his impeccable clothes and to his dynasty's commerce), and, as such, as justifies Ortega's condemnation of "señoritos" as "la especie más despreciable y estéril que puede haber."[21]

In another age and in accord with the possibilities and necessities of his station, Juanito would have converted the infidels by force of arms, or, failing that, would have excelled in tournaments like Calisto. At the very least, he would have had to kill a bull in order to establish the cleanliness of his lineage.[22] But now he has been brought up to do absolutely nothing. His amateur and flighty interest in politics only serves to bring out the irony of his name, of being a Santa Cruz without a crusading mission.[23] Of course, he is

[20] *Peñas arriba,* in *Obras Completas,* Madrid, 1895, vol. 15, p. 620. As a novel diametrically opposed both to *Fortunata y Jacinta* and to *Lo prohibido,* its theme is the redemption, not of a feminine victim, but (like *Captains Courageous*) of the "señorito" himself. In spite of his friendship with Pereda, Galdós (who believed that salvation was only possible for those sufficiently incited to find it for themselves) must have thought it hopelessly inane.

[21] "La moral del automóvil en España," in *Obras,* vol. 4, p. 86. Ortega goes on to observe in profound agreement with Galdós: "El señorito es el único ente de nuestra categoría zoológica que no *hace* nada, sino que toda su vida le es *hecha.* Incapaz de producir, todas las cosas del mundo, al llegar a él, se convierten en meros dijes y ornamentos, que pone sobre su persona para vanidoso lucimiento." ibid. Thus, our "hombre de trapo." Note the agreement of Juan de Mairena when he warns his students during the Civil War: "De ningún modo quisiera yo educaros para señoritos, para hombres que eluden el trabajo con que se gana el pan. Hemos llegado a una plena conciencia de la dignidad esencial, de la suprema aristocracia del hombre." "Consejos, sentencias y donaires de Juan de Mairena y de su maestro, Abel Martin," *Hora de España,* 1, 1937, pp. 10–11. Mairena, too, has his own "pícara idea"!

[22] Américo Castro, "De la España que aún no conocía," *EFil,* 5, 1969, pp. 13–15. The point of this is that Jewishness was equated with cowardice in the popular mind.

[23] "Porque Juan era la inconsecuencia misma. En los tiempos de Prim manifestóse entusiasta por la candidatura del duque de Montpensier . . . Vino don Amadeo, y el Delfín se hizo tan republicano que daba miedo de oirle." (*85*) This inconstancy is an evident reflection of the period and city into which he was born and extends to all phases of his being. Thus, his "love" life is compared to a "sucesión de modas," a situation that results when a person (or a society) has as its highest aspiration manipulation and enjoyment of "las cosas materiales." The history of styles, in other words,

305

gossiped about; of course, he never loses his diminutive (only his doting parents believe in him with intact faith), but, even so, he was admired by a society that seems to have no further purpose than to have produced him. On the one hand, he is socially speaking a hero as authentic as the Cid ("a todos alcanza brillo . . ."), and, on the other, he serves Galdós as a means of showing and showing up the emptiness of contemporary history—that Spanish gilded age, which he describes in feminine terms as "nuestra edad de seda." (*155*) Were Juanito the true hero, his novel would perhaps have resembled the "literatura de salones," which Galdós hated precisely because of its emphasis on "todo lo concerniente a vestidos, peinados, adornos modas y lazos."[24] Such were the feelings that underlay the bland and apparently objective presentation of the world of this "hombre de trapo." The gauze and silk and lace that Becquer adored, Galdós could not abide.

But Juanito is not the protagonist, let alone the hero. For, as we have seen, Galdós after reading *La Regenta* understood instinctively what Américo Castro was later to explain to us: that the highest form of novelistic life is that which is endowed with "incitation." Of this quality Juanito Santa Cruz, in spite of his name and in vivid contrast to Maxi and Fortunata, does not possess a single spark. His resulting novelistic triviality is already apparent in the opening paragraph. There Galdós brings him into being (his mother's much more interesting birth will occur a few pages later) first as an empty name ("la persona que lleva este nombre") and then as the subject of puerile and deservedly forgotten anecdotes of university mischief. These characteristic "mocedades" are introduced by an initial sentence that forsakes Cervantine irony ("de cuyo nombre no quiero acordarme") for total indifference: "Las noticias más remotas que

---

is a history of decorative art in cloth or veneer (hence, Dickens's Veneering family) rather than of creation or commitment to authentic values represented physically by solid flesh and solid wood.

[24] Shoemaker, *Cartas*, p. 68. Galdós was incensed not only at the possibly bad moral effects of this kind of writing (as in the case of Isidora) but also because Spain's contemporary "furor indumentario" (this was written in 1884) was inundating the language with "mil terminachos franceses." Cited in the dissertation of Alicia Graciela Andreu, "La *Mujer Virtuosa;* Galdós y la literatura popular," p. 214.

tengo . . ." It is almost as if the narrator were engaged in com-
piling a dossier. Only at the end of the stale résumé of "noticias"
do we first sense Galdós' malice. On the first page of a narrative
that was to continue for almost eight hundred more he writes:
"Otras muchas tonterías de este jaez cuenta Villalonga, las cuales no
copio por no alargar este relato." If Juanito's two other progenitors,
Barbarita and Restoration Madrid (the one representing heredity
and the other environment), respectively worship and admire him,
the author in his initial role as reporter disdains him so much that
he begrudges him even a paragraph of space. As he had found out
while writing *Lo prohibido,* the novel of "señoritismo" was not
worth the effort.

The Birth of an Angel

At this point our earlier question—why does Galdós exploit his
narrator's verbosity and allow him to supply so many apparently
unnecessary and seemingly endless "pormenores"?—may be rephrased more directly: why does Galdós dedicate chapter after
chapter to description of the Santa Cruz family, their manifold
friends and relations, and their heroically born but insignificant
heir? Why does he choose to "alargar su relato" in spite of the narrator's claim that he does not wish to do so? The obvious answer
that Juanito is structurally indispensable, that he serves as a fixed
and inert point of balance for his wife and his mistress is true and,
because the novel is a study of incitation as a phenomenon, relevant.
But it is not sufficient to explain the sheer length of the documentation. As was already insinuated, we must also realize that the
harshly emphasized disparity between Juanito's elaborate birth and
his spiritual futility is on both counts presented as antithetical to
Fortunata. Thus, the one casual sentence Galdós dedicates to her
genesis is designed to underline by its sheer contrast all the folderol
that accompanies the birth of her lover: "Who was the girl with the
egg? . . . Just an orphan living with her aunt who sold eggs in the
Cava de San Miguel." (*49*)

Unknown parentage is, of course, a familiar literary tradition for
such pathetic prostitutes as Sue's Fleur-de-Marie, who begins her

307

life story with an infantile rhyme about her parents: "Ni vus, ni connus; née sous un chou."[25] The difference in the case of Fortunata is that it is Galdós who chooses to tell us nothing. As we remember, he spends a considerable amount of time describing her uncle and aunt (the former in particular), but he feels no need even to mention her mother and father. In a novelistic world constructed upon genealogies, Fortunata has none; she is thus as unique in her own way as her princely seducer in his. He is determined by his genetic and social background and therefore admired, whereas she, as Galdós emphasizes repeatedly, has no background at all. She is a tabula rasa, sheer human raw material. Or as Villalonga says (citing Juanito ironically with specific reference not to Fortunata's soul or human potentiality but to her bosom), "The mass of [uneducated] people is like a quarry. Potentially it contains all great ideas and all beauty. But it needs intelligence and art to cut out the block of stone and to give it shape." (*152*) As befits the speakers, the comparison is superficial. Juanito, born a prince, ends by recognizing the emptiness of his own existence ("el vacío de la vida"), but Fortunata, emergent from nothingness, can finally proclaim with exaltation and a valid claim to our belief, "Soy angel." He is the one who has been "tallado" and discarded by the novelist-sculptor; she is the creator of herself. In a different way (and with more sympathy) we can detect the same incomprehension in Feijóo's enthusiastic comment: "Es un diamante en bruto esa mujer." (*330*)

If not born into the novel like some of the others, Fortunata is introduced in a fashion that is crucial to all that comes after. Her unexpected arrival in section 4 of chapter 3 of part 1 constitutes, in fact, what we termed earlier an "emblematic situation" comparable to don Quijote's joust with the windmill. As Northrop Frye would say, it is a "scene of exceptional intensity which moves up near the center of our memory" after we have finished reading, a scene which remains with us while other portions of larger and time-

---

[25] *Les Mystères de Paris,* vol. 1, p. 28. The cutthroat with a heart of gold called "le Chourineur" reemphasizes the point at the beginning of his life story: "Mes Parents? logés au même numéro que ceux de [Fleur-de-Marie]. Lieu de ma naissance? le premier coin de n'importe quelle rue, la borne à gauche ou à droite, en descendant ou en remontant vers le ruisseau." ibid., p. 41.

vulnerable novelistic experience fade away.[26] The selection of this scene is not purely subjective, for the notion of emblematic representation implies that generations of readers must agree that such scenes somehow stand for the book as a whole. To read a major novel is to belong to a community of past and future readers, who, in spite of individual and historical differences, are aware of sharing the same experience as well as of inheriting and bequeathing a treasure of favorite episodes.

In many cases (in addition to don Quijote and the windmills, familiar examples include Robinson Crusoe finding the footprint, Yossarian crouching naked on his branch, and Jim Hawkins hiding in the apple barrel), such situations are chosen spontaneously by the reading public, which perceives that each such scene sums up its novel in such a way that the dispersed meaning of the theme is therein condensed. But in others, most notably in the novels of Stendhal, the self-conscious novelist seems to have taken great pains to provide his future readers with appropriate emblems, to underline poetically and rhetorically those pregnant moments that he believes constitute the most revealing physical corollaries for his "postura hacia la vida."[27] That this is indeed the case when Juanito looks in from the staircase at Fortunata eating her raw egg is indicated both by the elaborate care Galdós takes in arranging and describing the meeting and by his equally elaborate pretense of carelessness.

Thus, although Fortunata seems to appear casually, she is in fact garlanded with a premeditated complexity of allusion and imagery, which in its significance surpasses by far the ironical hero-prince-messiah cluster that accompanied the birth and curriculum vitae of her lover. We have already discussed the contribution of certain passages from *Le Ventre de Paris* to the intensity of the scene, and indeed most of my readers probably remember it as well or better than I. Nevertheless, let us review the circumstances once again. Estupiñá has been taken ill for the first time in his life. Juanito has been sent by Barbarita to visit him in his rooms "en lo más último de arriba" of an ancient edifice opening (like the two-faced church

[26] *Myth and Symbol,* ed. B. Slote, Lincoln, Neb., 1963, p. 8.
[27] For further discussion of the notion of "emblematic" scenes or episodes and of its applicability to Stendhal, see my *The Tower as Emblem.*

of San Sebastián in *Misericordia*) both on the Plaza Mayor and on the Cava de San Miguel three stories and thirty stairs below. Unaware of the possibility of entering at the plaza level, he chooses the lower portal, a "tienda de aves" where chickens are killed and cleaned and eggs are sold. The fastidious "señorito," at once repelled and excited by the crudity of the spectacle, hastens through to the stone stairs. He pauses one flight up to look curiously through an open doorway, where there is a girl who impresses him as being "bonita, joven, alta." Lo and behold, Fortunata!

These three adjectives, corresponding to the rapid, predatory, and, as we have observed, eminently Naturalistic glance of the young male, constitute the whole of Fortunata's description in part 1. As we shall see, it is a noteworthy and intentional departure from the sort of detailed physical characterization that began with Scott and became conventional in the nineteenth-century novel. But before we meditate on Galdós' descriptive reticence, we must try to comprehend why he arranges such an abrupt and unexpected encounter. The answer to that question has already been supplied: he wishes to emphasize as strongly as possible that Fortunata (as her name implies) appears in Juanito's life and in the novel by chance. The explanation is unambiguous: "The visit of the Delfín [Dauphin] to his old servant and household retainer is stressed here, because if Juanito Santa Cruz had not made that visit, this particular history would never have been written. Another could have been written, naturally (because wherever a man may go his novel goes with him), but not this one." (*40*) In the creation of Juanito all is or seems inevitable; in the creation of Fortunata all is or seems casual.

The paradox of such an explanation is that genuine chance does not and cannot operate in the novel, and least of all in the nineteenth-century novel. The novelist arranges for it with care and is, by definition the chance maker, the chance chooser. Hence the shrewdness of Robert Petsch's advice that critical examination of the operations of chance or hazard in a given novel is often the most direct path toward its comprehension.[28] In the case of *Fortunata y Jacinta*

---

[28] "Der 'sinnvolle' oder 'bedeutende Zufall' ist dann derjenige 'Punkt' der Handlung von dem aus auf einmal die hintergründigen Zusammenhänge

the suggestion is illuminating. For if Juanito's introductory omens and "mocedades" (unlike those of Julien Sorel and Fabrice del Dongo) are ironically insignificant, Fortunata's first, brief appearance is literally encased in layers of social, poetic, and mythological meaning. Precisely because she is an embodiment of chance, an apparition so unexpected and ostensibly transient that she is not worth the effort of description, her creator begins by dressing her in sheer significance.

Let us begin with the obvious, the social implications. When Juanito looks through the doorway (what reader at this point has not been tempted by the invitation to symbolic exegesis?), he is fascinated by the sight of Fortunata sucking a raw egg and afterwards throwing the empty shell against the wall. The contrast between his background and hers could not have been more underlined. The scion of a dynasty dedicated to commerce in dry goods, to the decorous and fashionable covering up of human life, suddenly and with ardent curiosity confronts it in its primitive condition.[29] As we saw in the case of young Marjolin and "la belle" Lisa, the Naturalistic scene along with the stimulating odor of "la tienda de aves" is a fitting prelude to the encounter, not merely because of the egg motif but more importantly because it prepares us for Juanito's novel-long ambivalence of feeling—simultaneous attraction and repulsion—for Fortunata. Juanito, being who he is and representing the society he represents, can neither accept Fortunata's state of nature nor leave it alone.

Let us put it in this way: like the age for which he is a hero, Galdós seems to imply, Juanito prefers to toy with life, to hide it and peek at it, to dress it and undress it, to cook it and nibble at it, to decorate it with bustles and good manners, but not to live it to

---

und Stosskräfte erhellt werden die zum epischen 'Ende führen'." Robert Petsch, *Wesen und Formen,* p. 150.

[29] It is ironically characteristic of don Baldomero that his gift to doña Guillermina's orphans is "cuatro piezas de paño del Reino para que les haga chaquetas." (*149*) Domestically manufactured and therefore relatively inexpensive covering is his idea of what is suitable for poor children. Thus clothed, he asserts fatuously, they are better off than those well-to-do children "que gastan levita." This is a man who lives with complete comfort inside his limited perspectives, in every way a modern version of the appropriately named and clothed "Caballero del Verde Gabán."

the full.[30] Thus, on those various occasions later on when he tires of Fortunata's naive directness of behavior and feeling, he reproaches her for her lack of seductive lingerie and her failure to posture lasciviously "con esos asqueos de un cuerpo pegadizo y sútil que acaricia el asiento." (*322*) So too, his reaction in their first conversation:

> "No sé cómo puede usted comer esas babas crudas," dijo Santa Cruz, no hallando mejor modo de trabar conversación. "Mejor que guisadas. ¿Quiere usted?" replicó ella ofreciendo al Delfín lo que en el cascarón quedaba. Por entre los dedos de la chica se escurrían aquellas babas gelatinosas y transparentes. Tuvo tentaciones Juanito de aceptar la oferta, pero no; le repugnaban los huevos crudos. "No, gracias."[31] (*41*)

Galdós' point of novelistic departure is thus located (as is appropriate for an author who intends to abandon Naturalism) at the social core "de esta historia."

The next task was to dress Fortunata metaphorically. It goes without saying that, when first spied, she could not be unclothed or partially unclothed, as she might have been in a novel by Zola. Such an introduction would have been much too obvious for Galdós as an artist and much too indecorous for his peninsular public. Instead,

---

[30] As our previous discussion might have led us to expect, in Juanito's consciousness clothing and language are structurally identical. On the morning after his drunken confession, he is described as follows: "Y después, cuando el despejo de su cerebro le hacía dueño de todas sus triquiñuelas de hombre leído y mundano, no volvió a salir de sus labios ni un solo vocablo soez, ni una sola espontaneidad de aquellas que existían dentro de él, como existen los trapos de colorines en algún rincón de la casa del que ha sido cómico, aunque sólo lo haya sido de afición. Todo era convencionalismo y frase ingeniosa en aquel hombre que se había emperejilado intelectualmente, cortándose una levita para las ideas y planchándole los cuellos al lenguaje." (*64*) Precisely because of his sartorial skill with words, Juanito is characterized by his fondness for the "naked" language of the streets and for a picturesque lack of decorum.

[31] " 'I don't know how you can swallow that raw goo,' said Santa Cruz, who could not think of any better way to engage her in conversation. 'Better than cooked. Here try it,' she replied, offering him what was left in the shell. The gelatinous and transparent egg white was dripping through the girl's fingers. Juan was tempted to accept her offer, but no, he thought raw eggs were disgusting: 'No, thank you.' "

he contrasts orphan and prince by presenting the former as an "animalito," specifically, a bird:

> La moza tenía un pañuelo azul claro por la cabeza y un mantón sobre los hombros, y en el momento de ver el Delfín se infló con él, quiero decir, que hizo ese característico arqueo de brazos y alzamiento de hombros con que las madrileñas del pueblo se agazapan dentro del mantón, movimiento que les da cierta semejanza con una gallina que esponja su plumaje y se ahueca para volver luego a su volúmen natural.[32] (*41*)

Thus, when we first see Fortunata she not only eats an egg with primitive gusto, she herself is a wild thing, a bird behaving according to instinct.

Other references confirm the intentional nature of the poetic metamorphosis. When Fortunata "sacaba del mantón una mano con mitón encarnado y . . . se la llevaba a la boca," it corresponds in color and location to the wattle.[33] Again, when she is called from downstairs, "la chica se inclinó en el pasamanos y soltó un *yiá voy,* con chillido tan penetrante, que Juanito creyó se le desgarraba el tímpano. El *yiá,* principalmente, sonó como la vibración agudísima de una hoja de acero al deslizarse sobre otra. Y al soltar aquel sonido, *digno canto de tal ave,* la moza se arrojó con tanta presteza por las escaleras abajo, que parecía rodar por ellas."[34] (Italics mine.) (*41*)

---

[32] "The girl had a blue kerchief on her head and a shawl over her shoulders, and, at the moment when she first saw the "Delfín," she ruffled it up. That is to say, she made that arm and shoulder gesture which is characteristic of lower class Madrid women when they draw their shawls around them [as if for protection]. It is an arching movement that bears a certain resemblance to a chicken stretching out its feathers with the result that it seems larger than it really is—afterwards returning to its true size." The term animalito is, of course, Juanito's. Jacinta has asked "¿Y cuál era la más guapa?" And Juanito replies, "La mía . . ., un animalito muy mono, una salvaje que no sabía leer ni escribir. . . . Como te digo, un animal; pero buen corazón, buen corazón." (*50*)

[33] "drew from her shawl a hand with a red mitt and . . . lifted it to her mouth." Galdós mentions the mitt again the next time we observe Fortunata directly (in the rooms of *Ulmus silvestris*): "'Habló Fortunata poco y vulgar, todo lo que dijo fue de lo menos digno de pasar a la historia: que hacía mucho frío, que se le había descosido un mitón. . . .'" (*165*)

[34] "the girl leaned on the banister and shrieked 'I'm coming now' with such a penetrating high pitch that Juanito thought it would rend his ear-

After her initial display of feathers and comb, Fortunata sings and almost literally flies away. She has as we read been transformed into a bird, at once wild and innocent, colorful and intensely alive. This is neither allegory nor a new form of representation; it is an image, a poetic transformation, which in the context of the narrative leads us to participate in the breathless intensity of an encounter with a marvel of nature.

Bird imagery is, of course, frequent in many of Galdós' novels (Isidora, as we remember is an imitation bird with "alas postizas"), just as it is in those of his fellow Naturalists.[35] Zola on one occasion reminded himself, "donner une place importante aux animaux dans les romans. Créer quelques bêtes; chiens, chats, oiseaux . . ."[36] Birds seem, however, particularly and significantly abundant in *Fortunata y Jacinta,* almost as if Fortunata's initial presentation had cast a poetic spell over the whole. Thus, Estupiñá has a parrot profile as well as a parrot head to his cane and parrotlike verbosity; Maxi's shoulder blades are like "alones de un ave flaca"; Jacinta vents her

---

drums. The word "yiá" ["now" misspelled in order to indicate her pronunciation] in particular sounded like the sharp grating of one steel blade rubbed against another. And after emitting that sound, the appropriate song for such a bird, the girl ran downstairs so fast that it seemed as if she were falling." In my opinion the phrase "digno canto . . ." is crucial because it adds an oral dimension to the previous visual image and at the same time prepares us for the suddenness of Fortunata's flight.

[35] In *La Fontana,* for example, Coletilla's nose is compared to the beak of an "ave de rapiña," his gaze to "la mirada de los pájaros nocturnos," and his fingers to "garras de pájaro rapaz." And glancing rapidly over a few pages of *La desheredada* we encounter such comparisons as that of the "patio de las locas" with a "gallinero," of Isidora with a "ruiseñora," and of the song of the birds in the Retiro with a "galimatías parlamentaria forestal." There is no point in multiplying such examples, in part derived from Spanish popular speech (a "mala mujer" is a "pájara" as early as *La Celestina*), in part from Galdós' love of caricature, and in part from Naturalistic observations. In *Fortunata y Jacinta,* however, the identity of woman and bird becomes crucial.

[36] Ruiz Salvador called my attention to this Naturalistic recipe from Zola's annotations to Prosper Lucas' *Traité de l'hérédité naturelle* (Paris, 1850). Cited by Henri Massis, *Comment Zola composait ses romans,* Paris, 1906, p. 45. As already noted, bird imagery was of thematic importance in *La Regenta,* the novel Galdós had just finished reading before embarking on *Fortunata y Jacinta.* Nevertheless, Clarín's utilization of it, along with other animal comparisons such as the toad at the end, is less purely verbal and more deeply related to the semirural environment of the novel.

"rabia de paloma"; Ido swallows his porkchop like a turkey and resembles one in his jealous fits;[37] and as we shall see later, Madrid itself (as if framed by the visual images of the poultry store at the beginning and doña Desdémona's aviary at the end) is tacitly presented as a giant and twittering "república de las aves," to borrow the Calderonian expression appropriately cited by Segismundo Ballester.[38] It is, however, around Fortunata herself that such images cluster most thickly, as if the metamorphosis, once suggested, not only spreads by contagion to her world and to her companions but also remains with her as a subterranean metaphor, which emerges and reemerges along the anguished "chemin" of her residence on earth. The special quality of her way of being alive, both of rebelling against captivity and of celebrating freedom, is winged.

Let us begin with the honeymoon, where, as we remember, Jacinta feels equally sorry for ill-paid and uneducated factory girls (who are forced to the conclusion "Vale más ser mujer mala que máquina buena") (54) and the two dozen songbirds that she devours greedily on the train. If Fortunata's fate is only implicit in these two examples of incongruous bourgeois compassion, she is remembered explicitly a few pages later on (with sentiment that is comparably maudlin) by her seducer as a mother of doves feeding them at her breast and singing them to sleep. Later we learn such details as that her one piece of jewelry is a brooch in the shape of a swallow, that she prays to the Virgin "de la Paloma," and that, while in "las Micaelas," she and her companions are referred to as "Filomenas." More convincing than these minutiae, however, are two references to her sudden winging away and unpredictable changes

---

[37] Many more examples can be found in the articles by R. L. Utt (who stresses caged-bird imagery) and A. M. Gullón. Utt, " 'el pájaro voló': Observaciones sobre un leitmotif en *Fortunata y Jacinta*," *AG*, 9, 1974, pp. 37–50. Gullón, "The Bird Motif and the Introductory Motif: Structure in *Fortunata y Jacinta*," *AG*, 9, 1974, pp. 51–75. A definitive list would surely be even larger. I keep noticing new bird references, both veiled and obvious, every time I reread a chapter.

[38] The technique of embroidering the action ironically with "Siglo de Oro" nomenclature (Torquemada as a usurer, don Francisco de Quevedo as a humorless "comadrón" married to doña Desdémona) is further developed by having Segismundo Ballester cite *La vida es sueño* (Act 2, line 1055) unintentionally, although on other occasions he repeats the lines of his "tocayo" on purpose.

of direction. When, for example, Fortunata arrives at the Santa Cruz residence with the idea of forcing a confrontation, she suddenly stops short: "Just to see the front door was for the 'Wench' exactly the same as when a blinded and desperate bird flies headlong against a wall." *(324)* Or again, Ballester compares her sudden departure from the Rubín family to a "pigeon flying to the neighbor's rooftree." But most significant of all is the birdlike nature of her consciousness: ". . . allowing her idea to flutter across the ceiling" *(417)*; "an idea crossed her consciousness like a transient bird across the immensity of the sky" *(332)*; as well as the climactic announcement, "that's my idea, and I have been nurturing it for a long long time, like a bird sitting on an egg that finally hatches." *(504)*

It is of course to be expected that the other characters should refer to Fortunata with the idiomatic expression "pájara," as, for example, when doña Lupe comically imagines the ghost of Jáuregui threatening her: "Si no arrojas de tu casa a esa pájara, me voy yo . . ." *(473)* When doña Desdémona uses the same word as a kind of oral cipher, however, the intentional humor of Galdós' reference to the initial metaphor can hardly be denied. As we remember, she is trying to send a message concerning the birth of Fortunata's son to doña Lupe through Maxi without letting him in on the secret: "Do me the favor of telling doña Lupe that the naughty bird's egg hatched this morning. . . . It's a beautiful chick . . . and everything went perfectly." *(497)* And if Fortunata is once again for devious reasons compared to a bird, her "polluelo," by another idiomatic transformation, becomes a "canario de alcoba." It is a phrase that prepares us for the aural identity of bird and child when the mother is dying: "Bird song filled the somber room along with Juan Evaristo's screams for his bottle." *(536)* Until the very end Fortunata is accompanied poetically by bird song and the fluttering of wings.[39]

[39] We have already noticed the tacit metaphorical opposition of Fortunata and Jacinta, a devourer of songbirds with feline maternal instincts. This indirect method of suggesting the former's poetic identification with bird life becomes explicit when she is literally stalked by her maid, Patricia, in the form of a hunting cat: "La sirviente clavaba en la señora sus ojos de gato" *(271)*; "Patricia se acercaba pasito a pasito pisando como los gatos" *(272)*; etc.

As far as possible mythographic patterns are concerned, the most obvious and most superficial is that of the encounter of knight and shepherdess (usually referred to in Spanish as a "serranilla"). We begin to suspect what Galdós is up to when he remarks: "The stairways of those dwellings, because they were made of stone all the way from the entrance on the Cava [of San Miguel, a passageway leading into the Plaza Mayor] to the garrets, make a lugubrious and monumental impression as if they were in a castle in a fairy story."[40] (40) But what about Fortunata? Juanito as a modern version of the young knight who gives way to amorous temptation and forgets his obligations as a "caballero" and "hidalgo" is self-evident,[41] but how can she, as a totally urban creature, resemble a shepherdess? Juanito's drunken portrait of her provides a satisfactory answer: "Fortunata tenía las manos bastas de tanto trabajar; el corazón lleno de inocencia. . . . Fortunata no tenía educación; aquella boca tan linda se comía muchas palabras y otras las equivocaba. Decía *indilugencias, golver, asín*. Pasó la niñez cuidando el *ganado*. ¿Sabes lo que es el ganado? Las gallinas."[42] (60) Innocence, natural beauty, mispronunciation (the "sayagués" of Madrid), the care of "ganado" —all the essential elements are present. Medieval poetic play with the themes of innocence and class distinction is alluded to, but with the

---

[40] The comparison is repeated a few paragraphs later: "Efectivamente parecía la subida a un castillo o prisión de estado" (40); and at the end when Fortunata returns, "cogió . . . una llave enorme que parecía llave de un castillo." (477)

[41] "Seamos francos: la verdad ante todo . . . me idolatraba. Creía que yo no era como los demás, que era la caballerosidad, la hidalguía, la decencia, la nobleza en persona, el acábose de los hombres . . . ¡Nobleza! ¡qué sarcasmo! Nobleza en la mentira; digo que no puede ser . . . y que no, y que no. ¡Decencia porque se lleva una ropa que se llama levita!" (60-61) Without specially underlining the evolution, Galdós uses our memory of this youthful and useless remorse to communicate Juanito's progressively greater cynicism in the course of the novel.

[42] "Fortunata's hands were coarsened by hard work, but her heart was a repository of innocence. . . . She had no schooling, and it seemed that her pretty mouth either chewed up her words [rather than pronouncing them] or got them confused. She would say "indilugencias" [instead of "indulgencias" meaning "indulgences"], "golver" [instead of "volver" meaning "to return"], "asin" [instead of "así" meaning "so"]. She spent her childhood taking care of her "cattle." Can you guess what her "cattle" were? Chickens."

addition of a nineteenth-century guilty conscience. As Juanito proclaims in his fit of alcoholic remorse, "we men, I mean, we young dandies, are all curs; we treat the honor of lower class girls as if it were a plaything." (*60*)

Beneath this transient effort at medieval embroidery, however, there is, I suspect, a reference to classical mythology as calculated as those to be found in *Doña Perfecta* and *La de Bringas*.[43] Overt allusions to Aristophanes' famous description in *The Birds* of the birth of "graceful Eros with his glittering golden wings" from a "germless egg" may be missing,[44] but the entrance of Procne just prior to that passage nevertheless bears a significant resemblance to our first vision of Fortunata. I cite the 1880 translation by Federico Baraibar y Zumárraga, which appeared in the widely circulated Biblioteca clásica collection and which Galdós had surely read:

> *Pistetero:* ¡Oh venerado Júpiter! ¡Qué hermosa avecilla! ¡Qué brillante!
>
> *Evélpides:* ¿Sabes que la estrecharía con gusto entre mis brazos?
>
> *Pistetero:* ¡Cuánto oro trae sobre sí! Parece una doncella.
>
> *Evélpides:* Tentado estoy de darle un beso.
>
> *Pistetero:* Pero, desdichado, ¿No ves que tiene por pico dos asadores?
>
> *Evélpides:* ¿Qué importa? ¿Hay más que *quitarle la cascarilla que le cubre la cabeza como si fuese un huevo,* y besarla despues.[45] (Italics mine.)

The probable relation to Fortunata is reinforced by one of Baraibar's footnotes: "Según el Escoliasta, el atavío de Procne imitaba el traje de las cortesanas y el plumaje del ruiseñor."[46] What an intricate and marvelous combination of literary and mythological materials have been fused in the creation of the emblematic encounter!

Merely to exclaim at this extraordinary juncture of Zola, Aristophanes, and the Marqués de Santillana is, of course, insufficient,

---

[43] See Appendix and W. H. Shoemaker, "Galdós' Classical Scene in *La de Bringas,*" *HR,* 27, 1959, pp. 423–434.

[44] W. J. Oates and E. O'Neill, Jr., *The Complete Greek Drama,* New York, 1938, vol. 2, p. 762.

[45] *Aristophanes,* Madrid, 1880, pp. 250–251. Evélpides' first line is more obscene in the original and is rendered in Latin.

[46] Ibid.

and to prove it to skeptics is impossible. If Galdós did have Procne in mind, however, when he introduced Fortunata into the novel (as he very probably did), he could have also intended to refer to the birth of Eros or perhaps even of Helen of Troy who was hatched from the divine swan's egg laid by Leda. These are admittedly speculations based only on speculations, but they are nonetheless well worth mentioning. For even if they are not true, they suggest a possibility about Fortunata's birth that we otherwise might have overlooked. They suggest that she, the one character in the whole of the novel utterly lacking in genealogy, has been hatched (ab ovo) from the egg that she holds in her hand. On the literal as well as on the social level she, of course, eats it, but on the level of myth she emerges from it. She then casts it aside, and, as an infant without infancy, as a candid bird in her ruffled "mantón," she sets forth undetermined on her hazardous and airy "chemin."

In conclusion, whether or not we accept myths of origin as an intentional substratum of meaning, we do know that Galdós, ever since the composition of *La desheredada,* had been as preoccupied as his fellow Naturalists with myth fabrication. And Fortunata, who was to free him from the negative exigencies of the school, is surely the most profound and autonomous mythological creature to have appeared in Spain since 1615. She is neither Eros nor Helen, of course, in spite of her erotic impact on Juanito Santa Cruz. Rather, as she announces, as doña Guillermina admits may be possible, as Segismundo Ballester affirms, and as Maxi proclaims quixotically,[47] by the time of her death she has transformed herself into that most exalted of winged beings—an angel. The myth of origins has become a myth of metamorphosis. Hatched from an egg, condemned by society to the vain fluttering of captivity, Fortunata at long last flies to heaven accompanied by a chorus of bird song: "el piar de pájaros también se precipitaba en aquel sombrío confín." Only those who no longer believe in the novel and in its capacity to give "seres imaginarios vida más humana que social" would dare to doubt her salvation.

---

[47] "Era un ángel—gritó Maxi dándose un fuerte puñetazo en la rodilla— ¡Y el miserable que me lo niegue o lo ponga en duda se verá conmigo!" (547) Those who attempt to convert the novel into a defective Marxist treatise had better watch out!

CHAPTER XI

The Art of Consciousness

Fortunata in Mind

For passionate readers and rereaders of *Fortunata y Jacinta,* Fortunata is the woman who, among all women, is the most profoundly known. We know her from within, and we know her at length, from spiritual birth to physical death and believed-in resurrection. We know her in a way we can never know women of flesh and blood—our mothers, our sisters, and our wives. Yet it would not be easy to explain to a reader of, say, *Madame Bovary* what it *is* that we know about Fortunata, to explain to him, as he could explain to us about Emma, just what she is like. In so saying, I do not refer to the self-evident difficulties of determining character or of reducing ongoing life to static résumé. Far more than other fictional peers, an Emma Bovary, a Becky Sharpe, a Gina Sanseverina, or a Gervaise Lantier, Fortunata's way of being herself seems to evade the categories in terms of which we habitually comprehend the inhabitants of novels. It is not that she is more complex or more contradictory than the others mentioned. Instead, in the very naiveté and forthrightness that we came to know so well there is an element of mystery. Her changes, feelings, preoccupations, and decisions are powerful and direct, yet when we ask the question "Why?" or "Why at this point?" the answer is never self-evident.

In part this is because Galdós, like Zola, much prefers presentation to description. In the manuscript he systematically deletes the rudimentary comments on happening and character, which earlier versions had contained. But to a far greater extent it is because of Galdós' unusual angle of creative vision. He sees Fortunata in a way quite different from the way he sees the characters who surround her. How is she presented? To find out we must try to follow the awkward instructions of Virginia Woolf to common read-

320

ers: "All alone we must climb on the novelist's shoulders and gaze through his eyes . . ."[1] Upon so doing, as Montesinos remarks, we realize that neither Galdós nor we really *see* Fortunata at all. In sharp contrast to Jacinta, whose taste for clothes ("el polisón" and the "pardessus color de pasa"), expressively mobile face with premature wrinkles, and parts of the body (as intimate an assortment as those years could possibly allow) are etched in our memory, her rival's overpowering beauty lacks a specific visual image. On the occasion of Galdós' first description of her, when Juanito Santa Cruz sees her from the stairway, the three adjectives of the sentence "Juanito vio algo que de pronto le impresionó: una mujer bonita, joven, alta . . ." (*41*) are noncommittal. The contrast between this succinct introduction and the treasures of shared experience that the novel has in store for us could not be greater or more powerful.

Immediately, as we have seen, a process of verbal metamorphosis sets in, which transforms Fortunata's typical gesture with her "mantón" into the ruffling up of a bird. At the very moment of her novelistic birth, the physical presence, which other novelists might well have tried to make us visualize, is converted into an impression of natural force, into a primitive exhibition of vitality, which captivates us just as it captivates the "señorito" who stands there staring. In fact, as we remarked, it has captivated so many readers that this scene has become a deservedly famous emblem of the novel as a whole, comparable to don Quijote and the windmill or Robinson Crusoe and the footprint.[2]

In a different way, the same effect of disguise is achieved in the next description, when Fortunata, at the beginning of part 2, becomes conscious of herself while gazing at her own mirror image. She attempts to put the beauty she sees into words, but at that linguistically underprivileged beginning of her existence she can do little more than exclaim, "¡Vaya un pelito que Dios me ha dado!" or take refuge in such grotesque popular commonplaces as "Tengo los dientes como pedacitos de leche cuajada" and "[Mis

[1] From the essay on *Robinson Crusoe* in *The Second Common Reader,* New York, s.d., p. 43.
[2] See Frye in *Myth and Symbol,* p. 8.

ojos negros] le daban la puñalada al Espíritui Santo."[3] (*185–86*) Again words have been used more to conceal than to reveal; again we have been given only the impression of a marvelous presence, a presence to be sensed or at best glimpsed briefly (abundant black hair, firm white flesh, calloused hands, bosom slightly pockmarked by the beaks of pigeons, etc.) but never to be examined closely or possessed in memory. Only much later do we see, through the complacent and experienced eyes of her wisest lover, Feijóo, a few characteristic postures and facial gestures.[4] But if we stop to think about them, we get the uncomfortable feeling of having been transported from fiction into a tacit autobiography of the author.

Why does Galdós proceed in this way? One answer, and a true one, would be that he here (as he can be observed doing elsewhere) has imitated instinctively the narrative practice of Homer as ana- lyzed by Lessing in one of the most justly esteemed paragraphs in the entire history of literary criticism: "Let us recall the passage where Helen steps into the assembly of the Elders of the Trojan people. The venerable old men looked on her and one said to the other: 'We cannot rage at her, it is no wonder / that Trojans and Akhaians under arms / should for so long have borne the pains of war / for one like this. / Unearthliness. A goddess / the woman is to look at.' What can convey a more vivid idea of Beauty than to have frigid age confessing her well worth the war that had cost so much blood and so many tears? What Homer could not describe in its component parts, he makes us feel in its working."[5] So For- tunata, too, is all the more splendid when seen not directly but in

---

[3] "What a gift from God my hair is!"

"My teeth are like bits of coagulated milk."

"[My black eyes] are enough to transfix the Holy Ghost with love [as if she were the Virgin Mary]."

[4] For example: "¡Práctica—replicó ella arrugando la nariz con salero, como hacía siempre que afectaba no comprender una cosa y burlarse de ella al mismo tiempo." (*328*) The chapter is replete with similar observations of gestures and facial expressions. Maxi's vision of her as an "hermosa figura de salvaje" (*178*) is not that of a connoisseur. He can only compare her to illustrations he has seen of Old Testament women.

[5] Gotthold Ephraim Lessing, *Laocoön,* trans. W. A. Steel, Everyman's Library, London and New York, 1930, p. 131. I have substituted Fitzgerald's translation for Lessing's Greek quotation. *Iliad,* p. 72.

terms of the overwhelming impression she makes first on Juanito and then on herself.

But there is more to it than this. Between these two moments of transformed and transient description, Fortunata, as Sherman Eoff has noted, disappears in a way that suggests the deeper intention of Galdós' reluctance to paint her portrait in words.[6] As we learn in passing later on, after the death of Juanito's child, she sinks into a sexual underworld, where she undergoes the sordid adventures that Naturalists naturally reserve for innocent lower class girls who have been seduced and abandoned. But unlike her precursor, Isidora Rufete, these experiences do not touch her or affect her. The conventional degradation in her biography is tangential both to the story as a whole and to the integrity of her existence. What does matter is that, in spite of her physical disappearance in part 1, she nevertheless maintains her post of honor at the center of the novel. As *the* protagonist, in spite of the title, she continues to be present in the remorseful and lascivious memory of Juanito and in the apprehensive and curious imagination of Jacinta. Fortunata is not only the underlying subject of their cloying honeymoon dialogue (no matter what they pretend to be talking about) but also the incorporeal inhabitant, the uninvited guest, of their consciousness of each other. In this sense it could be said that she constitutes, precisely because she is *not* described from without, the *real* reality of part 1.

If this seems paradoxical in such a documentary narrative, it is because Galdós meant it to. The long, Naturalistic overture of *Fortunata y Jacinta* may seem out of proportion to some readers. The endless "pormenores," the genealogies, the investigation of the way Madrid dressed, ate, and found shelter, the background of urban scenery, types, and current events from the recent past are "constructed" (as my late teacher, Augusto Centeno, used to term it) with infinitely patient expertise.[7] As mentioned earlier, Galdós in his *Memorias* recalls the burdensome task of "gathering elements," and, when he started to write, he clearly did not intend to discard or abbreviate them. But we should not be fooled; this external Naturalistic realism is not there just because Madrid was *like* that. Instead it functions as a solid external point of departure for the

[6] *The Modern Spanish Novel,* New York, 1961, p. 131.
[7] See chapter 8, note 6.

basic inward movement of the novel. Even at the very moment of maximum display, in the very midst of all the infinite picturesque particularities of urban life, we find performing as if on a bare classical stage a figure of the mind that is more real both to those obsessed with her and to the reader than the mercantile and genealogical realities described at such length.

The point I am trying to make has already been made in another context. Galdós, following an experimental path that began with *El amigo Manso* (in apparent reaction against the Naturalistic determinism he had played with in *La desheredada*), had now decided to undertake what might be called a major Cervantine offensive against Emile Zola.[8] Heredity and urban environment are no longer to be allowed to determine individual lives and to distort or shrink their consciousnesses. Rather there is to be a return to don Quijote's open-ended quest for values to rehabilitate and to defend. This is why Fortunata is virtually invisible; she is not merely an exceptionally conscious protagonist but a champion of invisible consciousness at war with "race, milieu, et moment" and, in ultimate victory, an avenging angel who renders them impotent.[9]

The innovation was so great and the use of a standard Naturalistic victim such as Fortunata so startling that Galdós prepared the way with all possible caution. On the one hand, he built a verbal Madrid as solid as the Paris of Balzac or of Zola, and, on the other, he separated his heroine from her wretchedly topical biography and amplified her as a creature of the joint consciousness of the newly married couple. By the end of part 1 the unsuspecting reader has been prepared to know her in terms of her extraordinary attraction *for* and presence *in* a whole gallery of other minds—Maxi, doña Lupe, Mauricia, Feijóo, Segismundo Ballester. The substitution of

---

[8] See Raimond, *La Crise du roman*, p. 29.

[9] It should be clear by this time that Galdós' determination to transcend Naturalism has little to do with its rejection by those Spanish literati who found it distasteful, immoral, and ill-conceived. For example, González Serrano, who had praised *Doña Perfecta* and who admired certain aspects of the Rougon-Macquart saga, rejects Naturalism as a kind of "idealism in reverse." "El arte Naturalista," *Revista de España,* 105, 1885, p. 54. Although portions of these novels may at times be "bellas y geniales," a typical character, as Zola remarked with his "habitual franqueza," amounts to nothing more than a "cadáver humano." Ibid., pp. 43 and 37.

a novel premised on consciousness as such for novels premised on physical urges and on things could only be attempted slowly and indirectly.

The physical reappearance of Fortunata at the beginning of part 2, thus, initiates a continuation and amplification of the dialectic of consciousness and world that had begun in part 1. Galdós now is concerned with the multiple juxtaposition of individual consciousnesses: the several different Fortunatas who exist for those who know her and, at the same time, the others as they appear to her. From these contrasts there emerges a Cervantine novel of overlapping perspectives, that is, a novel of mutually involved minds, some narrowed by vice or social constraint, others exalted and on fire with idealism, and still others foreshortened by reason or twisted with insanity and all grouped around that of Fortunata. She acts as the magnetic pole of their acute or dim awareness of the health of her consciousness, a health that endows her with freedom and ultimately with the possibility of choosing between damnation and salvation. Characteristically she will choose both, but the reader cannot yet predict so much. He is gradually learning to know and celebrate the epic heroine of that faculty—not reason but self-awareness—that makes us different from other living creatures.

This, I think, is why Galdós chose not to paint Fortunata's enchanting portrait in words and why we, in spite of our intimacy with her, remain in awe of her mystery. Like those who live with her on Galdós' pages, our consciousnesses feel themselves pulled unaccountably in her direction. Other novelists present a character in much the same way that we meet people in so-called reality—as a fixed initial image, which we gradually penetrate and come to know better by a habitual process of observation and deduction. But in the case of Fortunata, we are disconcerted to find that the familiar technique has been put in reverse. We are primarily concerned with her mind, and we witness it from within. The more it grows (and we grow with it), the more marvelous the experience becomes. Fortunata is nothing less than what we might be, *if* we were true (today the commonplace word would be "authentic")—not crippled, self-serving, overtrained, cowardly, lazy, sophisticated, and generally alienated.

Without listing more of the deadly sins of consciousness (whether they be those of a Bueno de Guzmán or of critics of Galdós) let us simply stress Fortunata's transcendence of the dichotomies of flesh and spirit (thus, "naturalismo espiritual"), of intellect and life, which we have been taught to accept unthinkingly, or, even worse, to defend as if our very existence depended on them, when they actually cut it in two. As a result, she is strangely characterless, a creature of almost threatening naiveté whose seemingly limitless possibilities for growth, transparency of experiential intake, and capacity for passion make her into a candidate for the part of ultimate novelistic heroine. Her relationship to the Spanish people is not representational, as in the case of some of Galdós' earlier feminine creations, but rather like that of Huck Finn to the American people. By this I mean that the "neo-krausista" interpretation, which would explain the novel as an allegory of the salvation of decadent Restoration Spain by the uncorrupted "pueblo" in the person of Fortunata, if not completely untrue, *is* foreshortened and misleading.[10] Like Huck, Fortunata is more importantly a touchstone, a living, particular consciousness, which reveals to the reader what

---

[10] Galdós is nowhere near as simplistic in his view of the people as this interpretation would require. In his early novels he seems to have been profoundly ambivalent—almost as changeable as Juanito Santa Cruz—in his opinions. We have already discussed *La Fontana* in that connection (the would-be "menistros"), but in *El audaz* he seems to agree with Muriel's affirmations: "Hoy la plebe, con todos sus vicios, vale más que las otras clases y con ella simpatizo más" and "solo en la plebe hallo un resto de nobleza y virtud". (267) This attitude is affirmed in such "episodios" as *Zaragoza,* but in the second series the pendulum swings in the opposite direction. As for the Naturalistic novels, Clarín's observations are, as far as I can see, not wide of the mark: "Para Galdós como para Zola, la mayor miseria del pueblo, de la plebe, para que nos entendamos, es su podredumbre moral, y a lo primero que hay que atender es a salvar su espíritu. Para eso no hay mejor medio que pintar su estado moral tal cual es, junto a la miseria del cuerpo la del alma." *Galdós,* p. 101. In *Fortunata y Jacinta* both attitudes are present, the ultimately incorruptable heroine's uncle being the pathetically corrupt "revolutionary" Izquierdo. Fortunata is explicitly identified as *representing* "el pueblo" (as against being a member of it) for the first time when Juanito and Villalonga cynically discuss the new prominence of her bosom after she has learned how to mold it with a stylish French corset: "El pueblo es la cantera . . . el arte saca el bloque y lo talla. . . ." (152) As noted, the allegorical dimension here as opposed to previous novels is ironical.

he has become and perhaps what he still can aspire to be.[11] As Roy Harvey Pearce phrases it, "[Huck] exists not to judge his world but to furnish us the means of judging it—and also our world as it develops out of his."[12]

Conscience Abandoned

Until this point I have elaborated upon Sherman Eoff's notion of Fortunata's novel as a "deification of the conscious process" but with differing emphases.[13] What remains is to try to grasp how Galdós as an artist of the novel, as a ceaseless experimenter with structure and style, developed his changed intention in the course of the narrative. Another approach would have been to go outside the boundaries of fiction and to examine the concepts of consciousness that were available to Galdós: that of the positivistic psychology of the time ("mecánica espiritual")[14] and above all that of the "krausistas," who

[11] John Sinnigen makes much the same point. "Individual, Class, and Society in *Fortunata y Jacinta*," pp. 64–65.

[12] "Huck Finn in his History," *EA*, 24, 1974, p. 294.

[13] I cite the title of his chapter on *Fortunata y Jacinta* in *The Modern Spanish Novel*.

[14] This notion referred to frequently in the novel has its origins in the eighteenth century in Lamettrie's *L'Homme machine* and later contributes in Bergsonian fashion to the comedy of *Jacques le fataliste*. In *César Birotteau*, however, when Balzac tells us that "Madame Birotteau subit alors quelques-unes des souffrances en quelque sorte lumineuse qui procurent ces terribles décharges de la volonté répandue ou concentrée par un mecanisme inconnue," it seems to be a serious metaphor for mental processes conceived of along the lines of the new scientific psychology. *Comédie*, vol. 5, p. 325. Thus, too, Zola, who says: "Les corps vivants, dans lesquels admettaient encore une influence mysterieuse, sont a leur tour ramenés et réduits au mécanisme général de la matière. . . . Quand on aura prouvé que le corps de l'homme est une machine . . . il faudra bien passer aux actes passionels et intelectuels." *Le Roman expérimental, Oeuvres complètes*, ed. H. Mitterand, Paris, 1968, vol. 10, p. 1182. Clarín follows Zola when he says that Ana in *La Regenta* "notó unas ruedas que le daban vuelta dentro del craneo se movían más despacio y con armónico movimiento." *Obras*, vol. 1, p. 108. In a novel such as *Fortunata y Jacinta*, dedicated to a major voyage of exploration into the interiority of human lives, one cannot but suspect that a sentence such as "su espiritu . . . girando sobre un pivote" (526) is residual, evasive, or tinged with irony. It seems now to be a metaphor for inexplicability, just as when Galdós describes in the *Memorias* the project of the "epi-

believed that the reform of consciousness would bring Utopia, the "greening" of Spain that was gently mocked by Galdós in *El amigo Manso.* This approach was not taken because, in addition to my lack of preparation for the enterprise, I suspect strongly that it would be pointless, that what goes on inside *Fortunata y Jacinta* is really autonomous. When Galdós cites what clearly appears to be a Krausist definition of consciousness learned by Juanito at the university ("la intimidad total del ser racional consigo mismo"),[15] he does so with ill-concealed irony. Far more revealing for our purposes is Fortunata's popular phrase "lo que sale de entre mí," which embraces not only self-enclosed neo-Cartesian or neo-Kantian rationality but also the eruption of passion, remorse, vocational conviction, and all the other components of what Castro termed "incitation."

Having refused to enter this—to my mind—critical blind alley, let me now attempt a description of our heroine's novel-long discovery of herself derived entirely from the text and the news it brings us. To begin with, whenever Galdós employs the term "conciencia," he uses it ostensibly in the sense of the English "conscience." As we know, in the Romance languages "conscience" and "consciousness" as substantives are homonymous and without clear demarcation. Therefore, it is not surprising that Galdós consistently presents the latter as an extension or outgrowth of the former. The first occurrence of the word in connection with Fortunata is to be found in the chapter called *"Las Micaelas* por dentro" when, influenced by her woman-made milieu, she undertakes an "examen de conciencia." The results are illuminating: Saint Paul's *"con-*

---

sodios" as resulting from "un impulso maquinal que brotaba de lo más hondo de mi ser." (*1657*) Galdós may not have had any other language at his disposal, but he clearly did not believe, as did Taine, that there is no difference between a "souvenir" and a "vibration." See Taine, *De l'Intelligence,* Le Havre, 1873, p. 4.

[15] The first use of the word in the novel has to do with don Baldomero's theories of modern, nineteenth-century education (once again we are confronted with Galdós as an ironical prophet): "El hombre se educa sólo en virtud de las suscepciones constantes que determina en su espíritu la conciencia, ayudada del ambiente social." (*27*) The dry-goods merchant's formula for this is, of course, "el mundo marcha," but we are here told explicitly that for him society as such ("el ambiente social") is the other component of *"con-*scientia." This is precisely what Fortunata discovers is *not* true.

scientia," consciousness "shared" with some external and morally imperative entity (whether society or God),[16] is given voice by what she calls "la idea blanca." In the penitent's prayerful imagination, the host, sharing her "scientia," speaks to her in her own language and convinces her of the correctness of the conventional and social destiny that has been prepared for her. In other words, she becomes aware of herself as a moral being by projecting her thoughts into the supernatural symbol she has just been taught to worship.

Let us listen again briefly to Fortunata expressing herself for the first time as she is, confronting herself, talking to herself in language that is noble in its very humility:

> A ti, Fortunata, te miré con *indilugencia* entre las descarriadas, porque volvías a Mí tus ojos alguna vez, y Yo vi en ti deseos de enmienda; pero ahora, hija, me sales con que sí, serás honrada, todo lo honrada que Yo quiera, siempre y cuando que te dé el hombre de tu gusto. . . . Vaya una gracia! . . . Pero, en fin, no me quiero enfadar. Lo dicho, dicho: soy infinitamente misericordioso contigo dándote un bien que no mereces, deparándote un marido honrado y que te adora, y todavía refunfuñas y pides más, más, más. . . .[17] (249)

Consciousness, Galdós wants us to realize, begins with conscience, because the latter forces us to observe and judge our own thoughts and feelings from without.

Later, after her second seduction, Fortunata's more experienced conscience fills its most familiar and most disagreeable role, that of prosecuting attorney: "Overwhelmed by her conscience, Fortunata

---

[16] I have learned this from an unpublished lecture of my colleague in Classics, Zeph Stewart. In this case, just as in *Huck Finn,* God is implicitly identified with society, an identification which is the basis for both authors' condemnation of their times.

[17] "Among all the girls who have gone astray, I regarded you, Fortunata, with special 'indilugencia,' because once in a while you remembered Me, and I saw in you signs of a desire to repent. But now, child, it suddenly occurs to you that, yes, you will be an honest woman, fully as honest as I demand, when and if I bestow on you the man of your choice. . . . How laughable that is! But I don't want to get angry. A bargain is a bargain; I have been infinitely merciful to you by giving you a reward you don't deserve; finding you an honorable man who adores you and wants to marry you. But you grumble, and demand more and more. . . ."

couldn't say a word." (*289*) But when Juanito excuses his intention to abandon her for a second time by claiming to be conscience-stricken, she reacts in an antithetical way: " 'I deserve all I got,' she exclaimed in an outburst of grief mingled with rage, 'because we both have been bad, but I have been worse than you. . . . In comparison to me all other [sinful] women are pikers.' " (*323*) No longer a hapless and passive victim, Fortunata, in her newly discovered capacity for anger, uses her guilt both as an expressive weapon and as a form of self-assertion. Juanito's self-serving and patently false remorse for having violated "las leyes divinas y humanas" has incited in his mistress a sense of her authenticity as a sinner.

We should not, however, for that reason accept at face value Maxi's facile, and in its own way self-serving, explanation of Fortunata's later capacity to think for herself and about herself: " 'You think too in your own way,' Maxi said gently. 'You think because you feel; you understand me because you are in love. You've sinned; you've suffered; and sinning and suffering are really two ways of experiencing the same thing; you have a need for liberation. If I may express myself by a parable: the shackles of life are chafing your wrists.' " (*432*) But Maxi is wrong. It was not the pain of a bad conscience that impelled Fortunata's self-exploration; it was rather the fundamental discovery (made while separated from both husband and lover) that conscience does not tell the truth. Guilt had provided only a glimmering of rebellious selfhood, and by the time Fortunata returns to Maxi, her consciousness has grown to monumental proportions.

At first Fortunata's questioning of conscience had amounted to little more than resigned self-acceptance.

The place and the way it had happened made what she had done all the more reprehensible, and she realized that after a rapid examination of her conscience. Nevertheless, her ancient and constantly renovated passion was so strong and vigorous that the specter of guilt fled without leaving a trace behind. Fortunata conceived of herself as a blind mechanism turned on by a supernatural hand. What she had done had been done in her opinion as a necessary result of those mysterious energies

330

that govern the workings of the universe—as inevitable as sunrise or gravity. She couldn't stop herself from doing it again; she didn't try to persuade herself to change; and she didn't make excuses. She wasn't very clear about her own personal responsibility, and even if she had been, she was a person so determined that no possible consequences could deter her. She was *perfectly willing*—as she expressed it to herself—*to go to hell*. (277)

But later, when explaining her past misbehavior to herself and to Feijóo, she explicitly denies the validity of imperative messages from imposed codes of morality: "her conscience appeared to her to be unblemished, transparent, and strong. In her own self-judgment she was not guilty, innocent of all evil, as if her deed had been the result of obedience to an imperative and irresistible order from above. 'But I'm not bad,' she thought. 'What is there bad about me here inside? Really nothing.' " (*332*)

At this point our earlier comparison of Fortunata with Huck Finn becomes specific and textual. As we remember, after a long struggle with his conscience, which reproaches him for thievery (i.e. helping Jim escape), Huck is finally faced with a definitive choice. He has written a letter to Miss Watson informing her that Jim has been captured and is being held at the Phelps farm where she can now reclaim him. But he thinks back over the life he and Jim had shared on the river: "I took the letter up and held it in my hand. I was a-trembling, because I'd got to decide forever betwixt two things, and I knowed it. I studied a minute, sort of holding my breath, and then says to myself: 'All right, then, I'll *go* to hell'—and tore it up."[18] Writing in the same decade (and in that of Nietzsche's *Jenseits von Gut und Böse*) (1886) the two novelists, both deeply influenced by Cervantes, converge on an identical truth: society itself is hypocritical or, as Lukacs would say, in a state of axiological degeneration. Only a stripping away of conventional patterns of moral self-castigation can save the nineteenth-century person as a person. Only by rejecting "conscience" can "consciousness" find the freedom and the self-confidence necessary for the just estimation of received values and at the same time derive meaningful experi-

[18] Chapter 31.

ence from surrounding landscape, whether human or natural. Both Mark Twain and Galdós want us to realize that in order to see the river as it is and the Guadarrama or the Plaza Mayor as they are, the seer must first see himself as he is. From the point of view of the novel, consciousness is indivisible.

Both Huck, the outcast, and Fortunata, the castoff, are archetypically naive, but their revelatory innocence is not of the simple and passive sort that amused, or tearfully bemused, the eighteenth-century mind and provoked its own seduction.[19] We are not dealing with Candide or Mignon but rather with warriors (at once conscious and unconscious) against society, warriors tempered in novelistic battle whose heroism is their capacity for experience.[20] Clear vision, full reporting, implacable judgment, and unerring intuition are their arms. For these two illiterates "la incitación" emerges, not from magnificent printed prevarications projected comically on an ungratefully prosaic world, but from resolute rejection of "conscientia" understood as the antagonist of truth. Unlike the don Quijote of part 1, they are paladins, not of fantasy or romance, but of life in the present at its most alive and free. In these novels, so antithetical to everything their century took for granted, society is a liar, history a trap, and naiveté, rather than being charmingly irrational, man's only hope for spiritual survival. How heartily Galdós would have applauded Mark Twain's perverse and belated allusion to the "antimoral" of *Huck Finn:* "It shows that that strange thing, the conscience—that unerring monitor—can be trained to approve any wild thing you *want* it to approve, if you begin its education early and stick to it."[21]

Thematic rapprochement of our carnal "dos historias de casadas" to the sexless *Adventures of Huckleberry Finn* is confirmed by the strong resemblance of the contrast of Fortunata and Juanito to that

[19] See H. Petriconi's thematic study, *Die verführte Unschuld,* Hamburg, 1953.

[20] As Pearce puts it, Huck is a "witness to the full panoply of people and institutions which, as we see, even if he does not, would deny freedom not only to Jim but to themselves." "Huck Finn in his History," p. 285. The entire essay is deeply relevant to *Fortunata y Jacinta*—or at least to my interpretation of it.

[21] Ibid., p. 287. Cited by Pearce from an 1895 notebook.

of Huck and Tom. Both novels are structured humanly on a plurality of such contrasts: Fortunata against Juanito, then Maxi, and finally Jacinta, while Huck's invulnerable naiveté is placed between the primitive animism of Jim and the perverse sophistication of Tom. It is in terms of this last contrast that we can comprehend the deep resemblance of Tom and Juanito. Both are actors, stylists, manipulators, connoisseurs of life, inventors of "rasgos," intellectual puppeteers who take pleasure in role performance. In a word, fakes! And both present vivid and purposeful antitheses to the spiritual integrity of their partners in play or love. Mark Twain once remarked that he would have liked to have written the life of a boy growing up to manhood, but that Tom Sawyer would never do. A current English term roughly equivalent to "señorito" is "playboy," which is what a forty- or fifty-year-old Tom would inevitably have become. And as we have observed, novels about such hollow individuals—by definition, unincited—are at best self-defeating (*Lo prohibido*) and at worst sentimentally false (*Peñas arriba*).[22]

Returning now to Fortunata, we soon find her free of the fears and self-doubts that accompanied her initial assertions of guiltlessness. Unlike Huck, who at the end abandons civilization (as he had earlier abandoned conscience) as a hopeless enterprise, Fortunata aspires to nothing less than its reform. Her burning desire to be "honrada" on her own terms eventually leads her to the formulation of "la pícara idea." As we remember, this bold and assertive successor to the timid acquiescence of "la idea blanca" is based on love

---

[22] Our view of *Lo prohibido* as the "dialectical" antithesis of *Fortunata y Jacinta* leads us to the realization that the special naiveté of such nineteenth-century novel heroes and heroines as these two (or of a Pierre and a Fabrice, "señoritos" who refuse to live as such) is complementary to Castro's incitation. For Bueno de Guzmán (and for Juanito) sophistication and lack of any authentic mission go hand in hand; but for "heroes" who can save us and at the same time show us the world as if seen for the first time (Shklovsky's "ostranenie"), the opposite is the case. As Ortega says not only of "señoritos" but of all of us who get along as well as we can in our roles: "solemos hacer que vivimos, pero no vivimos efectivamente nuestro auténtico vivir, el que tendríamos si, deshaciéndonos de todas esas interpretaciones recibidas de los demás entre quienes estamos y que suele llamarse 'sociedad,' tomásemos de cuando en cuando enérgico, evidente contacto con nuestra vida en cuanto realidad radical." *El hombre y la gente,* Madrid, 1957, p. 127.

as self-justifying ("querer a quien se quiere no puede ser cosa mala") and on childbirth as the only true sacrament ("esposa que no tiene hijos no es tal esposa"). "Con la inspiración de un apóstol y la audacia criminal de un anarquista," as Galdós phrases it, Fortunata replaces her earlier acceptance of hellfire with advocation of a new "natural" society and a new "natural" moral code. That is, although he surely would not have employed such terms, a society based on what Ortega two generations later was to call "valores vitales."

Galdós the novelist, however, is less interested in Fortunata's never-to-be-realized Utopia as such than in portraying her conscious commitment to it. A heroine who dares autonomously to preach such a revolution is by definition remote from the hapless, hopeless, and virtually speechless victim we met at the beginning. Instead of being an unconscious "bête humaine" ("la pájara mala" as doña Desdémona puts it), the final eloquence of her exaltation expresses a distilled awareness of self at once fiery and clear.

As was suggested earlier, Fortunata's last dialogue with Maxi may remind us of certain of the more than human conversations to be found in *The Brothers Karamazov* or in *The Possessed*. But, as we also remarked, Galdós arrived at this intensity in a fashion far more decelerated than Dostoievsky. Fortunata's hysterical oral ferocity and her mad decision to mend the world are functions, paradoxically, of a long process of more or less tranquil meditation beginning in "las Micaelas" (an institution of conscience as stultifying as the household of the Widow Douglas) and ending with the "juicios claros" of her final review of her life. Alone in her room over the Plaza Mayor, she inhabits a second and far more elevated (Stendhalian?) convent: "She saw her whole life clarified by the light of reason, at that [temporal] distance which permits one to perceive without distortion the shape and form of things. Thus, similarly, the peace of the cloister permits fugitives from the world to realize the errors and sins they had committed while still living there." (*482*) But Galdós' emphasis on Fortunata's final rationality implies a certain surprise on his part. As her life as a whole demonstrates, revalidation of values (the greatest achievement of the greatest inhabitants of novels) depends on the will more than it does on Aristotle's other two faculties of the soul, memory and reason.

Jacinta in Mind

We cannot truly comprehend how Fortunata arrived at her quixotic resolve to reshape society without considering both her relationship with Jacinta and her triumph over another form of divided consciousness resulting from that relationship. I refer now, of course, to the self-consciousness (a form of spiritual foreshortening and self-torment that is more painful to most of us than conscience) that arises from her admiration of her rival. Here we must forego further comparison with Huck Finn, for he was created, blessedly, as immune from social hypochondria. When he does occasionally think about himself in comparison to others, it is either because he intends to deceive them or because he pities them. The rest of the time he is who he is as carelessly as an angel or as an animal. Fortunata, on the other hand, by the very juxtaposition of her name to that of Jacinta in the title, is condemned to a life of self-survey. The shape of the whole is one of mutuality, each woman being forced by circumstances to keep the other in mind. It should be added immediately, however, that Jacinta's jealousy and apprehension are less of a burden than Fortunata's admiration and insecurity.

Galdós is exceptionally explicit about this aspect of his theme, and we can afford to be no less so. Most of us think about self-consciousness in Stendhalian terms, that is, as a more or less prolonged early stage in life, during which we are condemned to observe ourselves critically in specific social situations: reciting in class, teaching, making conversation with an attractive hostess, dancing, explaining symptoms to a physician, etc. We are, or remember having been, the interior audience of our own wretched performance of some unavoidable (in some cases desirable) and unspeakably demanding role. This, however, is not the case for Fortunata, who does not aspire to social success and who is happiest when out of the limelight. Society and its judgment only matter to her insofar as they are embodied by Jacinta or by those close to Jacinta, particularly doña Guillermina. Otherwise, Fortunata is as natural, as unconcerned, and as candid (although never as sly) as Huck Finn. It is the being and existence of her rival that make her wonder if "su lenguaje no sería bastante fino" and that stimulate that continuity of meditation and worry about herself that is essential to the growth of her consciousness. It is not by accident that Fortunata undertakes her first "examen de consciencia" and allows the "idea blanca" to persuade her of the merits of marriage and honor immediately after her first encounter with Jacinta. Although separated here for purposes of clarity, conscience and self-consciousness are hardly distinguishable for her.

We all remember the beginning of Fortunata's novel-long voyage through self-consciousness toward self-discovery. When the charitable society matrons visit "las Micaelas" and doña Manolita points out Jacinta among their number, the wide-eyed heroine absorbs "aquella simpática imagen" for good. She is, of course, jealous and envious, but beneath these negative feelings there is admiration: "It was a burning desire to look like Jacinta, to be like her, to give the same impression, that special air of sweetness and ladylike gentility." (*243*) Afterwards, fantasy and "ensueño" suggest possible intimacy, transmigration of souls, and even a prophetic dream of the "rasgo," still so many pages and years in the future. (*246*) Jacinta in mind has been added to Fortunata in mind.

But there is no need to continue. The novel tells us explicitly and clearly all that we can possibly know concerning the development of the interpersonal relations of the two women. Only at the end is there an element of mystery, when it turns out that it is Jacinta, of all people, who confers significance on Fortunata's rebellious "pícara idea." By being "honrada" herself, Jacinta proves that honor is possible and so elevates Fortunata's program of self-justification far above the level of mere biological capability:

> Oh no! . . ., Fortunata exclaimed from the depths of her soul, for if she is not virtuous, it would seem to me that there would be no virtue in the world and that anybody could do whatever he pleased. It would seem to me to break all the threads that hold us in place and that white and black would be the same thing. . . . Ah, you have no idea what kind of thoughts I have at the end of the day. What goes through my mind is inexpressible. (*466*)

It is thus crucial both to Fortunata and to the intention of the novelist that Jacinta be what she is reputed to be: honest, honorable, faithful, loving, charitable, in short, a "proper" lady. This is to say, Fortunata's project of sacramental revolution is not really as revolutionary as it seems to doña Guillermina. It is not a Nietzschean negation or overturning of traditional values but rather a profound revalidation of those eternal values to which Restoration society paid lip service but in practice betrayed. And as long as there is one person who can be trusted, one exemplary being, the notion that any individual (even as adulteress) can aspire to worth ("honradez") is conceivable. Jacinta in a sense is the Amadís of Fortunata's "incitation."

Substituting a Hegelian comparison for that suggested by the *Quijote,* we might say that Fortunata and Jacinta, presented novelistically as antithetical, nonetheless aspire to eventual synthesis. Fortunata's progress is toward an autonomous state of consciousness, which will incorporate the values admired in Jacinta while retaining her own identity. And in this she succeeds. By the end of the end, self-consciousness, jealousy, emulation, and fear of inferiority are all surpassed, just as conscience had been surpassed long before. Her selfhood is not just satisfied but, in the sense proposed by Erik Erikson, completed. And the sign that the "reciprocal transmigration" of souls that she had dreamed of long before in "las Micaelas" has at last taken place is not merely the generosity of her living legacy nor even the style of the letter, which in its humility and striving for truth could only have been written by a consciousness that, having redeemed itself, is fully in command of language. What finally matters is the way Fortunata's final self continues to live in Jacinta.

John Sinnigen underlines this change when he points out how at the very end Galdós returns to the theme of Fortunata in mind,[23] observing that her self-redemption depends at least in part on having elevated Jacinta to a new level of awareness:

> She [Jacinta] couldn't stop thinking about the person who had ceased to exist that morning, and it surprised her to find in her heart something more than pity for that unfortunate woman. Her feelings did not arise solely from solidarity or sorority based on shared unhappiness. . . . the final stages of their enmity

---

[23] "Individual, Class, and Society in *Fortunata y Jacinta,*" p. 63.

and the incredible legacy of the *Pituso* involved an enigma beyond the reach of intelligence—a reconciliation. Cut apart by
death, the one alive in the visible world and the other in the
invisible looked at each other from opposite shores, each desiring to embrace the other. (542)

Earlier the "generoso corazón [de Jacinta] se desbordaba en sentimientos filantrópicos" at the spectacle of the exploitation of the
young women in Catalonian textile factories. But now she realizes
that she too has been as exploited as any of them or as Fortunata
herself. Thus, despite the gift of the heir, the end of the novel is not
a triumph for the bourgeoisie. Instead, ironically, insofar as that
class is personified in Juanito, it loses all that really matters: Fortunata and Jacinta joined in consciousness after having "worked
themselves free."

Consciousness Expanded

All that has been said so far is tainted with a grave critical fallacy,
i.e. the discussion of Fortunata's consciousness as if it were real
rather than fictional. It is, therefore, necessary now to retrace our
steps and to observe the growth of Fortunata's consciousness as a
composition, that is, as set forth by Galdós in narrative space and
time. Let us begin with space, if only because Galdós as early as
La segunda casaca (1876) has Carlos Navarro (in a moment of remarkable insight) call attention to the smallness of his own soul
with the anguished exclamation: "May God forgive me, but how
difficult it is to solve the enigma of the size of souls!" (1405) Fortunata, however, arrives at the opposite extreme. If we think, as is
our wont, of consciousness as inside and the dimensional world as
outside, it is natural to view the former as if it were a kind of inner
space, the boundless inner space of Hamlet's nutshell: "An idea
passed through her mind like a bird in flight across the immensity
of the sky." (332) It is because of this that the personages of Galdós'
later novels, like those of Dostoievsky, Joyce, and Virginia Woolf
(all of them creatures of consciousness, even though no birds soar
through the skies of their minds), seem so much larger than life.

Speaking specifically of Fortunata, Montesinos observes with wonder her "modo de agigantarse," which, of course, implies a process.[24] Fortunata's consciousness at the beginning is little more than a tiny bubble, which rises from her mirror image, but quite soon, by the time of her residence in "las Micaelas," it has expanded to a metaphorical "volume" far larger than that attained by most of us. The phenomenal growth, Galdós makes clear, is not due to an avid and tender sensibility of the sort possessed by Rousseau's alter egos, or even due to a specially keen intelligence, but rather to a fundamental quality of transparency. To educate her is a task of enormous difficulty for Maxi, and, as far as we can tell, even at the end she still "takes no stock in dead people" (for example, Columbus) and does not know how to spell. What has happened is something very different from learning lessons, drawing the proper conclusions from experience, or "Bildung" (she eventually rejects Feijóo's "sagesse" too). Instead, as our earlier comparison of her with Huck Finn suggested, all that she has met has become a part of her without distortion, honestly, as it was without overestimation or underestimation. It is in this, the evaluation of experience, that she excels. How well she knows who people are and what they amount to—even Juanito, in spite of her love for him.

The contrast between Fortunata as novelistic heroine and Maxi as novelistic hero is in this sense both striking and intentional. The latter, who begins with an exalted sense of the interior space of his consciousness, seems to us ever more diminished as we go on reading. Not only do his illusions about himself and others cut him off from experience, but he actually seems to grow backwards. By the end he has shrunken himself to a purely rational autonomy, encaged in a mind as self-sufficiently sick as Fortunata's is healthy. In other words, his very lucidity as well as his earlier paranoia are conditions of experiential incapacity: "All he wanted to do was to sit by the windows of the balcony contemplating the passers-by absent-mindedly." (442) And precisely because Maxi is the antithesis of his wife as far as his "inwardness" is concerned, Galdós constantly and with unrelenting cruelty delights in describing him from without. In a sense, it is his novelistic way of explaining why we are not allowed to see Fortunata.

[24] *Galdós,* vol. 2, p. 264.

These remarks should not be taken to mean that Galdós in his movement inwards abandons the external techniques of Naturalistic, and at the end melodramatic, storytelling. It is obvious that he does not. As the characters press ever more closely against an ever more incited Fortunata and as their mutual presence in each others' minds become more and more intense, the more *we* become aware that the meaning of the novel is what is going on in her consciousness. Hence the impression of a size not limited to the feet and inches of physique.

At the same time, Madrid, which loomed large and powerful at the beginning, is gradually diminished both by a process of acceleration (its inhabitants move in and out of the pages faster and faster) and by caricature.[25] For example, the device used in *La desheredada* of comparing groups of human beings to animal collectivities (the Pez family of politicians and bureaucrats) is further developed. Oysters, mollusks, rats, and, above all, birds are utilized. Like the chickens in the "tienda de aves" at the beginning and like doña Desdémona's noisy aviary at the end (the framing images), the population of Madrid is visualized as a flock of caged birds, twittering incessantly with their "picos de oro," giving birth to "canarios de alcoba," storing up deposits of "guano" or money. As Fortunata expands from within, Madrid shrinks from without; the city reminds us again of the verse from Calderón misquoted by Segismundo Ballester: "la inquieta república de las aves."

From time to time, of course, Galdós returns to his initial neo-Naturalistic comparison of Fortunata to a wild and errant bird (in intentional contrast to all the others), but as we remember and as those who witness her death observe unanimously, she ends as a creature still winged but by definition surpassing outwardness and size itself, an angel. As such, she is a creature of pure spirit (or consciousness) and of absolute meaning. In more general terms, the theme of *Fortunata y Jacinta* is the theme of all great novels ever

[25] At first glance, this process of acceleration appears to resemble Scott's technique as analyzed admirably by Bardèche. See chapter 1 in his *Balzac romancier*. But it is actually the opposite. The scurrying citizens of Madrid are used by Galdós to suggest the insignificance of all that had seemed so important at the beginning, whereas Scott shows us that what had seemed to be pointless historical details reveal their purpose and organic integration as the action accelerates.

since the *Quijote:* the creation of significance out of insignificance or, as Lukacs has taught us, a quest for values, a quest that in apparent failure nevertheless succeeds. Hence, Fortunata's physical death and her lonely funeral, attended by only four or five mourners, does not belie our certainty that in some sense she has found salvation for herself and perhaps also for us. In Lukacs' terms, to have thus "forgiven" Madrid can be interpreted as the seemingly impossible "metaphysical" deed necessary for the recovery of the lost spirituality of our novelistic times. Admittedly, even within the subjunctive history of this novel, society goes on as before. But who knows? It is conceivable that the sharing of her consciousness (and her firm rejection of conscience) with her readers on the printed page may save some of us from historical and social damnation: from pointless ambition, from mindless conformance, from stale topics, from sterile dogmatism, in short, from all the charades and façades that disguise the debasement of our community. We may not accept it, but what novels such as *The Brothers Karamazov, La Chartreuse de Parme, Huck Finn,* and *Fortunata y Jacinta* have to offer is nothing less than humanistic therapy, the possibility of "working ourselves free," escaping from society's "charnel house of dead interiorities," and returning to life.[26]

The structure of such a complex organism as *Fortunata y Jacinta* can be, and indeed has been, visualized in many ways: as a series of interlocking triangles of personal relationship, as a conflict of classes, etc. But I think that to describe it as a confrontation of inwardness

[26] I know of no better analysis of the dilemma of Fortunata than Lukacs' description of social "nature" (the social "out there") as opposed to natural nature:

> It is not silent or unaware, rather it consists of complex petrification of meaning, which have *become alien* and which are no longer capable of awakening our inner selves (Innerlichkeit); it is a charnel house (Schädelstatte) of dead interiorities; this is why—were it possible—it could only be resuscitated by a metaphysical act springing from a reawakening of the spirit that created it in the first place. . . . It is too much like the soul's aspirations to be treated as simple raw material and too foreign to constitute an adequate expression of one's true self."

Die Theorie, p. 62. My translation is more a paraphrase than a literal rendering, but this is essentially what the text says. I have checked myself against the French and Spanish versions. Fortunata's gift and the forgiveness it implies can be interpreted as the hypothetical "metaphysical" deed here imagined.

341

and outwardness (which includes within its terms expansion and contraction, freedom and servitude, sickness and health, prevarication and truth, perdition and redemption, etc.) is more valid, because it relates to Galdós' basic intention in the novels written between 1881 and 1887, that is, the intention to castigate the Spain of the Bourbon Restoration for its hypocrisy, its pompous triviality, its empty historical optimism, and above all its crass materialism. Like many major novelists before and after his time (from Cervantes to Joyce), Galdós' vision is moral and existential rather than psychological and aesthetic (*Madame Bovary*) or revolutionary (*Germinal*). When in the person of Fortunata he completes his earlier criticism with a spiritual solution, the resulting structural duality not only concerns us deeply (as frantic heirs of the decaying values of the nineteenth century) but also restates in a new way the crucial theme that has been built into the genre of the novel ever since the *Quijote,* that is, our possible significance as individuals living in a culture and a society primarily dedicated to insignificance.

This spatial concept of consciousness represents at best a series of cross sections; we must also take into account Galdós' art of inner time, his sequential composition of Fortunata's growth. In trying to do so, I must confess that I have found it unrewarding to try to utilize rigid schemes of the sort proposed by mystics and philosophers. Sherman Eoff is undoubtedly correct when he points out that Hegel must have influenced Fortunata's "climb" from initial unconsciousness. As mentioned previously, the title itself suggests as much. Since Hegel was concerned himself to resolve once and for all the pre-Socratic dilemma which had plagued philosophy from its beginning, he suits the intention of *Fortunata y Jacinta*. But to conceive of the whole as a kind of Hegelian *Pilgrim's Progress* would be as misleading as to read it as a Naturalistic "document humain" concerned with prostitution. After long meditation I propose instead that a number of allusive references to Hegel are used ironically by Galdós in order to illustrate or underline moments of decisive change in his heroine.

The most significant example occurs at the end of the chapter entitled appropriately "Naturalismo espiritual." As we remember, at that point Fortunata senses that "la simpatía misteriosa que le había inspirado Mauricia se pasaba a Guillermina," after which there occurs a synthesis in her mind of the two antithetical beings. This is expressed verbally by her confusion of their names: "Doña Mauricia, digo Guillermina la dura." It is, I think, licit and suggestive to interpret this as an intentional reference to transition from the "subjective" to the "objective spirit." This means, stated with startling oversimplification, that from now on, instead of being wrapped up in her own impulses and her passion for Juanito, Fortunata will be, in Hegelian terms, disposed to create an autonomous "institution": the new family based on nature rather than supernature. And when she puts her "pícara idea" into words ("A wife who can't bear children is not a real wife"), Galdós again expresses her synthesis of Mauricia, the subjective anarchist, and Guillermina, the apostle of traditional social order: " 'It's my idea,' she insisted with the inspiration of an apostle and the criminal audacity of an anarchist." (405) Fortunata's passion has been channeled into a project for the authentification and renewal of society.

Nevertheless, because this kind of interpretation is so tempting, let me insist again that such novelistic allusions to the concepts of thesis, antithesis, and synthesis should not be understood with allegorical rigidity. As an allegorist, Galdós here is much closer to Juan Ruiz than to Berceo, and, as a result, Hegel, mentioned only once, slyly and in passing,[27] serves him more as a means of allusion and evasion than as a solution to the mysteries of consciousness.[28]

[27] As we remember Manso translates Hegel with a prologue and Federico Ruiz writes a treatise on him in *El doctor Centeno*. Galdós lauds Fabié's translation of Hegel's *Logic* in a 15 May 1872 article as a "síntoma que han de prevalecer los estudios serios." *Crónica de la quincena,* ed. W. H. Shoemaker, Princeton, 1948, p. 131. In our novel the one ironical and tangential reference occurs in a café conversation:

" 'En verdad os digo que no hay Infierno ni Cielo—afirmó Rubín con acento apostólico—animada por la fuerza . . .' " . . .

" 'Llámelo usted *hache*—repuso doña Nieves—. La fuerza, el alma . . ., la . . ., como quien dice la idea.' "

" 'Doña Nieves, por amor de Dios . . .—dijo Rubín con desesperación de maestro—. Que está usted volviendo muy *hegeliana.*" (307)

All the interruptions, with the single exception of my omission after the quotation marks in line 3, correspond to Galdós' effort to reproduce the rhythm of the conversation.

[28] In the early chapters Galdós seems to flirt with a number of such allusions. W. T. Stace's analysis of Hegel's "self-consciousness" in the *Philosophy of Mind* triad will remind readers of certain aspects of the initial formation

Galdós obviously realized that, given his intention in creating Fortunata, certain of her abrupt changes and new stages of growth were susceptible to Hegelian interpretation,[29] but it would be hard to prove that his philosophical play is more serious than the historical play that led him to portray Juanito ("el hombre del siglo") as alternating between revolution and restoration. After all, it is not Fortunata but Maxi who, in a final flourish of Galdosian irony, ends up by living "en la pura idea." The point is that Hegelian consciousness is ultimately rational, while Fortunata's is ultimately voluntary—and so are her two "ideas." She is a vessel, not of thoughts, but of creative passion, undistorted perception, and true value judgment. To "explain her" as Hegelian is to ignore irony, just as if we believed in Cide Hamete Benengeli.

The shape of Fortunata's ascending biography (for Castro the soaring of incitation, for Madariaga a sequence of repression and explosion) can only be visualized ex post facto by its readers or intuited post mortem by Segismundo Ballester, its most reliable witness. As far as Fortunata is concerned, the temporality of her consciousness is manifest as ours is manifest, within the borders of

---

of Fortunata's consciousness: sheer impulsiveness of desire, the mirror image, the "subject" desiring to consume the "object" (apparently Hegel himself uses the communion comparison), the final consciousness of oneself in the other and in terms of the other. *The Philosophy of Hegel,* New York, 1955, pp. 350–359. These examples may seem coincidental, but the dialogue between Feijóo and Fortunata in the chapter entitled "Un curso de filosofía práctica" is clearly Hegelian. It corresponds to that moment in the dialectics when "practical reason" confronts "impulses"—humorously translated by Galdós as "rasgos." Then, when Fortunata declares her desire to "cambiar todo mi ser natural hasta volverme tal y como [Jacinta] es," (*336*) and Feijóo, failing to understand her, feels the first signs of his coming physical decline, Galdós ironically uses the Naturalistic change to express what might be called the dialectical abandonment or superseding of a kind of reason no longer needed by the spirit on its way toward self-completion. (Stace 368–372) However, the Guillermina-Mauricia synthesis is just as convincing or perhaps more so.

[29] In comprehending this aspect of *Fortunata y Jacinta,* we should keep in mind that in the 1872 article on the Spanish translation of the *Logic,* Galdós refers to it as a "libro oportunísimo" insofar as it provided an antidote to "los estragos que en entendimientos muy ilustrados hace la escuela positivista." *Crónica de la quincena,* ed. Shoemaker, p. 131. As against the unproblematical stasis of d. Baldomero's "entendimiento," that of Fortunata grows.

instant, hour, and day. As such, it is expressed, not in the structure of the novel, but in the style of appropriate paragraphs. In these essays and elsewhere I have frequently cited one of those remarks of Américo Castro that plunge to the heart of problems to which most of us merely lay siege: "The novel does not consist in telling what happens to a person, but instead how that person feels himself existing in a happening."[30] The meaning is clear: great novelistic characters, as against the heroes of romance, are not just swept along from adventure to adventure (each temporally isolated from the next, according to Simmel and Ortega)[31] but rather experience a communion of their inner "durée" (how it feels to exist) with the time that relentlessly "happens" out there in the "más allá de veras" of plots and clocks, rivers and orbits, seasons and tides. Castro is saying that, unlike the spatial image with its built-in dichotomy, temporal consciousness *unites* what is inside and what is outside. The river scenes in *Huck Finn,* the ride through the forest of Fontainebleau in *L'Education sentimentale,* and the dark night of the "batanes" are all familiar examples.

The first instance of such experiential communion in *Fortunata y Jacinta* occurs when the incarcerated and newly conscious Fortunata looks at the view of the Guadarrama from "las Micaelas por dentro." As we remember, she not only perceives its beauty but also observes how it is gradually "engloutie" as the wall of a church under construction arises day after day. Her own sense of vital repression, the institutional damming up of her flow of internal time, becomes one with the temporality of the scene: the fleeting clouds, the implacable growth of the wall. If we read as we should read, that is, if we supplement her experience with our imagination, we come to know exactly *how* it felt to exist within that particular happening. We know Fortunata profoundly, because in some sense the art of Galdós enables us to *be* Fortunata.

Since I commented earlier on the significance of this passage, let me cite instead one of the last records of a similar temporal experience. As in the case of don Quijote at the end of the third sally, the full circle of Fortunata's life has been completed: she has returned

[30] *De la edad conflictiva,* p. 202.
[31] See my "The Novelist and His Readers; Meditations on a Stendhalian Metaphor."

to a room overlooking the Plaza Mayor on the floor above the landing where she first saw Juanito; and now she is waiting for the birth of his second child. She looks out of the window, not with "la incierta mirada" of Maxi, but with remarkable intensity:

Una mañana al levantarse, vio que había caído durante la noche una gran nevada. El espectáculo que ofrecía la plaza era precioso: los techos enteramente blancos; todas las líneas horizontales de la arquitectura y el herraje de los balcones, perfilados con durísimas líneas de nieve; los árboles ostentando cuajarones que parecían de algodón, y el rey Felipe III, con pelliza de armiño y gorro de dormir. Después de arreglarse volvió a mirar la plaza, entretenida en ver como se deshacía el mágico encanto de la nieve, como se abrían surcos en la blancura de los techos, como se sacudían los pinos de su desusada vestimenta, como, en fin, en el cuerpo del rey y en el del caballo se desleían los copos y chorreaba la humedad por el bronce abajo. El suelo, a la mañana tan duro y albo, era ya al mediodía charca cenagosa, en la cual chapoteaban los barrenderos y mangueros municipales, disolviendo la nieve con los chorros de agua y revolviéndola con el fango para echarlo todo a la alcantarilla. Divertido era este espectáculo sobre todo cuando restallaban los airosos surtidores de las mangas de riego y los chicos se lanzaban a la faena armados con tremendas escobas. Miraba esto Fortunata cuando de repente. . . .[32] (*483*)

[32] "One morning when she got up she saw there had been a big snowstorm during the night. The Plaza was a marvelous thing to see; the roofs were entirely white; all the horizontal lines of the buildings and the iron railings of the balconies were outlined in dead white; the trees seemed proud of their little gobbets of snow, which looked like cotton balls; and there in the middle was the statue of Phillip III wearing an ermine cape and a nightcap. After she got dressed, she looked at the Plaza again and was entertained by the way the magic enchantment of the snow was disappearing: the white rooftops began to be laced with little waterways; the pine trees shook off their unaccustomed dress; and from the bodies of the king and his horse the melting snowflakes dripped down the bronze. The pavement, which in the morning had looked so hard and white, by midday was a muddy pool in which the street sweepers and hosemen attacked what was left of the snow with streams of water and, mixing it with the mud, sent it into the sewers. It was an entertaining show, particularly when the hoses squirted like fountains and the sweepers launched themselves into the fray armed with enormous brooms. Fortunata was looking at all this, when suddenly. . . ."

As we read, we become increasingly aware of the rapprochement of exterior time (daytime) with the interior time of consciousness. Fortunata's view of the urban metamorphosis worked by the snow-storm (a sight she had probably never seen before) and of its grad-ual disappearance under the morning sun and at the hands of the street cleaners is combined both with the candor of her idle amuse-ment and with an underlying melancholy. Instead of damming up (as from the window of "las Micaelas"), there is here a draining away of life, an inevitable dissolution of beauty. The whole tone of the final phase of Fortunata's existence is represented emblematically with a clarity that is at once visual and emotional.

In such scenes Fortunata's consciousness is antithetical to that of her predecessor, the Naturalistic antiheroine, Isidora Rufete. It is not just that the former has been exempted by authorial fiat from de-terminism but more importantly that she has been endowed with an ample, slow, Mississippi-like inner time that is completely lack-ing in the latter. We have already discussed the stylistic results of the difference. The sequence of verbs in the imperfect tense in the passage we have just read does not correspond to Flaubertian and Zolaesque "dialogue indirecte libre": "También ella era una reina que se iba." To refract experience through the character's mind and to reshape it in her unspoken words amount essentially to a closing off of inner time. Here it is the opposite; by sharing words with Fortunata the value of the experience as it happens is opened to us. Instead of an anguished succession of unrelated instants, half-thoughts, frustrated whims, and fleeting images all observed in the mind of the experimental subject, a tenderly humorous author unites his "manto de armiño" with her "gorro de dormir," his rhetorical "desusada vestimenta" with her "cuajarones que parecían de algo-dón,"[33] with the result that time outside and time inside, time ob-

---

[33] Galdós has, thus, adapted to what Dorrit Cohn has recently called "psycho-narration," an age-old device of comic discourse: stylistic eleva-tion followed by sudden descent (a verbal form of pulling out the rug from under one's feet). *Transparent Minds,* chapter 1. Cervantes performs the trick more gently and slyly than does Rojas, as, for example, in Cipión's in-troductory sentence: "Berganza amigo . . . retirémonos a esta soledad y entre estas esteras." Fielding's description of Sophia Western (book 4, chapter 2) culminating in "Sophia, then, . . . was a middle-sized woman" is a bravura piece in the same tradition, whereas Dickens returns to Cervan-

served and time experienced, coalesce. There is, of course, a certain amount of complacency to Galdós' tenderness, but I think he would be the first to recognize that it is the quality of Fortunata's experience that permits such treatment.

Let me try to explain in different terms: unlike the insomniac Isidora, whose consciousness is invaded by the ticking of the clock and the accelerated striking of the hours, Fortunata is not subject to the relentless movement forward of the homogeneous time that is out there. Her interior time is autonomous and, according to Ricardo Guillón, "excepcionalmente lento," and it can therefore be offered generously to meaningful "happening" rather than being submitted helplessly to meaningless sequence. Instead of surrendering to a stream of consciousness, a duration of consciousness takes over and joins the morning—in both character and author indistinguishably. And we too can become members, if we know how to accept the priceless gift we have been offered. The melting of the snow in the Plaza Mayor is like nothing so much as the thunderstorm over Jackson's Island or the opening of the clouds over wounded Prince Bolkonski. It is the sheer marvel of conscious life, at once immediate and temporally whole, which is what novels are about when they are at their best.

Consciousness Besieged

To speak of a temporal and spatial art of consciousness is at best an instructive form of vivisection. For consciousness "works," as Luis Vives would have phrased it, in immediate and uninterrupted relationship to what it is not: the consciousnesses of others and the unconscious that lies beneath it or around it. To begin with the first, it is Fortunata's incomparable openness to experience and her unerring judgment, the lack of distortion in her mental mirror or tabula rasa, that makes her so attractive to the other inhabitants of the novel. A Juanito Santa Cruz, who loved her least of all, might have been initially enchanted not only with the beauty Galdós hides from us but also with the primitive and unconscious vitality

---

tine subtlety when at the beginning of chapter 5 he describes Mr. Pickwick "contemplating nature and waiting for breakfast."

of her actions and reactions. But he, like the others, Maxi, Feijóo, doña Lupe, thinks of her as conscious raw material, as possessing the sheer potentiality of freshly quarried granite from "la cantera del pueblo." They are all small-time creators, would-be sculptors even less imaginative than poor León Roch (who naively thought of María Egipciaca as being composed of "un barro exquisito") (779), each concerned with shaping her into his or her own image.

Both interpretations, however, the primitive Fortunata and the potential Fortunata, are woefully inadequate. They correspond to the warped understanding of interpreters who cannot bring themselves to admit her possession of virtues they themselves lack; health, truthfulness, and freedom, more specifically, what her consciousness has in common with those of Stendhal's more sophisticated and complex heroes and heroines: the ability to look sharply, to see what is there clearly, and to react with spontaneous integrity. The others may believe that they want to shape, educate, and assist Fortunata, but we come to sense in all of them, even in Feijóo, who is the best of the lot, an underlying desire, if not to destroy her, at least to bring her down to their level. Angels in their midst are at once irresistible and intolerable.

Luckily, Fortunata is impervious to pedagogy. But not because she is as unintelligent as Montesinos seems to think. Rather it is because her "incitation," if not a source of Quixotesque illusion, does keep her from paying attention to lessons that do not matter to her. Her consciousness is not the passive granite that others imagine it to be;[34] in metaphorical terms, it is made of steel, and its powerful magnetic properties are beyond the comprehension of those who surround her. As a result, in addition to being an inner space and an open duration, in relation to others it generates uncontrollable forces of "simpatía" and "antipatía." Primary among these are her love for Juanito, the repugnance she feels for Maxi, and her powerful ambivalence of feeling toward Jacinta. But even more interesting is her apparently inexplicable attraction to Mauricia la Dura, which is later transferred to doña Guillermina.

Ironical references to Hegel aside, what are we to make of these determining forces at the very center of freedom? To my mind the

[34] Sinnigen has perceptive remarks on this subject. "Individual, Class, and Society in *Fortunata y Jacinta*," p. 50.

most illuminating answer is to be found in the literary tradition behind Galdós. Centuries before, another great artist of consciousness
and temporality named Fernando de Rojas had meditated creatively
on the inner magnetism that impelled his lonely speakers into an
unrelenting search for each others' company. "Amistad" (Friendship), "solaz" (relaxation), "deleite" (sensual pleasure), and, most
prized and intimate of all, "gozo" (sensual joy) are the only anti-
dotes to the solitude of the human condition, the isolation of one
consciousness from another. In contemplating these anxieties,
Rojas went on to discover something else upon which Galdós was
to elaborate to a much greater extent. He discovered that Sempronio,
who despised Calisto, had nonetheless absorbed the latter's image
into himself: "Here's the person," he says about his beloved Elicia,
"who for a long time had me behaving like another Calisto, sere-
nading at dawn, jumping over walls." Sempronio's identity has been
so remodeled that he is even infected by his master's passion for
Melibea. As Celestina shrewdly observes, "Be quiet little fool. I can
see it in your sudden pallor. You'd rather taste the prize itself than
just smell your share of the rewards." Rojas was, thus, the first to
comprehend the phenomenon of consciousness that is somewhat
illogically called "projection" by followers of Freud.

After Rojas, Cervantes (both in don Quijote's literary emulation and in Sancho's human "quijotismo" continued the tradition
and presented Galdós with a fully developed novel of consciousness
in this as in other aspects. And Galdós, just as much or as little a
precursor of twentieth century psychology as either of his two predecessors, centers his study of Fortunata on her "projection" of three
women, Mauricia, doña Guillermina, and, above all, Jacinta. As
we have seen, from the moment of their first encounter in "las
Micaelas" until Fortunata's last comprehensible words ("yo también . . . *mona del cielo*"), Jacinta exists within her in a way that
transcends our usual notions of jealousy and emulation. As for
Guillermina, Galdós invents an even more explicit comparison:
"She felt the other woman inside herself, almost as if she had taken
her in communion." (*399*) This is the only form of determination
that now interests Galdós. Instead of being a gross impingement on
consciousness by society, history, or heredity, determinism is an operation from within.

Having dared to mention Galdós' contemporary, Freud, I realize that I cannot bring these remarks to their conclusion without referring briefly to the recurrent encounter of Fortunata's consciousness (and Jacinta's too for that matter) with that other region of the self that looms so large today, the unconscious. In this, Galdós' technique resembles that of his treatment of spoken language. As we remember, Galdós was able to create a universe of speech, because he knew how to keep his readers aware of the frontiers of that universe: silence, noise, the defective enunciation of drunks, foreigners, infants, lovers, and illiterates, passion with its cries and moans, death with its asphyxiation. And so too, as has often been observed, he keeps us aware of his programmatic attention to consciousness by probing dreams and moments of symbolic recognition for what is going on beneath the surface or, avoiding misleading verticality, on the other side of the frontier.

Many of these will seem elementary to the latter-day amateur psychoanalysts, which Freud has made of us all. But for that very reason we should admire all the more Galdós' prescience in exploring what was at that time, at least in Spain, an absolutely unknown region. The first example I have noted occurs during the honeymoon, when Jacinta is suddenly and inexplicably reminded of her rival by the street cry of a fishmonger: "It was a sudden thing triggered by who knows what, by those mysterious associations of memory that seem to have no rhyme or reason. One remembers things completely illogically, and at times the way ideas are linked together is so ridiculous as to be grotesque. Who would believe that Jacinta suddenly remembered Fortunata when she heard a street vendor crying his wares: "Bocas de la Isla"." [Literally "Mouths of the Island," a special kind of Andalusian crab claws.] (63) Then later, skipping perforce Jacinta's dream of motherhood after having been put to sleep by Wagner, we find another similarly instantaneous revelation of Fortunata's unconscious mind. She and Maxi are seated contentedly at the dining table of their first apartment when suddenly her mood changes: "These sudden changes of mood were not infrequent with her, but none had been as violent as the one which occurred at that moment, the exact moment when she put the spoon into the rice in order to serve her future husband. She would not have been able to say how it happened or why that feeling came into her soul and took charge of it; all she knew was that she looked at him and suddenly felt such antipathy for the poor boy that she had to struggle to hide it." (*188*)

In contrast to novels of our century dealing with the same problems, *Fortunata y Jacinta* is particularly chaste and reticent about what is really going on. Even by the standards of a time that found Zola to be obscene, Galdós is surprisingly reserved. I, of course, do not refer to his failure to depict the sexual intercourse of Fortunata and Juanito (which was obviously out of the question), but rather to the absence of the sensual recollections and libidinal longings that fill the pages of *La Regenta* ("Hay en la obra de Vd. demasiada lascivia," Galdós writes Clarín on 6 April 1885) and *Lo prohibido*. In a sense I think this self-imposed restraint (he excised from the manuscript a number of such allusions) operates in the same way alexandrine couplets operate on the passion of Racinian characters. Galdós restraint augments and makes us appreciate, particularly when accompanied by such apparently inexplicable references as those just cited, the force of the carnal demands with which these consciousnesses must cope.

The most extreme example of juxtaposition of underlying and symbolically concealed erotic compulsion to conscious decision is the dream that results in "la pícara idea." As we have seen to be typical of climactic moments in the biographies of Galdosian female protagonists, the stuff of the dream is a compulsive walk through the streets of Madrid. But unlike the representational and implicitly allegorical "paseos" of Isidora at the end of part 1 of *La desheredada* or of Clara in *La Fontana,* Fortunata's is replete with oneiric symbols that would have interested Freud.[35] I refer, for instance, to the "tubos" she sees in a window display ("llaves de

---

[35] One can compare this dream with the simple reverie of Denise in *Au Bonheur des Dames* during which she perceives the department store as a giant machine. *Les Rougon-Macquart,* vol. 3, p. 402. Since Zola has no real belief or interest in individual consciousness as such, encounters with the unconscious are rare, rudimentary, and assimilated to his "dialogue indirecte libre." Galdós' extraordinary originality in this connection becomes evident when we realize that such leading contemporary psychologists as Wundt rejected the concept of the unconscious as "entirely unproductive." See A. Peñuel, "Galdós, Freud, and Humanistic Psychology," *H,* 55, 1972, pp. 66–75. Madariaga was, of course, the first to mention Freud in connection with Galdós. (See chapter 2, note 32.)

bronce, grifos y multitud de cosas para llevar y traer agua") (*409*), which significantly come back to her mind when she once again rejoins Juanito: "I dreamt I saw you near the plumber's supply shop full of pipes, so many pipes." (*412*) And who knows if her later pleasure at watching the street cleaners removing the snow with their hoses and "tremendas escobas" does not correspond to an identical symbolic appeal? In addition, in the same dream she notices a vendor of "the strongest pencils in the world (so strong you could slam the points against hard wood without breaking them)" (*410*), and she describes the sensation she shares with Saint Teresa of being transfixed by a dart. Even the "id" itself—probably this is far-fetched—appears as "a dwarf, a little monster dressed in a red cassock and a turban, Darwin's missing link between orangutans and men." (*409*)

It is natural to wonder to what extent Galdós himself was aware of the sexual significance of such symbols. My personal answer, based on his emphases and repetitions, would be that he knew exactly what he was about. Unlike Montalvo when he described the green sword of Amadís and the flowery hoop of Oriana, Galdós was overtly concerned with the workings of the unconscious. At the same time, however, given the lack of a literary tradition comparable to that pertaining to consciousness, I can only guess that these dreams and recognitions were taken from life, perhaps without a fully developed scheme for their interpretation. Otherwise we should have to assume not merely that Freud would have appreciated Galdós as a novelistic precursor (which he surely would have) but that the latter had discovered independently a central aspect of contemporary psychoanalytical theory. Berkowitz alludes to a mysterious model for Fortunata,[36] and perhaps the ambulatory dream just analyzed was told to Galdós by that good friend. As indicated previously, I am aware of the critical fallacy inherent in such suppositions, but I hope that my very awareness will render them harmless.

Origins aside, it is essential to remember that Fortunata's Freudian dream was conceived artistically as a structural counterpart to Jacinta's dreamlike descent in part 1 into the social hell of the

---

[36] H. Chanon Berkowitz, *Pérez Galdós, Spanish Liberal Crusader*, Madison, Wisc., 1948, p. 105.

"cuarto estado."[37] Each in her own way is in search of fulfillment and salvation, but the infernal imagery of Fortunata's journey ("la gran parrilla," "el fuego," "blasfemia," etc.) is interior. She has descended into a "hell," which, as we now know, we all carry within us: that of the unconscious mind. And if Jacinta encounters a socially calculated lie (the spurious "Pituso"), Fortunata's self-analysis encounters the deep truth of her own passion.[38] She emerges with her consciousness at once purged and enlarged, capable of founding the new institution of "la pícara idea." The myth of self-renewal (specifically in *both* cases by means of the new life of a child) after a journey to the underworld that was attempted in part 1 has now been fulfilled.

To conclude hastily, let us return to our previous comparison of Fortunata with Isidora. The latter, we suggested when considering *Fortunata y Jacinta* as still in prospect, is a precursor of the former, just as her lover and seducer, Joaquinito Pez, is a specifically identified precursor of Juanito Santa Cruz. Nevertheless, in spite of their parallel Naturalistic lives, they are antithetical to each other. Isidora's consciousness is chronically ill (the disease is different from that of Bueno de Guzmán, but she is just as sick) and could only have been cured if she had been treated early enough by those "verdaderos médicos" called "maestros de escuela." In Fortunata's

[37] See chapter 10, note 14. There is, however, a crucial difference between the two. Jacinta, as we remember, was only concerned with gaining her heart's desire, whereas Fortunata's descent corresponds to the traditional myth pattern as described by H. W. Clarke: the hero "detached from the burden of his obsessions [is] gathered to a new vision, prepared for a different destiny." *The Art of the "Odyssey,"* Englewood Cliffs, N.J., 1967, p. 60.

[38] Mircea Eliade compares psychoanalysis to the myth of "initiatory descents into hell" where "ghosts" and "monsters" are encountered. *The Sacred and the Profane,* New York, 1961, p. 208. In attempting to relate such extraneous observations to our novel, we must realize that its sheer density of human significance constantly tempts the interpreter to go too far. Imagine the dangers lurking for unwary "galdosistas" in the following paragraphs from Erich Neumann's neo-Jungian *Origins and History of Consciousness:* "The round is the egg, the philosophical World Egg, the nucleus of the beginning, and the germ from which, as humanity teaches everywhere, the world arises. It is also the perfect state in which opposites are united—the perfect beginning because the opposites have not yet flown apart and the world has not yet begun, the perfect end because in it the opposites have come together in a synthesis and the world is once more at rest." New York, 1954, p. 8.

case, however, Galdós set out to explore a completely healthy consciousness, impervious to education, immune to society, untainted by
ambition, resistant to history—a consciousness that, in spite of passionate excess, grows, flourishes, exercises freedom, revalidates values, and radiates truth. Placed against it in well-calculated counterpoint is another consciousness, that of Maximiliano Rubín, condemned first to the isolation of clinical insanity and afterwards to
that of self-sufficient reason, which is the greatest sickness of all. It
would be possible to interpret the creation of this latter-day "loco
cuerdo" as Galdós' final and most profound attack on "Quijotismo"
before going over definitively to the other side. But we should not
for that reason force Fortunata into the role of a triumphant
Sancho, a creature of good sense, folk humor, and practical judgment. She, no less than her husband, is also impelled by passion, incitation, and a sense of mission, the only difference being that she
is blessed and saved by a consciousness that integrates truth with
life, vitality with value.

CHAPTER XII

Retrospect

Novel and Memory

During the decade of the 1920s three major critics proposed a revolutionary definition for an upstart genre, which had in the course of the preceeding century captured the citadel of Western literature—the novel. Writing in different languages and, as far as I know, unaware of each other's existence, all three were initially surprised by the peculiarly "formless" quality of fictional experience. The first of the trio was Georg Lukacs, who, stimulated by Wilhelm Dilthey's *Das Erlebnis und die Dichtung*,[1] observed in 1920: "So erscheint der Roman im Gegensatz zu dem in der fertigen Form ruhenden Sein anderer Gattungen, als etwas Werdendes, als ein Prozess." For that reason it is frequently "als Halbkunst bezeichnet."[2] Then, in the following year, Albert Thibaudet, stimulated by Bergson, explained to readers of *La Nouvelle Révue Française* why they ought not to heed certain contemporary critics (notably Paul Bourget) who insisted upon "la composition dans le roman": "Le vrai roman n'est pas composé, parce qu'il n'y a composition que là où il y concentration. . . . Il . . . est déposé, déposé à la façon d'une durée vécue qui se gonfle et d'une mémoire qui se forme."[3]

But perhaps the most suggestive and surely the most autodidactic

---

[1] Leipzig, 1905.

[2] "As opposed to other genres which seem to rely on traditional forms which are essentially stable, the novel appears to be a becoming, a process." *Die Theorie*, p. 71. In his 1962 "Vorwort" Lukacs informs us that, although *Die Theorie* appeared in book form in 1920, it first appeared in a review in 1916. Its underlying pessimism, he implies, was generational, i.e. a reaction to the war.

[3] "Genuine novels are not 'composed,' because composition depends on concentration. . . . Instead it is 'deposed' like a swelling accumulation of experience and memory." *Réflexions sur le roman*, p. 159.

356

expression of the same critical realization was that of our own Percy Lubbock in 1926: "Though we readily talk of the book as a material work of art, our words seem crossed by a sense that it is rather a process, a passage of experience, than a thing of size and shape."[4] What Lubbock saw more clearly than his predecessors concerning that once strange and familiar rendering of lived and living experience called a novel is its temporal duality, that it is simultaneously a "now" and an "afterwards." He who would understand critically what he has read must reconcile both these times in his mind, no matter how mutually exclusive they are or appear to be. Since then, Américo Castro and Northrop Frye (to mention two of the most distinguished among recent theorists of the novel) have shown us how fruitful such a double awareness of time can be.[5]

Let us rephrase this invaluable critical legacy (now half a century old): the crucial difference between lives in novels and those we live on earth is that our immediate experience and final retrospect (our last self-judgment, assuming that we are serene enough at the grim moment of departure to contemplate ourselves as an autobiographical whole) are separated by irreversible time and irrevocable death. Fictional biographies and autobiographies, on the contrary, as J. V. Cunningham points out, do not come to an end when they are over.[6] To begin with, as we noticed when *Fortunata y Jacinta* was still in prospect, fictional biographies and autobiographies are emblematically or fragmentarily preserved in what we called the novelistic consciousness of the reading public. But more significant from the point of view of Lukacs, Thibaudet, and Lubbock is the pos-

[4] *The Craft of Fiction*, New York, 1957, p. 15.

[5] For Castro see the introduction to the Porrúa edition of *Don Quijote*. There he begins by proposing the substitution of the notion of "structure" with an evaluative sense of the whole: "So it is that the literary phenomenon has a dual and simultaneous manifestation, first, as an open and flowing form; second, as a *state*, as a situation stabilized with respect to the scale of values of the [reader]." Ibid., p. 80. We have already discussed Frye's fruitful and suggestive presentation of emblem formation in *Myth and Symbol*.

[6] After citing Saint Augustine's striking comparison of the spiritual wholeness of a human life to the poetic wholeness of a psalm, Cunningham goes on to comment that in contrast to our lives, "it is the peculiar nature of a composition that the experience . . . may be repeated." *Tradition and Poetic Structure*, Denver, Colo., 1960, p. 24.

sibility that such lives can be—and indeed must be by anyone who takes them seriously—relived by being reread. Even a reader who opens a recognizedly great novel for the first time is subliminally aware of the readings of those who have preceded him, that he too in a sense is a rereader. And as a result, the remembered whole (or the to-be-remembered whole) and the immediately experienced part exist in a state of continual confrontation.

Admittedly some rereaders reread only in order to reexperience cherished moments of episodic "happiness," as Stendhal termed it. As famished disciples of Alonso Quijano and Emma Bovary, they read novels as if they were romances; they pay no attention to the gathering significance of the whole and prefer to identify themselves with the pulsating and entrancing "now," "now," and "now again" of their favorite pages. And admittedly, too, there are others (we know them only too well in our profession) who, being excessively cerebral disciples of Paul Bourget or Roland Barthes, only reread in order to dissect the cadaver of the whole according to their neo-rhetorical or neo-Saussurian notions of narrative anatomy. But anyone who aspires adequately to relive a novel such as *Fortunata y Jacinta* must try to relate its ongoing fictional experience to its final configuration. Like a symphony, as Vernon Chamberlin proposes, it is at once a composition and a seemingly infinite number of moments of auditory joy.[7] The completed experience of the whole and the sequential experiences of the interlaced biographies are interdependent.

It is precisely this that I have tried to demonstrate as well as I could in the preceding chapters. Specifically, omens and premonitions, manipulations of chance, symbolic and mythographic messages, significant segmentations, chapter titles, ironical insinuations and many other such ways of communicating the larger structure and the guiding intention have been related as intimately as possible to the experience of being immersed in the consciousness of Fortunata, a consciousness which, according to the scornful definition of the novel of Cervantes' Canon, provides us with nothing less than a "nuevo modo de vida." This notion is curiously confirmed by another literary authority, the Innkeeper (who loves

---

[7] *Galdós and Beethoven: "Fortunata y Jacinta," a Symphonic Novel.*

novels for the same reason the Canon suspects them of heresy),
when he says that listening to them "nos quita mil canas" (they
give us so much new life that our gray hair returns to its original
color). There are all sorts of novels, however, and it is our duty as
ex post facto critics to ascertain whether the feat has been achieved
by an authentic transfusion of vitality or with hair dye. Although
the illiterate Innkeeper may have more fun as he listens breathlessly
to adventure after adventure, we cannot professionally evade the
critical imperatives expounded by the Canon. And conversely, in
posing pompously as latter-day Canons, we should never forget that
when we began to read novels we were juvenile Innkeepers.

Nevertheless, there does come a time (hence Unamuno's profound and anguished realization that reading fiction is a "prepa-
ratio mortis") when we at last must inevitably close the book and
remember its "passage of experience" as a past tangential to our own.
I mean both when it is finished and when, sadly, we are finished
with it and look back on it only as a whole and as an afterwards.
This, as we have just learned from Lukacs, Thibaudet, and Lubbock, is not a valid critical point of view for judging novels, even
though many critics (either for doctrinaire reasons or because they
are used to other genres) prefer it intellectually. Nevertheless, retrospective contemplation of the completed experience, aside from its
being inevitable, is often interesting. It offers possibilities for confessional and comparative meditation, which, however subjective,
can discover aspects of a given novel that proper criticism (the kind
that lives in and with what is going on and at the same time takes
into account the shape of the "durée vécue qui se gonfle") might
overlook or interpret differently. Paragraphs we thought we had
accounted for suddenly seem mysterious; passages we rightly paid
little attention to now stand out in our memory; and above all we
become aware of what we believe to be the hidden suppositions and
quality of the author's way of understanding and reproducing life
in a fashion he himself could not know.

Fortunata y Jacinta, like all major novels, has or will have an
afterwards for each of its readers. Each in retrospect will take from
it what he needs and what he can.[8] The time has now come for me

[8] Thus, Raymond Williams, instead of emblems or scenes, retains from
Dickensian novels an impression of sheer movement: "As we stand and look

to close the novel and to make a closing statement, which may or may not be of interest to others. Let me say, then, simply that now at the end of July 1977, having laboriously rewritten and corrected the preceding chapers and having reread *Fortunata y Jacinta* at least two dozen times in forty years, I find that what strikes me most vividly about its "afterwards" is its beginning. I do not refer now to the meeting of the future lovers on the stairs below Estupiñá's lodgings, which effectively initiates the happening and which is so deeply etched in the memories of most readers that it has become an emblem of the whole. Rather I remain uneasily preoccupied by the very first page. The contrast, already mentioned several times, of Galdós' pretense of preliminary carelessness, unconcern, and frigid superficiality with the intricate construction, the life-or-death commitment, and the white-hot intensity of the novelistic future he has in store for us is all the more shocking when considered in retrospect. Before committing this book to print, it may serve by way of epilogue to meditate once more on the anomaly of "Las noticias más remotas . . ."

Novel and History (III)

Meditation on a novel "afterwards" is a mournful task, but it does have one advantage over experiencing a novel in its immediacy as a "now." It permits unexpectedly illuminating comparisons with the assembled "afterwards" of other novels, primarily comparisons with those of the same novelist and secondarily with those of other novelists that we remember well enough to compare. Let us, therefore, begin by trying to recall whether the offhand and careless overture of *Fortunata y Jacinta* has precedents in prior or posterior novels of Galdós.

My first impression, subsequently confirmed by rapid rereading,

---

back at a Dickens novel the general movement we remember—the characteristic movement—is a hurrying seemingly random passing of men and women, each heard in some fixed phrase, seen in some fixed expression: a way of seeing men and women that belongs to the street." *The Country and the City,* p. 155. Since this in *my* memory more resembles Baroja in retrospect than Dickens, it serves to alert us afresh to the purely subjective and arbitrary nature of the present conclusion.

is that our introduction to Juanito offers a more puzzling discrepancy than meaningful comparison with the beginnings of those "novelas contemporáneas" that readers of Galdós remember most vividly. Indeed, the first pages of *La desheredada, Tormento, El amigo Manso, Nazarín, La de Bringas,* and *Misericordia,* to choose virtually unforgettable examples, show their author to have been a past master of the art of arresting novelistic initiation. By "educating the responses and guiding the collaboration of the reader," they confirm Martin Price's observation that "the openings of novels serve to set the rules of the game to be played by the reader."[9] Abrupt literary echoes (the mad monologue of Rufete, at once Cervantine and Zolaesque, or Ido's theatrically Romantic encounter with Centeno), elaborate emblematic descriptions (the two-faced church of San Sebastián or Bringas' myopic mosaic), and challenging disavowals of point of view (Manso's "yo no existo" or the unidentifiability of the narrator of Nazarín's haphazard martyrdom) all contrive to remind us by means of surprise, provocation, or recollection that in each case we must once again try to learn the ever-changing rules of the novelistic game.

In *Fortunata y Jacinta,* however, Galdós employs an antithetical procedure. Rather than trying to guide us by catching our attention, he seems purposefully to be inviting our disinterest. Here is the long, first paragraph, which I reproduce for the benefit of those whose recollections of it may not be as sharply etched as mine:

Juanito Santa Cruz

The most remote information I have been able to gather concerning the person who bears this name came from Jacinto María Villalonga and dates back to the time when that friend of mine and his buddies, Zalamero, Joaquinito Pez, Alejandro Miquis, were to be seen in the lecture rooms of the University. The were not all members of the same class, and although they all met in Camus' course, they were at different levels when it came to Roman law. The Santa Cruz boy was a student of

---

[9] Martin Price, "The Irrelevant Detail and the Emergence of Form," in *Aspects of the Narrative: Selected Papers from the English Institute,* ed. J. Hillis Miller, New York, 1971, p. 82.

Novar's and Villalonga of Coronado's. Nor did they show the same degree of scholarly dedication: Zalamero, serious and solemn, was the sort of fellow who sits in the front row looking at the professor with an appreciative expression and nodding his head approvingly at every affirmation. Santa Cruz and Villalonga did just the opposite; they would sit as far up the aisle as possible, wrapped up in their capes, and looking more like conspirators than students. There they passed the time talking in low voices, reading novels, drawing funny pictures, or whispering the answer to each other whenever the professor would ask them a question. Juanito Santa Cruz and Miquis took a skillet one day (I am not sure whether to Camus' lecture or to that of Uribe's on metaphysics) and proceeded to fry some eggs. Villalonga has told me a lot more of such mischief, which I shall not repeat in order not to lengthen this account unnecessarily. All of them (with the exception of Miquis, who died in '64 dreaming of being worthy of Schiller's fame) took part in the celebrated scuffle of the night of Saint Daniel. Even goody-goody little Zalamero got excited on that noisy occasion and whistled and screamed like a wild man, for which he got his ears boxed by a veteran law officer but with no further consequences. Villalonga and Santa Cruz, however, had a harder time. The former was laid up by a saber thrust in the shoulder for two endless months, while the latter was caught on the corner by the Royal Theater and taken to the lockup with a group of other prisoners, students as well as various delinquents of shadier background. They kept him on ice there for almost twenty-four hours, and his captivity might have been longer if on the eleventh his papá, a very respectable person with excellent connections, had not arranged for his release.

The technique employed at the very beginning of this passage is particularly curious. By using the name Juanito Santa Cruz as the chapter title and then referring to him in the text as "la persona que lleva este nombre," Galdós projects into our minds a virtual image of the manuscript page and of himself laboriously composing it. When we come to the indentification we have to glance back and *up* to the title in order to understand it, a glance that makes us aware of the page itself as an undifferentiated unity. The title is not merely the author's name for a segment of narration (to be remembered subliminally during the reading process as if enclosed in brackets) but rather becomes a part of it, as if it were the heading of a report. This, in turn, tacitly defines the narrator as a reporter, a private detective, or a hired scholar, whose duty it is to collect and submit in writing information concerning an individual under investigation. Thus, also, the tone of carelessness, which disconcerts us in retrospect. As pointed out in an earlier chapter, the narrator-reporter's collection of fragmentary facts and snippets of anecdotes seems even to him so boring and pointless that, before the paragraph has ended, he decides to omit data "para no alargar este relato." Not only may the reader be put off by such stale stuff, but also the presumably mercenary "relator" himself does not hesitate to express his ennui.

Irony aside (the "relato" will, like the Restoration itself, continue to grow in spite of the "relator's" desire to stop it), what Galdós has accomplished is clear. He has used a facsimile of documentation, not to provide verisimilitude, but to diminish the interest of the opening statement. We have already spoken of the so-called documentary pretense (excitingly "true" manuscripts discovered in bottles, vaults, or flea markets and in more recent years excitingly "relevant" psychiatric tapes, dossiers, or trial transcripts) designed to help us suspend our disbelief. Galdós, on the other hand, by means of the somewhat paradoxical act of pretending to be the writer of his own document, cunningly subverts the age-old device. He has suspended our potential concern for what he has to tell us, and at the same time he has clearly distinguished the narrator from himself.

Why should he do so? In order to understand the malice of Galdós' unexpected return to and sardonic internalization of this novelistic pawn to Queen's four, further comparison is necessary. The documentary pretense is, if we stop to think about it, a primordial version of another, equally familiar opening gambit: that corresponding to what might be called the historical pretense. The opening sentence of Dumas' *Le Vicomte de Bragelonne* will serve to remind us of all the novels of this sort that we have loved and lost: "Towards the middle of the month of May, in the year 1660, at nine o'clock in the morning, when the sun, already high in the sky, was fast absorbing the dew from the ravenelles of the castle of Blois, a little cavalcade composed of three men and two pages re-entered the city by the bridge . . ." Nothing is new under the sun (meaning that I do not dare rule out categorically the possibility of examples prior to the nineteenth century), but it seems obvious that this—to us—standard beginning corresponds to Sir Walter Scott's view of history as an "elsewhere" to be excavated archae-ologically and revived artistically. Accordingly, the historical novel does not begin with a birth (*Lazarillo de Tormes*), a self-introduc-tion (*Moby Dick*), nor a generative action (the meeting of Calisto and Melibea) but with a threshold: an inviting entryway into an-other time and space. Instead of a physical document, documented history incites our belief and entices our participation.

The rise of the nineteenth-century novel from its Scottian origins requires no further presentation here, but it should be pointed out that the historical pretense with its initial threshold was not aban-doned when novelists turned from the Middle Ages and the Scottish Highlands to the great cities of their own time. The "little cavalcade" and the "lone riders who might be seen" on the first pages of Western fiction were to become railroad passengers (*Doña Perfecta, The Idiot*) and even more recently lone couples getting undressed in suburbia. Once Scott and his emulators had shown how effective it could be to pinpoint a specific intersection of time and space other than ("elsewhere" than) the "now" of our watch and the "here" of our hammock, the practice became habitual. My point is obvious: it was precisely such a beginning accompanied by its customarily seductive expectations that Galdós, in launching *Fortunata y Jacinta,* sought to avoid at all costs. Instead of the mysterious past of the Middle Ages or the mysterious present of the metropolis (as perilous and unexplored as Cooper's American wilderness), he chooses to introduce his reader to his own only-too-familiar and only-too-trivial Madrid. And for this a documentary pretense, suitably familiarized and trivialized, would serve far better than a "little cavalcade" of "señoritos" who might have been seen on their way to the University on a fine morning in the Spring of 1864.

Another factor to be considered is that the documentary pretense enables a fictional narrator to be present as writer or discoverer of the document whereas the historical pretense tends to eliminate him. Thresholds such as that of *Le Vicomte de Bragelonne* are usually presented without overt stylistic intervention on the part of the narrator's voice. The essential facts—location, date, time of day or night, weather conditions, mode of locomotion, personal identity or identities—are stated without irony, lyrical enthusiasm, or rhetorical intentionality of any sort. The reason is clear. The irresistible enticement of a surrogate world consists in its very existence, in that unquestioned illusion of reality, which would inevitably be diminished by the slightest intimation of an intrusion on the part of the storyteller. Indeed, the sooner we forget that Dumas or Scott (or their surrogates) exists, the sooner we are able to enjoy what Ortega y Gasset called our liberating "submersion" in the "then" and "there" of their novels. Instead of a fictional document discovered, glossed, or edited by a discoverer, commentator, or editor (activities which necessarily imply interpretation), the page itself is presented as if it were documentary. It becomes a document, which the reader himself discovers in the act of opening the novel to its first page. Galdós, however, makes us aware of the pretense, and, in so doing (in spite of the growing unobtrusiveness of his narrator as the novel progresses), he is far closer to Defoe and the Cela of *Pascual Duarte* than he is to the historical and realistic novelists of his century.[10]

In other words, it was what we might term inherent novelistic believability the comfortable habit of automatically attributing historical truth to fiction on the fragile basis of a date and a place name, that Galdós could not accept. He wants to be present and on the scene (in the persona of his bored narrator) in order to warn us against himself and against the easy magic he has at his command. Instead of letting us (with prefabricated naiveté and experienced "voluptuousness") believe in his "historia de dos casadas" just because it *seems* historical, he prefers to teach us to recognize

[10] The first page of *Wuthering Heights* seems to have been designed to have a similar effect:

Wuthering Heights

CHAPTER I

1801–

I have just returned from a visit to my landlord—the solitary neighbor that I shall be troubled with.

it for what it is (or what it would be if it were): a compilation of more or less reliable and interesting facts by a more or less reliable and disinterested investigator. At the beginning of *La desheredada* Galdós indicates that all lives are potential novels; but now, having just finished *Lo prohibido,* he realized that biography, that is, personal experience understood historically, has no necessary significance. History for Scott and Balzac was a fascinating new revelation; for Stendhal and the mature Galdós, on the contrary, it represented the degeneration of the human condition in the nineteenth century. At best, in their view, it could be justified only when it challenged or "incited" the potential greatness of such exceptional individuals as heroes, villains, saints, and self-proclaimed angels.

The two characteristics just discussed, presentation of the prosaic Madrid that was familiar to his readers and self-presentation of the narrator as critic of his own narrative, inevitably remind us of the most famous of all novel beginnings. The flaunted carelessness, the tone of weary acquiescence, and the half-veiled scorn for the future hero and his world all amount to saying: "En un lugarón de España . . . no ha mucho tiempo . . . vivía un señorito de los de . . . de cuyas mocedades no quiero acordarme."[11] Just as in the *Quijote,* the intentional insignificance of the initial documentation in *Fortunata y Jacinta* constitutes a negative point of departure for the immense significance that was waiting to be discovered and explored novelistically. At the same time, the critique of contemporary history as such (the wretched university ambiance, the ironical reference to "aquella célebre noche de San Daniel" almost as if it were an "antiepisodio") reveals tacitly a more fundamental similarity. Just as the *Quijote* on one level is a reply to those Romances of Chivalry that compensate for their exaggerations by pretending to be chronicles (the documentary pretense is inherent in the genre), so *Fortunata y Jacinta,* as we remarked earlier, is to be an antihistorical novel. Not a parody, but an answer to the kind of fiction that began with Scott and seemed to have exhausted its authentic innovation—its "novelty"—with the saga of the Rougon-Macquarts.

I am not trying to suggest that Galdós did not dote on the major

[11] "In an overgrown village in Spain . . . not too long ago . . . there lived one of those dandies who usually . . . and whose youthful exploits I have no desire to recollect."

novels of his century, or that his considered opinion of their literary worth was as negative as that of the Cervantes of the Romances of Chivalry (who in the "escrutinio," in addition to applying critical theory, nevertheless revealed how hopelessly addicted he was to popular fiction). Rather *Fortunata y Jacinta's* nineteenth-century echo of "En un lugar de la Mancha . . ." corresponds to its author's intention to turn his immediate novelistic tradition inside out, to create a deicidal weapons-system capable of finishing off the latter-day divinity called history. Just as Cervantes satirized the Romances of Chivalry as a means of relieving his readers of the burden of their history and society (insofar as they conformed to stereotyped neo-chivalric roles), so Galdós in creating Fortunata proposed to relieve his readers of the burden of their historicism. The qualified historical optimism of *La Fontana* and of the first series of "episodios" was, as we saw, soon replaced by the bleak pessimism of Salvador Monsalud and later by the uncanny prophecy of doom, which constitutes part 2 of *La desheredada*. And now, twelve years ahead of his time, Galdós anticipates the Generation of '98 with a Cervantine attack on the central bastion of nineteenth-century awareness. Hence, a novel that is to end with ironic transfiguration and transcendence begins with what Roland Barthes might have called "le degré zéro de l'histoire," the deservedly forgotten, time-vulnerable reminiscences and anecdotes of a class reunion.

Novel and Time

Is it necessary, however, to insist once again so exclusively on the polemical intention, the negative thesis, that is implicit in the neo-Cervantine first paragraph? Could not its surprising recent "remoteness" also serve to introduce the reader to the novel's profound and positive concern with time itself as the medium of life? Had not, in other words, novelistic overemphasis on history (political and social time) tended to distract nineteenth-century novelists from temporality as a phenomenon? I do not mean to suggest that the Galdós of *Fortunata y Jacinta* resembles Proust or Azorín, but I do think that their common point of departure is a redefinition of the acute temporal preoccupation of their contemporaries. Ezra

Pound once remarked with superlative literary insight that when "Lope becomes ornate, irony is never far distant,"[12] and, similarly, when Galdós' narrative style seems careless or hasty, it frequently conceals a plurality of ironical messages. It will not do to underestimate him, as has so frequently been the case, nor to congratulate ourselves on having discovered a single and definitive interpretation.

Again, retrospective comparison will help, if not to answer the above questions, at least to assess their potential importance. As we remember, in many subsequent novels the noncommittal Scottian threshold is replaced by stylized emphasis either on its temporal or on its spatial vectors. The purpose seems to be to introduce us to the dimensional peculiarities of the strange new worlds we are invited to inhabit. As far as space is concerned, we may mention the horizontal and geographical presentation of Cooper's wide wilderness,[13] the vertical lines drawn by the soaring skyscrapers of Zenith,[14] or the perilous perspective of the highway leading to Mason City in *All the King's Men*.[15] Such beginnings not only initiate Lubbock's "process" but also prepare us to perceive what he called (avoiding the controversial notions of structure and form) the "size and shape" of the whole. In saying this, he might just as well have said "theme." As Georges Poulet, Jean-Pierre Richard, Joseph Frank, and Virginia Woolf (whose critical ideas are authenticated by her creative achievement) have all taught us, the

---

[12] *The Spirit of Romance,* New Directions, New York, n.d., p. 204.

[13] See the "bird's-eye view of the whole region east of the Mississippi" in the first paragraph of *The Deerslayer*.

[14] "The towers of Zenith aspired above the morning mist, austere towers of steel and cement and limestone, sturdy as cliffs and delicate as silver rods."

[15] We may notice how Warren uses a device similar to that of Galdós and Emily Brontë in order to communicate neither temporal remoteness nor human relations but a spatial perspective:

CHAPTER I

Mason City.

To get there you follow Highway 58, going northeast out of the city, and it is a good highway and new. Or was new that day we went up it.

I should add immediately that, when I asked Warren personally how he had conceived of such a splendid opening (the whole paragraph is a marvel), he told me with a smile that his original version had been different and that the editors (or editor) had amputated the manuscript at precisely this point. .

dimensional peculiarity of a given fictional world is a representation of its meaning. In a sense, it *is* the meaning.[16]

As against the spatial vestibules just alluded to, *Fortunata y Jacinta* begins temporally, and in a way worthy of meditation. Unlike the nostalgic duration ("le passé vécu") of Proust's "Longtemps je me suis couché . . .," the hilarious mechanical chronometry of Tristram Shandy's conception, the enchanting seasonal stasis of Tom Sawyer's endless summer,[17] or the depressing biological time of Updike's aging bodies, Galdós prefers the least significant form of temporal awareness: the "remote news" of recent, half-forgotten local history. Was his name Quijada or Quijana? Was it in the lectures of Uribe or Camus? Are we remembering characters from previous novels or professors who have taught us (or whom we have read about in histories of "krausismo")? All is uncertain; all is unimportant; and yet from the seed of this initial passage to oblivion there was to grow one of the most remarkable time-novels ever written.

Time, being a single and irreversible dimension, does not offer the obvious choices (across, up, or away) that are available to those who open their novels spatially. Instead, its varieties are sorted more subtly into levels—perhaps it would be better to say concentric spheres—of individual experience. That is, varieties of time are sorted in accordance with our way of relating them to our own existence. Thus, we recognize instinctively psychological time, biological time, seasonal and meteorological time ("el tiempo de sembrar," "el tiempo malo"), sidereal time,[18] and (as the outermost

[16] See Poulet's essay on *Madame Bovary,* in *Les Metamorphoses du cercle,* Paris, 1961; Richard's essay on Stendhal in *Littérature et sensation;* Frank's classic article, originally published in *The Sewanee Review,* on "Spatial Form in Modern Literature," reprinted in *The Widening Gyre,* New Brunswick, N. J., 1963; and Virginia Woolf's essay on *Robinson Crusoe* in *The Second Common Reader.*

[17] I am, of course, aware that the story begins with the directly quoted scolding of Aunt Polly; however, Mark Twain (I think in order to establish the precedence of present comedy over narrative nostalgia) reverses the usual order and locates his "seasonal" opening at the beginning of chapter 2.

[18] The familiar distinction drawn by Hans Meyerhoff between the objective time of "nature" (meaning the physical world) and the "qualitative," "existential," and "significant" time of experience obviously does not exclude

sphere?) social time, by which I mean the conventional and datable time of biography and history. Although Galdós, for reasons we have tried to reconstruct, began with the last, he was singularly endowed with that time-vision or time-sensibility which, according to Robert Petsch, constitutes "das Wesen der Epischen," and he went on to envelop his initial "noticias" with every conceivable variety of temporal experience. Psychological time, historical time, and the rest are not contemplated in a state of isolation but are presented interdependently, as inevitable companions or phases of each other. The result is a marvelous symphony of memory and prediction, of birth and death, of seasons and sunsets, of social and historical change.

Let us begin with the creation of urban time, which is the basic rhythm of this as of so many other nineteenth-century novels. In retrospect we remember the Madrid of *Fortunata y Jacinta* not so much as a place as an immense organism. In the words of the first Spaniard to be blessed or cursed with time-vision, "Who can explain that change of styles of clothing, the constant tearing down and re-edification of buildings, and the many other such effects and mutations to which weak humanity is vulnerable?" And now, four centuries later, the renovating flow of clean water through the recently opened Canal de Lozoya,[19] the importation of foodstuffs and cloth from ever more distant regions, the arrival of immigrants from the provinces, the invisible entry of new ideas and styles from beyond the Pyrenees all combine to create a rapidly changing society that is antithetical to Orbajosa's stagnation.

Readers of Balzac and Zola are familiar with the economic aspects of novelistic mutability: the plans of merchants (Isabel Cordero's prediction of the future demand for "el género blanco"), the rising

---

sidereal time from the novel and particularly from the nineteenth-century novel, in which night and day, sun and moon, sunset and dawn combine with weather as a central aspect of milieu. *Time in Literature,* Berkeley and Los Angeles, 1955.

[19] Two years before beginning *Fortunata y Jacinta* Galdós had mentioned the changes due to the new water supply in an article in *La Prensa:* "El acueducto de Lozoya, dotando a esta capital de una gran riqueza de aguas, ha influído de tal modo en la higiene y en las costumbres que los viejos no conocen el Madrid de su tiempo en la villa moderna." Shoemaker, *Cartas,* p. 107.

and falling fortunes of individuals, families, and entire classes, wise and foolish investment, and the worship of interest. But Galdós' time-vision is even more acute and inclusive. Instead of presenting a more or less fixed environment or milieu, he creates a Madrid that resembles nothing so much as an airport terminal. The city is conceptually in a state of endless construction and destruction and infested with scurrying multitudes. The horizontal growth of new "barrios," the vertical growth of buildings,[20] the ceaseless stop-and-go procession of drays and carriages are reported on incessantly. Everything is seen in terms of time, right down to such infinitesimal details (why this one comes to mind now I cannot imagine) as the shack in the courtyard of "las Micaelas," which had been built for a pig the nuns *used to* own.

We should not, however, equate this portrait of Madrid's temporality with Baroja's impressionistic, Pisarro-like sketches of directionless urban dynamism: "el eterno ir y venir de la gente."[21] Instead, Galdós' metropolis has emerged from an explicitly recorded historical "whence": the genealogical roots of its inhabitants in the seventeenth and eighteenth centuries. References abound to a past that was different in its social structure and values, i.e. the past represented symbolically by the monumental dwelling on the Plaza Mayor. As for the future, the tacit question of "whither?" is present on every page but is never satisfactorily answered. Don Baldomero, like M. Homais, smugly prates of progress—"el mundo marcha"— but neither author nor reader dares to be so confident. Instead of progressing erratically towards capitalistic pseudoabundance or moving inevitably towards social justice, the swiftly flowing and optimistic world of the novel seems destined to swirl down the drain of history into some unspeakable "pozo negro" of axiological

[20] In another article also written in the same year (1886) he stresses Madrid's extreme susceptibility to historical change: "Madrid es una población que se está transformando rápidamente. Ya hacia 1860, rompió aquella corteza villanesca que la envolvía, se dotó abundantes aguas, de sus plazoletas pedregosas hizo jardines, destruyó las antiguas tapias para emprender edificaciones en grande escala, y desde entonces sus progresos han sido mayores en cada década.

"Ninguna otra población ha pasado en menos tiempo de la categoría de villorrio grande a la capital populosa y bella." Shoemaker, *Cartas,* p. 47. One wonders what he would say today.

[21] Such was Sacha's first impression of Seville in *El Mundo es Ansí.*

degeneration. Hence, both the prescience of Galdós (whose historical pessimism has been more than confirmed since 1936) and the epic mission of Fortunata. The larger meaning of her deed of conciliation is ultrahistorical, history as it should or still could be.

Intimately harmonized with this novelistic dirge for Spain's nineteenth century, other rhythms are less disheartening. Nightfall with tinted clouds fleeing like escaping animals, sudden daybreak, and the daily drift of white and blue weather roof the city with ever-repeated and ever-new beauty. Air pollution would literally have destroyed the *Fortunata y Jacinta* we treasure in memory, just as it would have destroyed *L'Assommoir*. Aside from the visual beauty of "el tiempo" (to which all of the citizens except one are indifferent), welcome and unwelcome changes in temperature and humidity insist on being noticed. Heat, rain, sunshine, and snow mark the changing seasons, just as do recurrent holidays, which serve as an excuse for lavish or modest display of gourmandise. Galdós' recognition, however, that alimentary time is primarily and most urgently diurnal and only secondarily annual is evident in his almost obsessive attention to marketing, cooking, dining, and (in the case of Ido) digesting. In this he is as Naturalistic as his mentor. In preceding chapters, I fear I have overemphasized the novel's concern for cloth and clothing(buying and selling, concealing and revealing) as compared to food. The truth is, I think, that both *Au Bonheur des Dames* and *Le Ventre de Paris* (so immediately present in Galdós' mind) are temporally influential.[22] Lessing might well have liked *Fortunata y Jacinta* almost as much as he liked the Homeric poems.[23]

Alongside daily and seasonal repetition of experience, biological time, the time to be born and the time to die, commands the lives of these fictional "madrileños" as imperiously as it commands ours.

[22] As we remember the initial novelistic exploration of this kind of economic time was undertaken by Balzac in *La Maison du Chat-qui-pelote*.

[23] In addition to his portrayal of Fortunata as if she were Helen of Troy, earlier descriptions of which Lessing would have approved might include that of the Bringas apartment as Rosalía shows it off room by room and artifact by artifact. Similarly, in *Middlemarch* we learn how an English family lives through the auctioning off of its possessions. By the 1870s and the 1880s novelistic techniques had evolved remarkably. Even when most insistently descriptive, as in part 1, Galdós almost never describes intemporally.

As we have observed, the framing image (in parts 1 and 4) for this ultimate form of temporality is a giant genealogical tree with its ever-falling leaves and its incessant sprouting. But for the meta-physically careless inhabitants of the novel, each engaged in living his or her own life as best as he or she can, this is perhaps a too deliberate and a too dreadful allegory. Rather, Galdós presents most of them as experiencing an almost frantic confrontation of youth and age. Instead of facing death (as indeed they do), in their minds they face childhood.

The list is convincing. With the exception of Fortunata, whose infancy is nonexistent and whose inner time—consciousness—is clear and slow, as Montesinos notes, almost all the major characters are defined by their ways of retaining the past as they grow older. Don Baldomero knows himself in terms of his strict commercial education; Juanito's juvenile fads predict his later inconstancy; Barbarita's "chifladura de las compras" emerges from her infantile frustration at not being allowed to play with the Chinese figurines; Moreno Isla anguishes over his infancy during his final agitation as does Mauricia if only momentarily (374); Maxi pouts and struts like the grotesque child he was and is; and there is even something little-girlish about the way Guillermina bustles about preparing for Mauricia's last rites. These fluttering subjectivities correspond per-fectly to their time-fraught milieu. They are as literally made of time as Estupiñá is made of history anecdotally relived. When Segismundo Ballester cites incorrectly the image from *La vida es sueño* that we have referred to on several occasions, "la inquieta república de las aves" (thereby suggesting unwittingly that doña Desdémona's aviary is an emblematic scale model of the metropolis), the comparison is quite clearly founded on the accelerated, restless "bird time" of the featherless bipeds who are its inhabitants.

Along with their superlative adjustment to the time of urban ex-istence (Barbarita and doña Lupe, like Rosalía de Bringas, feel un-comfortable when obliged to leave their customary "barrios"), the assembled characters suffer from an atrophied sense of eternity. Re-ligious observance is routine and external: the unforgettable ex-ample is Barbarita's recital of the Ave Maria while whispering with Estupiñá about food bargains. The priests, with the notable excep-tion of old Padre Nones (left over from *Tormento*), are phrase makers and timeservers. And even doña Guillermina, when on occasion she turns her attention from practical charity to spiritual concerns, enjoys the rose-colored aspects of worship as childishly as Belén and Felisa. The grim, traditional, lacerated-Christ piety of doña Perfecta or of the various fanatics of the "episodios" has completely disappeared.

Other forms of timelessness, such as mountains and stars, are of course there, but only Fortunata looks at them. The Prado has been built and opened to the public, but nobody thinks of visiting it. Indeed, it is unfortunate for those of us who still possess some remnant of novelistic consciousness (meaning those of us who, in spite of ourselves, believe in novels) that Fortunata's wedding party did not imitate the hilarious visit to the Louvre of Gervaise and her guests. For surely Fortunata would have greatly enjoyed herself there. As for literature, the only genuine reader is the Alonso Quijano-like Maxi. And music serves mostly as a social occasion for dressing up and showing off. Again, only Fortunata (and on one occasion Jacinta), entranced with the "organillos" that fill the city with melody, really listens; for the others music is at best a pleasant variety of noise. Thus it is that she alone, among all the inhabitants of the novel-city, discovers vitally how to incorporate her life with timeless values and in the end achieves the eternity of angelic metamorphosis. The others, however much they may prate of heaven, live lives that are in every sense temporal and secular.

These memories, triggered by the first, past-laden sentence and paragraph of the novel, in their stress on time as against space may seem excessively personal or capricious to readers who interpret *Fortunata y Jacinta* as a replica or map of Madrid. For as we remember, Galdós, even before embarking on *La Fontana,* had proposed to reform the genre in terms of its superb adaptability to the spatial dimensions of urban life. Thus, in his 1866 manifesto entitled *Desde la veleta,* a piece which both recalls *El diablo conjuelo* and possibly influences (as remarked earlier) the opening of *La Regenta,* he proposes that the novel of the future should use vertical space as a way of presenting simultaneous cross sections of social time. The ambitious minister, the adulterous lovers, the squalid loser at cards would be seen as miniature components of the model metropolis, each observed living his life in his own way. The bird's-eye view of the novelist congeals time and actually makes it visible.[24]

In *Fortunata y Jacinta,* however, the opposite situation obtains: time is used to suggest space. Unlike *El doctor Centeno* with its initial bird's-eye (or child's-eye) view of Madrid from above,[25] the outlines of the city are traced by movement through the streets. Thus, for example, when Galdós describes Maxi's espionage in part 4, he does not have him ascend to rooftops. Rather, in his penultimate role as an insane Sherlock Holmes (that contemporary paragon of urban intelligence), he shadows his suspects down in the streets scurrying after them from lamppost to doorway. And in exactly the same way the circular honeymoon journey puts Madrid in its place by tracing temporally the outlying geography of Spain. There must be exceptions, but on those occasions, as I remember, when a character looks at space from on high (Fortunata out of the window of "las Micaelas" or of her last apartment), it is time (the rising wall or the melting snow) that defines the experience.

From the determinism of personal history, through the divergent rhythms of urban and biological life, and into the duration of her consciousness, Fortunata's experience of time is unique. What might be termed her temporal authenticity (that slow passage of experience, which is the corollary of her authenticity as a person) illustrates by contrast the temporal haste and triviality both of the city as a whole and of its individual citizens. It is hardly surprising, therefore, that what critics (prior to contemporary redefinition of the concept) used to call the structure of the novel should be the time of her life. By the end, the other characters wander off along whatever tangential paths they can find for themselves or others have found for them. Their drift down the rapid stream of urban time has been and is random and meaningless (or "structureless"), even though a few of them realize dimly that with Fortunata's death they have lost something of incomparable and incomprehensible worth. Her biography, on the contrary, reveals a hidden pattern as it draws to its mortal conclusion. It represents, as we sug-

---

[24] Jean-Pierre Richard contrasts Balzac to Flaubert in terms of the former's "goût des eminences" and "survols." *Etudes sur le Romantisme,* p. 115.

[25] In a seminar paper that should have been published, Michael J. Ruggerio pointed out the continuing emphasis on vertical space following this moving introduction.

gested previously, nothing less than the great circular journey of sally and return that is to be found in the *Quijote* and in the epics and romances that preceded it. Specifically and significantly, Fortunata returns to a higher level of the same high dwelling where we and Juanito first encountered her.

And if there she dies as she must die, she also brings to liberating perfection the passion that had so long enslaved her. From blindness to insight, from "eros" to "agape," from spiritual subjection to revalidation of values, from determinism to freedom—these are all unsatisfactory ways to describe the victory of Fortunata's consciousness over E. M. Forster's "naked worm" of value-devouring time. As for all truly great protagonists of novels, her "passage of experience" *is* the "shape" of the whole. When dealing with novels of this human magnitude, Lubbock's initial surprise becomes a revelation.

It is not only Fortunata who undergoes metamorphosis in the course of the narrative. Galdós, too, as he accompanies her on her quest and homecoming, gradually relinquishes his initial posture as the half-titillated, half-bored chronicler of her times and personal history. This rather contrived point of view (as we suggested, a nineteenth-century historical version of Cide Hamete), so intentionally ostensible at the beginning, reappears whenever it suits Galdós to interrupt the reader's vicarious flow of present "experience" and to remind him that what is being told is all over and long vanished. The narrator has met Barbarita; he has read Federico Ruiz' monograph on the "converso" background of the Rubín family, he has seen Feijóo at a distance in a café. On these occasions, the Madrid of his careless memory suddenly and disconcertingly invades the Madrid of our vivid imagination.

As was suggested earlier, the apparent function of such echoes of Cervantine interruption is to alert the reader to the far more profound Quixotesque metamorphosis of the standard nineteenth-century novel pattern. What concerns us now, however, is that as Galdós progresses through parts 3 and 4, the fictional role or narrative persona of reporter or gossip monger is increasingly difficult to maintain. What is happening inside Fortunata demands from her author an ever deeper creative commitment. Because she increasingly asserts her own presence, a presence as commanding as that of the Cid or of Charlemagne, she requires less and less "presentation" of the sort that made possible part 1 of the *Quijote*. The result is that the fictional narrator, unlike Cide Hamete in part 2, recedes from view. What was described metaphorically as "the third clause of the narrative sentence" is about to be pronounced.

To conclude, "noticias . . . remotas" excavated from an ephemeral past by an unconcerned scribe have gradually been transformed into a new novelistic gospel. The tedious, ostensibly Naturalistic "historia de dos casadas" is now a novel in the fullest nineteenth-century sense—a salvation of experience from historical time. As Lukacs phrases it, "Zeiterlebnisse, die zugleich Überwindungen der Zeit sind."[26] This signifies with German complexity the same thing as Eliot's simple "Only through time time is conquered." Like Huck Finn, Fortunata is intended, not to redeem our souls from sin, but to liberate our consciousnesses from temporal slavery. In Fortunata Galdós at long last found a creature for whom movement and meaning are not contradictory. In acting as she acts and in experiencing as she experiences, she means what she means.

There remains one last question more important than any yet broached: does Galdós achieve what he wanted to achieve? Do we as readers, after loving Fortunata at least enough to read her "history" to the last of so many pages, change as the text shows her narrator-enchanter to have changed? Galdós tried as hard as he could (in a sense, the reverential disappearance of the "Ich-Erzähler" is a form of negative rhetoric designed to influence us positively); but the novel with its special ironies and its plot and its hallucination (suspense is not the right word) can only go so far. Each of us, all alone, one by one, and from the depth (or shallowness) of his or her soul, must answer as best he or she can. As for myself, I must confess that I am dismayed by the realization that the existential change sought for by the novel seems almost patently necessary in our horrendously accelerated and historically hopeless late twentieth century, as contrasted to the Madrid of don Baldomero, and at the same time, cults, fads, and other therapeutic shortcuts aside, immeasurably harder to achieve.

[26] *Die Theorie*, p. 127.

Classical References in *Doña Perfecta*

At the moment of revising this essay, its subject is just a century old.[1] Nevertheless, despite the dignity of its greater age, the literary fortunes of *Doña Perfecta* have been, and still are, more contradictory and controversial than those of Galdós' later experiments in "contemporary" fiction. Although the novel was received enthusiastically in 1876,[2] it has since then been bitterly attacked, at least in part as a result of the *Electra* polemic.[3] Its critics, however, have included not only those offended by the thesis but also lovers of Galdós, who, while agreeing completely or partially with his sociological analysis, find it overinsistent. Considered a masterpiece in the Soviet Union,[4] it presents a kind of ideological Flatland to

[1] I am now writing early in June 1976 and the novel appeared in April 1876.

[2] As is noted by Leo J. Hoar, *Doña Perfecta* was greeted by an "outburst of applause." Clarín, Palacio Valdés, doña Emilia, González Serrano, and others all contributed rhapsodic reviews to the daily press. "Critics," pp. 38–56.

[3] The first overt clerical reaction against Galdós' novels was that of Fray Conrado Muiños Saenz writing in *Ciudad de Dios* between 1890 and 1892. This party line became institutionalized only after the *Electra* controversy, a full twenty-five years after Galdós' vivisection of Orbajosa. Recent criticism, according to Hoar, has been misled by the apparently unfounded statements of L. B. Walton in *Pérez Galdós and the Spanish Novel of the Nineteenth Century* (London, 1927) and Andrenio (E. Gómez de Baquero) in *El renacimiento de la novela española en el Siglo XIX* (Madrid, 1924) that *Doña Perfecta* stirred up a critical storm anticipating that of *Electra*. Hoar, "Critics," pp. 56–59.

[4] For this statement I rely on the testimony of my good friend, the Russian Hispanist, Georgy Stepanov, as well as on the recent article by Vernon Chamberlin on "El interés soviético por los *episodios* y *novelas* de Galdós (1935–40)," *Actas del Primer Congreso Internacional de Estudios Galdosianos, Ediciones del Excmo Cabildo Insular de Gran Canarias*, 1978, p. 4. See also Chamberlin, "A Soviet Introduction to *Doña Perfecta*," *AG*, 10, 1975, pp. 64–81.

those of us who inevitably compare it with *Fortunata y Jacinta* or *Misericordia*.

Finally, the continued utilization of *Doña Perfecta* as a schoolroom classic for foreign students of Spanish should not be forgotten. For this purpose it is, or was until recently, assigned to intermediate courses that excluded Galdós' later and undeniably greater works. As the author himself may have suspected would occur, through both ideological commitment (pro and con) and habitual sloth *Doña Perfecta* is the novel that readers most frequently associate with Galdós. In view of these anomalies, it may now be appropriate to reread the novel critically in the light of its internal relationships to both series of "novelas contemporáneas": that which it initiated and that which began in 1881 with *La desheredada*.[5]

A detail remembered by many casual readers of *Doña Perfecta* is the calculated opposition of two fictional etymologies: the ironically historical "Urbs Augusta > Orbajosa" as against the comically popular "Orb ajosa > Orbajosa." This provision of conflicting explanations for an imaginary place name would seem to be a clever touch of realism. The very fact that the narrator stresses disagreement means that there is something objectively real to disagree about. Orbajosa, in other words, has been doubly documented; it has existed, does exist, and will continue to exist in Spain forever. Yet that "Urbs Augusta" is just one among many similar references in the novel to antiquity has been generally overlooked. Parallel instances that come readily to mind are: Pepe Rey's provocative and indeed somewhat Shavian transposition of the Pantheon into nineteenth-century equivalents; don Inocencio's fondness for quoting Horace and Virgil; and the antiquarian lore of don Cayetano. There are many other less obvious examples, which further examination will discover. Since in matters of this sort chance may be ruled out, the question of the significance of this pattern of allusions deserves meditation. Do they represent an effort at stylistic decoration by an inexperienced author still impressed by the classical education he received in secondary school and at the University?[6] Or do they

---

[5] For a detailed discussion of Galdós' various "maneras" and "series," see, of course, Robert Ricard, *Galdós et ses romans*.

[6] The most thorough study of this aspect of Galdós' education is Josette Blanquat's excellent article, "Lecturas de juventud," *Homenaje*, pp. 161–220.

have an organic relationship to the novel as a whole? Should the latter be the case, their investigation will provide us with a convenient point of departure.

The reader's initial encounter with Orbajosa's classical affectation occurs when Pedro Lucas, Pepe Rey's peasant escort, remarks that "me llaman el tío Licurgo."[7] At first glance we are tempted to interpret this "apodo" as an allusion to the native virtue and illiterate sagacity of men of the soil. As we read on, however, and as this rustic Lycurgus reveals more about himself, this explanation becomes more dubious. To be sure, he is shrewd and a mouther of proverbs, the traditional oral wisdom of his kind, but he is virtually, if not openly, dishonest. It eventually turns out that the namesake

---

In addition to a secondary school education in Las Palmas heavily weighted in this direction, the influence of Camus (one of the faculty members mentioned at the beginning of *Fortunata y Jacinta*) on Galdós and his generation is discussed at length. Camus' lively and profound humanistic course on the classics (of a quality and orientation unique in the history of Spanish higher education) seems to have been a kind of general education requirement for law students. Classical references abound in Galdós' early works, usually in comic juxtaposition with Spanish nineteenth-century reality. Typical of such neo-Quevedesque rapprochement is the comparison in the "Crónica de Madrid" of those who celebrate the "fiesta de San Isidro" to Venus, Mercury, and Bacchus. (*1546*) Later in *La Fontana de Oro* Galdós compares "Doña Teresa de Burguillos . . . dama . . . de formas colosales" to "Minerva" and calls Gil de Carrascosa (who was about to be slashed by the razor of her husband) "el Agamenón de la covachuela." The surrounding references are at once Quixotesque and (as we shall see in the case of Pepe Rey) statuesque. (*17*) This kind of burlesque rhetoric is still to be found in *La desheredada*, where Galdós repeats the epithet used for Caballuco with even more sarcasm in his description of Luis Pez, equestrian, bureaucrat, and "señorito": "Iba nuestro galán centauro a la oficina lo menos que podía." (*1036*) In the same novel he describes his own chapter title "Flamenca Cytheria" as "la unión nefanda de . . . dos vocablos." (*1092*) Later, classical references become much more complex in their intentionality (for example, the beginning of *Halma*), but the principle is the same: to accentuate the particularities of history, personality, and locality by means of contrast with universal norms. It is only in *Doña Perfecta* (and in the dream of antiquity in *La sombra*), however, that this contrast is structurally and thematically central. W. H. Shoemaker's pertinent article on "Galdós' Classical Scene in *La de Bringas,*" as the title indicates, discusses a classical reference confined to a single episode.

[7] In the preliminary MS (which I have only seen in a photocopy at the BN) his original name seems (as far as I could make it out) to have been "el tío Tardío," which would seem to indicate that the use of classical references was more crucial to the finished creation than to the initial conception.

of the Athenian lawgiver is a typical rural "pleitista," the leader of a group of squatters on Pepe Rey's land who attempt to cover up their depredations with an interminable countersuit. Thus, it would seem that the cunning and legal unscrupulousness of "el tío Licurgo" is placed in ironic contrast with the intelligence and legal rectitude of his classical model. The general characteristics are the same, wisdom and interest in the law, but the Castilian possessor of the name represents them in a degenerate form. This contrast is further underlined when "el tío Licurgo" mentions the second nickname of a fellow "pleitista," "el tío Pasolargo." He is called "el filósofo" because of his "mucha trastienda"!

It is tempting to try to relate this ironic discrepancy between name and reality to the quixotic Castilian place names, which Pepe Rey criticizes in chapter 2. Cerrillo de los Lirios, Villarrica, Valdeflores, and Valleameno are the most desolate spots imaginable; yet their very barrenness gives rise to a merciful nomenclature that the newcomer attributes to "horrible irony." Galdós had previously referred to Pepe Rey and his guide as "señor y escudero," but in this instance it is the "señor" who takes the role of Sancho, while the regional population is intent on turning windmills into giants. Nevertheless, the possibility of making a Cervantine point in connection with Castilian toponymy was probably suggested by the nature and the conjunction of the two speakers.[8] It is a tiny example of the progressive exploration and deepening that characterizes Galdosian creativity at every level. In any event, it is clear that the intention of those who coined such toponyms does not resemble that which led Galdós to accumulate classical references. In the one case, the rather pathetic fancy of popular baptism does not alude to *any* perceptible relationship between the name and the named reality. In the other, Galdós insinuates the betrayal of the name by the person: an apparent suitability or congruence is in the long run seen to be betrayed.

The encounter with the "cacique faccioso" of Orbajosa suggests the possibility of an overall pattern of irony of this latter (non-Quixotic) variety. Nicknamed Caballuco and baptized Cristóbal Ramos, he accosts Pepe Rey and "el tío Licurgo" on their journey

[8] The echo was first heard by Madariaga in his 1924 reevaluation of Galdós.

from the station to Orbajosa and exchanges some rather haughty words with the man he is later to murder. Galdós describes him as so well mounted on a "soberbio caballo de pecho carnoso semejante a los del Partenón" that he resembles a "centauro." It is a comparison that reappears on several occasions and leads us to suspect that the designation Caballuco with its pejorative suffix may have been maliciously invented by Galdós as Orbajosa's version of the mythological "horse-man." Again we have, as in the case of the two etymologies, a classical reference undermined by a local and folkloric substitute.

Furthermore, as for the peasant guide, there is a certain equivalence between the myth and the reality. To begin with, the fierce independence and the traditional arrogance that are attributed to centaurs are not lacking in this Castilian "macho." The classical characterization is tacitly identified in the novel with the Castilian values of "entereza" and "honra," for Caballuco typically mutters repetitions of the "Siglo de Oro" formula, "yo soy quien soy," and the like. For example, when he aggressively asks Pepe Rey, "¿Sabe Vd. quien soy yo?", the answer, "Ya sé que Vd. es un animal," reminds us at once of the centaur comparison.

But the significant resemblance to "el tío Licurgo" emerges when we learn more about the rustic centaur. In spite of his pretensions to honor, he is baited by doña Perfecta into breaking his promise and declaring factional war on the troops from Madrid. Furthermore, he displays an unmanly jealousy of Pepe Rey that reminds us, not of "el caballero de Olmedo," but rather of his assassin, don Rodrigo. Caballuco's is a poor nature incapable of withstanding the slightest assault on his pride. Just as "el tío Licurgo" represents the degeneration of the traditional peasant sage, so Caballuco shows us the epic integrity of the "ome en si" (or "caballero") in a state of advanced decay.

A pattern of the classical references is now visible. An antique personage or mythological figure is interpreted as embodying a traditional set of Spanish values; his name or a variation of it is given to a character who might be expected to incarnate those values; and the inevitable result is that defective fulfillment of those expectations is vividly emphasized by the contrast. There is at once ironic harmony and ironic discrepancy in the relation of the classical norm with its provincial nineteenth-century avatar. But it should once again be emphasized that the specific and heavy-handed authorial intervention that is required by this technique will be alien to the far more Cervantine ironist of the mature novels.

A second variety of classical reference, which displays the same caustic pattern, is the characters' fondness for bucolic imagery in order to celebrate the peace and simplicity of life in Orbajosa. This ever-present litany is to be heard in different contexts and with differing degrees of literary affectation, depending on the individual orator. Pepe Rey's father begins by citing Virgil prior to his son's journey into the "el corazón de España." Then, once there, don Inocencio (a complacent reader of Classical Latin, like so many of the priests of Galdós, Zola, and Clarín) alludes to Horace's *Beatus ille* whenever his "patria chica" is mentioned. Less pedantic but in the same vein, both doña Perfecta and Rosarito respectively hope and fear that Pepe Rey will be bored by the "peaceful and pastoral life" of Orbajosa. And even he, in his efforts to discourage the one and reassure the other, speaks of having found solace in "la soledad y el sosiego del campo." (*419*) It is an illusion he does not cherish for long and about which he was somewhat dubious from the moment he left Villahorrenda with "el tío Licurgo." While on his way across the barren "meseta" to Orbajosa, his experience of its landscape is as foreign to that of *La Diana* as it was to be to the nostalgic Castile of Antonio Machado. Where were the "montes, lagos, ríos, poéticos arroyos, oteros pastoriles" (*409*) that had filled his childish imagination?

As Pepe Rey soon realizes, life in Orbajosa, rather than peaceful, is endlessly monotonous; rather than calm, it is petty in its incessant activity and gossip; and rather than offering Petrarchan solitude, it only provides spiritual isolation. Galdós' most explicit and striking portrait of existence in this anti-Vaucluse occurs in chapter 12, entitled "Aquí fue Troya." There he describes "la casa de las Troyas," where three indigent orphan girls ("las niñas de Troya") live in a kind of perpetual social "siege," suspected, maligned, despised, and isolated by all respectable citizens. Although they hardly have a chance to misbehave, they lack "honra" by definition. The classical reference in this case is so clear as to need no comment, particularly when Galdós tells us that the unique outlet for their youthful good spirits is to wander through the galleries and rooms of the old house laughing at trifles and responding to their ostracism by flinging pebbles at the passers-by. It is a corrosive "cuadro de costumbres," an account of small-town repression and frustration that is reminiscent of Sherwood Anderson's *Winesburg, Ohio*. But aside from the Homeric connotations, we may on our own intuit another betrayal of life modeled classically. Are not the poor Troyas the potential shepherdesses of the pastoral Orbajosa that never was?

Don Cayetano, the local antiquary and brother-in-law of doña Perfecta, provides another variation of the same pattern. This well-intentioned but hapless individual spends his time perusing old tomes, transcribing manuscripts, and worshiping relics of past glory, but he never guesses that ongoing history requires a new sort of historian. Like the ancestral pride of the Porreño sisters, don Cayetano's erudition is no longer meaningful. When he exclaims, "The ancients called our city "augusta"; today I dare call it "augustíssima," because now even more than then honor, generosity, valor, and nobility are its patrimony" (*437*),[9] he reveals the total lack of historical insight that vitiates his learning. Scornful of an incorrectly dated edition, he accepts the myth of Orbajosa at face value, that is, according to its complacently arrogant evaluation of itself. In so doing he naturally overlooks the popular "counter-etymology," which alludes to the town's most renowned agricultural product. The candid satisfaction of don Cayetano in the Roman origins of his birthplace suggests what Galdós had in mind. Each of the two etymologies presents its own perspective on municipal pride. Agricultural achievement on a very non-Virgilian level of decorum is used to suggest social and human failure. In a town as proud of its garlic as this one is Lycurgus is appropriately a "tío"!

We may penetrate more deeply into Galdós' intentions if we ask ourselves directly why he chose classical references for the presentation of his theme. Why should he not have compared Orbajosa's desiccated nineteenth century to the burgeoning Middle Ages or to the "Siglo de Oro," when provincial Castile, in spite of economic decline, was still capable of producing "conquistadores," mystics, poets, and even exemplary novelists, all of them exemplifying

[9] Incomprehensibly, in the MS Galdós' first version seems to have been "Urbs Excelsa."

apogees of human fervor and dignity? Or why not stress more emphatically the chasm separating this regressive "scène de province" from forward-looking life in Madrid? My answer would have to be that Galdós chose the ancient world because he was no longer primarily interested in studying historically the decline of Castile or in underlining sardonically the contrast of liberalism and reaction. Those had been the aims of *La Fontana de Oro* and of certain "episodios" in the first two series; now he was more interested in direct investigation of the imperfection of Spanish society as such and as a whole.

This definition of the intention underlying *Doña Perfecta* suggests in turn that the Balzacian dichotomy of capital city versus provinces, which had been the manifest point of departure for this initial experiment with contemporaneity, became almost immediately irrelevant.[10] All Spain, Madrid included, in spite of its deceptive façade of progress, was a province, with all the characteristic provincial vices that were to be expected. As Galdós remarked explicitly in an 1896 letter to the painter, Aureliano de Beruete, thanking him for a rather desolate "Vista de Orbajosa" in oils: "ya no hay en España provincia ni capital que no sea más o menos Orbajosoide. Orbajosa encontrará Vd. en las aldeas, Orbajosa en las

---

[10] In view of the substitution of the name "el tío Licurgo" for "el tío Tardío" (see note 7 above), I can only surmise that Galdós either read or suddenly recalled Balzac's *Les Paysans* while in the process of composition. See *Comédie,* vol. 8, p. 11. The basic plot or scheme of the novel, as we observed, seems clearly to have been derived from *Eugénie Grandet,* but the notion of using classical references as a means of debunking costumbristic sentimentality was already present in the opening letter of *Les Paysans,* in which the Burgundian countryside (which, as we already suspect, will be the scene of a grim, rural drama) is described fatuously as the new Arcadia. *Comédie,* vol. 8, p. 19. Chapter 2 follows, entitled with an irony identical to that of Galdós, "Une Bucolique oubliée par Virgile," a title that prepares us for our introduction to "le père Fourchon" (who, as we saw in chapter 7, note 8, may have been a precursor of Fortunata's uncle) as a "Diogène campagnard." Ibid., p. 34. Both in this classical comparison and in his role as a "maraudeur" against the estate of "Les Aigues," he foreshadows "el tío Licurgo." A number of other classical references follow. A coincidence that comes to my attention long after writing the above is Edward Thomas's *Heart of England,* which is replete with serious regional classicism including a centaur. See Raymond Williams, *The Country and the City,* p. 255. The contrast with Balzac and Galdós could not be greater.

ciudades ricas y populosas. . . . Todo es y todo será mañana Orbajosa, si Dios no se apiada de nosotros . . . que no se apiadará." The
letter is significantly identified at the end as having been written
in "Madrijosa . . . Marzo 96."[11] That Galdós was well aware of the
same devastating truth twenty years earlier is evident in the novels
that followed *Doña Perfecta: Gloria* and *La familia de León Roch.*
Most of the Spaniards they describe are in as wretched a state of
"degeneración lastimosa" as Caballuco himself. The merciless description of the latter, "Se parecía a los grandes hombres de don
Cayetano, como se parece el mulo al caballo" (476), could easily be
rephrased to fit almost all the assertive and devalued existences in
these novels.

The ironical use of doña Perfecta's name for the title is in itself
indicative of the renovated theme. Orbajosa, as represented by its
priest, its "cacique," its peasant, and its lady of quality, is a manifestly *imperfect* social organism, and each of those who represent it
contributes to it his or her particular variety of imperfection. These
are not vicious or perverted individuals, as Galdós is careful to let
us know; rather they do not measure up to their images of themselves, to the traditional "forms" of their existences. Their lives do
not fill their age-old types, and almost in spite of themselves, as they
interact against the intruding foreign body known as Pepe Rey,
they become a blind force for evil. It is precisely because Galdós
wanted to compare his characters to themselves (meaning the way
they see themselves) and not to other possibilities of being human
that he employed classical references. In the three or four so-called
"novelas contemporáneas de la primera época" Galdós' dominant
intention was to examine evil in Spain, that is, the tragedy of being
Spanish. He was no longer concerned with asking how we got
where we are now (as in the "episodios"), but instead asked who
we are and how it is possible to be that way. In this particular novel,
as we have seen, classical perfection is used as a reagent to reveal
the vital imperfection that transforms the human complex called

[11] See Leo Hoar, "Galdós y Aureliano de Beruete; Visión renovada de
Orbajosa," *Anuario de Estudios Atlánticos,* 20, 1974, p. 15. Clarín in his review in *El Solfeo,* 3 October 1876, agreed: "un pueblo en su sepultura . . .
el autor estudia el alma de aquel pueblo y la encuentra degradada, enferma
. . . Orbajosa es toda España." Hoar, "Critics," p. 44.

Orbajosa into a collective assassin.[12] Orbajosa, in summary, is not a place but a defective and destructive way of life.

If this is true of the antagonist, Orbajosa as a functioning whole, how can it be related to the person of the protagonist and victim, Pepe Rey? Although at first it might appear to be useless to look for a similar pattern of reference for this overexemplary character, let us glance at Galdós' initial description of him:

> The age of this excellent young man verged on thirty-four. His constitution was robust and his muscles were almost Herculean; in fact he was so perfectly built and so arrogant in his bearing that, had he worn a military uniform, he would have been the perfect image of a warrior. His hair and beard were blond, but his face was not phlegmatic and expressionless like that of a typical Anglo-Saxon. Quite to the contrary, he was so vital and full of life that his eyes seemed black, although in fact they were not. All in all he could well have qualified as a symbol [for heroic young manhood], and if he had been a statue, his sculptor might have written on his pedestal "Intelligence and Strength." Yet even though he had not been labeled in this fashion, one could easily read the same words in his gaze, in his special attraction for others, and in the way others reacted to that affectionate magnetism. (*416*)

Pepe Rey is, thus, a statue, in his physical being a formal and perfect representation of moral qualities. Little insight into Galdós' conception of antique sculpture (or nineteenth-century imitation thereof) is needed in order to comprehend that Pepe Rey has been defined by his positive relation to a classical model. Unlike his enemies, he fills his form, that is, his perfection, to the brim, a condition that helps greatly to explain his peculiar novelistic lifelessness.

Galdós goes on to tell us something more about this unwelcome paragon from the metropolis:

> He refused to condone falsehood, hoaxes, or the kind of intellectual sophistries of which certain intellects given to extreme

---

[12] Among the many classical references in the novel here left unmentioned because they do not function in this fashion is the unkind comparison of don Juan Tafetán to Antinoüs and the "escrutinio" of don Inocencio's library.

metaphorical rhetoric [modern reincarnations of the Baroque poet Góngora] are so fond. And when confronted with such, Pepe Rey was not averse to the employment of irony and offensive sarcasm in responding, perhaps even a bit excessively. This could almost be described as a defect of his, and his many admirers would have agreed that he was disrespectful of certain situations and kinds of behavior that most people were inclined to let pass without remark. (*416*)

A "casi . . . defecto" in an exemplary being, a certain intolerance, a sarcastic arrogance—can this not be a nineteenth-century version of the tragic flaw? From this point onwards the progressive enmeshment of Pepe Rey in the fatal web of Orbajosa is shown to be the result of this total lack of tact. The relentless sarcasm and the unthinking aggressiveness of our hero at once provoke and play into the two thousand and two hands of his collective antagonist, with the fatal results that we know and that we dreaded helplessly on the occasion of our first reading.

All of this suggests, not another classical reference, but a classical structure, that of tragedy. The social destiny of Pepe Rey, his victimization by a malign collective imperfection, is nothing less than a new and novelistic expression of Aristotelian prescriptions—the inevitable doom of flawed perfection portrayed in a series of extended narrative acts. In all brevity, these may be outlined as follows: first, introduction and initial encounter (chapters 1 through 7); second, increasing tension, moves and countermoves (8 through 12); third, intervention of external factors, "las niñas de Troya," don Juan Tafetán, and the political situation, which sharpen the conflict (13 through 18); fourth, Pepe's discovery (tragedy must have a discovery) of the full extent and perverse nature of what he is up against (19); fifth, his final struggle and death (20 through 31); and sixth, the epilogue (32 and 33). Aside from this tentative comprehension of structure, the notion of tragedy explains something else essential to a novel literally based on nomenclature: his baptism as "Pepe Rey." For as Shakespeare tells us with unquestionable authority, "sad stories of the death of kings" are the raw material of the genre.

Thematically a cardiogram of "el corazón de España" and in

structure a tragedy, *Doña Perfecta* is nonetheless a manifestly "imperfect" novel. Its calculated dramatic progression (indicated by such awkward chapter titles as "La existencia de la discordia es evidente" and "La discordia crece") directs the reader's attention to what is for E. M. Forster the most facile aspect of all novels, the story. Although at their best stories can be entrancing journeys through artificial time, this one is painful to read. As Cervantes teaches us, the reader of story-novels inevitably tends to identify himself with the hero. And to the extent that Pepe Rey can so be defined, his repeated blunders and unawareness of what is going on render the identification uncomfortable. A "tragic flaw" in a novel is not compensated for by the poetic overscale and the elevated poetic diction that are possible in the drama. The catastrophic fate of that other "Rey" called Oedipus is cathartic; but that of the engineer from Madrid is indigestible. As for the other characters, we understand them, and we may even be interested in them as representative of the failure of Spanish life, but they do not provoke the hatred or fear that are the obverse of identification. They are simply not supposed to be villains.

Similar difficulties impede our experience of the world of the novel. The equation of Orbajosa as a collectivity with tragic fate (in *León Roch* Galdós was to coin the phrase "el hado social") (*891*) effectively inhibits the creation of an environment with which we can participate in our imagination. Fate is by definition elusive and mysterious, and hence Galdós repeatedly avoids presenting Orbajosa directly. Such archly Cervantine evasions as "Those who gave us the information necessary for the composition of this history do not refer to that dialogue, undoubtedly because it was too secret" (*427*) seem almost designed to prevent submersion in the "elsewhere" of the novel. With the exception of the initial ride across the "meseta" and such fortunate sketches as those of don Juan Tafetán and "las niñas de Troya," Orbajosa is a nebulous entity. We understand it, but we do not experience it. Local particularities, social structure, even the plotting of doña Perfecta and her fellow conspirators all remain in the shadows. They are manifested indirectly, but they are not often witnessed. We have been taught painstakingly the social geography of Orbajosa, but we have not been allowed to explore it.

In this sense Galdós forsook consciously the advantages of the regionalistic novel as cultivated by his friend and rival, Pereda. The latter, who in *Don Gonzalo González de la Gonzalera* had attempted to answer the thesis of *Doña Perfecta* (a liberal Madrid outsider disrupts and corrupts rural beatitude), is able to develop his more simplistic view of good and evil in Spain by creating a literary world of inherent and manifest virtue, "la Montaña."[13] Values, as it were, are embodied in local color and provincial customs with the result that the reader experiences the regional world of the novel in a fashion fully as genuine, though not as stark, as he experiences the fictional Wessex of Thomas Hardy. Pereda's thesis may seem childish and even foolish when compared to the acute sociological analysis of *Doña Perfecta,* but it does serve to reveal milieu rather than conceal it. Quite simply, the very success of Galdós' contemporary "roman à thèse" (he would have been pleased and proud had he known that *Doña Perfecta* was to be prohibited during the early decades of the Franco regime) is the condition of its artistic failure.

What Galdós might have done had he proceeded otherwise is suggested by a character so far unmentioned, Rosario, the Ophelia-like daughter of doña Perfecta. Galdós begins by describing her in terms quite different from those used for the other inhabitants of Orbajosa:

> The genuine beauty of doña Perfecta's daughter consisted in a kind of transparency . . . through which the depths of her soul could be seen clearly, depths not cavernous like those of the sea but rather like those to be found in the gentle flow of a crystalline river. But nonetheless she was not a complete person: she needed a well-defined channel with shores. The vast volume of her spirit was always on the verge of flooding, of inundating the river banks. (*417*)

Here finally is a character who, rather than failing to live up to a traditional image (or existing in a state of perfect self-sufficiency), threatens to overflow the fragile limits of her identity.

Like a river, Rosario's ongoing awareness is unpredictable in its ever-present threat of irrational inundation. Although at this point

[13] See chapter 3, note 26.

(chapter 4) we only see her as she is interpreted by Galdós, his description is open-ended rather than enclosed by rigid classical definitions. As such it enables us to follow the course of her existence as it grows and changes after her initial exposure to amorous "incitation." From our point of view the causation of her inner metamorphosis, a mad passion for Pepe Rey, may seem as unconvincing as the flood of insanity that his murder produces in her. But such judgments are clearly tangential (Galdós does not offer her much choice as far as suitors or characterization are concerned); the real significance of Rosario is that she is the only person in Orbajosa who lives novelistically: she is the only person who lives in time from within herself. Her life is an authentic accumulation of experience, and, as such, it is worth contrasting the naturalness, length, and fervor of her declarations of love with the static and short replies of the tragic hero on the occasion of their first clandestine rendezvous (chapter 17).

Later, when Rosario's passion has been further crystallized by increasingly severe maternal repression and she is already on her way to madness, she provides the reader with the novel's most intense passage of shared experience. She has returned from a secret tryst with her beloved; she has been discovered by doña Perfecta; and "transfixed with the cold steel of an immense pain," she prays in a fashion that in some ways anticipates Fortunata's rejection of conscience: "To love, to love passionately, is that evil?" (478) But no, she realizes, she *is* evil, because polar to her love for Pepe Rey there has grown an equally passionate hatred of her mother. What happens next is what matters to us. Torn with conflicting feelings, she falls into a state of lethargy, and "in her fleeting dreams her imagination reproduced all that she had done that night, transforming it without changing it in essence." (478) Dreamed repetition of experience is an obvious device, but it does enable Galdós to achieve fully for the first time in *Doña Perfecta* the special kind of nineteenth-century suspension of disbelief that Balzac, Flaubert, Mark Twain, Tolstoy, and many others used in their communal elevation of the ci-devant genre to imperial dignity. I mean our awareness of being included in and contributing to the experience of what I called earlier a "presence" (Huck Finn, Fabrice, Fortunata, or even Gervaise Lantier and Emma Bovary) as against breathless or tearful identification with the adventures of flat, prefabricated surrogates such as Amadís, the Continental Op, or Fleur-de-Marie. In addition to such heroes and victims of romance and although there is no such personage in the novel at present under discussion, I would append to the second category, the comic or ridiculous figure—the butt—as a vehicle for realism. As Cervantes soon discovered, the belief we derive from laughing at fictional creatures is in no way superior to that we derive from identifying ourselves with them as they speed from adventure to adventure. The novel is truly significant when it invites us to a communion of consciousness and so enables us to participate in the otherness of another life and in the uniqueness of its temporal experience.

Confirmed addicts of the novel at its best, from "les bons stendhaliens," who spend their happiest moments incarcerated in "la tour Farnése," to "les bons joycéens," who spend theirs at liberty in Nighttown, will need no further explanation. Neither will any reader who has lived above the Plaza Mayor with Fortunata. Nevertheless, in conclusion let us again scrutinize Galdós' early experimentation with the possibilities of the new novel. In the preceding chapter of *Doña Perfecta* Galdós had presented directly the meeting of the local conspirators, their surreptitious gathering, their dialogue, and their characteristic betrayals of imperfection. But now through Rosario's oneiric re-creation of what she had seen on her way to meet Pepe Rey (the reader had not been informed that she was looking through the window), Galdós communicates in experiential terms the true horror of the sinister reunion:

> She could hear the clock in the steeple strike nine . . . and she left her room on tiptoes in order not to make a sound. . . . She was drawing close to the glass door of the dining room. . . . By the light of the lamp she could see her mother's back. The confessor was at her right, and his profile was strangely distorted. His nose had grown and looked like the beak of an imaginary bird. His whole body was transformed into a foreshortened shadow, thick, black with unexpected angles where it was not bare and thin. Caballuco was opposite and looked more like a dragon than a man. To Rosario his green eyes looked like two great lanterns with convex lenses. Their shine and his great

animal body frightened her. Uncle Lycurgus and the other three looked like grotesque figurines. She had undoubtedly seen at some fair those misshapen clay dolls that smile with the same grimace and look at you just as stupidly. The dragon revolved his arms like a windmill, and his green orbs resembled a lighthouse or bell jars in a pharmacy. His glance was blinding. . . . The conversation seemed to be interesting. The confessor flapped his wings. He was a presumptuous bird who wanted to fly but could not. His beak grew longer and then got twisted. His feathers ruffled up to express his anger, and after calming down and pulling them in, he hid his shaven head under his wing. Then the clay figurines got excited, pretending that they were persons too . . . *(478–479)*

At this point Galdós breaks in with an explanatory comment of his own: "Rosario was inexplicably terrified by the spectacle of that friendly gathering." He may speak of terror, but the mood is broken by the jocose irony of the phrase "amistoso concurso," an expression reminiscent of his archly written "revistas de la semana." Prior to this inappropriate interruption, what Erich Kahler has termed the generic tendency of the novel toward "Innerwendung" is clearly manifest for the first time.[14] The imagery of Rosario's dream sequence is no longer classical and external; now reminiscent of a fairy tale, it corresponds to the personal experience and frightened agitation of a young girl who is still in many ways a child. The novel for a brief moment has become fully alive in Rosario's consciousness.

Thus, doña Perfecta's passive and sensitive daughter, who contributes almost nothing to the impetus of the action, reveals the relationship of this first "novela contemporánea"[15] to the great novels that were to come. In them, Galdós' major human creations, like

---

[14] *The Inward Turn of Narration,* Princeton, 1973.

[15] When Madrid becomes Orbajosa in *León Roch,* it is the "monstrous" character of the Spanish nineteenth century as such that takes the blame, probably more justly, and not provincialism: "¡Monstruosa síntesis de los tiempos, no se sabe donde irá a parar, barajando con sus propias invenciones y prodigios nuevos las reliquias y curiosidades que ha conservado de aquel atrás remoto!" *(812)* Here a belated and pessimistic echo of Musset's generational quandary is clearly audible.

those of Cervantes and Dostoievsky, are going to live in a state of overflow. The swift and broad current of their continuing experience will surpass their containing social dikes and self-definitions. The principal characters of *Doña Perfecta,* on the other hand, by the failure of their lives to fill their types or archetypes (a failure communicated by the author's imposition of classical references), are antithetical to Fortunata, to Maxi Rubín, to Benita, and even to Torquemada. Galdós began his exploration of the Spain of his time with an "antinovel," which was nonetheless a below-zero point of departure for an ascending trajectory. For in the ordeal of Rosario we glimpse how Galdós, like Cervantes long before, was to replace the rigidity of fable and the hermeticism of adventure with lives in time, lives which in their very temporality become immortal.

In the index that follows, real and fictional persons are listed together without distinction. The thesis of the book it was designed to serve—that the nineteenth-century novel is not realistic fiction but rather a generic erasure of the frontier between the real and the fictional—may justify this procedure. Individual titles with a few exceptions are listed under the heading of their authors. Character indices for the authors discussed at most length—Galdós, Balzac, Cervantes, Clarín, Dickens, Twain, and Zola—have for the sake of convenience been appended at the end.

Achilles, 4
Adams, Henry, 14, 14 n22
Agamemnon, 380 n6
Ahab, Captain, 164
Alarcón, Pedro Antonio de, 23, 194, 195
Alcántara García, Pedro de, 125 n69
Alcott, Bronson, 79 n47
Aleixandre, Vicente, 25, 25 n46, 286
Alfonso XII, 88
Allende, Salvador, 6, 6 n7
Allison, G. H., 192 n9, 213 n49
Allworthy, Squire, 73 n40
Alonso, Amado, 40, 40 n20, 50, 252, 252 n10
Alonso, Dámaso, 30 n5, 31 n5
Amadeo de Saboya, 69, 90, 101, 205 n23, 283 n61
Amadís de Gaula, 159, 163, 234, 337, 353, 392
Anderson, Sherwood, 384
Andrenio [E. Gómez de Baquero], 378 n3
Andreu, Alicia, 112 n46, 306 n24
Antinoüs, 387 n12
Antúnez, Nemesio, 6 n7
Araya, Guillermo, 6 n8
Arenal, Concepción, 125 n69

Aristophanes, 318, 318 n45
Aristotle, 334, 388
Auden, W. H., 260, n31
Augustine, Saint, 357 n6
Austen, Jane, 173, n26, 270
Avellaneda, Fernández de, 116 n53, 127, 193 n13
Ayguals de Izco, Wenceslao, 112 n46
Azaña, Manuel, 162
Azorín [José Martínez Ruiz], 53 n6, 88 n7, 251 n9, 367

Bacarisse, Salvador, 189 n3
Bacchus, 380 n6
Bakunin, Mikhail, 168, 168 n21, 264
Baldensperger, Fernand, 20 n36
Baldwin, James, 273
Bally, Charles, 98 n24
Balmaseda, José Manuel, 6, 6 n7
Balmes, Jaime, 120, 120 n61, 120, n62, 121
Balzac, Honoré de, 5, 8, 9–11, 13, 15 n23, 16, 17, 17 n27, 23, 25 n48, 27, 30, 30 n3, 46, 46 n29, 55, 55 n11, 63–67, 70, 73 n40, 74 n40, 75, 77, 89 n8, 91–94, 94 n17, 95 n19, 103 n31, 104 n34, 104 n35, 105 n35, 112, 112 n47, 133, 133 n2, 147 n18, 147

n19, 148 n19, 155, 156, 161 n10,
165, 165 n17, 166 n19, 168 n22, 172,
173, 173 n26, 176–80, 180 n37, 181–
84, 188, 189 n3, 190–92, 195, 196,
196 nn17–19, 197 n20, 198, 198 n24,
199, 199 n27, 200–208, 210, 214,
n50, 215, 218 n58, 229, 235, 236,
237 n7, 238, 246, 249 n14, 256, 266
n38, 274 n49, 291, 292 n2, 296, 299
n14, 340 n25, 366, 370, 372 n22, 375
n24, 385, 385 n10, 391; *Avant-
propos,* 9 n10, 64 n27, 73 n40, 91,
173 n20, 192 n10, 199, 199 n25, 291;
Bal de Sceaux, Le, 94 n17, 104 n35;
Béatrix, 15 n23, 16, 19, 19 n32, 25
n48, 64 n27, 213, n50, 214 n50;
César Birotteau, 327 n14; *Comédie
humaine,* 6, 6 nn5–6, 9, 30, 42, 73,
91, 161 n10, 176, 178, 195, 195 n17,
196, 196 n19, 198, 199, 215;
Comment aiment les filles, 178,
179, 180 n37; *Employés, Les,* 46
n29; *Eugénie Grandet,* 27, 46 n29,
63, 63 n25, 64, 65, 93, 155, 155 n1,
156, 385 n10; *Fille aux yeux d'or,
La,* 299 n14; *Illusions perdues,* 17
n27, 19 n31; *Jésus-Christ en Flandres,* 64 n27; *Maison du chat-qui-
pelote, La,* 30, 161 n10, 215, 303
n18, 372 n22; *Maison Nucingen,
La,* 296; *Mémoires de deux jeunes
mariées,* 214 n50; *Ménage de garçon, Un,* 46 n29; *Paysans, Les,* 63,
65, 93, 156, 218 n58, 385 n10; *Père
Goriot, Le,* 13 n19, 147 n19, 196
n17, 198; *Pierrette,* 6 n6; *Splendeurs et misères des courtisanes,*
5, 112 n47, 122 n65, 133 n1, 176,
177, 179, 180, 184, 187, 292
Baquero Goyanés, Mariana, 143 n15
Baráibar y Zumárrage, Federico, 318
Barbéris, Pierre, 21 n37, 176 n32, 198
n24
Bardèche, Maurice, 11, 30, 55 n11,
64 n27, 74 n40, 147 n19, 161 n10,
172 n26, 173 n26, 195 n17, 196
n17, 196 n18, 197 n20, 199, 199 n27,
205 n37, 208, 237, 237 n7, 266 n38,
340 n25

Barnum, Samuel, 129
Baroja, Pío, 7, 20 n34, 360 n8
Barraclough, Geoffrey, 10, 16
Barthes, Roland, 98 n24, 358, 367
Barzun, Jacques, 60 n9
Baudelaire, Charles, 144, 176 n32, 259,
259 n25, 289, 289 n71
Bazarov, 64 n26
Bécquer, Gustavo Adolfo, 89 n8, 95
n19, 203, 203 n34, 306
Beethoven, Ludwig van, 231 n3, 358
n7
Béguin, Albert, 203, 203 n33, 204 n35,
292
Bellesort, André, 195 n17, 196 n18
Bénichou, Paul, 20 n36, 21 n37
Berceo, Gonzalo de, 250, 343
Bergamín, José, 249 n4, 260 n29
Bergson, Henri, 69, 73, 74 n41, 327
n14, 356
Berkowitz, H. Chonon, 51 n3, 169
n22, 200 n28, 353, 353 n36
Berlin, Isaiah, 60 n19
Bernard, Claude, 82, 93
Bertault, Philippe, 17 n27, 204 n35
Beruete, Aureliano de, 385, 386 n11
Beser, Sergio, 46 n29, 85 n1, 86 n5,
99 n25
Blaine, Amory, 20, 20 n34
Blanco Aguinaga, Carlos, 127, 229 n1
Blanquat, Josette, 27 n51, 379 n6
Blasco Ibáñez, Vicente, 88 n7
Block, Haskell, 103 n31, 260 n29
Bloom, Molly, 102
Bolkonski, Prince, 146, 348
Bonafoux, Luis, 161
Bonet, Laureano, 15 n23, 22 n39, 22
n40, 29 n1, 80 n50, 89 n8, 173 n28,
291 n1
Bonnard, Sylvestre, 128
Borges, Jorge Luis, 185
Bourgeois, Réné, 82 n25
Bourget, Paul, 356, 358
Bousono, Carlos, 25
Bouteron, Marcel, 6 n5, 196 n17, 197
Bovary, Emma, 114, 146, 161, 162,
166, 169, 171, 172, 177, 178, 244,
246, 358, 391
Brandes, Georg, 19 n33, 20 n33

Bravo Villasante, Carmen, 25 n45, 35
 n12, 64 n26, 81 n52, 85 n3, 95 n19,
 150 n23, 157 n5, 188, 188 n2, 209
 n42, 213 n48, 256 n19, 261 n32
Brentano, Clemens, 203 n33
Bridoux, André, 23 n42, 197 n20
Brontë, Emily, 368 n15
Buckley, Jerome, 28 n54
Buffon, Comte de (George Louis
 Leclerc), 266
Buñuel, Luis, 252
Burguillos, Tomé de, 201, 201 n31
Burke, Kenneth, 113
Byron, Lord (George Gordon), 111

Caballero de Olmedo, 382
Caesar, Julius, 37
Calderón de la Barca, Pedro, 162, 201
 n31, 315, 340
Calisto, 305, 350, 364
Calvin, John, 70
Camus, Alfredo Adolfo, 361, 362,
 369, 380 n6
Candide, 332
Cánovas del Castillo, Antonio, 69,
 88, 88 n6, 113, 183, 269
Cardona, Rodolfo, 27 n51, 114
Carlyle, Thomas, 21 n36
Carr, Raymond, 4 n3
Carroll, Lewis [Charles L. Dodgson],
 266 n39
Casalduero, Joaquín, 40, 40 n20, 53
 n9, 59, 118, 122 n65, 129, 136 n5,
 158, 252, 252 n10, 284
Castelar, Emilio, 4, 287, 287 n68, 288
Castro, Américo, 9, 11 n18, 52, 56, 56
 n13, 67, 67 n34, 72, 79 n48, 122
 n64, 162–64, 165 n16, 167, 168, 168
 n21, 193 n11, 201 n31, 240, 263
 n36, 265, 271, n47, 288, 292, 304
 n22, 306, 328, 333 n22, 344, 345,
 357, 357 n5
Cedric the Saxon, 236, 236 n6
Cela, Camilo José, 365
Celestina, La, 273, 350
Centeno, Augusto, 187, 188, 225, 233,
 323
Cernuda, Louis, 51, 51 n4, 52 n4
Cervantes, Miguel de, 11, 12 n19, 24,
 24 n44, 26, 30 n5, 48 n32, 56, 57,
 67, 73 n40, 83, 90, 95 n19, 96, 98,
 100, 110–12, 114, 116–19, 119 n58,
 127–29, 135, 137, 142, 148, 153, 154,
 156 n3, 158, 161 n10, 162, 162 n11,
 162 n15, 163, 165 165 n16, 165 n17,
 167, 169, 170, 170 n23, 171, 173
 n28, 177, 179, 180, 182, 184–87,
 193, 193 n11, 193 n13, 197, 198,
 200 n29, 208, 210, 223, 224, 224 n66,
 230, 231, 233, 234, 236, 238, 239,
 243, 245, 255, 256, 259, 262, 263
 n36, 265, 270, 273, 281, 288, 289,
 291, 293, 296, 302, 306, 324, 325,
 331, 342, 347 n33, 350, 358, 361,
 367, 376, 381, 383, 389, 392, 394;
 Don Quijote, 8, 12, 30 n5, 31, 48,
 60, 83, 85 n1, 97, 110, 116–18, 119
 n58, 129, 148, 158–62, 162 n12, 163,
 164, 164 n15, 165, 165 n16, 166, 168,
 170, 170 n23, 173 n28, 182, 184, 187,
 190, 193, 208, 230–34, 236, 240, 247,
 263 n36, 265, 274, 288, 302, 337, 341,
 342, 357 n5, 366, 376, 377, 380 n6;
 Galatea, La, 83; *Novelas ejemplares,* 119; *Numancia, La,* 263
Chamberlin, Vernon, 64 n26, 231
 n3, 358, 378 n4
Chanteau, Lazare, 91 n10
Charlemagne, 377
Chateaubriand, F.A.R., 21 n37
Chatman, Seymour, 175 n30
Chekhov, Anton, 72 n39
Chourineur, 308 n25
Christie, Agatha, 191
Chueca Goitia, Fernando, 251 n9
Cid, El [Ruy Díaz de Vivar], 79
 n48, 98 n24, 240, 244, 306, 377
Cinderella, 175
Clarín [Leopoldo Alas], 13, 46, 46
 n29, 85 n1, 86, 86 n5, 93, 93 n16,
 94, 99, 99 n25, 122 n65, 145, 149,
 149 n22, 150 n23, 155–57, 157 n4,
 158, 159, 159 n7, 160–62, 164, 165
 n18, 166, 166 n19, 167, 168, 170, 171,
 172 n25, 176, 177, 177 n33, 178–
 85, 188, 201 n31, 210, 252, 254, 255
 n15, 277 n53, 289, 314 n36, 326 n10,
 327 n14, 352, 378 n2, 383, 386 n11;

Mis plagios, 161; *Regenta, La,* 43, 80 n49, 93 n16, 94, 112 n47, 117 n55, 139, 140 n12, 145, 150 n23, 151, 156, 157, 158, 160, 161 n9, 168 n22, 170, 176, 177, 177 n33, 179–82, 182 n40, 185, 186 n43, 187, 206, 277 n59, 280, 306, 314 n36, 327 n14, 352; *Reyerta, La,* 93 n16

Clarke, H. W., 354 n37

Clavería, Carlos, 10, 11, 13, 16

Cohen, Hermann, 231, 231 n3

Cohen, Robert, 224 n66

Cohn, Dorrit, 98 n24, 347, n33

Columbus, 339

Comte, Auguste, 11

Conti, Fabio, 45

Continental Op, 392

Cooper, James Fennimore, 92, 195, 364, 368

Corneille, Pierre, 104

Coronado, Carolina, 362

Correa, Gustavo, 236 n6

Cortazar, Julio, 249 n5

Cortés, Hernán, 252

Cossío, J. M. de, 248 n2

Cossío, Manuel Bartolomé, 85 n2, 86 n4

Costa-Gavras, Constantín, 67

Couffon, Claude, 194 n15

Cousin, Victor, 21 n37

Crusoe, Robinson, 309, 321

Cruz Rueda, Angel, 53 n6

Culler, Jonathan, 191 n8, 192 n8, 211 n43, 284 n63

Cunningham, J. V., 357, 357 n6

Curtius, E. R., 103 n31

Cytheria, 380 n6

Damourette, Jacques, 98 n24

Daniel, Glyn, 26 n50

Dante (Alighieri), 277 n53

D'Artagnan, 56

Darwin, Charles, 353

Deffand, Mme. du, 173 n29

Defoe, Daniel, 198, 365

del Río, Angel, 68 n35

de Man, Paul, 190 n5

De Sanctis, Francesco, 18 n28

D'Esneval, Aurée, 105 n35

Díaz, Elías, 76 n42, 78 n46, 78 n47

Dickens, Charles, 7, 8, 11, 12 n19, 13, 30, 31, 39 n19, 40, 41 n21, 55 n11, 90, 91, 94, n17, 95 n19, 96, 105 n35, 111 n45, 112, 124, n68, 137 n7, 139 n11, 147 n18, 150, 165, 166 n19, 174, 190, 192 n10, 198, 201, 202 n32, 203, 205, 205 n37, 210, 218, 218 n58, 223, 249, 249 n4, 250 n6, 251, 259, 266, 266 n38, 278, 281, 292, 293, 306 n23, 347 n33, 359 n8, 360 n8; *Battle for Life, The,* 137 n7; *David Copperfield,* 11, 62 n22, 124 n68; *Dombey and Son,* 101 n28; *Great Expectations,* 40; *Little Dorrit,* 62, 94, 122, 139 n11, 174, 218 n58, 271 n46; *Nicholas Nickleby,* 40 n21; *Our Mutual Friend,* 218, 258 n24, 278 n54; *Pickwick Papers, The,* 7, 30, 90, 165 n17, 192, 192 n10, 274, 278; *Tale of Two Cities, A,* 19 n31

Diderot, Denis, 165 n17, 193, 193 n14, 202 n32

Diego, Don, 215

Dilthey, Wilhelm, 11, 11 n17, 13 n20, 23, 23 n41, 356

Diogenes, 385 n10

Dongo, Fabrice del, 20 n36, 42, 152, 239–41, 245, 311, 333 n22, 391

Doolittle, Eliza, 272

Dos Passos, John, 20 n34

Dostoievsky, Fyodor, 135, 137, 151, 183, 184, 205 n37, 251, 334, 338, 394

Dumas, Alexandre (père), 363, 365

Dumas, Alexandre (fils), 181

Dupin, Charles, 21 n37

Dupuy, Aimé, 125 n69

Du Val, M., 180

Eça de Queiroz, J. M., 176

Eddy, Mary Baker, 79 n48

Eliade, Mercea, 354 n38

Elicia, 350

Eliot, T. S., 18 n29, 258 n24, 377

Enrique IV, 24 n44

Eoff, Sherman, 323, 327, 342

Erickson, Effie, 94 n17

Erikson, Erik, 11, 11 n18, 337
Eros, 220, 319
Espina, Antonio, 249
Espronceda, José de, 17 n26, 29, 57
Estébanez Calderón, Serafín, 96 n21, 255
Eulenberg, Herbert, 16 n25
Evelpides, 318, 318 n45

Fabié, A. M., 343 n27
Fanger, Donald, 52 n5, 205 n37, 259 n26
Faulkner, William, 206
Faust, Dr., 164
Felipe II, 199 n58
Filipe III, 346, 346 n32
Fernán Caballero [Cecilia Böhl de Faber], 23, 29, 31, 32, 70, 73, 96 n21, 195, 202 n32, 255
Fernández, Ramon, 246
Fernández Almagro, Melchor, 249 n4
Fernández Seín, Ana, 97 n23, 115, 119, 199 n59
Fernández y González, Manuel, 111, 167, 213 n49, 235
Fernando VII, 23, 29, 38, 51, 52 n4, 57, 58, 60, 247
Ferrante Palla, 45
Fichter, W. L., 248 n1
Fielding, Henry, 11, 35 n12, 41, 73 n40, 95 n19, 158, 165 n17, 173, 173 n29, 185, 193, 200, 202 n32, 223, 231, 254, 259, 267, 270, 288, 347 n33
Fishtine, Edith. See Helman, Edith
Fitzgerald, F. Scott, 20, 20 n34
Fitzgerald, Robert, 295 n8, 322 n5
Flammarion, Camille, 162 n22
Flaubert, Gustave, 34 n10, 72 n39, 75, 82, 84, 95 n19, 98 n24, 99, 103, 103 n31, 104, 104 n34, 114, 122 n64, 155, 161, 164, 165 n18, 166, 166 n19, 177, 182, 184, 189 n3, 250, 251, 255 n15, 259, 270, 274 n48, 289, 347, 391; *Education sentimentale, L',* 19 n31, 34 n10, 345; *Madame Bovary,* 34, 34 n10, 103, 147, 161, 163, 166, 170, 246, 289

n71, 320, 342, 369; *Salammbó,* 34, 34 n10, 224
Fletcher, Angus, 39 n19
Fleur-de-Marie, 111, 166, 167, 301, 302 n17, 307, 308 n25, 392
Fontanella, Lee, 9 n10, 17 n28, 24 n44
Forster, E.M., 38, 376, 389
Foucault, Michel, 146 n17
France, Anatole [Thibault], 103, 103 n31, 127 n73
Franco, Francisco, 390
Frank, Joseph, 368, 369 n16
Freud, Sigmund, 12 n18, 82, 350-52, 352 n35, 353
Frye, Northrop, 308, 321 n2, 357, 357 n5
Fuente, Vicente de la, 201 n31, 202 n31
Fussell, Paul, 20 n34

Gadex, Dorio de, 248-50, 260
Galdós, Benito Pérez, 3-10, 12-16, 20-28, 31-39, 41-71, 73-77, 79-89, 91-107, 109-29, 133-60, 164-77, 179-85, 187-92, 194, 195, 198-225, 229-31, 233, 235-45, 248-72, 274-87, 289-303, 305-309, 311-15, 317-29, 332, 334, 335, 337-40, 342-45, 347, 348, 350-55, 358, 360-87, 389-94; *Abuelo, El,* 53; *Aita Tettauen,* 237; *Amigo Manso, El,* 126, 127 n71, 128, 128 n73, 136, 139, 177 n33, 210, 212 n45, 324, 328, 361; *Angel Guerra,* 3 n2, 248; *Apostólicos, Los,* 57, 59, 87, 97 n23, 115 n50, 167, 218 n57, 280 n56, 294 n7; Artículos de Galdós en *"La Nación,"* 36, 116 n52, 192 n10, 263, 271 n46; *Audaz, El,* 34 n9, 49, 68, 326 n10; *Batalla de los Arapiles, La,* 53, 58; *Bodas reales,* 256 n19; *Bringas, La de,* 139, 142, 149, 158, 188, 217, 318, 318 n43, 361, 380 n6; *Cádiz,* 58, 69, 162; *Cánovas,* 9 n9, 121 n64; *Cartas desconocidas de Galdós en "La Prensa" de Buenos Aires,* 4 n4, 109 n42, 167 n20, 175 n30, 250 n7, 253 n12, 256, 269, 269

n45, 292 n2, 305 n24, 370 n19, 371 n20; *Centeno, El doctor,* 114 n49, 133, 139, 158, 217, 343 n27, 375; *Cien mil hijos de San Luis, Los,* 66 n31, 100, 207 n40; *Condenados, Los,* 86 n5; *Crónica de la quincena,* 343 n27, 344 n29; *Crónica de Madrid,* 3 n2, 43, 303, 380 n6; *"Desde la veleta,"* 43, 374; *Desheredada, La,* 8, 25, 45, 47, 50, 75, 79 n48, 84, 85 n1, 86, 86 n5, 87, 88 n6, 89, 90 n9, 91–94, 96, 97, 97 n23, 100, 102–105, 109, 110, 111 n43, 111 n44, 112 n47, 113–15, 115 n50, 116, 116 n52, 116 n53, 117, 117 n53, 117 n55, 118, 119 n59, 121 n64, 122, 122 n65, 123, 123 n66, 125, 125 n69, 126–29, 133, 134, 134 n3, 136, 137, 137 n7, 139, 140 n13, 141, 146, 147, 147 n18, 148, 149, 151, 153, 154, 158, 175 n30, 176, 187, 189 n4, 206, 207 n40, 212 n45, 217, 230, 235, 250, 273, 274 n48, 282 n58, 293 n6, 303, 314 n35, 319, 340, 352, 361, 366, 367, 379, 380 n6; *19 de marzo y el 2 de mayo, El,* 6 n6, 61 n20; *Electra,* 378, 378 n3; *Ensayos de crítica literaria,* 15 n23, 22 n39, 22 n40, 29 n1, 80 n50, 89 n8, 173 n28, 291 n1; *Episodios nacionales,* 8, 9 n10, 13 n19, 16, 25, 27 n51, 28, 28 n53, 31, 32, 39, 47 n30, 49, 51 n3, 53, 53 n7, 53 n8, 54, 54 n10, 55 n12, 59, 59 n18, 60, 61, 61 n20, 63, 71, 75, 86, 87, 89, 90, 91, 93, 95, 97, 100, 109, 112–15, 119, n57, 121 n64, 158, 189 n4, 206, 208, 215, 229, 236 n6, 256 n19, 261 n32, 264 n34, 265 n37, 269, 271 n46, 276 n52, 293, 303 n18, 326 n10, 327 n14, 328 n14, 367, 374, 378 n4, 385, 386; *"Escenas de Madrid,"* 89 n8; *España trágica,* 108, 265; *Faccioso más y algunos frailes menos Un,* 61, 62 n23, 95, 100 n26, 261 n32; *Familia de León Roch, La,* 63, 64 n27, 79 n48, 85, 89, 90, 97, 97 n23, 149, 181, 212 n45, 386, 389, 393 n15; *Fontana de Oro, La,* 3, 5, 6,

6 n6, 6 n8, 7, 8, 21 n36, 23–26, 28, 29, 31, 32, 32 n7, 33, 34, 34 n11, 37, 38, 38 n18, 39, 40, 40 n20, 41 n23, 43–46, 47 n30, 48, 49, 51, 54 n10, 55, 56, 58, 60, 61, 62 n21, 64, 71, 73, 75–77, 82, 84, 87, 108, 109, 112 n47, 113, 114 n49, 123, 125, 137 n7, 146, 176, 195, 207, 212, 214 n50, 236 n6, 261 n32, 293 n6, 303 n18, 314 n35, 326 n10, 367, 374, 380 n6, 385; *Fortunata y Jacinta,* 3, 12 n18, 22 n40, 25, 33, 42, 42 n24, 44, 46, 49, 52 n5, 75, 81, 86, 86 n4, 93, 96, 96 n20, 98, 102, 112 n47, 118, 119 n59, 120, 120 n60, 121 n63, 133–38, 138 n7, 138 n8, 138 n9, 138 n10, 139, 142, 148, 151, 152, 156, 158, 159, 161, 167, 171, 172, 174 n30, 176, 179, 182, 185, 186 n43, 187, 189 n4, 192 n9, 194, 199, 201 n31, 204, 206, 208, 209, 211 n44, 212, 213 n49, 213 n50, 214 n50, 215, 216, 219, 221, 222, 225, 229, 230, 231 n3, 233, 235–39, 243, 245, 249, 254, 257 n22, 260, 260 n28, 261, 262, 262 n34, 264, 269, 269 n45, 271 n46, 273, 277 n53, 282 n58, 283 n61, 284, 286, 287, 289, 291, 292, 293 n6, 301, 303 n18, 305 n20, 310, 314, 314 n35, 314 n36, 315 n37, 320, 323, 324 n10, 327 n11, 327 n13, 327 n14, 328, 332, 333 n22, 337 n23, 340–42, 344 n29, 345, 349 n34, 352, 356, 357, 358 n7, 359–61, 364, 366, 367, 369, 370 n19, 372, 374, 375, 379, 380 n6; *Gloria,* 63, 137 n7, 167 n20, 209 n42, 386; *Grande Oriente, El,* 61, 63 n23; *Halma,* 35 n12, 48 n32, 288 n68, 303 n18, 380 n6; *Madrid,* 201 n30, 254; *Marianela* (drama), 191; *Memorias de un cortesano de 1815,* 52 n4, 58, 59, 143; *Memorias de un desmemoriado,* 26, 27, 50, 54, 200, 202, 204, 204 n36, 224, 282, 323, 327 n14; *Mendizábal,* 253, 277 n52; *Miau,* 137 n7, 257 n22; *Mi calle,* 43 n26; *Miseriocordia,* 86, 86 n4, 136, 151, 168, 275, 283 n61, 310,

361, 379; *Mintes de Oca*, 80 n52, 119 n57; *Nazarín*, 23 n43, 35 n12, 79 n48, 168, 361; *Novela en el tranvía*, 91 n10, 201; *Novelas españolas contemporáneas*, 84, 86, 109, 119 n57, 158, 229, 277 n52, 298, 303 n18, 379, 386; "Observaciones sobre la novela contemporánea," 22 n39, 201; *Perfecta, Doña*, 48 n31, 49, 61, 63, 63 n25, 64 n26, 67, 68, 70, 71, 72, 72 n38, 75–78, 82–85, 87, 89, 93, 97 n23, 137 n7, 146, 154, 155, 155 n1, 166, 167, 210, 318, 324 n9, 364, 378, 378 nn2–4, 379, 380 n6, 385, 386, 389, 390, 392, 394; *Prohibido, Lo*, 33, 133, 139, 142, 143, 144 n16, 146, 146 n17, 149, 150, 150 n23, 151, 154, 158, 187, 188, 217, 230, 249 n5, 250 n8, 256 n20, 305 n20, 307, 333 n22, 352, 366; "Prólogo a la tercera edición de *La regenta*," 80 n49, 117 n55, 151, 157; *Razón de la sinrazón, La*, 129; *Segunda casaca, La*, 36 n13, 51 n4, 62 n23, 66 n31, 67, 69, 69 n36, 70, 87, 338; *Siete de julio, El*, 83; *Sombra, La*, 380 n6; *Tormento*, 12 n19, 90, 139, 158, 217, 229, 265, 361, 373; *Torquemada en la hoguera*, 90; *Torquemada en el pergatorio*, 255 n15; *Trafalgar*, 34 n9, 49, 55, 110, 129; *Tristana*, 188; *Tristes destinos, La de los*, 28 n54, 58, 287; *Vergara*, 25 n47; *Viaje redondo, Un*, 200 n28; *Vuelta la mundo en la Numancia, La*, 266 n39; *Zaragoza*, 53, 58, 58 n15, 324 n10

Galdós, Doña María, 119 n59
Gallegos, Rómulo, 64 n26
Gamallo Fierros, Dionisio, 150 n23, 157 n4
Gaos, José, 120 n61, 120 n62
García Blanco, Manuel, 37 n17, 88 n7
García Lorca, Federico, 48 n32, 286, 286 n66, 287 n66
García Márquez, Gabriel, 194
Gaspar Media-noche, 167, 213 n49

Gautier, Marguerite, 180
Generation of 1898, 51, 53 n6, 88 n7, 122 n64, 251, 253, 253 n11, 367
George, A. J., 31 n6
Gilman, Stephen, 11 n18, 58 n15, 67 n34, 74 n41, 98 n24, 156 n2, 164 n15, 173 n28, 190 n6, 193 n13, 231 n2, 309 n27, 345 n31
Gil y Carrasco, Enrique, 29
Gil y Zárate, Antonio, 9 n10
Gimeno Casalduero, Joaquín, 38 n18, 47, 253, 253 n11, 254, 255, 255 n17, 256
Giner de los Ríos, Francisco, 77, 77 n44, 78 n47, 79 n48, 82, 83, 85, 85 n1, 85 n2, 86, 86 n4, 127, 127 n72
Gissing, George, 205 n37
Glaser, Edward, 193
Gloucester (Shakespeare), 208
Goethe, Johann W., 12, 13, 45 n28, 114 n49, 159 n10, 165, 168
Goffman, Erwin, 72
Gogol, Nikolai, 31, 52 n5, 116, 116 n52, 158, 159, 159 n6, 165, 165 n17, 259 n26
Goldman, Peter, 119 n58
Góngora, Luis de, 388
González Arias, Francisca, 157 n4
González Serrano, Urbano, 72 n38, 77, 324 n9, 378 n2
Goya, Francisco, 57, 61, 61 n20
Gravina, Carlos, 50, 58
Green, Martin, 57 n4
Grimm, J.L.K., 246
Groethuysen, Bernard, 11 n17, 23 n41
Guillén, Claudio, 289 n72
Guillén, Jorge, 112 n48, 276, 283
Guinard, Paul J., 195 n16
Gullón, Agnes Moncey, 315 n37
Gullón, Ricardo, 55, 59 n18, 88 n7, 123, 257, 257 n22, 258, 348
Gutenberg, Johann, 193
Guzmán de Alfarache, 143

Hafter, Monroe, 32 n7, 127 n73
Halévi, Daniel, 14 n22
Hamburger, Käthe, 231, 243
Hamlet, 286, 338

Hapsburgs, 28
Hardy, Thomas, 161 n10, 390
Harris, Derek, 51 n4
Hatin, Eugène, 18 n28
Hayek, F. A. von, 17 n27
Hegel, Georg Wilhelm Friedrich, 11, 76, 81, 135 n5, 137, 149, 337, 342–44, 349
Heine, Heinrich, 15, 16, 16 n25, 19, 20, 58, 111, 203
Heinz, Peter, 168 n21
Helen of Troy, 319, 322, 372 n23
Helman, Edith Fishtine, 61 n20, 255 n15
Hemingway, Ernest, 20 n34, 189 n3, 223, 224 n66
Hemmings, F.W.J., 95 n18, 125 n69, 147
Henderson the Rain King, 165 n17
Henry, O. [William Sydney Porter], 107 n39
Heraclitus, 46, 46 n29, 48, 49, 55, 71
Hercules, 387
Hesiod, 103
Hinterhäuser, Hans, 13 n19, 27 n51, 28, 51 n3, 55, 55 n11, 61 n20, 80 n52, 256 n19, 261 n32, 262 n34, 265 n37, 277 n2
Hoar, Leo, 43 n26, 86 n5, 149 n22, 177 n33, 303 n18, 378 n2, 378 n3, 386 n11
Hoffmann, E.T.A., 203
Hohlfeld, Paul, 78 n46, 79 n48
Holmberg, Arthur, 168 n22, 180 n37, 213 n49, 274 n49
Holmes, Sherlock, 375
Homais, M., 216, 371
Homer, 77 n44, 258, 295, 322, 372
Horace, 379, 383
Howells, William D., 117
Hoyo, Arturo del, 287 n66
Hudson, W. H., 224 n66
Hugo, Victor, 16, 20, 21, 21 n37, 23, 58, 199
Huidobro, Vicente, 276
Humphrey, Robert, 98 n24
Huntington, A. M., 58 n15
Hutter, A. D., 19 n31

Huysmans, J.-K., 148
Hyman, Diane, 42 n24, 138

Imaz, Eugenio, 11 n17
Immerwahr, Robert, 82 n55, 184 n41
Inés, Doña, 162
Isabel I, 14
Isabel II, 4, 140 n14, 205, 287
Ivanhoe, 56

Jackson, Robert, 161, 166
Jasinsky, Réné, 18 n29
Jaspers, Karl, 175
Jobit, Pierre, 76 n42
Johnson, Carroll, 41
Jones, C. A., 48 n31
Jones, Tom, 22
Jouffroy, Théodore, 21 n36
Joyce, James, 18 n29, 98 n24, 102, 242, 251, 276, 338, 342, 392
Jung, Carl, 72
Jupiter, 318

Kahler, Erich, 98 n24, 393
Kant, Immanuel, 11, 328
Karamazov, Alyosha, 184
Karamazov family, 164
Kasabal [José Gutiérrez Abascal], 303 n18
Keats, John, 252
Kecskimeti, Paul, 19 n30
Kempf, Roger, 259, 259 n25, 289 n71
Kempis, Thomas à, 168
Kermode, Frank, 246
Khrushchev, Nikita, 120
King, E. L., 11 n18, 164 n15
Kraus, Karl, 260
Krause, K.C.F., 76, 77, 78 n46, 79 n48
Krow-Lucal, Martha, 111, 112, 112 n48, 116 n53, 119 n59, 140 n13, 207 n40, 226 n67
Küpper, Werner, 177 n33

Laín Entralgo, Pedro, 45, 67, 68, 68 n35, 70
Lamartine, Alphone de, 20, 20 n36, 22
Lamartine, Marianne, 20 n36
Lamettrie, J. O. de, 327 n14

Lamiel, 170
Lammenais, Felicité de, 21 n37, 176 n32
Lampedusa, G. T., 200 n29
Lanoux, Armand, 100 n26
Lapesa, Rafael, 17 n26
Larra, Mariano José de, 17 n26, 29, 32, 51, 51 n5, 57, 61, 61 n20, 98, 120, 121, 124 n68, 126, 126 n70
Laurencia, 255
Lasswell, Harold, 92
Lavisse, Ernest, 125 n69
Lazarillo de Tormes (novel), 12, 91 n10, 117, 255, 364,
Lazarillo de Tormes, 48, 140 n12, 143, 163
Leda, 319
Leo, Ulrich, 64 n26
Lerch, Eugen, 98 n24
Leriano, 163
Lessing, Gotthold E., 62, 322, 322 n5, 372, 372 n23
Levin, Harry, 55 n11, 93, 95 n18, 103, 104 n33, 129, 173 n26, 199 n27
Lida, Clara, 53
Lida, Denah, 81 n54, 275 n51
Lida, Raimundo, 299 n14
Lips, Marguerite, 98 n24
Littré, M.P.E., 17 n8
Livingston, Leon, 127 n73
Llorens, Vicente, 21 n37
Lomba y Pedraja, J. R., 126 n70
López Barbadillo, Joaquín, 282 n58
López-Morillas, Juan, 34, 34 n11, 54 n10, 76–77, 79 n48, 83 n57
Lord, Albert, 211
Löwith, Karl, 10 n15
Lubbock, Percy, 225, 357, 359, 368, 376
Lucas, Paul, 314 n36
Lucena, Juan de, 14 n21
Lucena, Luis de, 24
Luengo, José, 205, 206, 223, 270
Lukacs, Georg, 15, 15 n24, 16, 19, 19 n31, 28, 33, 58 n16, 59, 66, 66 n30, 74 n40, 92, 161 n10, 173 n26, 190, 190 n5, 197, 206 n39, 331, 341, 341 n26, 356, 356 n2, 357, 359, 377
Lukacs, John, 31, 31 n6

Luther, Martin, 70, 299 n14
Lycurgus, 380 n6, 384

Macbeth, 164
Machado, Antonio, 260 n30, 289, 383
Machado y Álvarez, Antonio, 282 n58
MacIvor, Fergus, 59 n17
Madariaga, Salvador de, 48 n32, 243 n12, 252, 344, 352 n35, 381
Main, Pierre Emmanuel, 301
Mairena, Juan de, 201 n31, 305 n21
Mallarmé, Stéphane, 260
Malón de Chaide, Pedro, 193
Mann, Thomas, 103 n31
Mannheim, Karl, 18
Manrique, Jorge, 192
Manrique, Rodrigo, 121
Manuel, D. Juan, 79 n48
Marañón, Gregoria, 192, 192 n9
Marceau, Félicien, 133 n2, 196 n19, 207 n40
Marcus, Steven, 144 n16
Marías, Julián, 17 n26, 18 n29
Marichal, Juan, 162 n12
Maristany, Luis, 51 n4
Martín, Abel, 260, 305 n21
Martínez Cachero, J. M., 159 n7
Marx, Karl, 11, 122 n64
Massis, Henri, 314 n36
Maupassant, Guy de, 64 n27
McCarthy, Mary, 30, 31, 35 n12, 42
McLuhan, Marshall, 191, 231
Medusa, 204 n35
Meister, Wilhelm, 161 n10, 240
Melibea, 350, 364
Melville, Herman, 135, 137, 236
Menéndez Pelayo, Marcelino, 120 n62, 193 n13
Menéndez y Arranz, Juan, 260 n28
Mercury, 380 n6
Merleau-Ponty, Maurice, 10, 161 n10
Mesonero Romanos, Ramón de, 17 n26, 24 n44, 29, 32, 34, 92, 98, 270 n46
Meyerhoff, Hans, 369 n18
Michelet, Jules, 14 n22
Mignon, 332
Mill, John Stuart, 17 n28, 21 n36
Miller, J. Hillis, 361 n9

Minerva, 380 n6
Miñano, Sebastián de, 143 n15
Mitterand, Henri, 100 n26, 212 n46, 327 n14
Molière [Jean-Baptiste Poquelin], 72
Molina, Tirso de [Gabriel Téllez], 145
Montalvo, Garci de Rodríguez, 353
Montesinos, José F., 29, 30, 30 n2, 33, 34, 34 n9, 53, 54, 54 n10, 68 n35, 75, 103, 103 n30, 139, 195, 271 n47, 321, 338, 349, 373
Montpensier, Duque de, 305 n23
Moratín, Leandro F. de, 260, 260 n28
Morínigo, Marcos, 193 n12
Mosca, Count, 45
Moses, 232, 243
Moses, Grandma, 31
Mucklewrath, John, 96
Muiños Saenz, Conrado, 378 n3
Muñón, Sancho de, 282 n58
Musset, Alfred de, 19, 20, 25, 25 n48, 57, 393 n15
Myshkin, Prince, 184, 245

Nabokov, Vladimir, 185, 251
Nadeau, Maurice, 19 n31, 34 n10, 122 n64
Napoleon, 15, 17, 21, 67, 172 n26
Napoleon III, 122 n64
Narváez, R. M. de, 28
Navarro Tomás, Tomás, 99 n25
Neider, Charles, 226 n67
Nerval, Gérard de, 203 n33
Neumann, Erich, 354, n38
Nicol, Eduardo, 18 n29
Nicolson, Nigel, 156 n3
Nietzsche, Friedrich, 331, 337
Nora, Pierre, 125 n69
Noulet, E., 13 n19

Oates, W. J., 318 n44
Ochoa, Eugenio de, 51 n3
O'Donnell, Leopoldo, 69
Oedipus, 389
Oleza, Juan, 41
O'Neill, Eugene, 318 n44
Ophelia, 390
Oriana, 163, 353

Orlando, 166
Ortega, Soledad, 157 n4, 166 n19
Ortega Munilla, José, 149 n22
Ortega y Gasset, José, 18 n29, 57, 88 n6, 109, 162, 210, 231, 248, 249, 260, 293, 305 n21, 333 n22, 334, 345, 365
Ortiz, Gloria, 159 n 7

Palacio, J. M., 289
Palacio Valdés, Armando, 31, 93, 93 n16, 117 n55, 251, 378 n2
Palafox, 58
Pardo Bazán, Emilia, 93, 93 n16, 115, 158, 169, 188, 188 n2, 213 n48, 257, 258, 261, 378 n2
Parmenides, 46, 55, 71
Parry, Milman, 211
Pattison, Walter, 47 n30, 93 n14, 93 n16, 117 n54, 137 n7
Paul, Saint, 328
Paz, Octavio, 247
Pearce, Roy Harvey, 11 n18, 288, 327, 332 n20, 332 n21
Pedro I el Cruel, 24 n44, 205
Peñuel, Arnold, 352 n35
Pepys, Samuel, 12
Pereda, José María de, 23, 31, 64 n26, 70, 73, 80, 85, 88 n7, 150, 155, 157, 201 n31, 209, 213 n48, 251, 255, 305, 305 n20, 390
Pérez de Ayala, Ramón, 235, 263 n36
Pérez Galdós, Benito. See Galdós
Pérez Vidal, José, 3 n2, 37 n15, 91 n10, 255 n16, 269 n45
Petit, Marie-Claire, 6 n6, 213 n50, 214 n50
Petrarch, 210, 383
Petriconi, Helmut, 332 n19
Petsch, Robert, 9, 15 n23, 136 n6, 310, 311 n28, 370
Peyre, Henri, 18 n29
Picasso, Pablo, 260
Pichon, Edouard, 98 n24
Piel, Gerard, 14 n22
Pinciano, El [Hernán Núñez de Toledo], 82
Pisarro, Camille, 371
Pistetero, 318
Pleberio, 140 n12, 208

Poe, Edgar Allan, 62 n22, 144, 203
Poema del Cid, 57, 79 n48, 233, 244, 280 n6
Poirot, Hercule, 191
Poulet, Georges, 368, 369 n16
Pound, Ezra, 367, 368
Poux, Pierre, 21 n36
Pretender, The [Charles Stuart], 59 n7
Price, Martin, 361, 361 n9
Prim, Juan, 47, 47 n30, 62, 66, 91, 108, 109, 256 n18, 269, 294 n7, 305 n73
Procne, 318, 319
Proprischin, 116
Proust, Marcel, 55 n11, 74 n41, 98 n24, 186, 242, 367, 369

Quasimodo, 213 n49
Quevedo, Francisco de, 238, 255 n15, 277 n53, 299 n14, 380 n6
Quinet, Edgar, 21, 25

Racine, Jean, 104, 191, 352
Raeburn, Sir Henry, 61 n20
Raimond, Michel, 148 n20, 324 n8
Raskolnikov, 184
Renoir, Auguste, 217, 220, 300
Revilla, Manuel de la, 9 n10
Reyes, Alfonso, 252, 252 n10
Ribbans, Geoffrey, 270 n46
Ricard, Robert, 124 n68, 138 n8, 256 n20, 283 n61, 379 n5
Richard, Jean-Pierre, 178, 178 n36, 250 n6, 368, 369 n16, 375 n24
Richard the Lion-Hearted, 56
Richardson, Samuel, 41, 193, 193 n14
Richelieu, Cardinal, 56
Riego, Rafael del, 36
Riesman, David, 191, 191 n8
Risley, William, 236 n6
Ritter, Paul, 13 n20
Robert, Guy, 103 n21
Robert, Marthe, 27 n52, 173
Robespierre, Maximilien de, 67, 68
Rodgers, Eamonn, 117 n55, 129
Rodolphe, 301, 302 n17
Rodrigo, D., 382
Rodríguez Moñino, Antonio, 85 n1

Rodríguez Puértolas, Julio, 229
Rogers, Will, 291
Rogerson, T. F., 19 n33
Rojas, Fernando de, 12, 24, 57, 67 n34, 95 n19, 96, 100, 101, 145, 210, 221, 235, 254, 259, 266 n39, 270, 274, 276 n52, 347 n33, 350; *Celestina, La,* 119, 170, 221, 255, 258, 276 n52, 280, 314 n35
Rossini, G. A., 293
Rousseau, Jean-Jacques, 12, 65, 339
Rovetta, Carlos, 122 n65
Ruggerio, Michael, 375 n24
Ruiz, Juan, 343
Ruiz Ramón, Francisco, 201 n31, 284 n63
Ruiz Salvador, Antonio, 28 n54, 90, 91, 92 n12, 108, 123, 123 n67, 125 n69, 126, 314 n36
Russell, Robert, 111 n44

Sacha (Baroja), 371 n21
Sackett, Theodore, 251 n9
Saez de Melgar, Faustina, 111 n46, 112 n46
Sagasta, Práxedes, 108
Saint-Preaux, 12, 172 n26, 240
Saint-Simon, Claude H. de, 17 n28, 18 n28, 199
Salper de Tortella, Roberta, 206 n38
Sand, Georges [Aurore Dupin], 16, 25 n48, 214 n50
San Pedro, Diego de, 24
Sanseverina, Gina, 320
Santillana, Marqués de [Iñigo López de Mendoza], 318
Sanz de Río, Julián, 76, 78, 78 n46
Sarraute, Natalie, 254 n14
Sartre, Jean-Paul, 67, 254, 301
Schäffle, Albert E. F., 78 n46
Scheler, Max, 116 n64
Schelling, Friedrich, 12, 78 n46, 190
Schelling, K.F.A., 12 n19
Schlegel, August W. von, 11, 37, 37 n16
Schlegel, Friederich, 11, 12 n19, 81, 82 n55, 184
Scott, Sir Walter, 9 n10, 12, 15 n24, 16, 24, 26, 29, 33, 37, 46, 49, 54, 55,

59, 59 n17, 61 n20, 77, 92, 147 n18, 161 n10, 165 n16, 189 n4, 193, 194, 195, 197, 198, 199, 203, 225, 226, 227, 229, 266, 310, 340 n25, 364, 365, 366, 368; *Waverley,* 18 n29, 29, 33, 59 n17, 61 n20, 189 n4, 193 n14, 233

Seco Serrano, Carlos, 9 n10, 47 n30, 121 n64, 124 n68

Sempronio, 270

Shakespeare, William, 168, 388

Shandy, Tristram, 369

Sharp, Becky, 172, 320

Shaw, George Bernard, 272, 379

Shklovsky, Viktor, 33 n27, 333 n22

Shoemaker, William H., 4 n4, 85 n1, 109 n42, 116 n52, 127 n72, 167 n20, 175 n30, 192 n10, 201 n31, 250 n7, 253 n12, 256 n18, 263 n35, 269 nn44–45, 271 n46, 292 n2, 306 n24, 318 n43, 343 n27, 344 n29, 370 n19, 371 n20, 380 n6

Simmel, Georg, 231, 345

Singleton, Charles, 74

Sinnegan, John, 174 n30, 327 n11, 337, 349 n34

Sisto, D. L., 64 n26

Smith, Alan, 47 n30, 206, 207

Sobejano, Gonzalo, 177 n33

Socrates, 110

Sollers, Philippe, 191 n8, 192 n8, 256

Sorel, Julien, 161 n10, 164, 172, 199 n27, 311

Sorolla, Joaquín, 245

Stace, W. T., 343 n28, 344 n28

Stanislavski, K. S., 180

Stavrogin (Dostoievsky), 38, 184

Steele, Sir Richard, 30

Steele, W. A., 322 n5

Stendhal [Henri Beyle], 8, 16, 20, 20 n36, 32, 45, 46, 74 n41, 75, 82, 90, 111, 115, 156, 156 n2, 161 n10, 165, 165 n17, 172 n26, 173 n26, 179, 183, 185, 189 n3, 190 n6, 196, 199 n27, 200 n29, 231 n2, 233, 235, 243, 245, 250, 250 n6, 251, 270, 292, 309, 309 n27, 334, 335, 345 n31, 349, 358, 369 n16, 392; *Chartreuse de Parme,*

La, 46, 53, 234, 341; *Rouge et le noir, Le,* 19, 83, 199 n27

Stepanov, Georgy, 378 n4

Sterne, Laurence, 162 n17, 202 n32, 223, 231

Stewart, Zeph, 329 n16

Sue, Eugène, 96 n21, 111, 166, 235, 302, 302 n16, 307

Surville, Laure, 195, 195 n17, 196 n17

Swann, 38

Swedenborg, Emanuel, 168 n22

Swift, Tom, 192, 203

Taine, Hippolyte, 11, 328 n14

Tarr, F. Courtney, 29

Tenorio, D. Juan, 142, 145, 182

Teresa, Saint, 16, 168, 353

Terrón, Eloy, 78 n46

Terry, Arthur, 144 n16

Thackeray, William M., 14 n22

Thibaudet, Albert, 72 n39, 95 n19, 96 n20, 98 n24, 103, 104, 356, 357, 359

Thomas, Edward, 385 n10

Thomas, Russell, 49 n1

Thoreau, Henry David, 13 n19

Tierno Galván, Enrique, 24 n44, 253 n11, 255 n17

Todorov, Tsvetan, 284 n63

Tolstoy, Leo, 8, 53, 60, 160, 292, 391

Torquemada, Tomás de, 67

Torrente Ballester, Gonzalo, 249 n5

Toscanini, Arturo, 143

Tracy, M. de, 199 n27

Trautmann, Joanne, 156 n3

Trilling, Lionel, 60, 155, 165 n17, 262

Truel, Juana, 63, 63 n25, 64 n26, 155, 155 n1

Turgenev, Ivan, 19

Twain, Mark [Samuel Clemens], 46, 50, 90, 95 n19, 96, 165, 167 n17, 171, 183, 226 n67, 238, 240, 242, 245, 250 n6, 259, 264, 332, 333, 369 n17, 391; *Adventures of Huckleberry Finn, The,* 170, 183, 189 n4, 218 n58, 234, 262, 281, 329 n16, 332, 341, 345; *Adventures of Tom Sawyer, The,* 189 n4; *Celebrated Jumping Frog of Calaveras*

County, The, 95 n19; Connecticut Yankee in King Arthur's Court, A, 291; Life As I Find It, 226 n67

Ucelay, Margarita, 30 n4
Ullman, Joan C., 192 n9, 213 n49
Ullman, Stephen, 98 n24
Unamuno, Miguel de, 37, 37 n17, 88 n7, 111, 163, 209, 251 n9, 257, 258, 261, 284 n63, 295, 359
Updike, John, 369
Utt, R. L., 315 n37

Valera, Juan, 112, 115, 251
Valle-Inclán, Ramón del, 206, 206 n38, 248, 248 n1, 248 n2
Valverde, J. M., 249 n5
Varey, John, 144 n16, 249 n4
Vega, Lope de, 25 n47, 193 n13, 200, 205, 210, 265, 295 n9, 368
Venus, 380 n6
Vercingetorix, 73
Verde Pérez-Galdós, Benito, 47 n30
Vico, G. B., 23 n41
Vida, Jerónimo, 78 n46
Vigny, Alfred de, 20, 20 n36
Vindeuil, Mme. de, 193
Virgil, 299 n14, 379, 383, 384, 385 n10
Vives, J. L., 348
Voltaire [François-Marie Arouet], 23, 173, 173 n29, 193

Wagner, Richard, 277 n53, 298, 351
Walton, L. B., 378 n3
Warren, Robert Penn, 75 n41, 368 n15
Watt, Ian, 173 n26
Waverley, Edward, 12, 96, 161 n10, 193, 240
Weber, Robert J., 137 n7, 174 n30
Weiner, Jack, 64 n26
Weinrich, Harold, 98 n24
Wenger, Jared, 147 n18
Western, Sophia, 347 n33
Western, Squire, 73 n40
Whiston, James, 245 n13
Whitehead, Alfred N., 14, 14 n22
Williams, Raymond, 124 n68, 173 n26, 257, 257 n22, 359 n8, 385 n10
Wilson, Edmund, 122 n64

Woolf, Leonard, 19 n29, 156, 192, 235 n5
Woolf, Virginia, 18 n29, 98 n24, 156, 156 n3, 166, 189 n4, 192, 235, 251, 320, 338, 368, 369 n16
Wright, Chad, 40, 40 n20, 123, 123 n67, 123 n68, 137 n7
Wundt, Wilhelm, 252 n35
Wünsche, August, 78 n46, 79 n48

Yeats, W. B., 14
Yerma, 298, 300
Ynduráin, Francisco, 248 n2
Yossarian, 309

Zambrano, María, 252, 252 n10
Zola, Emile, 13, 27, 42, 73, 74 n40, 75, 81 n53, 82, 93–99, 104, 104 n35, 109–111, 115, 117, 117 n55, 118, 119, 122 n65, 125 n69, 128, 129, 135, 135 n5, 140, 142, 143, 146, 147, 147 n18, 148, 155, 158, 166 n19, 175–79, 184, 198 n24, 206, 210, 212, 213 n49, 215 n51, 217, 218 n58, 219–24, 236, 236 n6, 245, 250, 254, 260, 261, 265, 288, 293, 301, 312, 314, 314 n36, 318, 320, 321, 324 n9, 326 n10, 327, 347, 352, 352 n35, 361, 370, 375; Assommoir, L', 46 n29, 92, 93 n14, 94–97, 99, 115, 118, 125 n69, 129, 156, 246, 274, 372; Au Bonheur des dames, 104 n35, 215 n51, 216 n54, 303 n18, 352 n35, 372; Bête Humaine, La, 284; Conquête de Plassans, La, 161, 176, 177, 177 n33; Fortune des Rougons, La, 46 n29; Germinal, 342; Nana, 93 n14, 104, 118, 146, 147; Page d'amour, Une, 93 n14; Pot Bouille, 146; 198 n24, 212, 219; Roman expérimental, Le, 327 n14; Rougon-Macquart novels, 217, 324 n9; Thérèse Raquin, 212 n46, 213; Ventre de Paris, Le, 216, 217, 220, 222, 223, 309, 372
Zorilla, José 145
Zurbarán, Francisco de, 249 n4
Zweig, Stefan, 14 n22

CHARACTER INDICES

Listings are grouped under the Authors Galdós, Balzac, Cervantes, Clarín, Dickens, Twain, and Zola, respectively.

Galdós

Adoración, 266

Albrit, Conde de, 287 n66

Almudena, 275 n51

Ambrosia, Doña, 303 n18

Ansúrez, Jerónimo, 237

Araceli, Gabriel, 51, 52, 55, 56, 58, 59, 70, 90, 143, 240, 270 n46

Aransis family, 111

Aransis, Marquesa de, 101, 105, 112, 112 n48

Arnaiz family, 262 n34, 294

Arnaiz, El gordo, 304

Arnaiz, Gumersindo, 294 n7

Babel, Dulcenombre, 122 n65

Ballestre, Segismundo, 168 n22, 267 n40, 281, 315, 315 n38, 316, 319, 324, 340, 344, 373

Baraona, Jenara de, 71

Baraona, Miguel de, 70

Batilo, 101 n28

Belén, 241, 374

Benigna (de Casia), 183, 289, 394

Bou, Juan, 123

Bozmediano, Claudio, 35, 44, 125 n69

Bringas family, 140 n14

Bringas, Francisco, 361

Bringas, Rosalía Pipaón de, 91 n10, 140, 140 n14, 141, 144, 175, 215 n51, 303 n18, 372 n22, 373

Bueno de Guzmán, Camila, 149, 149 n22, 150–52, 154, 272

Bueno de Guzmán, José María, 142–50, 160, 203, 207, 219, 301, 326, 333 n22, 354

Burguillos, Doña Teresa de, 380 n6

Caballuco [Cristóbal Ramos], 380 n6, 381, 382, 386, 392

Calpena, Fernando de, 25 n47

Canencia, 91, 92, 206, 207 n40

Carnicero, D. Felicísimo, 61–62, 69, 97 n23

Carrascosa, Gil de, 380 n6

Casa-Muñoz, Marqués de, 121 n63

Centeno, Felipe, 139, 361

Clara (Chacón), 6, 39–41, 44, 50, 75, 101, 101 n28, 102, 105, 352

Coletilla (Elías Orejón), 5–7, 38–40, 44, 62, 62 n21, 69, 72, 75, 183, 207, 207 n40, 314 n35

Cordero, D. Benigno, 83, 97 n23, 100, 100 n26, 215, 293, 294 n7

Cordero, Cruz, 280 n56

Cordero, Elena, 294 n7

Cordero, Isabel, 259, 293, 294, 294 n7, 298, 300, 370

Cordero, Juan Jacobo, 218 n57

Desdémona, Doña, 277–79, 315 n38, 316, 334, 340, 373

Emperador, Amparo Sánches, 112 n46, 139, 175, 240, 265

Emperador, Refugio Sánchez, 120 n60

Estupiñá, Plácido, 204–206, 223, 229, 268–70, 270 n46, 271, 271 n46, 273, 293, 296, 296 n10, 302, 303, 304 n19, 309, 314, 360, 373

Feijóo, D. Evaristo González, 281, 282, 288, 292, 308, 322, 324, 339, 344 n28, 349, 376

Felisa, 241, 374

Fenelon, 266 n39

Fortunata (Izquierdo), 27, 35 n12, 38 n18, 48, 98, 101, 102, 115 n50, 129, 135, 135 n5, 136–38, 138 n7, 138 n8, 140, 142, 146, 148–51, 151 n23, 152, 159, 160, 164, 168–72, 174 n30, 175, 176, 180, 183, 185, 204, 207, 208, 214 n50, 216, 217, 219, 220, 229, 229 n1, 230, 235, 237, 239–45, 245 n13, 247, 262, 264,

265, 267–74, 274 n49, 275, 276, 277 n53, 278, 279, 279 n55, 280, 280 n56, 281–83, 283 n58, 283 n60, 283 n62, 284–86, 288, 289, 292, 293, 293 n5, 297, 297 n12, 298 n13, 299, 300 n14, 300 n15, 301, 302, 304, 304 n19, 306–13, 313 n33, 314, 314 n34, 315, 316, 316 n39, 317, 317 n42, 318–28, 328 n15, 329, 329 n17, 330–41, 341 n26, 342–44, 344 n28, 344 n29, 345, 346, 346 n32, 347–54, 354 n37, 355, 358, 367, 372, 372 n22, 373–77, 385 n10, 391, 392, 394

Francisca (Gutiérrez de Cisniega), Doña, 58

Germán, D., 296, 296 n10

Gonzalete, 118

Halconero, Vicente 58

Hillo, Pedro, 277 n52

Ibero, Santiago, 28 n54

Ido del Sagrario, José, 24 n44, 50, 112 n46, 120 n60, 144, 149, 162, 201, 201 n31, 204–206, 218, 239, 265, 266, 299 n14, 315, 361, 372

Ido del Sagrario, Nicanora, 162

Inés, 6 n6, 39, 105

Inocencio, D., 379, 387 n12

Irene, 127

Izquierdo family, 295

Izquierdo, José (Platón), 218 n58, 256, 256 n18, 262 n34, 266, 271 n46, 280, 281 n57, 282, 284, 300 n15, 326 n10

Izquierdo, Segunda, 261

Jáuregui, D. Pedro Manuel de, 316

Javier "el Doctrino," 114 n49

Juan Evaristo, 278, 316

Juárez el negro, 274 n49

Lázaro, 6 n6, 7, 8, 36, 36 n14, 37, 39, 41, 44, 47, 47 n30, 52, 56, 87, 126, 158

Majito, El, 282 n58

Manolita, Doña, 336

Manso, Máximo, 80–82, 125, 125 n69, 127, 127 n72, 128, 128 n73, 129, 137, 143, 151, 202 n32, 343 n27, 361

María Egipcíaca (Sudre), 168, 181, 349

Marianela, 191

Martín, Juan (el Empecinado), 59

Mauricia la dura, 135 n5, 138 n8, 204, 208, 241, 243, 259, 266, 280 n56, 281, 281 n57, 284, 292, 300, 324, 342, 343, 344 n28, 349, 350, 373

Miquis, Alejandro, 114 n49, 133, 134, 361, 362

Miquis, Constantino, 150

Monsalud, Salvador, 52, 61, 62, 70, 87, 105, 114, 367

Moreno family, 294

Moreno Isla, Manuel, 149, 208, 267 n40, 284, 286, 292, 295, 373

Morton, Daniel, 167 n60

Muriel, Martín Martínez, 68, 326 n10

Navarro, Carlos (Garotte), 70, 338

Navarro family, 158

Nazarín, 48 n32, 122 n65, 361

Nieves, Doña, 343 n27

Nones, Padre Juan Manuel, 286, 373

Olmedo (*Ulmus sylvestris*), 313 n33

Orozco, Tomás, 287 n66

Paca, La, 244

Pacheco, Guillermina, 135 n5, 152, 218, 266, 267, 267 n41, 268, 273, 283 n61, 288, 299 n14, 300 n15, 302, 311 n29, 319, 335, 337, 342, 343, 344 n28, 349, 350, 373, 374

Paoletti, Padre, 181, 182

Papitos, 205, 273 n48, 282, 283 n60

Patricia, 316 n39

Peña, Manuel, 82

Perfecta, Doña, 54 n9, 66, 67, 71–73, 76, 102, 112, 168, 374, 382–84, 386, 389, 391, 393

Peri, La (Leonor), 122 n65, 287 n66

Pez family, 92 n12, 340

Pez, Joaquín, 108, 109, 133, 134, 134 n3, 140, 140 n13, 145, 160, 207 n40, 214 n50, 219, 303, 354, 361

Pez, Luis, 380 n6

Pez, D. Manuel José Ramón del, 94, 140, 140 n13

Pimentosa, La (Nazaria), 95, 95 n19

Pintado, D. León, 259, 264, 280

Pipaón, Juan Bragas, 69

Pituso, El, 217, 218 n57, 219, 282, 295 n5, 300, 300 n15, 304 n19, 338, 354

Polo, Pedro, 160
Polentinos, D. Cayetano, 53, 73, 379, 384, 386
Polentinos, Rosario, 39, 105, 383, 390–94
Porreño, Doña Paulita, 48, 168
Porreño family, 39–41, 46, 50, 62, 73, 384
Quevedo, Francisco de, 315 n38
Quijano-Quijada, Santiago, 116, 119, 125, 126
Regato, José Manuel, 61, 183
Relimpio, José de, 106, 106 n37, 108
Requejo, D. Mauro, 6 n6
Rey, Pepe, 52, 64 n26, 65, 66, 68, 127, 379, 380, 380 n6, 381–83, 386–89, 391, 392
Riquín, 105 n36, 124, 304
Roch, León, 81, 82, 156, 183, 349
Rodrigo, D., 69, 162
Rubín family, 174 n30, 237, 281, 316, 376
Rubín, Juan Pablo, 186 n43, 222, 222 n65, 224, 261, 267 n40, 273 n48, 343 n27
Rubín, Maximiliano, 111 n46, 120 n60, 138 n8, 142, 152, 159–61, 168, 168 n22, 169, 169 n22, 171, 172, 185, 204, 204 n36, 207, 212, 213, 213 n49, 215, 222, 239–41, 243, 262, 272, 274, 275 n49, 276, 276 n52, 277, 278, 282, 283 n58, 284, 297, 302, 302 n17, 306, 314, 316, 319, 319 n47, 322 n4, 324, 330, 333, 334, 339, 344, 346, 349, 351, 355, 373–75, 394
Rubín, Nicolás, 180–82, 186 n43, 188, 204 n35, 211, 266, 276 n52, 280, 284
Rubín de Jáuregui, Doña Lupe, 174 n30, 204, 206, 255, 266, 268, 272, 273 n48, 274 n48, 274 n49, 276 n52, 280, 282, 283 n60, 284 n64, 287 n67, 316, 324, 349, 372
Rufete, Captain, 100 n27
Rufete family, 111, 118, 121, 143
Rufete, Isidora, 40, 48, 88, 90, 94, 96, 97, 101, 101 n28, 102, 104, 105, 106, 106 n37, 107–109, 111, 111 n44, 112, 112 n47, 113, 114, 114 n49, 116, 118, 119, 120 n59, 121, 122, 122 n64, 123, 123 n67, 124–29, 134 n3, 135, 135 n4, 137, 139, 140, 140 n14, 144, 149, 151, 158, 171, 176, 244, 269, 279, 299 n14, 303, 306 n24, 314, 314 n35, 323, 347, 348, 352, 354
Rufete, Mariano (Pecado), 96 n20, 118, 119
Rufete, Tomás, 91, 91 n10, 92, 114–16, 116 n52, 123, 167, 206, 254, 361
Ruiz, Federico, 343 n27, 376
Rumblar, Condesa de, 112
Samaniego, Aurora, 266, 266 n39, 277, 280 n56, 282 n58, 283 n61, 285
Samaniego family, 262 n34, 294
Samaniego, Olimpia, 277
Sanguijuelera, La (Encarnación Guillén), 97, 111, 111 n43
Santa Cruz, Baldomero I, 303
Santa Cruz, Baldomero II, 214–16, 238, 264, 301, 303, 311 n29, 328 n15, 344 n29, 371, 373, 377
Santa Cruz, Bárbara Arnaiz de, 91 n10, 214, 215 n51, 216 n54, 282 n58, 296, 296 n12, 300 n15, 304, 307, 309, 373, 376
Santa Cruz family, 42, 139, 174 n30, 175 n30, 229, 237, 239, 244, 246, 261, 294, 294 n7, 295, 298, 302, 304 n19, 307, 316
Santa Cruz, Jacinta Arnaiz de, 149, 151 n23, 174, 186 n43, 204, 214 n50, 215, 217, 218, 218 n57, 239, 240, 244, 247, 264, 266 n39, 267, 271 n47, 275, 275 n50, 277 n53, 280, 282, 283 n62, 284, 287 n66, 288, 292, 293, 293 n5, 296, 297, 297 n12, 298, 298 n13, 299, 299 n14, 300, 300 n14, 300 n15, 302, 304 n19, 313 n32, 314, 315, 316 n39, 321, 323, 333, 335–38, 344 n28, 349–351, 353, 354, 354 n37, 374
Santa Cruz, Juanito, 3, 25, 25 n48, 120, 121, 133, 134, 134 n3, 136, 137, 138 n8, 145, 159, 160, 183, 186 n43, 204, 207 n40, 214 n50, 216 n54, 219–21, 237, 243, 264, 268–71, 271 n46, 271 n47, 277, 277 n53, 280, 281, 283 n58, 284, 285, 287, 288, 293, 293 n5, 296 n12, 297 n12, 298, 298 n13, 300–304, 304 n19, 305, 305 n23, 306–312,

312 n30, 312 n31, 313, 313 n32, 313 n34, 317, 317 n41, 318, 319, 321, 323, 326 n10, 328, 330, 332, 333, 333 n22, 338, 339, 343, 344, 346, 348, 349, 352–54, 361, 362, 373, 376
Sarmiento, Patricio, 101 n28, 158
Severiana, 300
Sola (Gil de la Cuadra), 101 n28
Sor Marcela, 278
Sor Natividad, 280 n56
Tablas (Pedro López), 95
Tafetán, D. Juan, 387 n12, 388, 389
Tal, La, 122 n65
Tía Roma, 256
Tío Licurgo (Pedro Lucas), 66, 380–83, 385 n10, 393
Tío Pasolargo, 381
Tío Tardío, 380 n7, 385 n10
Torquemada, Francisco de, 122 n64, 123 n68, 183, 186 n43, 204, 205, 248, 256, 266, 267, 280, 315 n38, 394
Troyas, Las, 72, 383, 384, 388, 389
Trujillo family, 294
Villalonga, Jacinto, 133, 236, 273, 280, 307, 308, 326 n10, 361, 362
Villaamil, Ramón, 266
Zalamero, 133, 134, 361, 362
Zarapicos, 118

Balzac

Bianchon, Horace, 191
Birotteau, César, 73 n40, 214, 215, 215 n51
Birotteau, Mme., 327 n14
Brigant, 6 n6
Canquöelle, Le père [Peyrade], 5, 6 n6
Esther (Gobseck), 112, 112 n47, 176, 179–81
Félicité, 19 n32
Fontaine, Comte de, 94 n17
Fourchon, Le père, 66, 219 n58, 385 n10
Gobseck, 174
Goriot, Le père, 161 n10
Grandet, Le père, 65
Guénic, Calyste, 16, 214 n50
Guénic, Sabine de, 214 n50

Guillaume, Augustine, 161 n10, 215
Guillaume, M., 215, 216
Guillaume, Mme., 215
Herrera, D. Carlos [Vautrin], 176, 178–81
Lambert, Louis, 168 n22, 213 n49, 274 n49
Maupin, Camille, 16, 23, 25 n48
Mouche, 218 n58
Nucingen, Baron, 174
Peyrade, Lydie, 6
Pierrette, 6 n6
Rastignac, Eugène de, 208, 240
Rochefide, Mme. de, 214 n50
Rubempré, Lucien de, 17 n27, 133, 173 n26, 177, 179, 180, 244
Vautrin, 161 n10, 164, 176–81, 183, 208

Cervantes

Benengeli, Cide Hamete, 82, 116, 201 n31, 232, 344, 376, 377
Berganza, 346 n33
Canon, The, 148, 190, 231, 232, 358, 359
Carrasco, Sansón, 160
Cipión, 346 n33
Cortadillo, 118
Dorotea, 173 n28, 190
Juan Haldudo, 73 n40
Miranda, D. Diego de, 30
Panza, Sancho, 73 n40, 111, 128, 136, 164, 182, 184, 233, 234, 272, 281, 284, 350, 355, 381
Quijada, 369
Quijana, 369
Quijano, Alonso, 58, 116, 127, 166, 169, 194, 223, 230, 243, 244, 358, 374
Quijote, Don, 22, 73 n40, 82, 111, 114, 116, 118, 128, 128 n73, 136, 145, 152, 156, 158–61, 161 n10, 162–64, 167, 169, 171, 172, 173 n28, 180, 182, 184, 186, 190, 192 n10, 215, 219, 232–34, 239, 240, 263, 264, 284, 308, 309, 321, 324, 332, 345, 349, 350, 355, 376, 381
Rinconete, 118

Verde Gabán, Caballero del, 159 n6, 311 n29

Vizcaíno, El (D. Sancho de Azpeitia), 232

Yangüeses, Los, 284

Clarín (Leopoldo Alas)

Anacleto, 186 n43

Carraspique family, 179

Carraspique, Rosa, 179

Fortunato, D. (Camoirán), 177 n34

Mesía, Alvaro, 145, 159, 159 n7, 160, 167, 186 n43, 203, 219, 222 n65

Orgaz, Joaquín, 186 n43

Ozores (de Quintanar), Ana, 80, 159, 159 n7, 160–62, 166–69, 171, 172, 176–79, 182, 183, 185, 186 n43, 222 n65, 244, 327 n14

Ozores, Doña Anunciación de, 186 n43

Pas, Fermín de (Magistral), 43, 80 n51, 159, 159 n7, 160, 160 n8, 168, 172, 172 n25, 176–83, 185, 186 n43, 188, 211

Quintanar, Víctor, 160, 162, 168 n22, 169, 201 n31

Ripamilán, D. Cayetano, 177 n34, 186 n43

Somoza, Robustiano, 179

Dickens

Barnacle family, 94

Boffin, Henrietta, 218

Boffin, Noddy, 218

Casby, Christopher, 218 n58, 271 n46

Chillips, Mr., 124 n68

Clennam, 62, 62 n22, 122

Copperfield, David, 234

Cuttle, Captain, 101 n28

Diogenes, 101 n28

Dombey, Florence, 101, 101 n28, 111 n45

Gowan, Henry, 174

Havisham, Miss, 40

Higden, Betty, 218, 258 n24

Meagles, Pet, 174

Pickwick, Mr., 348 n33

Secretary, The (John Rokesmith), 218

Sloppy, 258 n24

Spenlow, Mr., 62 n22

Veneering family, 306 n23

Twain

Finn, Huckleberry, 146, 152, 164, 171, 232, 240, 243, 245, 326, 327, 327 n12, 331, 332, 332 n20, 333, 335, 339, 377, 391

Hawkins, Jim, 309

Jim, 331, 332 n20, 333

Mary Jane (Wilks), Miss, 245

Phelps family, 331

Polly, Aunt, 369 n17

Sawyer, Tom, 170, 264, 332, 333, 369

Watson, Miss, 232, 243, 331

Douglas, Widow, 334

Zola

Boche family, 100, 100 n26

Campardon, 219

Coupeau, "Cadet-Cassis", 115, 115 n50, 116, 156

Denise, 352 n35

Faujas, L'abbé, 178

Florent, 222, 224

Gavard, 220

Gervaise (Macquart Lantier Coupeau), 94, 99, 100, 100 n26, 101 n28, 124, 171, 216, 226, 240, 246, 266 n39, 320, 374, 391

Goujet family, 100, 100 n26

Grivet, M., 212

Lalie, 226

Lantier, Auguste, 99

Lantier family, 96 n20

Lebigre, M., 222

Lisa, La belle, 220, 221, 311

Louiset, 123 n68

Marjolin, 220, 221, 311

Marty, Mme., 215

Mignot, 104 n35

Mouret, Marthe, 177, 178

Mouret, Octave, 147, 177, 216 n54, 219

Mouret, Serge, 177

Muche, 217, 218, 218 n58
Nana (Coupeau), 94, 103 n31, 122 n65, 123 n68
Pauline, 218
Pichon, Marie, 198 n24
Raquin, Camille, 212, 274 n49
Raquin, Mme., 212
Raquin, Thérèse, 212
Rougon, Eugène, 94, 216
Rougon-Macquart family, 118, 244, 366
Vabré, Théophile, 212, 213
Valagnose, 216 n54

Library of Congress Cataloging in Publication Data

Gilman, Stephen.
  Galdós and the art of the European novel, 1867–1887.

  Includes index.
  1. Pérez Galdós, Benito, 1843–1920—Criticism and
interpretation.   I. Title.
PQ6555.Z5G5   863'.5   80-8550
ISBN 0-691-06456-3   AACR2